Complex Evolutionary Dynamics in Urban-Regional and Ecologic-Economic Systems

J. Barkley Rosser

Complex Evolutionary Dynamics in Urban-Regional and Ecologic-Economic Systems

From Catastrophe to Chaos and Beyond

Springer

J. Barkley Rosser
James Madison University
Department of Economics
South Main St. 800
Harrisonburg, VA 22807, USA
rosserjb@jmu.edu

ISBN 978-1-4419-8827-0 e-ISBN 978-1-4419-8828-7
DOI 10.1007/978-1-4419-8828-7
Springer New York Dordrecht Heidelberg London

Library of Congress Control Number: 2011928060

Printed on acid-free paper

Springer is part of Springer Science+Business Media (www.springer.com)

Preface

This is, therefore, the intensest rendezvous.
It is in that thought that we collect ourselves,
Out of all the indifferences, into one thing:

Within a single thing, a single shawl
Wrapped tight round us, since we are poor, a warmth,
A light, a power, the miraculous influence.

Here now, we forget each other and ourselves.
We feel the obscurity of an order, a whole...
Wallace Stevens, 1950, Final Soliloquy of the Interior Paramour

Within the past decade we have seen on the one hand the majority of the world's population come to reside in urban areas for the first time in world history, while on the other we have seen a dramatic rise in average global temperature widely thought to be mostly due to the economic activities humans carry out in those urban areas. Nonlinear complex dynamics are profoundly involved in both of these related developments. This book will open with considering the historical forces behind this rise of cities, including some critiques of certain recent ideas of "new economic geography," and will conclude (except for a mathematical appendix) with a consideration of the science and economics of global warming and how to deal with it in the face of the uncertainties arising from these nonlinear complex dynamics, which will reflect the unique perspective of this author having been involved with climatological research for more than 35 years. In between there will be discussions of broader regional economic dynamics, the foundations of evolutionary theory, and the dynamics of ecologic-economic systems. A deep theme is that in all of these areas, nonlinear complex dynamics can result in discontinuities, such as sudden changes of urban growth patterns or the sudden crashes of biological populations harvested by human beings. These discontinuities can appear with little warning and can serve as the basis for the theories of unexpected events such as "black swans" as proposed by Nassim Taleb (2010).

This book has been many years in the writing, having been contracted for originally over a decade ago by Kluwer, which was bought out some years later by Springer, who is publishing it now. It was originally supposed to be the second volume of the second edition of my 1991 book, *From Catastrophe to Chaos: A General*

Theory of Economic Discontinuities, published by Kluwer. That book was rejected by 13 publishers before Zack Rolnick at Kluwer took it up, after which it did quite well for such a monograph, leading to the contract for a second edition. Originally written as a critique of standard economic theory, after it came out it came to be viewed by many as a kind of reference work for nonlinear dynamics in economics. It was with this in mind that it was decided to break up the second edition into three volumes, given that I was thinking in such terms. It was in this vein that the first volume of the second edition was written and published in 2000 by Kluwer, expanding on the material in the first eight chapters of the first edition. I wrote the Preface for that book on September 9, 1999, exactly 11 years ago from my writing this Preface on September 9, 2010.

As it is, this book does fulfill in many ways the original intention of being that second volume, expanding on Chapters 9–14 of the 1991 book, which in fact are reproduced essentially directly in this book as, respectively, Chapters 1, 3, 4, 6, 8, and 10. In turn, the final chapter, Appendix A, which serves as a Mathematical Appendix here, is the second chapter from the first volume of the second edition from 2000. The remaining chapters are brand new, with each generally expanding on the chapter that precedes it.

Despite this, for various reasons this book does not carry the originally planned title. This is really a result of how long it has taken me to complete it, having gotten distracted by other projects and responsibilities during most of the past decade. One reason is that there has been such an explosion of literature in the areas of interest of this book that making this a reference book for all this has simply become undoable, at least as originally envisioned. Thus, the topics of urban-regional and evolutionary-ecological economic systems have been approached by focusing more on specific matters of particular interest in connection with the deeper themes of the original book, without attempting to be fully comprehensive.

There is also the matter that most economists now understand much better and are more open to the nonlinear complex dynamics mathematics that was the focus of the 1991 and 2000 books. Thus, there is less need to emphasize in this book an exposition of the mathematical techniques involved. This reinforces the idea of shifting more to focus on the issues of the topics themselves, even as nonlinear and complex dynamics continue to be an ongoing theme, including the original focus on discontinuities in economic systems. In any case, the relegation of the purely mathematical chapter to an appendix at the end symbolizes this shift, which fits with the change of title for this book.

I wish to thank the following for giving either advice, insights, or materials or general support for this book: Ehsan Ahmed, Craig Allen, Tim Allen, Åke Andersson, Dann Arce, Brian Berry, Gian-Italo Bischi, Buz Brock, Dan Bromley, the late Reid Bryson, Ken Button, Ping Chen, Carl Chiarella, Paul Christensen, David Colander, Bob Costanza, James F. Crow, Herman Daly, Herbert Dawid, Dick Day, Dee Dechert, Christophe Deissenberg, Domenico Delli Gatti, Dimitrios Dendrinos, Peter Dorman, Debbie Dove, Bill Duddleston, Steve Durlauf, Gustav Feichtinger, Duncan Foley, Carl Folke, Jamie Galbraith, Mauro Gallegati, Laura Gardini, Herb Gintis, John Gowdy, Steve Guastello, Roger Guesnerie, Weihong

Huang, Don Hester, Geoff Hodgson, Buzz. Holling, Cars Hommes, John Horgan, Bob Horn, Jean-Charles Hourcade, Yannis Ioannides, Börje Johansson, Jim Kahn, Shashi Kant, Steve Keen, Ali Khan, Alan Kirman, Michael Kopel, Roger Koppl, Ingrid Kubin, Honggang Li, Akio Matsumoto, Pat Michaels, Phil Mirowski, Peter Nijkamp, Dick Norgaard, Charles Perrings, Jason Potts, Tönu Puu, Otto Rössler, Kenshi Sakai, Larry Samuelson, Bill Sandholm, Tom Schelling, Frank Schneider, Willi Semmler, Ajit Sinha, Gene Smolensky, Michael Sonis, Roger Stough, Nassim Taleb, Vela Velupillai, Alessandro Vercelli, Nick Vriend, Florian Wagener, Dave Warsh, Wolfgang Weidlich, Roy Weintraub, Martie Weitzman, Ulrich Witt, Bill Wood, and Wei-Bin Zhang. Of course, none are responsible for any errors or misinterpretations that are contained in it.

I wish especially to thank my publisher, Jon Gurstelle, as well as his assistant, Talia Winch, and others at Springer involved in the production of this book. It was Jon who finally pushed me to complete this book after my long gathering of materials and writing papers without putting it together to make the effort. I went through several publishers at both Kluwer and Springer after Zack Rolnick stepped aside and before Jon took over who did not push me, although I cannot complain of their friendliness or sympathy. However, it was Jon who forced me to finally choose whether to do this or not, and I chose to do it.

Finally, I wish to thank my wife and colleague, Marina Rosser, source of much deep and wise advice. She also exhibited the tolerance that a writer of a book must have from a spouse for the distractions and disruptions of normal life that the writer of a book necessarily generates for those around and close. She has been my strong support throughout the long period of this endeavor and its many ups and downs. I am deeply grateful to her for all this and more.

I dedicate this book to my three lovely and loving daughters: Meagan, Caitlin, and Sasha. More than any other book I have written, this one is concerned with the future, their future, and that of their children and their childrens' children, on and on, hopefully.

Harrisonburg, VA
9/9/10

J. Barkley Rosser, Jr.

Contents

1 Discontinuous Evolution of Urban Historical Forms 1
1.1 Introduction 1
1.2 Agglomeration and the Formation and Sudden Growth of Cities 4
1.2.1 The Debate 4
1.2.2 Instability and Agglomeration 5
1.3 Long-Distance Trade and Instability 13
1.3.1 Another View: Open Versus Closed Cities 13
1.3.2 The Mees Version of Pirenne's Hypothesis 14
1.3.3 Comparative Advantage and City Size 16
1.3.4 Logistical Networks and Long-Distance Trade 17
1.4 A Possible Synthesis: The Role of Technological Change 18
1.4.1 Agglomeration, Logistical Networks, and Technology . 18
1.4.2 Rome Was Not Built in a Day 20
Notes 22

2 The New Economic Geography Approach and Other Views 23
2.1 The Setting 23
2.2 The Three Returns to Scale 26
2.3 The Dixit–Stiglitz Model of Monopolistic Competition 28
2.4 Bifurcations of the NEG Core–Periphery Model 30
2.5 The Core–Periphery Model at the Global Level 34
2.6 Chaotic Dynamics in a Discrete Version of the Core–Periphery Model 36
2.7 Criticisms of the New Economic Geography 38
Notes 41

3 Discontinuities in Intraurban Systems 43
3.1 Some General Remarks 43
3.2 The Role of Transportation in Urban Structural Bifurcations . . 44
3.2.1 Modal Choice in Transportation 44
3.2.2 Urban Retail Structure 46
3.3 An Ecological View 48
3.3.1 Density–Rent Cycles 48
3.3.2 Intraurban Lotka–Volterra Instability 50

3.4 Static and Dynamic Boundary Discontinuities 52
3.4.1 Neighborhood Boundary Dynamics 52
3.4.2 Land Use Boundaries 56
Notes 61

4 Morphogenesis of Regional Systems 63
4.1 The Continuous Flow Model 63
4.1.1 Linear and Nonlinear Variations 63
4.1.2 Structural Change of the Flow Pattern 65
4.1.3 Wave Patterns in the Continuous Flow Model 67
4.1.4 Multiplier–Accelerator Cycles in the Continuous Flow Model 67
4.2 Evolution of Urban and Regional Systems 69
4.2.1 Predator–Prey Cycles in Single Cities 69
4.2.2 Interregional Predator–Prey Cycles 71
4.2.3 The Emergence of Chaotic Dynamics 74
4.3 Self-Organizing Regional Morphogenesis 76
4.3.1 Order Through Fluctuations 76
4.3.2 Time Scales and Slaves 78
4.3.3 A Fractal Synergesis 80
Notes 82

5 Complex Dynamics in Spatial Systems 85
5.1 Complexity and Socioeconomic Spatial Systems 85
5.2 The Generality of the Schelling Model 86
5.3 An Evolutionary Game Theoretic View of the Schelling Model . 88
5.4 Network Analysis of the Schelling Model 89
5.5 Zipf's Law and Urban Hierarchy 93
5.6 Urban Hierarchy with Discrete Levels 97
5.7 Bottom-Up or Top-Down Development of Urban Hierarchies? . 100
Notes 104

6 Perspectives on Economic and Ecologic Evolution 107
6.1 Historical Perspectives 107
6.1.1 Origins 107
6.1.2 Dialectical Difficulties 108
6.1.3 Evolution and the Equilibrium Concept 110
6.1.4 Cycles and Chaos 111
6.2 Continuous Versus Discontinuous Theories of Evolution 112
6.2.1 Gradualism 112
6.2.2 Saltationalism 113
6.3 Hypercyclic Morphogenesis of Higher-Level Structures 115
Notes 117

7 Evolution and Complexity 121
7.1 The Ups and Downs of the Darwinian View of Evolution 121
7.2 The Ups and Downs of Darwinian Evolutionary Economics . . 126

7.3 The Multilevel Complication 128
7.4 Self-Organization and Natural Selection 131
Notes 136

8 Ecosystems and Economics 139
8.1 Nonlinear Bionomic Dynamics 139
8.1.1 Single-Species Models with Density Dependence . . . 139
8.1.2 Two-Species Lotka–Volterra Models 142
8.1.3 Complexity and Stability in Multispecies Ecosystems . 145
8.2 The Bioeconomics Synthesis 147
8.2.1 The Perversities of Open-Access Renewable Resource Use 147
8.2.2 The Special Problem of Extinction 156
Notes 160

9 Complex Ecologic-Economic Dynamics 163
9.1 The Intertemporally Optimal Fishery 163
9.2 Complex Expectational Dynamics in the Optimal Fishery 166
9.3 Complexity Problems of Optimal Rotation in Forests 169
9.4 Problems of Forestry Management Beyond Optimal Rotation . . 174
9.5 Complex Lake Dynamics 176
9.6 Stability and Resilience of Ecosystems Revisited 180
Notes 184

10 The Limits to Growth and Global Catastrophe Revisited 187
10.1 Neo-Malthusian Collapse Models 187
10.2 Renewable Versus Nonrenewable Resources 189
10.3 Managing Potential Catastrophe 190
10.4 The Entropy Argument 192
10.4.1 Entropy as the Ultimate Limit 192
10.4.2 Entropy and Value 194
10.4.3 The Vision of the Steady-State Economy 194
Notes 195

11 How Nonlinear Dynamics Complicate the Issue of Global Warming 197
11.1 Prologue on the Science of Global Warming 197
11.2 Could a Combined Global Climate–Economic System Be Chaotic? 199
11.3 Competing IAM Models 201
11.4 The Discounting Issue Again 204
11.5 Positive Feedbacks, Fat Tails, and Fundamental Uncertainty . . 206
Notes 209

Appendix A 213

References 263

Index 313

Chapter 1
Discontinuous Evolution of Urban Historical Forms

It was in permanent containers that neolithic invention outshone all earlier cultures: so well that we are still using many of their methods, materials, and forms. The modern city itself, for all its steel and glass, is still essentially an earth-bound Stone Age structure. . . . With storage came continuity as well as a surplus to draw on in lean seasons. The safe setting aside of unconsumed seeds for next year's sowing was the first step toward capital accumulation.
Lewis Mumford (1961, The City in History, p. 16)

As far as the present record stands, grain cultivation, the plow, the potter's wheel, the sailboat, the draw loom, copper metallurgy, abstract mathematics, exact astronomical observation, the calendar, writing and other modes of intelligible discourse in permanent form, all came into existence at roughly the same time, around 3000 B.C. give or take a few centuries. The most ancient urban remains now known, except Jericho, date from this period. This constituted a singular technological expansion of human power whose only parallel is the change that has taken place in our own time.
Lewis Mumford (ibid., p. 33)

1.1 Introduction

Perhaps more than any other human institution, the city reflects the tension between continuity and discontinuity in our social existence. It is simultaneously the vessel of continuity containing the deep structures of the past (symbolized by the longevity of many urban buildings, roads, and other infrastructure) as well as the staging ground for most of the revolutionary upheavals of human history. This conflict is manifested in the above pair of quotations from Mumford (1961).

The scope and variety of possible discontinuities in urban systems can be seen from the following quote from J.C. Amson (1975, p. 178):

> Specific illustrations of the structural singularities typical of urban systems spring readily to mind: the onset of preurban clustering in a primitive dispersed society; the tenfold enlargement of an already large city within one generation; the emergence 'almost overnight' of a

J.B. Rosser, *Complex Evolutionary Dynamics in Urban-Regional and Ecologic-Economic Systems*, DOI 10.1007/978-1-4419-8828-7_1,

suburban fringe to a provincial town; the relatively instantaneous depopulation of its inner core after centuries of lively inhabitation; the reversals of income patterns, social patterns, or ethnic zoning patterns in a metropolis; the counterreversal of that zoning half a century later; the exchange of dominance roles between rival cities; the spontaneous formation of a conurbation from its constituent towns; and many more.

Amson (1974, 1975) initiated the formal use of discontinuous techniques of analysis in urban economics with catastrophe theory by analyzing urban density as a function of rent and "opulence" (an index of the attractiveness of a city) within a cusp catastrophe context. Casti and Swain (1975) modeled central place orders and urban property prices as Zeeman's (1974) cusp catastrophes and as butterfly catastrophes. Mees (1975) modeled the revival of cities in medieval Europe as a butterfly catastrophe. Wilson (1976)[1] examined transportation mode choice as a fold catastrophe and Poston and Wilson (1977) did so for retail center size. Isard (1977) modeled population related to agglomerative and deglomerative tendencies as a cusp catastrophe, which prefigured more rigorous models by Casetti (1980), Dendrinos (1980a), Papageorgiou (1980), and Papageorgiou and Smith (1983) explaining sudden urban growth.[2] Smith (1977) used the fold catastrophe to model the decline in the number of banks post-1920s that occurred due to the spread of automobiles.[3] Wagstaff (1978) tried to explain Greek settlement patterns between the second and seventeenth centuries as a result of changes in agricultural land quality and "external threat" using a cusp catastrophe model.[4] Dendrinos (1978) modeled intraurban manufacturing and residential activities as a five-dimensional hyperbolic umbilic catastrophe, and in 1979, he modeled the formation of slums in cities with the six-dimensional parabolic ("mushroom") catastrophe. Puu (1979, 1981a, b, c) used the five-dimensional hyperbolic and elliptic umbilic catastrophes to model changes in regional trading patterns. Nijkamp and Reggiani (1988) have shown that a generalized optimal control model of nonlinear, dynamic spatial interaction can generate a catastrophe theoretic interpretation.

In contrast to the largely deterministic approach of catastrophe theory, the synergetics approach emphasizes self-organization of systems through nonequilibrium phase transitions arising from stochastic fluctuations near critical bifurcation points. Foreshadowed by Fuller (1975, 1979), this approach was developed by Nicolis and Prigogine (1977) and Haken (1977, 1983) and first suggested as applicable to urban and regional systems by Isard and Liossatos (1977). The latter explicitly link this approach to the more deterministic catastrophe theory approach through the common emphasis on systemic structural changes arising from transitions through bifurcation points.

The major application of these ideas in urban and regional modelling has been due to members of the "Brussels School," particularly Allen and Sanglier (1978, 1979, 1981), Sanglier and Allen (1989), and their associates under the direct influence of Ilya Prigogine, winner of the 1977 Nobel Prize in chemistry, who was himself located in Brussels. Also influenced by Forrester (1969), their efforts have generally focused on the construction of large-scale simulation models of urban and regional systems, incorporating stochastic processes, nonlinear feedback effects, and threshold levels for specific economic activities. Model simulations tend to exhibit dynamic self-organization with some cities growing and others declining as they pass upper or lower economic thresholds, respectively. Intraurban variations of this approach[5] have been used to model the development of specific cities in France (Pumain, Saint-Julien, and Sanders, 1987).

Yet another approach of a deterministic nature has been that of mathematical ecology, focusing on applying Lotka–Volterra equation systems of predator–prey cycles to model urban and regional cycles. Such an approach was initiated by Dendrinos (1980b) and Dendrinos and Mulally (1981) and summarized by Dendrinos with Mulally (1985). Sonis (1981, 1983) used it to analyze technological diffusion in regional spaces. Dendrinos and Mulally (1983) empirically tested such a model for many US cities and found it useful as did Dendrinos (1984) for US regional systems. Haag and Weidlich (1983) developed such a model for interregional migration which also contains elements of the synergetics approach. The onset of instability or structural change in such dynamic systems can be studied using bifurcation theory and catastrophe theory.

Furthermore the work of May (1976) and May and Oster (1976) has shown that Lotka–Volterra systems can generate chaotic dynamics given certain parameter values in the equations. This directly inspired analysis of chaotic dynamics in urban and regional systems. The first such application was an intraurban one of retail and residential systems attributed to Beaumont, Clarke, and Wilson (1981a). But most have focused on multiple-region models, either involving migration or population more generally (Rogerson, 1985; Day, Dasgupta, Datta, and Nugent, 1987; Dendrinos, 1982, 1985; Dendrinos and Sonis, 1987, 1989, 1990) or generalized interregional business cycles (White, 1985; Puu, 1987, 1989, 1990). However, White (1985) combines the original Beaumont, Clarke, and Wilson (1981a) intraurban retail model with a Brussels School synergetics approach to argue that chaotic fluctuations near a bifurcation point can engender the self-organization process. Thus, it would seem that the practitioners in the urban and regional fields have generally been more willing to see the links between different methods of discontinuous analysis rather than focusing on what distinguishes them from each other.

It may well be that urban and regional economics is a subdiscipline more open to the use and application of discontinuous techniques than others in economics. One reason may be the obvious existence of spatial discontinuities in land use, land values, social classes, and other such categories. Another may be the multidisciplinary links to geography, urban and regional planning, environmental science, political science, sociology, and other areas. This has led to the multidisciplinary fields of "urbanology" and "regional science," which while frequently using neoclassical methods can be argued to possess no central theory and thus to be more open to alternative methodologies. This lack of a clearly defined central theory has led on occasion to analyses entirely lacking any rigorous foundation and notable for their extreme ad hocracy and general uselessness. Notorious examples of this have been some of the more flagrantly off-the-wall and out-of-the-blue catastrophe theory applications.

Although it might seem that a defense of openness toward new and different approaches in the advance of knowledge should be unnecessary, nevertheless I shall do so by quoting the godfather of nonequilibrium phase transitions (which can also occur in the structure of knowledge itself), Ilya Prigogine and his coauthor Isabelle Stengers from their 1984 book, *Order Out of Chaos*, p. 206:

> We believe that models inspired by the concept of 'order through fluctuations' will help us with these questions and even permit us in some circumstances to give a more precise formulation to the complex interplay between the individual and collective aspects of behavior. From the physicist's point of view, this involves a distinction between states of the system in which all individual initiative is doomed to insignificance on the one hand, and on the other, bifurcation regions in which an individual, an idea, or a new behavior can upset the global state. Even in those regions, amplification obviously does not occur with just any individual, idea, or behavior, but only those that are 'dangerous'—that is, those that can exploit to their advantage the nonlinear relations guaranteeing the stability of the preceding regime. Thus we are led to conclude that the same nonlinearities may produce an order out of the chaos of elementary processes and still, under different circumstances, be responsible for the destruction of this same order, eventually producing a new coherence beyond another bifurcation.

1.2 Agglomeration and the Formation and Sudden Growth of Cities

1.2.1 The Debate

According to Braudel (1967, p. 373), "The town-country confrontation is the first and longest class struggle history has known." It is "the oldest and most revolutionary division of labor." (ibid.) The depth of this division, this contradiction, has inspired an array of thinkers and actors who wished to overcome it somehow: from the utopian socialist, Fourier (1840), the "scientific socialists," Marx and Engels (1848), and the anarchist, Kropotkin (1899), through the seminal "new town" advocate of garden cities and greenbelts, Ebenezer Howard (1902), and his modern disciples such as the Goodmans (1960), James Rouse, the developer of Columbia, Maryland, and Robert E. Simon, the developer of Reston, Virginia. We shall not seek how to achieve this goal, but rather to explain why this division exists.

Much debate exists over why cities exist. Are they merely central places of regional trading areas where markets occur, such as the German tradition of von Thünen (1826), Christaller (1933), and Lösch (1940) believes? Or do they arise, especially large cities, from agglomerative external economies such as argued by Adam Smith (1776, Part III),[6] Marshall (1890, Chap. 8), Hotelling (1929), and Chinitz (1961)? And why do we observe in history sudden changes in city sizes during particular periods such as the original "urban implosion," (Mumford, 1961), 5,000 years ago, or the sudden growth of cities noted in Europe by Pirenne (1925) after 1000 A.D.? We shall begin by discussing the case for agglomeration.

1.2.2 Instability and Agglomeration

1.2.2.1 A General View

Let us contemplate the clustering out of an initially uniform distribution of population as resulting from an instability in the balance of agglomerative and deglomerative forces. We view our units or agents as households rather than as individuals since the sexual and reproductive drives provide a fundamental source of agglomeration at this lowest level. But for a primitive agricultural or hunting society without trade, the self-sufficient household (possibly an extended family group or even clan) will be dominated by a deglomerative dynamic in its behavior, relative to other households. It will seek to maximize the amount of land available to itself for its farming or hunting activities. Thus on a homogeneous plane with identical households, there will tend to be an even distribution of those households as congestion costs (deglomerative force) predominate.

The origins of agglomeration beyond the household unit were probably not originally economic. Mumford (1961) argues that the first fixed gathering points were ancestral burial grounds of tribes or clans, often in caves which became the sites of religious ceremonies and artistic endeavors (i.e., Lascaux). "The city of the dead predates the city of the living" (Mumford, 1961, p. 7). But such agglomerations tended to be temporary rather than permanent, except for the corpses themselves (the "city of the dead").

Economic agglomeration came about from the discovery of the advantages of some collective labor in agriculture, most likely in the building and maintenance of irrigation and drainage systems. Such activities become the basis for small agricultural villages. But congestion costs remained high, especially due to public health problems associated with human excretion which are not totally relievable by recycling as fertilizer of "nightsoil."[7]

The likely critical element leading to a shift in the balance was probably the greater development of hydraulic systems in all their variety, as has been argued by Wittfogel (1957): not only the extensive building of dams, irrigation canals, and drainage ditches which allowed the expansion of population, but also the construction of water supply systems for direct human use, and, most important of all, for reducing congestion costs, *sewers* for removing human waste products. An old cliche goes, "sewers are the foundation of civilization." As Mumford notes (1961, p. 18), all these systems are ultimately containers, and so, "a city is a container of containers." Once this crucial barrier was passed, technological changes could occur more rapidly, which tended to increase the strength of the agglomerative advantage and the further expansion of cities.

1.2.2.2 A Local Instability Model

However, let us return to the initially even distribution of identical households on the homogeneous plane and consider a general model of the effects described above. In so doing, we shall initially follow the model of Papageorgiou and Smith (1983) in which the switch from deglomeration (or congestion costs) outweighing agglomeration effects (positive, locational, external economies) to just the opposite occurs at a bifurcation point where the dynamic system becomes unstable (Amson's "structural singularity").

They consider a homogeneous square plane, transformed into a torus, with M cells and N identical actors. Let n_1 = population in cell 1 and the externality generated by those in 1 to someone in cell j to be given by

$$E1_j = \phi_{1j} n_1, \tag{1.1}$$

where ϕ_{1j} is a distance-response function whose sign indicates whether a cell-to-cell relation is agglomerative (positive) or deglomerative (negative). Given the homogeneity of the plane, the signed "volume" of the spatial interaction field,

$$Z = \sum_t \phi_{tj}, \tag{1.2}$$

will be constant for all cells j. However, the total externality experienced by someone in j depends on the distribution of population and is given by

$$E_j = \sum_t {}_{tj}. \tag{1.3}$$

Agents are assumed to migrate stochastically, obeying a rational expectations utility maximization condition where utility of an agent at 1 is given by

$$u_1 = f[q_1, E_1(n)], \tag{1.4}$$

with $\partial f/\partial q_1 > 0$ and $\partial f/\partial E > 0$, and q_1 is land per capita consumed at 1. Assuming no transportation costs and letting u and n, respectively, represent vectors of the distributions over cells of utility and population, the probability of moving to cell j is given by

$$p_j = h_j[u,\ n] \ \text{ with } \sum_j p_j = 1 \text{ and } p_j \geq 0. \tag{1.5}$$

Letting $\mathrm{d}n_1/\mathrm{d}t$ be the expected net population change (assumed to be due purely to migration) in 1 at time t, a steady state will be given by $\mathrm{d}n_1/\mathrm{d}t = 0$ for all 1 and a spatial equilibrium by $u_1 = u$ for all 1. The latter occurs when

$$\mathrm{d}n_1/\mathrm{d}t = n_1 \left[N \middle/ \left(\sum_k n_k u_k \right) \right] (u_1 - u). \tag{1.6}$$

It readily follows from this that a uniform distribution of population (u, n) will be such a steady-state equilibrium.

Stability of this equilibrium can be examined by considering perturbations given by $n = 0_1$ such that

$$\begin{bmatrix} dn'_1/dt \\ \vdots \\ \vdots \\ dn'_M/dt \end{bmatrix} = \begin{bmatrix} c_0 c_1 c_2 \cdots c_1 \\ c_1 c_0 c_1 \cdots c_2 \\ c_2 c_1 c_0 \cdots c_3 \\ \vdots \qquad \vdots \\ c_1 c_2 c_3 \cdots c_0 \end{bmatrix} \begin{bmatrix} n'_1 \\ \vdots \\ \vdots \\ n'_M \end{bmatrix} \tag{1.7}$$

and

$$\sum_1 n'_1 = 0. \tag{1.8}$$

The elements of the C matrix are given by

$$c_0 = \alpha + \beta\phi_0 - (\alpha + \beta Z)/M, \tag{1.9}$$

$$c_k = \beta\phi_{M-k} - (\alpha + \beta Z)/M, \tag{1.10}$$

for all 1 and $k \geq 1$, where

$$\alpha = (n/u)(\partial f/\partial q_1)(\mathrm{d}q/\mathrm{d}n_1)|_n, \tag{1.11}$$

$$\beta = (n/u)(\partial f/\partial E_1)|_n. \tag{1.12}$$

The equilibrium will be stable if the real parts of all the eigenvalues of C, $\lambda_j < 0$, form the well-known Lyapunov theorem. Papageorgiou and Smith show that if $M \to \infty$ and $\phi_k > 0$ for only a finite number of cells (the spatial externality extends only over a limited area), then $\lambda_0 = 0$ and $\lambda_j = \alpha + \beta Z$ for all 1 and for $j \geq 1$. Thus, the condition for stability of the uniform distribution of population is $\alpha + \beta Z < 0$. This is equivalent to

$$(\partial f/\partial q_1)(\mathrm{d}q_1/\mathrm{d}n_1)|_n + (\partial f/\partial E_1)(\mathrm{d}E_1/\mathrm{d}n_1)|_n = \mathrm{d}u/\mathrm{d}n_1|_n < 0, \tag{1.13}$$

which admits a helpfully intuitive interpretation.

The first term is the marginal effect of increased congestion from greater population on utility and is always negative because $\partial f/\partial q_1 > 0$ and $\mathrm{d}q_1/\mathrm{d}n_1 < 0$ and thus is the congestion cost. The second term is the marginal effect on utility of the spatial externality whose sign depends on the sign of Z because $\partial f/\partial E_1 > 0$. Thus if the spatial externality is negative ($Z < 0$), the uniform distribution will be stable. However, for the distribution to become unstable, the spatial externality must become *sufficiently positive* to outweigh the negative congestion effect. The bifurcation point beyond which clustering will begin occurs where the two effects are evenly balanced. Papageorgiou and Smith see the positive agglomeration effect increasing as population rises and technology improves.

1.2.2.3 A Catastrophe Theory Interpretation

Although Papageorgiou and Smith did not do so, it is straightforward to generate a catastrophe theory interpretation of this model. The state variable could be the maximum rate of population growth in any cell. Control variables could be Z, the agglomeration variable, and the marginal cost (negative marginal utility) of congestion. The combination of these two variables for which the maximum eigenvalues of C equals zero traces out a bifurcation set at which discontinuities in the rate of maximum cell population growth would occur.

It can also be argued that this model provides a more solid foundation for the sort of model developed by Walter Isard (1977). His is of a cusp catastrophe surface for a single center with population as the state variable and parameters representing the agglomerative externality factor and the level of technology, respectively, as the control variables. The surface represents a social welfare maximum and the control variables are claimed to operate through their impact on the marginal productivity of labor, although the surface is not derived more explicitly from an underlying theoretical model. In Isard's formulation, the cusp catastrophe manifold comes from the canonical Thom (1972) equation:

$$W = -1/4x^4 + 1/2\alpha x^2 + \beta x + C, \tag{1.14}$$

where W is social welfare, x is population, α is the agglomerative parameter, β is the technological parameter, and C is a constant. Setting $\mathrm{d}W/\mathrm{d}x = 0$ for utility maximization gives the manifold

$$-x^3 + \alpha x + \beta = 0. \tag{1.15}$$

Isard interprets the first term as representing deglomerative diseconomies of scale which conflict with the agglomerative second term. Removing the third term would give something not all that different from what Papageorgiou and Smith derived more rigorously in a more disaggregated form. And the way the third term enters is not inconsistent with the verbal story Papageorgiou and Smith tell about the impact of technological change within their model. For a certain range of β, an increase in α (Z for Papageorgiou and Smith) will eventually lead to a discontinuous leap in population. This Isard cusp catastrophe manifold is depicted in Fig. 1.1.

It should be noted that a major difference between these approaches is that Papageorgiou and Smith emphasize migration between areas whereas Isard emphasizes production at a single site.

1.2.2.4 Some Further Variations

The Papageorgiou and Smith model has inspired several other efforts emphasizing the emergence of instability and the appearance of multiple equilibria. Anas (1988) has examined a variety of complex dynamics in a very similar model but shows that the presence of taste heterogeneity with respect to location can perform the same function as congestion costs do in the Papageorgiou and Smith model.

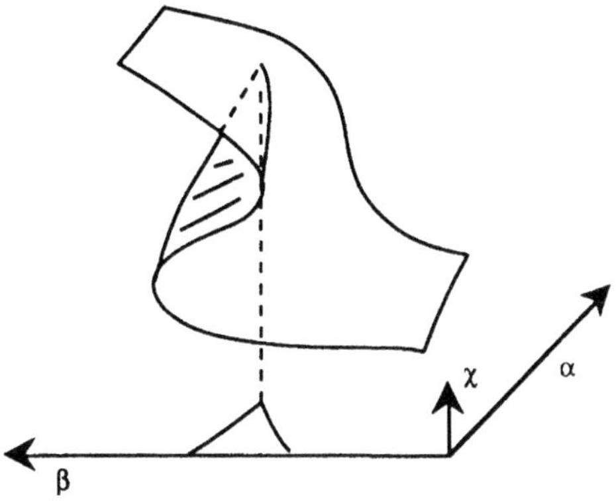

Fig. 1.1 Agglomerative instability as a cusp catastrophe

Weidlich and Haag (1987) present a three-region model with nonlinear migration equations driven by a single agglomeration parameter. They analyze their model in terms of equations of motion of the system, given by

$$\mathrm{d}n_1(t)/\mathrm{d}t = \mathrm{e}^{kn_1(t)} \sum_{i=1}^{L} kn_i^{(t)} \mathrm{e}^{-kn_i(t)} - kn_1(t)\mathrm{e}^{-kn_1(t)} \sum_{i=1}^{L} \mathrm{e}^{kn_i(t)}, \tag{1.16}$$

with the constant

$$\sum_{l=1}^{L} kn_1(t) = kN, \tag{1.17}$$

where $n_1(t)$ is the population in region 1 at time t, N is total population (assumed to be constant), k is the agglomeration parameter, and L is the number of regions (assumed to equal 3 in this case). They depict this dynamical system graphically with flux lines in a space of agglomeration-weighted, regional populations. They derive three separate cases for low, middle, and high values of k, the agglomeration parameter. These are depicted in Figs. 1.2, 1.3, and 1.4, in which each vertex represents a situation where all the population is in a single region and each side where one region has zero population.

In Fig. 1.2, $k < k_c{}^1$; the agglomeration parameter lies below the lower of the two bifurcation values of k. In this situation from any initial point the system moves to the center, representing our uniform distribution of population case, which happens to be a globally stable equilibrium.

In Fig. 1.3, $k_{c1} < k < k_c$; the agglomeration parameter lies between its two bifurcation values. In this situation the uniform distribution (center) is still locally stable but has lost its global stability. If the initial situation is sufficiently nonuniform, the system will converge on an equilibrium with agglomeration occurring (a city forms) in the nearest region to the initial point. In fact there are four basins of attraction

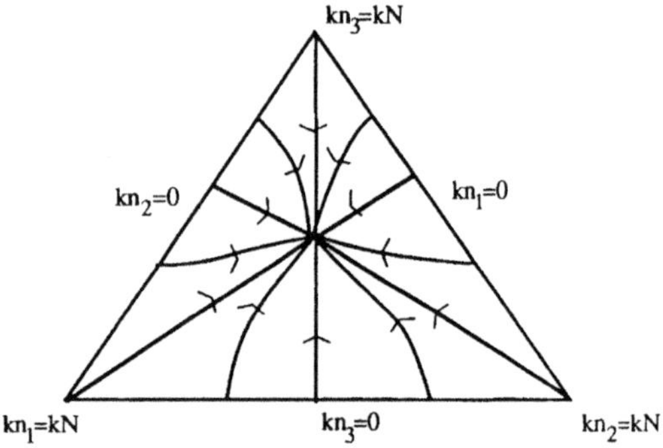

Fig. 1.2 Weidlich–Haag migration with weak agglomeration

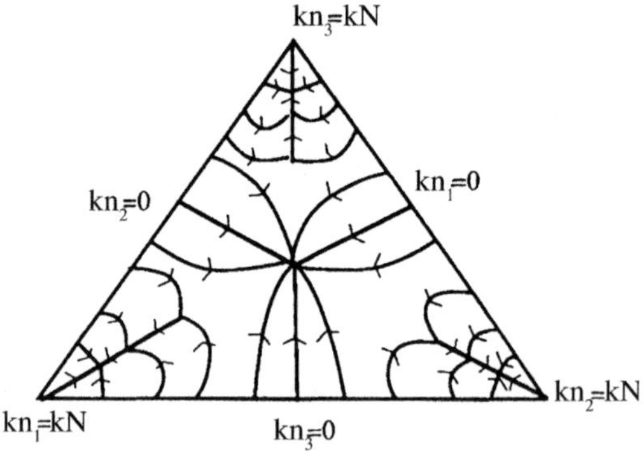

Fig. 1.3 Weidlich–Haag migration with intermediate agglomeration

around four, locally stable, stationary states, separated by lines intersecting at three unstable saddle points.

In Fig. 1.4, $k > k_c$; the agglomeration parameter now exceeds the upper bifurcation point. The uniform distribution has become an unstable node. In addition there are still three stable stationary states, each representing a "city" existing in a different region, and three unstable saddle points.

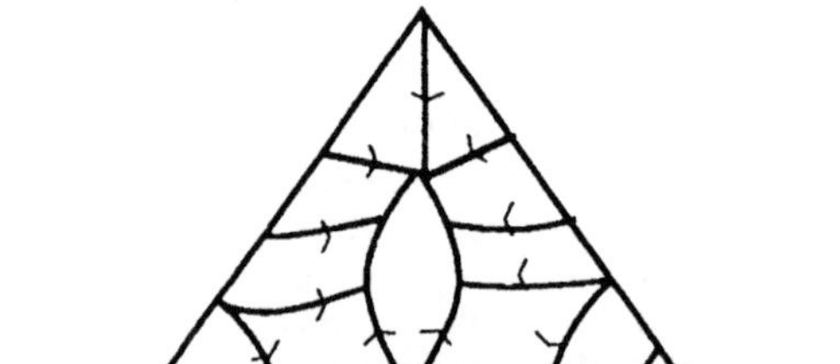

Fig. 1.4 Weidlich–Haag migration with strong agglomeration

We can directly compare this result with that of Papageorgiou and Smith. The upper bifurcation point in Weidlich and Haag corresponds to the condition given by Papageorgiou and Smith for the appearance of instability of the uniform distribution, and hence the condition for the original formation of cities. The lower bifurcation point may correspond with the value of Z, the locational externality in Papageorgiou and Smith, becoming positive. In their model, the uniform distribution remains locally stable, even when Z is positive, as long as marginal congestion costs remain greater. However, the Weidlich and Haag result suggests that if Z is high enough in the Papageorgiou and Smith model, one might find agglomerative behavior if the initial situation is sufficiently nonuniform (some sort of a city already exists), even though the uniform distribution is still locally stable.

Leonardi and Casti (1986) have examined a variation that includes moving costs in the form of "spatial discount factors." Assuming that P_i = relative population in zone i, $P_i \geq 0$, $\Sigma i P_i = 1$, Q_i = dwelling space in zone i, f_{ij} = spatial discount factor associated with a move from zone i to zone j, $0 \leq f_{ij} \leq 1$, α_1, α_2 = elasticity parameters, and K = a nonnegative constant, the interzone migration equation is

$$P_i = Q_i\left(\sum_j f_{ij}P_j\right)^{\alpha} \Big/ \sum_k Q_k\left(\sum_j f_{kj}P_j\right)^{\alpha}, \tag{1.18}$$

where $\alpha = \alpha_1/\alpha_2$. This equation closesly resembles equations studied by Beckmann (1976), Harris and Wilson (1978), and Andersson and Ferraro (1982). Although they do not make it at all clear, it would seem that α, the elasticity ratio, might be interpreted as an agglomerative parameter, and the f_{ij} "locational friction" parameters might also reflect congestion costs or other deglomerative effects. In any case they examine a dynamic generalization of this model in which the matrix Q is given by

$$q_{ij} = f_{ij}P_j \Big/ \sum_m f_{im}P_m. \tag{1.19}$$

The condition for a unique and stable equilibrium then becomes

$$\alpha < 1/\sup \mathrm{Re}\lambda_Q, \tag{1.20}$$

where the λ_Qs are the eigenvalues of Q. For α greater than this critical bifurcation value there will be multiple equilibria, stable ones alternating with unstable ones in the usual manner. They further argue that the smaller the locational friction parameters, the wider the zone of α for which there exists a unique and stable equilibrium. They conclude that this contradicts Papageorgiou and Smith, but this seems unclear due to basic differences between their respective models.

1.2.2.5 The Role of Production Made Explicit

An approach that combines elements of the Isard approach with those of a model of Casetti (1980) was developed by Papageorgiou (1980, 1981). Nonlinear productive returns to city size are modeled through their impact on the marginal product of labor. Migration depends on a comparison of equilibrium urban utility (u) with equilibrium rural utility (v) where the latter has linearity of that relation. If N is urban population, X is the urban good, and the ms are positive constants derived from various input costs (Papageorgiou, 1980, pp. 1039–1040), then the change in equilibrium urban utility with urban population is given by

$$dU/dN = -m_1 + m_2[d/dN(\partial X/\partial N)]. \quad (1.21)$$

The term $d/dN(\partial X/\partial N)$ describes how the marginal product of labor used in the urban good changes with city size. It is assumed that it increases initially at an increasing rate and later at a decreasing rate. For a sufficiently large m_1, this gives relations as shown in Fig. 1.5.

It is then posited that over time technological change will raise this u more rapidly than it raises the equivalent v for agriculture. In a world of constant population, this can be seen in Fig. 1.6.

In this system, urban population leaps discontinuously from N_3 to N_4. There is a hysteresis effect here in that if v were to rise more rapidly (or u were to decline), there would be a discontinuous drop from some urban population considerably below N_4 down to some level considerably below N_3. For u_1 and u_2, there are three equilibrium states with the outer two being stable and the middle one unstable.[8]

Despite its slightly different formulation, this model reflects the basic characteristics we have already seen. The nonlinear utility–population relation embodies the conflicting forces of agglomeration and congestion with the former "winning" at lower population levels and the latter winning at higher ones.[9] Changes in this "net

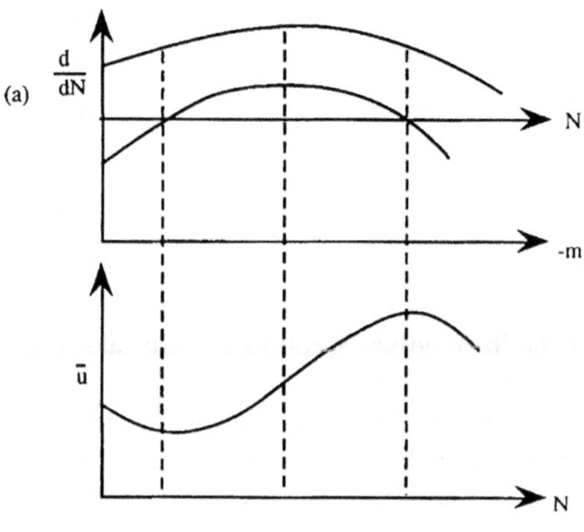

Fig. 1.5 Marginal and total urban utility as a function of population

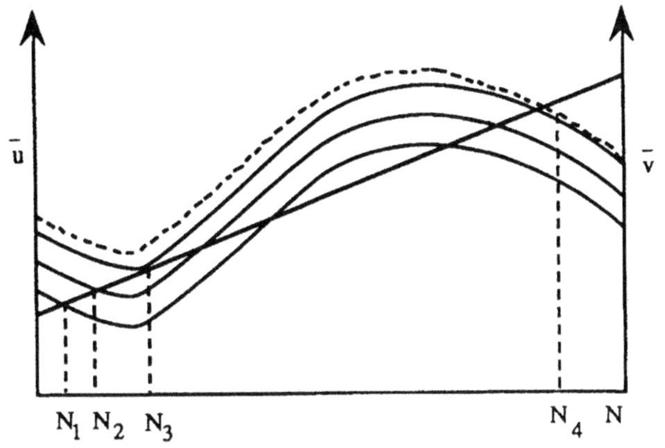

Fig. 1.6 Urban–Rural population distributions equilibrium

agglomerative tendency" are associated with changes in stability and number of equilibria, with discontinuous changes in equilibrium urban populations occurring as the tendency crosses certain critical levels. Thus, sudden changes in urbanization arise from interactions between agglomeration and technology in nonlinear systems.

1.3 Long-Distance Trade and Instability

1.3.1 Another View: Open Versus Closed Cities

An alternative to agglomeration as the driving force of urban formation and sudden growth is the expansion of long-distance trade. The German tradition view of cities as central places of trading areas naturally fits in with the idea that as the trading area expands, so does the city serving as its central place, irrespective of the presence or absence of agglomerative economies per se. In particular, the development of large cities is associated with the expansion of *long-distance trade*. It is Pirenne (1925) who is most frequently cited in this regard, due to his arguments linking the reemergence of long-distance trade and the relatively sudden expansion of medieval cities in Europe after 1000 A.D. But the argument has deeper roots than that.

Let us return to the question of the original formation of cities out of a uniform distribution, rather than the later question of the expansion of medieval European cities. Braudel (1973) distinguishes between "open" cities and "closed" cities. This distinction does not depend on the presence or absence of a wall, although a closed city is more likely to have one than an open city. An open city is one that is intimately connected economically to its immediately surrounding hinterland, archetypally, the self-sufficient neolithic village, recycling its night soil. The closed city is separated from its immediate hinterland and depends largely upon long-distance trade to sustain itself, archetypally, Renaissance Venice (also Singapore and Hong Kong). For Braudel, it is the existence of long-distance trade that allows for the separation of town and country and the "closure" of cities from their immediate hinterlands.

V. Gordon Childe (1942) argued that it was the ability to rely on long-distance trade that allowed ancient cities in Egypt and Mesopotamia to *dominate* their hinterlands in an exploitative manner, from the palace, the temple, and the granary, hidden within the walled citadel. Thus, it was not the economic externality of agglomeration, but the surplus accumulated from long-distance trade that allowed for the initial formation and growth of cities.[10] Braudel clearly sympathizes with this view in his remark, "[T]he town-country confrontation is the longest, running class struggle history has known."

Braudel refined this view and linked it explicitly to the German tradition through his vision of the hierarchy of central places. At the bottom are (open) agricultural villages, then the small town with its subordinate villages, then the provincial city with its ring of small towns, and then the national-imperial center, dominating the provinces and trading with the world at large.[11] Braudel (1984) eventually expanded this to a view of the entire world economy as a "set of sets," a series of such hierarchies, dominated by an ultimate central core (the "leading world city") with an ultimate periphery in the poorest and most isolated areas, a view further developed by Wallerstein (1979). Oscillations between core and periphery at this scale became for him the source of the longest of economic cycles, "la longue durée" (or long-term secular trend), lasting hundreds of years, an idea further discussed by Goldstein (1988). Without denying the association between large cities and long-distance trade, the advocates of the agglomerative perspective argue that the growth of long-distance trade followed the initial development of urban areas based on local agglomeration. Thus Mumford (1961) criticizes Pirenne explicitly for his theory of long-distance trade as the ultimate source of the growth of medieval European cities. Instead Mumford saw peace and protection of *local* markets afforded by the Church as the basis of medieval European, urban development.

> But note: the regular market, held once or sometimes twice a week under the protection of Bishop or Abbott, was an instrument of local life, not of international trade. So it should be no surprise that as early as 833, when long-distance trade was mostly in abeyance, Lewis the Pious in Germany gave a monastery permission to erect a mint for a market already in existence. The revival of trade in the eleventh century, then, was not the critical event that laid the foundations of the new medieval type of city: as I have shown, many new urban foundations antedate that fact, and more evidence could be added. Commercial zeal was rather a symptom of a more inclusive revival that was taking place in Western civilization; and that was partly a mark of the new sense of security that the walled town itself had helped to bring into existence. (Mumford, 1961, p. 254)

Of course an obvious response by Pirenne and his allies might be to agree that agglomeration laid a necessary foundation but that it was still the appearance of long-distance trade that was the stimulus and trigger of the actual urban growth.

1.3.2 The Mees Version of Pirenne's Hypothesis

A major effort to model the Pirenne hypothesis is due to Mees (1975). We begin with open, small towns in a localized landscape, after the Moorish and Viking invasions had broken apart the long-distance trading patterns of Western Europe. For a given region, population, P, is initially assumed to be constant and divided between farming, p_f, and towns, p_g. U_f and U_g are country and town utility levels, respectively, and t is the long-distance transportation cost. Above a certain level of t, there will be no long-distance trade, but as t declines below that level, such trade will appear and expand. Demographic dynamics depend on utility-maximizing migration, given by

$$\mathrm{d}p_f/\mathrm{d}t = p_f p_g \left(U_f - U_g\right) = -\mathrm{d}p_g/\mathrm{d}t. \tag{1.22}$$

Mees shows that when t is high and there is no trade, these dynamics can be depicted as in Fig. 1.7, where the only stable equilibrium is E_m, representing a mixture of town and country. He argues that as t declines, this curve shifts and may end up either as Fig. 1.8 or as Fig. 1.9, depending on the overall population density, the average productivity of the region, and the town–country productivity difference.

In Fig. 1.8, a region with high population density and a high town–country productivity difference has E_g as its only stable equilibrium and has completely specialized in urban production for long-distance trade.

In Fig. 1.9, just the opposite occurs because E_f is the only stable equilibrium and the region specializes in farming for long-distance trade. If the average level of

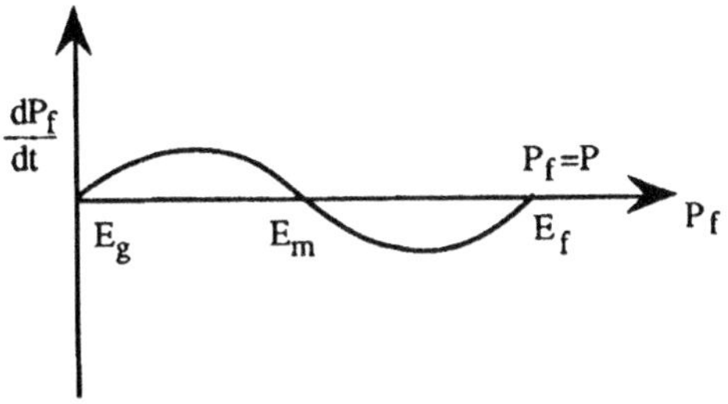

Fig. 1.7 No long-distance trade urban–rural equilibrium

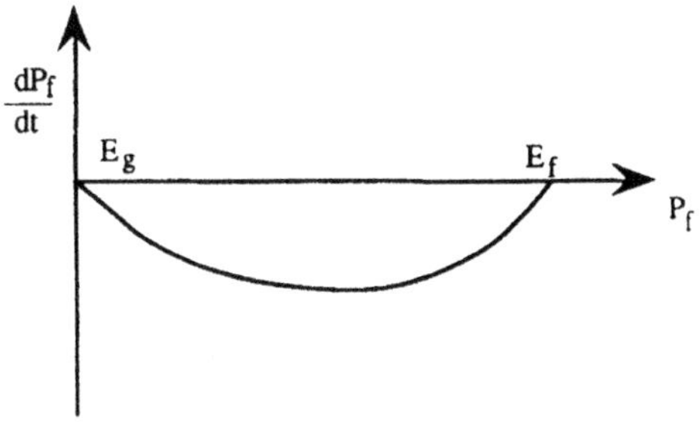

Fig. 1.8 Long-distance trading urban center

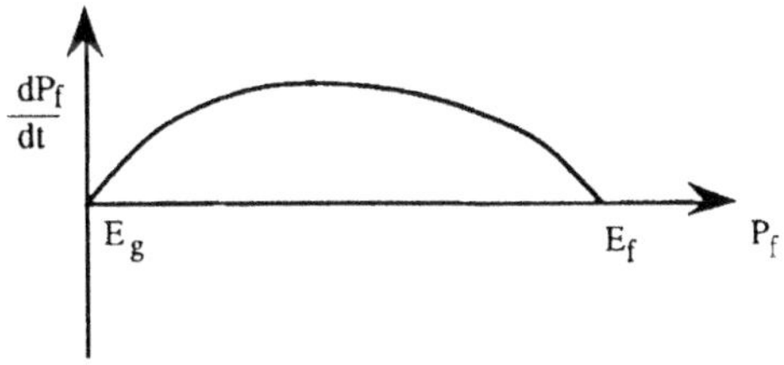

Fig. 1.9 Long-distance trading rural area

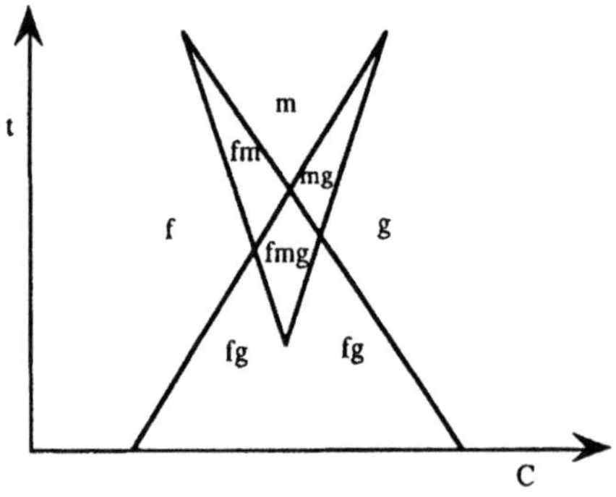

Fig. 1.10 Butterfly bifurcation set for long-distance trade model

productivity is high enough, and the other variables are at intermediate levels, then any of the three kinds of equilibria may be viable.

Mees argues that these results can be depicted in a Thom-type (1972) butterfly catastrophe whose four control variables form a four-dimensional bifurcation set. A projection of this set into the two-dimensional *t* and *C* space (where *C* is population density) is depicted in Fig. 1.10, with the possible equilibria, f, m, g, depicted for each zone of the space. The average productivity, q, produces the butterfly effect in which the triple equilibria occur. The sectoral productivity difference, Δq, is the bias factor that determines the tilt of the butterfly zone one way or the other.

Thus when *t* is high, the equilibrium will be m. But as *t* declines, it could become f or g, depending on *C* and the other factors, or even just remain mixed in the butterfly portion. Exogenous population change, by changing *C*, could trigger such shifts. In any case, it is the sudden shift of many local areas from all being mixed (small open towns in localized farming areas) to either purely urban (g) or purely rural (f); the decline in *t* represents the implicit dynamics of Pirenne's hypothesis.

1.3.3 Comparative Advantage and City Size

That there exist thresholds in the trading relations with the rest of the world which can be associated with sudden shifts in city size may reflect changes in the city's comparative advantage situation. Dendrinos (1980a) developed a model of such discontinuous city size changes arising from continuous changes in comparative advantage.

Given a production function and a position in the larger economy, the maximum utility level associated with different amounts of labor (and hence city sizes) is given by

$$V^* = v(L^{\mathrm{d}}), \tag{1.23}$$

where the inverse of v can be interpreted as the demand for labor, L^{d}. This V^* may be nonlinear, due to economies and diseconomies of urban scale (possibly reflecting variations in agglomerative effects), and even characterized by multiple local maxima.

Labor supply depends on factor rewards (v^s) and the level of comparative advantage of the city denoted by s. Thus L^s is labor supply

$$L^s = S^{-1}(s, V^s), \tag{1.24}$$

with S^{-1} smooth, twice differentiable, and possessing a smooth inverse. For a given s and L, there will be associated V^* and V^s. If $V^* > V^s$, there will be immigration and vice versa. When $V^* = V^s$, there will be an equilibrium. This s could depend on transportation costs of trade, thus linking this model to that of Mees.

If V^* has more than one local maximum, there can be multiple equilibria. In such cases, smooth changes in s, the level of comparative advantage, can lead to discontinuous changes in L, the equilibrium city labor force. This is depicted in Fig. 1.11.

The s curves represent labor supply curves for different levels of s. If labor supply were to increase from s_5 toward s_1, the city labor force would smoothly increase from L_5 to $L(b)_2$, beyond which it would discontinuously leap to slightly more than $L(a)_2$, and then on smoothly to L_1. In reverse, a decline in labor supply from s_1 to s_5 would see the labor force smoothly decline to $L(a)_4$, after which it would discontinuously decline to just below $L(b)_4$, beyond which it would smoothly decline to L_5. Clearly there is a hysteresis effect here. Also, of the three equilibria associated with s_3, the middle one is unstable. This model has a family resemblance to that of Papageorgiou (1980), as argued by Dendrinos and Rosser (1990).

1.3.4 Logistical Networks and Long-Distance Trade

Åke Andersson (1986) has proposed a major extension of the Pirenne–Mees hypothesis to the much broader context of what he calls "logistical networks." These are all

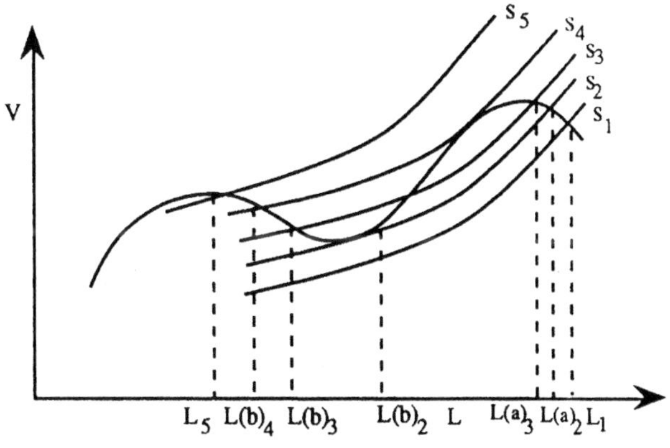

Fig. 1.11 Discontinuous urban comparative advantage and labor supply shifts

Fig. 1.12 Logistical revolutions

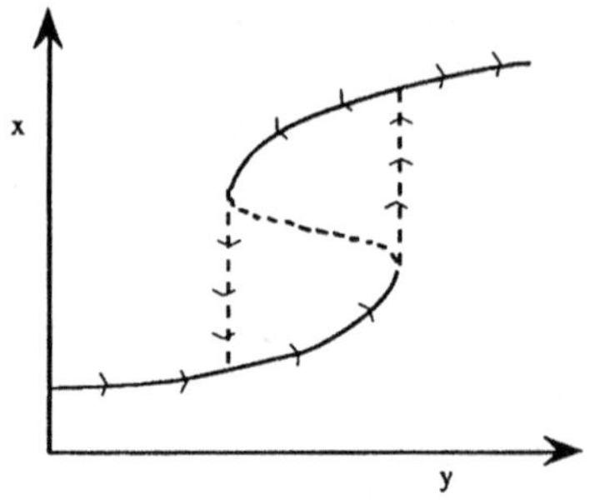

the factors that can facilitate interurban or interregional economic interactions, not just trade, but also financial transaction mechanisms and communication systems for information transfers. Andersson declares (1986, p. 1), "The great structural changes of production, location, trade, culture, and institutions are triggered by slow but steady changes in the logistical networks." In particular he argues that four such "logistical revolutions" have morphogenesized urban and regional structures over the last 1,000 years.

The first of these was that of Pirenne, a lowering of long-distance transportation costs and the rapid growth of cities such as Florence and Brussels from the eleventh century. The second logistical revolution arose from the development of state-backed, reliable banking and its associated transformation of trade relations, beginning in the sixteenth century, especially benefiting Amsterdam and London. The third involved a greater international division of labor based on the production technologies of the Industrial Revolution, beginning in the eighteenth century. Manchester especially manifested this. Finally in the late twentieth century we have the communications–information revolution with its headquarters in San Francisco and Tokyo. Each of these revolutions has been associated with a complete restructuring of the world system of city hierarchies.

To summarize this, he presents a general model of changes in commodity production, x, knowledge infrastructure, z, and network infrastructure, y, as functions of each other, depreciation rates, and various other constants and control variables. He argues that discontinuous changes in production, x, can arise from continuous changes in network infrastructure, y. This is depicted in Fig. 1.12 as a Thom-type (1972) fold catastrophe with hystersis effects. He argues that this represents the general form of a logistical revolution, with the actual path of commodity production following a logistic during a discontinuity.

1.4 A Possible Synthesis: The Role of Technological Change

1.4.1 Agglomeration, Logistical Networks, and Technology

The preceding discussion has not resolved the debate between the advocates of agglomeration and the advocates of long-distance trade as to the principal driving force of urbanization or de-urbanization. Both are important and are affected at different times and in different ways by technological change. Thus the development of economies of scale in sewage treatment plants encourages agglomeration, while improved septic tank technologies encourage deglomeration. Economies of scale in manufacturing might encourage urban specialization and expansion along with increased long-distance trade (the third logistical revolution), whereas the spread of computers and fax machines might encourage de-urbanization and localization (the fourth logistical revolution).

So we seek a synthesis, taking into account both effects and the impact of technological change upon the urbanization process. We consider a synthesis of several of the models discussed earlier with a model by Nijkamp (1983), although some of the earlier models already possess the potential for such a synthetic interpretation. Thus in the Isard (1977) model, if the technology parameter is assumed to represent the impact on long-distance trade of technological change, then it fits the bill. Also in the Mees (1975) model, if the urban–rural productivity difference (the bias factor) is viewed as reflecting urban agglomerative economies, then that model might fit the bill.

We shall consider our model in per capita terms and assume that total, but not urban, population is constant. Also we shall assume that the urban sector is measured relative to the rural sector, thus allowing us to ignore explicit modelling of the latter. Let $U =$ utility, $X =$ the export base (assumed to be related to total urban output by a fixed multiplier, $b > 1$), $L =$ the logistical network determining ease of long-distance trade and other interurban interactions, $I =$ infrastructure (assumed to drive the net agglomerative effect), $T =$ the technology or information level, $K =$ capital stock (indexed by sector), $C =$ consumption, and δ_i equals the ith sector's depreciation rate (assumed to be zero for sector T).

$$U = U(C, K, I), \tag{1.25}$$

$$X = X(I, L, T, K_x), \tag{1.26}$$

$$I = I(T, K_1), \tag{1.27}$$

$$L = L(T, K_{\mathrm{L}}^{-}), \tag{1.28}$$

$$T = T(K_{\mathrm{T}}), \tag{1.29}$$

$$K = K_x + K_1 + K_{\mathrm{L}} + K_{\mathrm{T}}, \tag{1.30}$$

$$bX = \mathrm{d}K/\mathrm{d}t + C + \Sigma\delta_i K_i. \tag{1.31}$$

Following Nijkamp (1983), the production relations are considered to be nonlinear in all arguments, with zones of increasing marginal productivity alternating with zones of decreasing marginal productivity beyond critical inflection points and also including time asymmetries that generate hysteresis effects. A presentation of

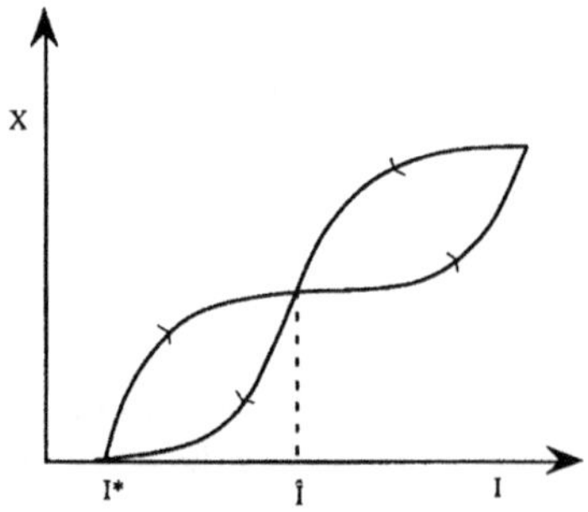

Fig. 1.13 Asymmetric nonlinear urban dynamics

such a partial effect can be seen in Fig. 1.13, with the relationship between I and X, drawn from Nijkamp. Changes in T can change the position of I, the critical inflection point, as well as I^*, the basic threshold level.

The dynamics will be driven by the solution to

$$\max U = \int_{t=0}^{\infty} U(C, K, I)\mathrm{e}^{rt}\mathrm{d}t, \tag{1.32}$$

where r is the time discount rate. Nijkamp presents a simpler version of this model because he has output purely as a function of technology (R & D), infrastructure, and capital, without any other interactions between sectors except for the intersectoral allocation of capital. His solution is that the shadow prices (marginal products) of capital in each sector should be equal. That holds here also, but the expression of these marginal products is more complicated because of the greater number of interactive effects between sectors.

Even in the simpler Nijkamp model, the presence of threshold effects, varying degrees of economies of urban scale, and time asymmetries lead to the possibility of "bang-bang" solutions to the optimal control problem, with discontinuous changes and patterns of growth followed by decline as technology and agglomeration interact, at times cooperatively and at times in conflict with each other. With our more complex model, these effects can also lead to chaotic dynamics as well.

1.4.2 Rome Was Not Built in a Day

And neither did it fall in a day.

Let us apply this synthetic view to one of the most spectacular of all urban expansions and declines, the rise and fall of Rome and the cities of its empire. This directly relates back to our discussion of the Pirenne hypothesis in which he argued that the political collapse of Rome itself in the fifth century did not cause the collapse of the Roman system of long-distance trade or the disappearance of Roman provincial cities. De-urbanization did not occur until the Moorish and Viking invasions finally broke down this trading system in the eighth century. However, we shall argue that what happened occurred in stages and involved both deglomerative effects as well as the decline of trade.

According to Edward Gibbon (1788), the city of Rome achieved a maximum population of around one million during the second and third centuries A.D. It declined to a minimum of 33,000 in the fourteenth century, after which growth resumed. At the "meridian," the large population was sustained by both a prodigious system of trade, supported by an impressive system of roads, and also over time increasingly an imperialistic exploitation of the provinces, along with an impressive system of hydraulic infrastructure undergirding the positive net agglomerative tendency.[12] The building and maintenance of such hydraulic infrastructure occurred throughout the empire at its "meridian" and can be considered one of its major positive achievements.

In his concluding chapter, Gibbon explicitly lists the decay and lack of maintenance of public buildings and public works as one of the major reasons for the "decline and fall" of Rome. The growth triggered by trade with and exploitation of the provinces led Rome to overexpand to the point that congestion overwhelmed the capacity of the infrastructure. This exacerbated the internal social and political conflicts which in turn fed the inability to defend against the "barbarians."[13] The inability to defend borders reduced the surplus available to Rome and further exacerbated its infrastructure maintenance problem. To quote Mumford (1961, p. 216):

> In sum, in the feats of engineering where Rome stood supreme in the aqueducts, the underground sewers, and the paved ways, their application was absurdly spotty and inefficient. By its very bigness and its rapacity, Rome defeated itself and never caught up with its own needs. There seems little doubt that the smaller provincial cities were better managed in these departments, just because they had not overpassed the human measure.

We see the Roman urban decline as going in at least two stages: the first due to deglomeration effects arising from congestion and the breakdown of infrastructure, the second due to the later collapse of long-distance trade. As noted above by Mumford, the congestion problems were less severe outside of Rome itself, but there is little doubt that after the political defeat of Rome in the fifth century, infrastructure maintenance in these provincial cities was also neglected and that there was a gradual decay of net agglomeration. This paved the way for the final de-urbanization after the collapse of the trading system in the eighth century.

Thus we can declare both Pirenne and Mumford correct. The medieval revival of European cities depended upon both the reemergence of a positive net agglomerative tendency and the revival of long-distance trade. More generally we can conclude that the morphogenesis of urban historical forms reflects a complex interplay and evolution of population, technological change, internal net agglomerative tendencies in cities, and interurban logistical networks and trade.

Notes

1. See Wilson (1981) for an excellent survey of catastrophe theory models in urban economics and a foreshadowing of the use of chaos theory also.
2. See Dendrinos and Rosser (1992) for a formal linking of these models.
3. Obviously the Great Depression provides a likely alternative explanation.
4. This model was much criticized by Alexander (1979) and Baker (1979) on grounds of extreme vagueness and atheoreticity (how does one measure "external threat"?), following the more general criticisms of catastrophe theory by Zahler and Sussman (1977). Many of these urban applications can be criticized on similar grounds.
5. The intraurban variation draws heavily on the multidisciplinary model of Lowry (1964).
6. Smith recognized both agglomeration (external economies) and economies of scale (internal economies) as factors in the development of cities. He argued that an existing city could attract more economic activity related to its existing economic base (agglomeration); while his famous dictum, "the division of labor is limited by the extent of the market," emphasizes that a large city provides a large market and hence ample scope for the division of labor and the improved "wealth of nations" pertaining thereto.
7. Even today the major cause of infant mortality in less-developed countries is from water-borne diseases whose origins are from human waste.
8. Even without discontinuities in steady-state city sizes, such a model can generate chaotic migration dynamics as shown by Day, Dasgupta, Datta, and Nugent (1987) in an urban–rural model of the Harris–Todaro (1970) type.
9. This implies there is an "optimal city size," an idea with a long history in urban economics (Hirsch and Goodman, 1972).
10. Childe (1942) argued that it was the long-distance trade in copper and tin (not located together anywhere in the Mediterranean or Middle East) that was specifically responsible for the initial emergence of cities. Copper and tin make bronze, and thus the Bronze Age was the first urban age. And bronze weapons were useful for conquering, subduing, and enslaving the hinterland populace.
11. This four-level hierarchy corresponds to the original such model developed by the Abbasid geographer, al-Muqqadisi (Hassan, 1972). Christaller identified seven levels in Southern Germany and Lösch ten since he allowed overlapping ones.
12. The most impressive of all these was the Cloaca Maxima, the oldest, largest, and most central sewer, *still in use after 2500 years* (Mumford, 1961, p. 214).
13. This is consistent with Marx and Engels (1848) who saw the collapse of Rome as due to internal class struggle, culminating in the general collapse of Ancient Slavery and its replacement by feudalism.

Chapter 2
The New Economic Geography Approach and Other Views

To say that urbanization is the result of localized external economies carries more than a hint of Moliére's doctor, who explained that opium induces sleep thanks to its dormitive properties. Or as a sarcastic physicist remarked to an economist at one interdisciplinary meeting, "So what you're saying is that firms agglomerate because of agglomeration effects.
Paul R. Krugman (1995, Development, Geography, and Economic Theory, p. 52)

Paul Krugman has clarified the microeconomic underpinnings of both spatial economic agglomerations and regional imbalances at national and international levels. He has achieved this with a series of remarkably original papers and books that succeed in combining imperfect competition, increasing returns, and transportation costs in new and powerful ways. Yet, not everything was new in New Economic Geography.
Masahisa Fujita and Jacques-François Thisse (2010, "New Economic Georgraphy: An appraisal on the occasion of Paul Krugman's 2008 Nobel Prize in Economic Sciences," Regional Science and Urban Economics, Abstract).

2.1 The Setting

In the previous chapter we presented a wide variety of models showing how interactions between agglomeration and long-distance trade influenced the historical development of cities. The presence of nonlinearities most clearly associated with increasing returns of one sort or another lay at the foundation of the discontinuous bifurcations underlying this historical process and its actual historical ruptures. However, since 1991 a literature has appeared that emphasizes different aspects of these ideas, focusing on the increasing returns within a context of monopolistic competition as the source of the nonlinearities and agglomerative tendencies underlying the development of urban centers. This approach ultimately depends on demand-side effects rather than supply-side effects. Cities arise not due to production externalities, but due to consumers favoring a variety of goods, with greater

J.B. Rosser, *Complex Evolutionary Dynamics in Urban-Regional and Ecologic-Economic Systems*, DOI 10.1007/978-1-4419-8828-7_2,

product differentiation occurring within larger urban areas. Cities arise not because of production advantages, but because of the lure of "bright lights" in the big city.

The workhorse model of this approach since 1991 has been the model of monopolistic competition due to Avinash Dixit and Joseph Stiglitz (1977). It was used by Paul Krugman (1979, 1980) to provide an approach to analyzing increasing returns in international trade. This effort, in combination with related work by others (Brander, 1981; Grossman and Helpmann, 1991), would come to be called the New International Trade theory, and the first portion of the citation for Paul Krugman when he won the 2008 Nobel Prize in economics emphasized this breakthrough on his part. It was not illogical then that he would follow the path of the previous Nobel Prize winner in international trade theory, Bertil Ohlin (1933), in moving from international trade to regional economics, aka economic geography, in applying the same model.

While others applied the Dixit–Stiglitz model to regional economics prior to him (Abdel-Rahman, 1988; Fujita, 1988) in the field journal *Regional Science and Urban Economics*, it is not surprising that attention would go to him when he did so without citing their efforts when he made his own application of it in his 1991 article in the *Journal of Political Economy* that would be cited in the second part of the statement about his Nobel Prize, and he would be hailed as the "father of the new economic geography."[1] While he would later coauthor with Fujita on various occasions and then cite his work, he has never cited any of the work presented in the previous chapter, not one single item discussed in that chapter. In the world of Krugman, none of this ever happened, or if it did, it was of no importance whatsoever.

This author does not know exactly what to make of this, but can attest that on more than one occasion he made efforts to get Krugman to acknowledge the existence of this earlier literature, much of which the astute reader will realize was carried out by noneconomists and published in noneconomics journals, although not all of it. One such occasion was in a public setting in the early 1990s at an American Economic Association session that Krugman chaired on complexity economics in which he presented certain ideas related to this that would appear in his 1996 book *The Self-Organizing Economy*. In front of roughly 100 people I asked him if he would be willing to acknowledge some of the unmentioned sources of what he had presented, to which he replied, "We can discuss sources later, next question," and that was the end of that, to this very day. Later this author would send him a draft of my review of his book quoted above (Krugman, 1995), which appeared not too long afterwards (Rosser, 1996) and to which he never replied. This review took him to task much as he is being now for not mentioning any of this literature, and it concluded with the following sentence: "If Paul Krugman is the emperor of the new economic geography, then he is an emperor without clothes."

Indeed, his attitude is fairly well summarized in the quotation from the beginning of the chapter and from that book. While in his 1991 article and in various later writings he recognizes that many have invoked production effects and externalities, going all the way back at least to the work of Alfred Marshall (Marshall and

Paley Marshall, 1879; Marshall, 1919; Belussi and Caldari, 2009),[2] he dismisses such approaches for an alleged lack of mathematical and theoretical rigor, suggesting that they are ultimately circular and empty black boxes, despite a considerable empirical literature studying the subject. His quote from the sarcastic physicist about agglomeration being due to "agglomeration effects" amounts to the high point of this argument, but I leave it to the reader to decide if the sorts of arguments discussed in the previous chapter are totally lacking in mathematical or theoretical rigor.

Now it must be admitted that for some of these models part of Krugman's argument may hold. Thus, while in much of his 1995 book he dismisses earlier work by such figures as Pred (1966) as being not mathematical, he also argues (without citing any literature that he might be referring to) that arguments that can be fitted clearly into conventional neoclassical economic theory are superior. Indeed, this is the great advantage of the Dixit–Stiglitz model as he presents it, not that it is more realistic than other models (in places he admits that its realism is severely limited), but that it is a model that is consistent with standard economic theory, bringing the shaggy dog of increasing returns into the nicely kept house of that theory. Nevertheless, while none of these models invoke the demand-side effects associated with the Dixit–Stiglitz model, many are by economists and provide rigorous mathematical models based on production-side agglomerative effects that closely resemble results presented by Krugman in various of his later works, particularly Papageorgiou and Smith (1983) and Weidlich and Haag (1987). We shall consider his versions of some of this analysis but will note now that it remains a professional scandal that Krugman has to this day never acknowledged the existence of any of this literature, some of which have appeared in economics journals, notably Papageorgiou and Smith in *Econometrica*. There simply is no excuse for this.

Before moving on to discuss the details of how this approach works (and it is able to provide useful insights), I would like to mention how in his 1995 book Krugman dismisses both the earlier nonmathematical literature Pred (1966) while simply pretending that the literature from the 1980s (Papageorgiou and Smith, 1983; Weidlich and Haag, 1987) discussed in this book does not exist. He begins the book by comparing the earlier students of agglomeration (and of economic development as well) to explorers of the African coast in the 1500s. They had maps showing portions of the interior of Africa with real features shown, but also with many errors, such as the presence of nonexistent mythical creatures. Then as knowledge of mapmaking improved, later maps dropped all the information about the interior as it was deemed not to be sufficiently reliable. The pearls of wisdom were lost, until finally in the 1800s explorers with improved technology explored the interior and provided accurate maps that reinstated the previous knowledge, but on a solid foundation. Krugman openly compares himself to these later mapmakers, thereby implicitly not only putting down the earlier figures for their weak mathematics and theory but also simply ignoring all the other "mapmakers" who were working with advanced methods prior to him, but whom he conveniently ignored in his papers in the most widely read journals.

We shall dispense with any further polemics on this unfortunate matter and will proceed to consider the contents of and uses to which this Dixit–Stiglitz approach to the new economic geography (NEG) have been put in subsequent sections, along with some related controversies and issues.

2.2 The Three Returns to Scale

As discussed in the previous chapter, the emergence and existence of spatial concentrations of human population ultimately involves some form of economies of scale to be gained by their so concentrating. These returns to scale broadly take two forms, with one of those subsequently having a further subdivision. The first two are *internal* and *external* economies of scale, a distinction first clearly made by Alfred Marshall (1879), with external economies also taking on this other label of *agglomerative economies*. In turn, external economies of scale are divided between those that occur between firms within a single industry, often called *localization economies*, and those that occur across industries and are associated with the size of the urban area, also called unsurprisingly, *urbanization economies*. Marshall's discussion of the first of these tends to occur using the language of Adam Smith, attributing the internal economies of scale to the division of labor. Regarding external economies, he largely discussed those associated with localization economies, using the term *industrial districts* in most of his discussions. He did not analyze the larger-scale urbanization external economies, and this distinction became more fully developed later as by Hoover and Vernon (1959) and by Chinitz (1961).

The first of these can be characterized as follows. Let production by a firm of a given good i be given by

$$Q_i = f(L_1, \ldots, L_n), \tag{2.1}$$

with Q being output and the Ls being factor inputs. There will exist internal economies of scale for this good by this firm if for any $k > 1$,

$$f(kL_1, \ldots, kL_n) > kf(L_1, \ldots, L_n). \tag{2.2}$$

While Smith emphasized division of labor, the full development of such internal economies of scale in later industrial economies came to be associated with large-scale machinery worked on by many specialized workers, with the development of the assembly line bringing this to its culmination.

Most literature on urbanization does not emphasize this form of economies of scale much as a major source. Part of this is because this formulation is usually set at the firm level, and firms can operate in many locales, with the internal economies coming from organization in the form of managerial economies of scale. What is relevant for urbanization are such economies as they exist for a single production plant within a firm. If such a production facility produces a good that is exported from the area, thus constituting part of the *economic base* of the area, then the needs of its workers and their families for many goods and services of a local sort can lead to the development of the secondary economic activities associated with the export base through a standard Keynesian-style multiplier. Thus, if a plant can become sufficiently large, it can support an urban population that is somewhat larger than the number of its employees.

Probably the major reason that one does not read much regarding such internal economies for urbanization is that there are distinct limits to such internal economies ultimately in all industries. Indeed, it is unlikely that there has ever been a single production facility whose workforce has exceeded 100,000, although the Lenin Steel Works in Magnitogorsk in Siberia employed as many as 60,000 workers at the height of its production activities.[3] This can give us a likely outer limit for such economies as the source for urbanization. If the typical family has four persons, then the workers and their families at a plant the size of the Lenin Steel Works would directly support almost 250,000. Assuming an export base multiplier of 2, this means that a plant such as that could support a city nearly up to half a million people, a pretty good size, but certainly far below by that of the largest cities, indeed probably two orders of magnitude less than the most expansive estimates of the population of metropolitan Tokyo, the world's largest urban agglomeration. Of course, some of these heavy industries with substantial plant-level internal economies of scale also exhibit localization economies, such as in the auto industry in Detroit and the steel industry in Pittsburgh in the past.

Localization economies were the main focus of Marshall in his discussion of industrial districts, and in his 1919 *Industry and Trade* he contrasted them with internal economies not as sources of urbanization per se, but rather in a contrast with American industry, seen as the rival that was to be overcome in any effort to advance British industry in the aftermath of World War I. The US economy was characterized by firms exhibiting internal economies of scale, whereas the British economy was characterized by clusters of small firms and plants within the industrial districts for particular industries such as cotton textiles in Lancashire, woolen textiles in Yorkshire, or cutlery in Sheffield (Belussi and Caldari, 2009). Such localization economies can be characterized as existing for good i if

$$Q_{ix} = f(L_1, \ldots, L_n, Q_{iy}), \tag{2.3}$$

with Q_{ix} being the quantity of good i produced by firm (plant) x and Q_{iy} being quantity of good i produced by firm (plant) y, with these plants being located in the same urban area.

Between his books of 1879 and 1919 as well as in the various editions of his *Principles of Economics*, 8th edition being in 1920, Marshall identified most of the sources of these localization economies that exist, a point that Krugman (1993) largely recognizes. Belussi and Caldari (2009, p. 337) list the following such identifiable sources found in Marshall's work.

(1) Hereditary skill. "The mysteries of the trade become no mysteries; but are as it were in the air, and children learn many of them unconsciously" (Marshall, 1920, p. 271).
(2) The growth of subsidiary trades, usually of inputs. Subsidiary firms "grow up in the neighborhood, supplying it with implements and materials, organizing its traffic, and in many ways conducing to the economy of its material (ibid.).
(3) Use of highly specialized machinery, with high division of labor in a district "in which there is a large aggregate of production of the same kind, even though no individual capital employed in the trade be very large" (ibid.).
(4) Local market for special skill, wherein there is "a constant market for skill" (ibid.), and factories do not have a problem finding workers. Krugman (1993) emphasizes that this is a two-way street, with workers possessing the skill willing to work there even though the wages might be slightly lower because of the lower risk of losing a job. If the firm they work for closes, there are others to go to work for, as has been seen in Silicon Valley in California.
(5) Industrial leadership, which "derives from an industrial atmosphere" that stimulates "more vitality than might have seemed probable in view of the incessant change of techniques" (Marshall, 1919, p. 287).
(6) Introduction of novelties into the production process, with good ideas being quickly adopted because they are "in the air" of the district working through its social networks: "If one man starts a new idea, it is taken up by others and combined with suggestions of their own; and thus it becomes the source of further new ideas" (Marshall, 1920, p. 271).

Urbanization economies can be characterized at a simple level by changing (2.3) to be externalities across industries. However, they are more frequently simply modeled as economies for a given industry as a function of the size of the urban area itself directly, and Ellison, Glaeser, and Kerr (2010) show that this Marshallian industrial district's model empirically explains industrial location and urban-scale patterns quite strongly, without any reference to any use of the Krugman application of the demand-side Dixit–Stiglitz approach. We shall now turn to how the Dixit–Stiglitz model has been used to model this phenomenon more specifically.

2.3 The Dixit–Stiglitz Model of Monopolistic Competition

In discussing the Dixit–Stiglitz model, we shall draw from the approach of Fujita, Krugman, and Venables (1999, Chap. 4), henceforth to be labled "FKV." While they grant that the model is "grossly unrealistic," they aver that it is "tractable and flexible" and leads to a "very suggestive set of results" (FKV, p. 45). The key to the model is the idea that utility is tied to the diversity of products available, and this diversity increases with the size of an urban area, which becomes the basis for the agglomerative increasing returns. People move to the big city to work because of the diversity of products available for them as consumers, not because of any productive efficiency in the places of work that they might be employed in.

Central to the argument is the formulation of the utility function, assumed identical across agents, which is of the CES form. Letting A be agriculture consumed and $m(i)$ be consumption of the ith manufactured good with n the range of such manufactured goods, utility is given by

$$U = A^{1-\mu}\left[\int_0^1 m(i)^\rho \mathrm{d}i\right]^{\mu/\rho}, \quad 0 < \rho < 1. \tag{2.4}$$

As with CES functions, a crucial variable is the elasticity of substitution, σ, which happens to equal $1/1-\rho$. This determines the strength of the agglomerative effect and falls with σ.

The budget constraint is given by

$$Y = p^A A + \int_0^n p(i)m(i)\mathrm{d}i, \tag{2.5}$$

where the ps are the respective prices of agricultural and manufactured goods. A price index can be constructed as

$$G = \left[\int_0^n p(i)^{1-\sigma}\mathrm{d}i\right]^{1/(1-\sigma)} = p^M n^{1/(1-\sigma)}. \tag{2.6}$$

Given all this, maximizing (2.4) subject to (2.5) yields uncompensated demands

$$A = (1-\mu)Y/p^A, \tag{2.7}$$

$$m(j) = \mu Y p(j)^{-\sigma}/G^{-(\sigma-1)}, \quad \text{for } j \in [0, 1], \tag{2.8}$$

associated with indirect utility function

$$U = \mu^\mu(1-\mu)^{1-\mu} Y G^{-\mu}(p^A)^{-(1-\mu)}. \tag{2.9}$$

Introducing this into a spatial context to analyze regional economic activity, transportation cost must be considered, with Krugman in his key 1991 paper introducing the notion of the volume of goods arriving at a destination declining linearly with distance from their production site like an iceberg melting over a distance it travels in water.[4] If production is at site r, then transport cost of M from r to site s is given by ${T_{rs}}^M$, and the delivered price index is given by

$$G_s = \left[\sum_{i=1}{}^R n_r({p_r}^M {T_{rs}}^M)^{1-\sigma}\right]^{1/(1-\sigma)}, \quad s = 1, \ldots, R, \tag{2.10}$$

which implies that the quantity of r variety manufactured good consumed at s will be

$$q_r^M = \mu \sum_{i=1}{}^R Y_s({p_r}^M {T_{rs}}^M)^{-\sigma} {G_s}^{\sigma-1} {T_{rs}}^M. \tag{2.11}$$

Assuming Chamberlinian monopolistic competition, with F being fixed input requirement and c^M being marginal input requirement, the labor input for M will be

$$1^M = F + c^M q^M, \tag{2.12}$$

implying an equilibrium labor input of

$$1^* = F + c^M q^* = F\sigma, \tag{2.13}$$

derived from the profit-maximizing output

$$q^* = F(\sigma - 1)/c^M. \tag{2.14}$$

This implies a "home market effect" due to the nonexistent transport costs of home-produced goods (identified by Ohlin in 1933), which implies that as manufacturing increases, there is a gain in the real manufacturing wage at the production site r. Nominal manufacturing wage at r is expressed as,

$$w_r{}^M = \left[(\sigma - 1)/\sigma\right]\left[(\mu/q^*)\sum{}_{i=1}{}^R Y_s(T_{rs}{}^M)^{1-\sigma} G_s{}^{\sigma-1}\right]^{1-\sigma}. \tag{2.15}$$

Real wage, ω, is then given by

$$\omega_r{}^M = w_r{}^M G_r^{-\mu}(p_r{}^A)^{-(1-\mu)}. \tag{2.16}$$

If there is no limit on this effect, then the economy will simply collapse into a single point. This can be avoided by imposing a "no black hole condition," which can be assured by assuming that

$$(\sigma - 1)/\sigma = \rho > \mu. \tag{2.17}$$

With this assumption holding, a spatially dispersed economy can exist and persist, and we have the pieces in place to study the implications of the new economic geography.

2.4 Bifurcations of the NEG Core–Periphery Model

A major focus of the important 1991 paper by Krugman was to show the emergence of an urbanized area out of an even distribution of population through bifurcations of the system. This emerged urban area is viewed as a core in which manufacturing becomes concentrated, with the other areas containing only agricultural workers.

To carry out this analysis, we shall consider a two-region system. We introduce λ to represent the fraction of manufacturing workers that are in a region 1, implying that $(1-\lambda)$ is the share of manufacturing workers for region 2. Given this and (2.4)–(2.17), equilibrium for the system is given by the following eight equations, which represent, respectively, the incomes for the two regions, the price indices for the two regions, nominal wages for the two regions, and real wages for the two regions, with both nominal and real wages being those for manufacturing (without superscripts), again from Fujita, Krugman, and Venables (1999, p. 65).

$$Y_1 = \mu\lambda w_1 + (1-\mu)/2, \tag{2.18}$$

$$Y_2 = \mu(1-\lambda)w_2 + (1-\mu)/2, \tag{2.19}$$

$$G_1 = [\lambda {w_1}^{1-\sigma} + (1-\lambda(w_2T)^{1-\sigma}]^{1/1-\sigma}, \tag{2.20}$$

$$G_2 = [\lambda(w_1T)^{1-\sigma} + (1-\lambda){w_2}^{1-\sigma}]^{1/1-\sigma}, \tag{2.21}$$

$$w_1 = [Y_1{G_1}^{\sigma-1} + Y_2{G_2}^{\sigma-1}T^{1-\sigma}]^{1/\sigma}, \tag{2.22}$$

$$w_2 = [Y_1{G_1}^{\sigma-1}T^{1-\sigma} + Y_2{G_2}^{\sigma-1}]^{1/\sigma}, \tag{2.23}$$

$$\omega_1 = w_1{G_1}^{-\mu}, \tag{2.24}$$

$$\omega_2 = w_2{G_2}^{-\mu}. \tag{2.25}$$

Bifurcations of this system are driven by variations in transport costs, T. With high T, both regions supply themselves with manufactures. As T declines, a bifurcation occurs with multiple equilibria possible, and as T declines further, the definite pattern of one region specializing in manufacturing (and presumably urbanized) with the other purely agricultural emerges. This pattern is shown in Figs. 2.1, 2.2, and 2.3 (Fujita, Krugman, and Venables, 1999, pp. 66–67), with for all of them the horizontal axis being λ, the share of manufacturing in region 1, and the vertical axis being ω_1–ω_2, the real manufacturing wage in region 1 minus that in region 2.

In the intermediate case, the even distribution outcome still exists and is stable, but there exist two unstable equilibria on each side of it, so that if the share is beyond those on one end or the other, an uneven distribution will emerge. This pattern of bifurcations is shown in Fig. 2.4 (Fujita, Krugman, and Venables,

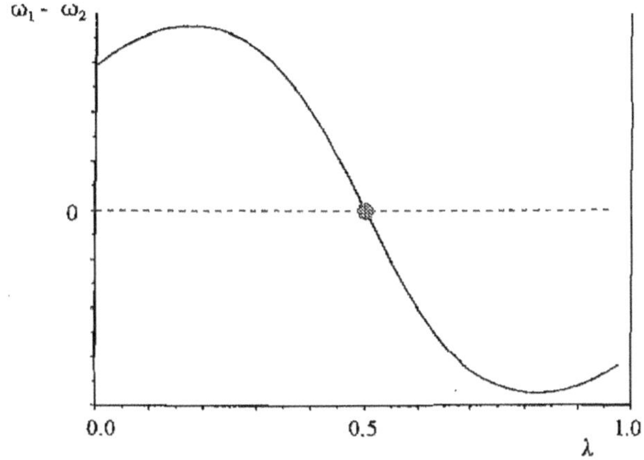

Fig. 2.1 Even distribution

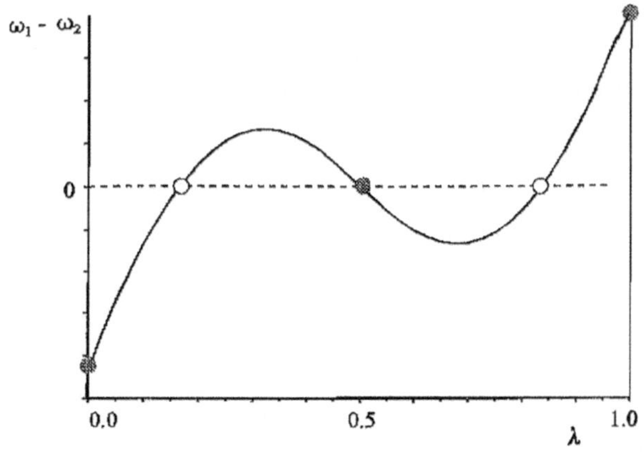

Fig. 2.2 Intermediate case (2 region case)

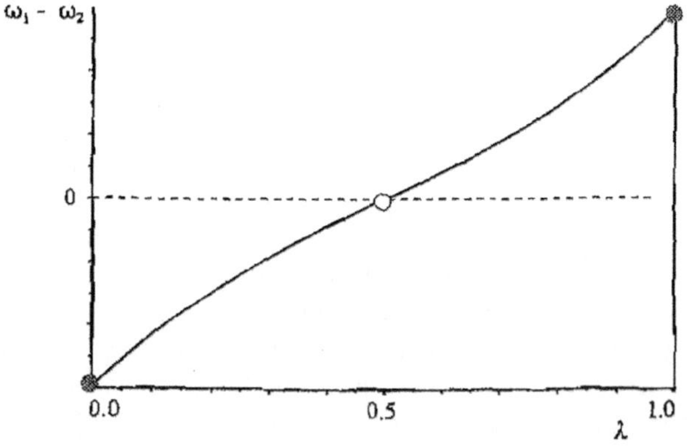

Fig. 2.3 Manufacturing concentrated in region 1

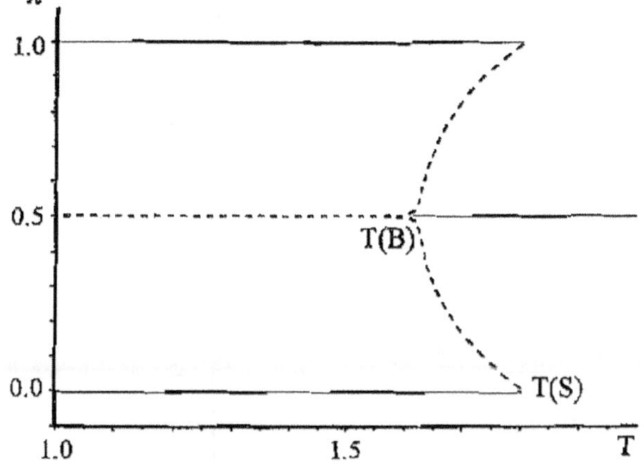

Fig. 2.4 Tomahawk bifurcation

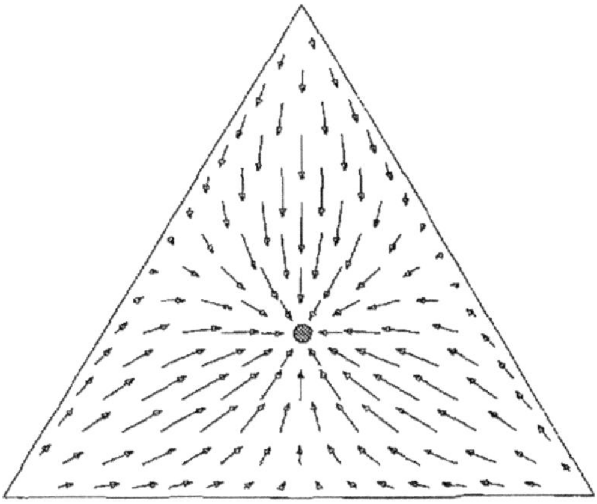

Fig. 2.5 Even distribution between regions

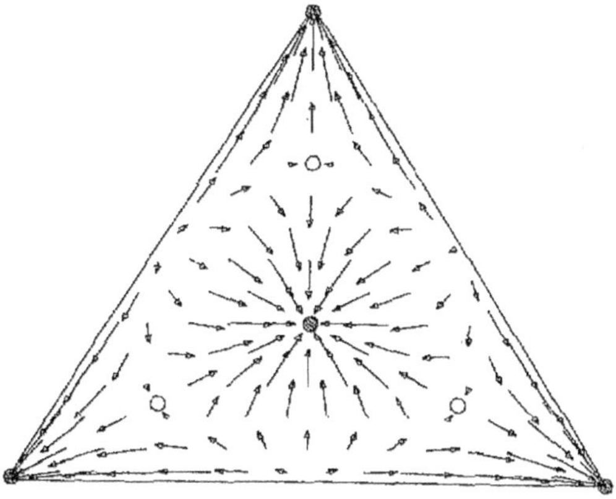

Fig. 2.6 Intermediate case (3 region case)

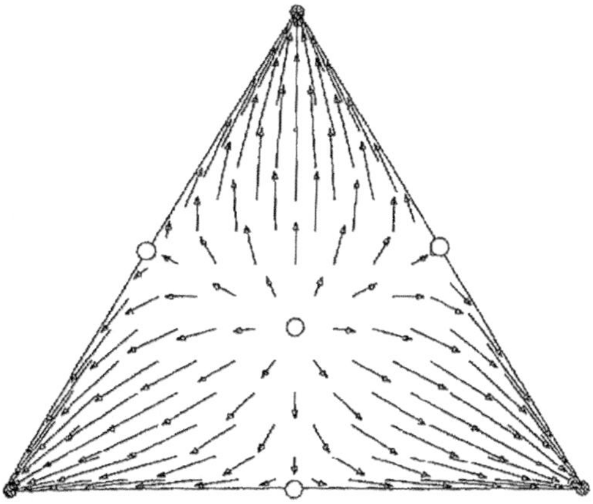

Fig. 2.7 Strong concentration in three regions

2003, p. 68), a "tomahawk" bifurcation, with transport cost on the horizontal axis and the manufacturing shares of the regions shown on the vertical axis.

If one extends this analysis to the three-region case, one gets a similar set of results, three cases ranging from even distribution, through an intermediate case of multiple equilibria, to one of a single region emerging as the core center. These are shown in Figs. 2.5, 2.6, and 2.7 (Fujita, Krugman, and Venables, 1999, pp. 80–81). Note the close similarity of this analysis to that of Weidlich and Haag (1987), as shown in Figs. 1.2, 1.3, and 1.4.

2.5 The Core–Periphery Model at the Global Level

The core–periphery model based on agglomeration reflects a long tradition of studying cumulative processes across trading regions (Rosenstein-Rodan, 1943; Perroux, 1955; Myrdal, 1957; Dendrinos and Rosser, 1992; Matsuyama, 1995; Fujita and Thisse, 2002). Closely linked to the models of endogenous growth, this idea has also been extended using models based on the Dixit–Stiglitz model as laid out above (Baldwin, 1999; Martin and Ottaviano, 1999; Puga, 1999), with these arguments being summarized in *Economic Geography and Public Policy* Baldwin, Forslid, Martin, Ottaviano, and Robert-Nicoud (2003), henceforth BFMOR. It is useful at this point before proceeding further to clarify some of the features of what has been derived so far, which are familiar from our earlier discussions of catastrophic processes in Rosser (2000a, Chap. 2), reappearing in this volume as Appendix A.

The first of these is *circular causality*. This arises from both demand-side features due to the positive feedback of increased diversity of goods and cost-side effects due to the magnifying home market effect, although in some broader applications one or the other of these may not be operative.

Another is *endogenous asymmetry*. This is the feature in which a lowering of transport costs brings about the bifurcation in which one region specializes in manufacturing while the other does not, with a divergence in real incomes arising from this. In the broader BFMOR view, this lowering of transport costs can also be associated with an increase in economic integration or freer trade at a global level in terms of international trade.

Another is *catastrophic agglomeration*. This is simply the process that develops after a bifurcation point is passed that results in the endogenous asymmetry. Symmetry of even development across regions is broken, and there is a concentration of the industrial growth in one of the regions.

Another is *locational hysteresis*. This is associated with the multiple equilibria arising from the tomahawk bifurcation. Once a bifurcation is passed and catastrophic agglomeration occurs, it is not so easily undone by a reversal of the underlying trends of parameter evolution.

Yet another is *hump-shaped agglomeration rents*. This is essentially a measure of the difference in real wages in the two regions that arises after the catastrophic agglomeration occurs. However, this reflects a feature we have not observed previously particularly. This feature implies that while initially there is an increase in the difference from zero to a positive number as transportation costs decline, eventually this difference will turn around and start declining after some point as the transportation costs continue to decline with it, disappearing again when those costs reach zero. After all, it is the existence of positive transportation costs that is crucial to the existence of the home market effect, which disappears if those transportation costs are zero. In effect, in this extreme case, the two regions have effectively collapsed into one from the standpoint of regional economics, as it is the existence of transportation costs that allows for the differentiation between regions in the first place.

Finally there is the possibility of *self-fulfilling expectations*. In a situation where the system is in the "overlap" zone of multiple equilibria from an initial symmetry, expectations of agents can put a region into one side or the other, with reallocations possible. That has been implicitly a matter of a random shock, but that shock may itself be due to some actions by agents in one or the other of the regions to make it move first to gain an edge in the industrialization process.

In BFMOR (Chap. 7), the model is expanded to bring in endogenous growth with investment in fixed capital and learning. A particularly interesting model is derived based on *local spillovers*, which differs in certain features from what we have seen previously.[5] In particular, the tomahawk bifurcation reverses itself so that there is no longer a zone of five equilibria. This is seen in Fig. 2.8 (Baldwin, Forslid, Martin, Ottaviano, and Robert-Nicoud, 2003, p. 179), in which S_K now represents the share of industrial capital stock in one region versus the other, and $\Phi = 1/T$ from the earlier analysis. That is, Φ can be viewed as the degree of "trade openness" or integration associated with lower transport costs.

This model has similar features as that of the basic core–periphery model, with the main exception being that there is no longer the ability for self-fulfilling expectations to effectuate a reallocation once the bifurcation point has passed. This

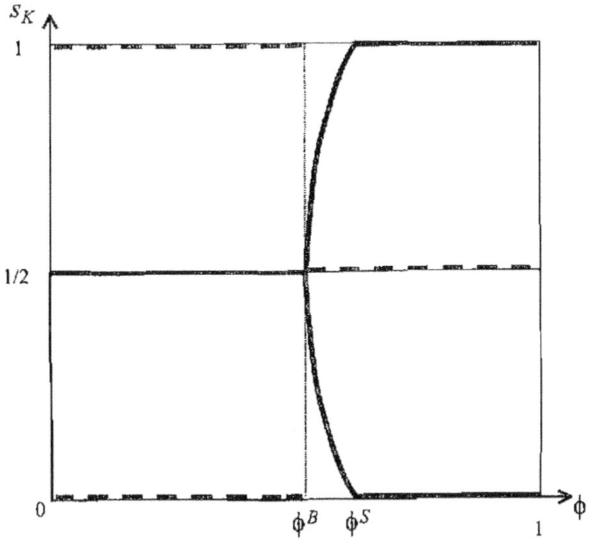

Fig. 2.8 Tomahawk bifurcation with local spillovers

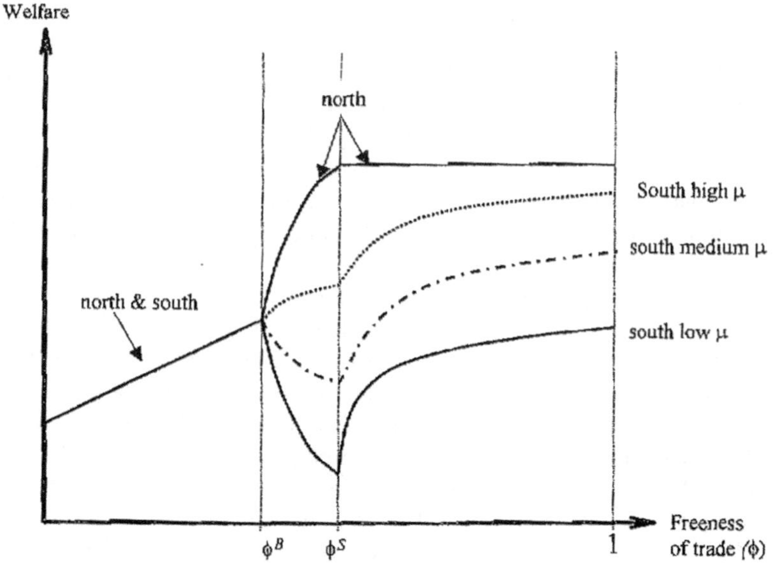

Fig. 2.9 Can the periphery gain from agglomeration?

is tied to the reversal of the tomahawk bifurcation. Intuitively, with fixed capital and reinforcement due to learning in the labor force, the distinct equilibria are now more seriously entrenched and cannot be so easily restructured.

Figure 2.9 (Baldwin, Forslid, Martin, Ottaviano, and Robert-Nicoud, 2003, p. 185) provides a broader picture of this outcome, with the industrialized region being labeled "north" and the agricultural region being labeled "south." The parameter μ is the same as in earlier equations in this chapter and plays an important role. Thus, in all cases the breaking of the symmetry at the bifurcation leads to a regional divergence of incomes with the north doing better than the south. However, whether the south actually experiences an initial decline in income or not depends on its relation to the industrial sector. It can fall or it can rise, but once the "sustain" point is reached, it will rise.[6] But it will more rapidly approach the income level of the north if μ is higher in the south. The more it purchases industrial goods, in effect the more it can take advantage of the economies of scale that are occurring in the agglomerating region, with its purchases reinforcing those returns to scale.

2.6 Chaotic Dynamics in a Discrete Version of the Core–Periphery Model

It is well known that for many systems that chaotic dynamics can occur for cases that are discrete with one less dimension than for the case of a continuous version. The literature we have discussed so far have involved continuous dynamics. None of the models discussed have been shown to exhibit chaotic dynamics. However, indeed, core–periphery models along the lines that have been presented here so far have been shown capable of exhibiting chaotic dynamics when in discrete form (Currie and Kubin, 2006; Commendatore, Currie, and Kubin, 2007; Commendatore, Kubin, and Petraglia, 2009; Commendatore and Kubin, 2010). While the second of these involves footloose capital between the regions, we shall look more closely at the first of these, which suggests that some of the generalizations made for the continuous model may not be robust considering a discrete version. In particular, destabilization may occur for the case of high transport costs in contrast with the continuous model.

Currie and Kubin (2006) draw on the FKV model as presented above for their analysis. Their change in the model involves two elements. One is to introduce a migration speed parameter, γ, and also to make migration a discrete process. It is the combination of these two changes that alters the qualitative dynamics of the system. It does not do so for the low transport cost case, where changing migration speeds within the discrete formulation merely changes how rapidly the system converges onto a particular core–periphery equilibrium pattern. However, for the high transport cost case, the qualitative dynamics change.

In particular, higher migration speeds can lead the system to overshoot the symmetric equilibrium if it does not start from there initially, which also emphasizes that the system is sensitive to starting-point conditions. If such an overshoot occurs, then it is possible for cycles to emerge where workers migrate back and forth, with the possibility of a core–periphery outcome also obtaining. As the migration speed increases or the transport costs increase, period-doubling bifurcations can occur, and chaotic dynamics can emerge. Such an outcome for rising transport costs for a given set of values of σ (the taste for diversity), μ (the share of manufacturing), and the labor supply, L, is shown in Fig. 2.10 (Currie and Kubin, 2006, p. 262), with 2.10a showing the starting point near a symmetric fixed point, while 2.10b shows the starting point far from a symmetric fixed point. In both cases, chaotic dynamics tend to emerge when transport costs are higher.

Regarding the role of migration speed, if it is slow enough, then for the high transport cost case, the symmetric fixed point of equal dispersion of industry can be a stable attractor, as in the continuous case. However, for a given set of other parameters for the high transport case, there will exist a bifurcation value of the migration speed, γ_p, such that for migration speeds exceeding this, the symmetric equilibrium becomes destabilized and cyclical and even chaotic dynamics can appear. This phenomenon arises from the discrete map of shares, λ_t and λ_{t+1}, becoming "stretched" as γ increases. There are actually two critical values, with another one appearing above which the system simply goes to an agglomeration outcome, γ_p. This stretching does not involve any change in the positions of the equilibrium outcomes, merely in the dynamic patterns going on around them. This is depicted in Fig. 2.11 (Currie and Kubin, 2006, p. 268), with 2.11a showing the stretching of the discrete map, and 2.11b showing how these critical values of γ vary with the transport cost, T.

Thus, in a discrete setting, substantially greater complexity of dynamics can be seen for the new economic geography model of core–periphery dynamics. The generalization that core–periphery outcomes appear only with low transport costs

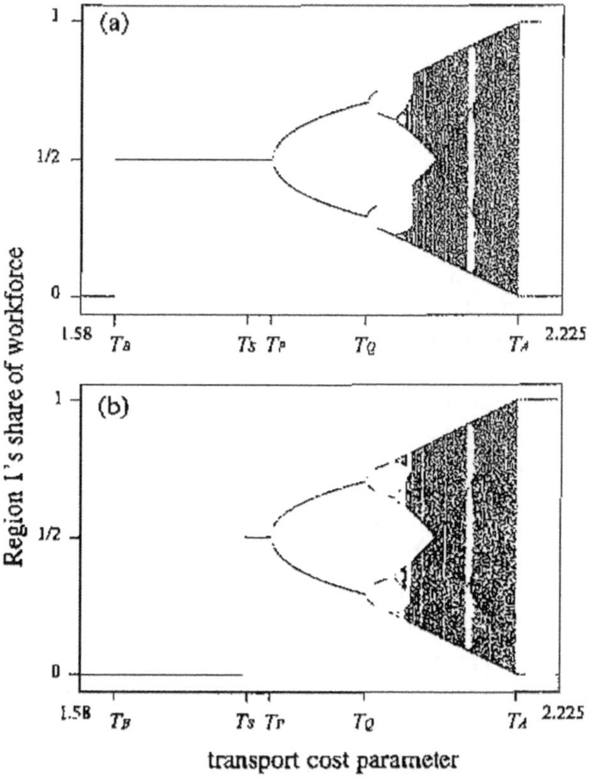

Fig. 2.10 Bifurcation diagrams for T from different initial points

disappears, and it is also clear that outcomes are dependent on such matters as migration speeds as well as initial conditions.

2.7 Criticisms of the New Economic Geography

It is not the author's intention now to revisit the points raised in the opening section of this chapter. Rather, given the widespread use that the new economic geography has come to have with numerous researchers investigating the implications and extensions of the model, we now wish to consider other critiques that have been raised regarding its use, noting that not all of these arguments the author necessarily agrees with.

Some of the criticisms represent ongoing debates between traditional geographers and economists, although others are more complicated. However, some of the arguments by traditional geographers involve criticizing the use of mathematical economic theory as opposed to studying specific cases and their circumstances, harking back to the old *methodenstreit* between the Neoclassicals and the Historical

Fig. 2.11 Significance of migration speed

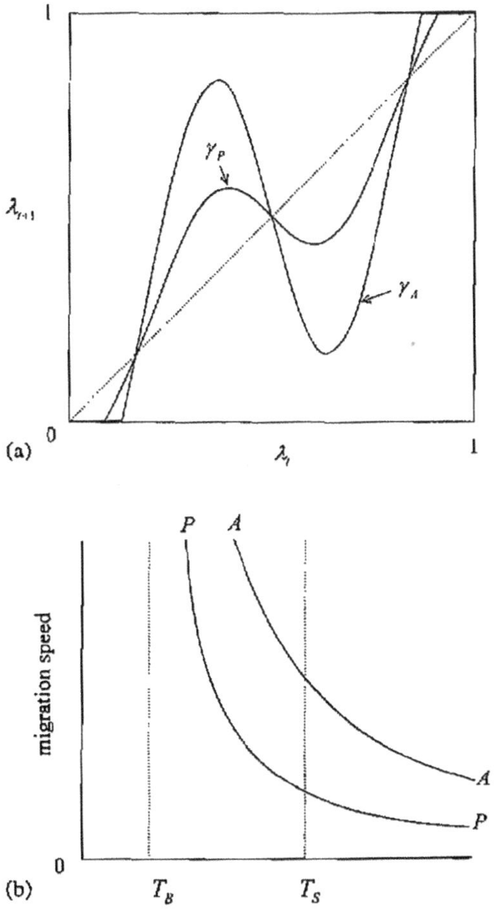

School in Germany in the late 1800s, which was replayed in the US in economics in the twentieth century, with the Institutionalists standing in for the Historical School.

Much in this vein was a critique by the geographer Ron Martin (1999), although published in an economics journal (the *Cambridge Journal of Economics*). Martin's aim is much broader than just the Fujita–Krugman version of new economic geography presented above. It is indeed all of formal mathematical theory, including the formal location theory of the German tradition from von Thünen (1826) through Weber (1909) to Christaller (1933) and Lösch (1940), although he seems to accept strictly geometric analysis coming out of this tradition. He sees this tradition as being broken into two strands by Walter Isard (1956) with his invention of *regional science*, which is seen as formal and mathematical. It is to be contrasted with *economic geography*, and Martin's position in favor of the latter is given by the following (Martin, 1999, p, 66).

> Economic geography, on the other hand, had by this time [1950s-60s] evolved into a more eclectic and empirically-orientated subject, in which formal neoclassically-orientated location theory had been largely displaced by concepts imported from other branches of economics: for example, Keynesian business cycle models, Myrdalian cumulative causation theory, and Marxian notions of uneven accumulation. Since the late 1980s, economic geography has undergone a further vigorous expansion, incorporating ideas from French regulation theory, Schumpeterian models of technological evolution, and institutional economics. And, even more recently, it has turned to economic sociology and cultural theory for inspiration.

It is not surprising given this that Martin concludes that the new economic geography is a "case of mistaken identity," with "too little region and too much mathematics." He accuses both regional science and the new economic geography of the sin of "positivism" and argues that proper economic geography is empirically based and builds "up from below" a view of what is going on in a particular area, following the precepts of critical realism instead (Lawson, 1997). He poses as good examples of the way to go the "Third Italy" movement of neo-Schumpeterian neo-Marshallians who empirically and institutionally and historically have studied industrial districts in Italy (Brusco, 1989; Antonelli, 1990), with the study by Buenstorf and Kappler (2009) of the Akron tire cluster fitting into this tradition as well.

Despite his criticism of the use of mathematics, Martin has since joined those advocating an *evolutionary economic geography* (Boschma, 2004; Boschma and Martin, 2007; Frenken and Boschma, 2007; Jovanović, 2009). While this approach does not use standard formal mathematics, this group tends to an interest in complexity and nonlinear dynamics approaches, although calling more on such figures as Beinhocker (2006) for inspiration than Puu, or Allen, or Weidlich. Nevertheless, Arthur (1994) is a strong inspiration, and Fujita provided a friendly Foreword to the book by Jovanović (2009). In any case, this group also continues to stress empirical study of specific cases from an eclectic perspective.

Perhaps a sharper critique comes from J. Peter Neary (2001) who does not have much sympathy for the arguments of Martin (1999), with Neary having no problems at all with conventional mathematical neoclassical theory. While he agrees with Martin that the new economic geographers have been very weak on doing empirical studies, he sees the approach advocated by Martin as being too much of a "case studies" approach that fools itself into thinking that it is "theory free." He does suggest that the few empirical studies attempting to support the new economic geography have provided mixed results, with Kim (1995) finding the story breaking down for the US after World War II, a result that Krugman himself now agrees with (2009).[7] At the same time Davis and Weinstein (1999) find support for it in regional patterns of industry within Japan.

Another is that there is effectively no theory of the firm arising from the Dixit–Stiglitz model. Free entry exists at all locations leading to "footloose cities" in principle, although variations of fixed or floating capital in the new economic geography models did come to be studied by Baldwin, Forslid, Martin, Ottaviano, and Robert-Nicoud (2003). But there remains no ability for firms to strategically interact with each other. The "myopic Chamberlinian firms" cannot engage in industrial strategies to "shore up their positions" (Neary, 2001, p. 50). "They cannot make strategic commitments to create artificial barriers to entry, nor vertically integrate to internalize the externalities arising from the combination of intermediate inputs with increasing returns. And, of course, out-sourcing or cross-border horizontal mergers in response to changes in trade, policy, technology, or market size are not allowed." (ibid) All this reduces the relevance of the model to industrial location theory, according to Neary.

Finally, Neary is unhappy about the simplification that the model is implicitly on a line rather than in a true space. While it is able to show the "shadow" of an emergent urban center on a neighboring area as a potential urban center, it does not present the full array of possibilities. This combines with some other simplifying assumptions, such as free transport of agricultural goods,[8] to place serious limits on the generality of the approach, especially given the weaknesses already mentioned regarding its lack of focus on the supply side and its weak theory of the firm. Nevertheless, in spite of all the criticisms, Neary in the end praises the new economic geography as harking back to the work of Bertil Ohlin that combined international and interregional trade theory.

Notes

1. Of the inventors of the model used by Krugman, of course Stiglitz had earlier won a Nobel Prize for his work on asymmetric information in 2001, while Dixit never has, which is true of Fujita as well.
2. Although Marshall had priority, the possibility of multiple equilibria when there are positive externalities of other firms in a region was recognized in the classical German industrial location theory of Weber (1909), as well as in Rietschl (1927), Ohlin (1933), and Palander (1935), as well as later literature such as Kaldor (1970) and Arthur (1986). Most of this literature was mathematical, assuming as in our analysis below that the externalities are production-related rather than deriving from the demand side as with Dixit and Stiglitz (1977), Fujita (1988), and Krugman (1991).
3. The Lenin Steel Works was named a Hero Plant by Josef Stalin for its role in producing steel for the tanks used in the decisive battles of Stalingrad and Kursk during World War II against the Germans, with their location east of the Ural mountains protecting them against the German invaders. It is a pathetic commentary on the problems of socialist central planning that when the Soviet Union finally collapsed at the end of 1991, the steel produced at the Lenin plant could only be sold on international markets as scrap metal, a symbol of its ultimate dysfunctionality in an age in which such internal economies have become far less important.
4. This "iceberg" analogy first appeared as such in Samuelson (1952), although it can be seen as similar to the idea found in von Thünen (1826) that animals eat grain as they are transported to a final consumption location.
5. Other models discussed by Baldwin, Forslid, Martin, Otaviano, and Robert-Nicoud (2003) include a footloose capital model, a footloose entrepreneur model, a constructed capital model with global spillovers, along with some other minor variations.
6. This corresponds in effect to the argument of Krugman (2009) in his Nobel Prize address in which he argues that the divergence between the core and the periphery between US regions reached a maximum during the 1920s and that in effect the declines in transport costs since then have been associated with a movement toward convergence between the regions rather than more divergence.

7. While the support for the Krugman-inspired use of the Dixit–Stiglitz model is weak, support for the supply-side approach of Marshall is strong (Ellison, Glaeser, and Kerr, 2010). This model is really kind of halfway between being a model of simply industry agglomeration and a broader urbanization model in that it looks at linkages across industries as explaining the agglomeration of a given industry cluster, thus providing the foundation for explaining how the presence of one industry can attract another closely related to it, much as in classic models of development looking at "forward" and "backward" linkages.
8. Davis (1998) shows that transport costs for nonindustrial goods are nearly as great as those for industrial goods and that this can break down the "home market effect" argument as it is presented by Krugman.

Chapter 3
Discontinuities in Intraurban Systems

But Petersburg is not merely imaginary; it can be located on maps—in the shape of concentric circles and a black dot in the middle; and this mathematical dot, which has no defined measurement, proclaims energetically that it exists: from this dot comes the impetuous surge of words which makes the pages of a book; and from this point circulars rapidly spread.
Andrey Biely (1913, St. Petersburg, p. xxii)

3.1 Some General Remarks

Historically there has been considerable unity of method in modelling the regional distribution of population and economic activities and the intraurban distribution of these. The most obvious example is that the standard neoclassical Mills–Muth model (Alonso, 1964; Mills, 1967; Muth, 1969) of intraurban land use and rent is essentially similar to the von Thünen (1826) model of land use and rent over a broader regional space.

This tendency to unity of approach extends to the analysis of discontinuous phenomena as well. Thus the earliest models using catastrophe theory to model intraurban discontinuities (Amson, 1974, 1975) emphasize a conflict between "attractive" forces (urban "opulence" in the Amson models) and "repulsive" forces (rent in the Amson models), similar to conflicts in the Papageorgiou and Smith (1983) and Isard (1977) models between agglomerative (attractive) and deglomerative (repulsive) forces in the formation of cities. This dialectic between attractive and repulsive forces lies at the heart of many intraurban models exhibiting discontinuous phenomena.

Yet another example of this tendency to unity of approach is in the work of the Brussels School. They have modeled both regional level models (Allen, 1978; Allen and Sanglier, 1978, 1979, 1981; Domanski and Wierzbiecki, 1983; Camagni, Diappi, and Leonardi, 1986; Sanglier and Allen, 1989) and intraurban level models (Allen, Denebourg, Sanglier, Boon, and de Palma, 1979; Allen, 1983; Allen, Engelen, and Sanglier, 1986; Pumain, Saint-Julien, and Sanders, 1987). In both

J.B. Rosser, *Complex Evolutionary Dynamics in Urban-Regional and Ecologic-Economic Systems*, DOI 10.1007/978-1-4419-8828-7_3,

cases the approaches are essentially identical. Simulation is carried out over a finely scaled grid, with a variety of activities or population groups, reflecting a variety of scale economies or diseconomies and threshold levels, with other attractive or repulsive characteristics, all driven by a stochastic process of exogenous variables. In both cases, development reflects the principle of synergistic "order through fluctuations" as the stochastic process determines the pattern of phase transitions near bifurcation points. The purely intraurban models of the Leeds School bear certain similarities to the Brussels School approach, although with certain crucial differences as well.

Nevertheless, there are some differences at times between the two kinds of systems. There seem to be sharper and more dramatic discontinuities in land use in intraurban systems; the divisions within a city into zones of different uses seem much clearer and more pervasive. Also within cities the residential segregation of income, class, and ethnic groups is a very pronounced feature and an important policy issue as well. And finally, as Dendrinos and Mulally (1985) have noted, there seems to be a greater tendency for cyclical and even chaotic dynamics for intraurban systems than for whole cities and even more so than for whole regions. Indeed they assert that "the closer we look at the intra-urban structure, the more likely we are to perceive it as an unstable system" (Dendrinos and Mulally, 1985, p. 117).

3.2 The Role of Transportation in Urban Structural Bifurcations

3.2.1 Modal Choice in Transportation

The University of Leeds in England has become a major center for the study of discontinuities in intraurban systems. The main leader of this group of scholars has been Alan G. Wilson, who has emphasized the role of nonlinearities and interactions related to transportation generating bifurcations in dynamic models of intraurban structure.

Wilson's (1976) initial foray into this area involved an analysis of the problem of modal choice in transportation. He considers a disutility function $E(x, a, b)$ where x represents choice between two alternative transportation modes and a and b are functions of the difference in transport cost between the two modes. From this a cusp catastrophe surface can be derived which translates to a simpler fold catastrophe in the space of mode and modal cost difference.

More Specifically,

$$\Delta c = c(2) - c(1), \tag{3.1}$$

where $c(2)$ and $c(1)$ are transport costs by modes 2 and 1, respectively, facing an individual. For $x > 0$, mode 2 is chosen and for $x < 0$ mode 1 is chosen. The disutility minimizing manifold will be given by

$$\partial E/\partial x = x^3 + ax + b = 0. \tag{3.2}$$

Wilson suggests that if k_1, k_2, and k_3 are positive constants, then a reasonable transformation might be given by

$$a = k_1(\Delta c)^2 - k_2, \tag{3.3}$$

$$b = k_3 \Delta c. \tag{3.4}$$

Wilson then hypothesizes the existence of a λ such that $|\Delta c| = \lambda$ constitutes the boundary of a critical region within which either mode could be chosen. This λ is given by

$$4\left[k_1(\Delta c)^2 - k_2\right]^3 + 9(k_3\Delta c)^2 = 0, \tag{3.5}$$

where $(\Delta c)^2 = \lambda^2$. This gives a fold catastrophe curve in the $(\Delta c, x)$ space as depicted in Fig. 3.1. Occurrence of the modal shift depends on modal shift costs (e.g., buying a car). The higher such modal shift costs, the greater the inertia and the likelihood of hysteresis effects.

Blase (1979) used the Wilson model as an explanation for "habit threshold" hysteresis effects in modal choice suggested by P.B. Goodwin (1977), using a data set on traffic flows, gas prices, and public transport fare levels in Greater London in the mid-1970s, gathered by Lewis (1977). Focusing on the weekend traffic component, he found in the traffic flow–gas price space that there were four distinct data clusters, which could be identified with two distinct demand curves. These demand curves could be identified with the two "arms" of Fig. 3.1. Blase estimated the "habit threshold" (equivalent to Wilson's λ), at which there would be a jump from one demand curve to the other, as being equal to a change of seven pence per gallon.

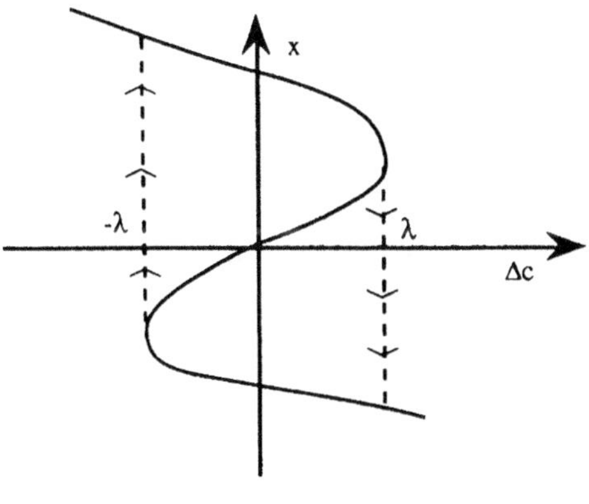

Fig. 3.1 Transportation mode shifts as a fold catastrophe

3.2.2 Urban Retail Structure

3.2.2.1 Economies of Scale Versus Transportation Costs

Wilson (1970) interpreted in an entropy-maximizing context a shopping model due to Huff (1964) and Lakshmanen and Hansen (1965). Beginning with Coelho and Wilson (1976) and continuing with Poston and Wilson (1977) and Harris and Wilson (1978), variations of the underlying parameters of this model were analyzed in a search for critical bifurcation points at which structural change might occur. Further extensions and explicit dynamic formulations of the model were considered in Wilson (1981a, b, 1982); Harris, Choukroun, and Wilson (1982); and Rijk and Vorst (1983). Although some of these models fit into the catastrophe theory framework, many did not possess a gradient interpretation and thus were analyzed with more general bifurcation theory.

The major focus of these models is the size of retail establishments and how this varies with economies of scale (from the consumer's perspective) and transportation costs. Bifurcation points in these models thus indicate some discontinuity in the size or pattern of retail outlets, the urban structure. A general form of this model follows.

Let the city be divided into discrete zones, e_i be per capita retail expenditures in zone i, P_i be the population in zone i, W_j be the size of retail outlets in zone j, W_k refers to other zones, c_{ij} be the travel cost between zones i and j, D_j be the total revenue in zone j, α be an economies of retail scale parameter, β be an ease of travel parameter, γ be a parameter based on the total retail market of the city, and ε be a speed of adjustment parameter, then the equilibrium condition is given by

$$D_j = (\gamma/\alpha)W_j \tag{3.6}$$

and the differential equation system is given by

$$\mathrm{d}W_j/\mathrm{d}t = \varepsilon\left(D_j - (\gamma/\alpha)W_j\right), \tag{3.7}$$

where

$$D_j = \sum_i \left[\left(\mathrm{e}_i P_i W_{j^\alpha} \mathrm{e}^{-\beta cij}\right) \Big/ \left(\sum_k {W_k}^\alpha \mathrm{e}^{-\beta cik}\right)\right]. \tag{3.8}$$

Bifurcation points of this system can then be derived based on variations of α, β, and (γ/α), the latter representing average supply costs per retail center. One very precise result, due to Rijk and Vorst (1983), is that for $\alpha \le 1$, there will be a unique and stable solution. In other words, it is only when economies of scale are present that multiple equilibria and large-scale shopping centers will arise.

More generally, for given values of β and γ, there will be a critical value of α *below* which the retail structure will be dispersed. Likewise, for a given α and γ, there will be a critical value of β *above* which the retail structure will be dispersed; if travel costs are too high everybody will shop locally. And for a given α and β,

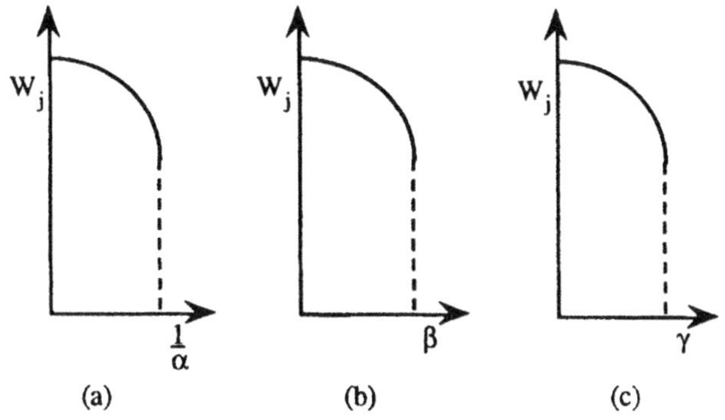

Fig. 3.2 Discontinuous urban retail agglomeration

there will be a critical γ *above* which retail structure will be dispersed. These are depicted in Fig. 3.2, where W_j is the dispersed solution.

This result parallels that of Papageorgiou and Smith (1983), with α acting as the "agglomerative" parameter and β as the "deglomerative" parameter. When scale economies outweigh transportation costs, given total city size, large-scale shopping centers appear.

3.2.2.2 Chaotic Dynamics

Simulation of a difference equation version of this model with many zones led to realizing the possibility of chaotic dynamics (Beaumont, Clarke, and Wilson, 1981a). Assuming growth or decline depends on profitability gives

$$W_{jt+1} = \left[(1 + \varepsilon D_{jt}) - \varepsilon(\gamma/\alpha)W_{jt}\right] W_{jt}. \tag{3.9}$$

For $0 \leq \varepsilon D_{jt} \leq 2$, there is a unique and stable steady state. For $2 < \varepsilon D_{jt} \leq 3$, there is oscillatory behavior with Feigenbaum period doubling, as εD_{jt} is increased with a transition to chaos occurring. For $\varepsilon D_{jt} > 3$, there is divergent behavior which means a collapse to the dispersed state in this model.

One of the reasons why it is difficult to analyze this model without simulation is that the D_js are interdependent, and their bifurcation values are also interdependent. Beaumont, Clarke, and Wilson (1981a) studied a 169-zone model. Holding population constant and $\alpha = \gamma$, they found that a single central retail center emerged eventually for $\alpha = 1.1$, $\beta = 0.1$, and $\varepsilon = 0.04$. For $\alpha = 1.5$, $\beta = 0.5$, and $\varepsilon = 0.06$, they eventually obtained four large retail centers alternating with four smaller ones in a circle around the center.

In another study, Beaumont, Clarke, and Wilson (1981b) simulated a 149-zone model with a Christaller-style hierarchy of goods as they varied β, presumably in response to changes in energy prices. As β declined, the pattern went from dispersed to two centers and eventually to one center. Adding on a congestion parameter led to a reduction and concentration of retail centers, but now the emergence of a single center was delayed.

3.2.2.3 Leeds Versus Brussels: A Comparison of Approaches

Clarke and Wilson (1983)[1] examine the relationship between the Leeds School approach and the Brussels School approach, arguing that a fundamental difference is that Leeds models lack stochasticity, they are purely deterministic. In this respect, for given parameter values and states of the rest of the city, bifurcations for individual areas can be specifically estimated. They argue that this is impossible in the Brussels School world, even though bifurcation points clearly exist. Furthermore the precise nature of transitions, as well as their locations, are indeterminable in a Brussels School model.

However, Wilson (1982) recognizes that the assumption of stochasticity is more realistic, given the unpredictable behavior of entrepreneurs and governmental agencies. But he still argues for the ultimate superiority of the analytical solution. Thus:

> Such developments (or lack of them) can be viewed as fluctuations around the equilibrium state evolutionary path at each point in time. However, we have seen that a given zonal development affects the calculation of criticality for all other zones. In this sense, fluctuations will drive the whole system to new states . . . In spite of this randomness, there is likely to be a degree of order in the spatial structure which evolves. For example, the number of centers in particular size groups and their average spacing may still be determined by the mechanism of evolution proposed. In this sense, the model proposed here generates order from fluctuations in the same sense as that of Allen and his coworkers (1978), even though the mechanisms are somewhat different" (Wilson, 1982, p. 171).

3.3 An Ecological View

3.3.1 Density–Rent Cycles

Dendrinos (1980b), Dendrinos and Mulally (1981), and Dendrinos with Mulally (1985) applied the Lotka–Volterra system of equations of competing populations to the analysis of urban cycles and evolution. Haag and Weidlich (1983) use the same approach to model the migratory patterns of two groups in a regional space.[2]

These approaches were combined in studies of intraurban migration by Haag and Dendrinos (1983) and Dendrinos and Haag (1984), the former largely theoretical and the latter largely empirical. They developed a stochastic Lotka–Volterra model to explain cyclical migrations between two intraurban zones, presumed to be a central area and a suburban ring, but concluded that this system can be represented and empirically estimated in its deterministic, mean-value form.

They posit zones i and j, land areas for each zone (z), population densities for each zone (n), occupancy levels supplied for each zone ($\tilde{n}$), demand-derived bid-rents (r) for each zone and supply-derived asking rents ($\tilde{r}$) for each zone, utility (U), N be half the total population, R half the total rent, and the as constants. Then the utility of moving from j to i is given by

$$U_{j\to i} = a_1[(\tilde{r}_i - r_i) - (\tilde{r}_j - r_j)] + a_2(n_i - n_j). \tag{3.10}$$

A profitability index of transferring rental value V_{ji} is given by

$$V_{j\to i} = a_3[n_i - \tilde{n}_i) - (n_j - \tilde{n}_j)]. \tag{3.11}$$

By adding individual transition probabilities, α and β, to these equations, Haag and Dendrinos (1983) derive a master probability equation linking micro-level transitions to macro-level shifts. They then consider the mean value form of this. Let

$$b_0 = a_1(\tilde{r}_i - \tilde{r}_j) - (a_1R - a_2N)[(1/z_i) - (1/z_j)], \tag{3.12}$$

$$b_1 = a_1[(1/z_i) + (1/z_j)] > 0, \tag{3.13}$$

$$b_2 = a_2[(1/z_i) + (1/z_j)], \tag{3.14}$$

$$b_3 = a_3\{(\tilde{n}_i - \tilde{n}_j) + N[(1/z_j) - (1/z_i)]\}, \tag{3.15}$$

$$b_4 = a_3[(1/z_i) + (1/z_j)] > 0. \tag{3.16}$$

Furthermore, let $x = n/N$ and $y = r/R$ be normalizations, and let $\tilde{b}_1 = b_1R$, $\tilde{b}_2 = b_2N$, and $\tilde{b}_4 = b_4N$. Then the dynamic deterministic mean value equations are given by

$$x = 2\alpha[\sinh(b_0 - \tilde{b}_1y + \tilde{b}_2x) - x\cosh(b_0 - \tilde{b}_1y + \tilde{b}_2x)], \tag{3.17}$$

$$y = 2\beta[\sinh(-b_3 + \tilde{b}_4x) - y\cosh(-b_3 + \tilde{b}_4x)]. \tag{3.18}$$

Extreme values are given by

$$x^* = \tanh(b_0 - \tilde{b}_1y^* + \tilde{b}_2x^*), \tag{3.19}$$

$$y^* = \tanh(-b_3 + \tilde{b}_4x^*), \tag{3.20}$$

which yields a transcendental equation in x^*:

$$x^* = \tanh[b_0 + \tilde{b}_2x^* - \tilde{b}_1\tanh(-b_3 + \tilde{b}_4x^*)]. \tag{3.21}$$

The qualitative properties of this system depend on the value of $\tilde{b}_2 - \tilde{b}_1\tilde{b}_4$. If this is less than one, there is a unique, stable equilibrium. When it equals one, there is a bifurcation, and if it exceeds one, there is an odd number of equilibria, alternating between stable and unstable.

Dendrinos and Haag (1984) estimated parameter values for these equations for 12 US SMSAs for 1950–1980. For all 12, they found that the values were consistent with the existence of unique equilibria and of sink-spiral behavior toward the equilibria in the normalized rent–density space.

3.3.2 Intraurban Lotka–Volterra Instability

3.3.2.1 Centralization Versus Suburbanization

Dendrinos with Mulally (1985) propose an alternative Lotka–Volterra formulation of central city–suburb interactions. Considering the zonal distribution of some activity with x the suburban share, w the central city share, and the as and bs all positive, they posit

$$dx/dt = (a_0 - a_1 x - a_2 w)x, \tag{3.22}$$

$$dw/dt = (-b_0 + b_1 x + b_2 w)w. \tag{3.23}$$

This makes the central city the "predator" and the suburb the "prey." Smooth variations in the value of b_0 can lead to shifts between suburbanization and centralization at critical values.

3.3.2.2 Slum Formation Versus Historical Preservation

Let q_1 be the quality level of housing in an older zone and q_2 be the quality level of housing in a newer zone with the older zone the predator and the newer zone the prey. Dynamics are given by

$$dq_1/dt = (-a_0 + a_1 q_1 + a_2 q_2)q_1, \tag{3.24}$$

$$dq_2/dt = (b_0 - b_1 q_1 - b_2 q_2)q_2. \tag{3.25}$$

In this case, a_0 performs the control variable function, causing the switching of the older zone from slum formation to historical preservation and back again.[3] They argue that such a shift of a_0 could arise from altered comparative advantages of the zones with respect to employment opportunities.[4] These dynamics are depicted in Fig. 3.3, with 3.3a the stable equilibrium E with $q_1 = 0$ showing slums in the older zone. As a_0 increases, 3.3b can arise which could lead to historical preservation of the older zone and deterioration of the newer zone.

3.3.2.3 Neighborhood Tipping and Gentrification

Clearly the question of slums versus historical preservation is closely related to questions of racially or class-based tipping of previously well-off neighborhoods into slummy ghettos and the reverse. Dendrinos with Mulally (1985) model this

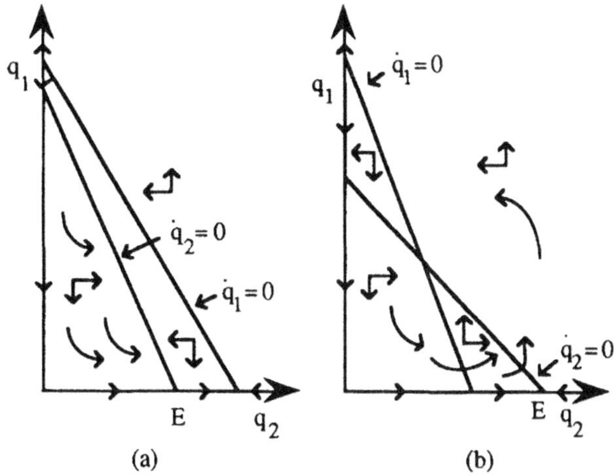

Fig. 3.3 Lotka–Volterra centralization versus suburbanization dynamics

process similarly to those above, in this case with the nonwhite (poor) group being the predators and the white (rich) group being the prey. Of course, this is meant in the migratory sense that nonwhites wish to move toward whites, while whites wish to move away from nonwhites, rather than that nonwhites exploit or otherwise socioeconomically prey on whites. In this case, w is white population share, x is nonwhite population share, and the dynamics are given by

$$\mathrm{d}x/\mathrm{d}t = (a_0 - a_1x - a_2w)x, \tag{3.26}$$

$$\mathrm{d}w/\mathrm{d}t = (-b_0 + b_1x + b_2w)w. \tag{3.27}$$

The two cases are shown in Fig. 3.4 with (a) showing E as the ghetto solution and (b) showing the gentrification solution. E is stable if $-a_0/a_1 < -b_0/b_1$. The bifurcation point occurs at $-a_0/a_1 = -b_0/b_1$, and E is unstable when the inequality is reversed.

3.3.2.4 A Note on Bifurcation Categories

In the previous three models, bifurcations have occurred within the so-called "predatory ecology" as one parameter has changed in value but not in sign. This predatory ecology will hold if either $a_2 < 0$ and $b_1 > 0$ or $a_2 > 0$ and $b_1 < 0$. In such cases, one group is predator and the other is prey.

However, two other broad types of ecological relationships may hold, symbiotic where the groups attract each other, given by $a_2 > 0$ and $b_1 > 0$, and competitive where the groups repel each other, given by $a_2 < 0$ and $b_1 < 0$. In these two cases, dynamics exhibit only nodes and saddle points, whereas spirals can also occur in the predator–prey case.

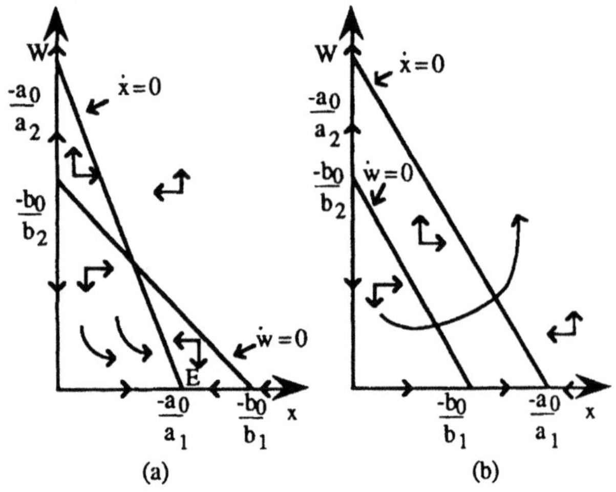

Fig. 3.4 Lotka–Volterra slums versus gentrification dynamics

The existence of these other types of ecological relationships creates another category of bifurcations, namely, those between the various states. Dendrinos with Mulally (1985) define the transition between symbiotic and predator–prey as "commensal." Such a bifurcation is given by $a_2 = 0$ and $b_1 > 0$ or by $a_2 > 0$ and $b_1 = 0$. The transition between competitive and predator–prey is "amensal," given by $a_2 < 0$ and $b_1 = 0$ or by $a_2 = 0$ and $b_1 < 0$. A direct transition from symbiotic to competitive (or vice versa) would require passing through the degenerate cusp at $a_2 = 0$ and $b_1 = 0$.

3.4 Static and Dynamic Boundary Discontinuities

3.4.1 Neighborhood Boundary Dynamics

3.4.1.1 A Static Model

Although the tipping[5] of one group to another can be analyzed using predator–prey models, it generally involves the accumulation to a critical percentage of minorities within a neighborhood (often thought to be around 40%), after which the neighborhood tips to nearly 100% minority. We shall examine an alternative view that focuses on conditions at a boundary, considering the case of complete segregation with a sharply defined boundary.[6]

A static model of this sort can be developed by combining the Bailey (1959) border model with a standard Mills (1967) and Muth (1969) model[7] and introducing elements of externalities on the demand side and land use controls on the supply side (Stull, 1974). Such a model has been analyzed by Rose-Ackerman (1975), Courant and Yinger (1977), White (1977), and Rosser (1978a).

Let U^{w} = utility of whites, U^{m} = utility of minorities, x = all nonhousing or transportation goods, q = housing quantity, D = distance in a homogeneous plane from a central business district (CBD) where everybody works, $\overline{D}$ = distance at edge of city, B = the neighborhood boundary position, T = travel costs (increasing with distance), y = income, H = number of households, $N(D)$ = number of households accommodatable at D, $P(d)$ = price of housing at D, $Q(D)$ = profit-maximizing supply at D, $r(D)$ = land rent at D, $\bar{r}$ = agricultural rent, s = price of structural inputs, S = quantity of structures, and L = quantity of land. Prejudice on the part of whites is a negative externality expressed as a linear function of their distance from the boundary, D–B.[8] We shall assume that whites are prejudiced but that minorities are not.[9] Households maximize utility subject to their budget constraints, which for the equal incomes case will lead to equal household utilities. Equilibrium will be given by

$$r(D) = p(D)(\mathrm{d}Q/\mathrm{d}L), \tag{3.28}$$

$$r(\overline{D}) = \bar{r}, \tag{3.29}$$

$$s = p(D)(\mathrm{d}Q/\mathrm{d}S), \tag{3.30}$$

$$N(D) = Q(D)/q(D), \tag{3.31}$$

$$H^{\mathrm{m}} = \int_0^B N^{\mathrm{m}}(D)\mathrm{d}D, \tag{3.32}$$

$$\mathrm{d}p/\mathrm{d}D|_{B<D} = (-1/q)(\mathrm{d}T/\mathrm{d}D), \tag{3.33}$$

$$H^{\mathrm{w}} = \int_0^D N^{\mathrm{w}}(D)\mathrm{d}D, \tag{3.34}$$

$$\mathrm{d}p/\mathrm{d}D|_{D>B} = (-\mathrm{d}T/\mathrm{d}D)/\mathrm{q}[\mathrm{d}U^{\mathrm{w}}/\mathrm{d}(D-B)/(\mathrm{d}U^{\mathrm{w}}/\mathrm{d}x)]/q. \tag{3.35}$$

This means that if whites are sufficiently prejudiced, their bid-rent gradient will increase with distance at the boundary. This will occur if

$$[\mathrm{d}U^{\mathrm{w}}/\mathrm{d}(D-B)]/(\mathrm{d}U^{\mathrm{w}}/\mathrm{d}x) > \mathrm{d}T/\mathrm{d}D, \tag{3.36}$$

that is, if their marginal disutility from proximity to minorities exceeds marginal transportation costs.

In this case, minorities will occupy more land and pay lower housing prices than in a case without prejudice. However, if whites are discriminatory and reduce the supply of minority housing, minorities will pay more, and a discontinuity in housing prices will exist at the boundary.[10] A comparison of these three cases is shown in Fig. 3.5 with (a) being the unprejudiced city,[11] (b) the prejudiced city without discrimination, and (c) the prejudiced and discrimination city.

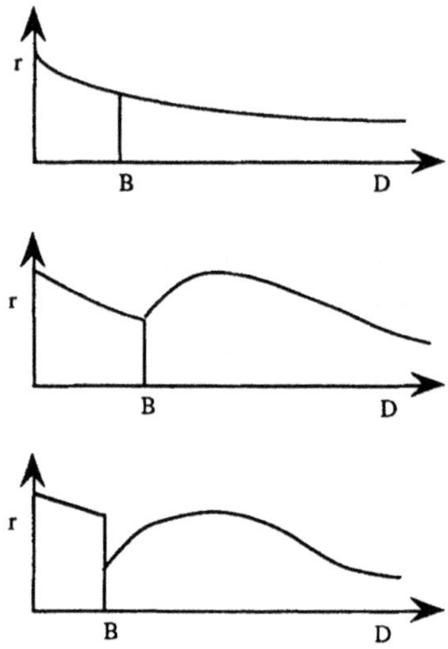

Fig. 3.5 (**a**) Rent gradient without prejudice or discrimination. (**b**) Rent gradient with prejudice but no discrimination. (**c**) Rent gradient with both prejudice and discrimination

Considerable debate exists about the shape of the minority ghetto that would transpire in such a static Mills–Muth–von Thünen city. Rose-Ackerman (1975) suggests that minorities would occupy a ring near the center. Yinger (1976) argues that a wedge-shaped ghetto would minimize the length of the boundary for minority populations between 15 and 90% of the population. This would correspond to the "finger ghetto" observed by Hoyt (1939) in Chicago.[12] However, Loury (1978) argues that such a model would produce a lens-shaped ghetto on the edge of the city, a pattern more frequently observed outside the US. Loury's solution may be avoided if minorities have lower incomes which could put them in the urban interior due to possessing steeper bid-rent gradients. Nevertheless, the question of how an elongated ghetto arises remains somewhat unclear in the static framework.

3.4.1.2 A Moving Boundary

An obvious way to model boundary dynamics is to assume that the minority population is increasing, that is, $dH^{m}/dt > 0$. Thus, the equilibrium path will reflect an intertemporal optimization based on expected future developments. Each group can be optimized by

$$\max \int_0^{\infty} U^{m}[x^{m}(t),\ q^{m}(t)]e^{\cdot\delta t}dt, \tag{3.37}$$

$$\max \int_0^{\infty} U^{w}[x^{w}(t),\ q^{w}(t),\ (D(t) - B(t))]e^{\cdot\delta t}dt, \tag{3.38}$$

subject to

$$x(t) + p(D,t)q(t) + T(D,y,t) - y(t) = 0, \tag{3.39}$$

holding for both groups with δ = time discount rate.

A solution for this problem can be found by using the Stefan (1891) moving boundary problem technique which was originally developed to explain the rate of melting of an iceberg.[13] The basic Stefan formulation is given by

$$\mathrm{d}V/\mathrm{d}t = \mathrm{d}/\mathrm{d}B(C\mathrm{d}V/\mathrm{d}B), \tag{3.40}$$

where V = temperature difference at the boundary, t = time, B = boundary position, and C is a diffusion relation. Furthermore if $A(V)$ = heat content and $A(V) = V$ for $V > 0$ and $A(V) = V - \lambda$ for $V < 0$ and $B = s(C,t)$, then the Stefan condition is

$$-\mathrm{d}s/\mathrm{d}B = \int_1^2 (C\mathrm{d}V/\mathrm{d}B)\mathrm{d}B, \tag{3.41}$$

where 1 and 2 represent the opposite sides of this boundary. This becomes

$$-\lambda\mathrm{d}B/\mathrm{d}t = C[\partial V/\partial B]_1^2. \tag{3.42}$$

Rosser (1980) has shown that this can be applied to the above problem by assuming that $V = p^{\mathrm{m}} - p^{\mathrm{w}}$ and that

$$\lambda = -\{[\mathrm{d}U^{\mathrm{w}}/\mathrm{d}(D-B)]/(\mathrm{d}U^{\mathrm{w}}/\mathrm{d}x)\}/q^{\mathrm{w}}. \tag{3.43}$$

This gives a general equation of motion of the boundary, assuming that diffusion is governed by minority household growth of

$$\begin{aligned}\mathrm{d}B/\mathrm{d}t = {} & C(\mathrm{d}H^{\mathrm{m}}/\mathrm{d}t)\{\mathrm{d}T/\mathrm{d}D[\mathrm{d}q^{\mathrm{w}}/\mathrm{d}B(\ln q^{\mathrm{w}}) - \mathrm{d}q^{\mathrm{m}}/\mathrm{d}B(\ln q^{\mathrm{m}})]\}/\\ & \{[\mathrm{d}U^{\mathrm{w}}/\mathrm{d}(D-B)]/[(\mathrm{d}U^{\mathrm{w}}/\mathrm{d}x)q]^{\mathrm{w}}\}\end{aligned}. \tag{3.44}$$

Thus boundary motion depends on the rate of growth of minority households, the housing supply response, and the degree of white prejudice.

Furthermore, V will be a function of the rate of motion of the boundary because of whites in the path of a moving boundary capitalizing into present value the future expected movement toward them of the boundary. Thus if the boundary begins to move more rapidly in one particular direction, that more rapid motion will be sustained if whites in the path of it expect it to continue. In this case, "white flight" becomes a self-fulfilling prophecy as prices fall in the direction of the more rapidly moving boundary, thus allowing it to continue moving more rapidly in that direction. Such a process can generate the elongated "finger ghetto." Stefan formalized such a feedback process as a "convection effect," given by $W(\mathrm{d}B/\mathrm{d}t)$ such that

$$\mathrm{d}V/\mathrm{d}t + W(\mathrm{d}B/\mathrm{d}t)\mathrm{d}V/\mathrm{d}t = \mathrm{d}/\mathrm{d}BC(\mathrm{d}H^{\mathrm{m}}/\mathrm{d}t)(\mathrm{d}V/\mathrm{d}B). \tag{3.45}$$

Stefan further argued that such convection can lead to an unstable, explosive reaction if the variables and functions are of sufficient values and strengths. Such explosions can occur when molten lead is dropped into water and the boundary accelerates outward as the water boils off rapidly. Rosser (1982) has suggested that such an unstable boundary motion can be modeled by a cusp catastrophe with the control variables being the rate of growth of the minority population, the degree of white prejudice, and the state variable being the rate of boundary movement.

3.4.2 Land Use Boundaries

3.4.2.1 Static Land Value Discontinuities

In the above instance the presence of a supply impediment in the form of discrimination can generate a discontinuity in land values at a neighborhood boundary in a static equilibrium. A variety of other factors can bring about such static discontinuities.

Rosser (1976, 1978a) summarizes a series of such factors that can bring about such discontinuities. Most of these factors involve some supply-restraining element, including discrimination, zoning, greenbelts or other extraterritorial land use controls at the urban–rural fringe,[14] private monopoly power, indivisibilities of public goods, and heterogeneity of land. A demand-side effect can be seen in the case of jurisdictional boundaries with different fiscal and income situations on each side of such a boundary, labeled "fiscal surplus" by Edelson (1975). Tiebout (1956) argued that perfect mobility should eliminate such discontinuities. But when one considers international boundaries, or boundaries between municipalities where entry is limited on an income basis through such devices as minimum lot size zoning, such mobility is by no means assured.

A final empirical oddity is that *nowhere* in the US are urban use value rents and agricultural use value rents even remotely close to each other. For Madison, Wisconsin, in the early 1970s, Rosser (1976) found a gap in present use value at the urban–rural fringe of between $5,000 and $650 per vacant acre. This latter represented prime agricultural land. Schmid (1968) found an average gap of 20 times for major urban areas in the US, an amount that has certainly increased in recent years.

Despite this curiosum, all theoretical models, such as the one above, assume that equalization of rents at the urban–rural fringe constitutes a closure condition necessary for establishing the urban equilibrium. This suggests a staggering lacuna in our understanding of what is actually determining urban land values. One possible explanation is a general limitedness of urban supply, although the size of these discontinuities would suggest that this limitation is quite severe. An alternative explanation might be that these persistent discontinuities reflect a much more profound, global level contradiction and imbalance between town and country than has generally been recognized.

3.4.2.2 Dynamic Discontiguities in Land Use and Polycentrism

Greenbelts

If there exist the sort of market imperfections described in the last section, then dynamic discontinuities and discontiguities in land use can arise. Thus, if a city through zoning or extraterritorial plat review is limiting development in a greenbelt, then there will be a discontiguity as development leaps over the preserved zone.

Rodriguez-Bachiller (1986) has reviewed various ways patterns of urban development with vacant land and other discontiguities can arise in dynamic models with a competitive market *without* resort to supply restrictions of either a public or private nature.

Intertemporal Problems

Boyce (1963) stressed the role of imperfect information and uncertainty in land markets. A speculator might hold land vacant within the urban boundary in the hope of developing it later at a higher intensity level if the city grows sufficiently rapidly. Ohls and Pines (1975) show that this can occur even with perfect foresight, if the discount rate is low enough (to make it worthwhile delaying development). They show that the delayed higher intensity use could be either residential or commercial, the latter requiring a delay in order to build up a critical mass of potential customers in the area to support a large-scale shopping center. Their solution is an efficient market solution brought about by speculators.

Externalities

Lessinger (1962) suggested the role of demand-side externalities due to the desire to be near open space and away from crowding, without developing a fully rigorous model. Richardson (1975) provides a formal model incorporating a desire for low density with an imposed maximum possible density, a specific version of a cusp catastrophe model developed by Amson (1974) producing discontinuities in the rent and density surfaces of the city, although not necessarily discontiguities in the form of vacant land. Richardson recognizes that the discontinuous rent boundaries may be unstable and ultimately falls back on supply limitation arguments to support their possible long-term existence.

A Hyperbolic Umbilic Catastrophe

The possible five-dimensional, hyperbolic umbilic catastrophe model suggested by Amson (1975) became the basis of a model by Dendrinos (1978) of the distribution of manufacturing and residential activities in an urban area with the possibility of vacant land occurring. The hyperbolic umbilic form generates a bifurcation set diffeomorphic to

$$V_j = 3x_j^2 + tx_k, \tag{3.46}$$

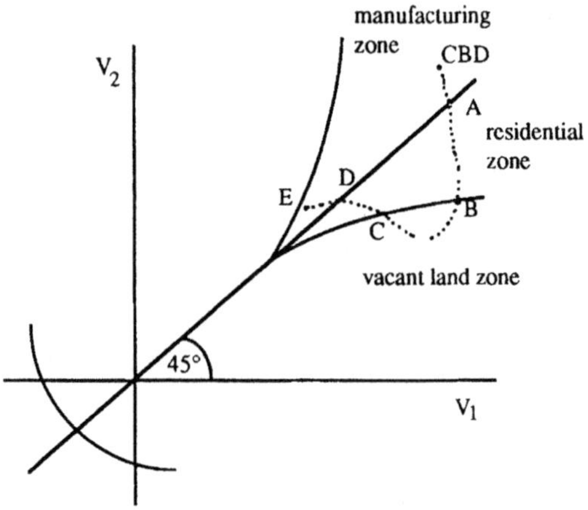

Fig. 3.6 Urban land use as a hyperbolic umbilic catastrophe

with $k \neq j$, k, $j = 1, 2$, V_1 = residential bid-rent, V_2 = manufacturing bid-rent, t = equilibrium utility level of all residents, x_1 = residential density, and x_2 = manufacturing density. The first three are control variables and the latter two are state variables. Although it is not formally derived, it is assumed that this reflects the minimizing of a potential reflecting social cost.

Dendrinos posits that the city will be structured in a ring pattern with significant nonlinearities in the rent gradient. A case with vacant land is shown in Fig. 3.6, assuming that $t > 0$, and this is a cross-section of the bifurcation set space with V_1 and V_2 being the respective residential and manufacturing rents. The dashed line represents the "areal path" of the rent gradient. The "northeast" end represents the high rent CBD and the "southwest" end the outer edge of the city. Solutions outside the cuspoid are imaginary and thus represent vacant land. Inside the cuspoid the zone above the 45° line contains manufacturing ($V_2 > V_1$) and below contains residences ($V_1 > V_2$). Thus the pattern displayed shows manufacturing from the CBD to A, residences from A to B, vacant land from B to C, residences from C to D, and manufacturing from D to E, the outer city boundary. Dynamics can occur as the control variables and the areal path shift over time, although the mechanics of this are not specified.

Vintage Models

Brueckner (1980a, b, 1981a, b) emphasizes the vintage nature of urban development and the role of redevelopment. Developers maximize expected present value of profits by comparing new land for development at the edge of the city with demolition and redevelopment of existing housing units, assuming that income from structures declines as the structures age. Thus rings of redevelopment move out from the center as rings of new development are added at the edge. He generates a "sawtooth" pattern of age and density replete with discontinuities from this model.[15]

There are two problems with this approach from our perspective. The first is that the discontinuous sawtooth depends on an assumed discontinuous pattern of the growth of urban population, possibly due to higher-level bifurcations. Take that away and both new development and redevelopment will smoothly proceed without sawteeth. The discontinuities do not reflect endogenous bifurcations.

Furthermore, as Rodriguez-Bachiller (1986) notes, the model does not directly generate discontiguities in the form of vacant land. However, Brueckner and Rabenau (1980) and Brueckner (1982) suggest the possibility of urban land being reconverted to agricultural land.

Land Use Reswitching

Yet another approach depends on the application of the neo-Ricardian approach of Sraffa (1960) to land use. Metcalfe and Steedman (1972) develop a version of the Sraffa model with technique matrices being chosen to maximize profits given a three-way division between profits, wages, and rents. As discussed in Rosser (2000b, Chap. 8), reswitching of techniques may occur between wages and profits, but according to Metcalfe and Steedman, this will not occur in either the rent–wage plane or the rent–profit plane. Letting α and β be alternative techniques, and w, r, and R wages, profits, and rents, respectively, such a case is depicted in Fig. 3.7.

This possibility has been used by Hartwick (1976), Schweizer and Varaiya (1977), Scott (1979), and Barnes and Sheppard (1984) to argue for the possibility of "reswitching" of land uses occurring across space, that is, of one use appearing for one zone, disappearing for another, and then reappearing at a further out location. Such reswitching could arise if transportation costs are wage intensive. In such a case, the rent–distance profile will be discontinuous at the switch points. If the intermediate land use is agricultural, then there will be a discontiguous pattern of development from the urban perspective.

A More Comprehensive Approach

An approach that combines a variety of the elements discussed so far is due to Fujita (1976a, b). This rather complex model combines the behavior of renters, both business and residential, builders and demolishers, building owners, both rent

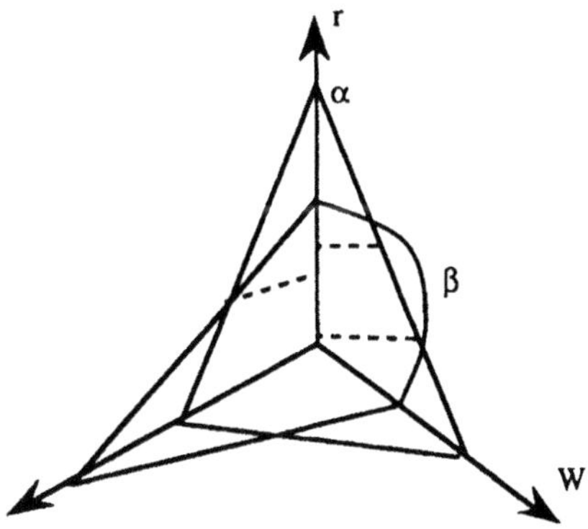

Fig. 3.7 Wage-profit–rent curves with reswitching

maximizers and speculators, and land speculators. All of these actors engage in intertemporal optimization within a vintage structures framework a la Brueckner. The resulting equilibrium reflects a "land-use sequence" for which each plot of land has certain building types at certain times, used for different purposes over time, all of this governed by an optimal set of "switching times."

This leads to a combination of the von Thünen (1826) ring model with the Hoyt (1939) wedge or sector model. Land uses will establish themselves at the most central point they can dominate at a point in time, based on the steepness of their bid-rent gradients, and develop outward along wedges. This leads to different rings being developed simultaneously with temporary gaps (discontiguities) appearing between rings as an inner land use grows to meet an outer one. The pattern existing at a point in time for three land uses is shown in Fig. 3.8, with the vertical axis showing the percentage of land use at a particular distance in each use and the horizontal one being the distance from the CBD.

Fujita (1981) placed this in an optimal control context to solve for an efficient pattern of zoning. Such a pattern in such a model is depicted for three land uses as shown in Fig. 3.9.

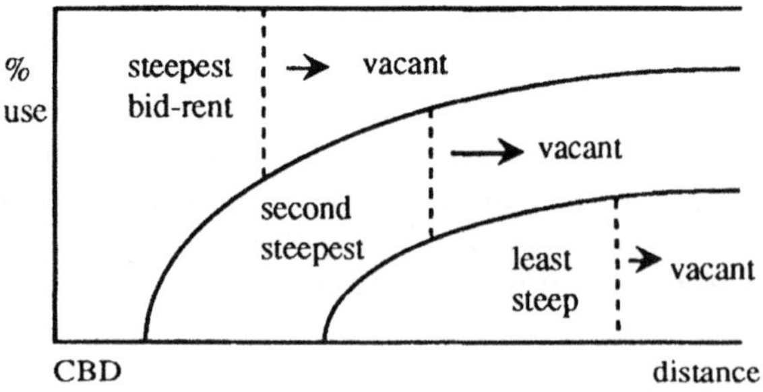

Fig. 3.8 Land use–distance relations in Fujita Ring-Wedge model

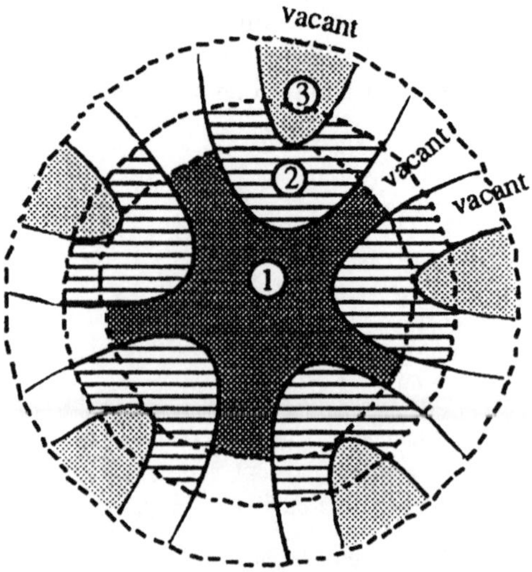

Fig. 3.9 Aeriel view of Fujita Ring-Wedge model

Polycentrism

Fujita and Ogawa (1982) use a similar model in a long narrow city to generate equilibria with multiple nuclei, the polycentric city originally envisioned by Harris and Ullman (1945).[16] Fujita and Ogawa rely on external economies among firms, arguing that structural shifts between monocentrism, duocentrism, tricentrism, and so on, will reflect bifurcations in a ratio of commuting to production parameter and an urban potential parameter. Thus, the model seems to reflect the old trade-off between agglomeration and congestion. If the centers represent a hierarchy, we have the basis for a Brussels-type model. In the discontiguous context, this suggests a mixing of town and country that might even please utopian socialists and garden city planners alike.[17]

Notes

1. They simulate a 729-zone model, concluding that a finer degree of resolution leads to greater multiplicity of solutions. This agrees with the arguments of Dendrinos with Mulally (1985).
2. Haag and Weidlich (1980) have used stochastic synergetics to model intraurban migration as well as more generally (Haag and Weidlich, 1983).
3. Thompson (1979) has posed the choice as "rat-infested slums or our glorious heritage" and used catastrophe theory to suggest that discontinuous shifts in architectural preferences could be the key variable in such switches ("rubbish" becomes "treasure" and vice versa).
4. Dendrinos (1979) models slum formation as a six-dimensional parabolic umbilic ("mushroom") catastrophe, with control variables being income, rental rate of return, rate of discount, and population to capital stock, and state variables being quality of stock and utility level of residents. Dendrinos (1981) also examines neighborhood stability when there are nonlinear lot size–lot quality relationships.
5. Tipping was first identified by Duncan and Duncan (1957) and Wolf (1963) with special reference to Chicago. Smolensky, Becker, and Molotch (1968) viewed it as "blockbusting," an unstable prisoner's dilemma, game theoretic outcome. O'Neill (1981) empirically confirmed racial tipping in Chicago whereas Woods (1981) did not for Great Britain, noting that this may be due to institutional barriers to residential mobility there.
6. Leung (1987) studies intermediate integrated forms between homogeneous zones using fuzzy set theory.
7. The Mills–Muth model is a neoclassically rigorous version for intraurban land use of the von Thünen (1826) model and like it (and the Burgess (1925) model) produces a ringlike structure of land uses.
8. Berry (1976) and Steinnes (1977) found empirical support for this formulation in Chicago.
9. Yinger (1976) shows that equilibrium does not exist in this kind of model if minorities want to live near whites while the latter are prejudiced. This resembles the predator–prey case of Dendrinos with Mulally (1985).
10. The relative size of this discontinuity should correlate with Becker's (1957) coefficient of discrimination. Similar discontinuities can occur due to zoning (Stull, 1974; White, 1975; Rosser, 1978a).
11. An additional assumption is necessary to obtain segregation without prejudice, such as a slight income differential between groups.
12. Other US cities exhibiting such ghettos include St. Louis, Milwaukee, and Los Angeles, to name a few more. Sometimes, such as in Milwaukee, ghetto boundaries may be influenced by local topographical or infrastructural features (rivers, railroads, etc.).

13. Other applications of this technique include internal physical–chemical structure of stars (Eggleton, 1974), volcanic eruptions (Tucotte, 1974), the impact of radiation on oxygen absorption in cancer cells and stress effects in heated polymers and metals (Crank, 1974), solving the optimal stopping decision of a gambler facing a given reward function (van Moerbeke, 1974), and modelling the penetration of an egg by a sperm (Perelson and Coutsias, 1986).
14. Rosser (1976) has shown how outside of Madison, Wisconsin, in the early 1970s, extraterritorial plat review was used within a three-mile limit to veto subdivision plats that could not be immediately hooked to an existing sewer interceptor. This led to leapfrog development beyond the three-mile limit and a reported discontinuity in vacant land values of $5,000 per acre just beyond the limit compared with $2,000 per acre just inside the limit. In short, "he who controls the sewers, controls the countryside" (Paul R. Soglin, Mayor of Madison, 1989, personal communication).
15. Brueckner (1981b) claims empirical support for such a sawtooth pattern from Milwaukee data. Yinger (1979) supports this for Madison and St. Louis without reference to Brueckner's model. Indeed, supply restrictions (Rosser, 1978a) are an alternative explanation.
16. Odland (1978) has empirically rejected monocentricity. Heikkila, Gordon, Kim, Peiser, Richardson, and Dale-Johnson (1989) show evidence for eight separate centers in metropolitan Los Angeles.
17. But not if what we are contemplating is an ugly exurban sprawl.

Chapter 4
Morphogenesis of Regional Systems

And if you share my personal taste, watch out especially for the breaks in continuity, the frontier zones. Be alert to the moment when the shape or the materials of the roofs change, or when the wells have a different structure (a revealing but rarely-noticed piece of evidence).
Fernand Braudel (1986, The Identity of France, p. 51)

4.1 The Continuous Flow Model

4.1.1 Linear and Nonlinear Variations

The most famous model of regional structure is the concentric ring model of von Thünen (1826) based on linear transportation costs, in a homogeneous plane, with a single urban market center. Subsequently this model was expanded by Christaller (1933) and Lösch (1940) to multiple market centers of different sizes and different commodities, while still assuming linear transportation costs on a homogeneous plane. For both Christaller and Lösch, the shape of a market area around a single center for a single commodity will be a hexagon. Thus the general structure of a regional hierarchy, based on a set of market areas for different commodities, will be a nested (Christaller) or overlapping (Lösch) set of hexagons.

An alternative way of deriving this model is due to an application of linear programming to transportation and location problems in the form of a continuous flow model by Beckmann (1952, 1953), based on earlier such work by Kantorovich (1942) and Koopmans (1949). This continuous flow framework was later extended to that of nonlinear transportation costs[1] (Puu, 1979, 1980, 1981a, b, c; Beckmann and Puu, 1985). In the nonlinear transportation cost case, quadrangular market areas arise as the optimizing solution rather than the hexagonal areas of the linear, Christaller–Lösch models.

Let us consider a general form of the continuous flow model for a single commodity. Let x_1 and x_2 refer to coordinates along the north–south and east–west axes, respectively, thus specifying locations. In such a space, trade flow vectors and price

J.B. Rosser, *Complex Evolutionary Dynamics in Urban-Regional and Ecologic-Economic Systems*, DOI 10.1007/978-1-4419-8828-7_4,

patterns can be given by flow equations determined, respectively, by a "divergence law" and a "gradient law."

Excess demand by location is given by

$$q = q(x_1, x_2). \tag{4.1}$$

Maxima will be sinks that are market outlets, and minima will be sources that are production points. Spatial equilibrium is given by

$$\iint q(x_1, x_2)\mathrm{d}x_1\mathrm{d}x_2 = 0. \tag{4.2}$$

The divergence law states that the local flow vector, $\phi(x_1,\ x_2)$, of commodity movements will be given by

$$-\ q(x_1, x_2) = \partial Ø_1/\partial x_1 + \partial Ø_2/\partial x_2, \tag{4.3}$$

with

$$Ø_n = 0, \tag{4.4}$$

holding normal to a trade-limiting, outer boundary.

If $k(x_1,\ x_2)$ is the unit transportation cost and $\lambda(x_1,\ x_2)$ is the price at location (x_1, x_2), then locational optimization is given by a potential function:

$$\mathrm{m}_{Ø} \iint k|Ø|\mathrm{d}x_1\mathrm{d}x_2 = k, \tag{4.5}$$

subject to (4.3) and (4.4) holding as constraints. This is solved by the gradient law solution,

$$kØ/|Ø| \quad = \mathrm{grad}\,\lambda, \tag{4.6}$$

which implies that flows move in the direction of steepest price increase (determined by transportation cost) and orthogonally cut equiprice lines.[2] The Christaller–Lösch hexagon pattern will arise when k is constant for all locations. Puu (1981a) has shown that labor flows may be just the opposite of commodity flows, when capital and labor are the only non-land inputs.

Puu (1981b) and Beckmann and Puu (1985, Chap. 4) argue that in the more general nonlinear case, the hexagonal pattern is structurally unstable and should disappear under perturbations, to be replaced by a structurally stable quadrangular pattern. In this pattern, a finite number of sinks and sources will alternate with a finite number of saddle points. Furthermore, in contrast to the Christaller–Lösch model, trade flows will tend to occur *along* boundary lines. Such a pattern is shown in Fig. 4.1.

Fig. 4.1 Beckmann-Puu quadrangular grid with nonlinear transportation costs

4.1.2 Structural Change of the Flow Pattern

Although such flow patterns are structurally stable, they may exhibit sudden structural changes in response to continuous changes in parameters underlying transportation cost. For the bifurcation set of underlying parameters, the system will be unstable as it passes from one state to another discontinuously.

Puu (1981a) suggests that road capacity, u, total traffic, v, and fuel prices, w, can be such control variables driving the potential function λ through the state variables, x_1 and x_2. Thus we have

$$\mathrm{d}x_i/\mathrm{d}k = \lambda x_i(x_1, x_2, u, v, w), \tag{4.7}$$

whose structural singularities (bifurcations) are determined by a Thom-type (1972) canonical form, which is either an elliptic umbilic catastrophe, diffeomorphic to

$$\lambda = x_1^3 - 3x_1x_2^2 + w\left(x_1^2 + x_2^2\right) - ux_1 - vx_2, \tag{4.8}$$

or a hyperbolic umbilic catastrophe, diffeomorphic to

$$\lambda = x_1^3 + x_2^3 + wx_1x_2 - ux_1 - vx_2. \tag{4.9}$$

The former case is shown in Fig. 4.2 with the upper portion showing the bifurcation set and the lower portion showing the flow patterns for different combinations of (u, v, w) with the middle one representing a completely unstable, degenerate hexagonal cusp, a "monkey saddle." This monkey saddle can be slit into either two ordinary saddles or a node surrounded by three saddles.

Fig. 4.2 Elliptic umbilic catastrophe of regional flow patterns

The latter case is shown in Fig. 4.3 with a similar layout. In this case, the most degenerate point is an isolated singularity in an otherwise structurally stable "laminar" flow. Parameter changes either eliminate the singularity entirely or split it into one saddle and one node or two saddles and two nodes.

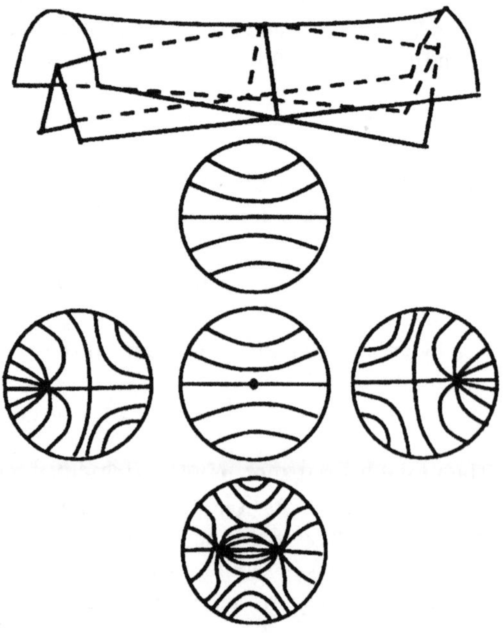

Fig. 4.3 Hyperbolic umbilic catastrophe of regional flow patterns

4.1.3 Wave Patterns in the Continuous Flow Model

Beckmann (1987) has shown how wave patterns can emerge in the above model under the appropriate dynamic specifications. Thus if λ represents equilibrium price, then flow adjustment will be given by

$$\partial \emptyset / \partial t = a \,\mathrm{grad}\, \lambda. \tag{4.10}$$

Likewise, if price adjustment is proportional to excess demand, we have

$$\partial \lambda / \partial t = b[q + (\partial \emptyset_1 / \partial x_1 + \partial \emptyset_2 / \partial x_2)]. \tag{4.11}$$

These combine to give

$$\mathrm{d}^2 \lambda / \mathrm{d}t^2 = bq' \mathrm{d}\lambda / \mathrm{d}t + ab\left(\partial^2 \emptyset_1 / \partial x_1^2 + \partial^2 \emptyset_2 / \partial x_2^2\right). \tag{4.12}$$

In the case where excess demand is independent of price (as in the simple continuous transportation model), this will generate undamped waves and prices will cycle forever, never converging to equilibrium. However, if excess demand is a strictly decreasing function of price, then the waves will diminish over time and converge on equilibrium. For specific values of a and b, singularities may emerge associated with the appearance of a growth pole or some other structural transformation.

4.1.4 Multiplier–Accelerator Cycles in the Continuous Flow Model

4.1.4.1 The Single-Region Case

The study of cycles in a continuous flow spatial context has been carried out by Puu (1982, 1986, 1989, 1990) and by Beckmann and Puu (1985, Chap. 8) for a single regional model. Initially Puu (1982) and Beckmann and Puu (1985) examined a continuous version, due to Philips (1954) of the linear multiplier–accelerator model of Samuelson (1939).

Let Y = income, I = investment, s = marginal propensity to save, v = accelerator, then the spaceless model is given by

$$\mathrm{d}Y / \mathrm{d}t = I - sY \tag{4.13}$$

and

$$\mathrm{d}I / \mathrm{d}t = v(\mathrm{d}Y / \mathrm{d}t) - I, \tag{4.14}$$

which can be combined to form

$$\mathrm{d}^2 Y / \mathrm{d}t_2 + (1 + s - v)(\mathrm{d}Y / \mathrm{d}t) + sY = 0. \tag{4.15}$$

Introduction of spatial income differences depends upon the Laplacian of income; $\overline{\upsilon}$:

$$\bar{\nu}^2 Y = \partial^2 Y/\partial x_1^2 + \partial^2 Y/\partial x_2^2. \tag{4.16}$$

Furthermore let m be the marginal propensity to import from a generalized outside and X = exports and M = imports. Thus at any location

$$X - M = m\bar{\nu}^2 Y, \tag{4.17}$$

which enters the model like induced investment. Thus our spatialized model becomes

$$\mathrm{d}^2 Y/\mathrm{d}t^2 + (1 + s - v)(\mathrm{d}Y/\mathrm{d}t) + sY - m\bar{\nu}^2 Y = 0. \tag{4.18}$$

This system can exhibit a variety of damped, explosive, or oscillatory patterns, depending on parameter values, much like the original multiplier-accelerator models. However, the spatial component can generate aperiodic cyclical behavior, *even in an essentially linear model*, an unusual occurrence.

Then Puu (1986) followed Hicks (1950) and Goodwin (1951) by adding a nonlinear investment function, possessing a floor and a ceiling, instead of the linear $v(\mathrm{d}y/\mathrm{d}t)$. He shows that a stable limit cycle in the $(Y, \mathrm{d}y/\mathrm{d}t)$ space exists for the spaceless version of this model. In the spatial version, the spatial coordinates bifurcate the temporal behavior of the system between damped and cyclical behavior. He (1990) has also examined chaotic behavior in this model with different strange attractors emerging for different savings rates.

4.1.4.2 The Two-Region Case

To analyze a two-region nonlinear case, Puu (1987) replaces the spatial element with adjustment speeds, λ for the multiplier and κ for the accelerator. If Y_2 is the income of the second region and f is the nonlinear investment function, then the system is given by

$$\mathrm{d}^2 Y_1/\mathrm{d}t^2 + \lambda\kappa S_1 Y_1 = \lambda\kappa v f(\mathrm{d}Y_1/\mathrm{d}t) - (\kappa + \lambda S_1)(\mathrm{d}Y_1/\mathrm{d}t) + \lambda\kappa m_2 Y_2 \lambda\kappa m_1 Y_1, \tag{4.19}$$

$$\mathrm{d}^2 Y_2/\mathrm{d}t^2 + \lambda\kappa S_2 Y_2 = \lambda\kappa v f(\mathrm{d}Y_2/\mathrm{d}t) - (\kappa + \lambda S_2)(\mathrm{d}Y_2/\mathrm{d}t) + \lambda\kappa m_1 Y_1 \lambda\kappa m_2 Y_2. \tag{4.20}$$

He examines this system from the standpoint of coupled oscillators.[3] Initially he considers a case where Y_2 drives $Y_1 (m_1 Y = 0)$, the "forced oscillator" case of the van der Pol (1927) type. In this case, the term $\sqrt{\lambda\kappa(S_2 + m_2)}$ becomes a forcing term of frequency whose value drives the system and bifurcates the patterns of cyclical behavior at certain values. Puu recognizes that as this term increases the system exhibits frequency "entrainment," followed by quasiperiodicity, and eventually chaotic dynamics.

For the general coupled oscillator case, behavior can be very complex, even for quite simple cases. Even letting $\lambda\kappa m_1 = \lambda\kappa m_2 = 1$, the system may have up to six equilibria, which can be a combination of stable or unstable limit cycles, as well as saddle points and sinks and sources. Obviously relaxing the above assumption can lead to almost anything, including chaotic dynamics, a result he examines in detail later (1989). Thus paired regional cycles may be very complex, even without the spatial component explicitly modeled.

4.2 Evolution of Urban and Regional Systems

4.2.1 Predator–Prey Cycles in Single Cities

An alternative tradition for modelling interacting cycles has long existed in the form of models of predator–prey cycles in ecology, as studied by Lotka (1920) and Volterra (1937).[4] The first to initiate such analysis of urban and regional systems were Dendrinos (1980b) and Dendrinos and Mulally (1981, 1983, 1985), for the case of individual cities relative to the nation as a whole. They argue that a city exists in an essentially ecological relationship with other cities, or more generally, the nation as a whole. For a given city, the national general equilibrium will imply a particular niche, as defined by a particular population and per capita income relative to the respective national averages for those variables, which will tend to be maintained over time as the nation as a whole grows.

Although some cities may remain in their relative steady-state niches, many exhibit oscillatory and other dynamic behavior patterns. Without modelling the underlying determinants, these dynamics are presumed to be captured in a pair of interacting differential equations of the relative (or normalized) population, x, and the relative per capita income, y. In particular, Dendrinos (1980b) proposed the following:

$$\mathrm{d}x/\mathrm{d}t = x(-a_1 - a_{11}x + a_{12}y) \tag{4.21}$$

and

$$\mathrm{d}y/\mathrm{d}t = y(a_2 - a_{21}x), a_1, a_{12}, a_2, a_{21} > 0. \tag{4.22}$$

The a_{11} parameter represents a growth-inhibiting congestion effect. When it is zero, as in the classical Lotka–Volterra model, the system harmonically oscillates around the equilibrium (orbital pattern). However, if $a_{11} > 0$, the system will spiral inward to the equilibrium (sink-spiral or stable focus) or converge directly on it without oscillation (stable node). Thus $a_{11} = 0$ represents a Hopf bifurcation point for this system.

Dendrinos and Mulally (1981) followed this up with a detailed empirical study of the data for 90 US SMSAs for the period 1940–1977. They found a variety of cases, including 64 oscillatory, 3 steady states (Bay City, MI, Shreveport, LA, and Syracuse, NY), 21 perturbed, and 2 unclassified (Clarksville-Hopkinsville, TN-KY and Boise, ID; these two possibly chaotic). Among the oscillatory, 23 showed sink spirals, 14 long-term oscillatory, 26 medium-term oscillatory, 1 orbital (Rochester, NY), and 0 limit cycles. Among the perturbed were 15 structurally stable switches of spiral pattern and 6 discontinuous changes of state, of which 4 (Anderson, IN, Chicago, IL, Buffalo, NY, and St. Louis, MO) shifted from steady state to unidentified, 1 (Bismark, ND) shifted from a sink spiral to unidentified, and 1 (Anchorage, AL) exhibited a "naked discontinuity" (unstable node) of explosive growth. But there were no Hopf bifurcations. Several of these patterns are shown in Fig. 4.4.[5]

Dendrinos and Mulally (1983a) expanded the set to 175 and sought to find patterns for the values of the parameters in the Lotka–Volterra system. No relation to age or region could be found. However, in general, population seemed to adjust about 100 times more quickly than income. Comparison of the steady-state population and income relation suggests a highly nonlinear relation along the lines hypothesized by Casetti (1980), Dendrinos (1980a), and Papageorgiou (1980). Furthermore, for most cities, the period of oscillation is negatively related to speed of population adjustment and the congestion effect ("urban friction coefficient").[6]

A modification of this single city, Lotka–Volterra approach has been investigated by Orishimo (1987) and extended by Zhang (1988). Instead of relative population and per capita income, he uses total population and average land rent, the latter reflecting environmental impacts of urban populations. He proposes and tests for Japanese cities a four-stage life cycle of cities, pre-urbanization, urbanization, sub-urbanization, and de-urbanization. The general pattern of this cycle is shown in Fig. 4.5.

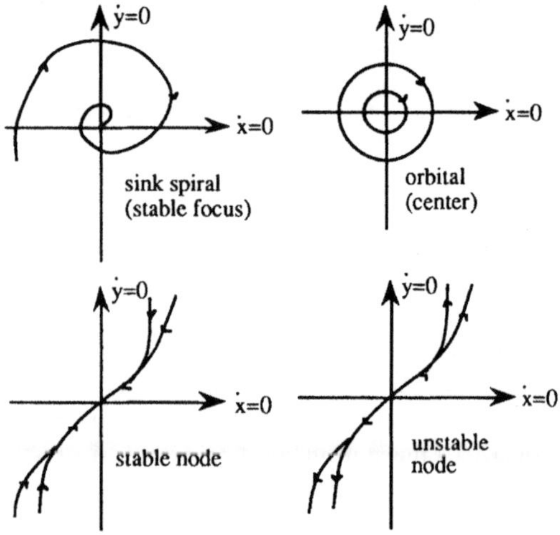

Fig. 4.4 Alternative Lotka–Volterra urban dynamics

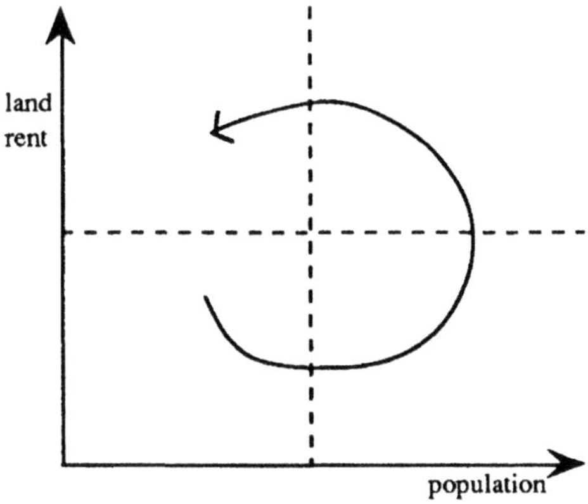

Fig. 4.5 Orishimo urban population–rent cycle

4.2.2 Interregional Predator–Prey Cycles

The Lotka–Volterra, "ecological" approach has been extended to regional and interregional systems and their evolution as well. Dendrinos and Sonis (1986) model relative population levels according to a "least action" principle, measured by a cumulative entropy, as suggested by Volterra (1937). They show that the only asymptotically stable solution is agglomeration into a single point, but note that this result certainly does not fit US data (or for that matter, that of any other country). They suggest that the pure Volterra relative dynamics need more interaction terms to avoid the single-point agglomeration result.

Another model focusing on Lotka–Volterra equations is due to Haag and Weidlich (1983). They study the behavior of two populations in a multiregion area. The Lotka–Volterra dynamics are driven by four control variables, namely, internal and external "sympathy" parameters for each population, whose values may be positive or negative. These Lotka–Volterra dynamics are embedded in a transition matrix migration model, subject to stochastic fluctuations. Numerical simulation suggests seven different outcomes as the control parameters are varied.

In the first case, all internal and external sympathy parameters are weak, leading to a stable node solution in the form of an even distribution of population. In the second, weak internal but strong external sympathies exist, leading to population concentration in one of two areas (stable nodes) while the uniform distribution is unstable. In the third, extremely strong internal and strong external sympathies exist. This resembles the second case except for the additional existence of weaker secondary stable nodes in which the populations are split between two distinct areas and four additional unstable nodes. In the fourth case, all sympathy parameters are positive, and both populations tend to prefer one particular area. This leads to a strong stable node at the preferred area, but a weak stable node at the opposite end of the area, and one unstable node. This means the populations will probably end up in the preferred area unless they initially begin sufficiently close to the other one in which case the positive sympathy effects may pull them there.

The remaining three cases all exhibit some cyclical phenomena. In the fifth case, there are weak internal sympathies and strong external sympathies of opposite sign, meaning one group likes to be near the other (predators), but the other group likes to be far from the first one (prey). This leads to a stable focus at the uniform distribution, but the convergence to that is a contracting spiral. The sixth case differs from the fifth in having stronger internal sympathies and thus more collective migrations, generating a bifurcation point where the uniform distribution has lost its stability. The result is a tendency for endless cycles as groups of "predators" chase groups of "prey" within a "zone of fluctuations," with no clear pattern, although they are bounded. In the final case, there are stronger internal sympathies than in the sixth case with the asymmetric and strong external sympathies as in Cases 5 and 6. This leads to a definite limit cycle where the "chase" will tend to converge on a particular "route." This final case resembles the classic Lotka–Volterra case with permanent, harmonic cycling.

In contrast to this approach, Dendrinos (1984a, b) extends the analysis of urban cycles (Dendrinos and Mulally, 1981) to regions of the US. Again the variables are regional population share and per capita income, normalized to national averages. He makes an empirical study of the New England (NE), Middle Atlantic (MA), East North Central (ENC), West North Central (WNC), South Atlantic (SA), East South Central (ESC), West South Central (WSC), Mountain (M), and Pacific (P) regions from 1929–1979. In contrast to the urban models, Dendrinos finds little cyclical behavior in this data set. Rather he finds a strong tendency for the regions to fall into two distinct groups, separated most clearly by population density. He argues that each group is converging on separated stable equilibria.

This led him to argue the strong position that there is an underlying structure, or "code," to the regional dynamics of the US economy.[7] The idea that there is a tendency toward a persistent regional division between developed and less-developed regions has been advocated by Casetti (1982)[8] and Sheppard (1983), and has a long history in economics. In this case, Dendrinos finds New England, Mountain, West North Central, and East South Central to be gravitating toward the less-developed node, whereas the rest are gravitating toward the more developed one. The estimated structure of this overall code, with its two stable equilibria (D_1, D_2), separated by an unstable one (D_3), and its phase dynamics, along with paths of each region (x is population share and y is normalized per capita income), are shown in Fig. 4.6.

The system generating this structure was given by

$$\mathrm{d}x_i(t)/\mathrm{d}t = \alpha_i[-ax_i(t)^3 + bx_i(t) + c - y_i(t)], \quad (4.23)$$

$$\mathrm{d}y_i(t)/\mathrm{d}t = \beta_i[-d + ex_i(t) - y_i(t)]. \quad (4.24)$$

In this system α_i and β_i are region-specific adjustment parameters. Dendrinos estimated national values for the other parameters as $b' = b/a = -27.09$, $c' = c/a = -30.78$, $d = 1.75$ and $e = 0.77$. He interprets (4.23) as being a demand process and (4.24) as being a supply process.

Stuctural stability can be analyzed using a cusp catastrophe of the form.

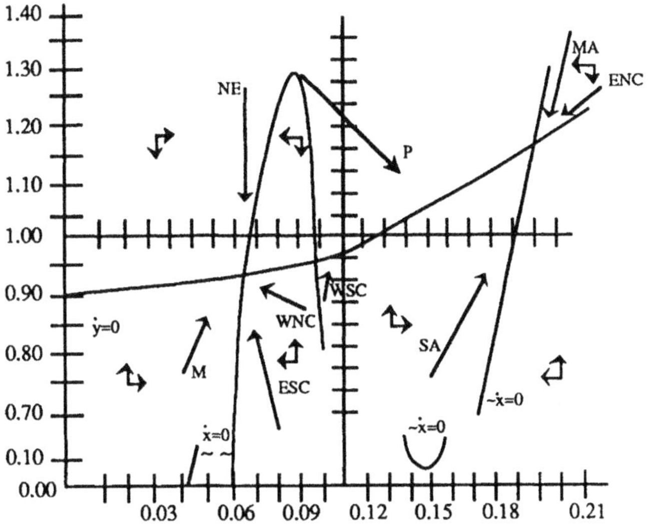

Fig. 4.6 Dendrinos US regional code

$$C = -x_i^3 + b'x_i + (c' - y), \tag{4.25}$$

which is consistent with the structure shown in Fig. 4.6. The broader structure with the isoclines of $x = 0$ and $y = 0$ in plane P is shown in Fig. 4.7.

Dendrinos (1984b) argues that the 50-year regional trajectories represent "fast dynamics," or adjustment to the equilibrium manifold. He then suggests that over a longer time horizon, "slow dynamics" changes in parameters will tend to bring the

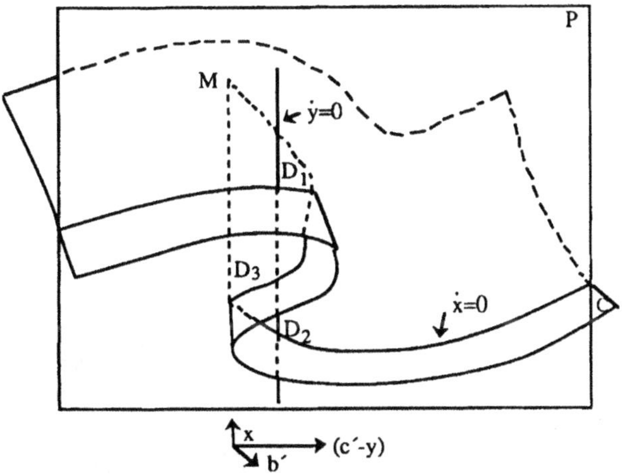

Fig. 4.7 Cusp catastrophe of Dendrinos US regional code

two stable equilibria nearer each other, thus reflecting the lesser regional inequality observable in more developed countries relative to LDCs generally. Except at the unstable cusp point, M, which is a uniform distribution, there will be multiple equilibria. Clearly, this ambitious effort by Dendrinos shows the possibility of analyzing the morphogenesis of regional evolutionary patterns, despite possible criticisms regarding model misspecification and econometrics.[9]

4.2.3 The Emergence of Chaotic Dynamics

4.2.3.1 Relative Stock Models

That Lotka–Volterra systems can exhibit deterministic chaos for certain parameter values was clearly demonstrated by May (1976) and May and Oster (1976). Dendrinos and Sonis (1987, 1988, 1989, 1990) and Sonis and Dendrinos (1987) have extended this to the study of relative stocks (population or income) in regions. They present a general specification for the I location, one stock case:

$$x_i(t=1) = A_i F_i / \Sigma_j A_j F_j, \tag{4.26}$$

with $A_i > 0,\ i,\ j = 1,\ 2,\ \ldots,\ I$, and

$$F_i = F_i[x_h(t);\quad h = 1, 2, \ldots, I] > 0. \tag{4.27}$$

The x_i is population in region i, the F_i is locational advantage for region i, and the A_is are control parameters driving the dynamics. They consider the J-stock case in Dendrinos and Sonis (1989).

Dendrinos and Sonis (1987) show that for certain values of the A_is, chaotic dynamics can occur for the two-location and three-location versions of the one stock model. They extend the terminology of chaos theory by showing the possible existence of large and dense "strange containers," within which the system may erratically oscillate. An example for the three-location case is shown in Fig. 4.8.

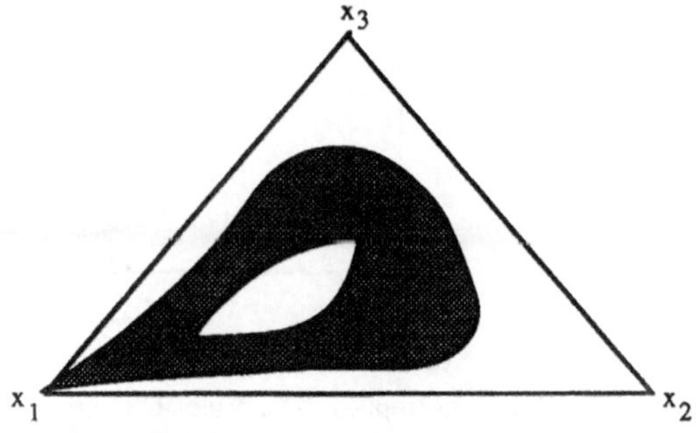

Fig. 4.8 Strange container for Dendrinos–Sonis model

It must be noted that the closer a strange container comes to filling the entire space, the closer the system is to pure randomness rather than deterministic chaos. If the attractor is the entire space, then there is no determinism.

Dendrinos and Sonis (1988) use a log linear form of the above to estimate the dynamics of a four-region breakdown of the US from 1850 to 1983. They conclude that the parameters are nowhere near the chaotic zone. They also predict long-term decline and "competitive exclusion" of the North. They suggest, following Dendrinos with Mulally (1985), that chaotic dynamics may be more likely for smaller units such as cities.[10]

Nijkamp and Poot (1987) have developed a very similar model to the above for New Zealand, although drawing on a theoretical foundation due to Alonso (1978). They present a series of simulations, including some exhibiting chaotic dynamics. However, they also suggest that the associated parameter values are unlikely.

The first model of chaotic interregional migratory dynamics was due to Rogerson (1985). Instead of a Lotka–Volterra mechanism, he took distance factors more into account by examining an unconstrained gravity model of the form

$$M_{ij}(t) = \alpha P_j(t) V_j(t) d_{ij}^{-B}, \qquad (4.28)$$

where M_{ij} is migration from i to j in time $(t, t+1)$, $P_j(t)$ is the population of j at t, $V_j(t)$ is the number of job vacancies in j at t, d_{ij} is the distance between i and j, and α, $\beta > 0$. Vacancies can be modeled from past migration to give a net migration equation with $\phi(t)$ being net migration in t. Thus

$$\emptyset(t+1) = \emptyset(t)[1 - \alpha(\Sigma_i P_i + \Sigma_i V_i)]. \qquad (4.29)$$

The term in the brackets determines the dynamics. If it is greater than 2, there are explosive oscillations, the equilibrium is unstable. Between 1 and 2 and also between 0 and -1, behavior is damped harmonic. Between 0 and 1, it is damped monotonic. Between -1 and -3.57 is the transition to chaos with period-doubling cycles. If the term is less than -3.57, there is chaos. Rogerson suggests that while the parameter values allowing chaos are limited and unlikely, a wide range of initial conditions are compatible with chaos.

4.2.3.2 A Production Model

Roger White (1985) has developed a generalized, multisector, multiregion model in which chaotic dynamics may appear. His model contains both sectoral and regional economies and diseconomies of scale. In general if there are no diseconomies, or if sectoral growth rates are very low, chaos will not emerge.

The basic equation is

$$X_{ij,t+1} = X_{ij,t} + r_j(\pi_{ij,t}), \qquad (4.30)$$

where $X_{ij,t}$ is production of the jth sector in the ith region at time t, r_j is the "intrinsic growth rate" of sector j, and $\pi_{ij,t}$ is profit generated. He then presents region- and sector-specific revenue and cost functions, the latter embodying both sectoral and regional economies and diseconomies of scale.

He simulates model behavior, varying the number of centers and sectors as well as r_js. The main conclusion is straightforward: Chaotic dynamics occur at lower levels of r_j when there are either more sectors or more regions, although the critical values of r tend to exceed 1.4 in all cases, a rather high number. He also notes the possibility of "degrees of chaos" and the appearance of "quasi-cyclical behavior" in zones of chaos. In any case, the greater likelihood of chaotic dynamics when there are more sectors and regions corresponds to the earlier observations regarding the greater likelihood of unusual cyclical behavior for cities as compared with regions (Dendrinos with Mulally, 1985; Dendrinos and Sonis, 1988).

4.3 Self-Organizing Regional Morphogenesis

4.3.1 Order Through Fluctuations

Regional morphogenesis can be studied by calibrating and simulating large-scale models. The first such large-scale model was the widely used and imitated model of spatially disaggregated, intraurban transportation networks, work locations, and residential locations, due to Lowry (1964).[11]

The next major development was due to Jay W. Forrester (1969), the inventor of "industrial dynamics" (1961), whose model has been much criticized, most notably for its lack of spatial disaggregation as well as for the ad hoc and empirically questionable basis of many of its equations, among other things.[12] Nevertheless, Forrester was responsible for a major breakthrough, namely, the recognition of the significance of nonlinearity, especially when combined with complex time-lag structures. He declares (1969, p. 108):

> Nonlinear coupling allows one feedback loop to dominate the system for a time and then cause this dominance to shift to another part of the system where behavior is so different that the two seem unrelated.

Although he later declared that such a complex system would be "highly insensitive to most system parameters" and "resistant to efforts to change its behavior" (ibid.), he nevertheless had uncovered the link between nonlinearity and discontinuity in dynamic systems.

A major synthesis of these two approaches has been that of the already mentioned "Brussels School." These models have focused on both intraurban and regional phenomena. Besides exhibiting nonlinear relationships between infrastructure, economic activity, and population, the latter group of these models are generally multisectoral with each sector exhibiting a critical threshold level of population necessary for it to function. This becomes the basis for the existence of a hierarchy of

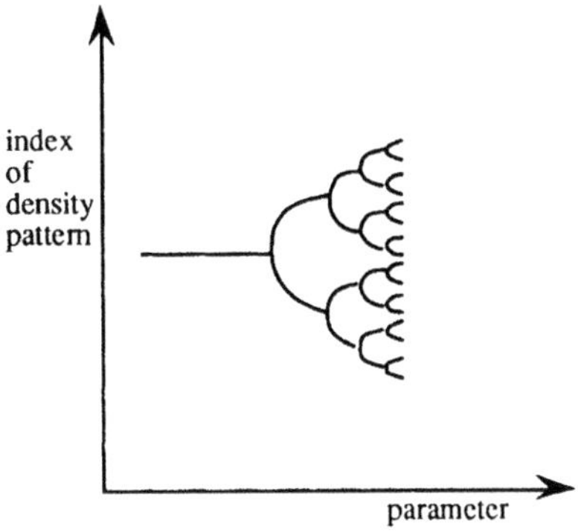

Fig. 4.9 Evolutionary bifurcation tree

cities in the classic Christaller–Lösch fashion, ultimately derived from al-Muqqadisi over a 1000 years ago (Hassan, 1972).

Another aspect of these models is that they are stochastic. System evolution can move along a "bifurcation tree," as in Fig. 4.9,[13] but through stochastic fluctuations that determine the outcomes of the phase transitions at the bifurcation points. Thus there is "order through fluctuations."

Furthermore, these branches, and the stochastic processes driving the actual outcomes, do not represent either equilibria or optimizing behavior in any necessary sense. Indeed, the emphasis is on the *out-of-equilibrium* nature of the fluctuations occurring at the bifurcating phase transitions, in contrast to the views of catastrophe theory and chaos theory in which it is the equilibrium *itself* that bifurcates. The inspiration for this approach has been from physical chemistry notions of the behavior of dissipative structures in open systems, obeying the laws of thermodynamics, as enunciated by Nicolis and Prigogine (1977). Structural change cannot occur in equilibrium. It is not just in "out-of-equilibrium" states, but in "far-from-equilibrium" states that the self-organizing, order-through-fluctuations process manifests itself. The Prigogine view has been further adumbrated by Jantsch (1979, 1982) to imply that "later" branches represent "higher" levels of organization, as in the process whereby particles became atoms became molecules became self-reproducing cells became structurally differentiated organisms became human beings became societies.[14]

A fairly standard version of this approach can be found in a model by Allen and Sanglier (1981). They argue that populations in particular urban subregions follow logistic equations related to unemployment wherein agglomerative externalities compete with congestion effects in conjunction with crucial sectoral threshold effects. Thus if x = population, i indexes location, k indexes sector, J = employment, d_{ij} = distance between i and j, b and m parameterize demographics, τ does so for congestion effects, and β does so for commuting costs, then

$$\mathrm{d}x_i/\mathrm{d}t = bx_i\left(\mathrm{J}_i^0 + \sum\nolimits_k J_i^k - x_i\right) - mx_i + \tau\left[\sum_{j\neq i} x_j^2 \exp(-\beta d_{ij}) - x^2 \sum \exp(-\beta d_{ij})\right]. \tag{4.31}$$

In turn, if α is a supply–response parameter, η is a labor–output ratio, ε is per capita demand at unit price, P is price, e is derived from elasticity of demand, ϕ is the transport cost of good k, and A_{ij} is the "attractiveness" of i to clients in j, then

$$\mathrm{d}J_i^k \Big/ \mathrm{d}t = \alpha J_i^k \left\{ \eta_i^k \left[\sum\nolimits_j \left(x_j \varepsilon^k \Big/ \left(p_i^k + \emptyset^k d_{ij} \right)^e \right) \left(A_{ij}^k \Big/ \sum\nolimits_i A_{ij}^k \right) \right] - J_i^k \right\}. \quad (4.32)$$

The attractiveness terms are given by

$$A_{ij}^k = \left\{ \gamma^- \left[1 \left(\delta + \rho \left(x_i - x_i^{th} \right) \right) \right] \right\} 1 \Big/ \left(P_i^k + \emptyset^k d_{ij} \right)^1, \quad (4.33)$$

where x_i^{th} is the threshold for which the function appears; γ, δ, and ρ are growth parameters of attractiveness; and I is population responsiveness to attractiveness.

In their simulations, which allow for a stochastic element, there is a strong tendency to "polarization." Although different cities rise and fall over time in response to the stochastic fluctuations and their interactive, nonlinear dynamics, there is a powerful tendency for the most rural zone to go into a permanent decline, unbudgeable by any fluctuation. They suggest that such a pattern appears in Belgium as a whole, where more urban Northern Belgium is growing and more rural Southern Belgium is declining. Within the Bastogne region of Southern Belgium, the smaller town of Libramont is growing while the others, including the larger Bastogne, are declining. They suggest that the growth of Libramont ("at the expense" of its neighbors) reflects "historical chance" because a railway stop was built only at Libramont, "initially by English speculators interested in travelling from Ostend to Trieste in order to take ship to India!" (ibid., p. 180).

According to Yannick Lung (1988), this tendency to polarization reflects the "dialectical discourses of French culture" in contrast to "Anglo-American approaches." In any case the morphogenetic transformation reflects the self-organizing principle of order through fluctuations.

4.3.2 *Time Scales and Slaves*

To fully understand the evolutionary morphogenesis of regional systems, it is important to distinguish between different timescales of activities or processes as well as different hierarchical levels. This effort links up with the synergetics ideas of Haken (1983), especially the idea of "adiabatic approximation" or the "slaving principle." The idea is that slower-moving variables ("order parameters") "slave" faster-moving variables, or more generally that unstable (or undamped) modes of oscillation determine the behavior of stable (or damped) modes. Thus, a hierarchy can be established of variables based on their time behavior, with slow ones driving fast ones, although there may be problems of interpretation as these are usually eigen combinations of observable variables (Medio, 1984).

Morphogenesis will be driven by bifurcations of the order parameters which will cause the slaves to jump to a new state or mode of behavior. Clearly, this concept closely relates to a catastrophe theory view of the world. Control variables can be viewed as order parameters slaving state variables which discontinuously jump at certain bifurcation values of their "masters." Haken, in line with the Prigogine view, sees a stochastic process laid on top of this deterministic structure. Fluctuations near bifurcation points may become the key to morphogenesis and synergetic self-organization.

Among those attempting to build models based on different time scales have been Wegener (1982) and Wegener, Gnad, and Vannahme (1986). Although not explicitly adopting the synergetics approach, they have built a multilevel model of the Dortmund region of West Germany, based on the idea that longer timescale processes fundamentally bound and determine the behavior of shorter timescale processes. They adopt the Lowry-type, tripartite division between industrial, residential, and transportation subsystems. They categorize processes for each of these subsystems into slow, medium, or fast timescales. Their categorization, including such factors as response duration, response level, and reversibility, are listed in Table 4.1.

They further enumerate greater detail in the medium-speed demographic change sector. Also it appears that the medium-speed "technological change" variable refers to the purchase or sale of media of transport, cars, buses, and so on, rather than what is more generally thought of as technological change, although such purchases are clearly the way by which embodied technological change in transportation (e.g.,

Table 4.1 Time structure of urban processes

Level	Change process	Stock affected	Response time (years)	Response duration (years)	Response level	Reversibility
Slow	Industrial construction	Industrial buildings	3–5	50–100	Low	Very low
	Residential construction	Residential buildings	2–3	60–80	Low	Low
	Transport construction	Transport system	5–10	>100	Low	Nearly irreversible
Medium	Economic change	Employment/ unemployment	2–5	10–20	Medium	Reversible
	Demographic change	Population/ households	0–70	0–70	Low/high	Partly reversible
	Technological change	Transport equipment	3–5	10–15	Medium	Very low
Fast	Labor mobility	Workplace occupancy	<1	5–10	High	Reversible
	Residential mobility	Housing occupancy	<1	5–10	High	Reversible
	Daily mobility	Traffic	<1	2–5	High	Reversible

Table 4.2 Space–time structure of regional processes

Time →	Fast	Medium	Slow
↓Space suburb	Local shopping trips	Household information	Segregation or similar social processes
Metropolitan region	Business trips	Relocation of offices or other facilities	Construction of buildings and infrastructure
System of regions	Information transfer	Migration	Establishing communication networks

more gas-efficient cars) diffuse into the subsystem. In the end, they emphasize the limits of their approach and cite Patrick Geddes (1915) on the "most manifest, yet most mysterious" nature of the patterns of urban evolution.

An effort to engage in such timescale classifications in conjunction with a view of hierarchies of scale is due to Batten and Johansson (1987). Furthermore, they explicitly link their approach to Haken's "slaving principle" and to the catastrophe theory idea that slower variables will control faster variables through their bifurcations. Their "doubly classified" processes are listed in Table 4.2.

This table reflects the influence of both Wegener, Gnad, and Vannahme (1986) and the logistical network theory of Åke Andersson (1986) regarding slow changes in logistical networks causing sudden changes in regional trading patterns and relative urban relationships.

A major caveat at this point is needed, one which relates to the conflict between a view of the world as essentially stable (the catastrophe theory view) and a view of the world as essentially unstable (the chaos theory view). The synergetics view usually coincides with the former, arguing that generally there is a stable structure, even if beset by stochastic fluctuations. At critical points, morphogenesis will occur as the structure shifts, driven by fluctuations near bifurcation points. What will matter here will be the change in the order parameters (control variables) as the slaving principle applies. However, Haken (1983, Chap. 12) notes that when there is a transition to chaotic motion, the slaving principle "fails." The damped fast modes or variables become destabilized, and there is no local or short-run stability whatsoever. Diener and Poston (1984) have labeled this phenomenon, the "revolt of the slaved variables," which "overthrow" the order parameters and engender chaos.

4.3.3 A Fractal Synergesis

We shall now synthesize both order and chaos in regional time and space by an abstract application of fractal geometry, the brainchild of Benoit Mandelbrot (1983). The concept of a fractal dimension allows for a way of measuring a degree of disorder and of scaling relationships both in time and space at different levels. We have seen that efforts have been made in this direction, but not fully developed. Among others, Beckmann and Puu (1985, Chap. 9), have recognized that the question of different levels of analysis severely complicates their continuous flow model. Indeed, they quote Mandelbrot on this problem, regarding the perception of a ball of thread:

> Indeed, at the resolution possible to an observer placed at 10 m, it appears as a point, that is, as a zero-dimensional figure. At 10 cm it is a ball, that is a three-dimensional figure. At 10 mm it is a mess of threads . . . At 0.1 mm each thread becomes a sort of column . . . At 0.01 mm each column is dissolved into filiform fibers. . . (1985, p. 254)

Mandelbrot has argued that fractal geometry provides a method for resolving the problem of scaling and relating processes at one scale with those of another scale. More formally, a fractal dimension is a Hausdorff–Besicovitch dimension, defined for a set S as d, such that d is the infimum of the numbers such that for any $\varepsilon > 0$, there is $\delta > 0$ and cover U of S such that the sets $B \in U$ (balls) all have diameter $< \delta$ and $\Sigma_{B \in U}$ (diam $B)^{\alpha} < \varepsilon$. This measure is similar to measures of dimension for the "determinateness" of "deterministically chaotic" processes.

Fractal measures in the form of Hurst coefficients of rescaled range analysis have been used to study long-term dependence in regional employment level in the US (Booth and Koveos, 1983). This method was developed by Mandelbrot (1969, 1972) and measures how the range of variation of a series divided by the standard deviation varies as the log of the scale as the scale is reduced.

Fotheringham, Batty, and Longley (1989) and Batty, Longley, and Fotheringham (1989) have investigated how fractal measures can be used to model urban growth patterns when not all land is developed simultaneously. This is the diffusion-limited aggregation process that generates density gradients as a historical outcome of development with resulting dendritic urban forms.[15]

Let us now propose a way of simultaneously characterizing the hierarchical structure as well as the evolutionary dynamics of a regional system. We shall contemplate a regional system with a total population, $P(t)$, that is growing at a natural rate, n, subject to some stochastic variability. There exists within the region a hierarchy of cities, each following a rank (i) specific logistic production function whose thresholds, K_i, depend both on infrastructure and the production function of the main commodity exported by a city of its rank, reduced in terms of population to

$$\mathrm{d}P_i(t)/\mathrm{d}t = n[1 - P_i(t-1)]/K_i. \tag{4.34}$$

Following a formulation of Mandelbrot (1965), due initially to Auerbach (1913) and Zipf (1941), the rank-size structure of the critical thresholds can be given by a fractal dimensionality, $d(K)$, such that

$$\Pr(K_i > K_j) = (K_j/K_0)^{-d(K)}, \tag{4.35}$$

where K_0 is the threshold level of the largest city.

Furthermore, the dynamics follow an attractor, R, whose fractal dimensionality is $d(R)$. As $d(R)$ increases, the dynamics will more closely approximate a random walk. Following May (1976), we can see that the "tuning parameter" of individual urban dynamics at any level will be given by n/K_i, which will be higher the lower down the ranks (the smaller is K_i) the city is. From the above authors, it is known that at a value of 3 for this parameter, the dynamics become two-period oscillations, leading to period doubling as it is increased, and becoming chaotic at 3.8284. This then corresponds with the much noted observation (Dendrinos with Mulally, 1985) that smaller population units are more likely to exhibit chaotic dynamics than larger ones.

Within this system, even without fractal change, cities will jump to new levels as they cross critical thresholds with general regional population growth. Thus, there will be an evolution of the system to greater complexity as new urban units form and old ones move to higher levels. Which specific ones will make the leap at any point will partly be determined by stochasticity.[16]

Now these fractal dimensions will depend on the whole array of factors that have been discussed so far as determining both dynamics (e.g., Dendrinos' "regional code") and hierarchies of central places (the pattern of threshold levels in the Allen and Sanglier analysis). These in turn will depend on the longer-term evolution of the underlying slow variables, most notably driven by technological change as well as infrastructure investment. Such changes will lead to regional morphogenesis if there is a discontinuous change in the fractal dimensions, that is, a bifurcation of the fractal structure of the deterministic chaos. Thus, even though the slaves might be free, synergetic morphogenesis through fluctuations at bifurcation points may still occur.

Notes

1. Although nonlinearity can arise from spatial heterogeneity, its most common source is "economies of distance" due to fixed loading and unloading costs with changes in transport modes with distance. Short hauls are carried by trucks with low fixed costs and high variable (distance-related) costs, while long hauls are by trains or ships with the opposite pattern.
2. The structure of a transportation network can be measured using "connectivity" indices (Casti, 1979).
3. Lorenz (1987b) has extended this model to the analysis of international trade.
4. Despite the obvious relevance for such phenomena as corn–hog cycles, economists were slow to utilize these models, Goodwin (1967) and Samuelson (1967, 1971) being the first with business cycle models.
5. Dendrinos (1985) has also investigated the possibility of chaotic dynamics for smaller urban areas.
6. Dendrinos (1982) and Dendrinos and Mulally (1984) modify this model to allow capital investment. Stability depends on the marginal effect of capital on population outweighing its marginal effect on urban "carrying capacity." Dendrinos and Mulally (1983b) also show that an optimal urban income tax can accelerate convergence to the steady state.
7. Dendrinos (1989) has carried out a similar study of regions in China.
8. Casetti (1982) distinguishes between those in a Malthusian trap and those that are not. He (1989) has estimated bifurcation points in Europe as nations went from the trap to growth with the Industrial Revolution.
9. Dendrinos himself recognizes that he fails to include other regions of the world, most notably those in neighboring countries into which US regions arguably extend (Garreau, 1981). It must

be admitted that he has made more effort to estimate his models than have the members of the Leeds or Brussels Schools.

10. This coincides with the general evidence that deterministic chaos is more likely to be found in microeconomic rather than macroeconomic data series (Baumol and Benhabib, 1989).
11. Anas (1986) has criticized this model for its linearity and lack of clear theoretical economic basis.
12. Rosser (1974) points out that "counterintuitive" policy conclusions emerging from Forrester's model, which he cited as evidence of the superiority of his method, clearly derive from questionable empirical relationships in his model.
13. This diagram is not a Feigenbaum cascade; there is no necessary chaos anywhere. It is more analogous to the branching of species in the "tree of evolution."
14. We can distinguish "morphogenesis," structural differentiation (Turing, 1952), from "autopoiesis," the self-renewal of a space–time structure (Maturana and Varela, 1975), from "anagenesis," the evolution of self-organizing dynamics to higher levels (Boulding, 1978; Jantsch, 1979). The crucial role of system openness for anti-entropic processes to operate in self-organizing contexts was stressed by Schrödinger (1944) and von Bertalanffy (1962). See Rosser (1990a) for further discussion.
15. It has been suggested in a personal communication by Daniel S. Friedman (the architect, 1986) that fractal measures can be used to measure intraurban design patterns.
16. This stochasticity depends on the vagaries of individual human acts and decisions. Thus, Moscow's rise to great size ultimately derived from its selection as the home of the Metropolitan of the Russian Orthodox Church, after Metropolitan Petr Of Vladimar died in Moscow in 1326 and Ivan I had his bones interred in the Kremlin, which led to it becoming the capital of the tsars and all that entailed in the highly centralized Russian system. Smolensk was far superior as a mid-Russian transhipment point from a purely economic–geographic perspective.

Chapter 5
Complex Dynamics in Spatial Systems

The unpurged images of day recede;
The emperor's drunken soldiery are abed;
Night resonance recedes, night-walkers' song
After great cathedral gong;
A starlit or a moonlit dome disdains
All that man is,
All mere complexities,
The fury and the mire of human veins.
William Butler Yeats, 1930, "Byzantium"

But evidently analysis of 'tipping' phenomena wherever it occurs — in neighborhoods, jobs, restaurants, universities or voting blocs — and whether it involves blacks and whites, men and women, French-speaking and English-speaking, officers and enlisted men, young and old, faculty and students, or any other dichotomy, requires explicit attention to the dynamic relationship between individual behavior and collective results.
Thomas C. Schelling (1971a, "Dynamic Models of Segregation," p. 186).

5.1 Complexity and Socioeconomic Spatial Systems

Dynamic complexity is a part of a broader meta-complexity that encompasses many different definitions of complexity, with the list of 45 provided by Seth Lloyd (Horgan, 1997) being the basic starting point (Rosser, 2009a). Dynamic complexity can be seen as consisting of four categories: cybernetics, catastrophe, chaos, and interacting heterogeneous agent-based complexity, which Rosser (1999b) previously labeled "small-tent complexity," the "big-tent complexity" being this overall dynamic complexity. However, given the vaguely insulting implication of this "small-tent" label, as well as the fact that dynamic complexity is hardly the totality of complexity, it seems better to use a more precisely descriptive term. Indeed, for many people when they hear the term "complexity," it is often this small-tent or agent-based complexity (also sometimes labeled "Santa Fe complexity") that they think of.

J.B. Rosser, *Complex Evolutionary Dynamics in Urban-Regional and Ecologic-Economic Systems*, DOI 10.1007/978-1-4419-8828-7_5,

Arthur, Durlauf, and Lane (1997, pp. 3–4) have famously identified characteristics associated with this sort of complexity as being dispersed interaction, no global controller, cross-cutting hierarchical organization, continual adaptation, perpetual novelty, and out-of-equilibrium dynamics. Crucial to this view of complex dynamics is the local nature of the dispersed interactions. These occur without any definite direction from some global level controlling force, particularly one that is driving toward some sort of equilibrium. Nevertheless, these local interactions do often produce higher-level emergent order that may sometimes come to resemble an equilibrium outcome, and the pattern of the local interactions may be influenced to some extent by feedback from these higher-order structures that they have created.

Within the social sciences broadly, one of the areas where this sort of vision is clearly highly appropriate is in spatial systems, particularly urban and regional systems in geographical space. It is thus not surprising that we have seen so many models in such systems that exhibit the sort of patterns of which we are speaking in earlier chapters. However, some of these operated directly at higher levels and did not truly reflect the sort of self-organizing form that we associate with true agent-based complexity.

Nevertheless, it is widely argued that the first example of this sort of complexity modelling was indeed from the area of spatial modelling, in particular urban socio-spatial modelling. The widely argued first example was the model of urban segregation due to Thomas Schelling (1969, 1971a, b, 1978).

5.2 The Generality of the Schelling Model

In his initial development of the model, Schelling did not formulate a mathematical model, per se. Rather he played "tabletop games" based on certain assumptions that did imply mathematical models. His initial effort (1969) involved a distribution of agents along a line, but then he expanded this to a two-dimensional setup using a chessboard or other rectangular boards with lattice structures on their surfaces (1971a, b, 1978).

In both of these setups, he assumed an initially random distribution of two types of agents, assumed to be white and black, in a more or less integrated situation. While he did not have any of the agents specifically favoring strictly segregated outcomes over integrated ones, he allowed both groups to have slight preferences for immediate neighbors like themselves. He also allowed for there to be vacant spaces. Within these fairly fixed spaces, he then allowed movements of agents, with them moving to preferred locations based on the slight preference to be next to others like oneself. The key was to have an agent move if she or he was in a condition of having more different neighbors than like neighbors. The result he found over time for both the linear and the two-dimensional lattice case was that a pattern of segregation would emerge over time as an apparently stable equilibrium outcome. Subsequent studies have found this general result to be amazingly robust to a variety of alterations.

The basic linear case can be seen in Fig. 5.1, with the upper line being the initially integrated case, and the lower one the fully segregated case that emerges (Schelling, 1971a, p. 151). In Fig. 5.2, one finds an initial distribution for the two-dimensional case (op. cit., p. 155), with Fig. 5.3 showing the segregated outcome (op. cit., p. 157).

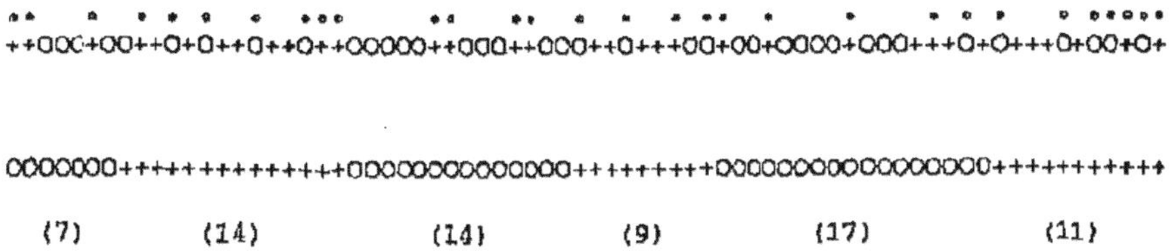

Fig. 5.1 Linear case for Schelling model

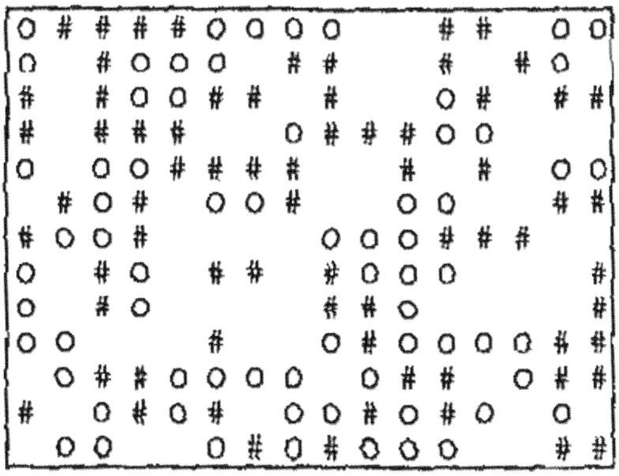

Fig. 5.2 Two-dimensional lattice case for Schelling model: initial distribution

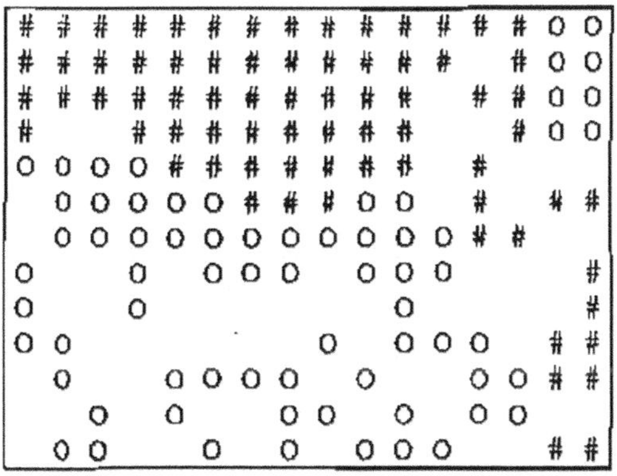

Fig. 5.3 Two-dimensional lattice case for Schelling model: segregated outcome

Many observers have found this to be a depressing result in the wake of moves to outlaw discrimination in housing. Sociologists (Clark, 1992; Clark and Fossett, 2008; Laurie and Jaggi, 2003) note that in reality there is asymmetry between whites and blacks in regard to their preferences. While blacks do not mind very much being in a 50–50 neighborhood, whites tend to mind quite a bit, more strongly preferring to be in solidly majority white neighborhoods. This tends to exacerbate the finding of Schelling, which comes about in the perfectly symmetric case regarding relative degrees of prejudice and presumably moves things closer to what one observes in the case of prejudice and discrimination. However, a strong outcome already discussed earlier is that when there is actual discrimination, the discriminated-against group pays more for equivalent housing than the discriminating group, whereas in the case of asymmetric prejudice without discrimination, it is the more prejudiced group that pays more for equivalent housing.

5.3 An Evolutionary Game Theoretic View of the Schelling Model

Following up on work by Young (1998), Zhang (2004a, b) shows how the Schelling result emerges as a general outcome of a wide class of evolutionary games played on a lattice within a torus. We follow the presentation in Zhang (2004a) here to see what is involved. A two-dimensional lattice graph is assumed to define the market, with agents located on the vertices, and there being a boundary. Agents may either be concerned about their four nearest neighbors, which is known as a *von Neumann neighborhood*, or they are concerned about their eight nearest neighbors, which is known as a *Moore neighborhood*, with the general results holding for either case. The total market must exceed the size of the neighborhood.

Zhang introduces prices for locations within given neighborhoods, which are determined solely by vacancy rates v_i, with there existing a "natural vacancy rate," $v^* > 0$. All agents are assumed to have identical incomes. A simple linear pricing rule is assumed for neighborhood i, given by:

$$P_i = a - b(v_i - v^*), \tag{5.1}$$

with $a, b > 0$. While this allows for a market mechanism, there is no assumption that the price will clear the market, given the assumption that there is a positive natural vacancy rate. This pricing mechanism also makes no distinction directly regarding the race of the owners within a neighborhood, which indeed is equivalent to simply being driven by the sum of the white and black owners in a neighborhood (the presumed two types of owners). Housing is assumed to be homogeneous, and all agents earn the same income, Y.

It is assumed that whites have some prejudice in that they suffer a loss of utility from living adjacent to blacks, whereas blacks do not have this prejudice. Thus, utility for a white as site i is given by

$$U_{wi} = Y + \theta W_i - B_i, \tag{5.2}$$

with $0 < \theta < 1$, and W and B are the respective numbers of white and black neighbors. Utility for a black at site j is given by

$$U_{bj} = Y - W_j - B_j. \tag{5.3}$$

Moving is an evolutionary stochastic process following rules laid out by Young (1998), which is governed by a potential function and a probabilistic behavioral rule. The potential function is derived from the sum of utilities over all the agents. Although the potential function shows how agents can increase their utilities, the random element in the evolutionary game allows for them to make mistakes and move to a lower utility situation. The behavioral rule for an agent to choose to make a move, A_1, rather than to make no move, A_2, is a probability given by

$$\Pr(A_1) = \left[e^{\beta u(A1)}\right] \Big/ \left[e^{\beta u(A1)} + e^{\beta u(A2)}\right], \tag{5.4}$$

with $\beta > 0$. This formulation follows the logit model of econometrics and has been elaborated further by Blume (1993, 1997) and Brock and Durlauf (2001a, b, 2002) as well as Young (1998).

Zhang then follows Foster and Young (1990) to define a *stochastically stable set* relative to a perturbed process, P^β, such that if $\lim(\beta \to \infty)\, u^\beta(x) > 0$. The stochastically stable set is the smallest set that contains all such sets, and it will be observed more frequently as both β and time go to infinity. Zhang then establishes that the probabilistic decision rule combined with the potential function guarantees that the evolutionary process will go to such a stochastically stable set and hence will be observed most of the time. This is a general result that shows the robustness of the Schelling model.

Zhang then goes on to find the well-established result for the case when there is prejudice but no discrimination. Segregation will emerge, and blacks will live in neighborhoods with higher vacancy rates and lower prices, while whites will live in neighborhoods with lower vacancy rates and higher prices. They will pay for their prejudice.[1]

5.4 Network Analysis of the Schelling Model

Given the use of a lattice framework since the early work of Schelling himself, it is somewhat surprising that it is only relatively recently that the idea of considering the model from the standpoint of network analysis has been followed. We have already seen a bit of a pointer in that direction in the distinction between von Neumann neighborhoods and Moore neighborhoods, although it seems that the basic insight of Schelling's holds irrespective of which of these holds in a simple lattice. While expanding the form of topology of the network in a set of Schelling neighborhoods does not undermine this fundamental tendency to an emergence of segregation even when most people favor integration over segregation in the abstract, allowing for broader forms does bring out some variations on the patterns that may be observed, with indeed real cities exhibiting different topological structures due to different geographies and physical features, matters usually assumed away in the standard economic models based on considering a homogeneous plane.[2]

A likely reason for this lack of application of network theory to the Schelling model for so long may well be that its application in economics for a long time was dominated by the study of spatial market structures and trading links rather than housing markets. The underlying theory for this is the mathematics of random graphs (Erdös and Renyi, 1959, 1960; Erdös and Spencer, 1974; Estigneev, 1988). The first effort in economics to draw on this vein of mathematics was Kirman, Oddou, and Weber (1986).[3] This would be followed by Ioannides (1990, 1997) and Estigneev (1991). Curiously while Ioannides has long been a student of urban economics, his focus was on market structures and relationships rather than housing patterns. However, it turns out that random graphs are just one of the several topologies possible in this network analysis, with key papers being by Pancs and Vriend (2007); Fagiolo, Valente, and Vriend (2007); and Banos (2010).[4] We shall draw principally on these last two in our discussion.

We now think of a non-directed graph (NDG) of M nodes with N agents occupying some of them, no more than one agent per node, with $M \geq N \geq 3$. Between any pair of nodes k and h, there may or may not be a connecting edge, with this pattern describable by a sociomatrix, W, where each w_{kh} will equal zero if the nodes are not linked and will equal 1 if they are linked. The neighborhood or interaction group of a node k will consist of the set of nodes to which it is linked. For our neighborhoods, the utility of an agent will depend on the proportion of her neighbors that are like her, with this equaling 1 if the proportion is less than a tolerance parameter, λ, and zero if the proportion is less than that.

A useful characteristic that varies across different network topologies is the clustering coefficient, C. If E is the number of connected pairs among neighbors of a node i, with k the degree of the node, then C is given by

$$C_i = 2E/\left[k_i\left(k_i - 1\right)\right]. \tag{5.5}$$

This can vary between zero and 1 as connectedness increases from none to a fully connected level, and a network as a whole can be characterized the average clustering coefficient for the entire network, as these may vary across nodes. A substantial variety of these topologies can be identified.

The two simplest are those we have already encountered, the von Neumann and the Moore neighborhoods, associated with a simple square or rectangular two-dimensional lattice setup (think of a rectangular grid pattern of streets as one finds in downtown Manhattan). Figure 5.4 (from Fagiolo, Valente, and Vriend, 2007, p. 320) shows these two patterns, with the von Neumann on the left and the Moore on the right.

These are examples of *regular* NDGs that are lattice grids characterized by spatial homogeneity and symmetry with roto-translation invariance. These particular

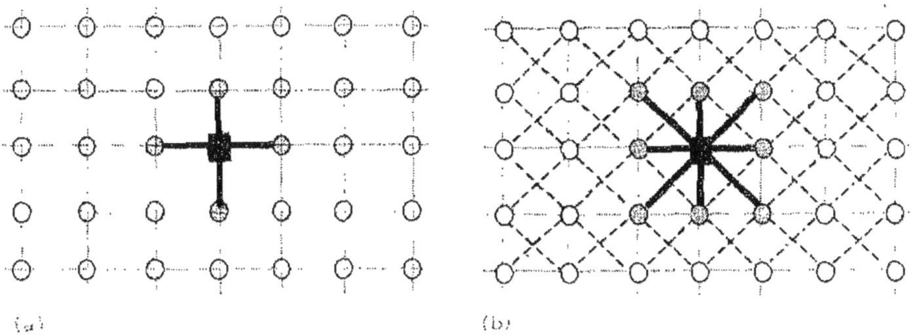

Fig. 5.4 von Neumann and Moore neighborhoods

Fig. 5.5 Regular graph of 20 nodes and 4 links per node

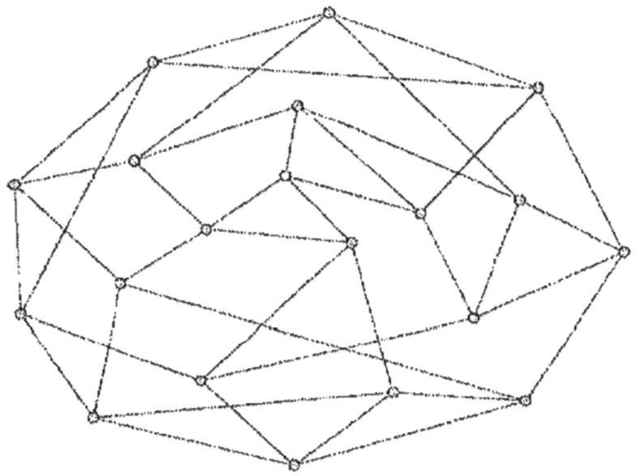

ones possess clustering coefficients of 0.55. However, regular NDGs may have more generalized shapes that are not grids. Regularity is given by every node having an identical cluster coefficient or number of links. Figure 5.5 (from op. cit., p. 321) shows a more generalized regular grid with 20 nodes for which each node is connected to 4 other nodes, but there is no grid or symmetry or roto-translation invariance.

From here the pattern can become more general still as we move to *random* graphs where the cluster coefficient can vary across nodes. Figure 5.6 (from op. cit., p. 321) shows such a case for 20 nodes for which the average is four links per node, but they can vary.

Rather different is the class of graphs known as *small world networks* that have substantially higher clustering coefficients and resemble a wide variety of social and economic networks, including market structures. These were fist studied by Watts and Strogatz (1998) and further by Watts (1999, 2003). These networks can be characterized by cliques, with different kinds of nodes that will have varying degrees of connectedness among each other. Figure 5.7 provides an example of such a network with 100 nodes, and the black ones more highly interconnected than

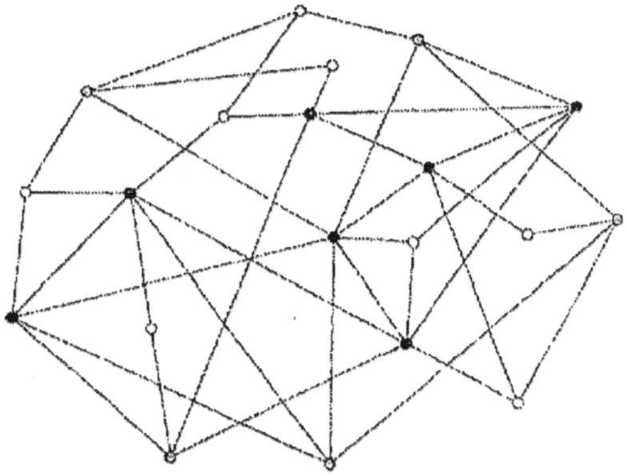

Fig. 5.6 Random graph with 20 nodes and average 4 links per node

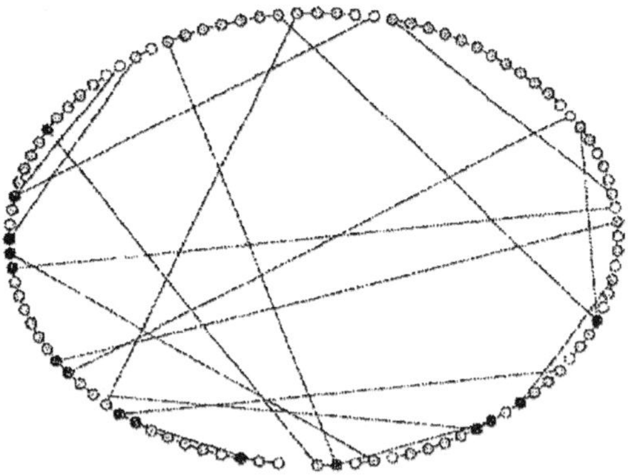

Fig. 5.7 Small world network with 100 nodes of varying clustering

the grey ones, which in turn are more highly interconnected than are the white ones (from Fagiolo, Valente, and Vriend, 2007, p. 322).

Another pattern is the *scale-free* network that can be characterized by hubs that are especially highly linked, with the pattern arising from a preferential attachment algorithm studied by Barabási and Albert (1999).[5] The average clustering will vary depending on the number of nodes, with this being a nonmonotonic relationship of the number of nodes, maximizing for about 40 nodes. Figure 5.8 provides an example of this sort of network (from Fagiolo, Valente, and Vriend, 2007, p. 323), with a high average clustering coefficient of 0.99.

Finally we observe the fractal network, which has a somewhat lower degree of clustering than the scale-free one, with an average clustering coefficient of about 0.95. This is given by a Sierpinski carpet pattern as depicted in Fig. 5.9 (from Banos, 2010, p. 10).

These different network patterns have been studied varying degrees of tolerance and forms of randomness in the allowing of movement of agents in simulations. While there are varying levels of bifurcations of patterns, the general robustness of the Schelling result has been confirmed across these many network structures.[6]

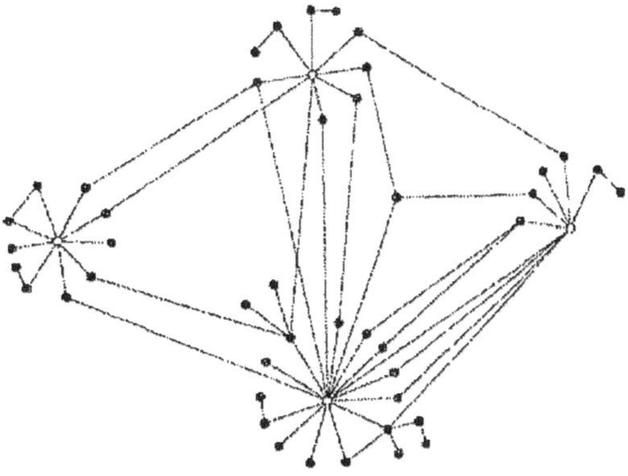

Fig. 5.8 Scale-free network

Fig. 5.9 Fractal Sierpinski carpet network

5.5 Zipf's Law and Urban Hierarchy

The emergence of real cities 5,000 years ago out of the nascent agricultural villages can be viewed as the historical analogue of the story implied in the model of the emergence of cities from a homogeneous plane. Corresponding with that emergence came the rise of agrohydraulic kingdoms and then empires in the great monsoon river systems of the Tigris–Euphrates, the Nile, the Indus, and the Hwang Ho. These systems were characterized by urban areas of varying size, going up from the agricultural villages at the base to great capital cities at the top of hierarchies of urban areas. From then forward such hierarchies have persisted, with only occasional breaks in certain areas, such as the collapse of cities in Europe for several centuries after the fall of Rome, although even in that period and place a ghost of the hierarchy persisted in the form of the Church and its hierarchy, with the cities with bishops and cardinals generally becoming prominent bases for expansion when cities revived during the Middle Ages, as discussed earlier in this book.

This urban hierarchy can also be viewed as a pattern of inequality, parallel in a sense to the inequalities in wealth and income that emerge among individuals in societies. This parallel was noticed quite early when Auerbach (1913) invoked Pareto (1897) as a possible source for a method to explain, or at least describe, the pattern of urban population inequality. Curiously, Pareto lies at the foundation of the approach of modern *econophysics* in describing modern economic phenomena through the use of power law distributions (Mantegna and Stanley, 2000; McCauley, 2004; Yakovenko and Rosser, 2009). While currently these distributions are being advocated strongly by physicists for use in explaining a variety of phenomena, including financial market returns,[7] their use was initiated by the economist and sociologist, Pareto, prior to their use by physicists, even if economists would essentially forget about these distributions[8] except in certain subfields, such as urban economics.

A form for the Pareto distribution as applied to city sizes due to Singer (1936) is given by

$$rP_r{}^{\alpha} = A, \tag{5.6}$$

where r is the rank of the city in size, P_r is the population of a city of rank r, and A and α are constants. Empirically, this is usually studied by fitting the relationship in a log–log form as given by

$$\ln r = \ln A - \alpha \left(\ln P_r\right). \tag{5.7}$$

It is typical of power law distributions that they are linear in log–log form.

Auerbach argued for a particular form of this to hold empirically, namely, that $\alpha = 1$. In that case, what is known as the *rank–size rule* holds that

$$P_r = P_1/r. \tag{5.8}$$

Even though Auerbach would argue first for this, this rule has come to be known as *Zipf's Law* after the work of George K. Zipf (1941, 1949), who applied it to many phenomena, although especially to cities. More strongly than Auerbach, Zipf argued that it was a universal law or empirical regularity.

Since then, many have argued that Auerbach and Zipf were right, that there is a nearly universal tendency for city sizes, or uban area sizes, to conform to Zipf's Law, with the rank–size rule holding across many societies and times (Krugman, 1996; Fujita, Krugman, and Venables, 1999; Batten, 2001). However, even as many argued for the universality of this presumed empirical regularity, many noted the lack of a theoretical explanation for it (Carroll, 1982; Krugman, 1996). While it has been argued to be a merely stochastic rather than fundamentally theoretical explanation, Gabaix (1999) has stepped forward to argue that Zipf's Law is a limit to processes conforming to Gibrat's Law (1931), also posed as with Pareto as a general explanation of patterns of inequality. Gibrat's law holds if the growth rates of cities are identically distributed independent of city size, with the distribution characterizable by mean and variance alone.

Even as a long tradition has argued for the universality of Zipf's Law, questioning voices have long raised doubts about this claim, starting with Alfred J. Lotka (1925), who estimated the value of α in Equation (5.7) to be 0.93 for an estimate based on the largest 100 cities in the US. While close to 1, it is not quite equal. The argument has continued ever since. Berry (2010) argues that there have been three phases of the debate, the first involving Auerbach and Lotka and Singer, the second starting with Zipf in the 1940s and ending with surveys by Rosen and Resnick (1980) and Carroll (1982), with a third phase coming out of the work of Gabaix (1999) and others (Batten, 2001; Dobkins and Ioannides, 2001; Ioannides and Overman, 2003).

Even as many have studied the relationship across nations and spaces (Rosen and Resnick, 1980), Batten (2001) argues that it has held over time within the US, drawing on the self-organizing sandpile model of Bak (1996). This historical pattern is exhibited in log–log form in Fig. 5.10 (Batten, 2001, p. 97), although as Batten admits, there are "kinks" in it from time to time.

A possible source for these kinks to emerge (and more general deviations from Zipf's Law) is if urban growth rates are not independent of size, and if cities of certain sizes tend to grow faster than ones at other sizes during certain historical periods. We shall return later to this argument. However, Gabaix (1999) recognized

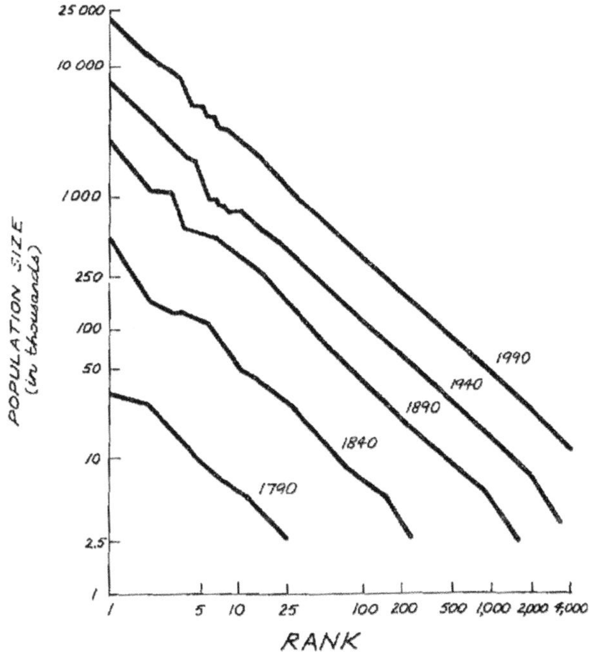

Fig. 5.10 Rank–size distribution of cities in the United States, 1790–1990

that the independence assumption might not hold in general (even though he thinks it holds approximately much of the time). If it does not, then it is still possible to characterize the pattern according to an instantaneous version of the distribution. Letting S_i be the ratio of city i to the total urban population (i.e., the normalized city size), with $\mu(S)$ the instantaneous mean of the growth rate of the city, $\sigma^2(S)$ be the instantaneous variance of the growth rate, and B_t a geometric Brownian motion, then city size at time t, S_t varies by

$$\mathrm{d}S_t/S_t = \mu\left(S_t\right)\mathrm{d}t + \sigma\left(S_t\right)\mathrm{d}B_t. \tag{5.9}$$

This leads to a limit distribution of city sizes with a local Zipf exponent, α, given by

$$\alpha\left(S\right) = 1 - 2\left[\mu\left(S\right)/\sigma^2\left(S\right)\right] + \left[\partial\sigma^2\left(S\right)/\sigma^2\left(S\right)\right]/\left[\partial S/S\right]. \tag{5.10}$$

Now Ioannides and Overman (2003) recognize this possible variability, following on Gabaix, nevetheless find that the basic Zipf Law still holds broadly, even as the local Zipf exponent may vary somewhat across city sizes.

A more recent meta-analysis of the empirical evidence has been carried out by Nitsch (2005). He reviews 29 studies ranging from Lotka's in 1925 to ones in 2002 (Song and Zhang, 2002; Davis and Weinstein, 2002), reporting minima, maxima, means, and standard deviations for each study, as well as estimating overall estimates using these studies as the database. A wide range of outcomes is found, especially in terms of the minima and maxima, with α being found to be as low as 0.54 (De Vries, 1984) and as high as 1.96 (Rosen and Resnick, 1980). Means varied from as low as 0.730 (Lagopoulos, 1971) to as high as 1.371 (Krakover, 1998).[9] While there is clearly considerable variation across the estimates drawing on varying data sources, the pooled estimate of α comes in at nearly 1.1, not too far from the figure for the classic version of Zipf's Law.

We conclude this section with an important caveat that is buried in this meta-study by Nitsch. Berry (2010) raises the important point that much depends on how one defines a "city" or "urban area." There are a variety of such measures, with the lowest being juridically defined cities. One can then move on up to more highly aggregated metropolitan units, Consolidated Metropolitan Statistical Areas, and on to Basic Economic Areas (BEA). Thus, there is the city of San Francisco, the CMSA around San Francisco, and the Economic Area that is the entire San Francisco Bay metropolitan region. In Berry's BEA analysis, he posits the largest US metropolitan area to be "Boswash," which extends from Boston to Washington,[10] with Los Angeles–San Diego as the second biggest. What Berry finds is that as one estimates α for the ever more highly aggregated units, which he considers to be the more appropriately integrated and meaningful in terms of the nationwide system of cities, it tends to converge on 1. Thus, he concludes that as one uses more consistent and meaningful measures of urban areas, one finds Zipf's Law tending to hold.

5.6 Urban Hierarchy with Discrete Levels

While size distributions of cities often fit power laws quite well, if not always exactly Zipf's Law rank–size rule, this approach ignores the basic approach implied in the opening paragraph of the previous section. This differs with the analysis by al-Muqaddisi as well as the nature of the hierarchy observed in the hierarchy of the Roman Catholic Church and its relation to the urban hierarchy. That is, there are discrete levels within the hierarchy that are clearly delineated from one another. In these two cases, one is considering a hierarchy of power or authority that is official and that encompasses a nested system of well-defined levels and sublevels. Al-Muqaddisi considered the hierarchy of the empire of the Abbasid caliphate, with Baghdad as capital, down through provincial capitals, to regional administrative centers, down to units below that at the base without authority, the fundamental agricultural villages. In the Church, one goes from Rome with the Pope through locations with cardinals through cities with bishops (and thus a cathedral), down to local units with priests. Likewise, in most countries one has a national capital, state or provincial capitals, down to county or other more local units of government to some basic village or township or city level. However, it must be noted that these politically or administratively defined hierarchies do not necessarily correspond with population hierarchies of urban areas, as the fact that only about a quarter of US states have as their capital city the largest city in the state.

Nevertheless, the idea of their being distinct levels within hierarchies that are identifiably distinct has long held sway in the analysis of urban hierarchies or in societies more broadly. Braudel (1979) has argued for the near universality of a three-level hierarchy system in which agricultural villages cluster about some local market town, with these towns in turn associating with a city. As one moves up this hierarchy, which is economically and demographically defined rather than politically, one sees more functions occurring at the higher levels. While Braudel was partly inspired by the German location theorist, von Thünen, it was another German location theorist who would lay this out more formally in his study of central places in Southern Germany, Walter Christaller (1933).[11] He identified seven levels of nested hieararchy there. In this model, higher-level units carry out all the functions contained in lower-level ones, whereas in the more complicated model of August Lösch (1940) with its nine levels, they are not necessarily nested, and a higher-level unit does not have to carry out all the functions of the lower-level ones.[12]

Whereas in the Gabaix version of a Zipf's Law urban hierarchy, the distribution arises out of a stochastic process across cities that on average are growing and having their growth vary in ways independent of the city size, the discrete hierarchy model suggests that something else or more is going on, even if ultimately there may be stochastic roots to how that something else gets distributed initially. The issue involves identifying distinct economic activities that are distinguished by differing degrees of economies of scale so that some activities occur in many small production facilities that are then scattered across the landscape in many different locations (and more likely in the lower-level units of a hierarchy) as opposed to activities that occur in a smaller number of usually larger production facilities (although this will vary with the size of the industry) that will be located in a smaller number of locations. These are more likely to locate in larger urban areas nearer the top of the hierarchy, even if this is not a perfectly correlated relationship as can occur in the non-nested hierarchies. Various efforts have been made to more formally describe the process of the emergence of urban hierarchies based on this underlying idea of different activities occurring in different numbers of cities.

An important one is due to Fujita and Ogawa (1982) and later Fujita and Mori (1997), described more fully in Fujita, Krugman, and Venables (1999).[13] In this latter formulation, it is tied to the previously discussed approach that relies on the Dixit–Stiglitz model based on product differentiation (1977). In that model, the source of economies of scale is not due to production conditions, but depends ultimately on demand conditions, particular the elasticity of substitution between varieties of the good in question, σ. One can recognize varying degrees of economies of scale across discretely defined industries based on this and then model market potential functions that also depend on share of consumption an industry has as well as transport costs, although industry variations in this are usually played down as important. These functions in turn depend on population, and as population rises, more production facilities can be sustained, with the result being more and more cities arising at the various levels.

In a world with h different manufacturing sectors, with ω being wages, μ the share of agriculture in the consumer's budget (assuming CES utility functions), σ the elasticity of substitution for the manufactured good and its varieties, t the per unit transport cost, being the aggregate of manufactured goods, A the agricultural good, f the outer limit of agricultural production, and r the distance from the nearest market city, the market potential function is given by[14]

$$\Omega^h(r) = \mathrm{e}^{\sigma h[1-\mu hMtA-\mu MtM]r}\left\{\left((1+\mu^M)/2\right)\mathrm{e}^{-(\sigma h-1)\mathrm{thr}} + \Psi^h(r,f)\left((1-U^M)/2\right)\mathrm{e}^{(\sigma h-\mathrm{thr})}\right\}, \tag{5.11}$$

where

$$\Psi^h(r,f) = 1 - \left\{\int_0^r \mathrm{e}^{-tAs}\left[1-\mathrm{e}^{-2(\sigma h-1)\mathrm{th}(r-s)}\right]\mathrm{d}s\right\} \Big/ \left(\int_0^f \mathrm{e}^{-tAs}\mathrm{d}s\right). \tag{5.12}$$

As long as this potential function is less than one, the activity h will only be located at the main central city. Complicated as this function is, which must be numerically estimated, it is in turn a function of N, the total population of the region, with it turning up at certain distances as N rises such that at critical levels of N and r it may reach 1, at which point the activity h can locate at a second city (or pair of flanking cities in this formulation). These distances tend to be shorter and the bifurcations occur more frequently as ρ declines, with $\rho = (\sigma - 1)/\sigma$. Different locations of bifurcations for two out of three sectors in a three manufactured goods model from a monocentric city are depicted for given values of the parameters in Fig. 5.11 (Fujita, Krugman, and Venables, 1999, p. 190).

This becomes further complicated when there become more than one city as the relations between them must be accounted for. An example for a particular case with three manufacturing sectors and a 9-city equilibrium (depicted on one side of the top

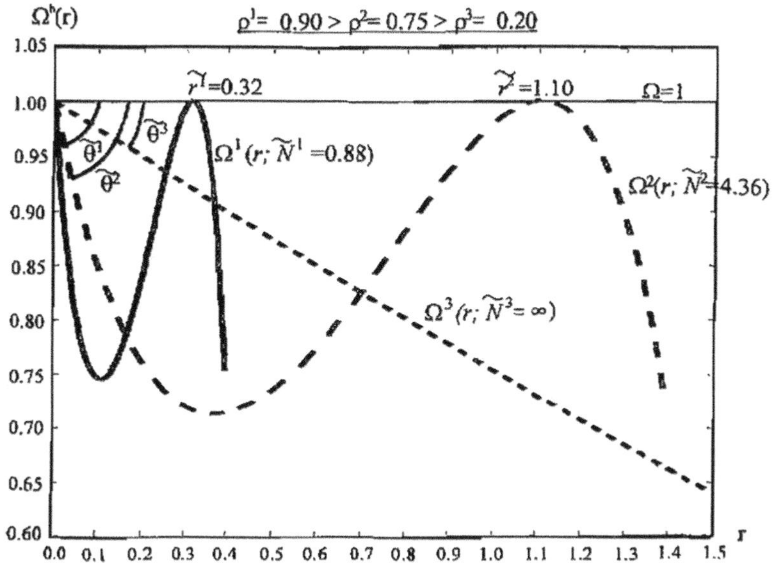

Fig. 5.11 Examples of critical potential curves for monocentric system

city only) for a given set of parameter values estimated numerically is depicted in Fig. 5.12 (Fujita, Krugman, and Venables, 1999, p. 199).[15]

We note for this figure that there are three levels represented. The point in the upper left corner is the primate central city with all three activities occurring in it. The one at the right is the first appearance of a city fully at the second level,

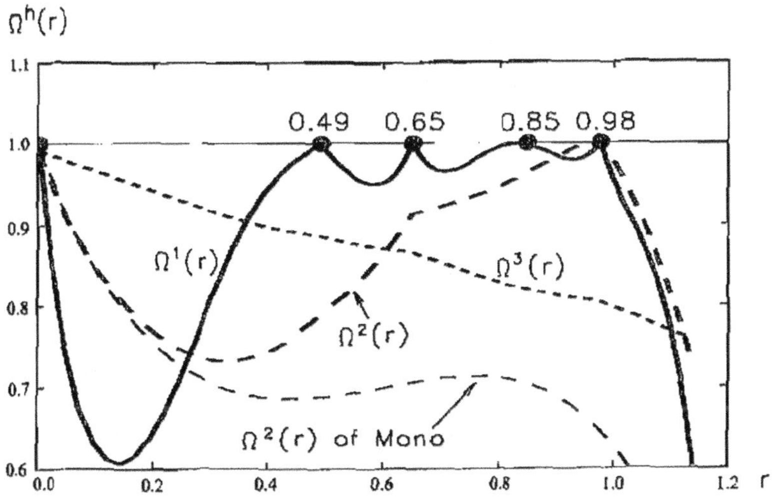

Fig. 5.12 Potential curves of the nine-city equilibrium

with the two lower-level activities in it and existing at the edge of the presumably growing system.[16] In between are three cities with the lowest level of activity only. The figure also shows the potential function for activity 2 without the other cities present as well as with, and without the other cities present, its curve will not rise to equal one, thus bringing about a city. It is the existence of the other cities in between the one at the right and the central city that allows for the one with second level of activity to exist along with the central city, where all the activities operate.

5.7 Bottom-Up or Top-Down Development of Urban Hierarchies?

The model discussed in the previous section is certainly an impressive achievement, but it would appear that there are still some loose ends left hanging by it. This is particularly so given some of the verbiage that accompanies the presentation, such as the following, made after quoting von Thünen (1826) on the emergence of a central city on a featureless plain in its "isolated state."

> Countless variants of this model have appeared since then [Samuelson, 1983; Nerlove and Sadka, 1991]. However, in all its variety, this literature simply assumes a crucial feature of the situation: the concentration of manufacturing in the central city. To our knowledge, there has never been a version of the von Thünen model that simultaneously derives the existence of the central city and the pattern of land use (Fujita, Krugman, and Venables, 1999, p. 133)

The authors are probably precisely and technically correct in this, as such papers examining the appearance of cities out of homogeneous plains as functions of degrees of economies of scale and other factors, such as Papageorgiou and Smith (1983) or Weidlich and Haag (1987), which have never been cited by any of these authors, do not also contain a model of the determination of bid-rent gradients over space as is in their presentation. It is indeed an impressive performance that captures important elements of the historical process of city formation in growing regions, with the US in the nineteenth century being a major focus of their attention, a period of both the emergence of the northeastern urban manufacturing belt along with the formation of new cities as the growing population moved westward.

Nevertheless, there are loose ends, as well as some unconvincing elements, for all the rigor and internal consistency of the model. One is the continuing reliance on the Dixit–Stiglitz framework for this modelling effort. That may be consistent with standard neoclassical foundations, but is it really applicable to the rise of such "industrial cluster" cities as Pittsburgh? Going back to Marshall, the focus has almost always been on the production side for the advantages of this sort of urban growth rather than the ultimately demand side approach from the desire of consumers for product diversity tied with monopolistic competition that is the foundation of the Dixit–Stiglitz approach. As this matter has been discussed earlier in this book, we shall not pursue it further here.

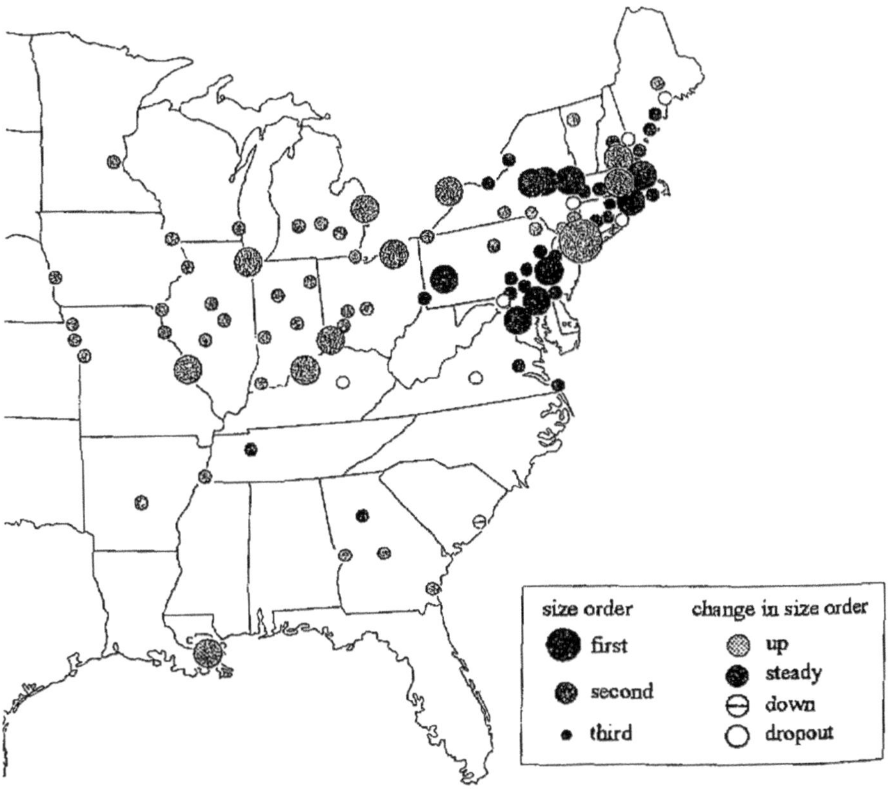

Fig. 5.13 Evolution of the US urban system, 1830–1870

However, there is another loose end that is not recognized by the authors, and, ironically, it somewhat goes back to their complaint about the lack of modelling of how central cities arise in the first place in the von Thünen model. So, let us consider a map of the history of urban development in the US that they present. This is Fig. 5.13, which is from Fujita, Krugman, and Venables (1999, p. 182).[17]

The problem is that while the presentation in Fujita, Krugman, and Venables does show rigorously how a monocentric city with one industry can arise out of a homogeneous plain with a single agricultural activity, it does not show how such a city arises initially with more than one manufacturing activity in it initially. And that is how the model discussed above is developed: an initial city with three activities occurring in it, which then begin to also appear in other cities as they appear. Figure 5.13 shows that indeed this is not a description of what happened historically in the US. The central city is New York, which is seen to emerge as such by 1870. However, it is not that in 1830. It is only a two-level activity city at that initial point. In this regard, the Fujita, Krugman, and Venables model is a top-down model, with the top city assumed to have all the functions initially, when there is not a clear reason why that should be the case. Historically, the story may be quite different: a bottom-up one in which higher-level cities develop as the higher-level activities appear and new levels of hierarchy appear, a process described by Kenneth Boulding (1978) as *anagenesis*.[18]

It is probably not the case that there is a definite answer to what is the best way to approach such a modelling effort. However, thinking about this tends to put this observer back into the mode of considering the supply side of the problem again, and the fundamental debate about the sources of agglomeration and generalized economies of scale in urban areas. While demand for product diversity undoubtedly does play some role in this agglomerative process in the rise of cities, other factors seem more important in the actual historical process that has happened, and not just in the United States. We are thrown back to the beginning of this book and the list of things that Lewis Mumford saw in the Neolithic village that would later play roles in such agglomerative processes, none of which are particularly tied to product diversity. The ancient primate cities of agrohydraulic civilizations depended on massive infrastructure publicly provided,[19] something not even in the models based on the Dixit–Stiglitz approach.

A variety of approaches have been used to model the role of infrastructure in urban development. A particular approach is that of Futagami and Mino (1995) that suggests the existence of threshold levels that induce multiple equilibria in city sizes, but with an urban area needing to get above a certain critical threshold of infrastructure and population that allows it to move to a substantially higher equilibrium. Rosser (1998) pursued this further, and it is implicit in the logistical revolutions argument of Andersson (1986), discussed earlier in this book. For Andersson these logistical revolutions can be seen as a sequence of ever higher-order catastrophic upsurges, although it must be recognized that a series of bifurcations are involved in this developmental process.

While infrastructure is not stressed, production side externalities are re-invoked in models that fit into the von Thünen framework, with human capital externalities tied to the spread of ideas being argued for particularly. A strong version of this recently has been Lucas (2001). Nevertheless, the evidence for a role of agglomeration in broader growth as argued by him also has its doubters who stress the limits of the approach. This is what we find with Brülhart and Sbergami (2009) who do find empirical support across countries for an agglomeration effect in economic growth, but find it tailing off in importance at about the level of $10,000 per capita, which is not at all that high a level of income and would seem not to fit into the Lucas type of argument.

It may be that the issue of how this alternative idea of a bottom-up formulation may work is best approached by considering the problematic case appearing in Fig. 5.13, the later emergence of New York in the US system of cities as a higher-level central city, which it is not shown as being as late as 1830. What happened and how did this come about? We can see it to some extent by looking at Fig. 5.10, where the 1840 line is noticeably differently shaped than the others, with a clear upward spike on the largest city. That would be New York. The evidence is there that this upward jump of New York may have been quite sudden, occurring between 1830 and 1840. What could have brought this about?

The obvious candidate for triggering such a change is the completion of the Erie Canal in 1825, and it is credited in most books on US economic history as playing precisely this role, of definitively putting New York into a dominant lead position among the cities on the US East Coast, which it barely had in 1790 over its near rival, Philadelphia, as can be seen in the 1790 line in Fig. 5.10. Now it can be asked why this jump had not happened by 1830, but we are talking about something that was not likely to happen instantly. Indeed, Fujita, Krugman, and Venables (op. cit., p. 183) briefly describe the upgrading of New York to being "the unparalleled first-order city of the United States providing the entire United States with the highest-order goods and services (such as major financial services and national newspapers)." They do not mention the role of the Erie Canal in this emergence, but this piece of public infrastructure first united the markets of the growing Midwest with those of the East Coast, reaching the coast at New York, with an urban agglomeration occurring as increasing warehousing activities supported increasing financial services and banking, which in turn supported other major activities such as the establishment of corporate headquarters, and the growth of related advertising and marketing services and information services, these supporting the newspapers, but also publishing more broadly, making the city also into a center of book publishing and intellectual activity, even as Boston would retain its lead in hosting the top academic institutions, with these sorts of intersectoral linkages as agglomeration sources studied by Ellison, Glaeser, and Kerr (2010). While some of these developments could be seen as expansions of product diversity a la Dixit–Stiglitz, they were very much driven by intersectoral spillovers on the supply side, arising from the increased volume of trade activity following the passing of a crucial threshold of public transportation infrastructure (or logistic infrastructure, to use the term of Andersson).

Another way of considering this interrelated outburst of expansion of interrelated sectors is to consider the theory of oscillations. Rosser (1994) provides such a model,[20] drawing on the work of Nicolis (1986, pp. 210–217). This allows for a set of interrelated oscillations at discrete levels. We can consider there to be m levels, each with income Y_i. Allowing $w_i(t)$ to be an external shock operator following an i.i.d. stochastic process with zero mean and standard deviation, σ, $w_{ij}(t)$ to be an element in a weighting matrix of environmental feedback operators and τ to be an expansion term, we can characterize the set of interacting multilevel oscillators by a set of coupled nonlinear differential equations of the form:

$$\mathrm{d}Y_i/\mathrm{d}t = h_i\left(Y_j, t\right) + w_i\left(t\right) + \sum\nolimits_{j=1}^{m} \int_0^t Y_i(t')w_{ij}(t' + \tau)\,\mathrm{d}t. \tag{5.13}$$

The third term on the right is a cross-correlation operator that is either off, indicating uncorrelated oscillations, or on, indicating some kind of frequency entrainment. Nicolis modeled this term as a "hard" van der Pol oscillator, and he was doing this in an effort to model the emergence of higher-order patterns within the brain.

A critical level of oscillator entrainment of this third right-hand term is determined by the probability distribution of the real parts of the eigenvalues of the cross-correlation operator, which occurs when the root-mean-square of the environmental fluctuations exceeds σ. It is this critical event that brings about the anagenetic emergence of a higher level of the hierarchy, a bottom-up process.

The value of this new variable at the $m + 1$ hierarchical level will be expressed as a set of nonzero terms for k levels having phase coherence for the portion of the third term on the right of (5.13) beginning with the integral sign, and the frequency entrainment itself is expressed as a nonzero sum of the entire third term on the right of (5.13).

The story here then becomes one of this representing a sufficiently large shock coinciding with a fortuitous set of interconnections across the levels and the sectors. For New York, that exogenous shock would have been the opening of the Erie Canal, with the set of sectoral interrelations being such that a combined growth of these sectors led to the emergence of new sectors and activities that operated at the higher hierarchical level.

Notes

1. O'Sullivan (2009) has carried out a somewhat similar analysis, although introducing full-blown bid-rent functions for blacks and whites. While it does not rely on evolutionary game theory, O'Sullivan arrives at the result that segregation arises, even when no household actually prefers a segregated outcome.
2. The author is aware from personal interactions with geographers that this tendency by economists to assume a homogeneous plane is a matter of some annoyance to them (Dendrinos and Rosser, 1992). They emphasize the role of physical peculiarities and specifics in the evolution of individual cities, including whether a city is more likely to have a von Thünen ring structure or a Hoyt sector structure often determined by such features. It is ironic that even in the original von Thünen (1826) model, which is often depicted or thought of as a homogeneous plane case, he had a river that the central estate was on and on which goods could be exported and imported out of and into the otherwise supposedly "isolated state."
3. While Kirman has mostly focused on studies of interconnections in nonhousing markets such as the fish market of Marseille, he turned to study the Schelling model eventually (Vinković and Kirman, 2006).
4. Besides networks, there have also been studies of Ising structures along statistical mechanics patterns (Stauffer and Solomon, 2007). This approach can be seen as part of *sociodynamics* (Weidlich, 2002) or *sociophysics* (Chakrabarti, Chakraborti, and Chatterjee, 2006).
5. More particularly, Barabási and Albert (1999) argue that the fraction of nodes that link to k other nodes, $P(k)$, rises with k according to a power law distribution such that $P(k) \sim k^{-\gamma}$, where $2 < \gamma < 3$, generally.
6. A further variation on the networks is due to Pollicott and Weiss (2001). In this, a dynamic system evolves with a defined Lyapunov function to minimize a variational nonlinear Laplacian whose Hamiltonian coincides with the Lyapunov function. Epstein and Axtell (1996) can be seen as a generalization of these agent-based models.
7. A particular feature of power law distributions is that they exhibit *kurtosis* or "fat tails" that are not observed in Gaussian distributions. Much of conventional financial theory assumes Gaussian distributions that are fully characterized by their mean and variance, including traditional CAPM analysis and the Black-Scholes formula for option pricing. That financial market returns ubiquitously exhibit kurtosis has long been a problem for this approach, as emphasized initially by Mandelbrot (1963).
8. Herbert Simon (1955) was an important exception during a period when few were studying them.

9. We note that as α rises, the distribution becomes flatter in the sense that the second biggest city's population is a rising proportion of that of the largest city, and so on.
10. Such a super-metropolitan area has been sometimes labeled a *megalopolis*. Berry initiated these arguments in Berry (1964).
11. In his historical discussion, the role of church hierarchy plays a role as it did in both Mumford and Pirenne, with the market towns being separated by the distance that a bishop could ride in one day to sit and observe the religious festivities associated with markets. This idea was affectionately labeled the "Bishop's Ass Hypothesis" in classroom presentations by Eugene Smolensky, the author's major professor, in the early 1970s at the University of Wisconsin-Madison.
12. In a Christaller world, the largest city will be a *primate city* where one finds all activities going on and where this city is clearly absolutely dominant. In a Lösch world, there may be competing top cities, with the "top functions" distributed among them. Nations such as Japan, France, and Mexico are examples with prominent primate cities, whereas China, India, and the US exhibit competing top cities versions, with this perhaps symbolized by the national capitals in these latter three not being in their largest cities.
13. The ultimate origin of market potential functions and theory is the von Thünen (1826) model. However, it was laid out more formally by Launhardt (1885) as the "economic law of market areas." A variation labeled the *law of retail gravitation* (Reilly, 1931) is closer still to the model discussed here. The work of Henderson (1988) is also closely related.
14. See Fujita, Krugman, and Venables (1999, p. 187).
15. See the citation for the specific parameter values used.
16. The theme of major new cities arising at the edge of the frontier is emphasized by William Cronon (1991) in his masterful study of the history of Chicago.
17. This analysis originally appeared in Fujita, Krugman, and Mori (1999).
18. See also Rosser, Folke, Günther, Isomäki, Perring, and Puu (1994) for further discussion.
19. The argument that state-provided agrohydraulic infrastructure underlay the ancient civilizations was due to Childe (1936), Steward (1949), and Wittfogel (1957). This argument has been challenged by Butzer (1976) and Park (1992), who argue that the relevant economies of scale were achieved at relatively local levels and did not require the full-scale empire, which was implicitly exploitative. This argument is advanced further by Allen (1997), who emphasizes the role of the desert in hemming in the growing population along the river, making it easier for the Pharoah to dominate a larger portion of the river basin.
20. For a more detailed discussion of this approach, see Rosser, Folke, Günther, Isomäki, Perrings, and Puu (1994).

Chapter 6
Perspectives on Economic and Ecologic Evolution

This natural inequality of the two powers of population, and of population in the earth, and that great law of our nature which must constantly keep their effects equal, form the great difficulty that to me appears insurmountable in the way to the perfectibility of society. All other arguments are of slight and subordinate consideration in comparison of this. I see no way by which man can escape from the weight of this law which pervades all nature.
Thomas Robert Malthus (1798, Essay on the Principle of Population, p. 16).

Man is to a considerable degree the artificer of his own fortune. We can apply our reflections and our ingenuity to the remedy of whatever we regret
William Godwin (1820, On Population, p. 615)

6.1 Historical Perspectives

6.1.1 Origins

The connection between economics and ecology[1] runs much deeper than the identical first two syllables of their respective names. Theories of evolution for each have directly and indirectly influenced each other for a long time in a symbiotic pattern. Both fields have shared a division between those theories of evolution emphasizing a gradualist continuity and those emphasizing a punctuationist discontinuity. We shall see how views on this division have moved between economics and ecology in an extended dialogue.

Although his ideas had existed in various forms long before him,[2] Malthus (1798) is the clear starting point of this dialogue because of the enormous influence of his vision of humanity limited by nature in contrast to that of most of his predecessors. Furthermore, it can be argued that he planted seeds that later germinated in the ecological literature and eventually ripened in the economics literature. Thus Day (1983) has argued that Malthus anticipated the theory of deterministic chaos

J.B. Rosser, *Complex Evolutionary Dynamics in Urban-Regional and Ecologic-Economic Systems*, DOI 10.1007/978-1-4419-8828-7_6,

in macrodynamics which was made explicit by such mathematical ecologists as May (1974, 1976),[3] May and Oster (1976), and Guckenheimer, Oster, and Ipaktchi (1977) from whom Day and others adapted it to economic models.

> Such a history would tend greatly to elucidate the manner in which the constant check upon population acts; and would probably prove the existence of the retrograde and progressive movements that have been mentioned; though the times of their vibration must necessarily be rendered irregular, from the operation of many interrupting causes; such as, the introduction or failure of certain manufacturers: a greater or less prevalent spirit of agricultural enterprise: years of plenty, or years of scarcity: wars and pestilence: poor laws: the invention of processes for shortening labor without the proportional extension of the market for the commodity: and, particularly, the difference between the nominal and real price of labor; a circumstance, which has perhaps more than any other, contributed to conceal this oscillation from common view. (Malthus, 1798, pp. 33–34)[4]

However, the most important role Malthus played as initiator of this dialogue lay in his direct influence on the independent codiscoverers of the theory of natural selection in organic evolution, Charles Darwin and Alfred Russel Wallace (1858). Thus Darwin declared in the introduction to his *Origin of the Species* (1859, p. 4):

> This is the doctrine of Malthus, applied to the whole animal and vegetable kingdoms. As many more individuals of each species are born than can possibly survive; and as, consequently, there is a frequently recurring struggle for existence, it follows that any being, if it vary however slightly in any manner profitable to itself, under the complex and sometimes varying conditions of life, will have a better chance of surviving and thus be *naturally selected*. From the strong principle of inheritance any selected variety will tend to propagate its new and modified form.

Interestingly this influence has been questioned (Schumpeter, 1954, pp. 445–446; Gordon, 1989) by claims that Darwin (and Wallace) either misinterpreted Malthus or were only peripherally influenced by him. However, others studying the record have strongly defended the view that Darwin's statements should be taken at face value (Jones, 1989). Whatever the case, the ironies and contradictions inherent in this influence showed up soon enough.

6.1.2 Dialectical Difficulties

It is with Marx and Engels that we find these contradictions most immediately manifest. On the one hand, they much admired Darwin, accepting his version of the theory of evolution as accurate with respect to organic evolution. They saw the transformation of species in evolution as a metaphor for the transformation of societies in history.[5] Furthermore, they saw the theory as a strong support for a materialist view of history, the continuous variability of species dialectically undermining the metaphysical idealism that identified species as distinct categories created in the mind of God (Engels, 1940, p. 234).

However, Marx and Engels faced a problem because of their profound dislike of Malthus and his works (Meek, 1954). Their solution to this problem was to distinguish between the human and nonhuman realms. Thus Engels (1940, pp. 208–209) accepts that the Darwinian "struggle for existence," within a Malthusian limits context, may be somewhat relevant to the plant and animal kingdoms, while arguing that animals merely "collect," whereas "man produces." This becomes the basis of their well-known technological and historical optimism that allows them to reject the Malthusian limits for human beings.[6]

Indeed both Marx and Engels tried to use Darwin against Malthus. Marx (1952) argued that Darwin's discovery of the general tendency of all populations to grow geometrically disproves Malthus's assertion of the arithmetic growth of food supplies supposedly limiting the geometric growth of human populations.[7] Engels declares (1940, p. 19):

> Darwin did not know what a bitter satire he wrote on mankind and especially on his countrymen, when he showed that free competition, the struggle for existence, which the economists celebrate as the highest historical achievement, is the normal state of the animal kingdom. Only conscious organization of social production in which production and distribution are carried on in a planned way, can lift mankind above the rest of the animal world as regards the social aspect, in the same way that production in general has done this for men as a species.

This contrasting of human and nonhuman systems allowed Marx and Engels to maintain otherwise contradictory views about the nature of evolution. Thus they accepted Darwin's "gradual evolution" of animals (Engels, 1940, p. 18) and reveled in the dialectical fuzziness implied by the continuous variability of species. On the other, the ability of humans to consciously decide and act allows for the discontinuous or punctuationist evolution of human society as revolutionary transformations occur, in this case a dialectical "transformation of quantity into quality." However, Engels further complicates things by arguing that the existence of discontinuous transformations in the *physical* world, such as the phase transitions from ice to water to steam at critical temperatures (an old example of Hegel's (1842, p. 217)), shows the general applicability of the dialectical method to all the sciences.[8] This argument in turn inspired the Marxist biologist Haldane (1940) to later develop arguments in mathematical genetics that helped support the non-Darwinian punctuationist theory of discontinuous organic evolution.

This contrast between human and nonhuman forms of evolution remains both influential and controversial even today. Boulding (1981, 1989) argues that the processes are very similar, that commodity types are like species (and individual commodities are like individuals, production being birth and consumption being death). The Social Darwinist, Herbert Spencer (1852), argued that ruling elites deserve their status because they are "the fittest," a judgment based on their having been "naturally selected." This argument has been updated in a more sophisticated form by the sociobiologist E.O. Wilson (1975).

However, others have emphasized the contrast, arguing that human evolution operates at the cultural level in a fundamentally different way from biological evolution. Nelson and Winter (1982) argue that "routines are genes," that it is industrial and economic *practices* that evolve in response to their perceived success or lack thereof. Routines and practices are linked to mental constructs which evolve along with them in an interactive fashion (Day, 1989). Ideas evolve as they translate into successful routines. This means that economic evolution has a much more self-aware and potentially self-controlled nature than purely ecological evolution.[9]

6.1.3 Evolution and the Equilibrium Concept

Arguably the greatest admirer of Darwin among economists was Alfred Marshall, accepting that the "struggle for existence" explains the evolution of market structures (1920, Book IV, Chap. VIII) and that human society gradually and continuously evolves. However, despite his assertion that "the Mecca of the economist lies in economic biology," (ibid., p. xiv) Marshall also declared, "But biological conceptions are more complex than those of mechanics; a volume on Foundations must therefore give relatively large place to mechanical analogies; and frequent use is made of the term 'equilibrium' which suggests something of a statical analogy." (ibid.) Thus he became the creator of the standard neoclassical model of static partial equilibrium, even as he criticized the limits of his own methodology.[10] It can be argued from the perspective of thermodynamics that Marshall overstated the contrast between mechanics and biology. Nevertheless, Marshall emphasized the distinction between the two views of equilibrium, for him the biological one consisting of the moment when growth and decay are evenly balanced in the life of an organism (or a firm), (1920, p. 323). Marshall's denigration of the applicability of the "mechanical statical" equilibrium concept to the biological realm was shared by biologists for a long time who generally did not use the concept in any sense similar to most economists. Needless to say, much of evolutionary economics has shared Marshall's antipathy to his creation (Veblen, 1898; Georgescu-Roegen, 1971; Nelson and Winter, 1974, 1982).

In any case, the concept of general equilibrium emerged on its own in ecology, although as Marshall noted, with much greater emphasis on dynamics. Much as one can see glimmerings of the idea of general equilibrium in the work of Adam Smith (1776), so Worster (1977) has claimed that one can see a general ecological equilibrium in Linnaeus's (1751) taxonomy of species. Worster argues that the Linnaean equilibrium combined the mechanical Newtonian image of a "well-oiled machine" with an almost medieval conception of a divinely ordered "great chain of being." Linnaeus's equilibrium of harmoniously interacting species was a repeating cycle and thus partially dynamic.

The first notion of a static or stationary state ecological equilibrium was due to Clements (1916). He identified such a condition with a climax ecosystem emerging at the end of a process of ecological succession. Clements, and also Lotka (1925), was strongly influenced by Spencer's (1899) concept of the synthetic unity of nature pursuing a moving equilibrium. This reflected Spencer's Social Darwinist view of a social equilibrium toward which society gradually moves. Spencer was a major two-way communicator between the social and biological sciences in his day, influencing Marshall both in his Darwinism and in his gradualism. Spencer (1852) coined the phrase, "survival of the fittest," a concept influential in evolutionary economics through Marshall (i.e., Alchian, 1950). It is ironic that Clement's defense of conservation was influenced by the laissez-faire Social Darwinism of Spencer who opposed government intervention in the economy on the grounds that it would impede the "progressive" nature of socioeconomic natural selection.

Odum (1953) extended the analysis of such equilibria with the concept of a "community matrix" showing all species interactions, a concept more fully developed by Levins (1968). This parallels the input–output model of economic analysis, the basis of the first fully rigorous, general equilibrium model, due to von Neumann (1937), and ultimately traceable to the physiocratic *Tableau Économique* of Quesnay which assumed a human economy subordinate to nature. Daly (1968) and Isard (1972) have proposed using input–output matrices for analyzing combined economic-ecologic systems.

But the most dramatic analysis of ecological equilibrium was due to Lotka (1925), who presented an analysis of static equilibrium and its stability more advanced than anything seen up to that time. He drew on Pareto as well as Poincaré, Le Chatelier, and Maxwell, among many others. Marshall might have objected to much of his analysis for being overly "mechanical." But Lotka resembled Marshall in that he recognized many different kinds and definitions of equilibria. Thus he distinguished stationary states from moving equilibria (ibid., Chap. 9). Furthermore, he noted a "kinematic" concept in which "velocities vanish," a "dynamic" concept in which "*forces* are balanced in which the *resultant force vanishes*" and an "energetic" concept in which "*virtual work* done in any small displacement compatible with the constraints *vanishes*", in short minimization of potential energy. It must be noted further that Lotka defined evolution as an irreversible process driven by the operation of the Second Law of Thermodynamics and labeled as "quasi-equilibria" those maintained by a "dissipation or degradation of available energy". Furthermore, he frequently used human–animal examples and argued explicitly that he was analyzing "the biological basis of economics" (ibid., p. 97).

6.1.4 Cycles and Chaos

If economics preceded ecology in developing the concept of static equilibrium, the reverse was the case for the development of cyclical models. More than a decade before the first formal business cycle models (Kalecki, 1935), Lotka (1920) developed the nonlinear predator–prey model, not recognized by economists until 47 years later (Goodwin, 1967; Samuelson, 1967). Furthermore he analyzed an amazing variety of possible dynamics for these systems. The eleven depicted on p. 148 of his 1925 book include saddle points and limit cycles, among others as yet undreamed of by economists. All that is missing is chaotic dynamics, although he recognized the fundamental concept of bifurcation. Thus (1925, p. 151):

> So it may happen that one of the roots λ of the characteristic equation vanishes. An example of this was encountered in dealing with the Ross malaria equations. It was found that as the number of mosquitos per head of the human population approaches a critical value, two singular points approach each other, and finally fuse, giving one 'double' point.

Although Lotka labeled this an "exceptional case," he would later argue that such states are sought out by human consciousness.

In any case Lotka's analysis of cycles (further adumbrated by Volterra, 1931) laid the foundation upon which Robert May and his associates developed models of deterministic chaos for population dynamics. As noted above it did not take economists 47 years to become aware of and utilize this development (e.g., Benhabib and Day, 1980).

6.2 Continuous Versus Discontinuous Theories of Evolution

6.2.1 Gradualism

Darwin strongly believed in a continuous gradualism in evolution, linking this to a denial of "cataclysm" and to a "confidence" that "[w]e may look to a secure future of equally inappreciable length as natural selection works solely by and for the good of each being, all corporeal and mental endowments will tend towards perfection" (p. 414).[11] Such sunny Victorian optimism certainly contrasts with the Hobbesian–Malthusian vision of a "struggle for existence."

This vision was adopted wholeheartedly by Darwin's most loyal economics follower, Marshall, the gradualism especially. In the Preface to the First Edition of his *Principles of Economics* (1890), he declares that the application to economics of the "Principle of Continuity" represents the "special character" of his whole book. Marshall is famous for placing on the title page of *all eight* editions of his *Principles* the motto "Natura non facit saltum"—"nature does not take a leap." What is less well known is that he borrowed this phrase from Darwin for whom it represented the very core of his gradualism. Thus:

> Natura non facit saltum. ... Why should not Nature have taken a leap from structure to structure? On the theory of natural selection we can clearly understand why she should not; for natural selection can only act by taking advantage of slight successive variations; she can never take a leap, but must advance by the shortest and slowest steps (Darwin, 1859, pp. 166–167)

In turn Darwin had borrowed this famous phrase from Leibniz, coinventor with Newton of the differential calculus, and thus incidentally of the "Principle of continuity." The general assumption of continuity in most economic analysis certainly reflects the powerful and continuing influence of the Marshallian apparatus.

In Darwin's own time, the greatest weakness of his theory was considered to be his lack of an explanation for the basis of the emergence of variations within populations. This was resolved by the development of Mendelian genetics and the discovery of mutations. Fisher (1930) provided a well-developed model of gradualistic Darwinian evolution based upon a stochastic model of Mendelian mutations, ecologic evolutionary orthodoxy until the 1970s.

In ecology, evolution is orthodoxy, but in economics it was the mechanistic legacy of Marshall that became orthodoxy rather than the evolutionary legacy.

Perhaps because of their relative unorthodoxy, there has been a tendency for evolutionary economists to be less wedded to gradualism and continuity than was Marshall. Nevertheless, some evolutionary economists have sided with Marshall on this issue, notably Georgescu-Roegen (1971) who has denounced the "discrete arithmomorphism" he associates with the alleged excessive quantification of the mechanistic approach. For Georgescu-Roegen, a biological approach necessarily entails a fuzzy dialectical qualitativeness, based ultimately on the alleged temporal continuity of human consciousness.

6.2.2 *Saltationalism*

6.2.2.1 Ecological

Saltationalism (or punctuationism) argues that "natura facit saltum," sometimes. One of the biggest problems for Darwin was the lack of intermediate transitional forms in the fossil record.[12] He explained this by claiming partly that transitional species populations would be low in number and partly that the geological strata themselves are discontinuous.

An alternative to these explanations is the saltationalist approach that speciation is a relatively rapid event in geological time, which explains the low numbers of transitional forms. This approach has been most dramatically revived by Eldredge and Gould (1972). Gould (1987, p. 122) presents a clear summary:

> Thus our model of punctuated equilibria holds that evolution is concentrated in events of speciation and that successful speciation is an infrequent event punctuating the stasis of large populations that do not alter in fundamental ways during the millions of years that they endure.

This view depends on the revival of two long-standing views. One, due to Goldschmidt (1940), was that a minor genetic mutation could lead to a major change in the adult form if the mutation affected the development of the organism at a very early (possibly embryonic) stage. Thus "hopeful monsters" might emerge in a single generation without intermediate forms.

The other was based on Sewall Wright's (1931) "shifting-balance" theory in which the environment defines a "selective surface" for different gene combinations in a species which has multiple local maxima. As local inbreeding occurs in small groups, random genetic drift (the "Sewall Wright effect") can combine with environmental change to move subgroups across "valleys" between "selective peaks." After this, intraspecies competition occurs which can lead to a rapid evolutionary change and speciation.[13]

That Wright's arguments can lead to discontinuous evolution has been further argued by Dodson (1976) who translates the "selective surface" into a "phenotype manifold" with multiple equilibria in certain zones. He uses Thom-type catastrophe theory to argue for rapid shifts at bifurcation points. Geiger (1983) has extended this argument to note that this could reconcile Fisher's (1930) argument for continuous shifts in gene frequencies with discontinuous changes in morphology asserted by saltationalism. In complex multispecies environments, it has been shown that the evolutionary dynamics can generate oscillatory dynamics in dissipative structures (Bazykin, Khibnik, and Aponina, 1983) and even chaotic dynamics (Smale, 1976).

In one of his final papers, Wright reconciles various approaches while defending his use of selective surfaces in the shifting-balance approach (1988, p. 122):

> It is to be noted that the mathematical theories developed by Kimura (1968), Fisher (1930), Haldane (1932), and myself dealt with four very different situations.
>
> Kimura's "neutral" theory dealt with the exceedingly slow accumulation of neutral biochemical changes from accidents of sampling in the species as a whole. Fisher's "fundamental theorem of natural selection" was concerned with the total combined effects of alleles at multiple loci under the assumption of panmixia in the species as a whole. He recognized that it was an exceedingly slow process. Haldane gave the most exhaustive mathematical treatment of the case in which the effects of a pair of alleles are independent of the rest of the genome. He included the important case of "altruistic" genes, ones contributing to the fitness of the group at the expense of the individual. I attempted to account for occasional exceedingly rapid evolution on the basis of intergroup selection (differential diffusion) among small local populations that have differentiated at random, mainly by accidents of sampling (i.e. by local inbreeding), exceptions to the panmixia postulated by Fisher. All four are valid.

6.2.2.2 Economics

Saltationalism became widely accepted in evolutionary economics at a time when it was very unfashionable in biology, probably because of Joseph Schumpeter, perhaps the most influential figure in modern evolutionary economics. Schumpeter was an explicit and thoroughgoing saltationalist.[14] For Schumpeter, the very essence of economic development lies in the discontinuities engendered by the innovative activities of entrepreneurs.[15] Thus he declares (1934, pp. 65–66):

> In so far as the 'new combination' may in time grow out of the old by continuous adjustment in small steps, there is certainly change, possibly growth, but neither a new phenomenon nor development in our sense. In so far as this is not the case, and the new combinations appear discontinuously, then the phenomenon characterizing development emerges.

For Schumpeter, such "new combinations" can consist of (1) new goods, (2) new methods of production, (3) new markets, (4) new sources of supply of raw materials or half-manufactured goods, or (5) new organization.

The legacy of Schumpeterian saltationalism lives on in his evolutionary economic successors, although generally with less force. Often both continuous and discontinuous processes are allowed. Thus Day (1974) proposes that adaptive economic processes may occur as continuous learning processes or as regime switches in which qualitative shifts occur, an approach considerably extended in Day and Walter (1989). Nelson and Winter (1974, 1982) model firm behavior as being a sequence of periods of little change, broken by occasional discontinuous transitions to new techniques. However, they argue that generally the new technique will not be "too far" from the old one, and furthermore, when all such behavior is aggregated, the result is a relatively smooth macroeconomic result.

Boulding (1978, 1981) also argues for a mix of continuous and discontinuous processes. Most evolutionary dynamics are continuous, with significant events leading to revolutionary change being rare events. Furthermore, Boulding emphasizes the role of instabilities in generating discontinuous events. Examples include unstable Lotka–Volterra cycles implying the extinction of a species, unstable prisoner's dilemma game situations that can lead to the outbreak of wars, and what he labels the "iceberg effect," comparable to the sudden turning upside down of an iceberg as its melting leads to a critical shifting of its center of gravity with respect to water displaced. Thus he argues that (1978, p. 330):

> [t]he more surprising changes in society are often the result of this kind of effect. The erosion of the invisible part of the consensus that assures social stability is often unseen and unnoticed until the equilibrium is destroyed and there is an unexpected, catastrophic overturn.[16]

This role of instabilities in economic evolution was recognized quite early on by the biologist Lotka (1925, pp. 407–408), arguing that human beings regularly encounter singular points, where they are on "unstable orbits, such as that of a ball rolling along the ridge of a straight *watershed* . . . where an imperceptible deviation is sufficient to determine into which of two valleys we shall descend." In such cases, "infinitesimal interference will produce finite, and, it may be, very fundamental changes." Lotka saw such a bifurcation as the basis of ongoing saltational economic evolution. Thus he declares (1925, p. 299), "the wholly unparalleled rapidity of our scientific and industrial evolution in past decades is itself the most brilliant example of instability and its cumulative power as a factor in evolution."

6.3 Hypercyclic Morphogenesis of Higher-Level Structures

A major theme of evolutionary theory in both economics and ecology has been teleology, a directed progressiveness to the process. Even though the idea of a divinely directed teleology with a preordained path has faded, the idea that evolution is an irreversible and progressive accumulation of greater complexity of structures has persisted. According to Jantsch (1982, p. 352), "Evolution is the open history of an unfolding complexity, not the history of random processes." The "progressiveness" of evolution was unquestioned by its nineteenth-century advocates, whatever their other differences, from the "tendency toward perfection" of Darwin through related ideas in Spencer and Marshall to even the projected emergence of socialism by Marx and Engels.

The shocks of the twentieth century have dissipated belief in the *inherent necessity* of the progressivity of evolutionary processes.[17] Nevertheless, it continues to be argued that the emergence of greater complexity and more levels of structure has been the historical reality at the physical, biological, and socioeconomic levels. A more recent twist on the teleological tendency has been the assertion that this reflects self-organizing processes emerging from the unidirectional operation of the law of entropy (Nicolis and Prigogine, 1977). A statement of this and a resolution of the apparent paradox involved is given by Boulding (1978, p. 10):

> ... we detect two processes that seem to have directionality in time's arrow-pointing toward irreversible change... The second law of thermodynamics points toward exhaustion, decay, loss of structure and uniformity, with the universe returning to chaos, a structureless homogeneity in which nothing more can happen. Evolution seems to point in the opposite direction, toward differentiation into structures of increasing complexity. The paradox may perhaps be resolved by looking at evolution as the segregation of entropy, the building up of little islands of order and complexity at the cost of still more disorder elsewhere.

The idea of a self-organizing morphogenesis was first proposed at the chemical level by Turing (1952). For him, self-organization occurs at bifurcation points in the degree of intermolecular interactions. The crucial step in the emergence of life was the emergence of self-reproducing molecules. Eigen and Schuster (1979, p. 87) have labeled this the "hypercycle ... the simplest system that can allow the evolution of reproducible functional links." The key to this hypercycle is the efficient transmission of information. Darwinian natural selection operates on these self-reproducing "quasi-species" according to their information-transmitting ability. This depends on their ability to stabilize themselves against the accumulation of errors in the self-reproductive process. Eigen and Schuster propose the existence of a "threshold of information content" for any given system which if exceeded will generate an "error catastrophe" and the "disintegration of information due to a steady accumulation of errors" (ibid., p. 25). They give this threshold as

$$V_{\mathrm{m}} < \ln \sigma_{\mathrm{m}}/(1 - q_{\mathrm{m}}), \tag{6.1}$$

where V_{m} = number of symbols, $\sigma_{\mathrm{m}} > 1$ = degree of superiority of "master copy" in selective advantage, and q_{m} = quality of symbol copying.[18]

One can see a direct analogy to the question of scale economies in production. Especially Marshall saw the life cycle of a firm depending on its taking advantage of increasing returns during the rapid growth phase (rising σ_{m} with V_{m}), but decreasing returns setting in due to managerial diseconomies of scale ultimately related to informational problems (declining q_{m}). This could explain "de-evolution," such as the collapse of the Roman Empire, the paralysis of the Soviet central planning mechanism, or the breakup of corporate conglomerates, as "error catastrophes."

The phenomenon of the emergence of a higher level of structure has also been examined by Garfinkel (1987) using the example of the slime mold which periodically forms out of isolated amoebae and then disintegrates back to its constituent cells after a period of time. In its organized state, cells group into specialized quasi-organs with their own subcenters. Garfinkel argues that the basis of the coordination between the cells is their mutual entrainment of harmonized oscillations in a coordination equilibrium (coherence) associated with wavelike phenomena occurring in the slime mold.[19] Garfinkel argues that the self-organization occurs at bifurcation points in the degree of entrainment and argues that this extends to social systems.[20] Thus (Garfinkel, 1987, p. 206):

In a model of cooperation as entrainment global attractors model overall equilibria. Because social conventions (like the working day, driving on the right, feudalism, or speaking English) are essentially coordination equilibria, the topology of various attractors in a given system provides the kinematic foundation for theories of social change. We might say, with apologies to Marx, that all history is the history of phase transitions of coordination equilibria.

In a social situation the entrainment or coherence can arise from common interests shared or by sets of mutually positive externality relations. The question of whether a hypercycle exists for a given level of organization has an answer very similar to whether or not a Buchanan-type (1965) "club" can form out of the constituent entities from a level below. Thus Rome lost coherence because the domination by the center ceased to give the periphery a reason for belonging to the club. Similar problems plagued the Napoleonic and Hitlerian enterprises from the start. But the emerging voluntary self-organization of the European Community may represent the formation of a sustainable club, the morphogenesis of a new hypercycle.[21]

Thus the sustainability of a club is determined by the condition asserted by takeover raiders regarding their corporate objects: Does the "breakup" value of the company exceed its value as a unified unit? If not, the synergy of its cohering component parts will sustain it. If so, the "managerial diseconomies" driven by the information-transfer problems will lead to the error catastrophe and the end of the hypercycle.

It may well be that the evolution of higher levels of structure ultimately involves transcendent self-referencing, much as the incompleteness of axiom systems shown by Kurt Gödel (1931) depends on self-referencing implying the existence of higher levels of organization or awareness (Hofstadter, 1979). The ability to reproduce an information structure (or to manage a group of subsidiaries successfully) depends on the ability of the system to reference (monitor) itself. Evolution gets more fully orchestrated into hierarchically structured levels that operate semiautonomously.

This question of transcendence through self-referencing becomes most evident in the evolution of the knowledge of evolution itself. Thus the emergence of the integrated field of bioeconomics (Clark, 1976) depends on the full recognition of the mutually interacting subparts, not merely the imposition on one part of the methods used in another part, as in the failed Social Darwinism of Herbert Spencer. Thus the fully aware dialogue between our ecologic and economic theories of evolution may provide the Gödelian self-referential key to a transcendent morphogenetic evolution of our hypercyclic human consciousness without limit.

Notes

1. The term "ecology" was neologized by Haeckel (1866). Prior to that, "economy of nature" was widely used (Worster, 1977).
2. The idea that population is limited by the ability to produce food can be found in Plato. Benjamin Franklin and Robert Townsend both developed fairly complete versions of the essential Malthusian model prior to 1798 (Rosser, 1978b).
3. May (1976) credits Samuelson (1942) with initially developing the graphical technique used by mathematical ecologists in analyzing difference equation systems.

4. It can be argued that many of these effects resemble the exogenous shocks of the real business cycle school rather than the endogenous fluctuations of the New Keynesian chaos models.
5. After initially reading Darwin's *Origin of the Species* near the end of 1860, Marx wrote to Engels that "although it is developed in the crude English style, this is the book which contains the basis in natural history for our view." (Marx and Engels, 1942, p. 126).
6. Their labor theory of value, circular model of expanded reproduction, and rejection of Malthusian limits have led to criticism that they did not understand nature (Georgescu-Roegen, 1971, p. 2). However, Perelman (1987) has argued that Marx distinguished between "value" and "wealth," with the former a relative concept based on labor time and the latter an absolute concept based at least partly on the bounty of nature.
7. See Rosser (1979) for further discussion of this point.
8. Unfortunately this argument provided the basis for Lysenko's suppression of Mendelian genetics on ideological grounds in the USSR. Lysenko carried out this atrocity in the name of "dialectical materialism," a phrase never used by either Marx or Engels.
9. See Rosser (1991) for a further discussion of this debate.
10. Marshall understood both the concept of multiple equilibria and the implications for stability as well (1923). Furthermore, in discussing oscillations around equilibria, he may have foreseen the possibility of chaotic dynamics.
    Thus he wrote (1920, p. 346):

    > But in real life such oscillations are seldom as rhythmical as those of a stone hanging freely from a string; the comparison would be more exact if the string were supposed to hang in the troubled waters of a mill-race, whose stream was at one time allowed to flow freely, and at another partially cut off. Nor are these complexities sufficient to illustrate all the disturbances with which the economist and the merchant alike are forced to concern themselves.
    >
    > If the person holding the string swings his hand with movements partly rhythmical and partly arbitrary, the illustration will not outrun the difficulties of some very real and practical problems of value.

11. Darwin did not originally hold this view when he began to formulate his theory (Worster, 1977, p. 159). Apparently it became more important to him to emphasize the ability of one species to evolve directly out of another, the most controversial core of his theory that contradicted the doctrine of Special Creation (by God) of species.
12. The discovery of the transitional reptile-bird, Archeopteryx, greatly aided the acceptance of his theory.
13. These processes are largely endogenous and do not require discontinuous changes in the environment, the "catastrophism" of Buffon and Cuvier (Worster, 1977, pp. 137–138). Of course saltationalism is enhanced by such events as the relatively sudden extinction of the dinosaurs, possibly due to a collision between the earth and an asteroid.
14. See Awan (1986) for a thorough discussion of Schumpeter's relation to Marshall and to evolutionary theory. Goodwin (1986) presents a Schumpeterian model capable of generating Long Waves of irregular periodicities.
15. > ... that kind of change arising from within the system which so displaces the equilibrium point that the new one cannot be reached from the old by infinitesimal steps. Add successively as many mail coaches as you please, you will never get a railway thereby. (Schumpeter, 1934, p. 64)

16. The recent events in Eastern Europe present a dramatic manifestation of this phenomenon.
17. See Williams (1966) for a critique of the belief in such inherent necessity in organic evolution.
18. Mosekilde, Rasmussen, and Sorensen (1983) have developed a simulation model of hypercycle formation. Silverberg, Dosi, and Orsenigo (1988) have used the hypercycle to model technological diffusion and the endogenous evolution of market structures, based on different rates of internal and external learning by firms.

19. He gives as other examples of entrainment the tendency of crickets in a field to chirp together and the tendency of women who live together to have synchronized menstrual cycles. Haken's (1983) "slaving principle" implies entrainment.
20. Drawing on Hayek (1948), Lavoie (1989) argues that in a pure laissez-faire economy, the free flow of information will self-organize spontaneous order from chaotic dynamics. Using a model of managerial evolution due to Rasmussen and Mosekilde (1988), using the Rössler attractor, Radzicki (1990) argues that institutional self-organization arises from chaotic dynamics.
21. This might vindicate the optimism of the "social supra-organismists" (Emerson, 1952).

Chapter 7
Evolution and Complexity

Darwin has, beyond all his cotemporaries [sic], given an impulse to the philosophical investigation of the most backward and obscure branch of the Biological Sciences of his day; he has laid the foundations for a great edifice; but he need not be surprised if, in the progress of erection, the superstructure is altered by his successors, like the Duomo of Milan, from the roman to a different style of architecture.
Henry Falconer, 1863, Quoted in Stephen Jay Gould (2002, The Structure of Evolutionary Theory, p. 2).

Evolution is not just 'chance caught on the wing.'[1] It is not just a tinkering of the ad hoc, of bricolage, of contraption. It is emergent order honored and honed by selection.
Stuart A. Kauffman (1993, The Origins of Order: Self-Organization and Selection in Evolution, p. 644).

7.1 The Ups and Downs of the Darwinian View of Evolution

In the previous chapter, our discussion of evolution focused on the matter of continuous versus discontinuous perspectives on evolution. Darwin was cast into the role of the defender and expositor of the continuous view. This would appear to put Darwin into a camp that would not view evolution as a dynamically complex process. Certainly, discontinuity can arise from dynamically complex processes, while at the same time discontinuities that arise from exogenous shocks as in the classic "catastrophism" of Cuvier (1818) and others are not considered to be part of a dynamic complexity perspective, even as we now know that such exogenous events as large meteor strikes from outer space have probably played major roles in mass extinction events that profoundly affected the course of evolution.[2]

While Darwin would reject even the exogenous catastophism of Cuvier, under the influence of his mentor, Charles Lyell (1830–1833), in favor of a *uniformitarianism* that saw large changes arising from a gradual acccumulation of small effects, increasingly current thinking is posing Darwin's view of evolution as involving a

J.B. Rosser, *Complex Evolutionary Dynamics in Urban-Regional and Ecologic-Economic Systems*, DOI 10.1007/978-1-4419-8828-7_7,

complexity perspective. The argument as posed by Hodgson and Knudsen (2006, 2010) is that Darwinian evolution is the ultimate complex system, as it supports a *generalized Darwinism*, which is in turn a slightly scaled-down version of the *universal Darwinism* advocated by Richard Dawkins (1983). Ironically, while he sharply disagreed with Dawkins on many things, Stephen Jay Gould (2002) also ends up defending Darwin against many critics as the fountainhead of all evolutionary theory and saw elements of Darwin's views as consistent with self-organizing complex dynamics approaches such as that of Kauffman (1993), even as he denied Darwin's relevance to other portions of the dynamic complexity view.[3] How did this curious convergence on admiring Darwin come about?

Let us approach this initially by considering how various elements of Darwin's view developed prior to him and how evolutionary theorists have subsequently moved him up and down with regard to these issues. In this discussion, it will be useful to keep in mind that there are arguably three crucial elements to Darwin's perspective: *variability*, *inheritance*, and *natural selection* (Hodgson, 1993). While we shall keep these mostly in the background, it is also important to keep in mind the relationship between views of evolution, and of Darwin and Darwinism in particular, and theology and broader social and political views as well.

Corsi (1988, 2005) as well as Gould (2002) provide useful discussions of the development of evolutionary views prior to Darwin. Curiously, the first to use the original word for evolution, the Latin *evolvere*, was the Swiss naturalist, Albrecht von Haller (1744). This word, and its close relatives, refers to the rolling up and unrolling of a scroll with a given answer written on it, and Haller prefigured Ernst Haeckel's famous observation that *ontogeny recapitulates phylogeny* (1866),[4] by applying the term to the development of embryos, arguing for a directed teleology of this development from a single homogeneous cell to a complex organism (Richards, 1992).

Given the linkage between political developments and evolutionary thought, it should not be surprising that a period of major development of evolutionary thought and recognition of species evolving out of each other over time on a materialist basis without any necessary divine direction came during the period of the French Revolution and its aftermath, although arguably a predecessor to this was the idea of languages evolving out of each other, which attracted attention after the 1786 hypothesis by William Jones of the descent of the Indo-European languages from a common ancestor, after realizing the parallels between Sanskrit, Ancient Greek, and Latin.[5] In Germany, there was von Goethe (1790); in England, there was Darwin's grandfather, Erasmus Darwin (1794–1796); in Italy, there was Giuseppe Gautieri (1805).[6]

However, it was in France itself that the term "evolution" would be applied to this process of the history of life on earth, with Virey (1803) going further than von Haller and more clearly prefiguring Haeckel by observing the succession of the embryo through all the stages of evolution, just as "nature has arisen from the most tenuous mould to the majestic cedar, to the gigantic pine, just as it has advanced from microscopic animals up to man, king and dominator of all beings" (Virey, 1803, p. 30), although he would retain a belief that all this was ultimately due to

Divine Providence. It would be Jean-Baptiste de Lamarck who in a lecture in 1800 first proposed a fully materialist version of evolution that he would subsequently develop into a full-blown theory (Lamarck, 1809) that many in France claim should be granted priority over Darwin's in the history of evolutionary theory.

While Darwin argued against many of the ideas in Lamarck, in this following Lyell, Gould argues (2002, Chap. 3) that Darwin drew heavily on many ideas of Lamarck, and in the view of many recent observers, some of the complexity elements in evolution that Darwin only hinted at, but did not fully develop, such as the role of hierarchy, appear in more fully developed form in Lamarck. What Lamarck and Darwin most strongly shared was the idea of adaptation to environmental changes.[7] However, they disagreed on the mechanism for this, with Lamarck posing his (in)famous inheritance of acquired characteristics, with Darwin denying this, although Darwin allowed for the possibility of it in the form of *pangenesis* operating out of somatic cells in the final chapter of the second edition of his *Variation in Plants and Animals under Domestication* (1875). Of course, evolutionary economics has often adopted the idea that in human cultural and economic evolution, such Lamarckian forces can operate (Hayek, 1967, 1979; Nelson and Winter, 1982). For Darwin, it would be natural selection that would bring about change over time, even as Darwin did not provide an explanation for exactly how this operated.

The other part of Lamarck's argument involved the idea of a progress to higher complexity through evolution. He was also accused of basing his adaptationism on some vitalist vision of a driving life force.[8] However, Gould argues that in the end Lamarck was not a full-blown teleologist and argued that this progress to a higher complexity was not a necessary outcome. Darwin more strongly emphasized this non-teleological view and the essential randomness of the underlying mechanism, although this is perhaps more strongly argued by the promulgators of the neo-Darwinian synthesis, such as Fisher (1930). Nevertheless, Lamarck presented the idea for a strong tendency to this, drawing on pre-Lavoisierian views of chemistry for this, combined with his belief in ongoing spontaneous generation of living things out of inorganic matter as the ultimate source of variation, something that Darwin did not agree with, but for which he did not have an alternative in the period preceding Mendel's work on discovering genes. While Mendel's initial research was going on in the 1860s, his results were not widely known or understood until many decades later.

Partly due to this lacuna in Darwin's theory, the lack of source of both variation and inheritance, many in his time and in the period following him preferred the ideas of Lamarck. Among the most prominent of these was Herbert Spencer, who introduced the term "survival of the fittest" and also readily used the term "evolution" (Spencer, 1864), which Darwin did not use at all in the first edition of his *Origin of the Species* (1859), although he introduced it into later editions in a limited way, largely under the influence of Spencer, who was one of his strongest supporters initially. Of course, Spencer was also a strong advocate of laissez-faire economics, and Gould (and Hayek also) sees Darwin as having been subtly but importantly influenced by Adam Smith's *Wealth of Nations* (1776),[9] as well as by the work of Malthus, as described in the previous chapter, even as Darwin avoided commentary on economics, per se, in contrast with Spencer.

Spencer would outlive Darwin by about two decades, and after Darwin's death in 1882, opinion shifted against him quite strongly, partly led by Spencer (1893) who advocated Lamarckian ideas in the absence of clear mechanisms for variability and inheritance within Darwin, although Spencer continued to stress natural selection, tying it into his advocacy of Social Darwinism.[10] Indeed, as has been widely reported (Hodgson, 1993; Gould, 2002), the centennial celebration of the birth of Darwin in 1909 in many ways marked a low point in his reputation. The accumulated criticisms from Spencer and many others, with no one having proposed the linking of Mendelian genetics to Darwinian evolution, led to this desultory outcome. Later, the understanding of Mendelian genetics and inheritance would bring about the revival of Darwin in the 1930s and 1940s, with the 1959 celebration of the centennial of the publication of *Origin of Species* marking a high watermark and hardening of the neo-Darwinian orthodoxy that came out of the 1930s. Since then, Darwin's reputation has fluctuated further, declining with the punctuated equilibrium controversy triggered by Eldredge and Gould (1972), but much more recently recovering substantially, due both to Gould's (2002) renewed defense of him as well as to the rise of the advocates of universal or generalized Darwinism.

The linking of Mendelian genetics with its mechanism of random mutations and inheritance into the neo-Darwinian synthesis is generally attributed to the trinity of Ronald Fisher (1930), Sewall Wright (1931, 1932), and J.B.S. Haldane (1932),[11] with their statistically based work being put into a codified form by the authoritative figures of Theodosius Dobzhansky (1937, 1940), Ernst Mayr (1942), and G.G. Simpson (1944, 1947). Fisher reinforced the uniformitarian and continuous perspective of Darwin, arguing for the rarity of substantial mutations that would be superior and survive. Evolution occurred at the single level of the gene as expressed in the organism in a continuous fashion. Open supporters of discontinuous ("punctuated") evolution (Goldschmidt, 1933, 1940) were criticized, as was the open advocate of "group selection," Wynne-Edwards (1962) by Williams (1966), with Richard Dawkins reinforcing this orthodoxy in his 1976 *The Selfish Gene*.

Curiously enough, seeds of doubt or future changes in views were present. The British Communist, Haldane, was open to the idea of group selection, especially among humans, although he did not pursue the matter.

More substantial was the idea of *random drift* that Sewall Wright introduced along with the idea of *fitness landscapes*, which has become a central concept in modern evolutionary theorizing. In his fitness landscapes, there are multiple local optima, and Wright theorized about how a species might evolve to move from one local optimum to another that would be higher in the landscape, "more fit," as it were. He allowed for the possibility of random movements of subpopulations to bring this outcome about, later to be called the "Sewall Wright Effect," which some have claimed to be a "non-Darwinian" form of evolution. It is worth noting that part of what motivated Wright to think in these terms was his long work for the US Department of Agriculture[12] on selective breeding, in which humans could in effect artificially induce a Sewall Wright Effect, something that Darwin himself had emphasized, pointing out artificial breeding as evidence for evolution by natural selection.

Nevertheless, the codifiers of the harder line form of the neo-Darwinian synthesis came to realize that the Sewall Wright Effect opened the door to both relatively rapid rates of evolution[13] as well as possibly forms of higher-level evolution, which led to the downplaying of this idea in much of the literature for a long time, as well as the perception that it was a "nonadpative" form of evolution. This led to disappointment and frustration on Wright's part (Gould, 2002, pp. 554–556). However, later elucidation and explanation of his views (Wright, 1978, 1988) would lead to the revival of his reputation during his long lifetime. This revival would also coincide with the emerging acceptance of the possibility of higher-level evolution and punctuated equilibria, which would raise doubts about Darwin, only to have Darwin's own position reconsidered in the light of these ideas more recently.

Figure 7.1 shows the original version of how Wright used his fitness landscapes, or "surfaces of selective value," to explain random drift through various patterns that could occur, which appeared initially in Wright (1932), but was reproduced in Wright (1988, p, 119). In A–C, the conditions for Fisher's theorem hold, with the population fully mixing. A and B show opposite effects of changes in mutation or selection, either spreading or concentrating the population around a peak. C shows a change in the landscape due to environmental changes,[14] so that the original peak disappears, and the population moves to another peak. In D–F, there is sampling and inbreeding of various degrees, with D being more intensive, E less intensive with slow mutation, and F with the emergence of a set of distinct subgroups.

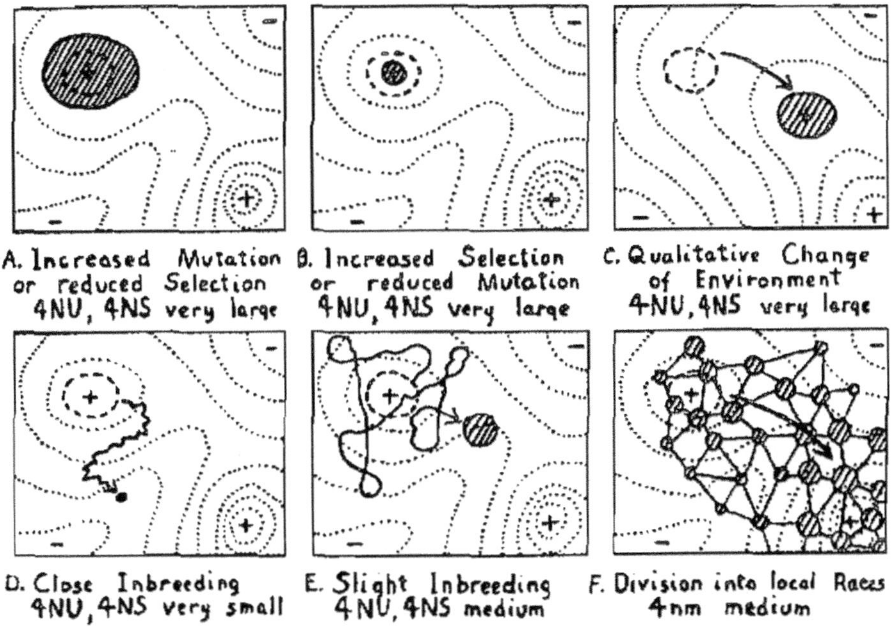

Fig. 7.1 Field of gene combinations in fitness landscapes with dynamics

7.2 The Ups and Downs of Darwinian Evolutionary Economics

E. Roy Weintraub (2002) has argued that one can trace the development of mathematical economics by observing the development of mathematics first, and then allowing for certain lags to occur after which one sees similar changes in the use of mathematics in economics. It is probably the case that one can argue for a similar process for attitudes toward Darwin and more broadly evolutionary theory within economics. The ups and downs described in the previous section have been reproduced to some degree within economics after some appropriate lags.

Just as in evolutionary theory there is a prehistory, so we can see such a prehistory in economics. In the previous chapter, we already discussed the important role of influence that Malthus had on Darwin himself as well as on Alfred Russel Wallace. Likewise, we have seen the rather complicated attitudes of Marx and Engels, who were Darwin's contemporaries, more or less, as well as Herbert Spencer and Alfred Marshall, with the later divergent views of Schumpeter, who in fact was not at all a fan of evolutionary theory as such due to his dislike of the continuity approach of Darwin, even as ironically some of the strongest advocates of an evolutionary approach to economics today are self-styled "neo-Schumpeterians" (Nelson and Winter, 1982; Potts, 2000; Foster and Metcalfe, 2001; Metcalfe and Foster, 2004; Dopfer, 2005).

As noted in the previous section, Darwin was not only influenced by Malthus but also by Adam Smith, indeed by both of his great works (Smith, 1759, 1776), with the tension between the cooperative and competitive aspects stressed in each of those works showing up in the long debate and struggle over cooperation versus competition within evolutionary theory, with the pacificist anarchist Kropotkin (1902) perhaps being the ultimate advocate of the more cooperative side of evolution. But Smith himself did not just jump out of a hat as is often depicted in simplified histories of economics but drew heavily on earlier influences.

These earlier strands have been discussed by Paul Christensen (1989, 2003), who points out that early protopolitical economists in various countries tended to have what we would now call an ecological economics perspective. This was substantially due to the enormous importance of agriculture in the preindustrial societies that these figures studied, and so they often drew on biophysical analogies or ideas quite substantially, especially as modern economic theory as such did not really exist. So, in Britain one has Hobbes (1651) and his *Leviathan*, in which society is seen as a single organic body. William Petty (1662) followed with a strong focus on the role of nature in agriculture. This in turn was the view in France of Boisguilbert (1695), considered by many to be the earliest precursor of general equilibrium theory, with his interrelations of economic sectors ultimately drawing on a foundation of nature in agriculture, being followed by the physiocrat Quesnay (1759) in his *Tableau Économique*, which in turn was read by Adam Smith as well as later figures such as Marx.

Adding a further note to the discussion from the last chapter, not only did Schumpeter fairly strongly disavow Darwinian evolutionary theory as such, despite his own work being readily interpretable within an evolutionary context (if of a saltationalist discontinuity version), but also Marshall, who though proclaimed his admiration for Darwin and for the "Mecca of biology," had his views of evolution more strongly taken from Herbert Spencer, including the Lamarckian and social Darwinist elements.

Another figure seen to have a strong evolutionary perspective was the founder of the Austrian School, Carl Menger. This is particularly in regard to his theory of the spontaneous emergence of money (Menger, 1892), which influenced Hayek in particular in his spontaneous emergence view of cultural evolution. However, it would appear that Menger himself was less concerned with the evolutionary aspect of this process, in contrast to Hayek, with not much to say about Darwin, Spencer, Haeckel, or any other figure promulgating evolutionary theory in one form or another at that time.

Thus, we have the situation that in the late nineteenth century, Darwin was relatively secondary in direct influence on evolutionary thinking in economics, with Spencer and Lamarck probably the more important figures. As already noted, this probably reflected the relative standing of Darwin and Spencer in particular in the broader view, as biologists saw limits to Darwin's theory, given the lack of knowledge of Mendelian genetics, and thus the underpinnings of variation through mutation and biological inheritance.

Hodgson argues in various places, including in an interview in Rosser, Holt, and Colander (2010, pp. 136–137), that it was Thorstein Veblen (1898, 1919) who was the first economist to really take on seriously the Darwinian perspective. He understood the distinction between Darwin and the then more popular Spencer, rejecting the teleology of Spencer as well as Social Darwinism. Veblen was one of the founders of the American Institutionalist tradition in economics, and he saw habits and institutions as the units of selection in the social sphere.

However, as Hodgson (2006) also argues, there is a curious twist in this link between Institutionalism and evolutionary economics. While Veblen supported Darwin, later Institutionalists would turn against him, at least partly for political reasons and because of a greater desire to focus on technological change, viewing institutions as barriers to progress. This was the view of Clarence Ayres (1932), who strongly rejected Darwin just at the time that he was being revived in biology by the promulgators of the neo-Darwinian synthesis. It is thus an even greater irony that while the main association for the "Old Institutionalists" is called the Association for Evolutionary Economics, this had nothing to do with Veblen or Darwinism, reflecting the fact that when it was founded in the 1960s, it was followers of Clarence Ayres who were responsible for naming it, and they wished to downplay the "institutionalist" aspect of it, while favoring their own version of evolutionary theory instead.

The initial revival of the Darwinian perspective came with the famous article by Armen Alchian (1950), followed by strong support for this view from Milton Friedman (1953), although this was also arguably a more Spencerian approach than Darwinian. Evolutionary theory was brought in as an "as if" factor in the process of economic competition. There had been much discussion that business managers did not know what their marginal costs were, and so presumably would be unable to optimize. However, Alchian argued that this did not matter, as those who did succeed in optimizing, however they achieved it, would be the ones who would do better than their competitors and would survive in competition. Friedman pushed this further to a fully instrumentalist view by suggesting that people know how to optimize intuitively, the way a billiard player knows how to play or a bicycle rider knows how to ride, without knowing the detailed mathematics or mechanics of what is involved. This strand of thought has continued and has had an outlet in the *Journal of Bioeconomics*, originally founded under the influence of Gordon Tullock, who has also advocated this view (Tullock, 2004). It is perhaps appropriate that the period of domination by the neo-Darwinian synthesis as an orthodoxy in biology would also be reflected by a very orthodox view of evolution's application to economics, but it remained largely not an approach used by most economists.

More recently there has been an explosion of multiple strands of interest in evolutionary economics. A harbinger of a more ecologically oriented approach would be Georgescu-Roegen (1971), but this view would be more strongly advocated by Kenneth Boulding (1978, 1981), whose work was also discussed in the previous chapter. This would be followed also by the more neo-Schumpeterian perspective of Nelson and Winter (1982) and their more recent followers mentioned above such as Dopfer,[15] Foster, Metcalfe, and Potts.

After, the curious hiatus of interest by Institutionalist economists in evolutionary theory, this has also turned around with the movement in this area being led by Geoffrey Hodgson (1993, 2006, 2009), founding editor of the *Journal of Institutional Economics*. So today, the Association for Evolutionary Economics has a more solidly based Darwinian evolutionary approach to it, albeit with many emphasizing competing ideas from punctuated equilibria and self-organizing dynamics.

Finally, and very influentially, has been the development of evolutionary game theory. This originally came out of biology with the introduction of the concept of an *evolutionarily stable strategy* by Maynard Smith and Price (1973), which was more properly mathematically formalized by Selten (1980). This has come to be viewed as a major approach within conventional game theory, offering a possible solution to the problem of equilibrium selection in dynamic games when there are multiple equilibria, as is often the case (Foster and Young, 1990; Binmore and Samuelson, 1999).

7.3 The Multilevel Complication

It is appropriate that we have just brought up the matter of evolutionary game theory, as this has played a central role in the more recent debates regarding the question of what is now carefully called *multilevel selection*, partly to avoid the more contentious older term "group selection." As noted earlier, in most of his writings Darwin advocated a single level of selection that operates at the level of the organism primarily. With the neo-Darwinian synthesis after the integration of Mendelian genetics into the Darwinian system, the fundamental level seemed to go down to the individual gene, a view most strongly emphasized by Williams (1966) and Dawkins (1976). Later when Dawkins (1983) introduced the idea of universal Darwinism that extends beyond just biology, he introduced the concept of the *meme*, the object upon which evolution operates, although this in turn has become a contentious topic (and a word stretched far beyond this original meaning to have become nearly gibberish), especially as it has been applied in economics and other social sciences. It continues to be the case that Dawkins and others hold to the view that biological evolution in particular fundamentally operates only at one level, the lowest level, and that the critique by Williams (1966) of the work of Wynne-Edwards (1962) and others was definitive.

Nevertheless, since these strong assertions, there has been a building of support for the idea that evolution sometimes operates at higher levels, with this most strongly argued once we get to human evolution, which as noted earlier was recognized by Darwin himself (1871), despite his general view. For humans, the equivalent of the supposedly hard-core neo-Darwinian view that Darwin did not accept was to focus on the individual, leading back to a focus on the gene. However, the fundamental mathematics behind understanding multiselection was developed by Crow (1955), Hamilton (1964, 1972), and particularly Price (1970, 1972). The broader arguments as applied to humans and how culture could be a part of the actual biological part of human evolution drawing on these earlier arguments has been laid out in Boyd and Richerson (1985), Wade (1985), Maynard Smith (1998), Sober and Wilson (1998), and Henrich and Boyd (1998), with economists getting into this more recently (Gintis, 2000; Fehr and Gächter, 2002). Hayek (1979) provided an early version of this for strictly cultural evolution. Henrich (2004) provides an excellent overview.

From the game theoretic standpoint, the issue of multilevel selection is deeply connected to the dilemmas within game theory about selfishness versus cooperation that show up in such examples as the prisoner's dilemma (PD) and the stag-hunt coordination games. While cooperation is a Pareto superior outcome, a more selfish strategy is the Nash equilibrium. As developed by Maynard Smith (1972) and Maynard Smith and Price (1973), evolutionarily stable strategies (ESS) are subsets of the larger set of Nash equilibria. Cheaters or selfish individuals can undermine cooperation both among humans and also in biological evolutionary systems. The question becomes that of how cooperation can evolve in the face of this powerful effect (Axelrod, 1984).[16]

Crucial to understanding the dynamics of multilevel selection, it is necessary to distinguish changes in fitness within a group versus those between groups. With regard to the question of cooperation, or as it is conventionally put, altruism, one must consider genes that lead to behaviors that are damaging to an individual but good for the group the individual is within. Following work of Crow (1955) on defining these elements and drawing on the work of Price (1970, 1972), Crow and Aoki (1982) determined a basic condition for the mean value of an altruistic gene to increase.

Let B_w the within-group genic regression on the fitness value of the trait as defined in the work of Sewall Wright (1951) and B_b be the between-group genic regression to the fitness value. Let V_w be the variance among individuals within a group and V_b the variance among means across groups. For an altruistic trait, one expects B_w to be negative while B_b to be positive. Given these, a sufficient condition for the altruistic trait to increase in frequency is given by

$$B_b / - B_w > V_w / V_b. \tag{7.1}$$

The expectation here is that V_w is likely to be substantially larger than V_b, which becomes an argument for the widespread skepticism regarding the ability of altruistic genes to increase relative to selfish ones. The between-group fitness effect must be substantially greater than the (negative) within-fitness effect, which can be tied to kin selection effects, the classic source of multilevel selection in purely biological evolution, with social insects a classic example.

Focus of discussion has often focused on variables that affect the right-hand side of this equation. Among those are the size of the groups and the degree of isolation of them, with the right-hand term tending to decline as groups are smaller and more isolated. This has led to skepticism that the condition can be met among human groups, given in particular tendencies to migration and interbreeding (keeping in mind that these equations were developed by people such as Wright much concerned with the matter of artificial selection and breeding). Nevertheless, Henrich suggests that a case observed by anthropologists of this working in a combined biological-cultural setting was the displacement during the nineteenth century in the Sudan of the Dinka group by the Nuer group, where the former killed their cattle to eat beef, while the latter used their cattle for milk and did not kill them.

When one shifts to the more purely cultural evolution aspect of this within a game theoretic setup, the matter of within group versus between group very much involves being able to identify who is a cooperator ("carries the altruistic gene") versus is not a cooperator. This has often been posed, as Henrich (2004) explains, as the "greenbeard problem." So, within a group cooperators may identify themselves by growing green beards. However, if a mutation allows defectors (noncooperators) to learn how to grow green beards and pass as cooperators, the evolutionary advantage of the cooperators (or carriers of the altruistic genes) will disappear, and the selfish defectors will take over. This can be seen as a matter of costly signaling. Among biologists those scoffing at the ability to maintain such signals have included Dawkins (1976) and Low (2000). Among social scientists, Frank (1988) and Frank, Gilovitch, and Regan (1993) have argued for this signaling to be able to occur, while skeptics have included Ekman (1992) and Ockenfels and Selten (2000).

We wish to note that the conditions being discussed here are not along the same lines as those advocated by Wynne-Edwards (1962) that were ridiculed by Williams (1966). Those involved independent adaptations occurring directly at the group level. Here the analysis is derived ultimately from the model of Fisher (1930) that underpins the neo-Darwinian synthesis and that such figures as Dawkins rely upon in their arguments, meaning that even the opponents of multilevel selection cannot simply rule it out a priori, but must contest the possibility on empirical grounds with regard to certain key parameters. We note at this point the link between this discussion and that regarding hypercyclic morphogenesis that occurred in the previous chapter. I also further note that at this level when we are discussing the more purely economic and social side of this, this condition is very strong in that it holds for true altruists, those who do not personally benefit from their own actions, the classic example recognized by Darwin of the tribal member who sacrifices his life for the good of his group.

A much weaker form of this, and thus more likely to develop, is the reciprocal altruism of Trivers (1971), in which there is an implicit expectation by the cooperator of future cooperation back by others. This is the mechanism underlying the tit-for-tat strategy in repeated PD games (Axelrod, 1984), and many have studied how punishment plays a role in enforcing these sorts of cooperation over time in groups, with Nowak and Sigmund (1998) agreeing with the earlier observation about group size that enforcing cooperation is harder as group size increases. This leads to arguments that mutations that lead to only allowing cooperation with punishment should be selected for (Boyd and Richerson, 1992; Gintis, 2000).

The distinction between purer altruism and more selfish sorts of reciprocity-based cooperation has become a matter of intense study. Fehr and Schmidt (1999) proposed a method of distinguishing the two. However, how easily this can be measured has become a matter of considerable debate among experimental economists (Binmore and Shaked, 2010; Fehr and Schmidt, 2010).

7.4 Self-Organization and Natural Selection

We now come to a matter of ongoing controversy within evolutionary theory, the relationship between complex self-organization and natural selection. A leading advocate of the self-organization idea in evolution has been Stuart Kauffman (1993, p. xiii), who argues that "this single force view [of Darwin's, e.g., natural selection]. . .fails to stress, fails to incorporate the possibility that simple and complex systems exhibit order spontaneously." Kauffman follows Eigen and Shuster (1979) in posing the emergence of higher-ordered structures in evolution as self-organizing processes along the lines of hypercyclic morphogenesis, with this providing an explanation for the origin of life itself, as well as the origin of multicellular organisms, with these processes only partially driven by natural selection as such.

The ultimate origin of this argument is traced to D'Arcy Thompson (1917) and his views on growth and form, who saw order arising as forms fit to optimal patterns, such as honeycombs being hexagonal as these compactly order volumes with minimal use of surface materials. This is seen as fitting in with the older pre-evolutionary theorists such as Paley and the idea of *rational morphology*, these older views consistent with creationism in which God has made all species fit into their environments in a rational and optimal way without any need for natural selection to form them to fit. This "order for free" has brought down considerable opposition from many evolutionary theorists, including Gould (2002, pp. 1200–1214), who does not suggest that Thompson or Kauffman or Goodwin (1994) are creationists.[17] He claims to admire the efforts of those at the Santa Fe Institute (where Kauffman is located) to study complex systems, agreeing that there may be some value in doing so.[18] But in the end, the Kauffman theory is too general and not very useful when one tries to understand the evolution of "such a phyletically localized, complex, and historically particular structure as the tetrapod limb" (Gould, 2002, p. 1213). Gould throws "complexity" back into the faces of those putting it forward as a complement to natural selection.

An underlying commonality of argument between Gould and Kauffman in their respective struggles with the conventional neo-Darwinian synthesis is their mutual reliance on the ideas of Sewall Wright. For Kauffman, he has developed the *NK* theory of adaptation to Wrightian fitness landscapes. In the *NK* model, N is the number of parts in a system, the genes in a genotype, the proteins in an amino acid, whatever, which, however are adapting to the fitness landscape. K is the number of other parts that the N parts are connected to and whose interaction is also involved in the adaptation process in the landscapes.

Drawing deeply on work of Crow and Kimura (1970) and Lewontin (1974), Kauffman derives various conclusions. If $K = 0$, then there will be a single peak in the fitness landscape. At the other extreme is the case of the largest possible value for K, namely, $N - 1$. In that case, the landscape becomes completely random. More generally, as N increases, the number of peaks in the landscape tends to increase while the heights of the peaks tend to diminish. Kauffman labels this phenomenon the *complexity catastrophe*. These two extreme cases are posed as extreme order and extreme disorder (or "chaos," although this is not proper mathematical chaos), with Kauffman eventually arguing that evolutionary advances and the emergence of higher-order structures occurs on the boundary between these zones, "at the edge of chaos."

Eventually, Kauffman would see this all being equivalent to computational problems and issues. This would be picked up by his Santa Fe Institute (SFI) colleague James Crutchfield (1994, 2003), who would pursue further the problems of the emergence of higher-order structures out of evolutionary processes from an essentially computational standpoint. This has involved the use of genetic algorithms and other methods. Crutchfield (2003) posits the existence of "mesoscales," where microscopic genotypes manifest themselves in forms of phenotypes. These then change over time in punctuated episodes of dramatic change in a process of "epochal evolutionary unfolding," in which on both the genotypical and phenotypical levels, there are leaps to new levels of order. This process is depicted in Fig. 7.2 (Crutchfield, 2003, p. 116), with the genotypes on the right moving upwards from one basin of attraction to a higher one, while on the left the phenotypes do so as well in a parallel pattern in response to an initial mutational innovation.[19]

This approach to evolutionary emergence reopens the door to the question of multilevel selection again from another direction, with the threat of "holistic" evolution posing as a possibility, which had supposedly been vanquished by Williams

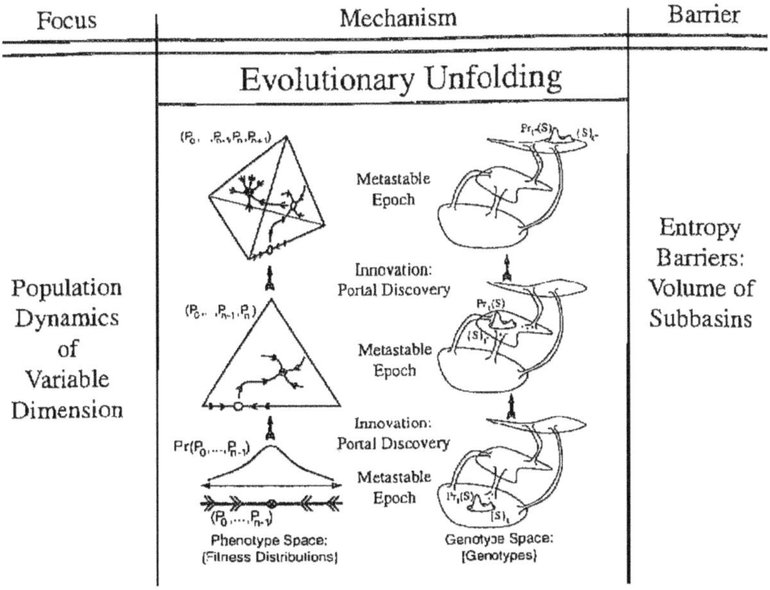

Fig. 7.2 Portrait of an evolutionary innovation

(1966). The idea of *emergence* in evolution is an old one, having achieved a peak of interest in the 1920s with the so-called British Emergentist School (Morgan, 1923; McLaughlin, 1992). Their approach has been argued to derive from John Stuart Mill's concept of "heteropathic laws" (Mill, 1843). In the hands of Crutchfield and Kauffman and their allies (Newman, 1997; Bornholdt, 2003; Eble, 2003; Gavrilets, 2003), this becomes a computational process.

This has led to criticism by yet others. Among those is Joseph McCauley (2005), who objects from a physics perspective. An advocate of econophysics (2004),[20] McCauley argues that true science involves the search for invariances and ergodicity in systems, which he argues does not appear in these biological and evolutionary systems. McCauley (2005, p. 77) accepts that we may know "how a cell mutates to a new form, but we do not know how a fish evolves into a bird." It is too complicated even for complexity theory. McCauley further cites Moore (1990, 1991a, b) who studied Turing machines without attractors that exhibit full unpredictability and surprise, declaring this to be the ultimate foundation of complexity theory.[21]

The questions of computability, emergence, and evolution has spilled into economics as well, particularly following the work of Mirowski (2007). He makes the controversial claim that markets are algorithms, thus reducing them to a computability issue.[22] He argues that over time markets develop hierarchies that have some resemblance to Chomsky (1959) or Wolfram (1984) hierarchies. So, futures markets emerge from spot markets, options markets emerge from futures markets, and higher-order derivatives markets emerge from options markets, and so on, with the higher-order markets embedding the lower-order ones in the way that a more evolved "higher-order" evolved system may contain that which it came out of anagenetically in the self-organizing evolutionary view with a fully teleological drive, perhaps connected to entropic processes working themselves out. In any[23] case, Mirowski sees these algorithmic market systems as competing with each other and evolving via natural selection, just as other evolutionary economists have focused on the evolution of technologies or firms. For Mirowski, the goal is some sort of universal Turing machine (Cotogno, 2003), but Zambelli (2007) argues that he is overreaching, and that his system collapses partly due to there being unbridgeable gaps in the hierarchies of Chomsky and Wolfram that he fails to deal with adequately.

We thus return to perhaps a deeper aspect of this debate between the neo-Darwinian synthesis and the advocates of complex self-organization. This is indeed the matter of teleology versus a sort of wandering randomness. There have been only a few evolutionary theorists who have advocated a full-blown teleological perspective, notably the Catholic theologian and evolutionist Teilhard de Chardin (1956) with his idea of evolution being a divinely driven process proceeding toward the noöspheric (Vernadsky, 1945)[24] Omega Point, although Davies (2003) and Morowitz (2003) provide somewhat lower-key examples as well. Most self-organization advocates such as Kauffman tend to eschew such exogenously driven processes, but nevertheless see some tendency for some sort of greater complexity to gradually emerge over time through evolution, even as it is not necessarily an inexorable or monotonic process, especially in the face of dramatic mass extinctions that have occurred from time to time. But, left on its own, the biosphere self-organizes to higher orders of greater complexity (Crutchfield, 2003), however defined. The ultimate argument for this is to point to the grand movement from the nonorganic through unicellular organisms through the hypercyclic morphogenesis of the multicellular and finally to organisms with larger and larger brains, finally achieving the self-consciousness of humanity.

Needless to say the neo-Darwinian response to this ultimate assertion of Thompson-Kauffman quasi-teleology is to reemphasize the stochastic nature of all this and the ultimately dominating role of natural selection within it. If we see more complicated, if not more necessarily more complex,[25] organisms over time on average, this is because that complicatedness has given these organisms a competitive edge in the coevolutionary landscape within which the landscape itself is coevolving with the species struggling within it for survival and reproduction. But there is no inherent tendency for this, and numerous examples can be brought forth of simplifications that have occurred at one point or another in evolutionary history, quite aside from the drastic simplifications enforced by the great mass extinctions of history such as the Permian. There is no fundamental teleology, even if it looks sort of like maybe there is, kind of.

There is no final resolution of this debate. However, we shall go out the door on this for now by presenting two figures that depict the alternative perspectives within a dynamic evolutionary context. A teleological vision would be one that sees higher-order multilevel structure, emerging inexorably from such processes, whereas a neo-Darwinian perspective would see a greater randomness, a process

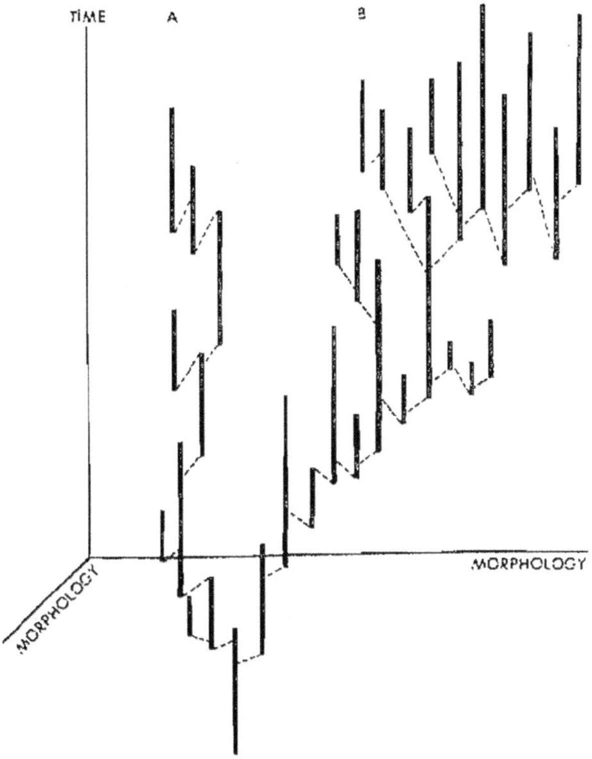

Fig. 7.3 Evololutionary tree with higher-order morphological complexity

that changes, but in which no strategy or structure permanently dominates as the system simply goes on and on in its evolutionary dynamic.

Figure 7.3 from Bornholdt (2003, p. 68) shows a branching pattern to more diverse and complicated forms of morphology developing in a classic evolutionary tree that is marked by sharp punctuations of Eldredge-Gouldian sort. While Lindgren and Johansson (2003) show outcomes that evolve to cooperation out of a dynamic prisoners' dilemma game, Fig. 7.4 from Lindgren (1997, p. 349) can

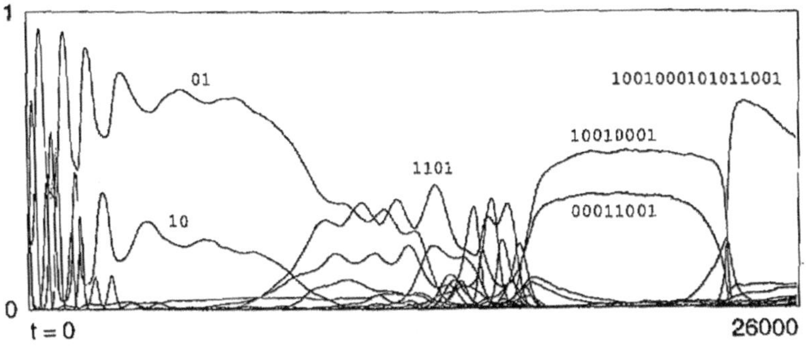

Fig. 7.4 Evolving prisoner's dilemma game tending nowhere particularly

be thought of as showing a neo-Darwinian vision, albeit with a touch of punctuationism. Showing the presence of competing strategies of cooperation or defection within a PD game, operating within a mean-field framework,[26] periods emerge when one or another strategy may dominate, but then these break down within fairly short periods during which there is a vigorous competition, followed by the emergence of a new structure, although none of these persist for too long, and the system simply moves along, a complex evolving system that does not necessarily self-organize itself into some sort of hierarchical teleological final steady state or noöspheric Omega Point.

Notes

1. The line "chance caught on a wing" is from Monod (1971) originally, who especially emphasized the stochastic element in evolution.
2. While the likely strike that wiped out the dinosaurs (that did not evolve into birds) is a dramatic example, a far more dramatic one was whatever triggered the Permian extinction much earlier that may have wiped out as much as 90% of the existing species of the time.
3. In the case of Gould, an aspect of this is connected with his finding Darwin open to multilevel selection despite the widespread view that he was unalterably opposed to it. He accepted it in regard to humans at the tribal level (Darwin, 1871). Thus, Gould (2002, p. 136) declares "Supporters of hierarchy theory – I am one... – are revising Darwinism into a multilevel theory of selection."
4. Haeckel was the main advocate of Darwin's theory in Germany, and he used the apparent passage of an embryo through a facsimile of the evolutionary process of an organism as evidence for evolution.
5. Curiously, although he fell short of a full-blown theory of this, Adam Smith discussed this aspect of languages in an appendix to the third edition of *The Theory of Moral Sentiments* (1767). See also Berry (1974). David Hume (1779) was also an influence on Darwin and arguably came closer to the idea of natural selection in his discussion of the idea of the evolution of laws and customs.
6. Corsi (2005, p. 77) argues that Gautieri posed a vision of life arising from nonliving matter, "Gautieri rapidly sketched a series of steps linking the inorganic to the organic, minerals to crystals, zoophytes to plants and animals, and finally to man."
7. It should be kept in mind that existing views such as the "natural theology" perspective of Paley (1802) accepted that species are adapted to their environments but saw this as part of the perfection of divine creationism, with no environmental changes of any significance having occurred to disrupt these adaptations, a word Paley used, but which Darwin would propose a different source for.
8. This life force supposedly was striving to satisfy "needs," or *besoins*, although a fairer reading of him would say that these "needs" simply reflected what helped an organism to be well adapted to an environment in order to survive and reproduce, which would make his argument much closer to Darwin's. That Lamarck held this "vitalist" view was largely a caricature due to Cuvier (Burckhardt, 1977).
9. In fact, the evidence from Darwin's *Descent of Man* (1871, p. 129) is that he read *Theory of Moral Sentiments* as well as *Wealth of Nations* (Haig, 2010; Schliesser, 2010). Both Smith (1759) and Darwin (1872) saw the origins of human morality in some primate behaviors (Brosnan, 2010), although most of these behaviors are of the more "selfish" sort associated with reciprocal altruism (Trivers, 1971; Brosnan, Freeman, and van der Waal, 2006; Burkhart, Fehr, Efferson, and van Schaik, 2007). Some argue that mirror neurons, observed in primates

in general (Gallese, Fadiga, Fogassi, and Rizzolatti, 1996), provide a basis for empathy and thus altruism and morality (Molnar-Szakacz, 2010).

10. Darwin's relation to "Social Darwinism" has been a matter of controversy. The leading critic of Spencer, Richard Hofstadter (1944), tended to absolve Darwin of what he viewed as the errors and sins of Spencer. However, more recent observers say that in his theory of human evolution, Darwin (1871) exhibited elements of an independent version of Social Darwinism (Ruse, 1980, 2009; Weikart, 2009; Leonard, 2009). Much of this debate became aggravated with the controversies over *sociobiology* (Wilson, 1975).
11. Kimura's (1968) "neutral" theory is often viewed as adding to this, albeit much later.
12. In his work for the USDA, Wright invented the method of path coefficients analysis, a form of structural equation modeling related to multiple regression (1918, 1921, 1923), and also was the first to use instrumental variables in his analysis of corn-hog cycles (1925), although it would be his father, Philip G. Wright, who showed how these could be used to solve the identification problem (Wright, 1928). The author wishes to thank James Crow for providing materials and discussion related to Sewall Wright's work. Crow is one of the last to be closely associated with those who formulated the neo-Darwinian synthesis, and he was responsible for bringing Sewall Wright to the University of Wisconsin-Madison in 1955.
13. Among advocates of the synthesis, one figure who allowed for varying rates of evolution was G.G. Simpson (1949).
14. While initially such environmental changes were thought of as being external to the biological system, such as climatic changes, it has come to be understood that they may also include changes in the relative populations of other species or even mutations and evolutionary changes of those populations, possibly in reaction to changes or behaviors of the population under question. This is then the system of *coevolution*, a term coined by Ehrlich and Raven (1964) and first applied in economics by Norgaard (1984), although it has since been recognized that Darwin discussed the concept without the name. In such a system, the fitness landscape itself coevolves with the species in it.
15. However, this group has pulled in many others at least as nominal allies, with Dopfer (2005) containing essays by such figures as Herbert Simon, Paul David, Joel Mokyr, Peter Allen, Gerald Silverberg, and Bart Verspagen.
16. While Axelrod touted Anatol Rapoport's tit-for-tat strategy as being the best performing in repeated games, this has since been superseded by other strategies, some of them basically variations on tit-for-tat.
17. It is ironic that Gould himself came under fire from other evolutionists initially for his punctuated equilibrium theory precisely because it seemed to provide ammunition for creationists against the theory of evolution, and it may be that Gould's monumental 2002 book was at least partly done in an effort to refute this allegation and to assert the consistency of his viewpoint with that of Darwin.
18. A more vigorous advocate of a dynamic view against traditional Darwinianism is the "Poincaréan epistemological pragmatist" James Barham (1992, p. 262) who declares "For the dynamicist, teleonomic or purposive behavior is an objective property of biological systems; for the Darwinian, the apparent purposiveness of living things is a subjective illusion, and the language of purposes and goals. . .is a mere convention or shorthand to help us describe certain complex but essentially mechanical processes."
19. We note that this approach assumes distinct levels of hierarchy in this process of evolution, in contrast to the Zipf's Law approach in urban economics where there is a continuous distribution of city sizes. This view of ecology more broadly as possessing well-defined hierarchical levels is discussed in Allen and Starr (1982).
20. McCauley (2004) decries what he labels as *econobiology*. Rosser (2010a) considers these comparisons and debates further. McCauley's usage calls to mind sociobiology more than say "bioeconomics" does.

21. Velupillai (2009) argues that complexity is ultimately defined as being computational. Rosser (2009b, 2010b) disagrees, arguing for the dynamic complexity view drawn on Day (1994) and Rosser (1999b), which Velupillai (2011) are now labeling "Day–Rosser complexity."
22. Conlisk (2007) and Kirman (2007) both dispute this view, arguing that ultimately a market is a social interaction between human beings.
23. We also note that Hayek (1948, 1952, 1967, 1979) was an advocate of this complexity view of evolution, and despite his strong methodological individualism, he also supported the idea of multilevel evolution within human societies (Caldwell, 2004).
24. A predecessor of Vernadsky's broader ideas within the Russian tradition, as well as of later general systems theory and cybernetics, was A.A. Bogdanov (1922) and his theory of organization, or *tektology*, which attempted a unification of the physical and social sciences. See also Stokes (1992).
25. Israel (2005) distinguishes between complexity and complicatedness, noting that they come from different Latin roots. Complexity comes from *complecti*, to "grasp, comprehend, or embrace," whereas complicatedness comes from *complicare*, to "fold or envelop." Usually the difference is that complexity implies some higher order arising from the elements, whereas complicatedness simply involves there being many elements. However, some have used the two interchangeably, such as von Neumann (1966). Herbert Simon (1962) was important in linking hierarchy and complexity.
26. See Brock and Hommes (1997).

Chapter 8
Ecosystems and Economics

She says, "I am content when the wakened birds,
Before they fly, test the reality
Of misty fields, by their sweet questionings;
But when the birds are gone, and their warm fields
Return no more, where, then, is paradise?"
Wallace Stevens, 1947, "Sunday Morning"

8.1 Nonlinear Bionomic Dynamics

8.1.1 Single-Species Models with Density Dependence

That populations of single species in simple environments may exhibit oscillatory patterns over time has been well understood since first being documented experimentally for sheep blowflies by Nicholson (1933), and by Hewitt (1921) and Elton (1942) for small mammals in boreal environments. In the latter case, the most famous example is the 4-year cycle of lemmings. Keith (1963) has documented the existence of 10-year cycles for other boreal, fur-bearing mammals, such as muskrats. Of course, the single-species model strictly holds only in a laboratory context.

Generally such populations are thought to grow exponentially but to face some well-defined carrying capacity, K, beyond which the population cannot be sustained. Such growth follows the S-shaped logistic equation, first developed by Verhulst (1838). The density dependence due to the upper bounding carrying capacity induces nonlinearity in the growth function.

Hutchinson (1948) investigated the case where there is a generational time delay in the function. Thus,

$$\mathrm{d}X/\mathrm{d}t = r[1 - X(t - T)/K], \tag{8.1}$$

where X is the population, r is the intrinsic net growth rate, and T is the lag of the feedback mechanism. $1/r$ is the "return time," the time it takes to return to equilibrium (carrying capacity) if the population is exogenously shocked. If $rT > 1$, then

J.B. Rosser, *Complex Evolutionary Dynamics in Urban-Regional and Ecologic-Economic Systems*, DOI 10.1007/978-1-4419-8828-7_8,

the population overshoots the equilibrium if shocked and tends to oscillate.[1] This led to a distinction between low rT, "K-adjusting" species and high rT "r-adjusting" species. The former tend to exhibit short-run stability, that is, relatively constant populations in the face of environmental fluctuations. However, they may have difficulty adjusting to a severe shock. On the other hand, the latter are likely to fluctuate in response to time-varying environmental shocks.[2] However, their relatively high intrinsic growth rates allow them to recover better from a severe shock, thus exhibiting a long-run resilience. This is the essence of the "stability-resilience" trade-off postulated by Holling (1973).

In the mid-1970s, it was realized that for such equations sufficient increases of r, or equivalent variables, would lead to period-doubling bifurcations, and eventually to chaotic dynamics (Li and Yorke, 1975; May, 1974, 1976; May and Oster, 1976; Guckenheimer, Oster, and Ipaktchi, 1977). Indeed, these were the studies that introduced the term "chaos" to the discussion of nonlinear dynamics. These models were the immediate influence upon economists for the study of chaotic dynamics, especially for single-equation macroeconomic growth models (Stutzer, 1980; Benhabib and Day, 1980; Day, 1982, 1983).[3] However, it must be noted that May (1976) not only acknowledged a direct influence from work in nonlinear economic models (Samuelson, 1942, 1947; Goodwin, 1951; Baumol, 1970) but also explicitly recognized the applicability of what was being done by him and his ecologist colleagues to economic modelling. Thus he declared (May, 1976, pp. 459–460):

> Examples in economics include models for the relationship between commodity quantity and price, for the theory of business cycles, and for the temporal sequences generated by various other economic quantities. The general equation also is germane to the social sciences, where it arises, for example, in theories of learning (where X may be the number of bits of information that can be remembered after an interval t), or the propagation of rumors in variously structured societies (where X is the number of people to have heard the rumor after time t).

Even though this particular article by May has been very widely cited in the economic literature on chaotic dynamics, it has rarely been recognized that May himself *explicitly* argued for an application to economic models.

Li and Yorke (1975) and May (1976) studied a simple form of the logistic equation:

$$X_{t+1} = aX_t(1 - X_t). \tag{8.2}$$

The bifurcation values of the "tuning parameter," a, are at $a = 3.0$, the stable equilibrium bifurcates to a two-period oscillation; at $a = 3.57$, it bifurcates to a four-period cycle with an accumulation of further period-doubling bifurcations following rapidly; and then at $a = 3.8284$, a three-period cycle appears which is the beginning of the zone of chaotic dynamics. The chaotic zone ends at $a = 4.0$, with all solutions going to $-\infty$ beyond there.

Most of the equations reviewed in May and Oster (1976) and most of the empirical studies of single-species models have involved insect populations (entomology). Among the first empirical efforts to find chaos was by Hassell, Lawton, and May

(1976) who estimated parameter values for 24 field and four laboratory populations of arthropod species, exhibiting nonoverlapping, discrete generations, according to the following equation:

$$X_{t+1} = \lambda X_t[1 + X_t]^{-\beta}. \tag{8.3}$$

For arbitrarily large β, the bifurcation values of λ are as follows: For $\lambda < 7.39$, there is a stable equilibrium; for $7.39 < \lambda < 12.50$, damped oscillations may occur; for $12.50 < \lambda < 14.77$, stable limit cycles exist with period-doubling bifurcations occurring as λ increases; and finally chaotic dynamics for $\lambda > 14.77$. Of the species in question, one lab population (blowflies) exhibited chaotic dynamics, two lab populations showed oscillatory behavior, and one showed monotonic damping to a stable equilibrium; whereas none of the field populations were chaotic, only two were oscillatory, and the remaining 22 exhibited monotonic damping to a stable equilibrium. These results are shown in Fig. 8.1, where the black dots represent field populations and the open circles represent laboratory populations.[4]

> The solid lines demarcate the stability domains for the density dependence parameter, β, and the population growth rate, λ, in equation (17); the dashed line shows where 2-point cycles give way to higher cycles of period 2*. The solid circles come from analyses of life table data on field populations, and the open circles from laboratory populations.

This apparent divergence of behavior between field and laboratory populations has occasioned much discussion, notably that field populations are in fact in complex, multispecies environments whose dynamics are not adequately captured by the single-species model. The apparent instability of "artificial" environments is a long theme in ecological literature. This split shows up even among the field populations as noted by May (1981a, p. 22):

> It is perhaps suggestive that the most oscillatory natural population is the Colorado potato beetle, Leptinotarsa, [labeled A in 8.1] whose contemporary role in agroecosystems lacks an evolutionary pedigree.[5]

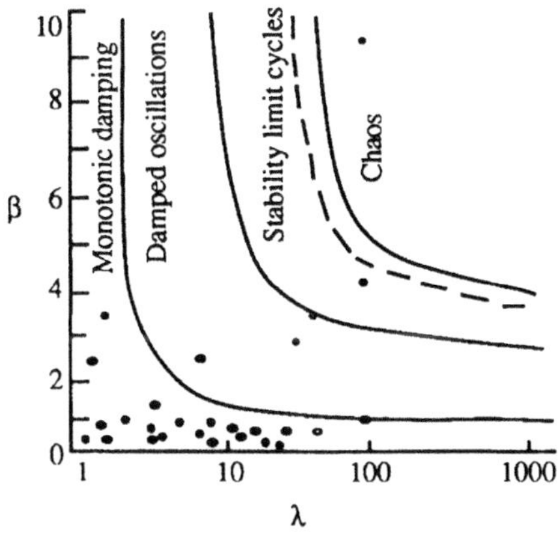

Fig. 8.1 Arthropod single-species dynamics

8.1.2 Two-Species Lotka–Volterra Models

A major difficulty with the single-species models involves the concept of carrying capacity. Except for photosynthesizing green plants, the "carrying capacity" for any particular species in any particular environment depends on the availability of those species upon which it feeds (prey). Furthermore, it can be limited in its growth by the presence of a predator that feeds on it. This set of relationships was analyzed initially by Lotka (1920, 1925) and Volterra (1931, 1937) with the famous predator–prey model.

Changes in the abundance of the lynx and the snowshoe hare, as indicated by the number of pelts received by the Hudson Bay Company. This is a classic case of cyclic oscillation in population density.

This model explains coupled oscillations that occur in nature. Perhaps the most famous of these is the approximately 10-year, interlinked, hare–lynx cycle in the Hudson Bay region, data for which goes back over 200 years because of the records of pelt purchases by the Hudson Bay Company from Cree–Ojibwa hunters.[6] This pattern is exhibited in Fig. 8.2 (from Odum, 1953) with Hewitt (1921) originally reporting some of this data.

The original ("classical") formulation of the model, due to Lotka (1920), takes the form

$$\mathrm{d}x/\mathrm{d}t = aX - \alpha XY, \tag{8.4}$$

$$\mathrm{d}y/\mathrm{d}t = -bY + \beta XY, \tag{8.5}$$

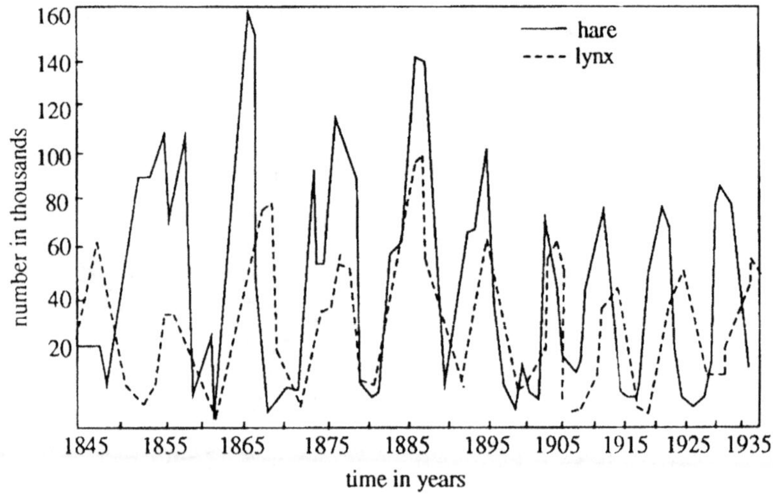

Fig. 8.2 Hudson Bay hare–lynx cycles

where X is the prey population, Y is the predator population, a is the intrinsic growth rate of the prey, b is the death rate of the predator, and α and β are the predator–prey interaction terms.[7] This model generates oscillations around an equilibrium with a period of $2\pi/\sqrt{ab}$ that exhibit the "neutral stability" of a frictionless pendulum. If the system is shocked, it will oscillate with a new amplitude. Lotka noted (1925, p. 92) that when the higher-order interaction terms are included, damped oscillatory behavior, spiraling toward the equilibrium, will occur.[8]

Kolmogorov (1936) showed for a general continuous form of this system with some form of density dependence that in the long run the system will converge to either an equilibrium point or a stable limit cycle.[9] The system reflects a tension between the stabilizing prey density dependence effect and the often de-stabilizing predator functional and numerical responses. A curious result of this is the "paradox of enrichment," due to Rosenzweig (1971), and supported by empirical evidence. As K rises (the ecosystem gets "richer"), stabilizing prey density dependence is lowered, and the system can bifurcate from a stable equilibrium point to a stable limit cycle.

Although the Kolmogorov theorem rules out chaotic dynamics for continuous Lotka–Volterra systems, they can occur in difference equation systems, appropriate for nonoverlapping generations species, such as insects and arthropods. Following May (1974), Beddington, Free, and Lawton (1975) examine chaotic dynamics in a density-dependent version of host–parasite equations, developed by Nicholson and Bailey (1935) of the form

$$X_{t+1} = X_t\{\exp[r(1 - X_t/K) - aY_t]\}, \tag{8.6}$$

$$Y_{t+1} = \alpha X_t[1 - \exp(-aY_t)], \tag{8.7}$$

with all variables defined as above. This is analogous to the predator–prey model; predators are parasites and prey are hosts. Beddington, Free, and Lawton find that the further a predator suppresses a prey below its carrying capacity, the lower is the growth rate required for chaos. This result is consistent with the "paradox of enrichment," where de-stabilization results from K rising relative to the prey rather than the prey declining relative to K.

May and Anderson (1983) study an epidemiological model due to Kermack and MacKendrick (1927) of the form

$$1 - \theta(X) = \exp(-X\theta(X)/\tilde{x}), \tag{8.8a}$$

where X is the host population, θ is the proportion of the host infected by the virus or bacteria, and $\tilde{x}$ is a threshold host density necessary for the disease to survive in the host population. This model exhibits what they label "pure chaos" in that there are no stable equilibria or stable cycles or period-doubling phenomena. Rogers, Yang, and Yip (1986) label this "complete chaos" and show that it will occur for any positive function whose logarithmic derivative exceeds $1/x$.

Epidemiological models and pest outbreak models exhibit "breakpoint" threshold phenomena that can result in catastrophic-style dynamic changes in population.[10] Ross (1911) first argued for the existence of a threshold for malaria, later confirmed by MacDonald (1957). May (1977) shows a "breakpoint" model for schistosomiasis, and Anderson (1981) shows one for hookworm infections in India. In Fig. 8.3, the Anderson hookworm model is shown with M^* being the mean hookworm burden per host and r being the reproductive rate of the hookworms.

The spruce budworm has exhibited a pattern of sudden outbreaks of population about every 40 years, as has been documented by Holling (1973) and by Ludwig, Jones, and Holling (1978). May (1977) models budworms (X) as a function of leaf area (S) and the leaf area as a function of the budworms, depicted in Fig. 8.4 showing cyclical behavior marked by periodic bursts of budworm population offset by much smaller crashes.[11]

Two other interspecies relationships that can arise from the Lotka–Volterra framework are competition and symbiosis. Competitive models are like the single-species models except that the carrying capacity for each species is reduced by the other species' consumption of its food supply. Competitive relations are common in nature and equilibria frequently exist. Generally, the greater the range of possible equilibria, the smaller is the degree of niche overlap between the species (May, 1981b).

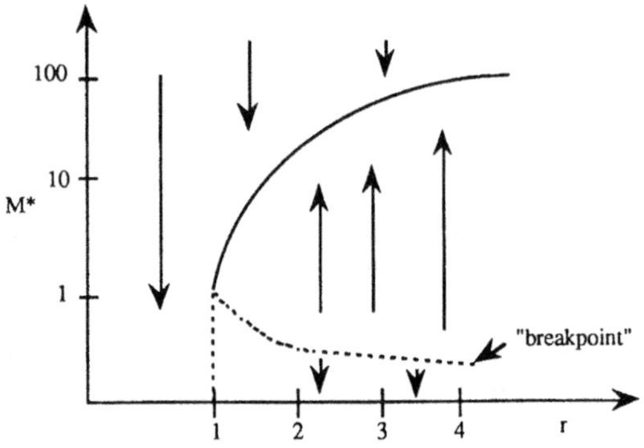

Fig. 8.3 Hookworm population dynamics

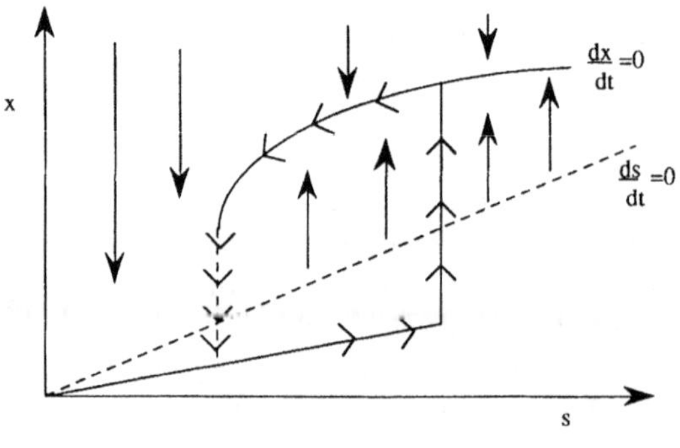

Fig. 8.4 Spruce budworm dynamics

Symbiotic (or mutualistic) relations between species tend to be de-stabilizing and can only exist if there is a saturation in the magnitude of the mutual benefits (May, 1981b). Such systems may exhibit multiple equilibria and thus be subject to discontinuous shifts as well as a greater propensity to chaotic dynamics. They are more common in the highly stable tropical ecosystems. Classic examples include plant pollination and seed dispersal by animals as well as the role played by bacteria in most larger animals. In one dramatic case, the fungus–algae symbiosis is so complete that it has virtually formed a higher-level species, lichens.

8.1.3 Complexity and Stability in Multispecies Ecosystems

Are more complex ecosystems more stable than simpler ones, such as those formed by human beings in their agricultural activities? In the 1950s, led by Odum (1953), MacArthur (1955), Elton (1958), and Hutchinson (1959), the answer appeared to be a resounding *yes*. MacArthur (1955) went so far as to propose a direct relationship between the logarithm of the number of links in a food web and the degree of stability.

Elton (1958) summarized the case for complexity breeding stability. He cited the mathematical argument of MacArthur. He noted the oscillatory behavior of populations in simple boreal environments and in laboratory populations and that, in the latter case, provision of cover tends to mitigate the fluctuations. He noted the extreme vulnerability of island ecosystems and crop monocultures to invasions by pests or nonlocal species.[12] He noted the apparent extreme stability of tropical rain forests, the archetypal complex ecosystem. And finally he noted the greater susceptibility to pest outbreaks of orchards that have been treated with pesticides in contrast with those that have not, although the former may achieve a greater yield and quality level of the desired fruit. He blamed the greater instability of pesticide orchards on the "upsetting of the relationships between pests and their natural enemies and parasites through differential effects of the poisons used." (ibid., p. 151).

These arguments came under attack in the 1960s and 1970s. Turnbull and Chant (1961) argued that a pest might be easier to control if it has only one predator than if it has many (e.g., the troublesome rodents, locusts, grasshoppers, and spruce budworms). Paine (1966) documented the collapse of an intertidal marine community from 15 invertebrate species to only 8 within 2 years of the removal of a single species. Such cases led to an argument by Gardner and Ashby (1970) that "an excessive degree of interconnectance in an ecosystem can lead to instability."[13]

The sharpest attack on the complexity-stability hypothesis came from May (1975) and May and Oster (1976) on mathematical grounds. They argue that, in general, greater complexity tends to *decrease* stability. May (1975) adapted Levin's (1968) version of the community matrix idea of Odum's (1953) to describe the equilibrium point of an ecosystem by

$$(A - \lambda I)x(t) = 0, \qquad (8.8b)$$

where A is the community matrix indicating the direct impacts of each species on every other one, and x is the vector of species populations. This equilibrium will be stable if real λ max < 0 (real λ max $<$ variance of fluctuations for stochastic environments). May's point is that as the number of species increases, the probability increases that one of them will be associated with a positive real eigenvalue and hence an unstable mode of oscillation. This is reinforced by May and Oster (1976) concluding that as the number dimensions (species) increase, the possibility of chaotic dynamics increases and will tend to occur for lower values of exogenous "tuning" parameters (e.g., intrinsic species growth rates).

May reconciles these arguments with the undisputed data of more oscillatory behavior in simpler boreal ecosystems than in more complex tropical ones by arguing that the causation is reversed. Thus (May, 1975, p. 76):

> ... although increased complexity makes for a more unstable system, it is advantageous on other grounds; for example, it may be conducive to a more thorough exploitation of the community's total resources. Then a stable environment may permit such complexity, and also be characterized by relatively unfluctuating populations. But an unstable environment may drive population instabilities which the complex system is in general ineffective in damping, with the consequence that such environments may be typified by relatively simple systems with unstable populations ... it could be that stability permits complexity.

Such a view is reinforced by the dual Pimentel (1968) argument that the long undisturbed coevolution of species in an environment tends to lead to both a greater stability of interspecies relationships as well as a greater complexity. Old and undisturbed ecosystems tend to be both more complex and more stable, at least in lacking fluctuations.

Another possible argument is Holling's (1973) contrast between the stability and resilience of ecosystems, the latter interpreted by Brauer (1984) to be global asymptotic stability. The trade-off is evident for individual species. High growth rate, r-adapting species (blowflies) may exhibit chaotically fluctuating populations, unstable locally, but bounded in the face of very large shocks. But low growth rate, K-adapting species (blue whales) may exhibit relatively unfluctuating populations that remain stable in response to local shocks but that may go extinct in the face of a severe shock. This led May (1981c, p. 227) to declare, "[T]he large and unprecedented perturbations imposed by man are likely to be more traumatic for more complex natural systems than for simple ones."

Nevertheless, it all depends on the specific relationships in systems under examination. Kindleman (1984) argues that the connectance–stability relationship may vary non-monotoncially with the number of species in a system. May (1975, p. 5) recognizes that the presence of time lags may complicate things and that "[u]nder certain conditions, which are commonly met in nature, the vegetation-herbivore-carnivore system is stable (with population fluctuations being damped out), while the vegetation-herbivore system with no predators is unstable." Thus the presence of time lags may, in some cases, lead to the complexity–stability relationship again, at least with respect to the number of trophic levels within the food web.

In other words, it all depends. Svirizhev and Logofet (1983, p. 312) conclude that "within the framework of mathematical models there is no use in looking for a *unique* relation between complexity and stability, that in particular cases is determined by peculiarities of structures under consideration and the specific character of mathematical formulations."[14] This latter point becomes all the more significant when we contemplate whether specific human interventions in ecosystems will lead to greater stability (and possibly efficiency) or to collapse and extinction of species.

8.2 The Bioeconomics Synthesis

8.2.1 The Perversities of Open-Access Renewable Resource Use

8.2.1.1 The Basic Tendency to Overexploitation

Gordon (1954) demonstrated the tendency for an open-access fishery to be economically,[15] and possibly biologically, overfished. This model has since been applied to other similar questions, such as grazing (Hardin, 1968; Libecap and Johnson, 1980). But it is the issue of fisheries[16] that has brought forth the development of a fully synthesized and integrated bioeconomics, with Colin W. Clark (1976, 1985) playing a crucial role in this effort.

Every complication from uncertainty through multiple species dynamics occurs with fisheries, and fisheries have dramatically exhibited the phenomenon of overexploitation and mismanagement. Clark (1985, p. 6) lists the following species whose catches have drastically declined in recent decades. Antarctic blue whales from a catch of 29,000 in 1931 to nil in 1981, Antarctic fin whales from a catch of 27,000 in 1938 to nil in 1981, Hokkaido herring from a catch of 850,000 tons in 1913 to nil in 1981, Peruvian anchoveta from a catch of 12.3 million tons in 1967 to 0.3 million tons in 1981, Southwest African pilchard from a catch of 1.4 million tons in 1968 to nil in 1981, North Sea herring from a catch of 1.5 million tons in 1962 to negligible in 1981, California sardine from a catch of 640,000 tons in 1936 to nil in 1981, Georges Bank herring from a catch of 374,000 tons in 1968 to nil in 1981, and Japanese sardine from a catch of 2.3 million tons in 1939 to 17,000 tons in 1973. Of course, such patterns can result in the ultimate discontinuity, the extinction of a species.

The standard dynamic analysis of an open-access fishery was developed by Smith (1968)[17] and clarified by Clark (1973b, 1976), drawing upon the static externality models of Gordon (1954) and Scott (1955) and the yield effort curve analyses of Schaefer (1957) and of Beverton and Holt (1957). The bionomic aspect is given by the simplest of one-species models, the logistic equation of Verhulst (1838), that is,

$$dX/dt = rX(1 - X/k) = F(X), \tag{8.9}$$

where the variables are identical to those above. Without harvesting, K is a stable equilibrium. This case is "pure compensation" with $r(X)$ as a decreasing function of X. If this is an increasing function for a certain zone, due to difficulties in reproducing with population too low, then there is a "depensation effect" (or Allee (1931)

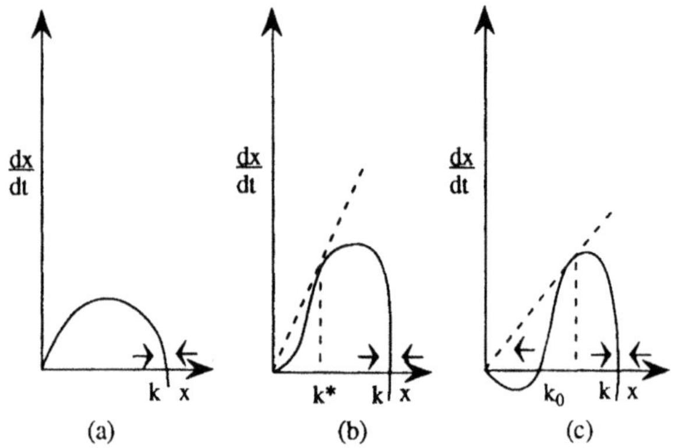

Fig. 8.5 Bionomic equilibria with compensation and depensation effects

effect). If $F(x) < 0$ for a zone, then there is "critical depensation" which can lead to extinction below K_0, the minimum viable population level. These are depicted in Fig. 8.5a–c, respectively.

Bionomic equilibrium or sustainable yield is given by

$$F(X) - h(t) = 0, \tag{8.10}$$

where $h(t)$ is the harvested yield and is given by

$$h = Y = EX = KE(1 - E/r), \tag{8.11}$$

where E is effort and $E < r$. In the pure compensation case, there will be a single equilibrium, but there will be multiple equilibria if there is depensation with the resulting possibilities of discontinuities and hysteresis effects. The bifurcation value will be $E = E^*$, where E^* is the maximum sustained yield (MSY) given by

$$E^* = \max r(x) = r^*, \tag{8.12}$$

where r^* is the intrinsic growth rate of the population. These cases (compensation, depensation, critical) are, respectively, exhibited in Figs. 8.6, 8.7 and 8.8, with (a) being the growth curve with the harvest function and (b) the effort–yield relationship.

The open-access, bioeconomic equilibrium will occur where $TC = TR$ (Gordon, 1954), where TC is a linear function of E and $TR = PX$. This will not coincide with the maximum sustainable rent $MR = MC$ because of the externality arising from each fisherman perceiving social average cost as his private marginal cost. This leads to economic overfishing and can lead to biological overfishing if there is depensation. This is depicted in Fig. 8.9 under the assumption that price is constant and that the cost curve is linear with zero fixed costs. E' is the open-access equilibrium; E_0 is the maximum sustainable rent equilibrium. With open access, the rent will be dissipated by overfishing.

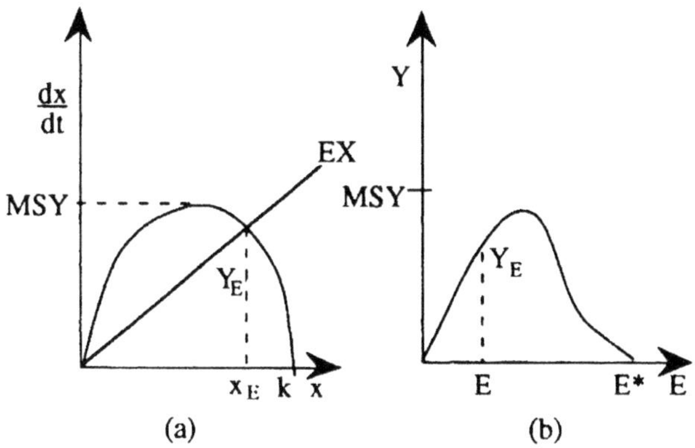

Fig. 8.6 Effort–yield relations with pure compensation

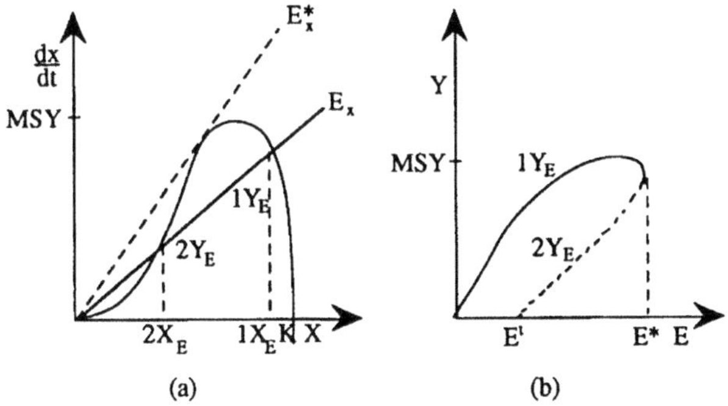

Fig. 8.7 Effort–yield relations with depensation

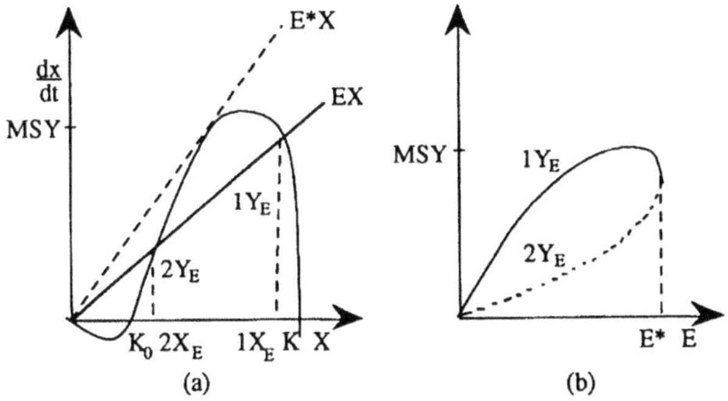

Fig. 8.8 Effort–yield relations with critical depensation

8.2.1.2 Sources of Dynamic Discontinuities and Instabilities

The Backward-Bending Supply Curve and "Demand Instability"

Besides bionomic depensation, "over-fishing catastrophes" (biological, not merely mathematical) can also arise from an economic cause, a combination of a backward-bending supply curve due to open access (Copes, 1970) and a sufficiently inelastic demand that shifts at a critical point (Anderson, 1973).

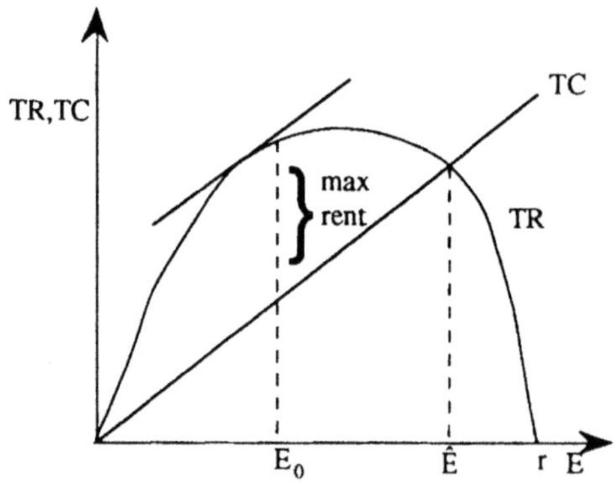

Fig. 8.9 Open-access bioeconomic equilibrium

Let the bionomic conditions be given by the basic Schaefer equation:

$$\mathrm{d}x/\mathrm{d}t = rX(1 - x/k) - EX, \tag{8.13}$$

variables defined as above.

Let rent, R, be given by

$$R = (pX - c)E. \tag{8.14}$$

The open-access bionomic equilibrium is given by

$$Y = EX = rX(1 - x/K) \tag{8.15}$$

and

$$pX - c = 0. \tag{8.16}$$

Thus sustained yield Y as a function of p, that is the bionomic equilibrium supply curve for the open-access fishery, is given by

$$Y = (rc/p)[1 - (c/pk)]. \tag{8.17}$$

$Y = 0$ for $p < c/k$, reaches MSY at $p = 2c/k$ and bends backward for $p > 2ck$, approaching zero as p goes to infinity. Thus if prices get too high, biological overfishing can occur.

Figure 8.10 depicts this case with inelastic demand that increases from D1 to D3, thereby generating a demand-induced overfishing catastrophe, as the bioeconomic equilibrium jumps from M1 to M3.

As D1 shifts to D2, there is a mathematical catastrophe, that becomes a biological catastrophe as it moves to D3. Hysteresis sets in as it would require a more substantial decline of demand to push the equilibrium back toward M1 and closer to the MSY.

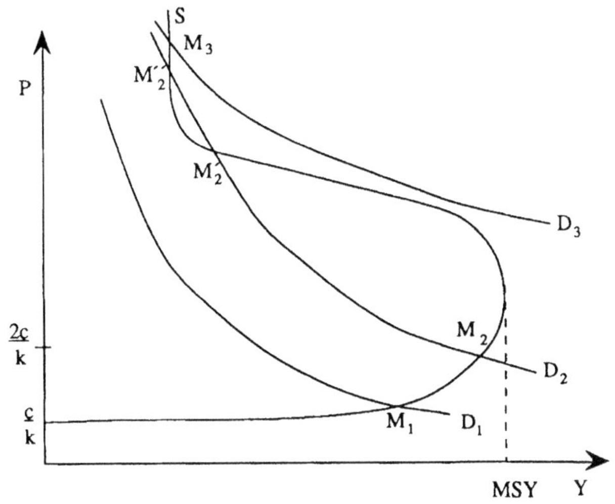

Fig. 8.10 Overfishing catastrophe with backward-bending supply

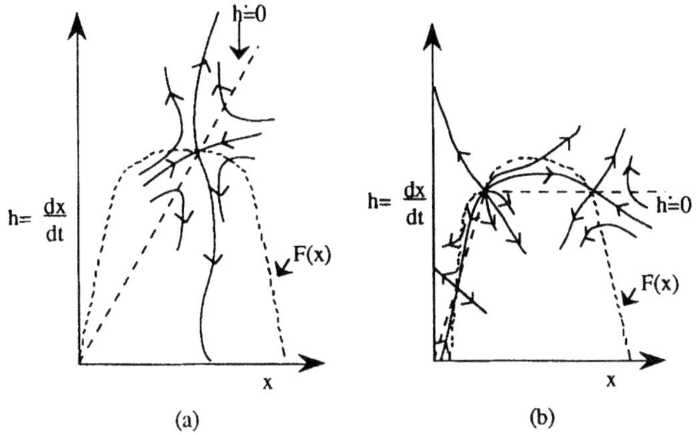

Fig. 8.11 Phase diagrams of bioeconomic equilibria. (a) Single-saddle equilibrium. (b) Multiple equilibria

Clark (1976, p. 201) has examined this bifurcation in terms of phase diagrams in the harvest (d*x*/d*y*) species stock (*X*), space. Figure 8.11a depicts the M1 equilibrium as a saddle point at the intersection of the $x = 0$ and $h = 0$ isoclines, and Fig. 8.11b depicts the multiple equilibria associated with D2, an unstable equilibrium surrounded by two saddle points.

Age Structure Effects

Ricker (1954) and Beverton and Holt (1957) initiated the study of multicohort fisheries with age-specific effects. This led to regulating mesh size of nets with the idea of only harvesting larger, older fish, thus maintaining the stock better. However, the age dependence of mortality, the interactions between age cohorts (e.g., the cannibalizing of young observed by Ricker (1954) among salmon) and the time lags involved can lead to nonlinearities and "overcompensation" effects that can induce chaotic dynamics and a rich variety of other oddities.

Blythe, Gurney, and Nisbet (1982) model adult population of a species assuming a fixed maturation time, birth rates depending on adult population, and adult and pre-adult death rates depending on the respective populations. This generates a set of differential-difference equations whose stability bifurcates as birth rate increases. Period doubling and a transition to chaos occur. These effects are more pronounced as time lags increase.

Brauer (1987a, b) and Brauer, Rollins, and Soudack (1988) examine more generalized forms of this model with constant-effort harvesting. A curious result is that as effort increases the stability of the equilibrium increases, *up to* the point where the system suddenly collapses from overfishing.

Capital Stock Inertia

Spence (1975) showed that the tendency of fishery capital stocks to adjust slowly further complicates time lags. This nonmalleability exacerbates any tendency to biological overfishing that might emerge, even if initially due to an unusual, environmentally induced perturbation.

Clark, Clarke, and Munro (1979) examine the extreme case of irreversible investment with positive depreciation. This leads to two sustained-yield equilibria, one purely temporary $X_{var}{}^*$ (based on variable costs) and one long-term $X_{tot}{}^*$ (based on all costs). These depend on the capital-species stock relation and are given by two "switching curves" (σ_1 and σ_2) which divide the space into three behavioral regimes as depicted in Fig. 8.12. In R1, both maximum fishing and investment occur; in R2, maximum fishing occurs but no investment; in R3, the fishery shuts down until

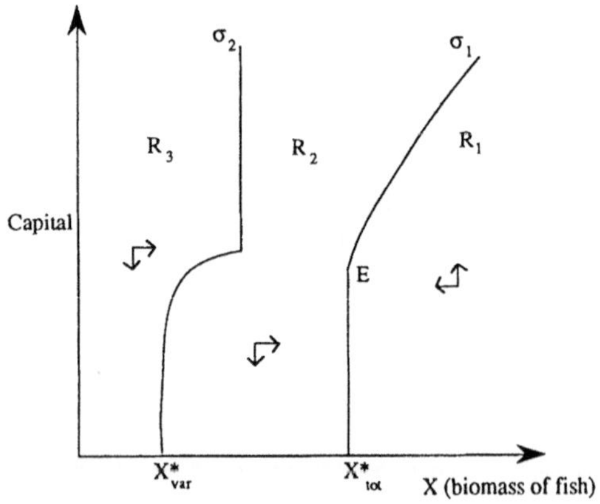

Fig. 8.12 Fishery adjustment with capital stock inertia

either the fish recover, or the capital stock depreciates, or both sufficiently.[18] E is the long-term equilibrium, coinciding with the perfectly-malleable-capital short-term equilibrium.

Berck and Perloff (1984) argue that capital adjustment will tend to be smoother if fishermen have rational expectations for entry behavior rather than myopic (adaptive) expectations, as assumed by Smith (1968) and others. Even so, cycles can still appear during the convergence to equilibrium, which equals the myopic adjustment equilibrium. The rational expectations assumption may be hard to maintain for fisheries behavior, given the extreme levels of uncertainty documented by Sissenwine (1984) and others.

"Pulse Fishing" as a Chattering Solution

The modern distant water fishing fleets of Japan and the USSR tend to be highly capital-intensive, large-scale operations—a factory vessel accompanied by many trawlers. Under these conditions, Clark (1976) argues there may be declining marginal costs of harvesting for a certain range. Then the bioeconomic optimum may be a "chattering solution,"[19] a bang-bang alternation between no harvesting and maximum harvesting known as "pulse fishing."

Clark's argument involves comparing constant harvest behavior versus the bang-bang chattering solution which produces the same total yield. For the bang-bang solution to be cheaper, the maximum possible harvest rate up to which marginal costs still decline is greater than the maximum sustainable yield level. This is a purely economic argument.

However, pulse fishing may be biologically superior to the MSY solution (Pope, 1973; Hannesson, 1975) if fishing gear is nonselective and it takes more than one generation for an age cohort to reach its maximum biomass. In such a case, the maximum yield will be achieved by harvesting all cohorts at a maximum rate once every n years, if $n =$ the average number of years it takes a cohort to reach maximum biomass. If gear can be made age selective through adjusting net mesh size, then the advantage of pulse fishing disappears as the fish of maximum biomass can be continuously harvested while leaving their younger peers for the future.[20]

Despite the possibility that the discontinuous pulse fishing may be bioeconomically superior to a sustained yield policy under certain conditions, such policies (followed by the Japanese and Soviet fleets) are unpopular with fishery biologists because they often involve taking fish of not only many different age cohorts but also every species in the area. Endangered species may be taken as well as those that are the main object of the harvesting effort. Given that the possible biological gains appear not to exceed 10% over MSY (Hannesson, 1975), the concerns of the fisheries biologists regarding a policy that is economically driven may be well founded.

Complexities with Competitive Species

Gause (1935) developed a Lotka–Volterra model of two competitive species:

$$dx/dt = rx(1 - x/K) - \alpha xy, \tag{8.18}$$

$$dy/dt = sy(1 - y/L) - \beta xy, \tag{8.19}$$

where s is the intrinsic growth rate of the y species, L is its carrying capacity, and all other variables are defined as above. This model admits either coexistence or competitive exclusion under different conditions. Gause considered cases where x has excluded y, but y still exists nearby as a "refugee," capable of returning if anything should happen to x. Clark (1976) argues that if x is harvested by an amount $= qEx$, its $x = 0$ isocline will be given by

$$y = (r/\alpha)(1 - x/k) - (q/\alpha)E. \tag{8.20}$$

As E increases, the system will bifurcate and a collapse of x can occur as it is competitively replaced by y at a value of $\hat{E} = s/\beta$. This might occur if fishery managers are unaware of the threat posed by the competitor species. Murphy (1967) analyzed the collapse of the Pacific sardine fishery in the late 1940s and its replacement by anchovies in a manner that suggests the above outcome as a possibility, although that event may also have been due to environmental disruption.

If $\hat{E} < r/2q$, the value of E associated with MSY of x without y, such a mistake could easily occur. The collapse of x could occur while its yield–effort curve is still increasing, as depicted in Fig. 8.13.

Complexities with Predator–Prey Systems

Brauer and Soudack (1979) derive a similar result for a Lotka–Volterra predator–prey model in which the predator is harvested. For harvest levels below the

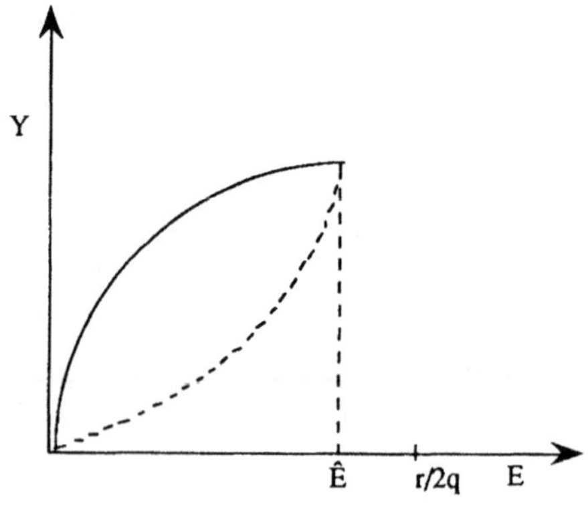

Fig. 8.13 Fishery collapse with competitor species

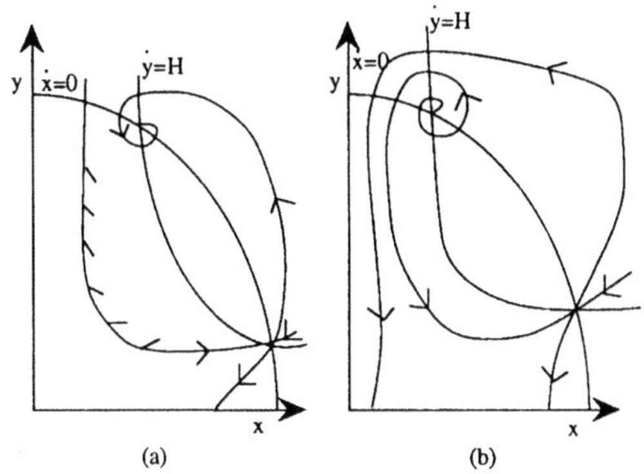

Fig. 8.14 Complex predator–prey dynamics with harvesting. (a) Stable situation. (b) Unstable situation

maximum for which an equilibrium might exist, two equilibria will exist: one a saddle point, the other either locally stable, unstable, or a limit cycle. Under certain conditions, the predator population may collapse at a harvest level less than the apparent maximum sustainable yield. This occurs as the nonsaddle equilibrium suddenly goes from being stable to being unstable, depending on a change in the behavior of the separatrices emanating from the saddle point. This is depicted in Fig. 8.14 with (a) being the stable situation and (b) the unstable collapse situation that emerges as the harvest rate increases, with x the prey and y the predator. The predator's isocline includes the effect of harvesting. In (a) any initial point inside the hatched zone will asymptotically approach the long-run equilibrium.

Brauer and Soudack (1985) show in the "fragile" case above that an optimal harvesting strategy that can approach the potential MSY is a bang-bang harvest cycle. In the predator–prey case such a strategy may also be optimal in the nonfragile case. They also show that if the harvest thresholds are sufficiently high, period-doubling and chaotic dynamics may emerge along the optimal trajectory of the two populations.

8.2.1.3 Management Approaches to Open-Access Fisheries

Conflicts of Objectives and Policies

Clark (1985) and Walters (1986) discuss the problems and alternatives involved in resolving the management problems raised by open-access fisheries subject to possible catastrophic discontinuities. Managers of fisheries face conflicting objectives compounded by inevitable uncertainty, especially when they clash with fishermen over access, income distribution, methods of fishing, and so on. Limiting access, preferably to a sole owner, resolves the basic problem. But this is rarely a possible outcome, especially with regard to freely migrating pelagic species. Taxes or quotas on effort can be effective, while quotas on catches can lead to highly nonoptimal behavior in the face of backward-bending supply curves (Hartwick and Olewiler, 1986). With efforts to restrict effort, cheating can occur which heightens uncertainty

(Milliman, 1986), and whose forms can range from nighttime poaching to "capital stuffing" (Stollery, 1986). Given the close-knit nature of fishing communities, "outsider" regulators may have great difficulties detecting such practices (Charles, 1988). Boat buybacks to draw down excessive capacity have been proposed, but these are resisted if unemployment is high in fishing communities and alternative sources of employment are not readily available. Johnson and Libecap (1982) suggest that informal practices or cooperatives may provide reasonable alternatives to government regulation, although Stollery (1987) argues that cooperatives may either overfish or overconserve depending on their management policy. Lawson (1984) argues that "traditional" communities handle such informal systems better but tend to break down as market economies develop.

In predator–prey situations, predator stocking may extinguish prey population (Brauer and Soudack, 1981). Prey stocking generally stabilizes population levels, but the increased predator populations may become dependent on continued prey stocking, and wild prey may get reduced or wiped out. Indeed, in some multi-species situations, subsidizing the catch of a species may be optimal (Hannesson, 1983). Walters (1986) argues that occasionally these conflicts and contradictions can be manipulated to overcome themselves. He discusses the Hilborn Plan for the Canadian salmon fisheries that involves both stocking and quotas simultaneously, two policies dangerous by themselves, made productive by being implemented together.

Exploiting Potential Catastrophe Through "Surfing"

In the Great Lakes, trout were nearly wiped out by a lamprey invasion coming through the St. Lawrence Seaway. Managers have stocked trout, but this predator–prey system is subject to "catastrophic dynamics"[21] of the Ludwig, Jones, and Holling (1978) type, according to Mehre (1981) and Walters (1986).

The latter suggest a so-called "surfing" strategy in order to obtain maximum yields from the trout fisheries. This involves varying harvest effort in a way that skates near the edge of the catastrophe, both to locate it and to maximize yield. This strategy reflects "Koonce's doughnut," (Walters, 1986) the idea that in the face of uncertainty there is an optimal variability of strategy: too little, and information will be insufficient for maximizing yields; too much, and a catastrophic collapse can occur. In the Great Lakes, the catastrophe would be a disappearance of the wild trout stocks, a "pathological" surfing, displayed in Fig. 8.15 as the larger cyclical pattern (b). The point to the left (c) is the conservative, low-yield strategy. The smaller cycle (a) represents the optimal, "productive" surfing strategy.

8.2.2 The Special Problem of Extinction

8.2.2.1 "Optimal" Extinction

One of the most troubling implications of the general tendency to overexploitation of open-access resources is the possibility of the extinction of a species occurring from a catastrophic population collapse or even from a gradual population decline.

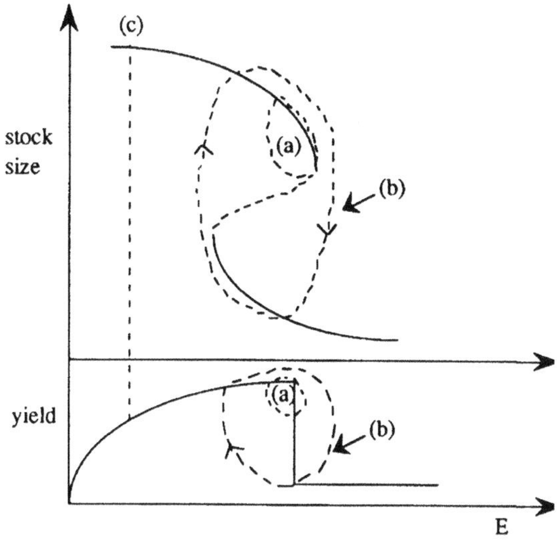

Fig. 8.15 Great Lakes trout dynamics under alternative strategies

This can happen if there is critical depensation, a "minimum viable population," or from interactions with other species. Unfortunately there is no way of knowing for sure for any population just what such a level might be. Thus, as noted by Bachmura (1971), a protected population of 2000 was insufficient for the preservation of the heather hen, whereas other endangered species have persisted with much lower population levels.

The extinction of species by human activity arouses very intense emotions. It is the most dramatic form of irreversibility there is, the clearest sign of humanity's "interference" with the natural order. Arguments are raised that even the "lowliest" endangered species has an intrinsic right to survival, that human-induced extinction is the ultimate in a "human imperialism" that is doomed to self-destruction. More prosaically, it is argued that such species should be preserved because they might have a value in the future that cannot be foreseen today.[22]

However, it is also argued that extinction is the very essence of evolution, the "way of all species," including eventually *Homo sapiens*, and that human activities themselves are part of the natural order. Even supposedly "harmonious with nature" societies have been responsible for extinction of species, such as the probable extermination of woolly mammoths, sabre-tooth tigers, and assorted other large mammals by Pleistocene hunters in the Americas (Smith, 1975).[23]

This issue is brought sharply into focus when it is suggested that such extinctions may not merely be the result of inefficience, open access, and overexploitation combined with inefficiently inertial capital stocks, but may sometimes be *optimal* from the perspective of society and efficient resource management. Such arguments may arouse such strong emotions because of the possible parallels to the extermination of one human group by another.

The first to present such arguments were Gould (1972) and Clark (1973a), although Clark explicitly denied any "social optimality" to his analysis of profit-maximizing extinction (1973a). Clark analyzed fisheries with partially linear economics, that is a constant price for the fish, although he allowed marginal cost to increase as population declines (they're harder to catch).

He derives conditions under which a present-value maximizing sole owner will fish the species to extinction. These conditions are that the discount rate be sufficiently greater than the natural rate of increase and that harvesting the last animal (or the last above minimum viable population) be immediately profitable.[24] The first raises the question of time horizon; extinction is more likely with fishermen having a present orientation, a high discount rate, and fishing a K-adapting species (like blue whales). The second provides a possible escape hatch—as a species gets reduced, it may be saved by the rising marginal cost of fishing it all the way to extinction, unless of course critical depensation kicks in and the species cannot maintain itself with low numbers. This argument suggests that larger, easier to catch species (woolly mammoths, blue whales) may be more vulnerable than smaller, harder to catch ones (cod, anchovetas). Also, the larger ones frequently have lower rates of natural increase.

Later modifications allow for nonlinear prices, namely that price increases as the species nears extinction, thus working against the "saving" element of rising marginal cost (Cropper, Lee, and Pannu, 1979). A much greater emphasis has been placed on the question of minimum viable population and critical depensation (Lewis and Schmalensee, 1977; Berch, 1979; Cropper, 1988). In the fully nonlinear fishery, the crucial relationship is between the minimum viable population size and the minimum that can be profitably exploited. One implication of an inverse harvest rate–price relation is that if the initial stock is sufficiently high, the species may survive even if the discount rate exceeds the intrinsic growth rate.[25] On the other hand, species we "need now," that are easily caught and are slow to reproduce, are the most likely candidates for perishing from this earth by the hand of man.

Clearly, if we wish to avoid "nonoptimal" extinction, caution must be exercised with such critical thresholds as minimum viable population sizes. This is because of both the general uncertainty about such thresholds and the natural environmental variability that may push an overharvested species down too far. It may be fine to explore "Koonce's doughnut" by "surfing" when one is dealing with a purely local population that can be restocked from elsewhere (i.e., Great Lakes trout). But when it is the entire species whose viability is at risk, then the surfboards should be put away and the doughnut left in its wrapper. The death of a species is more final and complete than the death of an individual.

8.2.2.2 The Complicated Role of the Discount Rate

The significant role of the discount rate fits in with a long-running theme in resource economics and capital theory—that lower discount rates indicate more concern for the future and thus presumably for the longer-term preservation of species. This parallels the theory of nonrenewable, depletable resources and the Hotelling (1931) rule that the discount rate indicates the rate at which such a resource will be optimally depleted. Ironically, endangered species more closely resemble nonrenewable resources than they do renewable ones.

Such a view has led to severe criticisms of the use of positive discount rates as a culprit responsible for intergenerational rip-offs.[26] Frank Ramsey (1928) wrote of the "ethical indefensibility" of positive discount rates. D'Arge, Schulze, and Brookshire (1982) argue that in contemplating potential long-term global catastrophes such as carbon dioxide accumulation, a Rawlsian (1972) view of intergenerational utility comparisons would call for the use of zero discount rates lest we ignore such possibilities entirely.

However, the dual role of the discount rate as a measure of the rate of time preference and of the opportunity cost of capital muddies the case considerably.[27] Even when only the first issue is to be considered, the complexity of the time streams of environmental and ecological effects can complicate such simple stories.

Farzin (1984) considers the dual-aspect issue for the extraction of nonrenewable resources and the Hotelling theorem, arguing that the opportunity cost of capital aspect comes into play through the capital-intensive nature of extraction processes and the cost of extraction of possible "backstop" substitute resources. If extraction processes are highly capital intensive, a rise in the discount rate could raise the cost of extraction enough to offset the time preference effect of desiring to extract more of the resource now. The offset will operate if the present values of capital requirements in the substitute and resource sectors exceed the present value of the resource stock. This will tend to occur either when the resource is very available or very scarce. The latter case suggests the paradoxical possibility of a lower discount rate accelerating the depletion of an extremely scarce resource.

Hannesson (1987) shows this argument may apply to renewable resources and to fisheries in particular. He argues that if harvesting costs depend on population size, then the impact of discount rate changes will be ambiguous but will tend to violate the standard story if the capital intensity is high. In such a case, the possibility of species extinction could be increased by a lowering of the discount rate.

Such anomalies connect to the paradoxes of capital theory. That Farzin found two ranges at the opposite extremes of the time horizon for his anomalies corresponds to the impact on relative valuation of respective time streams of net returns when multiple roots or reswitching are present (Fisher, 1930). The duality presented by Farzin compares to the case when there are both high front-end and high back-end costs. In the case of environmentally significant investment projects, the front-end costs are generally direct capital expenditures, whereas the back-end costs are delayed environmental external costs of one sort or another (Herfindahl and Kneese, 1974; Viscusi and Zeckhauser, 1976; Asheim, 2008; Fisher, 1981; Porter, 1982; Prince and Rosser, 1985).

Porter (1982) considers the implications of such paradoxes and anomalies for "preservation." In the US in the 1960s, most conservationists concerned with preserving the wilderness and endangered species with little immediate economic value argued for the use of high discount rates in the benefit–cost analyses carried out by the US Army Corps of Engineers. This was because such projects had high front-end capital costs while delayed environmental costs were not counted. Thus, high discount rates tended to lower estimated benefit–cost ratios and favored the conservationist position. In 1969, President Nixon's Chief of the Office of Management and Budget, Roy Ash, ordered the imposition of a uniform 10% discount rate for all US benefit–cost analyses,[28] based on estimates of then existing opportunity costs of capital (Stockfish, 1969). This reflected an "anti-Iron Triangle" alliance of convenience between environmentalists and antipork barrel budget cutters that has periodically appeared from time to time.

However, Porter (1982) and others realized that the reality of the delayed environmental costs associated with many such projects means that the reality expounded by Ramsey and Clark holds. Lower discount rates *are* more future-minded and can also weigh against these projects *if the future environmental costs are properly accounted for*. Thus we have the duality: Large-scale investment projects with high front-end costs and delayed environmental costs will tend to be relatively devalued under both very high and very low discount rates. Thus, we have the "ambiguity of future-mindedness" with conservation being potentially favored under both high and low discount rates.[29]

This complicates the discussion of the role of discount rate in dealing with the problem of uncertainty (Viscusi and Zeckhauser, 1976; Prince and Rosser, 1985). Most analysts argue that when there is greater risk, then higher discount rates should be used to reflect the greater risk premium, which holds for the relative valuation of purely private capital projects. But when a social analysis is considered, it all depends on how the risks, benefits, and payments are borne (Fisher and Krutilla, 1974; Arrow and Fisher, 1974; Mishan, 1976).

Such ambiguities turn up in the bioeconomic arena. Plourde and Bodell (1984) argue that if there is environmentally based uncertainty about the stock of a species, for example, it could be wiped out by bad weather, then a higher discount rate should be used in traditional risk premium fashion. Better to harvest some of it now rather than none at all, leading to a lower steady-state population than the certainty equivalent. However, if the uncertainty affects the growth process, for example bad weather inhibiting spawning, then concern about possible losses to future generations argues for a lower discount rate and a higher steady-state population under normal conditions (Ludwig, 1978; Ludwig and Varah, 1979; Smith, 1980).

Thus, we face profound ambiguity in evaluating the future in the face of environmental complexity and uncertainty when we are concerned about preserving endangered species. In short, the tangles and paradoxes of capital theory become the tangles and paradoxes of bioeconomic theory.

Notes

1. Greater time lags can induce chaotic dynamics (Blythe, Gurney, and Nisbet, 1982; Brauer, 1987a).
2. Seasonality is a source of regular shocks that may be consistent with the behavior of some predator–prey cycles (Blom, de Bruin, Grasman, and Vernon, 1987).
3. Rand's (1976) chaotic duopoly model, the first economics chaos model, appears to have been independent of this influence.
4. This particular model has been used to analyze Goodwin's (1967) macroeconomic Lotka–Volterra model (Desai, 1973; Vellupillai, 1978; Pohjola, 1981; Lorenz, 1987a).

5. That long coevolution of a group of species may lead to greater stability of an ecosystem has been argued by Elton (1958) and Pimentel (1968). The evolutionary pedigree of this idea traces at least to Alfred Russel Wallace (1860, 1876).
6. Winterholder (1980) argues that these cycles for some boreal species may be artifacts of the foraging practices of the native hunters but that the hare cycle is naturally occurring. Pease, Vowles, and Keith (1979) argue that the hare cycle may be driven by a two-to-three-year cycle in resistance to the hare by the plants upon which it feeds.
7. Lotka recognized that this is a simplified form in that the interaction term, α, would actually be a complicated power series function of X and Y. This form reflects a "convenient approximation" that the coefficients beyond the initial constant "are sufficiently small."
8. May (1981b) reviews extensions where higher-order terms depend on a prey logistic growth equation related to the system carrying capacity.
9. Based on this, May (1975, p. 92) argues that the hare–lynx cycle is a stable limit cycle.
10. Jeffers (1978) estimated an explicit catastrophe theory model of Dutch Elm disease outbreaks, using data of Gibbs and Howell (1972) and an empirical technique of Cobb and Zacks (1985).
11. Casti (1989) discusses the spruce budworm case as a catastrophe theory model. Svirizhev and Logofet (1983) show alternating population bursts and crashes for a predator–prey model under more complicated conditions.
12. Elton (1966) later recognized that vulnerability to invasion is not the same thing as instability. May (1975) notes the vulnerability to invasion by Dutch Elm disease, chestnut blight, and gypsy moths of the complex, North American deciduous forest.
13. This depends on mathematical specification. Siljak (1979) shows vulnerability reduced by greater subsystem autonomy, while Kindleman (1984) has shown the opposite for systems of 10 or 11 species while the result holds for a system of 30 species.
14. Rotenberg (1988) shows for n-species Lotka–Volterra systems that a "patchy" distribution of prey species may be more stable than a smooth distribution.
15. Gordon focused on the concept of "common property resource," but Ciriacy-Wantrup (1971) argues that "open access" is the essential problem. Rules limiting access can be established for a common property resource sometimes. See Ostrom (1990) for further discussion.
16. We use the term "fisheries" even though some species involved are not fish. Whales are mammals and crabs are crustaceans.
17. Smith's model is a Lotka–Volterra predator–prey model with man as the predator and the fish as prey, with a density-dependent logistic growth curve. Wang and Cheng (1982) show global stability for this model within an invariant region if there are no time lags in investment and the cost function is quadratic. Smith-type models have been empirically estimated for the North Sea herring fishery by Bjørndal and Conrad (1987) and for the bowhead whale by Conrad (1989).
18. With uncertainty, this model obtains lower yields (more conservationist) and larger fleet size if the resource stock is rapidly growing and capital is cheap as well as vice versa (Charles and Munro, 1985).
19. See Young (1969) for a detailed discussion of "chattering solutions."
20. McCallum (1988) argues that pulse fishing will be economically superior if gear selectivity costs are too high as with bottom-dwelling demersal species.
21. Jones and Walters (1976) use a cusp catastrophe manifold to explain the collapse of the Antarctic fin and blue whale stocks in response to improved size and efficiency of fishing fleets. Clark and Mangel (1979) show "catastrophic dynamics" associated with "depensatory predation."
22. See Rosser (1990b) for further discussion of these points.
23. It can be argued that this was an exceptional case of ecological disequilibrium because this was the initial ("Eltonian") human invasion of the hemisphere. There had been no long coevolution leading to stability of the ecosystem.
24. These conditions have been cited to explain deforestation and desertification in some less developed countries (Morey, 1985; Southgate and Runge, 1985; French, 1986; Hassan and

Hertzler, 1986; Perrings, 1989). Furthermore, some of these systems are fragile, and when people are starving, their discount rates are very high. The breakdown of traditional tenure systems and the appearance of new forms of open access, driven by global markets, can exacerbate these situations.

25. Tell this to the once highly numerous, but now extinct, passenger pigeon.
26. Rejection of positive interest rates is an old idea accepted by Aristotle, the Qu'ran, St. Thomas Aquinas, and Karl Marx, among others. Even so the USSR always paid positive interest on savings accounts in its state banks as does ultra-fundamentalist Saudi Arabia in its banks (Rosser and Sheehan, 1995). Hausman (1979) has shown evidence of personal discount rates as high as 39% for US consumers.
27. Possible sources of divergence between the two include the influence of macroeconomic policy, capital market imperfections, risk factors, taxation, public characteristics of savings, public–private sector trade-offs, and intertemporal externalities (Marglin, 1963; Baumol, 1968).
28. Water projects dear to the budget of the Corps of Engineers and projects of the US Forest Service soon received exemptions (Prince and Rosser, 1985).
29. Becker (1982) shows within a Rawlsian (1972) intergenerational equity model that simple consumption-environment trade-offs break down when paradoxical steady states are possible.

Chapter 9
Complex Ecologic-Economic Dynamics

We live on the border of two habitats. This is basic. We are neither one thing nor the other. Only birds and fish know what it means to have one habitat. They don't know this, of course. They belong. I doubt that man would meditate, either, if he flew or swam. To meditate, one needs a contradiction that does not exist in a homogeneous habitat — the tension of the border.

There is constant conflict and incident on this border. We are tense. We relax only in our sleep, in a kind of scavenged safety, as if under a stone. Sleep is our way of swimming, our only way of flying. Behold how heavily man treads the earth...
Andrei Bitov (1995, The Monkey Link, pp. 3–4)

A 'Public Domain,' once a velvet carpet of rich buffalo-grass and grama, now an illimitable waste of rattlesnake-bush and tumbleweed, too impoverished to be accepted as a gift by the states within which it lies. Why? Because of the ecology of the Southwest happened to be set on a hair trigger.
Aldo Leopold (1933, "The Conservation Ethic," Journal of Forestry, 33, 636–637)

9.1 The Intertemporally Optimal Fishery

In the previous chapter we examined the problems of management of an open access fishery. We saw that a general outcome for this case was that fishery supply curves can easily bend backwards, opening the possibility of catastrophic collapses of such fisheries as demand increases. We considered a number of management issues related to this problem, although we shall further consider these issues in this chapter. However, even when efficiently managed, fisheries may still exhibit complex dynamics, particularly when discount rates are sufficiently high. Just as species can become extinct under optimal management when agents do not value future stocks of the species sufficiently, likewise in fisheries, as future stocks of fish are valued less and less, the management of the fishery can come to resemble an open access fishery. Indeed, in the limit, as the discount rate goes to infinity at which point the future is valued at zero, the management of the fishery converges on that of the

J.B. Rosser, *Complex Evolutionary Dynamics in Urban-Regional and Ecologic-Economic Systems*, DOI 10.1007/978-1-4419-8828-7_9,

open access case. But well before that limit is reached, complex dynamics of various sorts besides catastrophic collapses may emerge with greater than zero discount rates, such as chaotic dynamics.

We shall now lay out a more general version of the model seen in the previous chapter that is based on intertemporal optimization to see how these outcomes can arise as discount rates vary, following Hommes and Rosser (2001).[1] We shall start considering optimal steady states where the amount of fish harvesting equals the natural growth rate of the fish as given by the Schaefer (1957) yield function:

$$h(x) = f(x) = rx(1 - x/k), \tag{9.1}$$

where the respective variables are the same as in the previous chapter: x is the biomass of the fish, h is harvest, $f(x)$ is the biological yield function, r is the natural rate of growth of the fish population without capacity constraints, and k is the carrying capacity of the fishery, the maximum amount of fish that can live in it in situation of no harvesting, which is also the long-run bionomic equilibrium of the fishery.

We more fully specify the human side of the system by introducing a catchability coefficient, q, along with effort, E, so that the steady-state harvest, Y, is also given by

$$h(x) = qEx = Y. \tag{9.2}$$

We continue to assume constant marginal cost, c, so that total cost, C, is given by

$$C(E) = cE. \tag{9.3}$$

With p the price of fish, this leads to a rent, R, that is

$$R(Y) = pqEx - C(E). \tag{9.4}$$

So far this has been a static exercise, but now let us put this more directly into the intertemporal optimization framework, assuming that the time discount rate is δ. All of the above equations will now be time indexed by t, and also we must allow at least in principle for non-steady-state outcomes. Thus

$$\mathrm{d}x/\mathrm{d}t = f(x) - h(x), \tag{9.5}$$

with $h(x)$ now given by (9.2) and not necessarily equal to $f(x)$. Letting unit harvesting costs at different times be given by $c[x(t)]$, which will equal c/qx, and with a constant $\delta > 0$,[2] the optimal control problem over $h(t)$ while substituting in (9.5) becomes

$$\max \int_0^\infty \mathrm{e}^{-\delta t}(p - c[x(t)](f(x) - \mathrm{d}x/\mathrm{d}t)\mathrm{d}t), \tag{9.6}$$

subject to $x(t) \geq 0$ and $h(t) \geq 0$, noting that $h(t) = f(x) - \mathrm{d}x/\mathrm{d}t$ in (9.6). Applying Euler conditions gives

$$f(x)/\mathrm{d}t = \delta = [c'(x)f(x)]/[p - c(x)]. \tag{9.7}$$

From this, the optimal discounted supply curve of fish will be given by

$$x(p, \delta) = k/4\{1 + (c/pqk) - (\delta/r) + [(1 + (c/pqk) - (\delta/r))^2 + (8c\delta/pqkr)]^{1/2}\}. \tag{9.8}$$

This entire system is depicted in Fig. 9.1 (Rosser, 2001a, p. 27) as the Gordon–Schaefer–Clark fishery model.

We note that when $\delta = 0$, the supply curve in the upper-right quadrant of Fig. 9.1 will not bend backwards. Rather, it will asymptotically approach the vertical line coming up from the maximum sustained yield point at the farthest point to the right on the yield curve in the lower-right quadrant. As δ increases, this supply curve will start to bend backwards and will actually do so well below $\delta = 2\%$. The backward

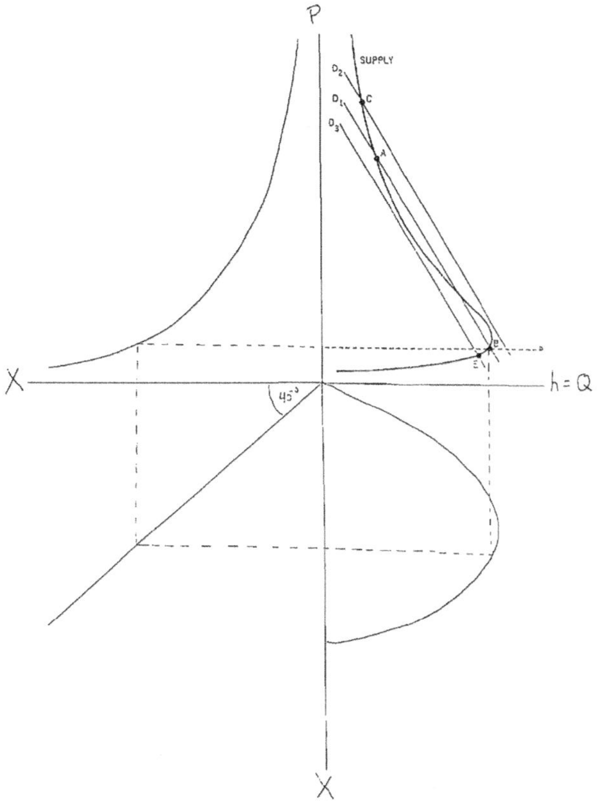

Fig. 9.1 Gordon-Schaefer-Clark fishery model

bend will continue to become more extreme until at $\delta = \infty$ the supply curve will converge on the open access supply curve of

$$x(p, \infty) = (rc/pq)(1 - c/pqk). \tag{9.9}$$

It should be clear that the chance of catastrophic collapses will increase as this supply curve bends further backwards. So, even if people are behaving optimally, as they become more myopic, the chances of catastrophic outcomes will increase.[3]

Regarding the nature of the optimal dynamics, Hommes and Rosser (2001) show that for the zones in which there are multiple equilibria in the backward-bending supply curve case, there are roughly three zones in terms of the nature of the optimal outcomes. At sufficiently low discount rates, the optimal outcome will simply be the lower price/higher quantity of the two stable equilibrium outcomes. At a much higher level, the optimal outcome will simply be the higher price/lower quantity of the two stable equilibria. However, for intermediate zones, the optimal outcome may involve a complex pattern of bouncing back and forth between the two equilibria, with the possibility of this pattern becoming mathematically chaotic.[4]

To study their system, Hommes and Rosser (2001) assume a demand curve of the form

$$D(p(t)) = A - Bp(t), \tag{9.10}$$

with the supply curve being given by (9.8). Market clearing is then given by

$$p(t) = [A - S(p(t)), \delta]/B. \tag{9.11}$$

This can be turned into a model of cobweb adjustment dynamics by indexing the p in the supply function to be one period behind the p being determined, with Chiarella (1988) and Matsumoto (1997) showing chaotic dynamics in generalized cobweb models.

Drawing on data from Clark (1985, pp. 25, 45, 48), Hommes and Rosser (2001) assumed the following values for parameters: $A = 5241, B = 0.28, r = 0.05, c = 5000, k = 400,000, q = 0.000014$ (with the number for A coming from $A = kr/(c - c^2/qk)$). For these values, they found that as δ rose from zero, at first a low-price equilibrium was the solution, but starting around $\delta = 2\%$, period-doubling bifurcations began to appear, with full-blown chaotic dynamics appearing at around $\delta = 8$.[5] When δ rose above 10% or so, the system went to the high-price equilibrium.

9.2 Complex Expectational Dynamics in the Optimal Fishery

The possibility of dynamically chaotic optimal equilibria in fisheries with backward-bending supply curves raises the question of whether or how fishers might be able to learn to such equilibrium paths. One can simply assume that they have rational expectations and that is that. Of course, this was why Muth (1961) proposed rational expectations for solving the problem of how farmers would figure how to overcome the nonchaotic cycles of garden variety cobweb dynamics. As it is, the empirical evidence is not strong that cobweb cycles have been eliminated for such agricultural markets as cattle or pork (Chavas and Holt, 1991, 1993; Aadland, 2004).[6] As it is, given the association of chaos with sensitive dependence on initial conditions, the problem of how agents can learn to rationally expect a chaotic dynamic seems far more serious.

This question has drawn considerable attention, with much of the discussion focusing on patterns of whether adaptive expectations can converge on such an optimal pattern through learning (Bullard, 1994). In particular, Grandmont (1998) suggested the idea that has come to be known as *consistent expectations equilibrium* (CEE). This was picked up and developed further by Hommes and Sorger (1998). They argued that agents might learn certain chaotic dynamics using rules-of-thumb decision making. A key to this approach is the understanding that a simple autoregressive (AR) process can mimic certain kinds of chaotic dynamics, with such AR(1) processes being examples of rule-of-thumb decision making. Following on Bunow and Weiss (1979), Sakai and Tokumaru (1980) observed that an example where an AR process could mimic a chaotic dynamic holds for the case of the asymmetric tent map. This is seen in Fig. 9.2 (Rosser, 2000c, p. 31).

A simple AR(1) formulation for adaptive expectations is given by

$$p^e(t) = \alpha + \beta(p(t-1) - \alpha), \tag{9.12}$$

with α and $\beta \in [-1, 1]$, although usually with the first positive and the second negative.

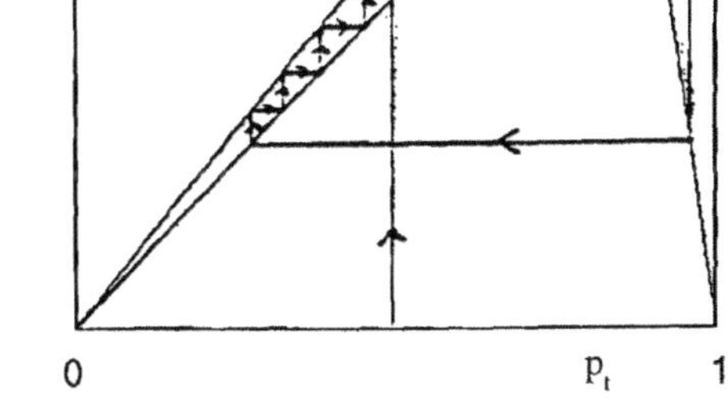

Fig. 9.2 Asymmetric tent map chaotic dynamics

Needless to say, simply randomly picking a particular pair of parameter values for such an AR(1) rule-of-thumb decision-making process is not at all likely to be able to mimic the underlying chaotic dynamic. The question arises if by some simple learning process the parameters of this rule of thumb can be changed in response to the performance of the decisions and in so doing converge on one that indeed does successfully mimic the underlying chaotic dynamic. The answer is yes, and the method by which this is done is by *sample autocorrelation* (SAC) learning. Hommes (1998) showed that this could come about and labeled the process *learning to believe in chaos*.[7,8]

An example of this from Hommes and Sorger (1998) is shown in Fig. 9.3 (Rosser, 2000b, p. 92). What one can see is that initially the agent guesses a particular price, which holds for awhile, but then the price begins to oscillate in a two-period cycle, as the parameters of the AR(1) process adjust with learning, with the cycle becoming gradually more complicated, and finally becoming fully chaotic as the parameter values approach those that lead to the AR(1) process accurately mimicking the underlying chaotic dynamic. Hommes and Rosser (2001) show that this can happen for their fishery model as well.

Foroni, Gardini, and Rosser (2003) study an extension of this model to that of a geometrically declining statistical learning mechanism. They focus particularly on the basins of attraction of the system and find that not only do the price dynamics become complex for certain regions of the discount rate, but the basins of attraction also become more complicated with the basins coexisting in certain zones and with the boundaries possessing lobes, holes, and other forms of heightened complexity that could induce greater likelihoods of unexpected catastrophic outcomes.[9] They note that this statistical learning mechanism is arguably more "sophisticated" than the simpler rule-of-thumb learning mechanisms studied by Hommes and Rosser and that they lead to greater possibilities of difficulties in the fishery than the simpler

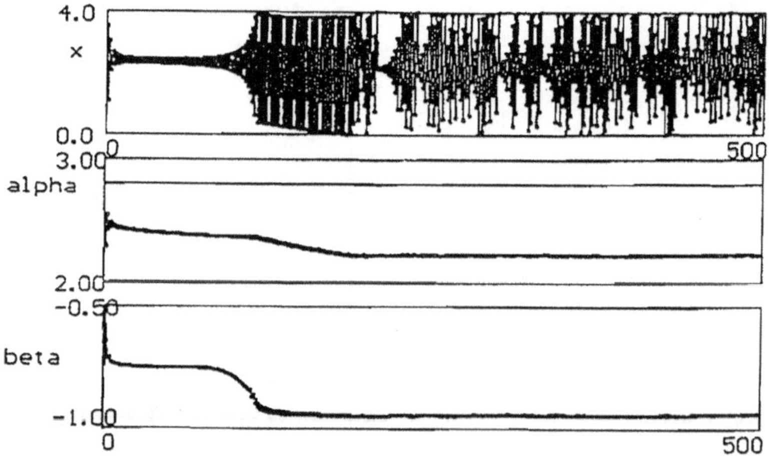

Fig. 9.3 Learning to believe in chaos

mechanisms. This suggests that it may be inadvertent wisdom for fishers to rely on rules of thumb, which given the immense vagaries and uncertainties surrounding fishing may be comforting in the face of the many difficulties that we face in the management of fisheries.

9.3 Complexity Problems of Optimal Rotation in Forests

Some complexities of forestry dynamics have been discussed in the previous chapter, notably in connection with the matter of spruce–budworm dynamics (Ludwig, Jones, and Holling, 1978).[10] In order to get at related sorts of dynamics arising from unexpected patterns of forest benefits as well as such management issues as how to deal with forest fires and patch size, as well as the basic matter of when forests should be optimally cut, we need to develop a basic model (Rosser, 2005). We shall begin with the simplest sort of model in which the only benefit of a forest is the timber to be cut from it and consider the optimal behavior of a profit-maximizing forest owner under such conditions.

Irving Fisher (1907) considered what we now call the "optimal rotation" problem of when to cut a forest as part of his development of capital theory. Positing positive real interest rates, he argued that it would be optimal to cut the forest (or a tree, to be more precise) when its growth rate equals the real rate of interest, the growth rate of trees tending to slow down over time. This was straightforward: As long as a tree grows more rapidly than the level of the rate of interest, one can increase one's wealth more by letting the tree grow. Once its growth rate is set to drop below the real rate of interest, one can make more money by cutting the tree down and putting the proceeds from selling its timber into a bond earning the real rate of interest. This argument dominated thinking in the English language tradition for over half a decade, despite some doubts raised by Alchian (1952) and Gaffney (1957).

However, as eloquently argued by Samuelson (1976), Fisher was wrong. Or to be more precise, he was only correct for a rather odd and uninteresting case, namely, that in which the forest owner does not replant a new tree to replace the old one, but in effect simply abandons the forest and does nothing with it (or perhaps sells it off to someone else). This is certainly not the solution to the optimal rotation problem in which the forest owner intends to replant and then cut and replant and cut and so on into the infinite future. Curiously, the solution to this problem had been solved in 1849 by a German forester, Martin Faustmann (1849), although his solution would remain unknown in English until his work was translated over a century later.

Faustmann's solution involves cutting sooner than in the Fisher case, because one can get more rapidly growing younger trees in and growing if one cuts sooner, which increases the present value of the forest compared to a rotation period based on cutting when Fisher recommended.

Let p be the price of timber, assumed to be constant,[11] $f(t)$ be the growth function of the biomass of the tree over time, T be the optimal rotation period, r be the real interest rate, and c the cost of cutting the tree. Fisher's solution is then given by

$$pf'(T) = rpf(T), \tag{9.13}$$

which by removing price from both sides can be reduced to

$$f'(T) = rf(T), \tag{9.14}$$

which has the interpretation already given: Cut when the growth rate equals real rate of interest.[12]

Faustmann solved this by considering an infinite sum of discounted earnings of the future discounted returns from harvesting and found this to reduce to

$$pf'(T) = rpf(T) + r[(pf(T) - c)/(e^{rT} - 1)], \tag{9.15}$$

which implies a lower T than in Fisher's case due to the extra term on the right-hand side, which is positive and given the fact that $f(t)$ is concave. Hartman (1976) generalized this to allow for nontimber amenity values of the tree (or forest patch of same aged trees to be cut simultaneously),[13] assuming those amenity values can be characterized by $g(t)$ to be given by

$$pf'(T) = rpf(T) + r[(pf(T) - c)/(e^{rT} - 1)] - g(T). \tag{9.16}$$

An example of a marketable nontimber amenity value that can be associated with a privately owned forest might be grazing of animals, which tends to reach a maximum early in the life of a forest patch when the trees are still young and rather small. Swallow, Parks, and Wear (1990) estimated cattle grazing amenity values in Western Montana to reach a maximum of \$16.78 per hectare at 12.5 years, with the function given by

$$g(t) = \beta_0 \exp(-\beta_1 t), \tag{9.17}$$

with estimated parameter values of $\beta_0 = 1.45$ and $\beta_1 = 0.08$. Peak grazing value is at $T = 1/\beta_1$. This grazing amenities solution is depicted in Fig. 9.4 (Rosser, 2005, p. 194).

Plugging this formulation of $g(t)$ into the Hartman equation (9.18) generates a solution depicted in Fig. 9.5 (Rosser, 2005, p. 195), with MOC representing marginal opportunity cost and MBD the marginal benefit of delaying harvest. In this case, the global maximum is 73 years, a bit shorter than the Faustmann solution of 76 years, showing the effect of the earlier grazing benefits. This case has multiple local optima, and this reflects the sorts of nonlinearities that arise in forestry dynamics as these situations become more complex (Vincent and Potts, 2005).[14]

Grazing amenities from cattle on a privately owned forest can bring income to the owner of the forest. However, many other amenities may not directly bring income, or may be harder to arrange to do so. Furthermore, some of the amenities may be in the form of externalities that accrue to others who do not own the forest. All of this may lead to market inefficiencies as the $g(t)$ are not properly accounted for, thus leading to inaccurate estimates of the optimal rotation period, which may be to not

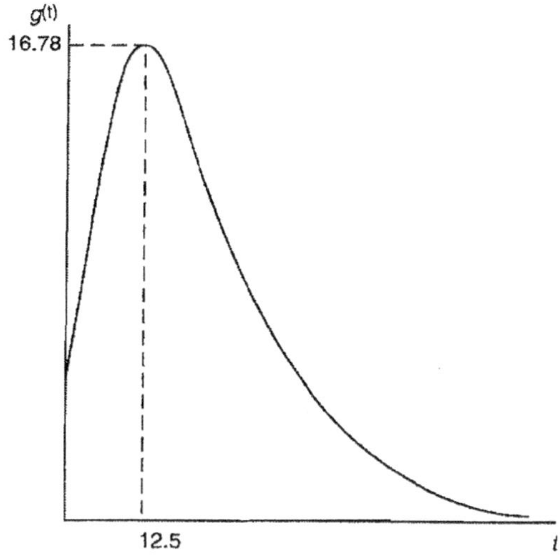

Fig. 9.4 Grazing amenities function

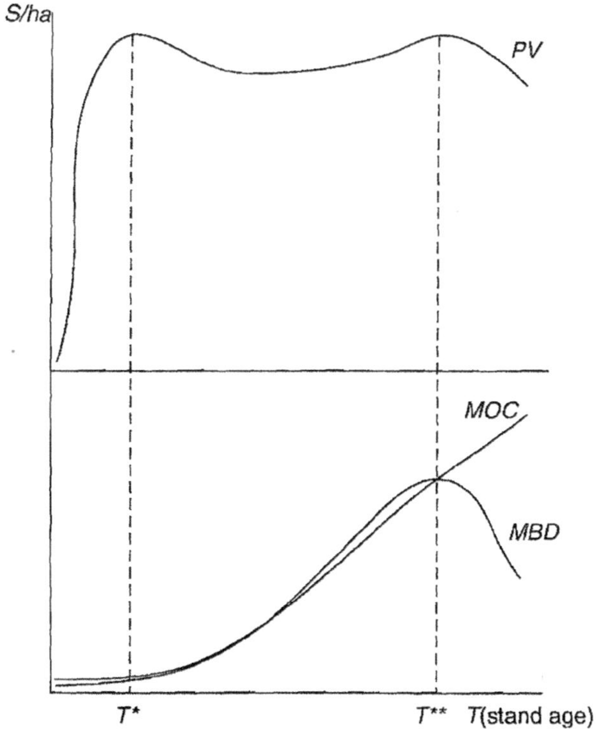

Fig. 9.5 Optimal Hartman rotation with grazing

rotate at all, to leave a forest uncut so that such amenities as endangered species or aesthetic values of older trees, or prevention of soil erosion, or carbon sequestration may be enjoyed, particularly, if the timber value from the trees in the forest is not all that great.

While private forest owners are unlikely to account for such externalities fully, it is generally argued that the managers of publicly owned forests, such as the National Forest Service in the US, should attempt to do so. Indeed, the US National Forest Service has been doing so now for several decades through the FORPLAN planning process to determine land use on national forests (Johnson, Jones, and Kent, 1980; Bowes and Krutilla, 1985). In practice, this is often done through the use of public hearings, with the numbers of people attending these meetings representing groups interested in particular amenities often ending up becoming the measure of the weights or implicit prices put on these various amenities.

Among the amenities for which it may be possible for either a private forest owner to earn some income or a publicly owned forest as well are hunting and fishing. Clearly, for a private forest owner to fully capture such amenities involves controlling access to the forest, which is not always possible, given the phenomenon of poaching, with there being an old tradition of this in Europe of peasants poaching on an aristocrat's forest (many of which have since become public forests), or of poaching of endangered species on public lands in many poorer countries. In many countries at least a partial capturing of income for these activities can come through the sale of hunting and fishing licenses. Likewise, many public forests are able to charge people for camping or hiking in particularly beautiful areas.

A more difficult problem arises with the matter of biodiversity. Here there is much less chance of having people pay directly for some activity as with hunting or fishing or camping. One is dealing with public goods and thus a willingness to pay for an existence value or option value for a species to exist, or for a particular forest or environment to maintain some level or degree of biodiversity, even if there is no specific endangered species involved. Some of these option values are tied to possible uses of certain species, such as medical uses, although once these are known, market operators usually attempt to take advantage of the income possibilities in one way or another. But broader biodiversity issues, including even the sensitive subject of endangered species, is much harder to pin down (Perrings, Mäler, Folke, Holling, and Jansson, 1995).

Among some poorer countries such as Mozambique, as well as middle-income ones such as Costa Rica, the use of ecotourism to generate income for such preservation has become widespread. While this can involve bringing economic benefits to local populations, some of these resent the appearance of outsiders. More generally the problems of valuing and managing forests with poorer indigenous or aboriginal populations, whose rights have often been violated in the past, is an ongoing issue (Kant, 2000; Gram, 2001).[15]

Another external amenity is carbon sequestration. This benefit tends to be strongly associated with cutting less frequently (Alig, Adams, and McCarl, 1998) or not at all, especially as in general any cutting involves burning of underbrush or "useless" branches, leading to large releases of carbon dioxide. However, the pattern of this varies, and one thing pushing for cutting sooner is that more rapidly growing trees, younger ones, tend to absorb more carbon dioxide than older, slower growing ones or alternative species that grow more rapidly (Alavalapati, Stainback, and Carter, 2002). Details of both the nature of the forest as well as such things as what it is replaced with if it is cut can also lead to possible conflicts with biodiversity initiatives (Caparrós and Jacquemont, 2003) or other amenities such as avoiding soil erosion or flooding (Plantinga and Wu, 2003).

How complicated these patterns of nonmarketed amenities can be is seen by an example this author had personal experience with, the George Washington National Forest in Virginia and West Virginia, for which he was involved in the FORPLAN planning process at one time. The normal pattern of ecological succession in the eastern deciduous forests found in the George Washington tends to favor different animal species at different times as the vegetation passes through various stages, with those wishing to hunt certain species thus finding themselves supporting different policies.

The first stage after a clear-cut of a section of forest involves new, small trees growing rapidly, with such an environment favoring grazing by deer, much as in the example of cattle grazing in Montana. This peaks out between about 5 and 10 years, and deer hunters, very numerous in the area, thus tend to favor more timber harvesting. The second stage is actually associated with the greatest biodiversity as there are many shrubs and other sorts of undergrowth beneath the middle-aged trees. In terms of hunting, this favors wild turkeys and grouse, peaking at around 25 years. The final stage is an old growth forest more than 60 years old, with lots of large fallen logs in which one finds bears, whose hunters tend to be highly specialized and also highly motivated and who thus unsurprisingly oppose the deer hunters' desire for more timber harvesting.[16] Figure 9.6 (Rosser, 2005, p. 198) depicts the time pattern of these net amenities, and this pattern opens up the possibility of multiple equilibria and associated possible complex dynamics and capital theoretic issues, just as the case of cattle grazing in Montana did.

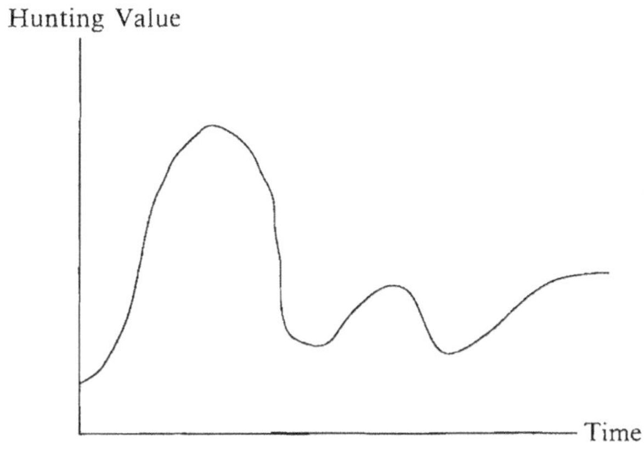

Fig. 9.6 Virginia deciduous forest hunting amenity

9.4 Problems of Forestry Management Beyond Optimal Rotation

Other problems associated with forestry management go beyond the model of optimal rotation period. One of these involves fire management, which has become very controversial in recent years. Traditional policy on the US national forests was to fight all fires at any point at any time. It has been argued that this leads to a stability-resilience trade off of the Holling (1973) type. Without humans in nature, fires occur naturally from time to time due to lightning. Actively stopping all fires can lead to an increase in vegetative density to the point that when a fire finally does break out, it can become enormously destructive (Muradian, 2001) as several have in the US in recent years in such areas as California and Yellowstone National Park. This has led in some areas to efforts to actually set controlled fires to thin out vegetation and dead branches, although the danger of these getting out of control has led many to oppose such policies, especially after such an effort in Arizona led to such a fire destroying property.

Besides setting smaller fires in order to avoid bigger fires, use of fires to manage forests and ecosystems more generally was done by the Native American Indians in many parts of the US for a long time prior to the arrival of the Europeans. One such usage is the one that has been directed at preserving endangered species that peak in population prior to the later stages of a succession, such as eastern bristlebirds in the US (Pyke, Saillard, and Smith, 1995). Stochastic dynamic programming has been used to study optimal fire management in such systems by Possingham and Tuck (1997) and Clark and Mangel (2000).

Clark and Mangel (2000, pp. 176–178) provide a more detailed analysis of an endangered species population, where habitat quality is given by $q(t)$ from the time of the fire, r is litter size, s_a is probability an adult survives in absence of fire, s_j is probability that a juvenile survives in the absence of fire, and $N(t)$ is the adult population in time t after the fire. Then population after a fire is given by

$$N(t+1) = [s_a + s_j rq(t)]N(t). \tag{9.18}$$

Clark and Mangel (2000, p. 178) estimate a specific trajectory of average population to follow a fire, which is depicted in Fig. 9.7, based on assuming that $r = 2, s_a = 0.7$, and $s_j = 0.2$. This leads to population reaching a peak about 10 years after the fire.

Clark and Mangel (2000, p. 181) further analyze what an optimal fire policy might be in such situations, bringing in a fitness parameter, f, which is the percent of the population that survives a fire. Figure 9.8 (Rosser, 2005, p. 200) depicts the time–population space divided between starting a fire and not starting a fire over 20 years for a population that can reach a maximum of 50, but must stay above a minimum of 3, with $f = 0.8$. The dividing line is based on the maximum probability of the survival of the species based on starting a fire or not starting a fire for the given population size at that time.

Another issue not related to optimal forest rotation per se involves the size of patches that are cut at a time in a forest. Private timber harvesters uninterested in

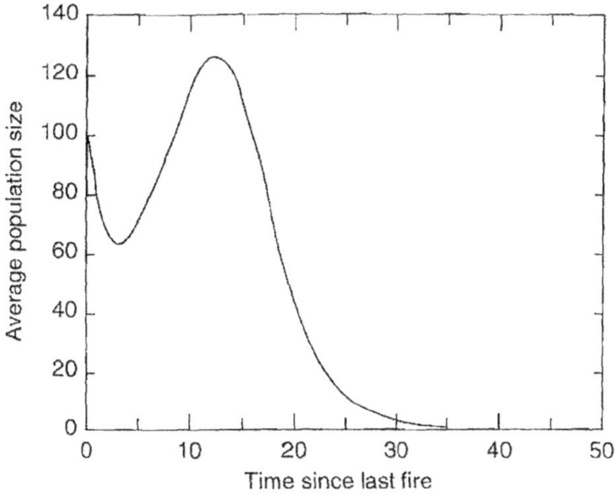

Fig. 9.7 Average population path after a fire

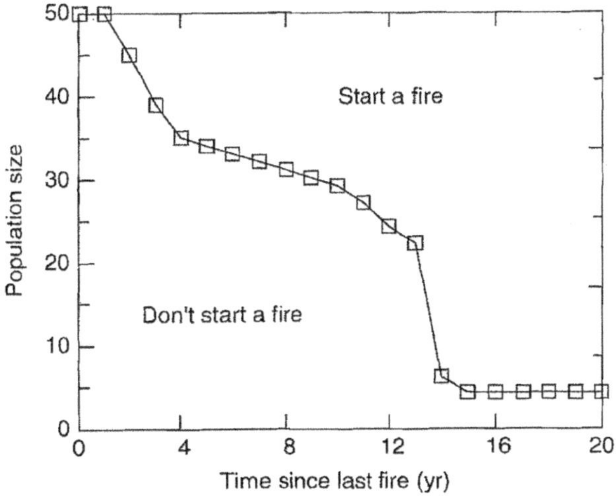

Fig. 9.8 Optimal fire management for endangered species

any externalities find their costs per quantity of timber obtained declining as size increases of clear-cuts of homogeneous species that are then replaced after cutting. However, large clear-cuts threaten the survival of fragile species, with this being a nonlinear relationship subject to a catastrophic decline of population for clear-cuts above a certain size (Tilman, May, Lehman, and Nowak, 1994; Bascompte and Solé, 1996; Metzger and Décamps, 1997; Muradian, 2001).

Figure 9.9 (Rosser, 2005, p. 202) depicts this situation. Its horizontal axis is the size of the harvest cut; the vertical one shows both the costs of cutting and the benefits of species preservation associated with a cut. Line A shows the benefits for species preservation of a certain sized cut. Line B shows the average costs of

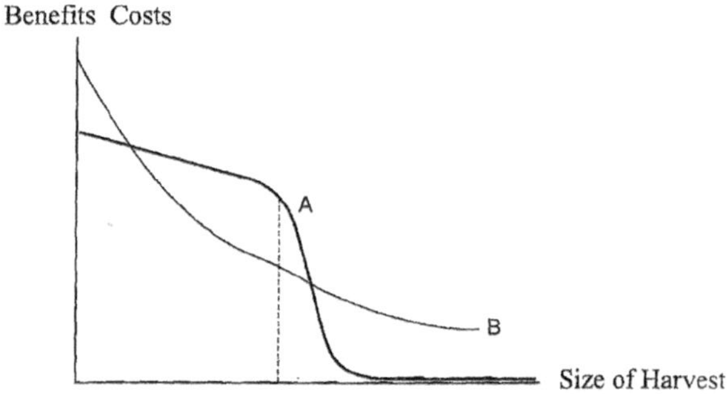

Fig. 9.9 Harvest cut size and habitat damage

cutting for a given size of cut. Clearly, given the gradually declining average cost of cut with the threat of a catastrophic decline in population beyond some point, the middle-sized cuts would be preferred in this case. We note that besides this issue there are many others associated with the size of clear-cuts, with aesthetic ones for cuts that are visible from outside the forest, as well as such things as soil erosion and flooding also important as well for this controversial matter that has long been debated vigorously in forest management circles.

9.5 Complex Lake Dynamics

There have been many ecologic-economic models of various hydrological ecosystems.[17] However, among the most intensively studied such systems have been of lakes, particularly shallow lakes whose state is sensitive to nutrient loadings, most often phosphorus from human agricultural activities (Hasler, 1947; Scheffer, 1989, 1998; Schindler, 1990; Carpenter, Kraft, Wright, He, Soranno, and Hodgson, 1992; Carpenter, Ludwig, and Brock, 1999; Carpenter and Cottingham, 2002; Scheffer, Westley, Brock, and Holmgren, 2002; Brock and Starrett, 2003; Mäler, Xepapadeas, and de Zeeuw, 2003; Wagener, 2003; Brock and Carpenter, 2006; Iwasa, Uchida, and Yokomizo, 2007; Kiseleva and Wagener, 2010). These systems attract special attention because they exhibit multiple equilibria and the possibility for fold catastrophic discontinuities as critical levels of phosphorus concentrations are reached, with resulting complications for public policy. Some of this policy discussion has involved analysis of repeated games (Brock and de Zeeuw, 2002; Dechert and O'Donnell, 2006; Wagener, 2009).

Although there are others that have been studied in detail, particularly in the Netherlands (Mäler, Xepapdeas, and de Zeeuw, 2003; Wagener, 2003), an early and ongoing focus of this research has been Lake Mendota in Madison, Wisconsin, where the University of Wisconsin is located, one of the earliest and leading centers in the world for limnology research (Hasler, 1947; Carpenter, Brock, and Ludwig, 1999). The lake is a scenic center of tourism and was long used for swimming as well as boating, but is also in the center of one of the world's richest areas in terms of soil for growing maize/corn, which intensively uses phosphorus as a fertilizer input. This fertilizer runs off these surrounding farmlands into the lake, which spurs algal growth (now so great that swimming has been reduced to a minimum) and has steadily worsened over a many decades period. Experience with other similar glacial lakes and modeling suggests that at a critical level of phosphorus concentrations, the lake will rather suddenly become *eutrophic* rather than *oligotrophic*, which it still is. Such a lake will have far more algae and few fish and will be essentially unusable for any recreation or tourism.[18]

A broad overview of the relationships within such a lake that is suffering a tendency to eutrophication is depicted in Fig. 9.10 (Carpenter and Cottingham, 2002, p. 56). The disturbed system is seen at different time (vertical axis) and space (horizontal) scales in terms of what is happening in it, moving from the lowest level of phosphorus accumulation up to broader climatic change.

We shall follow here the presentation in Wagener (2009) for a simplified version of shallow lake dynamics, who in turn draws largely on Scheffer (1998). Let $s = s(t)$ be the concentration of phosphorus in the shallow lake, $a = a(t)$ represent human action in the system, b be the sedimentation rate of the phosphorus in the lake (how rapidly it falls out of the lake to be absorbed in the lake bottom, with an assumption that it stays there once it goes there), and $a = g(s)$ give the response curve of the system to the human action (phosphorus inflow to the lake). The basic dynamics are given by

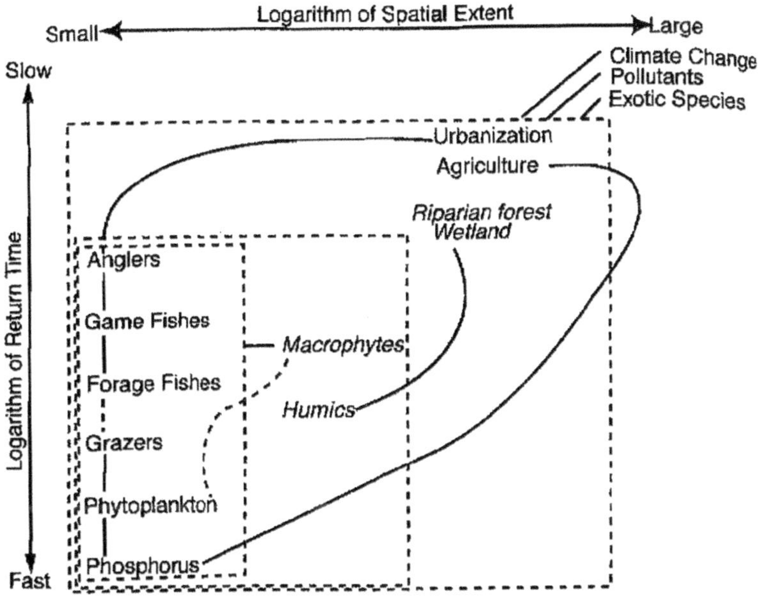

Fig. 9.10 Major interactions in pathological lake dynamics

Fig. 9.11 Shallow lake dynamics, monotone case

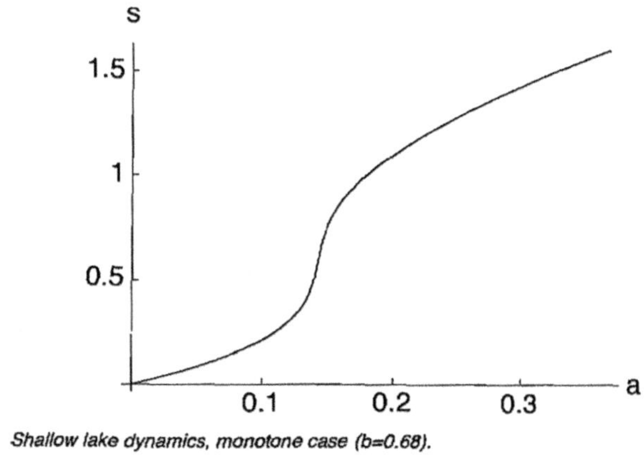

$$s' = a - g(s) = a - [bs - s^2/(1 + s^2)]. \tag{9.19}$$

At this stage the crucial parameter in terms of how the system behaves is b, the sedimentation rate. For high b, the response curve is monotonic, as depicted in Fig. 9.11 (Wagener, 2009, p. 4), for which $b = 0.68$.

As b declines below 0.65, the response curve bends sufficiently to set up a multiple equilibria situation that resembles the fold catastrophe (see Appendix A, this book). Figure 9.12 (Wagerner, 2009, p. 5) depicts a curve for $b = 0.52$, at which level the lake can suddenly and discontinuously jump to a much higher level of phosphorus concentration, possibly associated with eutrophication. However, if the level of phosphorus inflow is reduced, there is the possibility of this condition being reversed and the lake returning to its previously oligotrophic state, although at a much lower level of phosphorus loading than the one that triggered the initial shift to eutrophy. This is the standard hysteresis effect of catastrophe theory.

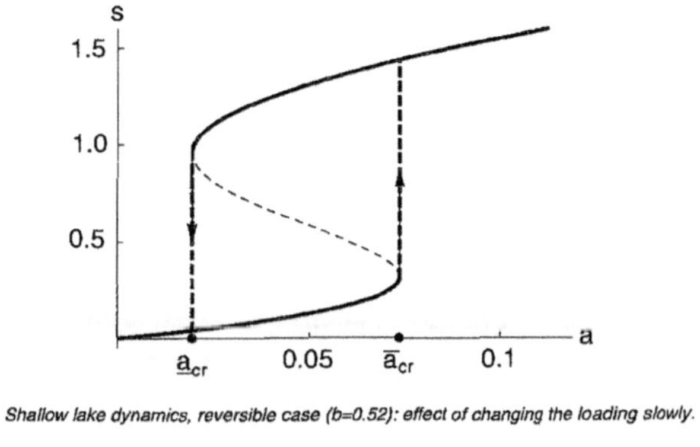

Fig. 9.12 Shallow lake dynamics, reversible case

Fig. 9.13 Shallow lake dynamics: irreversible case

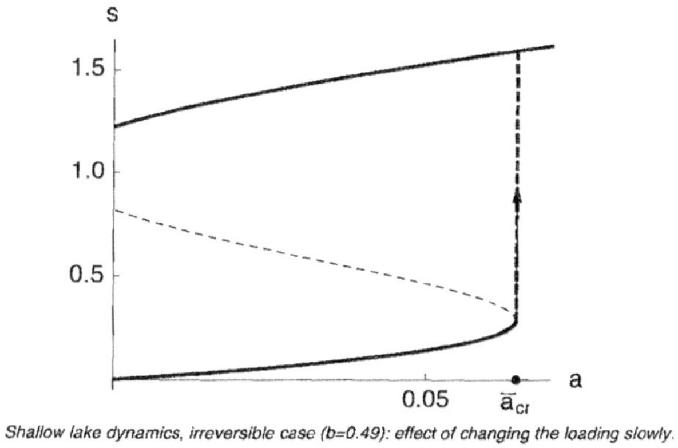

Finally, as b goes below about 0.50 or so, the sedimentation rate is so low that once the lake shifts to the eutrophic condition, this cannot be reversed. This is depicted in Fig. 9.13 (Wagener, 2009, p. 6), with $b = 0.49$.

Wagener then moves to consider welfare analysis in a more dynamic context of repeated game Nash equilibria. He assumes a relatively simple welfare function, which is an aggregation of identical individual utility functions driving the dynamic lake game, with c = cost of action, and the individual utility function for agent i given by

$$U = \log(a_i) - c_i s^2. \tag{9.20}$$

From this the intertemporal optimization for welfare, W, with a discount rate $= \delta$ and a shadow value of the lake, $p(t)$, is given by maximizing

$$W = \int_0^\infty \mathrm{e}^{-\delta t}[\log(a(t) - cs(t)^2)], \tag{9.21}$$

which implies a Pontryagin function of

$$P = \log(a) - cs^2 + p[a - g(s)]. \tag{9.22}$$

Applying Pontryagin's maximum principle generates solutions for $[a(t), s(t), p(t)]$, which satisfies the following conditions:

$$0 = \partial P/\partial a = (1/a) + p, \tag{9.23}$$

$$s' = \partial P/\partial p = a - g(s), \tag{9.24}$$

$$p' = \delta p - \partial P/\partial s = 2cs + [\delta + g'(s)]p. \tag{9.25}$$

Fig. 9.14 Typical solution of the dynamic lake problem

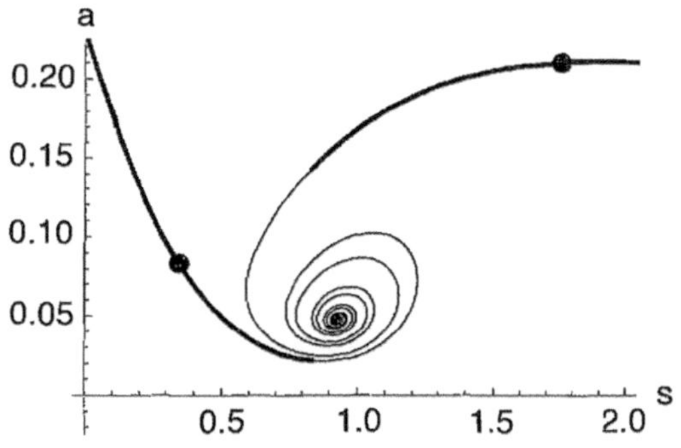

The solution involves for most combinations of parameter values two competing outcomes, a low-loading/low-phosphorus concentration one versus a high-loading/high-phosphorus concentration one in the long run. Unsurprisingly, the relative sizes of the basins of attraction for these two solutions depends crucially on the discount rate, δ, with the size of the basin feeding to the high-loading/high-phosphorus concentration increasing as the discount rate rises. As the agents become more myopic, they value the benefits of growing more food now (and loading more phosphorus) over having the benefits of an oligotrophic lake in the future.

A curious aspect of this solution is that what separates the basins of attraction is not a true separatrix, which would be an unstable equilibrium outcome. Rather it is an *indifference point*, or multistable point, where both of the equilibrium solutions coexist, and the agents are indifferent between them. Such a point has also been called a "Skiba point" (Skiba, 1978), a "Dechert-Nishimura-Skiba point" (Sethi, 1977; Dechert and Nishimura, 1983), a "Dechert-Nishimura-Skiba-Sethi point," and in the optimal control literature, a "shock point." Figure 9.14 (Wagener, 2009, p. 21) depicts a pair of solution points (the dots) with trajectories coming out of the indifference point for $b = 0.55, c = 0.5$, and $\delta = 0.03$. The thicker portions of the trajectories show welfare-maximizing portions. The indifference point is at $s = 0.85$. The point to the left is the low-loading/low-phosphorus outcome, and the point to the right is the high-loading/high-phosphorus outcome.

9.6 Stability and Resilience of Ecosystems Revisited

In the early portion of the previous chapter we encountered a discussion of the sources of stability within ecosystems. Whereas it was argued for quite some time that there is a relationship between the diversity of an ecosystem and its stability, this was later found not to be true in general, with indeed mathematical arguments existing suggesting just the opposite. It was then suggested by some that the apparent relationship between diversity and stability in nature was the other way around, that stability allowed for diversity. More broadly, it was argued that there is no general relationship, with the details of relationships within an ecosystem providing the key to understanding the nature of the stability of the system, although certainly declining biodiversity is a broad problem with many aspects (Perrings, Mäler, Folke, Holling, and Jansson, 1995).

Out of this discussion came the fruitful insight by C.S. Holling (1973) of a deep negative relationship between stability and resilience. This relationship can be posed as a conflict between local and global stability: that greater local stability may be in some sense purchased at the cost of lesser global stability or resilience. The palm tree is not locally stable as it bends in the wind easily in comparison with the oak tree. However, as the wind strengthens, the palm tree's bending allows it to survive, while the oak tree becomes more susceptible to breaking and not surviving. Such a relationship can even be argued to carry over into economics as in the classic comparison of market capitalism and command socialism. Market capitalism suffers from instabilities of prices and the macroeconomy, whereas the planned prices and output levels of command socialism stabilize the price level, output, and employment. However, market capitalism is more resilient and survives the stronger exogenous shocks of technological change or sudden shortages of inputs, whereas command socialism is in greater danger of completely breaking down, which indeed happened with the former Soviet economic system.

This recognition that ecosystems involve dynamic patterns and do not remain fixed over time led Holling (1992) to extend his idea to more broadly consider the role of such patterns within maintaining the resilience of such systems and also to consider how the relationships between the patterns would vary over time and space within the hierarchical systems (Holling and Gunderson, 2002; Holling, Gunderson, and Peterson, 2002; Gunderson, Holling, Pritchard, and Peterson, 2002). This resulted in what has come to be called the "lazy eight" diagram of Holling, which is depicted in Fig. 9.15 (Holling and Gunderson, 2002, p. 34) and shows a stylized picture of the passage of a typical ecosystem through four basic functions over time.

This can be thought of as representing a typical pattern of ecological succession on a particular plot of land.[19] Conventional ecology focuses on the r and K zones, corresponding to r-adapters and K-adapters. So, if an ecosystem has collapsed (as in the case of a forest after a total fire), it begins to have populations within it grow again from scratch, doing so at an r rate through the phase of exploitation. As it fills up, it moves to the K stage, wherein it reaches carrying capacity and enters the phase of conservation, although as noted previously, succession may occur in this stage as the precise set of plants and animals may change at this stage. Then there comes the release as the overconnected system now become low in resilience and collapses into a release of biomass and energy in the Ω stage, which Gunderson and Holling identify with the "creative destruction" of Schumpeter (1950). Finally, the system enters into the α stage of reorganization as it prepares to allow for the reaccumulation of energy and biomass. In this stage, soil and other fundamental factors are prepared for the return to the r stage, although this is a crucially important stage

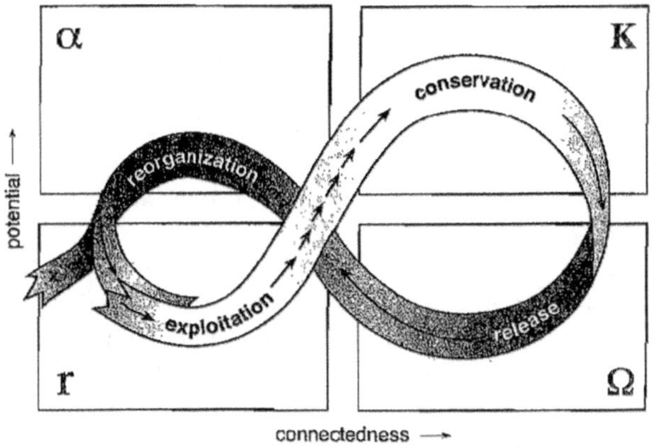

Fig. 9.15 Cycle of the four ecosystem functions

in that it is possible for the ecosystem to change substantially into a different form, depending on how the soil is changed and what species enter into it, with the example of the shift from buffalo grass and grama to rattlesnake bush and tumbleweed a possibility as described by Leopold (1933) in the second of the quotations at the beginning of this chapter.

This basic pattern can be seen occurring at multiple time and space scales within a broader landscape as a set of nested cycles (Holling, 1986, 1992). An example drawn on the boreal forest and also depicting relevant atmospheric cycles is depicted in Fig. 9.16 (Holling, Gunderson, and Peterson, 2002, p. 68). One can think in terms of the forest of each of the levels operating according to its own "lazy eight" pattern as described above. Such a pattern is called a *panarchy*.

Increasingly, policymakers come to understand that it is resilience rather than stability per se that is important for longer-term sustainability of a system. In the face of exogenous shocks and the threat of extinction of species (Solé and Bascompte, 2006), special efforts must be made to approach things adeptly. Costanza, Andrade, Antunes, van den Belt, Boesch, Boersma, Catarino, Hanna, Limburg, Low, Molitor, Pereira, Rayner, Santos, Wilson, and Young (1999) propose six principles for the case of oceanic management: Responsibility, Scale Matching, Precautionary, Adaptive Management, Full Cost Allocation, and Full Participation. Of these, Rosser (2001a) suggests that the most important are the Scale-Matching and Precautionary principles. We shall discuss the second of these in Chapter 11 of this book, but wish to further discuss the first of these at this point.

Scale-matching means that the policymakers operate at the appropriate level of the hierarchy of the ecologic-economic system. Following Ostrom (1990) and Bromley (1991), as well as Rosser (1995) and Rosser and Rosser (2006), the idea is to align both property and control rights at the appropriate level of the hierarchy.[20] Managing a fishery at too high a level can lead to the destruction of fish species at a lower level (Wilson, Low, Costanza, and Ostrom, 1999).

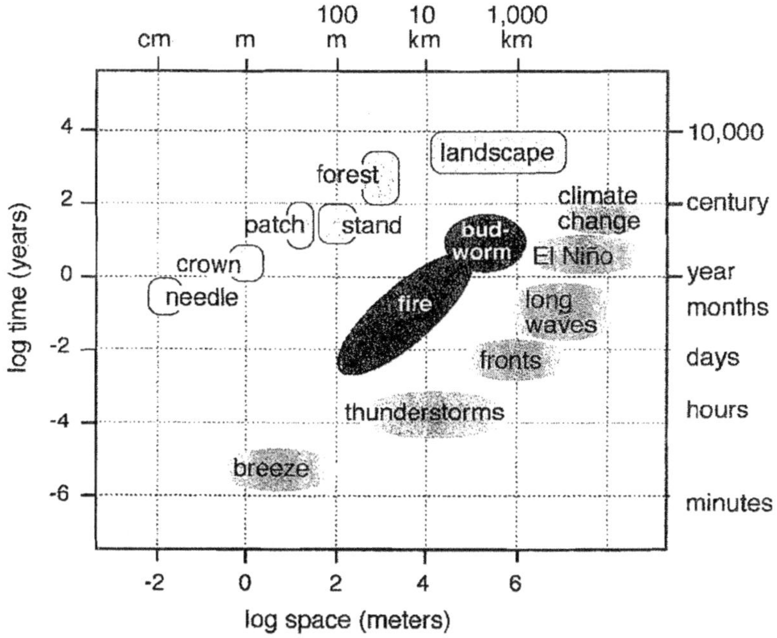

Fig. 9.16 Time and space scales of the boreal forest and the atmosphere

Assuming that appropriate scale-matching has been achieved, and that a functioning system of property rights and control has been established, the goal of managing to maintain resilience may well involve providing sufficient flexibility for the system to be able to have its local fluctuations occur without interference while maintaining the broader boundaries and limits that keep the system from collapsing. In the difficult situation of fisheries, this may involve establishing reserves (Lauck, Clark, Mangel, and Munro, 1998; Grafton, Kompas, and Van Ha, 2009) or system of rotational usage (Valderarama and Anderson, 2007). Crucial to successfully doing this is having the group that manages the resource able to monitor itself and observe itself (Sethi and Somanathan, 1996), with such self-reinforcement being the key to success in the management of fisheries for certain as in the case of the lobster gangs of Maine (Acheson, 1988) and the fisheries of Iceland (Durrenberger and Pálsson, 1987). Needless to say, all of this is easier said than done, especially in the case of fisheries where the relevant local groups are often quite distinct socially and otherwise from those around them and thus tending to be suspicious of outsiders who attempt to get them to organize themselves to do what is needed (Charles, 1988).

Notes

1. For further discussion see Rosser (2000c, 2001a, 2009c, 2011) and Foroni, Gardini, and Rosser (2003).
2. Constancy of the discount rate over time is not a trivial assumption. We know that for many people internal discount rates probably exhibit some form of hyperbolicity, with short-term rates very high (Strotz, 1956; Akerlof, 1991; Laibson, 1997), whereas in the discussions of intertemporally equitable environmental policy it has been argued that longer-term discount rates should be lower than shorter-term ones along the lines of the Green Golden Rule (Chichilnisky, Heal, and Beltratti, 1995). While these appear to resemble each other superficially, in the case of hyperbolic discounting the short-term rates are generally above real market interest rates, whereas in the Green Golden Rule case, the longer-term rates are generally below real market interest rates.
3. Other ecosystems exhibiting multiple equilibria and possible catastrophic discontinuities include the reportedly periodic mass suicides of lemmings (Elton, 1924), coral reefs (Done, 1992; Hughes, 1994), kelp forests (Estes and Duggins, 1995), and cattle grazing of fragile grasslands (Noy-Meir, 1973; Ludwig, Walker, and Holling, 2002).
4. While it did not involve an optimizing model, Conklin and Kohlberg (1994) showed the possibility of chaotic dynamics for fisheries with backward-bending supply curves. Doveri, Scheffer, Rinaldi, Muratori, and Kuznetsov (1993) showed the possibility within more generalized multiple-species aquatic ecosystems. Zimmer (1999) argues that chaotic cycles are more frequently seen in laboratories than in real life due to the noisiness of natural ecosystems, although Allen, Schaffer, and Rosko (1993) argue that chaotic dynamics in a noisy environment may help preserve a species from extinction.
5. This is well below the range that chaotic dynamics appear in Golden Rule growth models (Nishimura and Yano, 1996).
6. See Sakai (2001) for a broader overview of chaotic agricultural cycles. The corn–hog cycle is really a form of predator–prey cycles, first argued to be possibly chaotic by Gilpin (1979) in the hare–lynx case by Schaffer (1984), with an overview presented by Solé and Bascompte (2006, pp. 38–42), and lemmings and Finnish voles by Ellner and Turchin (1995) and Turchin (2003). Ginzburg and Colyvan (2004) argue that what many think are predator–prey cycles reflect inertial patterns within populations.
7. See also Sorger (1998).
8. Schönhofer (1999, 2001) has also studied this process.
9. Fractal basin boundaries have been studied for predator–prey systems by Gu and Huang (2006), with Kaneko and Tsuda (2001) studying even a broader array of possible complex dynamics in them. At a higher level, chaotically oscillating patterns of phenotype and genotype over long evolutionary periods within predator–prey dynamics have been studied by Solé and Bascompte (2006) and Sardanyés and Solé (2007).
10. See also Holling (1965) for a foreshadowing of this argument. For broader links, Holling (1986) later argued that these spruce–budworm systems in the Canadian forests could be affected by "local surprise" or small events in distant locations, such as the draining of crucial swamps in the US Midwest on the migratory flight paths of birds that feed on the budworms.
11. This is a nontrivial assumption, with a large literature existing on the use of option theory to solve for optimal stopping times when the price is a stochastic process (Reed and Clarke, 1990; Zinkhan, 1991; Conrad, 1997; Willassen, 1998; Sapphores, 2003). Arrow and Fisher (1974) first suggested the use of option theory to deal with possibly irreversible loss of uncertain future forest values.
12. Another related example by Fisher was for the optimal time to age a wine, a curious example for him given his teetotaling personal habits. In any case, one ages a wine until the rate of increase in its quality equals the real rate of interest, although now we might be more inclined to replace the real rate of interest with some sort of subjective intertemporal rate

of time preference, a concept that Fisher was aware of, although he saw these coinciding in equilibrium in a society with homogeneous agents.

13. A more general model based on Ramsey's intertemporal optimization that solves for an optimal profile of a forest was initiated by Mitra and Wan (1986), with follow-ups by Salo and Tahvonen (2002, 2003). One of their results was to take seriously Ramsey's idea that intertemporal equity implies the use of zero discount rates. In this case, management converges on the long-run maximum sustained yield solution. Khan and Piazza (2011) study this model from the standpoint of classical turnpike theory.
14. The existence of these multiple equilibria opens the possibility of capital theoretic paradoxes as the real rate of interest varies (Rosser, 2011). The problem this can pose for benefit–cost analysis was discussed in the final section of the preceding chapter. This matter also holds for the case of forestry management in the George Washington National Forest in the US, discussed below. See Asheim (2008) for an application to the case of nuclear power.
15. For more detailed discussion of the special problems of tropical rainforest deforestation and rights of indigenous peoples, see Barbier (2001) and Kahn and Rivas (2009).
16. This author can report a conversation from the time he was involved with this matter with the Forest Superintendant, a man ironically named Forrest Woods. He reported that the most difficult choice and conflict he faced in managing the forest was dealing with the conflict between the more numerous deer hunters and the more intense and motivated bear hunters, some of whom could be quite fearsome.
17. Examples include of the Florida Everglades (Gunderson, Holling, and Peterson, 2002; Gunderson and Walters, 2002), of the Baltic Sea (Jansson and Jansson, 2002), and of coral reef systems (McClanahan, Polunin, and Done, 2002).
18. Most of the lakes in Minnesota, Wisconsin, and Michigan, including the Great Lakes, are of glacial origin, dating from the most recent Ice Age that ended only about 10,000 years ago. The natural history of these lakes is to gradually become more and more full of nutrients and to eventually eutrophicate. The end result of this eutrophication process is for the lake to cease being a lake and to become simply a swamp. The nutrient loadings from farm runoff simply accelerates this inevitable process, and once a lake flips into the eutrophic state, it is extremely difficult to reverse this, a typical hysteresis effect of catastrophe theory. It should also be noted that not all the nutrients come from farm fertilizer runoff, with such things as fertilizer and wastes from urban lawns involved, as well as such things as urban pet feces.
19. We should note here the definition of an "ecosystem" as being a set of interrelated biogeochemical cycles driven by energy. In terms of scale, these can range from a single cell all the way to the entire biosphere. Thus we have a set of nested ecosystems that may operate at a variety of levels of aggregation.
20. As already noted, property rights and control rights may not coincide (Ciriacy-Wantrup and Bishop, 1975), with control of access being the key. Without control of access, property rights are irrelevant. The work of Ostrom and others makes clear that property rights may take a variety of forms. While these alternative efforts often succeed, sometimes they do not, as the failure of an early effort to establish property rights in the British Columbia salmon fishery demonstrates (Millerd, 2007). Some common property resources have been managed successfully for centuries, as in the case of the Swiss alpine grazing commons (Netting, 1976), whose existence has long disproven the simple version of Garrett Hardin's (1968) widely known "tragedy of the commons."

Chapter 10
The Limits to Growth and Global Catastrophe Revisited

like the aging of an organism, the working of the Entropy Law through the economic process is relatively slow but it never ceases. So its effect makes itself visible only by accumulation over long periods. Thousands of years of sheep grazing elapsed before the exhaustion of the soil in the steppes of Eurasia led to the Great Migration.
Nicholas Georgescu-Roegen (1971, The Entropy Law and the Economic Process, p. 19)

The main fuel to speed our progress is our stock of knowledge, and the brake is our lack of imagination. The ultimate resource is people—skilled, spirited, and hopeful people who will exert their wills and imaginations for their own benefit, and so, for the benefit of us all.
Julian Simon (1981, The Ultimate Resource, p. 348)

10.1 Neo-Malthusian Collapse Models

The possibility of extinguishing species by human action underlies the biggest fear of all, that the species we extinguish may be ourselves. To the extent that we are dependent on the biosphere, a major collapse of other species could be the trigger for our collapse, a forecast made by the most pessimistic of analysts (Meadows, Meadows, Randers, and Behrens, 1972).

Such models have been labeled "neo-Malthusian" because of their obvious link with the pessimism of Malthus regarding population and poverty. But a crucial difference is that although Malthus was aware of catastrophic collapses of population arising from his infamous "positive checks," war, famine, and pestilence, he generally did not forecast drastic and sudden declines in living standards. Ironically this was due to his pessimism; he saw little prospect of living standards ever being raised sufficiently high on a per capita basis that they could experience a drastic decline. When he wrote at the beginning of the industrial revolution, such a view was not all that unrealistic. The great mass of people did live, and always had lived, at or near the subsistence level.

J.B. Rosser, *Complex Evolutionary Dynamics in Urban-Regional and Ecologic-Economic Systems*, DOI 10.1007/978-1-4419-8828-7_10,

Thus, pessimistic "global catastrophism" depends partly on the fact that real per capita growth has occurred. But another crucial idea, only partly perceived by Malthus, is the cobweb, the overshoot of an equilibrium due to time lags. The original oscillatory version of such a model comes from ecology, the Lotka–Volterra, predator–prey model. Most modern, neo-Malthusian, global collapse models are essentially Lotka–Volterra models (Goodwin, 1978) with humanity as the predator, overexploiting the prey, or bionomic base, to the point of collapse by one means or another.

It is not widely known among economists that exactly such a possibility was envisioned by Alfred J. Lotka, the inventor of the predator–prey model, who expressed many ideas that have run through more modern discussions. Thus (Lotka, 1925, p. 279):

> The human species, considered in broad perspective, as a unit including its economic and industrial accessories, has swiftly and radically changed its character during the epoch in which our life has been laid. In this we are far from equilibrium—a fact which is of the highest practical significance, since it implies that a period of adjustment to equilibrium conditions lies before us, and he would be an extreme optimist who should expect that such adjustment can be reached without labor and travail. We can only hope that our race may be spared a decline as precipitous as is the upward slope along which we have been carried, heedless, for the most part, both of our privileges and of the threatened privation ahead. While such a sudden decline might, from a detached standpoint, appear as in accord with the eternal equities, since previous gains would in cold terms balance the losses, yet it would be felt as a superlative catastrophe. Our descendants, if such as this should be their fate, will see poor compensation for <u>their</u> ills in the fact that <u>we</u> did live in abundance and luxury.

Most would criticize and reject such a scenario, without necessarily being "extreme optimists." One can debate just what the long-run equilibrium we may have overshot actually is. But clearly Lotka had in mind an adjustment much more profound than that which occurred a few years after he wrote in the form of the Great Depression.

One final element in the more recent versions of this scenario that neither Malthus nor Lotka thought about is the role of pollution. We now know that pollutants can accumulate gradually in the environment with long lags. Such pollutants can serve as the crucial mechanism of the overshoot, achieving a critical destructive mass some time after their release. Thus in the Club of Rome model (Meadows, Meadows, Randers, and Behrens, 1972) several of the doomsday simulations crucially involve a negative, lagged feedback from industrially generated pollutants upon agriculture as the key to the overshoot and collapse. The global accumulation of carbon dioxide and of chlorofluorocarbons both suggest that such scenarios are not beyond the realm of possibility.[1]

Let us briefly review the arguments of the Club of Rome group. Whereas Malthus considered only population and food in a world of fixed land, the Club of Rome group modeled five variables: population, food, industrial output, nonrenewable resources, and pollution. They included many other variables in their rather complicated model,[2] but these were the five major state variables. Generally the model exhibits short-run exponential growth of population, industrial output, and food production, followed by a collapse of all three as either nonrenewable resources run out or pollution roars out of control. The presence in the model of numerous lags is crucial to this overshoot and collapse scenario. Assumptions of more resources, improved agricultural productivity or pollution control, and similar such concessions to the presumed virtues of technology merely serve to prolong the agony of the final collapse, but fail to avoid it entirely. Only a freezing of population and industrial output works, with food and pollution output constant while resources gently decline.

This effort now stands largely discredited, despite its phenomenal burst of influence in the early 1970s.[3] Standard critiques include noting that the combination of overaggregation and excessive lagging ignores the role of price signals in market economies as allocators of resources leading to the substitution of less scarce resources for scarcer ones (Stiglitz, 1979). Such price signals also induce technological changes directed toward relieving the scarcity, occasionally with dramatic results, such as the emergence of the coal-based industrial revolution from the firewood and charcoal "crisis" of Britain in the eighteenth century (Rosenberg, 1973). Furthermore, technological progress may be stimulated by greater human population (Simon, 1981), people as the "ultimate resource." And if that does not suffice we can go into space and mine the moon. Finally, careful studies of long-term relative price movements of most nonrenewable resources suggest that, despite short periods of upward motion such as the early 1950s and early 1970s, there exists a clear downward trend indicating the general success of substitution and technological improvements of various sorts at avoiding apocalypse (Barnett and Morse, 1963; Barnett, 1979; Baumol, 1986).[4]

10.2 Renewable Versus Nonrenewable Resources

However, these empirical studies contain an ironical fly in the ointment, one admitted even by the extremely optimistic Julian Simon (1981). Besides mercury, the one item whose real price appears to be rising in the long run is that of timber, a supposedly *renewable* resource. According to the theory, it is the nonrenewable resources whose prices should rise and which we should run out of (maybe, eventually), not the renewable ones. But we have examined in our discussion of the extinction of species many reasons why this might happen, including, when such resources are open access and subject to capital inertia or increased pollution which can inject dangerous lags a la the Club of Rome and Lotka–Volterra.

It is the possibility of extinction that gives the lie to the distinction between renewable and nonrenewable resources. If a "renewable resource" is made extinct, it suddenly becomes nonrenewable. Furthermore, in a broader perspective, most of our nonorganic resources are probably available within our solar system, the "mining the moon" remark (or perhaps Mars or the asteroids) being quite serious in the longer time horizon. But increasingly it appears that life does not extend beyond earth in our solar system, at least not in any form we can recognize. And as long as the speed of light is a barrier, that makes organic, supposedly renewable, resources the genuinely scarce ones in the broader context. This also applies to such not-easily-renewable biogenic resources as oil and coal.

Thus, in terms of the Club of Rome model, it is the pollution feedback that continues to raise questions, not the rundown of supposedly nonrenewable resources. If we destroy species, or life more broadly, either by pollution or by careless over-harvesting, we can certainly end up in a serious bind with no available substitutes and no hope. It is the threats of desertification, deforestation, and species extinction that constitute our most serious threat, as we are still dependent on the biosphere. And the most difficult-to-control source of a threat along these lines is probably a global level pollution, collectively produced, and operating with a long lag, such as appears to be the case with atmospheric chlorofluorocarbons.

10.3 Managing Potential Catastrophe

This is a complex and controversial topic for which we have no ultimate solution. Besides the profound uncertainties involved, there are serious differences between regions and nations over impacts and policies involving nontrivial distributional issues. Thus it may be easy to declare that "the polluter must pay" when said party is a well-off, industrialized region generating acid rain or toxic waste. But as Kosobud and Daly (1984) have noted, Latin America may be a net gainer from the greenhouse effect while North America may be the net loser. But proposals by the US to reduce Brazil's debt burden in exchange for reduced cutting of the Amazon rain forest have roused strongly nationalistic feelings that go well beyond either economic or environmental issues.

A traditional way of analyzing the uncertain possibility of catastrophic irreversibilities uses the concept of option value, due initially to Weisbrod (1964). This can be compared to an insurance premium concept. One (or society) is willing to pay an option value to preserve the species or avoid the catastrophe (Cicchetti and Freeman, 1971; Arrow and Fisher, 1974). Miller (1981) proposes that if the decision makers have a utility function for the species or resource, an option value can be derived as a shadow price from a "survival constraint" in an intertemporal optimization problem.

Ayres and Sandilya (1987) follow such an approach to consider the optimal behavior of nomadic herdsmen, concerned with survival in a fluctuating environment. The problems of nomadic herdsmen are exacerbated by a tendency to inertia in cattle stocks, which can lead to overgrazing in a drought, much as how capital stock inertia can exacerbate overfishing problems.[5] They recommend that following "pessimistic forecasts" will increase the chances of survival while lowering average grazing rates, in short a classic risk-rate-of-return trade-off.

But in fact things can be more complicated, making the measurement of option value more difficult. Cropper (1976) analyzes a model of pollution generation where there is a catastrophic level of pollution, P^*, which will drive utility and consumption to zero. This critical level fluctuates randomly according to a function $\Lambda(P)$ that gives the probability for any level of pollution, P, such that $P < P^*$, that is, that catastrophe has been averted. If $U(C)$ is the utility of consumption, $Z(C)$ is the pollution generation function, α is the exponential rate of decay of pollution, δ is the discount rate, and ψ is the negative of the marginal utility of pollution, then an optimal control solution includes the following equations:

$$\dot{\psi} = (\alpha + \delta)\psi - \Lambda'(P)U(C), \tag{10.1}$$

$$\dot{P} = Z(C) - \alpha P. \tag{10.2}$$

Analysis is rather straightforward if there is a single equilibrium point given by $\dot{\psi} = 0$, $\dot{P} = 0$. However, it is possible for there to be no equilibrium or multiple equilibria for this problem, both of which pose problems for potential planners. The multiple equilibria case arises if beyond a certain level of P, the probability of disaster increases at a decreasing rate. Such a case is depicted in Fig. 10.1. Cropper argues that the solution will depend on the initial point in this case.

In this case, equilibrium A is stable with relatively low levels of both pollution and consumption, whereas equilibrium B is an unstable focus tending to a limit cycle around higher levels of pollution and consumption. This could also be interpreted in the risk-rate-of-return framework.

Cropper further shows that inserting pollution *directly* into the utility function along with consumption guarantees that an equilibrium will exist, but also allows for three equilibria to exist of the following form as depicted in Fig. 10.2.

Now A and C are stable and the equilibrium, B, associated with intermediate levels of pollution and consumption, is an unstable focus tending to a limit cycle. In this case, the simple risk-rate-of-return trade-off breaks down. We are now back in the anomalous world of reswitching and situations involving ambiguous discount rate effects.

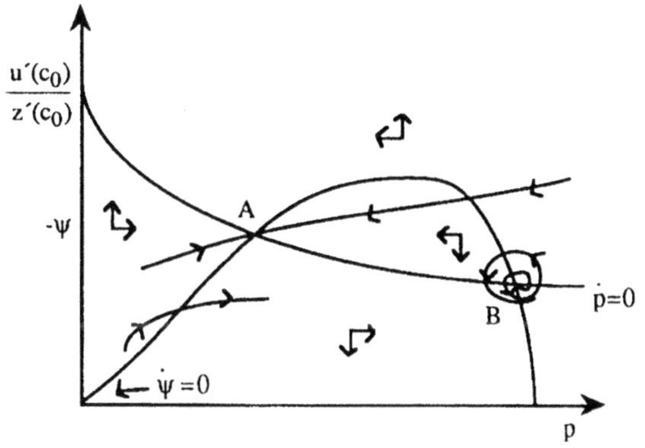

Fig. 10.1 Catastrophe pollution dynamics with two equilibria

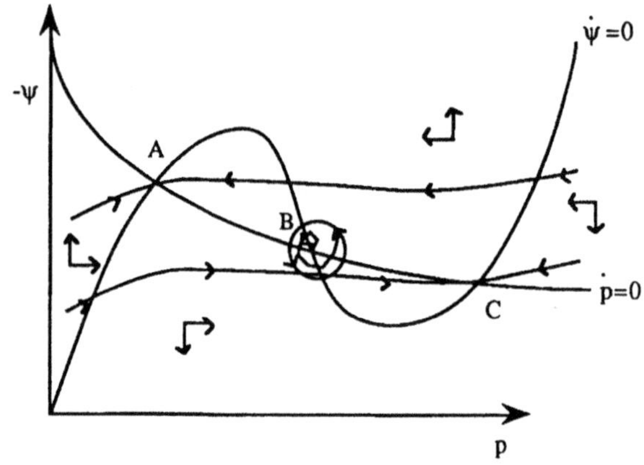

Fig. 10.2 Catastrophe pollution dynamics with three equilibria

Such paradoxical cases remind us that although in general caution is the best way to avoid catastrophe, sometimes caution should be thrown to the wind. In a Julian Simon–like manner more rapid growth may generate the technological changes which will avoid the possible catastrophe, the "solution to pollution" perhaps. But then the future possibilities of technological change remain one of the severest of uncertainties in the entire "limits to growth" debate.

10.4 The Entropy Argument

10.4.1 Entropy as the Ultimate Limit

Nicholas Georgescu-Roegen (1971) argues that the Second Law of Thermodynamics, also known as the Law of Entropy, represents the ultimate basis for scarcity in economic analysis and thus the ultimate limit to growth. The First Law of Thermodynamics is that of the conservation of matter and energy. The second has taken many forms. Ultimately derived from Carnot's study of the efficiency of steam engines, onc form asscrts that in a closed system available ordered energy tends to become unavailable disordered energy. Boltzmann (1886)[6] emphasized the universal aspect of this with the idea that entropy (disorder) increases throughout the universe. This has been interpreted as the basis of the unidirectionality of time (Prigogine and Stengers, 1984).

Open systems can temporarily resist this process by sucking low entropy from around themselves. Schrödinger (1944) argued that this is the essence of life. This is also the essence of many economic activities that create order out of chaos (i.e., the purification of metals from ores). Such processes can temporarily exist only by more rapidly increasing entropy around themselves. As argued by Georgescu-Roegen, the combination of the two laws of thermodynamics implies that "the economic process consists of a continuous transformation of low entropy into high entropy, that is, into *irrevocable waste* or, with a topical term, into pollution" (1971, p. 281). For him, this implies that the concepts of "production" and "consumption," common to both neoclassical and Marxian economics[7], are fundamentally flawed as bases for analysis.

Now the loophole of open systems was recognized by Georgescu-Roegen himself with respect to the earth and the sun. Although eventually the sun will entropically burn out, it is for a long time to come as an extraterrestrial source of low entropy. The scale of this source has led some observers (Gerelli, 1985) to ridicule Georgescu-Roegen's arguments and the limits to growth arguments more generally. Daly (1987) responds by arguing that on shorter time scales for which solar energy is constant, the law applies to the proximate resources of the purely terrestrial system.

Both Daly and Georgescu-Roegen (as well as many other ecologically oriented economists) have argued that such considerations should push us to a greater reliance on solar energy sources rather than our terrestrial stores of low entropy (e.g., fossil fuels). Thus, Georgescu-Roegen (1971, p. 303) hankers after an agriculture based on the use of draft animals rather than machines and on manure rather than chemical fertilizers.[8] The "substitution of capital for scarce natural resources" called for by Stiglitz (1979) and others will only serve to draw down more rapidly the ultimate scarce resources, terrestrial low entropy.

The severest critics of the limits to growth view deny the relevance of the entropy limit. Thus, Julian Simon (1981, p. 347) has argued, "[T]hose who view the relevant universe as unbounded view the second law of thermodynamics as irrelevant to the discussion," and places himself among those viewing knowledge and outer space as the keys to this unboundedness.

A more restrained view is that of Dasgupta and Heal (1979, Chap. 7). They recognize the validity of arguments regarding entropy. Placing this into the context of a CES production function with capital (K) and energy (R), they argue that allowing for the second law of thermodynamics can be done by assuming a minimum amount of energy $\mathrm{Rm}(Y)$, necessary for the production of any given level of output, Y.

Formally, if

$$Y = \left[\alpha_1 K^{(\sigma-1)/\sigma} + \alpha_2 R^{(\sigma-1)/\sigma} + (1-\alpha_1-\alpha_2)\right]^{\sigma/(\sigma-1)}, \quad 0 \leq \sigma < 1, \quad (10.3)$$

then as $K \to \infty$,

$$\mathrm{Rm}(Y) = \{[Y^{(\sigma-1)/\sigma}/\sigma_2] - [(1-\alpha_1-\alpha_2)/\alpha_2]\}^{\sigma/(\sigma-1)} > 0. \quad (10.4)$$

This implies an elasticity of substitution between capital and energy of less than one, a result that extends to the variable elasticity of substitution (VES) case. They conclude that this means that growth cannot occur without resource-augmenting technological change.

10.4.2 Entropy and Value

Given the usual neoclassical perspective of scarcity as the source of value, this suggests a possible role for entropy in the determination of value. Indeed Georgescu-Roegen has frequently been falsely identified as promoting an "entropy law of value" or perhaps an energy law of value.[9]

Such an idea has a long history, although generally pushed by noneconomists. Initiated by Helm (1887) and Winiarski (1900), who argued that gold was "socio-biological energy," it reached a more subtle elaboration with Ostwald (1908) who argued that the conversion factor from energy to value depends on the physical availability of specific forms of energy. Julius Davidson (1919) was the first economist to enter this fray by suggesting that the law of diminishing returns ultimately depends on the Law of Entropy. Harold J. Davis (1941) suggested that the utility of money might be "economic entropy," an argument criticized by Lisman (1949) on the grounds that it does not play the same role in the economy as does entropy in thermodynamics.

The critics have been legion. Samuelson (1972) dismisses such ideas as "crackpot."[10] Although sympathetic to the effort, Lotka highlighted a key problem, the variety of conversion factors necessary. Thus he noted (1925, p. 355), "The physical process is a typical case of 'trigger action', in which the ratio of energy set free to energy applied is subject to no restricting general law whatsoever (e.g., a touch of the finger upon a switch may set off tons of dynamite). In contrast with the case of thermodynamics conversion factors, the proportionality factor is here determined by the particular mechanism employed." This raises a problem associated with any "single-factor" theory of value, namely how to deal with its heterogeneity and also variations in its ratio to other things entering into production. For the Marxian labor theory of value, this latter point was encapsulated in the so-called transformation problem—why do the appropriate, single-factor value ratios not correspond to their respective price ratios?

Georgescu-Roegen (1971) further notes that social attitudes or utility can further complicate the problem of determining conversion factors. Thus, nobody wants the low-entropy poisonous mushroom, and some people value more highly the high-entropy beaten egg to the low-entropy raw egg. However, for Georgescu-Roegen this simply reflects the fact that value depends on utility, difficult as it is to measure, even while entropy remains the ultimate limit to growth.[11]

10.4.3 The Vision of the Steady-State Economy

The Club of Rome projected that zero population growth (ZPG) combined with zero economic growth (ZEG), the steady-state economy, could be sustained over a longer time horizon than any other. Fans of such a steady-state (or stationary state) economy[12] have included John Stuart Mill (1859), Kenneth Boulding (1966), and the especially eloquent Herman Daly (1977), many of whose arguments take on a moral-ethical cast,[13] although he relies on Georgescu-Roegen's argument regarding entropy as an ultimate limit to growth. Perrings (1986) shows that for a Sraffa-von Neumann system in a thermodynamically closed environment without innovations, the maximum rate of growth is zero.

But is this vision either ethically or ecologically sound? There is no clear answer to the first question. Those who argue that growth is necessary to improve the lives of those in poverty must respond to the arguments of Daly, citing Brazil, that growth may exacerbate poverty and that income redistribution is the solution to poverty. The critics might respond that *significant* income redistribution may require an oppressive state apparatus, as in China or Albania; although Sweden is a possible counter-example here, as well as to the argument that growth necessarily exacerbates poverty.

The answer to the second is more difficult, but it would appear that at best this vision is only provisionally possible. Ironically, it is Georgescu-Roegen (1979) who punches the sharpest hole from his deeper pessimism: The Law of Entropy *ultimately* rules out the steady state. In a von Neumann–Marxian model, simple reproduction can simply go on and on forever. But in the real world this involves the drawdown of low-entropy stores to a point where eventually it can no longer be sustained. Even in the Club of Rome scenario, natural resources are being depleted in the ZPG–ZEG case. They simply do not project beyond 2100, and the crash has not occurred by then for this case.

Despite his criticism of Daly, Georgescu-Roegen agrees with him that humanity should respond to the entropy problem by relying more on solar low entropy rather than terrestrial low entropy. But Georgescu-Roegen also sees change as inevitable and inextricably linked to the Law of Entropy. He agrees with Lotka's view of evolution as an "irreversible entropic process" and that the economy must perpetually "mutate" and "move into new realms." These are not the hallmarks of the steady state.

Thus we are thrown back upon the reality of economic evolution as the means of human evolution within the larger biophysical context. All equilibria are moving ones at best. The inevitable drawdown of low entropy becomes the spur to the morphogenesis of higher forms. Our economy can grow in quality but not necessarily in material quantity. As we approach bifurcations that lead to species extinction and the degradation of the biosphere, we seek the bifurcations of our technical knowledge and our social organization that will prevent a total collapse and allow for our survival and even for our improvement. Let us hope that as past crises have sometimes induced economic mutations, so our present ecologic crisis will lead us to mutate a new and better relationship with our environment and our world.

Notes

1. The potential for catastrophic impacts from these phenomena has been seriously questioned by some climatologists (Michaels, 1989a, b).
2. They argued that complicatedness is a virtue, following the arguments of their mentor, Jay Forrester (1971), and his love of "counterintuitive" results. Ironically "overaggregation," and

thus excessive simplicity of the main variables, was a source of considerable criticism of the model.

3. This influence was undoubtedly increased by the surges in both oil and food prices occurring in the 1972–1974 period. That those prices tended to decline in the 1980s certainly contributed to the fall of the Club of Rome's influence.
4. Such data tend to contradict the simple model of Hotelling (1931) that such prices should rise at the rate of interest in real terms.
5. Ironically, the word "capital" is etymologically derived from the Latin word for "cattle."
6. Boltzmann developed the measure of entropy as $\ln(N!/N_1!N_2!\ldots N_s!)$, where the N_is are distributions over possible states. This measure has been used in information theory and other fields.
7. Gowdy (1989) argues that Marxian economics can be reconciled with the law of entropy using Marx's distinction between "value" and "wealth" as emphasized by Perelman (1979).
8. Gowdy (1988) argues that Georgescu-Roegen apotheosizes the peasant agrarian economy as part of a Romanian version of the populist Narodnik philosophy.
9. See Burness, Cummings, Morris, and Paik (1980) and also the response by Daly (1987).
10. It could be argued that this is the pot calling the kettle black, given Samuelson's (1947) role as the most prolific translator of economic theory into equations of thermodynamics ever.
11. While accepting its validity as an "ultimate" constraint, Nordhaus (1988) argues that it is around $1/10^{12}$ less significant than technology and capital as a proximate constraint and thus irrelevant to any concept of value based on scarcity.
12. It is ironic that many advocates of growth have used the steady-state economy as an analytical fetish, that is, Marx (1893).
13. Schumacher (1973) also stresses this aspect, especially in his discussion of "Buddhist economics."

Chapter 11
How Nonlinear Dynamics Complicate the Issue of Global Warming

I sat upon the shore
Fishing, with the arid plain behind me
Shall I at least set my lands in order?
London Bridge is falling down falling down falling down
T.S. Eliot, "The Waste Land," 1922

11.1 Prologue on the Science of Global Warming

I have been involved with studies about global climate change since the early 1970s when I was working at the Institute for Environmental Studies at the University of Wisconsin-Madison on a project led by the late climatologist Reid Bryson.[1] This large multidisciplinary group was attempting to model the impacts on world food production of changes in global climate (there had been a big run-up in world grain prices that lasted for 2 years, due to drought in the USSR in 1972, the so-called "great world food crisis," now largely forgotten). Among the changes the group expected that I was working with was global cooling, and Bryson was among those who would later be labeled "global warming skeptics" (Bryson and Murray, 1977), as were some of his students, most prominently, Patrick J. Michaels (1992). This does not mean that I am one of those who wish to doubt the current science of global warming, and I am certainly not one of those who wish to ridicule science by pointing out how at an earlier time many were worried that we were in danger of experiencing global cooling, as some have done, only to have some of those concerned about global warming proceed to make themselves look foolish by denying that there was ever a time that anyone was worried about global cooling, except for a few "cranks" here or there.

Rather it is to remind the reader that things do change and that our knowledge is always limited, particularly in climatology (Schelling, 1992), even though we have made numerous advances in both our knowledge of data as well as of how the global climate system operates. For those who wish to dismiss as foolishness the concerns of the early 1970s regarding possible global cooling, two things should be kept in mind. One is that indeed average global temperature had been declining since reaching a peak in the mid-to-late 1930s, only to turn around and start rising again

J.B. Rosser, *Complex Evolutionary Dynamics in Urban-Regional and Ecologic-Economic Systems*, DOI 10.1007/978-1-4419-8828-7_11,

in the mid-1970s. The other was that scientific knowledge was less solid then, and many were concerned about a conflict between the cooling effect of rising particulate/aerosol emissions and the warming effect of rising carbon dioxide emissions and concentrations.

Among those seeing the outcome of this as uncertain was the late Stephen H. Schneider (Schneider and Rasool, 1971). Many have made fun of his uncertainty at that time, but in that year there was nearly an even balance of papers in the leading climatology journals between warning of global cooling versus warning of global warming. It was only later with improved data and methodology that the tide turned toward the idea that global warming was the greater danger, with Schneider changing his mind even prior to the appearance of actual global warming (Schneider, 1975). From the late 1970s on, the vast majority of papers published in the leading scientific journals have supported the idea that we face a highly likely trend to global warming, largely driven by anthropogenic causes, mostly due to increased emissions of carbon dioxide as well as certain other greenhouse gases (GHGs), notably methane.[2]

For the rest of this chapter, I shall be proceeding on the assumption that the mass of scientific evidence, which supports that we are in for a period of global warming largely due to human activity, is correct. Indeed, a major concern will be that the dangers of an upside error with globally exploding temperatures may be higher than has been estimated, even as the chance of a surprise move in the other direction might be greater as well, with the positive feedbacks inherent in nonlinear systems lying at the source of these concerns. The lesson I learned from Reid Bryson regarding the nonlinear and chaotic nature of the global climate system has stuck, even as I maintain respect for the more serious of those who get labeled "climate skeptics." Let me note two categories of these, given that there is now nearly no serious scientist who maintains that there has been no global warming at all during the past three and a half decades.

While that last statement is correct, there certainly were some skeptics who held out on the basic question for quite a long time. Among the most prominent and persistent of those was Fred Singer, the father of the US weather satellite program, and for a long time there was a disjuncture between temperature readings from the ground and those from space satellites, which appeared not to find any or much global warming. This was the basis of Singer's skepticism, although eventually the satellite data would be reinterpreted and found to support warming, even as some disjuncture persists.[3] However, as the data became unequivocal that global warming was indeed happening, Singer shifted to arguing that it was inevitable and due largely to natural causes, with humans having little ability to stop it (Singer and Avery, 2007).

A larger group is represented by the already mentioned Michaels (Michaels and Balling, 2009). For some time, Michaels has argued (along with Schneider, 1975) that to the extent warming was happening, it would be concentrated in the Arctic regions at night during winter months, and indeed we have seen the warming most prominently in the Arctic, with the noticeable shrinking of the Arctic ice cap, perhaps the most dramatic evidence of global warming available. However, Michaels has argued that of the variety of projections put forward in the intergovernmental panel on climate change (IPCC) reports (Stern, 2006; IPCC,2007), we are more likely to see one nearer the lower end of the spectrum. Very broadly he observes that what we have seen since 1975 has been quite close to a straight-line increase in global temperature and that despite all the complicated models that have been studied, such an outcome is what one would expect from the most prominent of aggregate trends and relations: that on the one hand carbon dioxide concentrations are rising exponentially, while on the other hand the main direct relation between CO_2 concentrations and global temperature is a logarithmic one (Augustsson and Ramanathan, 1977; Mitchell, 1983). The rough outcome of the combination of this trend and this effect is a straight-line increase, as we have been observing since 1975 approximately.

At this point, people begin debating the costs and benefits of doing anything about these trends, with some suggesting that even if it is happening, we should not work to combat it by reducing emissions but by some sort of adaptive policies (Lomborg, 2001, 2004),[4] including possibly geoengineering (Levitt and Dubner, 2009). I am not going to give a bottom line on either the scientific debate or this issue, with there certainly being many who think that it is worthwhile doing something about CO_2 emissions in a serious way (Cline, 1992; Nordhaus and Boyer, 2000; Stern, 2006, 2008, 2010), although there have been numerous debates over what is the best policy tool or set of policy tools to achieve this outcome (often an argument over carbon taxes versus "cap and trade" emissions permits tied to a quantity control). Rather, I shall consider the problems associated with the greater uncertainties for the whole issue arising from the nonlinearities and complexities of dynamics in the system.

In the meantime, whatever has been advocated, we live in a world since the Copenhagen summit of 2009 in which there is no longer any international agreement on doing anything globally in a coordinated way, for better or for worse, even as there continue to be efforts in many countries at action, many, but not all, of these initiated by the efforts arising from the Kyoto Accords of 1997 that are set to expire in 2012. This does not bode well, if indeed some of the more unpleasant possible scenarios come to pass.

11.2 Could a Combined Global Climate–Economic System Be Chaotic?

It has been widely believed since the dramatic model of Lorenz (1963) that the global climatic system is chaotic to some degree. Indeed, this has been viewed as consistent with the generally accepted inability of even the most sophisticated of meteorological models to forecast with any reliability beyond a week or so into the future. The flapping butterflies are just too numerous and insistent, messing things up, even if they are not causing hurricanes or tornadoes in Texas from their activities in Brazil as Lorenz (1993) once put it.[5] Even so, it has been thought possible to make more general forecasts of longer-term averages for global climate, in contrast with the shorter-term forecasting problems faced by meteorologists.

However, even if the climatic system is not chaotic in and of itself, interaction between it and the human economic system may lead to chaotic dynamics within a combined climate–economic system at the global level. This was demonstrated by Chen (1997), whose model we shall now consider. It is relatively simple and stylized, yet it shows clearly that the interactions between the systems need to be carefully considered. While there have been efforts to do this in many of the succeeding studies, it remains the case that these mutual feedbacks have not been fully modeled as thoroughly as they should be.

The basic climate model is linear in the relation between global average temperature and global manufacturing output at time t, based on a model due to Henderson-Sellers and McGuffie (1987). If c is positive but less than one, T_{n} is "normal" global mean temperature, $g > 0$, and $X_{\mathrm{m}t}$ is global manufacturing output in time t, then this basic relationship is given in difference equation format by

$$T_{t+1} = (1 - c)(T_t - T_{\mathrm{n}}) + T_{\mathrm{n}} + gX_{\mathrm{m}t}. \tag{11.1}$$

The economic system is posited as having two sectors, an agricultural one in addition to the manufacturing one, m, with the agricultural one, a, susceptible to the condition of the state of the global climate. We thus have the basic setup for how this interacting system works: manufacturing impacts climate, which in turn then impacts agriculture. It is assumed that the economic model proceeds by optimizing on a global CES utility function of the consumption, C of a and m. The elasticity of substitution is $\sigma = 1/(1 - \rho) < 1$. With $C_{\mathrm{i}t} = X_{\mathrm{i}t}$, utility is given by

$$U(C_{\mathrm{a}t}, C_{\mathrm{m}t}) = (C^{\rho}{}_{\mathrm{a}t} + C^{\rho}{}_{\mathrm{m}t})^{1/\rho}. \tag{11.2}$$

Sectoral outputs are linear in labor, $l_{\mathrm{i}t}$, which sum to one. Agricultural output is a quadratic function of global temperature, which provides the nonlinearity in the system. With p being the market clearing relative price, the rest of the economic system is given by

$$X_{\mathrm{a}t} = (-\alpha T^2{}_t + \beta T_t + 1)l_{\mathrm{a}t}, \tag{11.3}$$

$$X_{\mathrm{m}t} = bl_{\mathrm{m}t}, \tag{11.4}$$

$$p_t = (-\alpha T^2{}_t + \beta T_t + 1)/b. \tag{11.5}$$

All of this implies an equilibrium law of motion of global temperature given by

$$T_{t+1} = (1 - c)T_t + g[(bp^{1-\sigma}{}_t)/(1 + p^{1-\sigma}{}_t)]. \tag{11.6}$$

Chen simulates this model for parameter values of $\sigma = 0.5, \alpha = 8, \beta = 7, b = 1$, and $g = 0.6$, with c being the crucial control parameter that gets varied for different runs, the adjustment parameter for global temperature. For $c \in (0.233, 1)$, the system converges on a steady state. However, as c is lowered below 0.233, period-doubling bifurcations appear, with the system reaching an aperiodic chaotic state at $c = 0.209$, with the sensitive dependence on initial conditions, or the "butterfly effect," holding.

We note that this is a bounded condition. Therefore, it is not necessarily something that implies some terrible outcome in terms of the quality of life of people living within it. However, it is clear that it arises due to the interaction between the climatic and economic systems, with neither being chaotic on its own. This is a deep reminder that nonlinearities anywhere in the overall system can generate complexities for the dynamics of the entire system that would not otherwise occur.[6]

11.3 Competing IAM Models

In considering the possible impacts of global warming, integrated assessment models (IAMs) have been used.[7] In more recent discussions, two broad versions of these have played particularly prominent roles, with both of these having undergone substantial development and evolution over time. The older and more widely cited of the two has been the Dynamic Integrated model of Climate and Energy (DICE), developed out of an older set of energy production models under the direction of William Nordhaus (1994). A parallel version of DICE developed somewhat later has been the Regional Integrated model of Climate and Energy (RICE), first reported in Nordhaus and Yang (1996). Closely linked 1999 versions of these related models are presented in detail in Nordhaus and Boyer (2000) known as DICE-RICE-99, with further subsequent development of these continuing (Nordhaus, 2007).

An idea of what is involved with these can be seen by considering the list of variables that these models have in them, either exogenously or endogenously. For RICE-99and DICE-99, the following are the variables according to Appendix A of Nordhaus and Boyer (2000). Exogenous variables or parameters are population, social time preference discount factor, social time discount rate, growth rate of social time preference rate,[8] initial social time preference discount rate, growth rate of population, initial population growth rate, rate of decline of population growth rate, initial population, total factor productivity, elasticity of output with respect to capital, elasticity of output with respect to carbon energy, ratio of carbon energy to industrial carbon emissions, growth rate of the latter variable, initial growth rate of variable before last, rate of decline of previous variable, initial ratio of carbon energy to industrial carbon emissions, growth rate of total factor productivity, initial productivity growth rate, rate of decline of initial productivity growth rate, industrial carbon emissions permits, rate of depreciation of capital stock, initial capital stock, regional energy services markup, parameters of long-run industrial emissions supply curve, point of diminishing returns in carbon extraction, parameters of carbon transition matrix, land-use carbon emissions, initial land-use carbon emissions, rate of decline of land-use emissions, initial atmospheric concentration of CO_2, initial concentration of CO_2 in upper oceans/biosphere, initial concentration of CO_2

in deep oceans, increase in radiative forcing due to doubling of CO_2 concentrations from preindustrial levels, preindustrial CO_2 concentration, increase in radiative forcing over preindustrial levels due to exogenous anthropogenic causes, temperature dynamics parameters, climate sensitive or equilibrium increase in temperature due to CO_2 concentration doubling, initial atmospheric temperature, initial ocean temperature, and parameters of damage function. In addition, specific to the DICE model are coefficient on control rate in abatement cost function, exponent on control rate in abatement cost function, initial and subsequent rates of decline of these two variables, base-case ratio of industrial emissions to output and initial and subsequent rates of decline of such emissions and parameters determining those rates of decline, and initial value of base case.

Endogenous variables of the RICE-99 models are welfare, utility during period *t*, per capita consumption, output, climate-change damage factor on gross output, capital stock, carbon-energy services from carbon fuels, cost of carbon energy, industrial CO_2 emissions, industrial emission permit price [could be treated exogenously], consumption, investment, industrial emissions permit price in a given trading bloc, cost of extraction of industrial emissions, world industrial carbon emissions, atmospheric CO_2 concentration, world total CO_2 emissions, upper oceans/biosphere CO_2 concentration, lower oceans CO_2 concentration, radiative forcing increase over preindustrial level, atmospheric temperature increase over 1900 level, lower ocean temperature increase over 1900 level, climate damage function as fraction of net output, and in addition specific to the DICE-99 model, the industrial control rate. Clearly, this model is far more complicated than the simple one that can generate chaotic dynamics presented in the previous section, and it combines a three-level model of global climate (atmosphere, upper ocean, lower ocean) with an economic model.

While this is a very complicated model, it is not clear that it is one that fits into the definition of being "complex." Most relationships in it are linear, although not all are. Many have observed that it is a model that does not generate large changes or possess noticeable threshold effects. While it is consistent with accepted climate science, it is also very conventionally neoclassical in its economics, essentially a model that provides marginal answers to marginal questions, a model that fits well into a world in which global temperature is likely to gradually increase with a gradual increase in world output and industrial emissions of CO_2, with only gradual effects on the world at large. It is not surprising that such a model tends to be used to support marginal and relatively modest policy efforts to deal with global warming, with Nordhaus having long been associated with favoring a global carbon tax of relatively modest proportions.[9]

While this last paragraph may reek of dismissiveness, this model is widely respected and has been probably the most widely used IAM, or variations on it, in the world, used even by most of the groups issuing the various IPCC reports. It is formidable and respectable. Also, while Nordhaus himself (2007, p. 147) has said that "...models such as [DICE] have limited utility in looking at the potential for catastrophic event," it has been shown that by altering the nature of its damage function and its climate sensitivity function, one can generate catastrophic outcomes from an essentially minor variation on the DICE model (Ackerman, Stanton, and Bueno, 2010).[10]

Probably the most prominent rival to the RICE–DICE approach has been the PAGE modeling approach due to Hope (2006), with a version of this being used for the Stern Review (Stern, 2006), which has received much publicity. It is arguably both more complicated and more complex than the DICE model, with efforts to estimate critical thresholds for a variety of effects in it. The model then provides as part of its output, estimates of probabilities of going across these critical thresholds for each given possible increase in future global temperature. This is part of why the Stern Review led to somewhat more dramatic conclusions regarding the dangers of global warming, although both Nordhaus (2007) and Weitzman (2007) argue that the most important reason for the high benefit–cost ratios for strong action against global warming produced by Stern is the excessively low discount rates used in the analysis, a matter taken up in more detail below.

However, we note that the Stern report does recognize that for much of the world, the initial impact of increased global warming may well be on the whole favorable, largely due to reduced winter heating bills and reduced deaths due to hypothermia in winter. As some global warming skeptics, or at least critics of doing much about global warming, argue, we see a tendency for net migration in many parts of the world, including the United States, to go from colder regions to warmer ones, a pattern that cannot simply be dismissed as irrelevant to this discussion.

In any case, a sampling of what the Stern Review has to offer, and it must be noted that much of it draws on the most recent of IPCC reports prior to it, is given by the mean expected effects it forecasts as resulting from a 5°C increase in average global temperature, an increase in the upper range of the band possibly considered in the IPCC reports (Stern. table 3.1, pp. 66–67). Thus, such a temperature increase would lead to "possible disappearance of large glaciers in Himalayas, affecting one-quarter of China's population and hundreds of millions in India." Also, there would be "continued increase in ocean acidity seriously disrupting marine ecosystems and possibly fish stocks." Although lower rates of temperature increase would improve health due to the declines of hypothermia deaths, at a 5°C increase in temperature, there would be more than 3 million dying of malnutrition and over 80 million dying of malaria. Another effect would be "sea level rise threatens small islands, low-lying coastal areas (Florida) and major world cities such as New York, London, and Tokyo." At only a 4°C increase, as many as 300 million people might be affected by coastal flooding, with Bangladesh particularly hard hit. Also, there would be loss of up to half of the Arctic tundra, and half of the world's nature preserves failing to fulfill their objectives. Extinction rates of species might rise from 15 to 70%. There might also be collapses of the Atlantic thermohaline circulation, the Greenland and West Antarctic ice sheets, and abrupt changes in atmospheric circulation, possibly damaging the monsoons. Finally, at temperature increases above 5°C, destabilizing positive feedbacks could kick in, with the most dramatic associated with massive releases of the GHG methane stored in the permafrost of high-latitude regions (Harvey and Huang, 1995).

Finally, we note that all the IAMs agree that the most damaging effects will be on[11] poorer countries nearer the equator, while some higher-income countries such as Canada and the Scandinavian ones would generally gain from global warming. The most threatened countries would be the small, low-lying island states, such as the Seychelles Islands in the Indian Ocean, whose prime minister engaged in dramatic demonstrations at the 2009 Copenhagen conference to no avail. Some of these states could disappear entirely due to rising sea levels. Of the larger of the poorer states, the one most in danger of major severe impacts would be Bangladesh, with even the more intermediate ranges of forecast temperature increases leading to GDP declines ranging from 5 to 20% due largely to coastal flooding.

11.4 The Discounting Issue Again

In Chapters 8 and 9, the role of the discount rate was discussed, with potential complications such as the possibility of reswitching noted when future streams of benefits and costs become complicated. In these situations, ambiguity may arise regarding which alternatives will be favored as the time profiles of the alternatives themselves become essentially ambiguous. In the case of the global warming issue, however serious one thinks it is or whichever model or projection of future climate or costs and benefits of doing something about it is, the time profile at least is not ambiguous. In the near term, global warming may actually be beneficial on the whole, especially in higher-latitude countries. However, as time passes and temperature continues to rise, this changes to a net negative situation, with this even spreading to the highest-latitude countries if the temperature rises high enough. Thus, action to restrain global warming may have net costs in the near term but net benefits as one moves further into the future, just as with conventional investment projects. Thus, the lower the discount rate that one uses in the analysis, the stronger the case for engaging in action to offset global warming sooner and more vigorously. Given the long time horizons involved in many analyses, with the many IAMs running out at least 300 years in the future, the sensitivity of current estimates of conventional benefit–cost ratios become even more sensitive to the choice of discount rates used in the analysis.

In their critique of the Stern Review (2006), the matter of the choice of discount rate plays a central role, with both Nordhaus (2007) and Weitzman (2007, 2009) coming down hard and critically on the Stern Review for its discount rate choice. Therefore, let us reconsider the issues involved in the choice of discount rate or rates to be used in this analysis, given the sensitivity of the results to this important parameter. A very old debate has involved whether a social discount rate should equal some marginal rate of return on capital investment in the economy on opportunity cost/efficiency grounds, or whether due to incomplete markets (especially intertemporally) and various externalities, the discount rate should reflect some sort of social rate-of-time preference that may have little to do with such a measure of the marginal returns to capital. Generally, given the long time horizons involved in the global warming debate, the latter has generally been favored. The standard approach has been to use the Ramsey (1928) equation, namely,

$$r = \delta + \eta g, \tag{11.7}$$

where r is the discount rate, δ is a pure rate of social time preference, g is the per capita real growth rate of the economy, and η is the elasticity of marginal utility of income or, equivalently according to standard theory, the coefficient of relative risk aversion. That the pure rate of social time preference should be in here is pretty straightforward (even if what it should be is not at all so), but the other term may be less obvious. The argument is that if the economy is growing and will continue to grow (which the more apocalyptic of global warming worriers doubt), then there is less point in current generations sacrificing for the benefit of these future generations that will be better off than we are, with η modifying this somewhat, although some find the idea of the marginal utility of income to be a meaningless concept. In any case, this is a standard formulation, and Weitzman (2009) rather jocularly notes that some assume a "triple two" formulation of this, wherein each of these parameters is a 2% for δ and g, and just plain 2 for η, which would generate an r of 6%. This contrasts with the 1.4% used by Stern, which comes from assuming $\delta = 0.1, g = 1.3$, and $\eta = 1$, all of which both Weitzman and Nordhaus argue to be too low. In any case, this low discount rate assumed by Stern plays very significantly into his argument for strong action now against global warming.

Much of the focus of the debate is on the appropriate choice for δ. Stern invokes Frank Ramsey himself, along with a long line of subsequent distinguished economists and moral philosophers (Harrod, 1948; Broome, 1994), who argue that it should equal zero, that there is no moral justification for treating future generations as being less worthy than current ones.[12] Stern does allow that one must account for the possibility of the future extinction of the human species due to some extreme event such as nuclear war or a major asteroid strike on earth, which is the reason he uses a δ just barely above zero at 0.1.

While Nordhaus is not willing to go along with such arguments, Weitzman is more willing to allow for the possibility and indeed assumes a zero pure rate of time preference rate in his more recent study of fat tails (Weitzman, 2010). However, in Weitzman (2009), even with a zero δ, one can still easily end up with an $r = 6\%$, with not unreasonable values of the other parameters, such as $g = 2\%$ and $\eta = 3$. What begins to stick out is the degree of uncertainty involved in estimating these numbers. Even if we can agree on the deeply normative issue of the pure rate of social time preference, we do not know what future growth rates will be (the DICE model makes assumptions about these matters), and estimates of η are also widely varying. There is even the odd matter, not discussed by any of these, that the future growth rates may depend on which r society selects in effect, with an ineffective action in the face of more severe global warming due to an overly high g, which could in fact itself help trigger future lower growth.

Weitzman (2009) notes this potential variability of these latter two parameters and alters the Ramsey equation to find a risk-free discount rate, r^{f}, accordingly under the assumption that the future growth rate varies according to a normal distribution with mean of μ and variance of σ^2. This is then given by

$$r^f = \delta + \eta g - \frac{1}{2}\eta^2 g^2. \tag{11.8}$$

Unsurprisingly, worrying about possible future variability of the growth rate lowers the social discount rate somewhat, thus providing a measure of increased insurance for the future generations. Weitzman then proceeds to add further considerations and variations to this formulation, bringing in returns on equity in the abstract and other issues, leading to even more complicated formulations of what r should be. However, for what he considers to be reasonable formulations of this, including formulations that allow for r to decline over time into the future along Green Golden Rule lines, assuming reasonable parameters often lead to r being in the neighborhood of 6%, although there are some possibilities of it being substantially lower.

However, in the end Weitzman eventually views all of this as a sideshow to the real problem, which is the deeper uncertainties and nonlinearities that make for non-Gaussian distributions of outcomes likely, thereby throwing much of the underpinnings of these calculations out the window. Weitzman suggests that in the end, Stern may be "right but for the wrong reasons."

11.5 Positive Feedbacks, Fat Tails, and Fundamental Uncertainty

In more recent studies, Weitzman (2009, 2010) shifts his focus away from the matter of discount rates to the matter of risk and uncertainty regarding the future path of global temperature within the complex nonlinear dynamical system that combines climate, economy, and ecology. While there are some moderating effects such as the logarithmic direct relationship between CO_2 concentrations and global temperature, there are many nonlinear relationships in which there are positive feedback effects that can potentially get out of hand.[13] This argument suffuses the Stern Review with its various estimates of possible thresholds beyond which one or another effect might run out of control. We have noted in particular the matter of possible methane releases from tundra permafrost. However, there are others, with another generally left out of most of the IAMs discussed here being changes in albedo or reflectivity of the earth's surface with changes in ice and snow cover. As it gets warmer, and glaciers and ice caps melt, there is less reflection of sunlight back into space, thus further increasing warming.

We note that this effect can go in reverse as well. Indeed, it should be kept in mind that the possibility of global cooling and the scary stories about ice ages in the early 1970s were partly driven by exactly these concerns on the part of some climatologists (Bryson and Murray, 1977). Indeed, there is strong geological evidence to prove that the movements in and out of ice ages, particularly in terms of the basic temperature shifts, were quite rapid in geological time terms, occurring in periods possibly as short as 100 years (Bryson, 1974). It may well be that these changes were due to fully exogenous factors such as changes in solar flux, and there is no way to know for certain. But the known existence of such positive feedbacks as the albedo effect and the methane effect and others suggests the clear possibility that once a temperature change is initiated, strong positive feedback effects can kick in to make it go much further than it would otherwise without these effects operating. The geological record is certainly consistent with such a view. In any case, this suggests that if there are greater chances of extreme warming coming up, there may also be greater chances of the system going the other way as well, which would justify the simultaneous worry about both of these extreme outcomes that many have found silly at different times.

Weitzman (2010) performs a useful service to consider the implications of the probability distributions of future global temperatures possessing "fat tails," or positive leptokurtotic fourth moments, although he only focuses on upside chances of such outcomes rather than downside ones, which is not unreasonable given the current upward trend of average global temperatures, even if so far that trend has been largely linear. He assumes that a median expected outcome is an increase in average global temperature of 3°C. Then he considers three different distributions for possible outcomes above this median outcome: one based on a normal distribution, one based on a lognormal distribution, and one based on a Pareto distribution. The first of these does not exhibit fat tails, but the latter two do, with the Pareto distribution doing so more dramatically than the lognormal distribution.

Weitzman estimates the cumulative probability distributions for three specific formulations of these distributions (Weitzman, 2009) and finds dramatic differences. While the Stern Review found dangerous effects and serious probabilities of moving across thresholds when global temperatures rise by more than 6°C, few studies go much beyond this. However, Weitzman considers the probabilities of substantially worse and more catastrophic increases, up to 12 and even 18°C. According to Sherwood and Huber (2010), the former would involve a world where half the population would be subjected on average once a year to heat stress that would kill within 6 h of exposure, a situation that would "present an extreme threat to human civilization as we know it," if not necessarily to the survival of the human species itself (Weitzman, 2010, p. 8). However, the 18°C increase would be so extreme that it would threaten the survival of the human species and possibly more than that, a possible "global death temperature."

For his particular equations, the normal distribution generates a probability of reaching a 12°C increase of a miniscule 3×10^{-10} and an essentially infinitesimal probability of reaching the ultra-catastrophic increase of an even deadlier 20°C of 4×10^{-32}. The lognormal exhibits higher probabilities than these, but still ones that are very low: 2×10^{-4} for a 12°C increase and a 6×10^{-7} probability of the 20°C increase. However, for the Pareto distribution that we saw in Chapter 7, the probability of a 12°C increase is at 0.008 and of a 20°C increase is 0.002. Certainly these are small probabilities, less than 1%, but not all that much less than 1%. They are conceivable, not at the distinctly remote levels associated with the normal and lognormal distribution. For Weitzman, the problem becomes this: What to do about these small probabilities of very bad outcomes? For this, there is no simple answer, although concerns regarding the precautionary principle suggest that some thoughts should be given to such severe dangers.

While there is no definite answer, there have been vigorous attempts recently to deal with this problem of fat tails. It is a problem in the insurance industry where catastrophic insurance has become a big business (Posner, 2004). Increasingly it has also become a focus in financial economics, even though most textbooks, even many advanced ones (Cochrane, 2001), continue to present all their models and tools assuming that underlying distributions are Gaussian, when in fact it is a known and stylized fact that financial market returns exhibit fat tails.[14] Even though the official textbooks have tended to ignore this phenomenon, practitioners in the financial and insurance markets have not done so at all. A statistical tool that has come to be widely used in these fields has been that of the *copula*, or multivariate joint distributions derived from sets of marginal uniform distributions on the unit interval. Copulas do provide a way of modeling dependence across distributions that will exhibit kurtosis or fat tails (Joe, 1997; Nelson, 1999; Embrechts, McNeil, and Straumann, 2002; Genest and Favre, 2007).[15] There are several families of copulas, and it is a matter of judgment of which is most appropriate to use in which kind of situation. A particular danger is if participants in a market herd on a particular formulation and use it to the point that it breaks down in application and is unable to model dynamics changed by the use of it. It is widely believed that this happened on a global scale due to the popularity among issuers of high-level credit-default obligations (CDOs) of the bivariate Gaussian normal copula found able to generate a pricing formula for them, due to David Li (2001).[16] All of this is a warning that having a tool does not mean that it will work well, although some insurance companies have reportedly used this tool for pricing catastrophic insurance for coastal real estate threatened by the possibility of flooding due to global warming.

At this point, we finally must confront the deeper problem, the one first understood simultaneously in 1921 by Frank Knight (1921) and John Maynard Keynes (1921), namely, the distinction between risk and uncertainty. The former is measurable and knowable by some method or another, whereas the latter is not, either because sufficient data cannot be found or observed or perhaps more profoundly because there is in fact not a probability distribution to know at all.[17] Thus, to follow the famous line of Donald Rumsfeld, risk is the known unknown, whereas uncertainty is the unknown unknown. Non-Gaussian distributions with fat tails may not be as amenable to easy modeling as the standard Gaussian ones usually assumed in much of econometrics. But at least these are in principle measurable and knowable probability distributions. They are not associated with true uncertainty, which, despite various efforts, we still do not fundamentally know how to handle. Whether or not the problem of global warming is a matter of risk, if complicated risk involving fat tails arising from complex nonlinear dynamics as suggested by Weitzman, or is indeed such a complicated system that we really cannot determine the true probability distribution or even know if one exists, is I believe at this point itself unknown. It may be that we must accept that in this matter we are facing true uncertainty of the Knightian–Keynesian variety.

Nassim Taleb (2010) has characterized this general issue as being one of "grey swans" versus "black swans." Grey swans represent situations or events that exhibit power laws or fat tails, but are nevertheless potentially knowable by use of statistical methods. Black swans are truly unexpected and unforeseeable events, the unknown unknowns. Taleb has argued that the financial crash of 2008 was a grey swan that anyone intelligent should have seen coming. However, the apparently out-of-the blue crash on October 19, 1987, the single largest decline of the US stock market in percentage terms in its history, was a black swan. Events such as the attack on the Twin Towers on 9/11/01 would be another example of such a black swan, and he argues that such events can prove to be among the most important that happen. It may be that a runaway global warming disaster would not really be such a true black swan, because we can foresee its possibility, even if we think that it is a very low-probability event. But, it would be a very important event, and avoiding it may be very important, even if current politicians and policymakers have been unable to overcome their inertia and the power of interest groups to fashion much in the way of coordinated global action to deal with this problem.

In the face of such deep threats and difficulties and failures of inaction, it may be that we need to adopt a philosophical attitude until we are able to counteract such threats, a philosophical attitude that prepares us for the worst by recognizing what we have is good. In that regard, I shall close this chapter by quoting from Taleb (2010, p. 298) regarding this very issue of how to deal with the threat of such black swans.

> Imagine a speck of dust next to a planet a billion times the size of the earth. The speck of dust represents the odds in favor of your being born; the huge planet would be the odds against it. So stop sweating the small stuff. Don't be like the ingrate who got a castle as a present and worried about the mildew in the bathroom. Stop looking the gift horse in the mouth – remember that you are a Black Swan.[18]

Notes

1. Among other things that I learned from the polymathic Bryson was about chaos theory, which at that time was not yet being called that. However, he made me aware of the model of climatic change due to Edward Lorenz (1963), the father of the "butterfly effect," and this affected me quite profoundly in my intellectual development, quite possibly being the seed for not only this book but its two predecessors as well.
2. This does not mean that scientists do not recognize that this trend could be offset by some exogenous change of natural conditions, such as a massive outbreak of volcanic eruptions or a reduction of solar radiance. However, changes in such exogenous events have been largely ruled out as sources of the global warming that has been observed since 1975, despite the ongoing arguments by some.
3. One issue has long been the "urban heat effect," that over time certain recording stations have gone from being in rural areas to having urban settings built around them, and it is well known that cities are hotter than rural areas. However, the scientists behind the various Intergovernmental Panel on Climate Change (IPCC, 2007) reports made adjustments for this trend a long time ago.

4. As of August 30, 2010, rumors on the Internet report that Lomborg may have changed his mind substantially to support far greater expenditures on slowing CO2 emissions than he previously supported.
5. Many think that Lorenz made this remark in his original 1963 paper, but one finds no reference there to a "butterfly effect," much less the less colorful term "sensitive dependence on initial conditions," which he reported as an example of in that seminal paper. He first came up with this famous example in a 1972 speech to a group of meteorologists, recounted in Lorenz (1993). He noted that this example really drew on an older set of beliefs among meteorologists symbolized by the remark that someone sneezing in Korea could set off snowstorms in New York, which were prevalent in that discipline well before the conscious application of chaos theory to meteorology or climatology. See Rosser (2009d) for further discussion.
6. Another fairly simple model with nonlinearities is due to Greiner and Semmler (2005), which shows multiple equilibria, separated by Skiba points.
7. Rosser (2010a) has argued that it is only in studying the global system that we see full use of transdisciplinary perspectives cutting across physics, biology, and economics.
8. As this growth rate may be negative, this allows for "Green Golden Rule" sorts of intertemporal discounting that is supposed to avoid allowing either present people exploiting future people or vice versa.
9. Obviously an enormously important issue in terms of what to do or not do involves the costs of various actions. This matter will not be delved into in this work, with those cautioning against excessive action such as Lomborg invoking fears of very high costs of abatement, while others are more optimistic, even invoking "win-win" scenarios where strong policy induces technological change that reduces the costs of abatement. There are also many debates over alternatives to fossil fuels, with many pushing wind and solar alternatives, although van Kooten (2004) seriously questions their serious viability for substantially replacing coal and nuclear for large-scale electricity production. De Canio (2003) provides a broader critique of the economic models used.
10. Two alternative IAMs we shall not discuss in much detail are due to Mendelsohn, Morrison, Schlesinger, and Andronova (1998) who focus more on agriculture and related sectors and find relatively weak damages compared to DICE, and Tol (2002) who considers more markets and also models disease effects while finding net benefits to warming in the near term for many higher-income countries compared to DICE. The origin of all of these IAMs is the work of Cline (1992). Using a game theory approach, Dutta and Radner (2009) argue that a constant flow of carbon emissions is optimal.
11. Aside from arguments about discount rates or ethical theories, more technical details of the Stern Review have been criticized by Tol and Yohe (2006), Mendelsohn (2006), Seo (2007), Byatt, Castles, Goklany, Henderson, Lawson, McKitrick, Morris, Peacock, Robinson, and Skidelsky (2006), and Carter, de Freitas, Goklany, Holland, and Lindzen (2006).
12. A more radical critique that may lead to a zero discount rate is due to Marx, who saw such discount rates as tied to rates of surplus value and thus exploitation. While the image of Marx has long been that he was an anti-environmentalist, largely based on his known dislike of Malthus, Burkett (1999) and Foster (2000) offer a different view based on Marx's study of the organic chemist Justus von Liebig and his concerns about soil depletion within broader ecosystems.
13. See Hallegatte, Hourcade, and Dumas (2007) for a related study.
14. Given the prestige of his 2001 *Asset Pricing*, Cochrane's recent comments on the financial crisis are somewhat bizarre. He has publicly declared that as a student of Eugene Fama (and his son-in-law as well), he, Cochrane, and his cohort, all knew about fat tails from Fama, who was himself a student originally of Mandelbrot (1963), who was the first to emphasize that financial asset returns follow power law distributions such as the Pareto. Given these statements, it is all the more strange that he completely ignores this stylized fact in his famous and studied book.
15. The foundational theorem for understanding and constructing copulas is due to Sklar (1959).

16. See Brigo, Pallavicini, and Torresetti (2010) for a discussion of how this developed. Despite this disaster, copulas continue to be the workhouse for many financial traders and insurance actuaries attempting to manage extreme events.
17. See Rosser (2001b) for further discussion of this issue.
18. A broader perspective of this involving planets is the absence so far of any signals indicating life on other planets by the Search for Extra-Terrestial Intelligence (SETI) that has been going on for decades now (Armstrong and Johnson, 2009). The apparent rarity of life such as ours, at least in our region of our galaxy, suggests that we may face a greater responsibility than we thought for the proper care and stewardship of our planet and its global ecosystem and noösphere.

Appendix A
The Mathematics of Discontinuity

On the plane of philosophy properly speaking, of metaphysics, catastrophe theory cannot, to be sure, supply any answer to the great problems which torment mankind. But it favors a dialectical, Heraclitean view of the universe, of a world which is the continual theatre of the battle between 'logoi,' between archetypes.
René Thom (1975, "Catastrophe Theory: Its Present State and Future Perspectives," p. 382)

Clouds are not spheres, mountains are not cones, coastlines are not circles, and bark is not smooth, nor does lightning travel in a straight line.
Benoit B. Mandelbrot (1983, The Fractal Geometry of Nature, p. 1)

A.1 General Overview

Somehow it is appropriate if ironic that sharply divergent opinions exist in the mathematical House of Discontinuity with respect to the appropriate method for analyzing discontinuous phenomena. Different methods include catastrophe theory, chaos theory, fractal geometry, synergetics theory, self-organizing criticality, spin glass theory, and emergent complexity. All have been applied to economics in one way or another.

What these approaches have in common is more important than what divides them. They all see discontinuities as fundamental to the nature of nonlinear dynamical reality.[1] In the broadest sense, discontinuity theory is bifurcation theory of which all of these are subsets. Ironically then we must consider the bifurcation of bifurcation theory into competing schools. After examining the historical origins of this bifurcation of bifurcation theory, we shall consider the possibility of a reconciliation and synthesis within the House of Discontinuity between these fractious factions.

J.B. Rosser, *Complex Evolutionary Dynamics in Urban-Regional and Ecologic-Economic Systems*, DOI 10.1007/978-1-4419-8828-7,

A.2 The Founding Fathers

The conflict over continuity versus discontinuity can be traced deep into a variety of disputes among the ancient Greek philosophers. The most clearly mathematical was the controversy over Zeno's paradox, the argument that motion is unreal because of the alleged impossibility of an infinite sequence of discrete events (locations) occurring in finite time (Russell, 1945, pp. 804–806). Arguably Newton and Leibniz independently invented the infinitesimal calculus at least partly to resolve once and for all this rather annoying paradox.[2]

Newton's explanation of planetary motion by the law of gravitation and the infinitesimal calculus was one of the most important intellectual revolutions in the history of human thought. Although Leibniz's (1695) version contained hints of doubt because he recognized the possibility of fractional derivatives, an earlier conceptualization of fractals was in some of Leonardo da Vinci's drawings of turbulent water flow patterns, with Anaxagoras possibly having the idea much earlier. But the Newtonian revolution represented the triumph of the view of reality as fundamentally continuous rather than discontinuous.

The high watermark of this simplistic perspective came with Laplace (1814), who presented a completely deterministic, continuous, and general equilibrium view of celestial mechanics. Laplace went so far as to posit the possible existence of a demon who could know from any given set of initial conditions the position and velocity of any particle in the universe at any succeeding point in time. Needless to say quantum mechanics and general relativity completely retired Laplace's demon from science even before chaos theory appeared. Ironically enough, the first incarnation of Laplacian economics came with Walras' model of general equilibrium in 1874[3] just when the first cracks in the Laplacian mathematical apparatus were about to appear.

In the late nineteenth century, two lines of assault emerged upon the Newtonian–Laplacian superstructure. The first came from pure mathematics with the invention (discovery) of "monstrous" functions or sets. Initially viewed as irrelevant curiosa, many of these have since become foundations of chaos theory and fractal geometry. The second line of assault arose from unresolved issues in celestial mechanics and led to bifurcation theory.

The opening shot came in 1875 when duBois Reymond publicly reported the discovery by Weierstrass in 1872 of a continuous but nondifferentiable function (Mandelbrot, 1983, p. 4), namely,

$$W_0(t) = (1 - W^2)^{-1/2} \sum_{t=0}^{\infty} W^n \exp(2\pi b^n t), \tag{A.1}$$

with $b > 1$ and $W = b^h, 0 < h < 1$. This function is discontinuous in its first derivative everywhere. Lord Rayleigh (1880) used a Weierstrass-like function to study the frequency band spectrum of blackbody radiation, the lack of finite derivatives in certain bands implying infinite energy, the "ultraviolet catastrophe."[4] Max Planck resolved this difficulty by inventing quantum mechanics whose stochastic view of wave/particle motion destroyed the deterministic Laplacian vision, although some observers see chaos theory as holding out a deeper affirmation of determinism, if not of the Laplacian sort (Stewart, 1989; Ruelle, 1991).

Sir Arthur Cayley (1879) suggested an iteration using Newton's method on the simple cubic equation

$$z^3 - 1 = 0. \tag{A.2}$$

The question he asked was which of the three roots the iteration would converge to from an arbitrary starting point. He answered that this case "appears to present considerable difficulty." Peitgen, Jürgens, and Saupe (1992, pp. 774–775) argue that these iterations from many starting points will generate something like the fractal Julia set (1918) and is somewhat like the problem of the dynamics of a pendulum over three magnets, which becomes a problem of fractal basin boundaries.[5]

Georg Cantor (1883) discovered the most important and influential of these monsters, the Cantor set or Cantor dust or Cantor discontinuum. Because he spent time in mental institutions, it was tempting to dismiss his discoveries, which included transfinite numbers and set theory, as "pathological." But the Cantor set is a fundamental concept for discontinuous mathematics. It can be constructed by taking the closed interval [0, 1] and iteratively removing the middle third, leaving the endpoints, then removing the middle thirds of the remaining segments, and so forth to infinity. What is left behind is the Cantor set, partially illustrated in Fig. A.1.

The paradoxical Cantor set is infinitely subdividable, but is completely discontinuous, nowhere dense. Although it contains a continuum of points, it has zero length (Lebesgue measure zero) as all that has been removed adds up to one.[6] A two-dimensional version is the Sierpinski (1915, 1916) carpet which is constructed by iteratively removing the central open ninths of a square and its subsquares. The remaining set has zero area but infinite length. A three-dimensional version is the Menger sponge, which is constructed by iteratively removing the twenty-sevenths of a cube and its subcubes (Menger, 1926; Blumenthal and Menger, 1970). The remaining set has zero volume and infinite surface area.

Other ghastly offspring of Cantor's monster include the "space-filling" curves of Peano (1890) and Hilbert (1891) and the "snowflake" curve of von Koch (1904).[7] This latter curve imitates the Cantor set in exhibiting "self-similarity" wherein a pattern at one level is repeated at smaller levels. Cascades of self-similar bifurcations frequently constitute the transition to chaos, and chaotic strange attractors often have a Cantor set-like character.

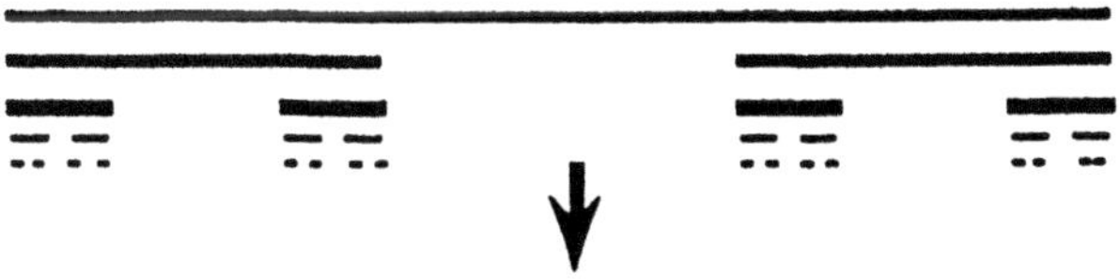

Fig. A.1 Cantor set on unit interval

Henri Poincaré (1890) developed the second line of assault while trying to resolve an unresolved problem of Newtonian–Laplacian celestial mechanics, the three-body problem (more generally, the n-body problem, $n > 2$). The motion of n bodies in a gravitational system can be given by a system of differential equations:

$$x_i = f_i(x_1, x_2, \ldots, x_n), \tag{A.3}$$

where the motion of the ith body depends on the positions of the other bodies. For $n = 2$, such a system can be easily solved with the future motions of the bodies based on their current positions and motions, the foundation of Laplacian naiveté. For $n > 2$, the solutions become very complicated and depend on further specifications. Facing the extreme difficulty and complexity of calculating precise solutions, Poincaré (1880–1890, 1899) developed the "qualitative theory of differential equations" to understand aspects of the solutions. He was particularly concerned with the asymptotic or long-run stability of the solutions. Would the bodies escape to infinity, remain within given distances, or collide with each other?

Given the asymptotic behavior of a given dynamical system, Poincaré then posed the question of structural stability. If the system were slightly perturbed, would its long-run behavior remain approximately the same or would a significant change occur?[8] The latter indicates the system is structurally unstable and has encountered a bifurcation point. A simple example for the two-body case is that of the escape velocity of a rocket traveling away from earth. This is about 6.9 miles per second which is a bifurcation value for this system. At a speed less than that, the rocket will fall back to earth, while at one greater than that, it will escape into space. It is no exaggeration to say that bifurcation theory *is* the mathematics of discontinuity.

Poincaré's concept of bifurcation concept is fundamental to all that follows.[9] Consider a general family of n differential equation whose behavior is determined by a k-dimensional control parameter, μ:

$$x = f_\mu(x); \quad x \in R^n, \mu \in R^k. \tag{A.4}$$

The equilibrium solutions of (A.4) are given by $f_\mu(x) = 0$. This set of equilibrium solutions will bifurcate into separate branches at a singularity, or degenerate critical point, that is, where the Jacobian matrix $D_x f_\mu$ (the derivative of $f_\mu(x)$ with respect to x) has a zero real part for one of its eigenvalues.

An example of (A.4) is

$$f_\mu(x) = \mu x - x^3, \tag{A.5}$$

for which

$$Dxf_\mu = \mu - 3x^2. \tag{A.6}$$

The bifurcation point is at $(x, \mu) = (0, 0)$. The equilibria and bifurcation points are depicted in Fig. A.2.

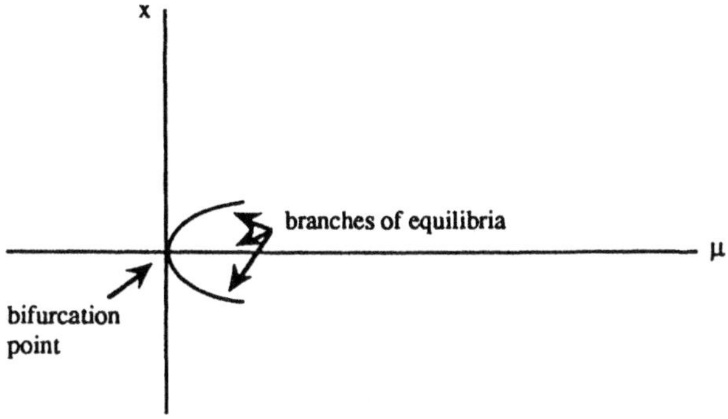

Fig. A.2 Supercritical pitchfork bifurcation

Table A.1 Main one- and two-dimensional bifurcation forms

Name	Type	Prototype map
Pitchfork (Supercritical)	Continuous	$x_{t+1} = x_t + \mu x_t - x_t^3$
Pitchfork (Subcritical)	Discontinuous	$x_{t+1} = x_t + \mu x_t + x_t^3$
Flip (Supercritical)	Continuous	$x_{t+1} = -x_t - \mu x_t + x_t^3$
Flip (Subcritical)	Discontinuous	$x_{t+1} = -x_t - \mu x_t - x_t^3$
Fold (Saddle-node)	Discontinuous	$x_{t+1} = x_t + \mu - x_t^2$
Transcritical	Continuous	$x_{t+1} = x_t + \mu x_t - x_t^2$
Hopf (Supercritical)	Continuous	$x = -y + x[\mu - (x^2+y^2)]\ y = x + y[\mu - (x^2+y^2)]$
Hopf (Subcritical)	Discontinuous	$x = -y + x[\mu + (x^2+y^2)]\ y = x + y[\mu + (x^2+y^2)]$

In this figure, the middle branch to the right of (0, 0) is unstable locally whereas the outer two are stable, corresponding with the index property that stable and unstable equilibria alternate when they are sufficiently distinct. This particular bifurcation is called the *supercritical pitchfork bifurcation.*

The supercritical pitchfork is one of several different kinds of bifurcations (Sotomayer, 1973; Guckenheimer and Holmes, 1983; Thompson and Stewart, 1986). Table A.1 illustrates several major kinds of local[10] bifurcations that occur in economic models of the one- and two-dimensional types. The prototype equations are in discrete map form (compare the supercritical pitchfork equation with (A.4) which is continuous), except for the Hopf bifurcations which are in continuous form.

The bifurcations can be continuous (*subtle*) or discontinuous (*catastrophic*). A bifurcation is continuous if a path in (x,μ) can pass across the bifurcation point without leaving the ensemble of the sets of points to which the system can asymptotically converge. Such sets are called *attractors*, and the ensemble of such sets is the *attractrix.*

In the fold and transcritical bifurcations, exchanges of stability occur across the bifurcations. Flip bifurcations can involve period doubling and can thus be associated with transitions to chaos. The Hopf (1942) bifurcation involves the emergence of cyclical behavior out of a steady state and exhibits an eigenvalue with zero real parts and imaginary parts that are complex conjugates. As we shall see later, this bifurcation is important in the theory of oscillators and business cycle theory.

The degeneracy of (0,0) in the supercritical pitchfork example in Fig. A.2 can be seen by examining the original function (A.4) closely. The first derivative at (0,0) is zero but it is not an extremum. Such degeneracies, or *singularities*, play a fundamental role in understanding structural stability more broadly.

The connection between the eigenvalues of the Jacobian matrix of partial derivatives of a dynamical system at an equilibrium point and the local stability of that equilibrium was first explicated by the Russian mathematician Alexander M. Lyapunov (1892). He showed that a sufficient condition for local stability was that the real parts of the eigenvalues for this matrix be negative. It was a small step from this theorem to understanding that such an eigenvalue possessing a zero real part indicated a point where a system could shift from stability to instability, in short a bifurcation point.

Lyapunov was the clear founder of the most creative and prolific strand of thought in the analysis of dynamic discontinuities, the Russian School. Significant successors to Lyapunov include A.A. Andronov (1929), who made important discoveries in bifurcation theory and who with Andronov and L.S. Pontryagin (1937) dramatically advanced the theory of structural stability; Andrei N. Kolmogorov (1941, 1954), who significantly developed the theory of turbulence and stochastic perturbations; A.N. Sharkovsky (1964), who uncovered the structure of periodicity in dynamic systems; V.I. Oseledec (1968), who developed the theory of Lyapunov characteristic exponents that are central to identifying the "butterfly effect" in chaotic dynamics; and Vladimir I. Arnol'd (1968), who most completely classified singularities. This exhausts neither the contributions of these individuals nor the list of those making important contributions to studying dynamic discontinuities from the Russian School.

Meanwhile returning to Poincaré's pathbreaking work, several other new concepts and methods emerged. He analyzed the behavior of orbits of bodies in a Newtonian system by examining cross-sections of the orbits in spaces of one dimension less than where they actually happen. Such *Poincaré maps* illustrate the long-run limit set, or "attractor set,"[11] of the system. Poincaré used these maps to study the three-body problem, coming to both "optimistic" and "pessimistic" conclusions.

An "optimistic" conclusion is the Poincaré-Bendixson Theorem for planar motions (Bendixson, 1901), which states that a nonempty limit set of planar flow which contains its boundary (is compact) and which contains no fixed point is a closed orbit. Andronov, Leontovich, and Gordon (1966) used this theorem to show that all nonwandering planar flows fall into three classes: fixed points, closed orbits, and the unions of fixed points and trajectories connecting them. The latter are *heteroclinic orbits* when they connect distinct points and *homoclinic orbits* when they connect a point with itself, the latter being useful to understanding *chaotic strange attractors*, discussed later in this chapter. The Poincaré-Bendixson results were extended in a rigorous set theoretic context by George D. Birkhoff (1927), who, among other things, showed the impossibility of three bodies colliding in the case of the three-body problem.

A "pessimistic" conclusion of Poincaré's studies is much more interesting from our perspective. For the three-body problem, he saw the possibility of a nonwandering solution of extreme complexity, an "infinitely tight grid" that could in certain cases be analogous to a Cantor dust. It can be argued that Poincaré here discovered the first known strange attractor of a dynamical system.

A.3 The Bifurcation of Bifurcation Theory

A.3.1 The Road to Catastrophe

A.3.1.1 The Theory

The principal promulgators and protagonists of catastrophe theory have been René Thom and E. Christopher Zeeman. Thom was strongly motivated by the question of qualitative structural change in developmental biology, especially influenced by the work of D'Arcy Thompson (1917) and C.H. Waddington (1940). Thom's work was summarized in his highly influential *Structural Stability and Morphogenesis* (1972) from which Zeeman and his associates at Warwick University drew much of their inspiration. But Thom's Classification Theorem culminates a long line of work in singularity theory, and the crucial theorems rigorously establishing his conjecture were proven by Bernard Malgrange (1966) and John N. Mather (1968).

This strand of thought developed from the work of "founding father" Poincaré and his follower, George Birkhoff. Following Birkhoff (1927), Marston Morse (1931) distinguished critical points of functions between nondegenerate (maxima or minima) and degenerate (singular, nonextremal). He showed that a function with a degenerate singularity could be slightly perturbed to a new function exhibiting two distinct nondegenerate critical points in place of the singularity, a bifurcation of the degenerate equilibrium. This is depicted in Fig. A.3 and indicates sharply the link between the singularity of a mapping and its structural instability.

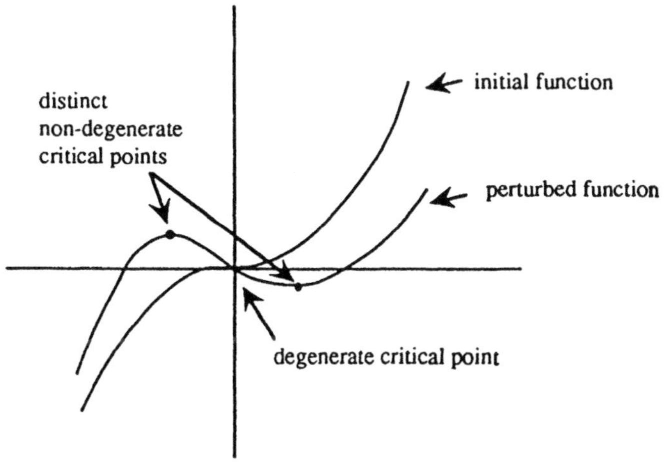

Fig. A.3 Bifurcation at a singularity

Hassler Whitney (1955) advanced the work of Morse by examining different kinds of singularities and their stabilities. He showed that for differentiable mappings between planar surfaces (two-dimensional manifolds) there are exactly two kinds of structurally stable singularities, the *fold* and the *cusp*. In fact, these are the two simplest elementary catastrophes and the only ones that are stable in all their forms (Trotman and Zeeman, 1976). Thus it can be argued that Whitney was the real founder of catastrophe theory.[12]

Thom (1956) discovered the concept of *transversality*, widely used in catastrophe theory, chaos theory, and dynamic economics. Two linear subspaces are transversal if the sum of their dimensions equals the dimension of the linear space containing them. Thus, they either do not intersect or intersect in an nondegenerate way such that at the intersections none of their derivatives are equal. They "cut" each other "cleanly." Following this, Thom (1972) developed the classification of the elementary catastrophes.[13]

Consider a dynamical system given by n functions on r control variables, c_i. The n equations determine n state variables, x_j:

$$x_j = f_j(c_1, \ldots, c_r). \tag{A.7}$$

Let V be a potential function on the set of control and state variables:

$$V = V(c_i, x_j), \tag{A.8}$$

such that for all x_j

$$\partial V/\partial x_j = 0. \tag{A.9}$$

This set of stationary points constitutes the equilibrium manifold, M. We further assume that the potential function possesses a gradient dynamic governed by some convention that tends to move the system to this manifold. Sometimes the control variables are called "slow" and the state variables "fast," as the latter presumably adjust quickly to be on M, whereas the former control the movements along M. These are not trivial assumptions and have been the basis for serious mathematical criticisms of catastrophe theory, as we shall see later.

Let Cat(f) be the map induced by the projection of the equilibrium manifold, M, into the r-dimensional control parameter space. This is the catastrophe function whose singularities are the focus of catastrophe theory.

Thom's theorem states that if the underlying functions, f_j, are generic (qualitatively stable under slight perturbations), if $r \leq 5$, and if n is finite with all but two state variables being representable by linear and nondegenerate quadratic terms, then any singularity of a catastrophe function of the system will be one of 11 types and that these singularities will be structurally stable (generic) under slight perturbations. These 11 types constitute the *elementary catastrophes*, usable for topologically characterizing discontinuities appearing in a wide variety of phenomena in many different disciplines and contexts.

The canonical forms of these elementary catastrophes can be derived from the *germ* at the singularity plus a perturbation function derived from the eigenvalues of the Jacobian matrix at the singularity. This "catastrophe germ" represents the

Table A.2 Seven elementary catastrophes

Name	dim X	dim C	Germ	Perturbation
Fold	1	1	x^3	cx
Cusp	1	2	x^4	$c_1x + c_2x^2$
Swallowtail	1^-	3	x^5	$c_1x + c_2x^2 + c_3x^3$
Butterfly	1	4	x^6	$c_1x + c_2x^2 + c_3x^3 + c_4x^4$
Hyperbolic umbilic	2	3	${x_1}^3 + x_2^3$	$c_1x_1 + c_2x_2^2 + c_3x_1x_2$
Elliptic umbilic	2	3	$x_1^3x_2^3$	$c_1x_1 + c_2x_2 + c_3(x_1^2 + x_2^2)$
Parabolic umbilic	2	4	$x_1^2x_2 + x_2^4$	$c_1x_1 + c_2x_2 + c_3x_1^2 + c_4x_2^2$

first nonzero components of the Taylor expansion about the singularity (the polynomial expansion using the set of ever higher-order derivatives of the function). Thom (1972) specifically named the seven forms for which $r \leq 4$ and described them and their characteristics at great length.[14] Table A.2 contains a list of these seven with some of their characteristics.

For dimensionalities greater than five in the control space and two in the state space, the number of catastrophe forms is infinite. However, up to where the sum of the control and state dimensionalities equals 11, it is possible to classify families of catastrophes to some degree. Beyond this level of dimensionality, even the categories of families of catastrophes apparently become infinite and hence very difficult to classify (Arnol'd, Gusein-Zade, and Varchenko, 1985).

Thom (1972, pp. 103–108) labels such higher-dimensional catastrophes as "non-elementary" or "generalized catastrophes." He recognizes that such events may have applications to problems of fluid turbulence but finds them uninteresting due to their extreme topological complexity. Such events constitute central topics of chaos theory and fractal geometry.

Among the elementary catastrophes, the two simplest, the fold and the cusp, have been applied the most to economic problems. Figure A.4 depicts the fold catastrophe with one control variable and one state variable. Two values of the control variable constitute the catastrophe or bifurcation set, the points where discontinuous behavior in the state variable can occur, even though the control variable may be smoothly varying. Figure A.4 also shows a *hysteresis cycle* as the control variable oscillates, and discontinuous jumps and drops of the state variable occur at the bifurcation points.

The dynamics presented in Fig. A.4 use the *delay convention* that assumes a minimizing potential determined by local conditions (Gilmore, 1981, Chap. 8). The most sharply contrasting convention is the *Maxwell convention* in which the state variable would drop to the lower branch as soon as it lies under the upper branch and vice versa. The middle branch represents an unstable equilibrium and hence is unattainable except by infinitesimal accident.

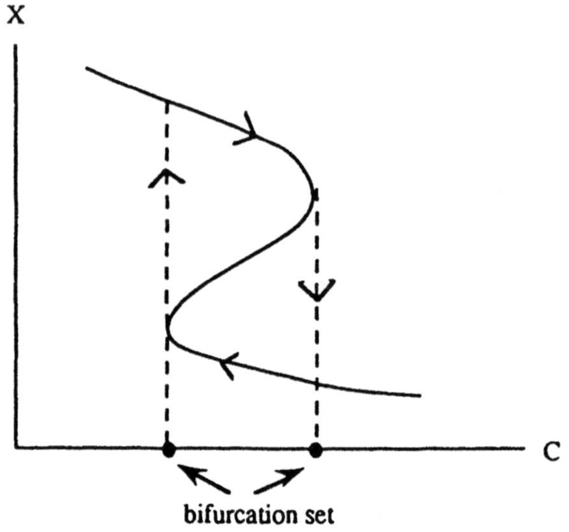

Fig. A.4 Fold catastrophe

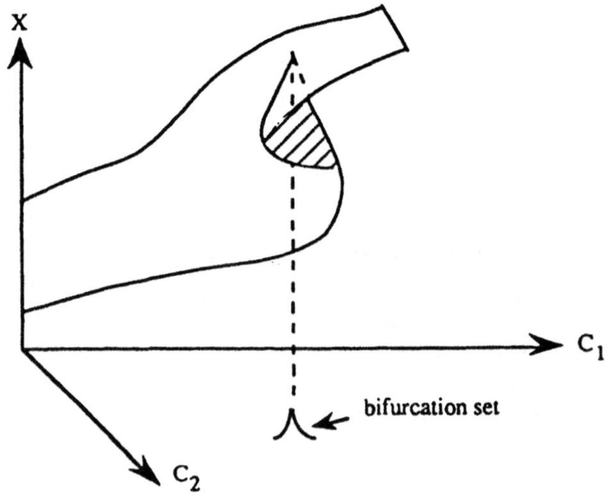

Fig. A.5 Cusp catastrophe

Figure A.5 depicts the cusp catastrophe with two control variables and one state variable. C_1 is the *normal factor* and C_2 is the *splitting factor*. Continuous oscillations of the normal factor will not cause discontinuous changes in the state variable if the value of the splitting factor is less than a critical value given by the cusp point. Above this value of the splitting variable, a pleat appears in the manifold and continuous variation of the normal factor can now cause discontinuous behavior in the state variable.

Zeeman (1977, p. 18) argues that a dynamic system containing a cusp catastrophe can exhibit any of five different behavioral patterns, four of which can also occur with fold catastrophes. These are *bimodality, inaccessibility, sudden jumps* (catastrophes), *hysteresis*, and *divergence*, the latter not occurring in fold catastrophe structures.

Bimodality can occur if a system spends most of its time on either of two widely separated sheets. The intermediate values between the sheets are inaccessible. Sudden jumps occur if the system jumps from one sheet to another. Hysteresis occurs if there is a cycle of jumping back and forth due to oscillations of the normal factor, but with the jumps not happening at the same point. Divergence arises from increases in the splitting factor with two parallel paths initially near one another moving apart if they end up on different sheets after the splitting factor passes beyond the cusp point.

A third form sometimes applied in economics is the butterfly catastrophe with four control variables and one state variable. Zeeman (1977, pp. 29–52) argues that this form is appropriate to situations where there are two sharply conflicting alternatives with an intermediate alternative accessible in some regions. Examples include a bulimic-anorexic who normally alternates between fasting and binging and achieves a normal diet[15] and compromises achieved in war/peace negotiations.

Figure A.6 displays a cross-section of the bifurcation set of this five-dimensional structure for certain control variable values. It shows the "pocket of compromise," bounded by three distinct cusp points. As with the cusp catastrophe, C_1 and C_2 are normal and splitting factors, respectively. Zeeman labels C_3 the *bias factor* which tilts the initial cusp surface one way or another. C_4 is the *butterfly factor* (not to be confused with the "butterfly effect" of chaos theory) that generates the pocket of compromise zone for certain of its values. Zeeman's advocacy of the significance and wide applicability of this particular catastrophe form became a focus of the controversy discussed in the next section.

The hyperbolic umbilic and elliptic umbilic catastrophes both have three control variables and two state variables, their canonical forms listed in Table A.2. Figures A.7 and A.8 show their respective three-dimensional bifurcation sets.

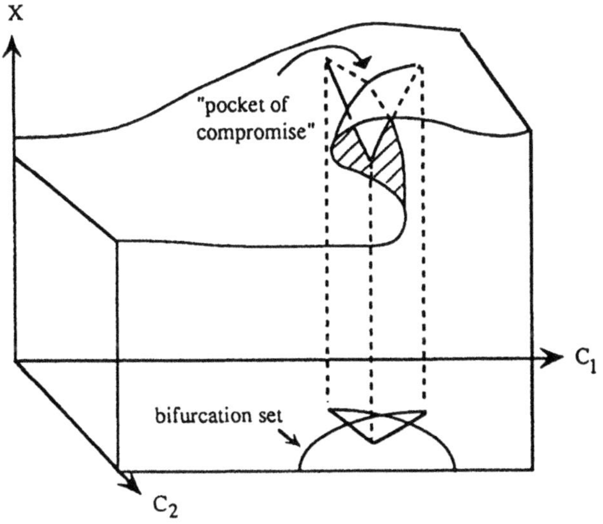

Fig. A.6 Butterfly catastrophe

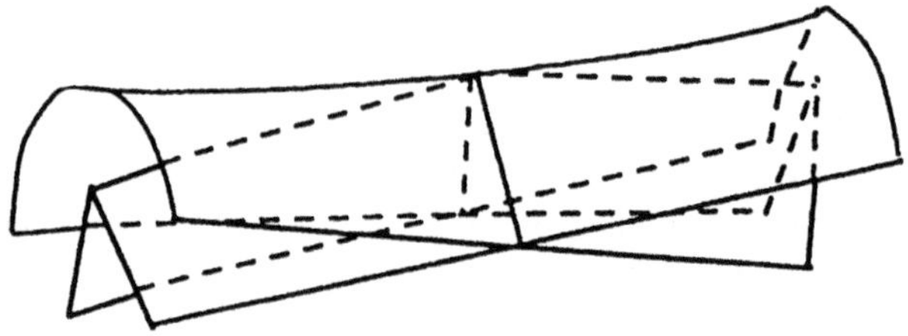

Fig. A.7 Hyperbolic umbilic catastrophe

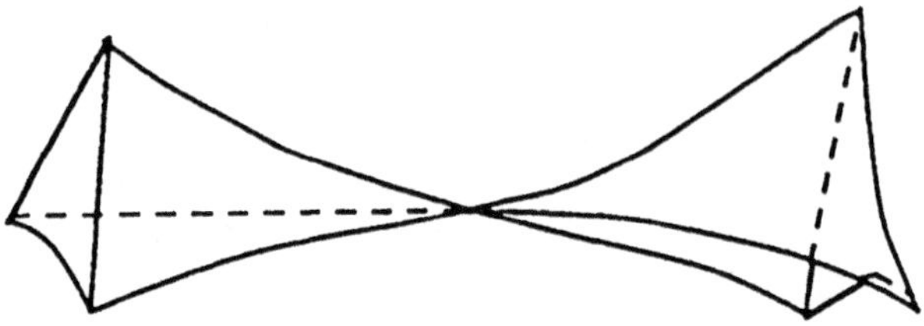

Fig. A.8 Elliptic umbilic catastrophe

Thom argues that an archetypal example of the hyperbolic umbilic is the breaking of the crest of a wave, and that an archetypal example of the elliptic umbilic is the extremity of a pointed organ such as a hair. The six-dimensional parabolic umbilic (or "mushroom") is difficult to depict except in very limited subsections. Guastello (1995) applies it to analyzing human creativity.

A.3.1.2 The Controversy

Thom (1972) argued that catastrophe theory is a method of analyzing structural and qualitative changes in a wide variety of phenomena. Besides his extended discussion of embryology and biological morphology, his major focus and inspiration, he argued for its applicability to the study of light caustics,[16] the hydrodynamics of waves breaking,[17] the formation of geological structures, models of quantum mechanics,[18] and structural linguistics. The latter represents one of the most qualitative such applications and Thom seems motivated to link the structuralism of Claude Lévi-Strauss with the semiotics of Ferdinand de Saussure. This is an example of what Arnol'd (1992) labels "the mysticism of catastrophe theory," another example of which can be found in parts of Abraham (1985b).

Zeeman (1977) additionally suggested applications in economics, the formation of public opinion, "brain modeling," the physiology of heartbeat and nerve impulses, stress,[19] prison disturbances, the stability of ships, and structural mechanics, especially the phenomenon of Euler buckling.[20] Discussions of applications in aerodynamics, climatology, more of economics, and other areas can be found in Poston and Stewart (1978), Woodcock and Davis (1978), Gilmore (1981), and Thompson (1982).

In response to these claims and arguments, a strong reaction developed, culminating in a series of articles by Kolata (1977), Zahler and Sussman (1977), and Sussman and Zahler (1978a, b). Formidable responses appeared as correspondence in *Science* (June 17 and August 26, 1977) and in *Nature* (December 1, 1977), as well as articles in *Behavioral Science* (Oliva and Capdevielle, 1980; Guastello, 1981), with insightful and balanced overviews in Guckenheimer (1978) and Arnol'd (1992), as well as an acute satire of the critics in Fussbudget and Snarler (1979). That the general outcome of this controversy was to leave catastrophe theory in somewhat bad repute can be seen by the continuing ubiquity of dismissive remarks regarding it (Horgan, 1995, 1997)[21] and the dearth of articles using it, despite occasional suggestions of its appropriate applicability (Gennotte and Leland, 1990), thus suggesting that Oliva and Capdevielle's (1980) complaint came true, that "the baby was thrown out with the bathwater."

Although some of the original criticism was overdrawn and inappropriate, for example, snide remarks that many of the original papers appeared in unedited Conference Proceedings, a number of the criticisms remained either unanswered or unresolved. These include excessive reliance on qualitative methods, inappropriate quantization in some applications, and the use of excessively restrictive and narrow mathematical assumptions. Let us consider these in turn with regard especially to their relevance to economics.

A simple response to the first point is that although the theory was developed in a qualitative framework as was the work of Poincaré, Andronov, and others, this in no way excludes the possibility of constructing or estimating specific quantitative models within the qualitative framework. Nevertheless, this issue is relevant to the division in economics between qualitative and quantitative approaches and also divides Thom and Zeeman themselves, a bifurcation of the bifurcation of bifurcation theory, so to speak.

Even scathing critics such as Zahler and Sussman (1977) admit that catastrophe theory may be applicable to certain areas of physics and engineering such as structural mechanics, where specific quantifiable models derived from well-established physical theories can be constructed. Much of the criticism focused on Zeeman's efforts to extend such specific model building and estimation into "softer" sciences, thus essentially agreeing that the proof is in the pudding of such specifically quantized model building.

Thom (1983) responded to this controversy by defending a hard-line qualitative approach. Criticizing what he labels "neo-positive epistemology," he argues that science constitutes a continuum between two poles: "understanding reality" and "acting effectively on reality." The latter requires quantified locally specific models, whereas the former is the domain of the qualitative, of heuristic "classification of analogous situations" by means of geometrization. He argues that "geometrization promotes a global view while the inherent fragmentation of verbal conceptualization permits only a limited grasp" (1983, Chap. 7). Thus, he sides with the critics of some of Zeeman's efforts declaring, "There is little doubt that the main criticism of the pragmatic inadequacy of C.T. [catastrophe theory] models has been in essence well founded" (ibid.). This does not disturb Thom who sees qualitative understanding as at least as philosophically valuable as quantitative model building.

Although the long-term trend has been to favor "neo-positive" quantitative model building, this division between qualitative and quantitative approaches continues to cut across economics as one of its most heated ongoing fundamental controversies. Most defenders of qualitative approaches tend to reject *all* mathematical methods and prefer institutional-historical-literary approaches. Thus, Thom's method offers an intriguing alternative for the analysis of qualitative change in institutional structures in historical frameworks.[22]

Compared with other disciplines for which catastrophe theoretic models have been constructed, economics more clearly straddles the qualitative–quantitative divide, residing in both the "hard" and "soft" camps. Catastrophe theory models in economics range from specifically empirical ones through specifically theoretical ones to ones of a more mixed character to highly qualitative ones with hard-to-quantify variables and largely ad hoc relationships between the variables.

Given this diversity of approaches in economics, it may well be best for catastrophe theoretic models in economics if they are clearly in one camp or the other, either based on a solid theoretical foundation with well-defined and specified variables or fully qualitative. Models mixing quantitative variables with qualitative variables, or questionably quantifiable variables, are likely to be open to the charge of "spurious quantization" or other methodological or philosophical sins.

This brings us to the charge of "spurious quantization." Perhaps the most widely and fiercely criticized such example was Zeeman's (1977, Chaps. 13, 14) model of prison riots using institutional disturbances as a state variable in a cusp catastrophe model with "alienation" and "tension" as control variables. The former was measured by "punishment plus segregation" and the latter by "sickness plus governor's applications plus welfare visits" for Gartree prison in 1972, a period of escalating disturbances there. Two separate cusp structures were imputed to the scattering of points generated by this data. Quite aside from issues of statistical significance, this model was subjected to a storm of criticism for the arbitrariness and alleged spuriousness of the measures for these variables. These criticisms seem reasonable. Thus this case would seem to be an example for which this charge is relevant.

For most economists, this will simply boil down to insuring that proper econometric practices are carried out for any cases in which catastrophe theory models are empirically estimated, and that half-baked such efforts should not be made for purely heuristic qualitative models. It is the case that Sussman and Zahler (1978a, b) went further and argued that any surface could be fit to a set of points and thus one could never verify that a global form was correct from a local structural estimate. This would seem indeed to be "throwing the baby out with the bathwater" by denying the use of significance testing or other methods such as out-of-sample prediction tests for *any* econometric model, including the most garden variety of linear ones. Of course there are many critics of econometric testing who agree with these arguments, but it is a bit contradictory of Sussman and Zahler on the one hand to denounce catastrophe theory for its alleged excessive qualitativeness and then to turn around and denounce it again using arguments that effectively deny the possibility of fully testing any quantitative model.

We note that although these have only been sparingly used in economics, there is a well developed literature on using multimodal probability density functions based on exponential transformations of data for estimating catastrophe theoretic models (Cobb, 1978, 1981; Cobb, Koppstein, and Chen, 1983; Cobb and Zacks, 1985, 1988; Guastello, 1995). Crucial to these techniques are data adjustments for location (often using deviations from the sample mean) and for scale that use some variability from a mode rather than the mean. There are difficulties with this approach, such as the assumption of a perfect Markov process in dynamic situations, but they are not insurmountable in many cases.[23]

With respect to the argument that catastrophe theory involves restrictive mathematical assumptions, three different points have been raised. The first is that a potential function must be assumed to exist. Balasko (1978) argued that true potential functions rarely exist in economics, although Lorenz (1993a) responded by suggesting that the existence of a stable Lyapunov function may be sufficient. Of course, most qualitative models have no such functions.

The second restrictive mathematical assumption is that gradient dynamics do not explicitly allow time to be a variable, something one finds in quite a few catastrophe theory models. However, Thom (1983, pp. 107–108) responds that an elementary catastrophe form may be embedded in a larger system with a time variable, if the larger system is transversal to a catastrophe set in the enlarged space. Thom admits that this may not be the case and will be difficult to determine. Guckenheimer (1973) especially notes this as a serious problem for many catastrophe theory models.

The third critique is that the elementary catastrophes are only a limited subset of the possible range of bifurcations and discontinuities. The work of Arnol'd (1968, 1992) demonstrates this quite clearly and the fractal geometers and chaos theorists would also agree. Clearly, the House of Discontinuity has many rooms.

Thus elementary catastrophe theory is a fairly limited subspecies of bifurcation theory, while nevertheless suggesting potentially useful interpretations of economic discontinuities and occasionally more specific models. But is this why it has apparently been in such disfavor among economists?

An ironic reason may have to do with Zahler and Sussman's (1977) original attack on Zeeman's work in economics. In particular, the first catastrophe theory model in economics was Zeeman's (1974) model of the stock exchange in which he allowed heterogeneous agents, rational "fundamentalists" and irrational "chartists." Zahler and Sussman ridiculed this model on theoretical grounds arguing that economics cannot allow irrational agents, 1977 being a time of high belief in rational expectations among economists. Today this criticism looks ridiculous as there is now a vast literature (see Chapters 4 and 5 in this book) on heterogeneous agents in financial markets. The irrelevance of this criticism of Zeeman's work has largely been forgotten, but the fact that a criticism was made has long been remembered. Indeed, the baby did get thrown out with the bathwater.

Clearly, catastrophe theory has numerous serious limits. Indeed, it may be more useful as a mode of thought about problems than for its classification of the elementary catastrophes per se. Nevertheless, economists should no longer feel frightened of using it or thinking about it because of the residual memory of attacks upon past applications in economics.[24] Some of those applications (e.g., the 1974 Zeeman stock market model) now look very up-to-date and more useful than the models to which they were disparagingly compared.

A.3.2 The Road to Chaos

A.3.2.1 Preliminary Theoretical Developments

General Remarks

Despite being plagued by philosophical controversies and disputes over applications, the basic mathematical foundation and apparatus of catastrophe theory are well established and understood. The same cannot be said for chaos theory where there remains controversy, dispute, and loose ends over both definitions and certain basic mathematical questions, notably the definitions of both *chaotic dynamics* and *strange attractor* and the question of the structural stability of strange attractors in general (Guckenheimer and Holmes, 1983; Smale, 1991; Viana, 1996). In any case, chaos theory emerged in the 1970s out of several distinct streams of bifurcation theory and related topics that developed from the work of Poincaré.

Attractors, Repellors, and Saddles

Having just noted that there are definitional problems with some terms, let us try to pin down some basic concepts in dynamic systems, namely, *attractor, repellor,* and *saddle*. These are important because any fixed point of a dynamic system must be one of these. Unfortunately there is not precise agreement about these, but we can give a reasonable definitions that will be sufficient for our purposes.

For a mapping G in n-dimensional real number space, $\mathbf{R^n}$, with time (t) as one dimension, the closed and bounded (compact) set A is an *attracting set* if for all $x \in A$, $G(x) \in A$ (this property is known as *invariance*), and if there exists a neighborhood U of A such that if $G(x)$ in U for $t \geq 0$, then $G(\mathrm{x}) \rightarrow A$ as $t \rightarrow \infty$. The union of all such neighborhoods of A is called its *basin of attraction* (or domain of attraction) and is the stable manifold of A within which A will eventually capture any orbit occurring there.

A *repelling set* is defined analogously but by replacing t with $-t$. If an attracting set is a distinct fixed point, it is called a *sink*. If a repelling set is a distinct fixed point, it is called a *source*. A distinct fixed point that is neither of these is a *saddle*. Basins of attraction of disjoint attracting sets will be separated by stable manifolds of nonattracting sets (*separatrix*).

A physical example of the above is the system of hydrologic watersheds on the earth's surface. A watershed constitutes a basin of attraction with the mouth of the system as the attractor set, a sink if it is a single point rather than a delta. The separatrix will be the divide between watersheds. Along such divides will be both sources (peaks) and saddles (passes). In a gradient potential system, the separatrices constitute the bifurcations or catastrophe sets of the system in catastrophe theory terms.

Although many observers identify *attractor* with attracting set (and *repellor* with repelling set), Eckmann and Ruelle (1985) argue that an attractor is an *irreducible* subset of an attracting set. Such a subset cannot be made into disjoint sets. Irreducibility is also known as *indecomposability* and as *topological transitivity*. Most attracting sets are also attractors, but Eckmann and Ruelle (1985, p. 623) provide an example of an exception, even as they eschew providing a precise definition of an attractor.[25]

The Theory of Oscillations

After celestial mechanics[26] the category of models first studied capable of generating chaotic behavior came from the theory of oscillations, the first general version of which was developed by the Russian School in the context of radio-engineering problems (Mandel'shtam, Papaleski, Andronov, Vitt, Gorelik, and Khaikin, 1936). This was not merely theoretical as it is now clear that this study generated the first experimentally observed example of chaotic dynamics (van der Pol and van der Mark, 1927). In adjusting the frequency ratios in telephone receivers, they noted zones where "an irregular noise is heard in the telephone receivers before the frequency jumps to the next lower value. . .[that] strongly reminds one of the tunes of a bagpipe" (van der Pol and van der Mark, 1927, p. 364).

Indeed prior to the generalizations of the Russian School, two examples of nonlinear forced oscillators were studied, the Duffing (1918) model of an electromagnetized vibrating beam and the van der Pol (1927) model of an electrical circuit with a triode valve whose resistance changes with the current. Both of these models have been shown to exhibit cusp catastrophe behavior for certain variables in certain forms (Zeeman, 1977, Chap. 9).

Moon and Holmes (1979) showed that the Duffing oscillator could generate chaotic dynamics. Holmes (1979) showed that as a crucial parameter is varied, the oscillator can exhibit a sequence of period-doubling bifurcations in the transition to chaotic dynamics, the "Feigenbaum cascade" (Feigenbaum, 1978), although period-doubling cascades were first studied by Myrberg (1958, 1959, 1963). Early work on complex aspects of the Duffing oscillator was done by Cartwright and Littlewood (1945), which underlies the detailed study of the strange attractor driving the Duffing oscillator carried out by Ueda (1980, 1991).

As noted above, van der Pol and van der Mark were already aware of the chaotic potential of van der Pol's forced oscillator model, a result proven rigorously by Levi (1981). The unforced van der Pol oscillator inspired the Hopf bifurcation (Hopf, 1942) which has been much used in macroeconomic business cycle theory and which sometimes occurs in transitions to chaotic dynamics. It happens when the vanishing of the real part of an eigenvalue coincides with conjugate imaginary roots. This indicates the emergence of limit cycle behavior out of noncyclical dynamics. The simple unforced van der Pol equation is

Fig. A.9 Hopf bifurcation

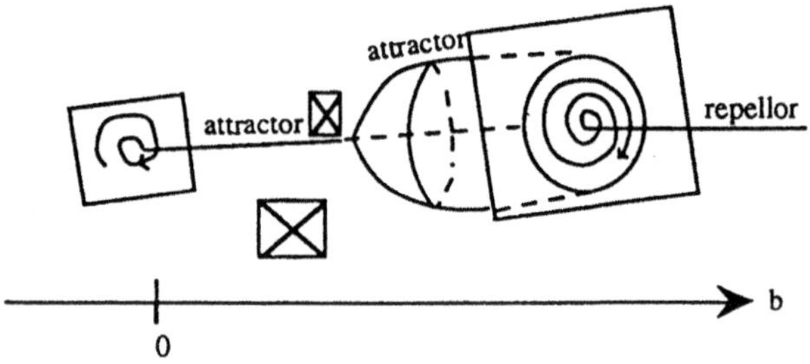

$$\ddot{x} + \varepsilon(x^2 - b)x + x = 0, \qquad (A.10)$$

where $\varepsilon > 0$ and b is a control variable. For $b < 0$, the flow has an attractor point at the origin. At $b = 0$, the Hopf bifurcation occurs, and for $b > 0$, the attracting set is a paraboloid of radius $= 2\sqrt{b}$, which determines the limit cycles while the axis is now a repelling set. This is depicted in Fig. A.9.

Noninteger (Fractal) Dimension

Another important development was an extension by Felix Hausdorff (1918) of the concept of dimensionality beyond the standard Euclidean, or topological. This effort was largely inspired by contemplation of the previously discussed Cantor set and Koch curve. Hausdorff understood that for such highly irregular sets another concept of dimension was more useful than the traditional Euclidean or topological concept, a concept that could indicate the degree of irregularity of the set. The measure involves estimating the rate at which the set of clusters or kinks increases as the scale of measurement (a gauge) decreases. This depends on a cover of a set of balls of decreasing size. Thus, the von Koch snowflake has an infinite length even though it surrounds only a finite area. The *Hausdorff dimension* captures the ratio of the logarithms of the length of the curve to the decrease in the scale of the measure of the curve.

The precise definition of the Hausdorff dimension is quite complicated and is given in Guckenheimer and Holmes (1983, p. 285) and Peitgen, Jürgens, and Saupe (1992, pp. 216–218). Farmer, Ott, and Yorke (1983), Edgar (1990), and Falconer (1990) discuss relations between different dimension measures.

Perhaps the most widely used empirical dimension measure has been the *correlation dimension* of Grassberger and Procaccia (1983a). To obtain this dimension, one must first estimate the *correlation integral*. This is defined for a trajectory in an m-dimensional space known as the *embedding dimension*. The *embedding theorem* of Floris Takens (1981) states that under appropriate conditions this dimension must be at least twice as great as that of the attractor being estimated ("reconstructed"). Such reconstruction is done by estimating a set of delay coordinates.[27] For a given radius, ε, the correlation integral will be the probability that there will be two randomly chosen points of the trajectory within ε of each other and is denoted as $C_m(\varepsilon)$. The correlation dimension for embedding dimension m will then be given by

$$D_m = \lim_{\varepsilon \to 0} \left[\ln(C_m(\varepsilon)) / \ln(\varepsilon) \right]. \tag{A.11}$$

The correlation dimension is the value of D_m as $m \to \infty$ and is less than or equal to the Hausdorff dimension. It can be viewed as measuring the degree of fine structure in the attractor. It can also be interpreted as the minimum number of parameters necessary to describe the attractor and its dynamics and thus is an index of the difficulty of forecasting from estimates of the system.[28] A dimension of zero indicates completely regular structure and full forecastibility, whereas a dimension of ∞ indicates pure randomness and inability to forecast. Investigators hoping to find some usable deterministic fractal structure search for some positive but low correlation dimension.

Much controversy has accompanied the use of this measure, especially in regard to measures of alleged climatic attractors (Nicolis and Nicolis, 1984, 1987; Grassberger, 1986, 1987; Ruelle, 1990) as well as in economics where biases due to insufficient data sets are serious (Ramsey and Yuan, 1989; Ramsey, Sayers, and Rothman, 1990).[29] Ruelle (1990, p. 247) is especially scathing, comparing some of these dimension estimates to the episode in D. Adams' *The hitchhiker's guide to the galaxy* wherein "a huge supercomputer has answered 'the great problem of life, the universe, and everything'. The answer obtained after many years of computation is 42."

For smooth manifolds and Euclidean spaces, these measures will be the same as the standard Euclidean (topological) dimension, which always has an integer value. But for sufficiently irregular sets, they will diverge, with the Hausdorff and other related measures generating noninteger values and the degree of divergence from the standard Euclidean measure providing an index of the degree of irregularity of the set. A specific example is the original triadic Cantor set on the unit interval discussed earlier in this chapter. Its Euclidean dimension is zero (same as a point), but its Hausdorff (and also correlation) dimension equals ln2/ln3.

The Hausdorff measure of dimension has become the central focus of the fractal geometry approach of Benoit Mandelbrot (1983). He has redefined the Hausdorff dimension to be *fractal dimension* and has labeled as *fractal* any set whose fractal dimension does not equal its Euclidean dimension.[30] Unsurprisingly, given the multiplicity of dimension measures, there are oddball cases that do not easily fit in. Thus, "fat fractals" of integer dimension have been identified (Farmer, 1986; Umberger, Mayer-Kress, and Jen, 1986) that must be estimated by using "metadimensional" methods. Also, Mandelbrot himself has recognized that some sets must be characterized by a spectrum of fractal numbers known as *multifractals* (Mandelbrot, 1988)[31] or even in some cases by negative fractal dimensions (Mandelbrot, 1990a, b).

As already noted, the use of such fractal or noninteger measures of dimension has been popular for estimating the "strangeness of strange attractors," which are argued to be of fractal dimensionality, among other things. Such a phenomenon implies that a dynamical system tracking such an attractor will exhibit irregular behavior, albeit deterministically driven, this irregular behavior reflecting the fundamental irregularity of the attractor itself.

Yet another application of the concept that has shown up in economics has been to cases where the boundaries of basins of attraction are fractal, even when the attractors themselves might be quite simple (McDonald, Grebogi, Ott, and Yorke, 1985; Lorenz, 1992).[32] In such cases, extreme difficulties in forecasting can arise without any other forms of complexity being involved. Figure A.10 shows a case of fractal basin boundaries arising from a situation where a pendulum is held over three magnets, whose locations constitute the three simple point attractors.

Both attractors with fractal dimension and fractal basin boundaries can occur even when a dynamical system may not exhibit sensitive dependence on initial conditions, widely argued to be the sine qua non of truly chaotic dynamics.

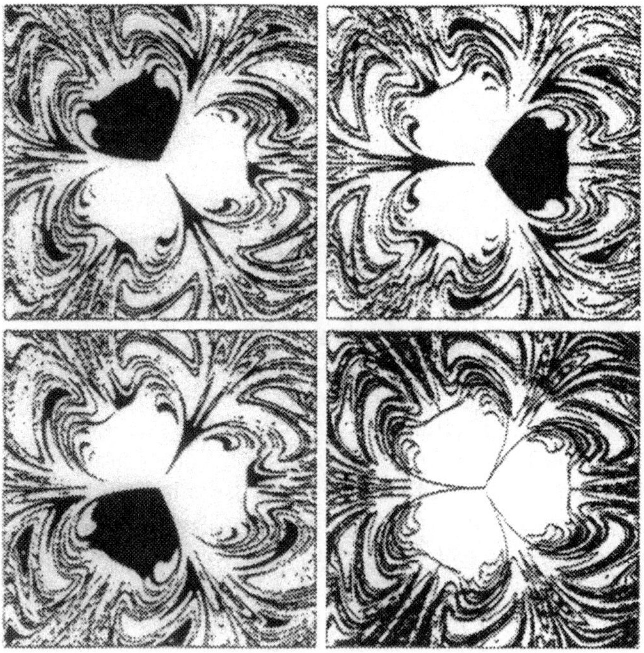

Fig. A.10 Fractal basin boundaries, three magnets. Basins of attraction for the pendulum over three magnets. For each of the three magnets, one of the above figures shows the basin *shaded* in *black*. The fourth picture displays the *borders* between the three basins. This *border* is not a simple line: but within itself it has a Cantor-like structure

A.3.2.2 The Emergence of the Chaos Concept

The Lorenz Model

As with the emergence of discontinuous mathematics in the late nineteenth century, the chaos concept emerged from the separate lines of actual physical models and of theoretical mathematical developments. Indeed, the basic elements had already been observed by early twentieth century along both lines, but had simply been ignored as anomalies. Thus Poincaré and Hadamard had understood the possibility of sensitive dependence on initial conditions during the late nineteenth century; Poincaré had understood the possibility of deterministic but irregular dynamic trajectories; Cantor had understood the possibility of irregular sets in the 1880s while Hausdorff had defined noninteger dimension for describing such sets in 1918; and in 1927 van der Pol and van der Mark had even heard the "tunes of bagpipes" on their telephone receivers. But nobody paid any attention.

Although nobody would initially pay attention, in 1963 Edward Lorenz published results about a three-equation model of atmospheric flow that contains most of the elements of what has since come to be called *chaos*. They would pay attention soon enough.

It has been reported that Lorenz discovered chaos accidentally while he was on a coffee break (Gleick, 1987; Stewart, 1989; E.N. Lorenz, 1993b). He let his computer simulate the model with a starting value of a variable different by 0.000127 from what had been generated in a previous run, this starting point being partway through the original run. When he returned from his coffee break, the model was showing totally different behavior. As shown in Fig. A.11, from Peitgen, Jürgens, and Saupe (1992, p. 716), trajectories that are initiallly separated will rapidly diverge. This was *sensitive dependence on initial conditions* (SDIC), viewed widely as the essential sign of chaotic dynamics (Eckmann and Ruelle, 1985).

Later Lorenz would call this the *butterfly effect* for the idea that a butterfly flapping its wings in Brazil could cause a hurricane in Texas.[33] The immediate implication for Lorenz was that long-term weather forecasting is essentially impossible. Butterflies are everywhere.

The model consists of three differential equations, two for temperature and one for velocity. They are

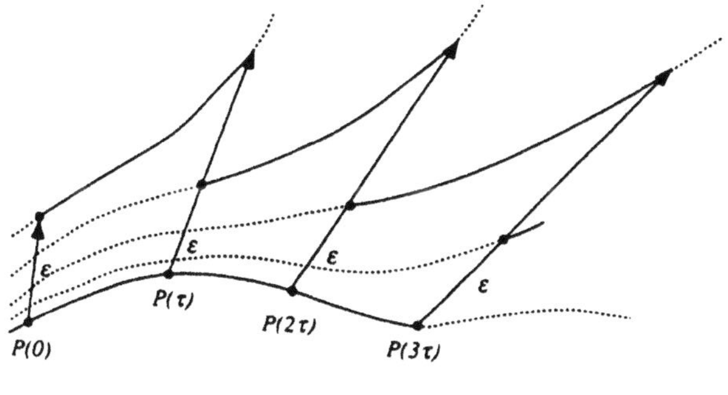

Fig. A.11 Divergent trajectories due to sensitive dependence on initial conditions

$$x = \sigma(y - x), \tag{A.12}$$

$$y = rx - y - xy, \tag{A.13}$$

$$z = -\beta z + xy, \tag{A.14}$$

where σ is the so-called Prandtl number, r is the Rayleigh number (Rayleigh, 1916), and β an aspect ratio. The usual approach is to set σ and β at fixed values (Lorenz set them at 10 and 8/3, respectively) and then vary r, the Rayleigh number. The system describes a two-layered fluid heated from above. For $r < 1$, the origin (no convection) is the only sink and is nondegenerate.

At $r = 1$, the system experiences a cusp catastrophe. The origin now becomes a saddle point with a one-dimensional unstable manifold while two stable attractors, C and C', emerge on either side of the origin, each representing convective behavior. This bifurcation recalls the discontinuous emergence of hexagonal "Bénard cells" of convection in heated fluids that Rayleigh (1916) had studied both theoretically and experimentally. As r passes through 13.26, the locally unstable trajectories return to the origin, while C and C' lose their global stability and become surrounded by local basins of attraction, N and N'. Trajectories outside these basins go back and forth chaotically. This is a zone of "metastable chaos." As r increases further, the basins N and N' shrink and the zone of metastable chaos expands as infinitely many unstable turbulent orbits appear. At $r = 24.74$, an unstable Hopf bifurcation occurs (Marsden and McCracken, 1976, Chap. 4). C and C' become unstable saddle points, and a zone of universal chaos has been reached.

Curiously enough, as r increases further to greater than about 100, order begins to reemerge. A sequence of period-halving bifurcations happens until at around $r = 313$, a single stable periodic orbit emerges that then remains as r goes to infinity. All of this is summarized by Fig. A.12 drawn from Robbins (1979). This represents the case with $\sigma = 10$ and $\beta = 8/3$ that Lorenz studied, but the bifurcation values of r would vary with different values of these parameters. These variations having been intensively studied by Sparrow (1982).

In his original paper, Lorenz studied the behavior of the system in the chaotic zone by iterating 3,000 times for $r = 28$. He found that fairly quickly the trajectories moved along a branched, S-shaped manifold that has a fine fractal structure. This has been identified as the *Lorenz attractor* and a very strange attractor it is. It has been and continues to be one of the most intensively studied of all attractors (Guckenheimer and Williams, 1979; Smale, 1991; Viana, 1996). Generally trajectories initially approach one of the formerly stable foci and then spiral around and away from the focus on one half of the attracting set until jumping back to the other half of the attractor fairly near the other focus and then repeat the pattern again. This behavior and the outline of the Lorenz attractor are depicted in Fig. A.13.

Structural Stability and the Smale Horseshoe

It took nearly 10 years before mathematicians became aware of Lorenz's results and began to study his model. But at the same time that he was doing his work,

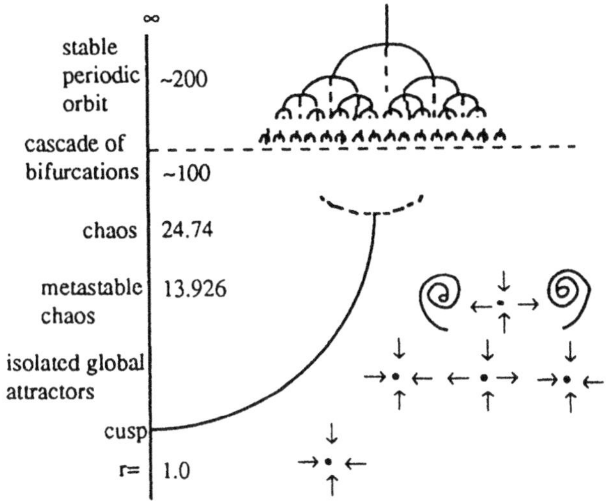

Fig. A.12 Bifurcation structure of the Lorenz model

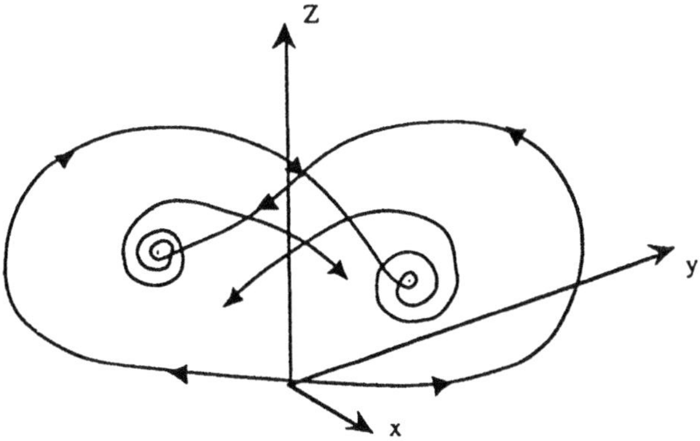

Fig. A.13 Lorenz attractor

Steve Smale (1963, 1967) was expanding the mathematical understanding of chaotic dynamics from research on structural stability of planar flows, following work by Peixoto (1962) that summarized a long strand of thought running from Poincaré through Andronov and Pontryagin.

In particular, he discovered that many differential equations systems contain a *horseshoe map* which has a nonwandering Cantor set containing a countably infinite set of periodic orbits of arbitrarily long periods, an uncountable set of bounded nonperiodic flows, and a dense orbit. These phenomena in conjunction with SDIC are thought by many to fully characterize chaotic dynamics, and indeed orbits near a horseshoe will exhibit SDIC (Guckenheimer and Holmes, 1983, p. 110).

The Smale horseshoe is the largest invariant set of a dynamical system; an orbit will stay inside the set once there. It can be found by considering all the backward and forward iterates of a control function on a Poincaré map of the orbits of a dynamical system which remain fixed. Let the Poincaré map be a planar unit square S and let f be the control function generating the set of orbits in S. The forward iterates will be given by $f(S) \cap S$ for the first iterate and $f(f(S) \cap S) \cap S$ for the second iterate and so forth. The backward iterates can be generated from $f^{-1}(S \cap f^{-1}(S))$ and so forth. This process of "stretching and folding" of a bounded set lies at the heart of chaos as the stretching in effect generates the local instability of SDIC as nearby trajectories diverge while the folding generates the return toward each other of distant trajectories that also characterizes chaos.

As depicted in Figs. A.14, A.15 and A.16, the set of forward iterates will be a countably infinite set of infinitesimally thick vertical strips, while the backward iterates will be a similar set of horizontal strips, both of these being Cantor sets. The entire set will be the intersection of these two sets which will in turn be a Cantor set of infinitesimal rectangles, Λ. This set is structurally stable in that slight perturbations of f will only slightly perturb Λ. Thus, the monster set was discovered to be sitting in the living room.

Many systems can be shown to possess a horseshoe, including the Duffing and van der Pol oscillators (Guckenheimer and Holmes, 1983, Chap. 2). Smale horseshoes arise when a system has a transversal homoclinic orbit, one that contains intersecting stable and unstable manifolds. Guckenheimer and Holmes (1983,

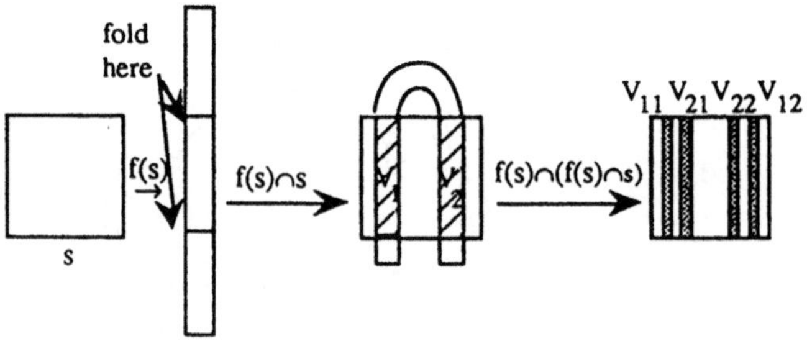

Fig. A.14 Forward iterates of Smale horseshoe

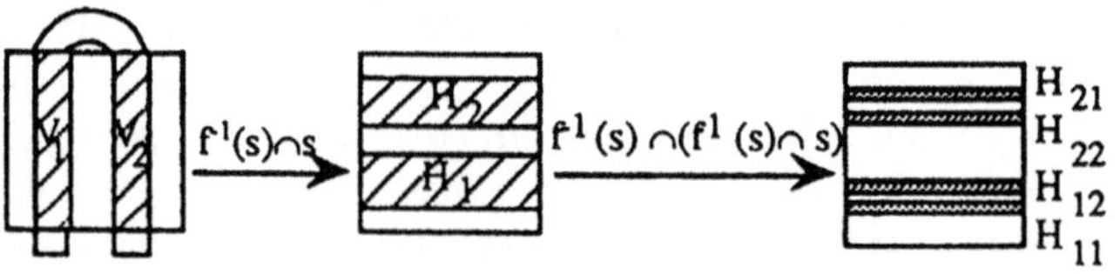

Fig. A.15 Backward iterates of Smale horseshoe

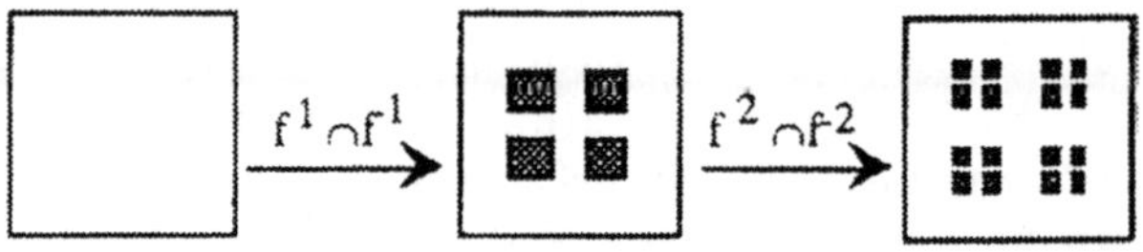

Fig. A.16 Combined iterates of Smale horseshoe

p. 256) define a *strange attractor* as one that contains such a transversal homoclinic orbit and thus a Smale horseshoe. However, we must note that this does not necessarily imply that the horseshoe is itself an attractor, only that its presence in an attractor will make that attractor a "strange" one. If orbits remain outside the horseshoe, they may remain periodic and well behaved, there being nothing necessarily to attract orbits into the horseshoe that are not already there. Nevertheless, the Smale horseshoe provided one of the first clear mathematical handles on chaotic dynamics,[34] and incidentally brought the Cantor set permanent respectability in the set of sets.

Turbulence and Strange Attractors

If the early intimations of chaotic dynamics came from studying multibody problems in celestial mechanics and nonlinear oscillatory systems, the explicit understanding of chaos came from studying fluid dynamics, the Lorenz model being an example of this. Further development of this understanding came from contemplating the emergence of turbulence in fluids (Ruelle and Takens, 1971).

This was not a new problem and certain complexity ideas had arisen earlier from contemplating it. The earliest models of turbulence with emphasis on wind were due to Lewis Fry Richardson (1922, 1926). One idea widely used in chaos theory, especially since Feigenbaum (1978), is that of a hierarchy of self-similar eddies linked by a cascade, a highly fractal concept. Richardson proposed such a view, declaring (Richardson, 1922, p. 66):

> Big whorls have little whorls,
> Which feed on their velocity;
> And little whorls have lesser whorls,
> And so on to viscosity
> (in the molecular sense).

In his 1926 paper, Richardson questioned whether wind can be said to have a definable velocity because of its gusty and turbulent nature and invoked the above Weierstrass function as part of this argument.[35]

Another phenomenon associated with fluid turbulence that appears more generally in chaotic systems is that of intermittency. Turbulence (and chaos) is not universal but comes and goes, as in the Lorenz model above. Chaos may emerge from order, but order may emerge from chaos, an argument especially emphasized by the Brussels School (Prigogine and Stengers, 1984). Intermittency of turbulence was first analyzed by Batchelor and Townsend (1949) and more formally by Kolmogorov (1962) and Obukhov (1962).

A major advance came with Ruelle and Takens (1971) who introduced the term *strange attractor* under the influence of Smale and Thom, although without knowing of Lorenz's work. Their model was an alternative to the accepted view of Lev Landau (Landau, 1944; Landau and Lifshitz, 1959) that turbulence represents the excitation of many independent modes of oscillation with some having periodicities not in rational number ratios of each other, a pattern known as *quasi-periodicity*

Fig. A.17 Ruelle–Takens transition to chaos

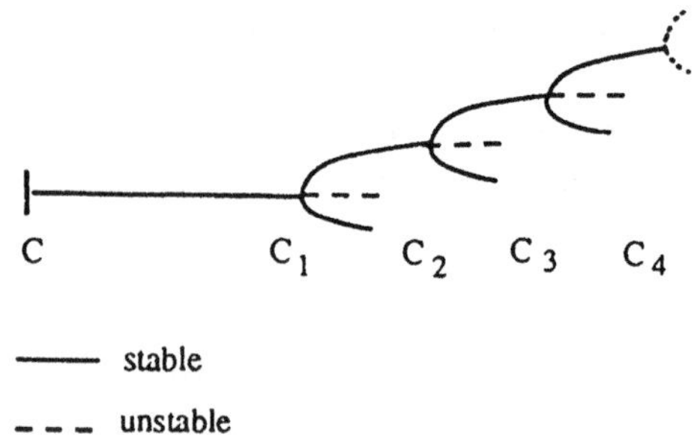

(Medio, 1998). Rather they argued that the modes interact with each other and that a sequence of Hopf bifurcations culminates in the system tracking a set with Cantor set Smale horseshoes in it, a strange attractor, although they did not formally define this term at this time.

Figure A.17 shows this sequence of bifurcations. The n-dimensional systems has a unique stable point at $C = 0$ which persists up to the first Hopf bifurcation at $C = C_1$ after which there is a limit cycle with a stable periodic orbit of angular frequency ω_1. Then at $C = C_2$, another Hopf bifurcation occurs followed by a limit torus (doughnut) with quasiperiodic flow governed by (ω_1, ω_2) as frequency components. As C increases and the ratio of the frequencies varies, the flow may vary rapidly between periodic and nonperiodic. At $C = C_3$, there is a third Hopf bifurcation followed by motion on a stable three-torus governed by quasiperiodic frequencies $(\omega_1, \omega_2, \omega_3)$. After $C = C_4$ and its fourth Hopf bifurcation, flow is quasiperiodic with frequencies $(\omega_1, \omega_2, \omega_3, \omega_4)$ on a structurally unstable four-torus with an open set of perturbations containing strange attractors with Smale horseshoes and thus "turbulence."

In 1975, Gollub and Sweeny experimentally demonstrated a transition to turbulence of the sort predicted by Ruelle and Takens for a rotating fluid. This experiment did much to change the attitude of the scientific community toward the ideas of strange attractors and chaos.

A major open question is the extent of structural stability among such strange attractors. Collett and Eckmann (1980) could not determine the structural stability of the attractors underlying the Duffing and van der Pol oscillators. Hénon (1976) numerically estimated a much-studied attractor that is a structurally unstable Cantor set. The first structurally stable planar strange attractor to be discovered resembles a disc with three holes in it (Plykin, 1974).

However, considerable controversy exists over the definition of the term "strange attractor." Ruelle (1980, p. 131) defines it for a map F as being a bounded m-dimensional set A for which there exists a set U such that (1) U is an m-dimensional neighborhood of A containing A, (2) any trajectory starting in U remains in U and approaches A as $t \to \infty$, (3) there is sensitive dependence on initial conditions (SDIC) for any point in U, and (4) A is *indecomposable* (same as irreducible), that is, any two trajectories starting in A will eventually become arbitrarily close to each other.

Although accepted by many, this definition has come under criticism from two different directions. One argues that it is missing a condition, namely, that the attractor have a fractal dimensionality. This is implied by the original Ruelle-Takens examples which possess Smale horseshoes and thus have Cantor sets or fractal dimensionality to them. But Ruelle's definition above does not require this. Others who insist on fractal dimensionality as well as the above characteristics include Guckenheimer and Holmes (1983, p. 256), who define it as being a closed invariant attractor that contains a transversal homoclinic orbit (and therefore a Smale horseshoe). Peitgen, Jürgens, and Saupe (1992, p. 671) simply add to Ruelle's definition that it has fractal dimension.

In the other direction is a large group that argues that it is the fractal nature of the attractor that makes it strange, not SDIC (Grebogi, Ott, Pelikan, and Yorke, 1984; Brindley and Kapitaniak, 1991). They call an attractor possessing SDIC a *chaotic attractor* and call those with fractal dimension but no SDIC *strange nonchaotic attractors*. It may well be that the best way out of this is to call the strange nonchaotic attractors "fractal attractors" and to call those with SDIC "chaotic attractors." The term "strange attractor" could either be reserved for those which are both or simply eliminated. But this latter is unlikely as the term seems to have a strange attraction for many.

"Period Three Equals Chaos" and Transitions to Chaos

Although a paper by the mathematical ecologist Robert M. May (1974) had used the term earlier, it is widely claimed that the term *chaos* was introduced by Tien-Yien Li and James A. Yorke in their 1975 paper, "Period Three Equals Chaos." Without doubt this paper did much to spread the concept. They proved a narrower version of a theorem established earlier by A.N. Sharkovsky (1964) of Kiev. But their deceptively simple version highlighted certain important aspects of chaotic systems, even as their definition of chaos, known as *topological chaos*, has come to be viewed as too narrow and missing crucial elements, notably sensitive dependence on initial conditions (SDIC) in the multidimensional case.

Essentially their theorem states that if f continuously maps an interval on the real number line into itself and it exhibits a three-period cycle (or, more generally a cycle wherein the fourth iteration is not on the same side of the first iteration as are the second and third), then: (1) cycles of every possible period will exist; (2) there will be an uncountably infinite set of aperiodic cycles which will both diverge to some extent from every other one, and also become arbitrarily close to every other one; and (3) that every aperiodic cycle will diverge to some extent from every periodic cycle. Thus, "period three equals chaos."

The importance of period three cycles was becoming clearer through work on transitions to chaos as a control ("tuning") parameter is varied. We have seen above that Ruelle and Takens (1971) observed a pattern of transition involving a sequence of period-doubling bifurcations. This was extended by May (1974, 1976), who examined in more detail the sequence of period-doubling pitchfork bifurcations in the transition to chaos arising from varying the parameter, a, in the logistic equation[36]

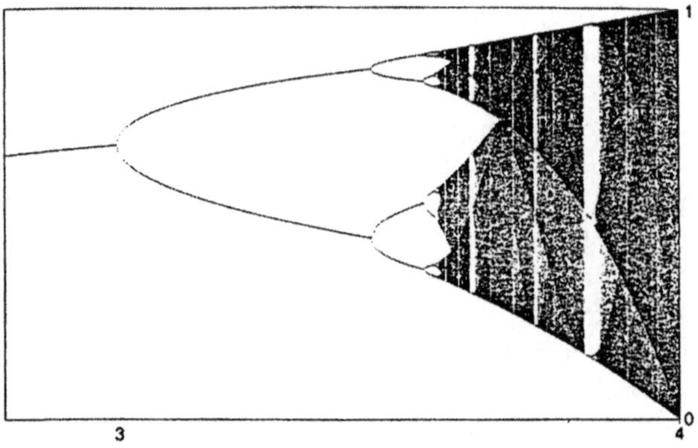

Fig. A.18 Logistic equation transition to chaos

$$x_{t+1} = ax_t(1 - x_t), \tag{A.15}$$

which is arguably the most studied equation in chaotic economic dynamics models.[37]

Figure A.18 shows the transition to chaos for the logistic equation as a varies. At $a = 3.00$, the single fixed point attractor bifurcates to a two-period cycle, followed by more period-doubling bifurcations as a increases with an accumulation point at $a = 3.570$ for the cycles of 2^n as $n \to \infty$, beyond which is the chaotic regime which contains nonzero measure segments with SDIC. The first odd-period cycle appears at $a = 3.6786$ and the first three-period cycle appears at $a = 3.8284$, thus indicating the presence of every integer-period cycle according to the Li-Yorke Theorem. The Li-Yorke Theorem emphasizes that three-period cycles appear in chaotic zones after period-doubling bifurcation sequences have ended. Interestingly, the three-period cycle appears in a "window" in which the period-doubling sequence is reproduced on a smaller scale with the periods following the sequence, 3×2^n.[38] This window is shown in more detail in Fig. A.19.

Inspired by Ruelle and Takens (1971) and work by Metropolis, Stein, and Stein (1973), the nature of these period-doubling cascades was more formally analyzed by Mitchell J. Feigenbaum (1978, 1980), who discovered the phenomenon of *universality*.[39] In particular, during such a sequence of bifurcations, there is a definite rate at which the subsequent bifurcations come more quickly as they accumulate to the transition to chaos point. Thus, if Λ_n is the value of the tuning parameter at which the period doubles for the nth time, then

$$\delta_n = (\Lambda_{n+1} - \Lambda_n)/(\Lambda_{n+2} - \Lambda_{n+1}). \tag{A.16}$$

Feigenbaum shows that as n increases, δ_n very rapidly converges to a universal constant, $\delta = 4.6692016\ldots$.

Closely related to this, he also discovered another universal constant for period-doubling transitional systems, α, a scaling adjustment factor for the process. Let d_n be the algebraic distance from $x = \frac{1}{2}$ to the nearest element of the attractor cycle of

Fig. A.19 Three-period window in transition to chaos

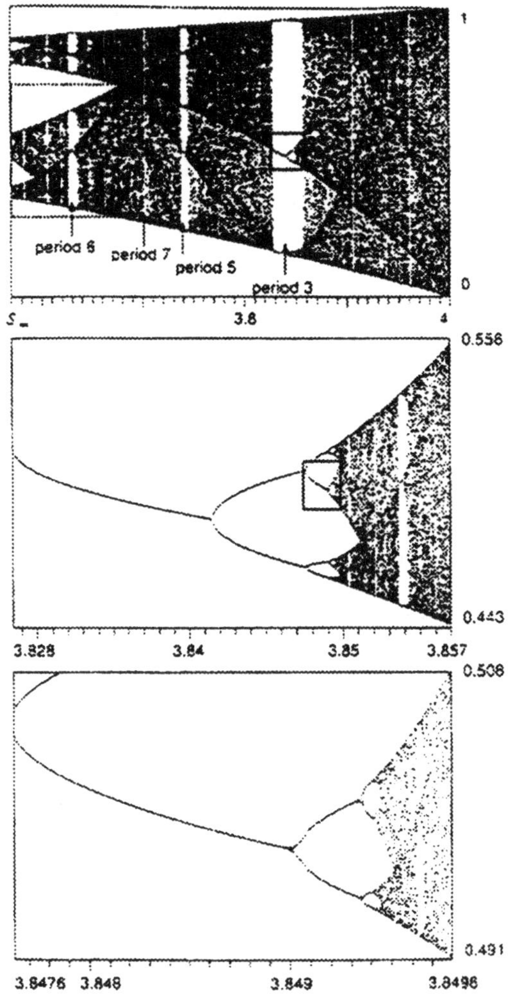

period 2^n in the 2^n cycle at λ_n. This distance scales down for the 2^{n+1} cycle at λ_{n+1} according to

$$d_n/d_{n+1} \sim -\alpha. \tag{A.17}$$

Feigenbaum discovered that $\alpha = 2.502907875\ldots$ universally. Unsurprisingly, cascades of period-doubling bifurcations are called *Feigenbaum cascades*.[40]

There are other possible transitions to chaos besides period doubling. Another that can occur for functions mapping intervals into themselves involves *intermittency* and is associated with the *tangent* or *saddle-node* bifurcation (Pomeau and Manneville, 1980), a phenomenon experimentally demonstrated for a nonlinearly forced oscilloscope by Perez and Jeffries (1982). As the bifurcation is approached, the dynamics exhibit zones of long period cycles separated by bursts of aperiodic behavior, hence the term "intermittency" (Thompson and Stewart, 1986, pp. 170–173; Medio with Gallo, 1993, pp. 165–169).

Yet another one-dimensional case is that of the hysteretic chaotic *blue-sky catastrophe* (or chaostrophe) initially proposed by Abraham (1972, 1985a) in which a variation of a control parameter brings about a homoclinic orbit that destroys an attractor as its basin of attraction suddenly goes to infinity, the "blue sky." This has been shown for the van der Pol oscillator (Thompson and Stewart, 1986, pp. 268–284) and is illustrated in Fig. A.20. A more general version of this is the *chaotic contact bifurcation* when a chaotic attractor contacts its basin boundary (Abraham, Gardini, and Mira, 1997).

The theory of multidimensional transitions is less well understood, but it is thought based on experimental evidence that transitions through quasi-periodic cycles may be possible in this case (Thompson and Stewart, 1986, pp. 284–288). In the case of two interacting frequencies on the unit circle mapping into itself, such a transition would involve avoiding zones of mode-locking known as *Arnol'd tongues* (Arnol'd, 1965). It remains uncertain mathematically whether such a transition is possible with the experimental evidence possibly having been contaminated by noise (Thompson and Stewart, 1986, p. 288).

The Chaos of Definitions of Chaos

We have been gradually building up our picture of chaos. Chaotic dynamics are deterministic but seem random, lacking any periodicity. They are locally unstable

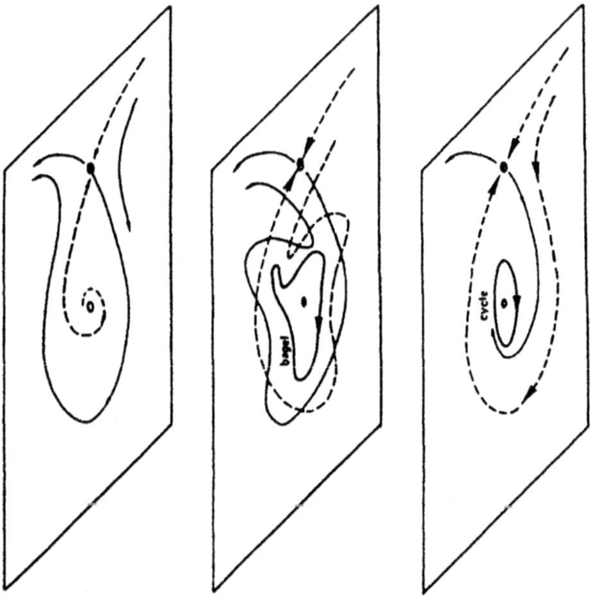

Fig. A.20 Blue-sky catastrophe (blue-bagel chaostrophe)

in the sense of the butterfly effect (or SDIC), but are bounded. Initially adjacent trajectories can diverge, but will also eventually become arbitrarily close again.[41] These are among the characteristics observed in the Lorenz (1963) model as well as those studied by May (1974, 1976) and in the theorem of Li and Yorke (1975) for the one-dimensional case.

However, despite the widespread agreement that these are core characteristics of chaotic dynamics, it has proven very difficult to come up with a universally accepted definition of chaos, with some surprisingly intense emotions erupting in the debates over this matter (observed personally by this author on more than one occasion).[42] Some (Day, 1994) have stuck with the characteristics of the Li-Yorke Theorem given above as defining chaotic dynamics, perhaps in honor of their alleged coining of the term "chaos." But the problem with this is that their theorem does not include SDIC as a characteristic and indeed does not guarantee the existence of SDIC beyond the one-dimensional case.[43] And of all the characteristics identified with chaos, the butterfly effect is perhaps the most widely accepted and understood.[44]

Yet another group, led by Mandelbrot (1983), insists that chaotic dynamics must involve some kind of fractal dimensionality of an attractor. And while many agree that fractality is a necessary component of being a strange attractor, most of these also accept that SDIC is the central key to chaotic dynamics, per se. Thus, Mandelbrot's is a distinctly minority view.

Perhaps the most widely publicized definition of chaotic dynamics is due to Robert Devaney (1989, p. 50) and involves three parts. A map of a set into itself, $f: V \rightarrow V$, is *chaotic* if (1) it exhibits sensitive dependence on initial conditions (SDIC, the "butterfly effect"), (2) is *topologically transitive* (same as indecomposable of irreducible), and (3) periodic points are *dense* in V (an element of regularity or "order out of chaos").

A formal definition for a map $f: V \rightarrow V$ of sensitive dependence on initial conditions is that depending on f and V there exists a $\delta > 0$ such that in every nonempty open subset of V, there are two points whose eventual iterates under f will be separated by at least δ. This does not say that such separation will occur between any two points, neither does it say that such a separation must occur exponentially, although some economists argue that this should be a condition for chaos, as they define chaos solely by the presence of a positive real part of the largest Lyapunov characteristic exponent which indicates exponential divergence (Brock, 1986; Brock, Hsieh, and LeBaron, 1991; Brock and Potter, 1993).

A formal definition of topological transitivity is that for $f: V \rightarrow V$ if for any pair of open subsets of V, U and W, there exists a $k > 0$ such that the kth iterate, $f^k(U) \cap W \neq \emptyset$. In effect this says that the map wanders throughout the set and is the essence of the indecomposability that many claim is a necessary condition for a set to be an attractor.

A formal definition of denseness is that a subset U of V is dense if the closure of $U = V$ (closure means union of set with its limit points). Thus, for Devaney, the closure of the set of periodic points of the map $f: V \rightarrow V$ must equal V. This implies that, much as in the Li-Yorke Theorem, there must be at least a countably infinite set of such trajectories and that they just about fill the set. Of the three conditions proposed by Devaney, this latter has been perhaps the most controversial. Indeed, it is not used by Wiggins (1990) who defines chaos only by SDIC and topological transitivity.[45]

A serious problem is that denseness does not guarantee that the periodic points (much less those exhibiting SDIC) constitute a set of positive Lebesgue measure, that is, are observable in any empirical sense. An example of a dense set of zero Lebesgue measure is the rational numbers. Their total length in the real number line is zero, implying a zero probability of randomly selecting a rational number out of the real number line.

This view of Devaney's is more topological and contrasts with a more metrical view by those such as Eckmann and Ruelle (1985), who insist that one must not bother with situations in which Lebesgue measure is zero ("thin chaos") and in which one cannot observe anything. There has been much discussion of whether given models exhibit positive Lebesgue measure for the sets of points for which chaotic dynamics can occur ("thick chaos"), a discussion affected by what one means by chaotic dynamics. Nusse (1987) insists that chaotic dynamics are strictly those with aperiodic flow rather than flows of arbitrary length, and Melèse and Transue (1986) argue that for many systems the points for these constitute measure zero, although Lasota and Mackey (1985) present a counterexample. Day (1986) and Lorenz (1993a) argue that arbitrary periodicities may behave like chaos for all practical purposes. Drawing on work of Sinai (1972) and Bowen and Ruelle (1975), Eckmann and Ruelle (1985) present a theory of *ergodic chaos* in which the observability of chaos is given by the existence of invariant ergodic[46] SRB (Sinai-Ruelle-Bowen) measures that are absolutely continuous with respect to Lebesgue measure along the unstable manifolds of the system, drawing on the earlier work of Sinai (1972) and Bowen and Ruelle (1975). One reason for the widespread use of the piecewise-linear tent map in models of chaotic economic dynamics has been that it generates ergodic chaotic outcomes.

Yet another source of controversy surrounding Devaney's definition involves the possible redundancy of some of the conditions, especially in the one-dimensional case. Thus, Banks, Brooks, Cairns, Davis, and Stacey (1992) show that topological transitivity and dense periodic points guarantee SDIC, thus making the most famous characteristic of chaos a redundant one, not a fundamental one. For the one-dimensional case of intervals on the real number line, Vellekoop and Berglund (1994) show that topological transitivity implies dense periodic points.[47] Thus both SDIC and dense periodic points are redundant in that case, which underlies why the Li-Yorke Theorem can imply that the broader conditions of chaos hold for the one-dimensional case. In the multidimensional case, Wiggins (1990, pp. 608–611) lays out various possibilities with an exponential example that shows SDIC and topological transitivity but no periodic points on a noncompact set, a sine function on a torus example with SDIC and countably infinite periodic points but only limited topological transitivity, and an integrable twist map example that shows SDIC and dense periodic points but no topological transitivity at all. Clearly there is still a lot of "chaos" in chaos theory.

The Empirical Estimation of Chaos

Despite its deductive redundance, sensitive dependence on initial conditions remains the centerpiece of chaos theory in most peoples' eyes. If it wasn't the bestselling account by James Gleick (1987) of Edward Lorenz's now immortal coffee break that brought the butterfly effect to the attention of the masses, it was "chaotician" Jeff Goldblum's showing water drops diverging on his hand in the movie version of *Jurassic Park*. Thus, it is unsurprising that most economists simply focus directly on SDIC in its exponential form as the single defining element of chaos, although it is generally also assumed that chaotic dynamics are bounded.

For observable dynamical systems with invariant SRB measures, the most important ones are the *Lyapunov characteristic exponents* (LCEs, also known as "Floquet multipliers").[48] The general existence and character of these was established by Oseledec (1968), and their link with chaotic dynamics was more fully developed by Pesin (1977) and Ruelle (1979). In particular, if the largest real part of a dynamical system's LCEs is positive, then that system exhibits SDIC, the butterfly effect. Thus Lyapunov characteristic exponents (or more commonly just "Lyapunov exponents") are the Holy Grail of chaoeconometricians.

Let $f^t(x)$ be the tth iterate of f starting at initial condition x, D be the derivative, v be a direction vector, $|| \; ||$ be the Euclidean distance norm, and ln the natural logarithm, then the largest Lyapunov characteristic exponent of f is[49]

$$\lambda_1 = \lim_{t\to\infty} \left[\ln(||Df^t(x) \cdot v||)/t\right]. \tag{A.18}$$

This largest real part of the LCEs represents the exponential rate of divergence or convergence of nearby points in the system. If all the real parts of the LCEs are negative, the system will be convergent. If λ_1 is zero, there may be a limit cycle, although convergence can occur in some cases.[50] A $\lambda_1 > 0$ indicates divergence and thus SDIC. If more than one λ has a real part that is positive, the system is *hyperchaotic* (Rössler and Hudson, 1989; Thomsen, Mosekilde, and Sterman, 1991) and if there are many such positive λ's but they are all near zero, this is *homeochaos* (Kaneko, 1995).

An important interpretation of a positive λ_1 is that it represents the rate at which information or forecastibility is lost by the system (Sugihara and May, 1990; Wales, 1990), the idea being that short-term forecasting may be possible with deterministically chaotic systems, even if long-term forecasting is not. This suggests a deeper connection with measures of information. In particular, Kolmogorov (1958) and Sinai (1959) formalized a link between information and *entropy* initially proposed by Claude Shannon in 1948 (Peitgen, Jürgens, and Saupe, 1992, p. 730). This Kolmogorov–Sinai entropy is rarely exactly computable but is approximated by

$$K = \lim_{m\to\infty} \lim_{\varepsilon\to 0} \{(1/\tau)[\ln(C_m(\varepsilon))/(C_{m+1}(\varepsilon))]\}, \tag{A.19}$$

where τ is the observation interval and $C_m(\varepsilon)$ is the correlation integral defined in paragraph before equation A.11 as being the probability that for a radius ε two randomly chosen points on a trajectory will be within ε of each other (Grassberger and Procaccia, 1983b).

This entropy measure indicates the gain in information from having a finer partition of a set of data. Thus it is not surprising that it (the exact measure of K) can be related to the LCEs. In particular, the sum of the positive Lyapunov exponents will be less than or equal to the Kolmogorov–Sinai entropy. If there is absolute continuity on the unstable manifolds, and thus a unique invariant SRB measure, this relationship becomes an equality known as the Pesin (1977) equality. For two-dimensional mappings, Young (1982) has shown that the Hausdorff dimension equals the entropy measure times the difference between the reciprocals of the two largest Lyapunov exponents.[51]

Unsurprisingly, a major cottage industry has grown up in searching for the best algorithms and methods of statistical inference for estimating Lyapunov exponents. Broadly there have been two competing strands. One is the direct method, originally due to Wolf, Swift, Swinney, and Vastano (1985), which has undergone numerous refinements (Rosenstein, Collins, and de Luca, 1993; Bask, 1998) and which focuses on estimating just the maximum LCE. Its main rival is the Jacobian method, due originally to Eckmann, Kamphorst, Ruelle, and Ciliberto (1986), which uses the Jacobian matrix of partial derivatives which can estimate the full spectrum of the Lyapunov exponents and which has been improved by Gençay and Dechert (1992) and McCaffrey, Ellner, Gallant, and Nychka (1992), although the latter focus only on estimating the dominant exponent, λ_1. However, this method is subject to generating spurious LCEs associated with the embedding dimension being larger than the attractor's dimension, although there are ways of partially dealing with this problem (Dechert and Gençay, 1996).

The problem of the distributional theory for statistical inference for LCE estimates has been one of the most difficult in empirical chaos theory, but now may have been partialy solved. That it is a problem is seen by Brock and Sayers (1988) showing that many random series appear to have positive Lyapunov exponents according to some of the existing estimation methods. An asymptotic theory that establishes normality of the smoothing-based estimators of LCEs of the Jacobian-type approaches is due to Whang and Linton (1999), although it does not hold for all cases, is much weaker in the multidimensional case, and has very high data requirements.

A somewhat more ad hoc, although perhaps more practical procedure involves the use of the moving blocks version of Efron's (1979) bootstrap technique (Gençay, 1996). In effect this allows one to create a set of distributional statistics from an artificially created sample generated from successive blocks within the data series.[52] Bask (1998) provides a clear description of how to use this approach, focusing on the direct method for estimating λ_1, and Bask and Gençay (1998) apply it to the Hénon map.

We shall not review the multitude of econometric estimates of Lyapunov exponents at this point, as we shall be referring to these throughout this book. We note, however, that beginning with Barnett and Chen (1988) many researchers have found positive real parts for Lyapunov exponents in various economic time series, although until recently there were no confidence estimates for most of these. Critics have argued, however, that what is required (aside from overcoming biases due to inadequate data in many cases) is to find low-dimensional chaos that can allow one to make accurate out-of-sample forecasts. Critics who claim that this has yet to be achieved include Jaditz and Sayers (1993) and LeBaron (1994).

One response by some of those who argue for the presence of chaotic dynamics in economic time series has been to use alternative methods of measuring chaos. Some of these have attempted to directly estimate the topological structure of attractors by looking at close returns (Mindlin, Hou, Solari, Gilmore, and Tufilaro, 1990; C. Gilmore, 1993; R. Gilmore, 1998). Another approach is to estimate continuous chaos models that require an extra dimension, the first model of continuous chaos being due to Otto Rössler (1976). Wen (1996) argues that this avoids biases that appear due to the arbitrariness of time periods that can allow noise to enter into difference equation model approaches. An earlier method was to examine spectral densities (Bunow and Weiss, 1979). Pueyo (1997) proposes a randomization technique to study SDIC in small data series as found in ecology.

Finally, we note that a whole battery of related techniques are used in the preliminary stages by researchers searching for chaos to show that linear or other nonlinear but nonchaotic specifications are inadequate.[53] A variety of tests have been compared by Barnett, Gallant, Hinich, Jungeilges, Kaplan, and Jensen (1994, 1998), including the Hinich bispectrum test (1982), the BDS test, the Lyapunov estimator of Nychka, Ellner, Gallant, and McCaffrey (1992), White's neural net estimator (1989), and Kaplan's (1994) test, not a full set. One found to have considerable power by these researchers and one of the most widely used is the BDS test originally due to Brock, Dechert, and Scheinkman (1987), which tests against a null hypothesis that series is i.i.d., that is, it is independently and identically distributed.[54] The statistic uses the correlation integral, with n being the length of the data series and is

$$\mathrm{BDS}_{m,n}(\varepsilon) = n^{1/2}\{[C_{m,n}(\varepsilon) - C_n(\varepsilon)^m]/\sigma_{m,n}(\varepsilon)\}, \tag{A.20}$$

with $C_n(\varepsilon)^m$ being the asymptotic value of $C_{m,n}(\varepsilon)$ as $n \to \infty$ and σ being the standard deviation.

Practical use of this statistic is discussed in Brock, Hsieh, and LeBaron (1991) and Brock, Dechert, LeBaron, and Scheinkman (1996).[55] It can be used successively to test various transformations to see if there is remaining unexplained dependence in the series. But it is not itself directly a test for chaotic dynamics or any specific nonlinear form, despite using the correlation integral.

Controlling Chaos

It is a small step from learning to estimate chaos to wanting to control it if one can. Studying how to control chaos and actually doing it in some cases has been a major research area in chaos theory in the 1990s. This wave was set off by a paper on local control of chaos by Ott, Grebogi, and Yorke (1990), one by Shinbrot, Ott, Grebogi, and Yorke (1990) on a global targeting method of control using SDIC, and a paper showing experimentally the control of chaos by the local control method in an externally forced, vibrating magnetoelastic ribbon (Ditto, Rauseo, and Spano, 1990).[56] Shinbrot, Ditto, Grebogi, Ott, Spano, and Yorke (1992) experimentally demonstrated the global SDIC method with the same magnetoelastic ribbon. Control of chaos has since been demonstrated in a wide variety of areas including mechanics, electronics, lasers, biology, and chemistry (Ditto, Spano, and Lindner, 1995).

One can argue that the control of chaos had been discussed earlier, that it is implicit in the idea of changing a control parameter in a major way to move a system out of a chaotic zone, as suggested by Grandmont (1985) in the context of a rational expectations macroeconomic model. But these methods all involve small perturbations of a control parameter that somehow stabilize the system while not moving it out of the chaotic zone.

The local control method due to Ott, Grebogi, and Yorke (1990), often called the OGY method, relies upon the fact that chaotic systems are dense in periodic orbits, and even contain fixed saddle points that have both stable and unstable manifolds going into them. There are three steps in this method, which has been extended to the multidimensional case by Romeiras, Ott, Grebogi, and Dayawansa (1992). The first is to identify an unstable periodic point by examining close returns in a Poincaré section. The second is to identify the local structure of the attractor using the embedding and reconstruction techniques described above, with particular emphasis on locating the stable and unstable manifolds. The final part is to determine the response of the attractor to an external stimulus on a control parameter, which is the most difficult step. The ultimate goal is to determine the location of a stable manifold near where the system is and then to slightly perturb the system so that it moves on to the stable manifold and approaches the periodic point. Ott, Grebogi, and Yorke (1990) provide a formula for the amount of parameter change needed that depends on the parallels and perpendicular eigenvalues of the unstable manifold about the fixed point, the distance of the system from the fixed point, and the responsiveness of the fixed point itself to changes in the control parameter.[57]

The main problems with this method are that once on the stable manifold it can take a long time to get to the periodic point during when it can go through a variety of complex transients. Also, given this long approach, it can be disturbed by noise and knocked off the stable manifold. Dressler and Nitsche (1991) stress the need for constant readjustment of the control parameter to keep it on the stable manifold and Aston and Bird (1997) show how the basin of attraction can be expanded for the OGY technique.

The global targeting method of Shinbrot, Ott, Grebogi, and Yorke (1990) avoids the problem of transients during a long delay of approach. It starts by considering possible next step iterates of the system as a set of points and then looks at further iterates of this set which will diverge from each other and begin wandering all over the space because of SDIC. The goal is to find an iterate that will put the system within a particular small neighborhood. If the observer has sufficiently precise knowledge of the system, this can then be achieved usually with a fairly small number of iterations.[58]

The main problems with this method are that it requires a much greater degree of knowledge about the global dynamics of the system than does the OGY method and that it will only get one to a neighborhood rather than a particular point. Thus, one gains speed but loses precision. But in a noisy environment such as the economy, speed may equal precision.

There have now been several applications in economics. Holyst, Hagel, Haag, and Weidlich (1996) apply the OGY method to a case of two competing firms with asymmetric investment strategies and Haag, Hagel, and Sigg (1997) apply the OGY method to stabilizing a chaotic urban system, while Kopel (1997) applies the global targeting method to a model of disequilibrium dynamics with financial feedbacks as do Bala, Majumdar, and Mitra (1998) to a model of tâtonnement adjustment. Kaas (1998) suggests the application of both in a macroeconomic stabilization context. The global method is used to get the system within the neighborhood of a stable manifold that will take the system to a desirable location, and then the OGY method is used to actually get it there by local perturbations.

Unsurprisingly, all of these observers are very conscious of the difficulty of obtaining sufficient data for actually using either of these methods and of the severe problems that noise can create in trying to do so. Given that we are still debating whether or not there actually even is deterministic economic chaos of whatever dimension, we are certainly rather far from actually controlling any that does exist.

A.4 The Special Path to Fractal Geometry

Fractal geometry is the brainchild of the late idiosyncratic genius Benoit Mandelbrot. Many of its ideas have been enumerated in earlier sections, and there is clearly a connection with chaos theory. Certainly, the notions of "fractal dimension" and "fractal set" are important in the concept of strange attractors, or "fractal attractors" as Mandelbrot preferred to call them. The very idea of attempting to measure the "regularity of irregularity" or the "order in chaos" is a central theme of Mandelbrot's work.

Like the late René Thom, Mandelbrot claims to have discovered an all-embracing world-explaining theory. This has gotten him in trouble with other mathematicians. Just as Thom claims that chaos theory is an extension of catastrophe theory, so Mandelbrot claims that it is an extension of fractal geometry. The reaction of many mainstream bifurcation theorists is to pretend that he is not there. Thus, neither he nor the word "fractal" appear in Guckenheimer and Holmes's comprehensive *Nonlinear Oscillations, Dynamical Systems, and Bifurcations of Vector Fields* (1983). At least Thom and Zeeman rate brief mentions in that book, even though Mandelbrot is probably closer in spirit to Guckenheimer and Holmes than are Thom or Zeeman.

But then Mandelbrot ignored Thom and Zeeman, not mentioning either or catastrophe theory in his magisterial *Fractal Geometry of Nature* (1983).[59] At least Thom at one point (1983, p. 107) explicitly recognized that Mandelbrot has presented what Thom labels "generalized catastrophes" and mentions him by name in this context.

But there is a deep philosophical divide between Thom and Mandelbrot that goes beyond the appropriate labels for mathematical objects or who had the prettiest pictures in *Scientific American*, a contest easily won by Mandelbrot with his justly famous Mandelbrot Set (see especially Peitgen, Jürgens, and Saupe, 1992).[60] It is also despite Thom and Mandelbrot both favoring geometric over algebraic or metric approaches, as well as less formal notions of proof, in contrast with the Russian School and mainstream bifurcation theorists such as Guckenheimer and Holmes. The latter are intermediate between Thom and Mandelbrot who divide on whether the world is fundamentally stable and well ordered or fundamentally irregular, with Thom holding the former position and Mandelbrot holding the latter. Mandelbrot is the vanguard of the radical chaos position, as Mirowski (1990) argues, in sharp contrast with the relative continuity and order of Thom's position. Both see reality as a balance of order and chaos, of continuity and discontinuity, but with the two sides operating at different levels and relating in different ways.

Although Thom paraded as the prophet of discontinuity, he was fixated on structural stability, part of the title of his most famous book. Between catastrophe points, Thom sees dynamic systems evolving continuously and smoothly. His major innovation is the concept of transversality, central to proving the structural stability of the elementary catastrophes, the basis for their claimed universal significance and applicability. For Thom to carry out his wide-ranging qualitative analysis of linguistic and other structures, he must believe in the underlying well-ordered nature of the universe, even if the order is determined by the pattern of its stable discontinuities.

But Mandelbrot would have none of this. For him, the closer one looks at reality, the more irregular and fragmented it becomes. In the second chapter of *Fractal Geometry of Nature*, he quotes at length from Jean Perrin (1906) who won a Nobel Prize for studying Brownian motion. Perrin invokes a vision of matter possessing "infinitely granular structure." At a sufficiently small scale finite volumes and densities and smooth surfaces vanish into the "emptiness of intra-atomic space" where "true density *vanishes* almost everywhere, except at an infinite number of isolated points where it reaches an infinite value." Ultimate reality is an infinitely discontinuous Cantor set.

Mandelbrot's vision of ultimate discontinuity carries over to his view of economics. Mandelbrot claimed that the original inspiration for his notions of fractal measures and self-similar structures came from work he did on random walk theory of stock prices and cotton prices (Mandelbrot, 1963). It has often been thought that the random walk theory was inspired by the Brownian motion theory. But Mandelbrot (1983) argues persuasively that Brownian motion theory was preceded, if not directly inspired, by the random walk theory of speculative prices due to Louis Bachelier (1900).

Thus Mandelbrot's view of price movements in competitive markets is one of profound and extreme discontinuity, in sharp contrast with most views in economics. His radically discontinuous view is exemplified by the following quotation (Mandelbrot, 1983, pp. 334–335):

> But prices on competitive markets *need not* be, continuous, and they are conspicuously *discontinuous*. The only reason for assuming continuity is that many sciences tend, knowingly or not, to copy the procedures that prove successful in Newtonian physics. Continuity should prove a reasonable assumption for diverse "exogenous" quantities and rates that enter economics but are defined in purely physical terms. But prices are different: Mechanics involves nothing comparable, and gives no guidance on this account.
>
> The typical mechanism of price formation involves both knowledge of the present and anticipation of the future. Even where the exogenous physical determinism of a price vary continuously, anticipations change drastically, "in a flash." When a physical signal of negligible energy and duration, "the stroke of a pen," provokes a brutal change of anticipations, and when no institution injects inertia to complicate matters, a price determined on the basis of anticipation can crash to zero, soar out of sight, do anything.[61]

We note again that despite his assertions of universal irregularity, Mandelbrot constantly seeks the hidden order in the apparent chaos.

A.5 The Complexity of Other Forms of Complexity

A.5.1 What Is Complexity?

John Horgan (1995, 1997) has made much in a negative light of a claimed succession from cybernetics to catastrophe to chaos to complexity theory, labeling the practitioners of the latter two, "chaoplexologists." Certainly such a succession can be identified through key individuals in various disciplines, but the issue arises as to what is the relationship between these? One approach is to allocate to the last of them the most general nature and view the others as subcategories of it. This then puts the burden squarely on how we define *complexity*. As Horgan has pointed out, there are numerous definitions of complexity around, more than 45 by the latest count of Seth Lloyd of MIT, so many that we have gone "from complexity to perplexity" according to Horgan.

Although some of our discussions above of entropy and dimension measures point us toward some alternative definitions of complexity, we shall stick with one tied more clearly to nonlinear dynamics and which can encompass both catastrophic and chaotic dynamics, as well as the earlier cybernetics of Norbert Wiener (1948) that Jay Forrester (1961) first applied to economics. Due to Richard Day (1994), this definition calls a nonlinear dynamical system complex if for nonstochastic reasons it does not go to either a fixed point, to a limit cycle, or explode. This implies that it must be a nonlinear system, although not all nonlinear systems are complex, for example, the exponential function. It also implies that the dynamics are bounded and endogenously generated. All of this easily allows for the earlier three of the "four C's."

But then we need to know what distinguishes "pure complexity" from these earlier three. Arthur, Durlauf, and Lane (1997), speaking for the "Santa Fe perspective," identify six characteristics associated with "the complexity approach": (1) dispersed interaction among heterogeneous agents, (2) no global controller, (3) cross-cutting hierarchical organization, (4) continual adaptation, (5) perpetual novelty (4 and 5 guaranteeing an evolutionary perspective), and (6) out-of-equilibrium dynamics. Of these the first may be the most important and underpins another idea often associated with complex dynamics, namely, *emergent structure*, that higher-order patterns or entities emerge from the interactions of lower-order entities (Baas, 1997). These ideas are reasonably consistent with those of older centers than Santa Fe of what is now called complexity research, namely Brussels, where Ilya Prigogine (1980) has been the key figure, and Stuttgart, where Hermann Haken (1977) has been the key figure, as discussed in Rosser (1999b).

Many of these characteristics also apply to cybernetics as well, but a notable contrast appears with both catastrophe and chaos theory. These two are often stated in terms of a small number of agents, possibly as few as one; there might be a global controller; there may be no hierarchy, much less a cross-cutting one; neither adaptation nor novelty are guaranteed, although they might happen, and equilibrium is not out of the question. So, there are some real conceptual differences, even though the complexity approaches contain and use many ideas from catastrophe and chaos theory. One implication of these differences is that it is much easier to achieve analytical results with catastrophe and chaos theory, whereas in the complexity models one is more likely to see the use of computer simulations[62] to demonstrate results, whether in Brussels, Stuttgart, Santa Fe, or elsewhere.

A.5.2 Discontinuity and Statistical Mechanics

An approach borrowed from physics in economics that has become very popular among the Santa Fe Institute (SFI) complexologists is that of statistical mechanics, the study of the interaction of particles. Such systems are known as *interacting particle systems* (IPS) models, as *spin-glass* models, or as *Ising* models, although the term "spin glass" properly only applies when negative interactions are allowed (Durlauf, 1997).[63] The original use of these models was to model phase transitions in matter, spontaneous magnetizations or changes from solid to liquid states,[64] and so forth. Kac (1968), Spitzer (1971), Sherrington and Kirkpatrick (1975), Liggett (1985), and Ellis (1985) present mathematical and physical foundations of these models and the conditions in them under which discontinuous phase transitions will occur.

Their first application in economics was by Hans Föllmer (1974) in a model of local interaction with a conditional probability structure on agent characteristics. Idiosyncratic shocks can generate aggregate consequences, a result further developed in Durlauf (1991) for business cycles. A major development was the introduction into this model by Brock (1993), Blume (1993), and Brock and Durlauf (1995) of the discrete choice theory by agents of Manski and McFadden (1981) and Anderson, de Palma, and Thisse (1992). A particularly influential version of this was the *mean field approach* introduced by Brock (1993).

Let there be n individuals who can choose from a discrete choice set $\{1,-1\}$ with m representing the average of the choices by the agents, J a strength of interaction between them, an intensity of choice parameter β (interpreted as "inverse temperature" in the physics models of material phase transitions), a parameter describing the probabilistic state of the system, h, which shows the utility gain from switching to a positive attitude, and an independent and identically distributed extreme value exogenous stochastic process. In this simple model, utility maximization leads to the Curie-Weiss mean field equation with tanh being the hypertangent:

$$m = \tanh(\beta Jm + \beta h). \tag{A.21}$$

This equation admits of a bifurcation at $\beta J = 1$ at which a phase transition occurs. Below this value $m = 0$ if $h = 0$, but above this value there will be two solutions with $m_- = -m+$. If $h \neq 0$ then for $\beta J > 1$ there will be a threshold H such that if βh exceeds it there will be unique solution, but if $\beta h < 0$ then there will be three solutions, one with the same sign as h and the other two with opposite sign (Durlauf, 1997, p. 88). Brock (1993) and Durlauf (1997) review numerous applications, some of which we shall see later in this book. Brock and Durlauf (1999) discuss ways of dealing with the deep identification problems associated with econometrically estimating such models as noted by Manski (1993, 1995). A general weakness of this approach is its emphasis on binary choices, although Yeomans (1992) offers an alternative to this. In any case, this approach exhibits discontinuous emergence, how interactions among agents can lead to a discontinuous phase transition in which the nature of the system suddenly changes. Figure A.21 shows the bifurcation for this mean field equation (from Rosser, 1999b, p. 179).

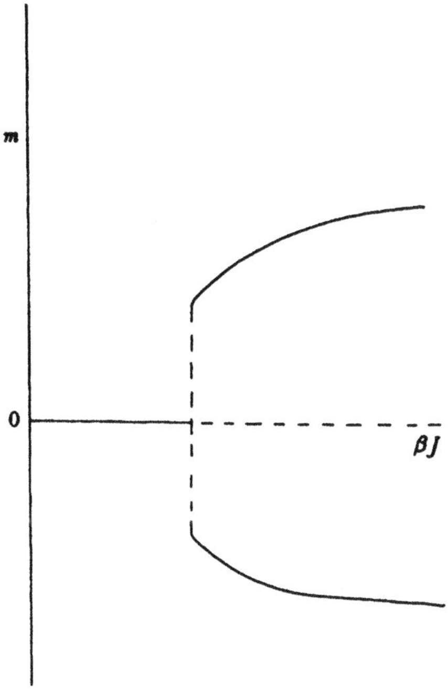

Fig. A.21 Interacting particle systems mean field solutions

A curious link between the mean field version of interacting particle systems models and chaotic dynamics has been studied by Shibata and Kaneko (1998). Kaneko (1990) initiated the study of globally coupled logistic map systems. Shibata and Kaneko consider the emergence of self-coherent collective behavior in zones of such systems with networks of entities that are behaving chaotically independently (from logistic equations). In the windows of periodicity within the chaotic zones, tongue-like structures can emerge within which this coherent collective behavior can occur. Within these structures *internal bifurcations* can occur even as the basic control parameters remain constant as the mean field interacting particle system dynamics accumulate to critical points. This model has not been applied to economics yet, but one possibility for a modified version might be in providing mechanisms for finding coherences that would allow overcoming the Manski (1993, 1995) identification problems in such systems as Brock and Durlauf (1999) note that nonlinear models actually allow possible solutions not available to linear models because of the additional information that they can provide.

A.5.3 Self-Organized Criticality and the "Edge of Chaos"

Another approach that is popular with the SFI complexity crowd is that of *self-organized criticality*, due to Per Bak and others (Bak, Tang, and Wiesenfeld, 1987; Bak and Chen, 1991) with extended development by Bak (1996). This approach shares with the Brussels School approach of Prigogine an emphasis on out-of-equilibrium states and processes. Agents are arrayed in a lattice that determines the structure of their interactions. In a macroeconomics example due to Bak, Chen, Scheinkman, and Woodford (1993), this reflects a demand–supply structure of an economy. There is a Gaussian random exogenous bombardment of the system with demand shocks that trigger responses throughout the system as it tries to maintain minimum inventories. The system evolves to a state of self-organized criticality where these bombardments sometimes trigger chain reactions throughout the system that are much larger than the original shock.

A widely used metaphor for these is *sandpile models*. Sand is dropped from above in a random way. The long-run equilibrium is for it to be flat on the ground, but it builds up into a sandpile. At certain critical points a drop of sand will trigger an avalanche that restructures the sandpile. The distribution of these avalanches follows a power law that generates a skewed distribution with a long tail out toward the avalanches, in comparison with the normal distribution of the exogenous shocks.

More formally for the Bak, Chen, Scheinkman, and Woodford (1993) macro model, letting y = aggregate output, n = the number of final buyers (which is large), τ be a parameter tied to the dimensionality of the lattice, and Γ be the gamma function of probability theory, then the asymptotic distribution of y will be given by

$$Q(y) = 1/n^{1/\tau}\{\sin(\pi\tau/2)\Gamma(1+\tau)/[(y/n^{1/\tau})^{1+\tau}]\}. \quad \text{(A.22)}$$

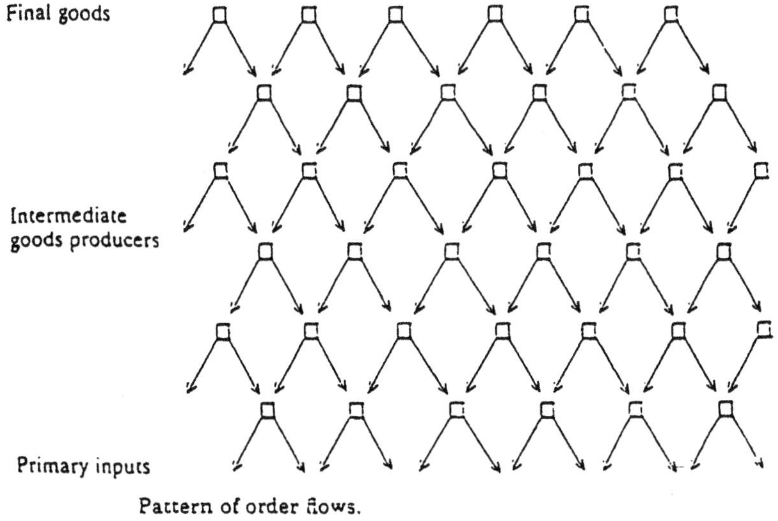

Fig. A.22 Lattice framework in Sandpile model

Figure A.22, from Bak, Chen, Scheinkman, and Woodford (1993) depicts the lattice framework of this model with the relations between different levels shown.

The borderline instability character of these models has led them to be associated with another class of models that have been associated with the Santa Fe group, although more controversially. This is the *edge of chaos* concept associated with modelers of artificial life such as Chris Langton (1990) and of biological evolution such as Stuart Kauffman (1993, 1995, and originally Kauffman and Johnsen, 1991). This idea has been identified by some popularizers (Waldrop, 1992) as the central concept of the SFI's complexity approach, although that has been disputed by some associated with the SFI (see Horgan, 1995, 1997).

Generally the concept of chaos used by this group is not the same as that we have been using, although there are exceptions such as Kaneko's (1995) use of homeochaos to generate edge of chaos self-organization. Rather it is a condition of complete disorder as defined in informational terms. The edge of chaos modelers simulate systems of many interacting agents through cellular automata models or genetic algorithms such as those of Holland (1992)[65] and observe that in many cases there will be a large zone of complete order and a large zone of complete disorder. In neither of these does much of interest happen. But on their borderline, the proverbial "edge of chaos," self-organization happens and structures emerge. Kauffman has gone so far as to see this as the model for the origins of life.

Although we shall see considerable use of the self-organization concept in economics, rarely has it directly followed the lines of the edge of chaos theorists, despite a few efforts by Kauffman in particular (Darley and Kauffman, 1997) and Kauffman's work exerting a more general influence.

A.5.4 A Synergetics Synthesis

Finally we contemplate how the Stuttgart School approach of *synergetics* (Haken, 1977) might offer a possible synthesis that can debifurcate bifurcation theory and give a semblance of order to the House of Discontinuity. Reasonable continuity and stability can exist for many processes and structures at certain scales of perception and analysis, while at other scales quantum chaotic discontinuity reigns. It may be God or the Law of Large Numbers which accounts for this seemingly paradoxical coexistence.

At the large scale where many processes and structures appear continuous and stable much of the time, important changes may occur discontinuously, perhaps as the result of complex emergent processes or phase transitions bubbling up from below, perhaps as high-level catastrophic bifurcations. In turn, chaotic oscillations can arise out of the fractal process of a cascade of period-doubling bifurcations, with discontinuities appearing at the bifurcation points and most dramatically at the accumulation point where chaos emerges.

These can be subsumed under the synergetics perspective which operates on the principle of *adiabatic approximation*, which in the hands of Wolfgang Weidlich (Weidlich, 1991; Weidlich and Braun, 1992) and his *master equation* approach can admit of numerous interacting agents making probabilistic transitions within economic models.[66] In the version of Haken (1983, 1996), a complex system is divided into "order parameters" that change slowly and "slave" fast moving variables or subsystems, usually defined as linear combinations of underlying variables, which can create difficulties for interpretation in economic models. This division corresponds to the division in catastrophe theory between "slow dynamics" (control variables) and "fast dynamics" (state variables). Nevertheless, stochastic perturbations are constantly occurring, leading to structural change when these occur near bifurcation points of the order parameters.

Let the slow dynamics be generated by a vector F and the fast dynamics by a vector q. Let A, B, and C be matrices and ε be a stochastic noise vector. A general locally linearized model is given by

$$q = Aq + B(F)_q C(F) + \varepsilon. \tag{A.23}$$

Adiabatic approximation allows this to be transformed into

$$q = -(A + B(F))^{-1} C(F). \tag{A.24}$$

Thus the fast variable dependence on the slow variables is determined by $A + B(F)$. Order parameters will be those of the *least* absolute value, a hierarchy existing of these.

A curious aspect of this is that the "order parameters" are dynamically unstable in possessing positive real parts of their eigenvalues while the "slave variables" will exhibit the opposite. Haken (1983, Chap. 12) argues that chaos occurs when there is a destabilization of a formerly "slaved" mode which may then "revolt" (Diener and Poston, 1984) and become a control parameter. Thus, chaotic dynamics may be associated with a deeper catastrophe or restructuring and the emergence of a whole new order, an idea very much in tune with the "order out of chaos" notions of the Brussels School (Prigogine and Stengers, 1984). And so, perhaps, a synergetics synthesis can pave the way to peace in the much-bifurcated House of Discontinuity.

Notes

1. There are cases where discontinuity replaces nonlinearity. Thus piecewise linear models of the variance of stock returns using regime-switching models may outperform models with nonlinear ARCH/GARCH specifications regarding volatility clustering, especially when the crash of 1987 is viewed as a regime-switching point (de Lima, 1998). Such models are of course nonlinear, strictly speaking.
2. Smale (1990) argues that this problem reappears in computer science in that modern computers are digital and discrete and thus face fundamental problems in representing the continuous nature of real numbers. This issue shows up in its most practical form as the roundoff problem, which played an important role in Edward Lorenz's (1963) observation of chaos.
3. Despite his Laplacian image, Walras was aware of the possibility of multiple equilibria and of various kinds of complex economic dynamics (see Day and Pianigiani, 1991; Bala and Majumdar, 1992; Day, 1994; Rosser, 1999a for further discussion). After all, "tâtonnement" means "groping."
4. It was actually from this case that René Thom adopted the term "catastrophe" for the current theory of that name.
5. Otto Rössler (1998, Chap. 1) argues that the idea of fractal self-similarity to smaller and smaller scales can be discerned in the writings of the pre-Socratic philosopher Anaxagoras.
6. That the Cantor set is in some sense a zero set while not being an empty set has led El Naschie (1994) to distinguish between zero sets, almost empty sets, and totally empty sets. Mandelbrot (1990a) developed the notion of negative fractal dimensions to measure "how empty is an empty set."

   The idea that something can be "almost zero" lay behind the idea of infinitesimals when calculus was originally invented, with Newton's "fluxions" and Leibniz's "monads." This was rejected later, especially by Weierstrass, but has been revived with nonstandard analysis that allows for infinite real numbers and their reciprocals, infinitesimal real numbers, not equal to but closer to zero than any finite real number (Robinson, 1966).
7. Mandelbrot (1983) and Peitgen, Jürgens, and Saupe (1992) present detailed discussions and vivid illustrations of these and other such sets.
8. Poincaré (1908) also addressed the question of shorter-run divergences, what is now called *sensitive dependence on initial conditions*, the generally accepted sine qua non of chaotic dynamics. But he was preceded in his recognition of the possibility of this by Hadamard's (1898) study of flows on negatively curved geodesic surfaces, despite the concept being implicit in Poincaré's earlier work, according to Ruelle (1991). Louçã (1997, p. 216) credits James Clerk Maxwell as preceding both Hadamard and Poincaré with his discussion in 1876 (p. 443) of "that class of phenomena such that a spark kindles a forest, a rock creates an avalanche or a word prevents an action."
9. Although Poincaré was the main formal developer of bifurcation theory, it had numerous precursors. Arnol'd (1992, Appendix) credits Huygens in 1654 with discovering the stability of cusp points in caustics and on wave fronts and Hamilton in 1837–1838 with studying critical points in geometrical optics, and numerous algebraic geometers of the late nineteenth century, including Cayley, Kronecker, and Bertini, among others, with understanding the typical singularities of curves and smooth surfaces, to the point that discussions of these were in some algebraic geometry textbooks by the end of the century.

10. A local bifurcation involves qualitative dynamical changes near the equilibria. Global bifurcations are such changes that do not involve changes in fixed point equilibria, the first known example being the *blue-sky catastrophe* (Abraham, 1972). The attractor discontinuously disappears into the "blue sky." Examples of these latter can occur in transitions to chaos, to be discussed later in this chapter. If the blue-sky catastrophe is achieved by a perturbed forced oscillation that leads to homoclinic transversal intersections during the bifurcation event, this is known as a *blue-bagel chaostrophe* (Abraham, 1985a). In three-dimensional maps, such an event is a *fractal torus crisis* (Grebogi, Ott, and Yorke, 1983). For more discussion of global bifurcations, see Thompson (1992) on indeterminate bifurcations, Palis and Takens (1993) on homoclinic tangent bifurcations, and Mira (1987) and Abraham, Gardini, and Mira (1997) on chaotic contact bifurcations.
11. Although we shall not generally do so, some observers distinguish *attractors* from *attracting sets* (Eckmann and Ruelle, 1985). The former are subsets of the latter that are indecomposable (topologically transitive).
12. For a complete classification and analysis of singularities, see Arnol'd, Gusein-Zade, and Varchenko (1985).
13. For the link between transversality and the classification of singularities, see Golubitsky and Guillemin (1973).
14. Apparently, this number is only true for the case of generic metrics and potentials. The number of locally topologically distinct bifurcations in more generalized gradient dynamical systems depending on three parameters is much greater than conjectured by Thom and may even be infinite for the case of such systems depending on four parameters (Arnol'd, 1992, Preface).
15. Although it has been rather sparsely applied in economics since the end of the 1970s, catastrophe theory has been much more widely applied in the psychology literature (Guastello, 1995).
16. Arnol'd (1992, Appendix) suggests that this application was implicit in some of Leonardo da Vinci's work who studied light caustics.
17. M.V. Berry (1976) presents rigorous applications to the hydrodynamics of waves breaking. Arnol'd (1976) deals with both waves and caustics.
18. See Gilmore (1981) for discussion of quantum mechanics applications of catastrophe theory.
19. See Guastello (1995) for studies of stress using catastrophe theory, along with a variety of other psychology and organization theory applications.
20. Thompson and Hunt (1973, 1975) use catastrophe theory to analyze Euler buckling.
21. Horgan's jibes are part of a broader blast at "the four C's," the allegedly overhyped "cybernetics, catastrophe, chaos, and complexity." However, he uses the supposedly total ill-repute of the first two to bash the second two, which he sardonically conflates as "chaoplexity." See Rosser (1999b) for further discussion of Horgan's ideas along these lines.
22. One such, advocated by Thom himself, is the dialectical approach that sees qualitative change arising from quantitative change. This Hegelian perspective is easily put into a catastrophe theory framework where the quantitative change is the slow change of a control variable that at a bifurcation point triggers a discontinuous change in a state variable (Rosser, 2000a).
23. Oliva, Desarbo, Day, and Jedidi (1987) use a generalized multivariate method (GEMCAT) for estimating cusp catastrophe models. Guastello (1995, p. 70) argues that this technique is subject to Type I errors due to the large number of models and parameters estimated although it may be useful as an atheoretic exploratory technique.
24. This is clearly idealistic. I am not so naive as to advise junior faculty in economics attempting to obtain tenure to spend lots of time now writing and submitting to leading economics journals papers based on catastrophe theory.
25. For more detailed analysis of problems in defining attractors, see Milnor (1985).
26. An apparent case of observed chaotic dynamics in celestial mechanics is the unpredictable "tumbling" rotation of Saturn's irregularly shaped moon, Hyperion (Stewart, 1989, pp. 248–252).

27. For generalizations of the Takens approach, see Sauer, Yorke, and Casdagli (1991). For problems with attractor reconstruction in the presence of noise, see Casdagli, Eubank, Farmer, and Gibson (1991). For dealing with small sample problems, see Brock and Dechert (1991). For an overview of embedding issues, see Ott, Sauer, and Yorke (1994, Chap. 5).
28. A related concept is that of *order* (Savit and Green, 1991; Cheng and Tong, 1992), roughly the number of successive elements in a time series which determine the state of the underlying system. Order is at least as great as the correlation dimension (Takens, 1996).
29. For more general limits to estimating the correlation dimension, see Eckmann and Ruelle (1991) and Stefanovska, Strle, and Krošelj (1997). In some cases, these limits are related to the Takens embedding theorem. Brock and Sayers (1988), Frank and Stengos (1988, and Scheinkman and LeBaron (1989) suggest for doubtful cases fitting an AR model and then estimating the dimension which should be the same. This is the *residual diagnostic* test.
30. One point of contention involves whether or not a "fractal set" must have the "self-similarity" aspect of smaller-scale versions reproducing larger-scale versions, as one sees in the original Cantor set and the Koch curve. Some insist on this aspect for true fractality, but the more general view is the one given in this book that does not require this.
31. For applications of multifractals in financial economics, see Mandelbrot (1997) and Mandelbrot, Fisher, and Calvet (1997).
32. Even more topologically complicated are situations where sections of boundaries may be in three or more basins of attraction simultaneously, a situation known as *basins of Wada* (Kennedy and Yorke, 1991), first observed by Yoneyama (1917). This can occur in the Hénon attractor (Nusse and Yorke, 1996).
33. Crannell (1995) speculates that the phrase dates to a 1953 Ray Bradbury story, "A Sound of Thunder," in which a time traveler changes the course of history by stepping on a prehistoric butterfly.

    Edward Lorenz (1993) reports that he was unaware of this story when he coined the phrase in a talk he gave in 1972. This talk appears as an appendix in E.N. Lorenz (1993). Lorenz (1993) also speculates that part of the popularity of the phrase, which he attributes to the popularity of Gleick's (1987) book, came from the butterfly appearance of the Lorenz attractor. He originally thought of using a seagull instead of a butterfly in his 1972 talk and reports (1993, p. 15) that it was an old line among meteorologists that a man sneezing in China could set people in New York to shoveling snow.
34. The Russian School was close on Smale's heels as Shilnikov (1965) showed under certain conditions near a three-dimensional homoclinic orbit to a saddle point that a countably infinite set of horseshoes will exist.
35. A curious fact about Richardson is that measurements he made of the length of Britain's coastline using different scales of measurement inspired Mandelbrot's concept of fractal dimension (Mandelbrot, 1983, Chap. 5).
36. Ulam and von Neumann (1947) studied the logistic equation as a possible deterministic random number generator.
37. May (1976) was the first to consciously suggest the application of chaos theory to economics and proposed a number of possible such applications that were later carried out by economists, generally with no recognition of May's earlier suggestions, although his paper has been widely cited by economists. Ironically, it was originally submitted to *Econometrica*, which rejected it before it was accepted by *Nature*.

    There was a much earlier paper in economics by Strotz, McAnulty, and Naines (1953) that discovered the possibility of business cycles of an infinite number of periods as well as completely wild orbits depending on initial conditions in a version of the Goodwin (1951) nonlinear accelerator model. But they did not fully appreciate the mathematical implications of what they had found, possibly the first demonstration of chaotic dynamics in economics, although arguably preceded by Palander's (1935) analysis of a three-period cycle in a regional economics model.
38. Shibata and Kaneko (1998) show for globally coupled logistic maps, tongue-like structures can arise from these windows of periodic behavior in the chaotic zone of the logistic map

in which self-consistent coherent collective behavior can arise. Kaneko (1990) initiated the study of such globally coupled maps.

39. See Cvitanovic (1984) for more thorough discussion of universality and related issues.
40. For more detailed classification of period-doubling sequences, see Kuznetsov, Kuznetsov, and Sataev (1997).
41. That a property that brings trajectories back toward each other rather than mere boundedness is a part of chaos can be seen by considering the case of *path dependence*, the idea that at a crucial point random perturbations can push a system toward one or another path that then maintains itself through some kind of increasing returns, a case where "history matters" with distinct multiple equilibria (Arthur, 1988, 1989, 1990, 1994). In this case, there is a butterfly effect of sorts, but there is not the sort of irregularity of the trajectories that we identify with chaotic dynamics. The trajectories simply move apart and stay apart. The same can be said for the sort of crucial historical accidents exemplified by: "For want of a nail the shoe was lost; for want of the shoe the horse was lost; for want of the horse the battle was lost; for want of the battle the kingdom was lost" (McCloskey, 1991).
42. Although only briefly dealing with the definition-of-chaos issue, the intensity of polemics sometimes surrounding this topic can be seen in print in the exchange between Helena Nusse (1994a, b) and Alfredo Medio (1994).
43. An example would be a map of the unit circle onto itself consisting of a one-third rotation. This would generate a three-period cycle but would certainly not exhibit SDIC or any other accepted characteristic of chaotic dynamics (I thank Cars Hommes for this example).
44. Even James Yorke of the Li-Yorke Theorem would appear to have accepted this centrality of SDIC for chaos given that he was a cocoiner of the term "nonchaotic strange attractors," for attractors with fractal dimension but without SDIC (Grebogi, Ott, Pelikan, and Yorke, 1984).
45. Another difference between Devaney and Wiggins is that the latter imposes a condition that the set V must be compact (closed and bounded in real number space) whereas Devaney leaves the nature of V open. Many observers take an intermediate position by requiring V to be a subset of n-dimensional real number space, $\mathbf{R^n}$.
46. A time series is "ergodic" if its time average equals its space average (Arnol'd and Avez, 1968). Many Post Keynesian economists object to this assumption as being ontologically unsound in a fundamentally uncertain world (Davidson, 1991). Davidson (1994, 1996) carries this further to criticize the relevance of ergodic chaos theory in particular. He is joined in this by Mirowski (1990) and Carrier (1993), who argue that such approaches merely lay the groundwork for a reaffirmation of standard neoclassical economic theory. Mirowski sees the approach of Mandelbrot as more fundamentally critical.
47. Crannell (1995) proposes an alternative to topological transitivity in the form of *blending*.
48. For discussions of measuring chaos in the absence of invariant SRB measures, see El-Gamal (1991), Domowitz and El-Gamal (1993), and Geweke (1993).
49. This equation gives the global maximum LCE defined asymptotically. There has also been interest in local Lyapunov exponents defined out to n time periods with the idea of varying degrees of local predictability (Kosloff and Rice, 1981; Abarbanel, Brown, and Kennel, 1991, 1992; Bailey, 1996). See Abarbanel (1996) for a more general discussion.
50. Nusse (1994a, p. 109) provides an example from the logistic map where one of the LCEs $= -1$, and there is convergence even though another LCE $= 0$.
51. The Kaplan–Yorke conjecture (Frederickson, Kaplan, Yorke, and Yorke, 1983) posits a higher dimensional analogue of Young's result with a relationship between Kolmogorov–Sinai entropy and a quantity known as the *Lyapunov dimension*. See Eckmann and Ruelle (1985) or Peitgen, Jürgens, and Saupe (1992, pp. 738–742) for more detailed discussion.
52. Andrews (1997) warns that bootstrapping can generate asymptotically incorrect answers when the true parameter is near the boundary of the parameter space. Ziehmann, Smith, and Kurths (1999) show that bootstrapping can be inappropriate for quantifying the confidence boundaries of multiplicative ergodic statistics in chaotic dynamics due to problems

arising from the inability to invert the necessary matrices. Blake LeBaron in a personal communication argues that the problems identified by them arise ultimately from an inability of bootstrapping to deal with the long memory components in chaotic dynamics.

Despite the problems associated with bootstrapping, LeBaron (personal communication) argues that it avoids certain limitations facing related techniques such as the method of surrogate data, favored by some physicists (Theiler, Eubank, Longtin, Galdrikan, and Farmer, 1992), which assume Gaussian disturbances, whereas bootstrapping simply uses the estimated residuals. Li and Maddala (1996) provide an excellent review of bootstrapping methods.

53. We note a view that argues that nonlinear estimation is unnecessary because Wold (1938) showed that any stationary process can be expressed as a linear system generating uncorrelated impulses known as a Wold representation. But such representations may be as complicated as a proper nonlinear formulation, will not capture higher moment effects, and will fail to capture interesting qualitative dynamics. Finally, not all time series are stationary.
54. Brock and Baek (1991) study multiparameter bifurcation theory of BDS and its relation to Kolmogorov–Sinai entropy using U-statistics. Golubitsky and Guckenheimer (1986) approach multiparameter bifurcations more theoretically.
55. One loose end with using BDS is determining σ, which might be dealt with via bootstrapping (I thank Dee Dechert for this observation).

    Another possible complication involves when data change discretely, as with US stock market prices which used to change in $1/8 increments (a "bit" or "piece of eight," reflecting the origin of the New York stock market as dating from the Spanish dollar period), then in $1/16 (a "picayune") increments, and now does so in decimal increments. Krämer and Rose (1997) argue that this discrete data change induces a "compass rose" pattern that can lead the BDS technique to falsely reject an i.i.d. null hypothesis, although the BDS test was verified on indexes which vary continuously (I thank Blake LeBaron for this observation). Ironically, this counteracts the argument of Wen (1996) that discreteness of data leads to false rejections of chaos in comparison with continuous processes.
56. In the same year, Pecora and Carroll (1990) developed the theory of synchronization of chaos. Astakhov, Shabunin, Kapitaniak, and Anishchenko (1997) show how such synchronization can break down through saddle periodic bifurcations, and Ding, Ding, Ditto, Gluckman, In, Peng, Spano, and Yang (1997) show deep links between the synchronization and the control theory of chaos. Drawing on earlier work of Lorenz (1987b) and Puu (1987) on coupled oscillators in international trade and regional models, Lorenz (1993b) showed such a process of saddle periodic bifurcations in a model of Metzlerian inventory dynamics in a macroeconomic model.
57. There are situations with lasers, mechanics of coupled pendulums, optics, and biology, and other areas where chaos is a "good thing" and one wishes to control to maintain it. One technique is a kind of mirror-image of OGY, moving the system onto the unstable manifolds of basin boundary saddles using small perturbations (Schwartz and Triandof, 1996).
58. Another method slightly resembling global targeting involves using a piecewise linear controller to put the system on a new chaotic attractor that has a specific mean and a small maximal error, thus keeping it within a specified neighborhood (Pan and Yin, 1997). This is "using chaos to control chaos."
59. In a personal communication to this author, Mandelbrot dismissed catastrophe theory as being only useful for the study of light caustics and criticized Thom for his metaphysical stance.
60. Blum, Cucker, Shub, and Smale (1998) demonstrate that the Mandelbrot Set is unsolvable in the sense that there is no "halting set" for a Turing machine trying to describe it. This is one way of defining "computational complexity" and is linked to logical Gödelian undecidability. See Albin (1982), Albin with Foley (1998), Binmore (1987) and Koppl and Rosser (2002) for discussions of such problems in terms of interacting economic agents.
61. For Mandelbrot's later work on price dynamics, see Mandelbrot (1997) and Mandelbrot, Fisher, and Calvet (1997).

62. A widely used approach for multiple agent simulations with local interactions is that of *cellular automata* (von Neumann, 1966), especially in its "Game of Life" version due to John Conway. Wolfram (1986) provides a four-level hierarchical scheme for analyzing the complexity of such systems. Albin with Foley (1998) links this with Chomsky's hierarchy of formal grammars (1959) and uses it to analyze complex economic dynamics. In this view, the highest level of complexity involves self-referential Gödelian problems of undecidability and halting (Blum, Cucker, Shub, and Smale, 1998; Rössler, 1998).
63. I thank Steve Durlauf for bringing this point to my attention.
64. Of course Hegel's (1842) favorite example of a dialectical change of quantity into quality was that of the freezing or melting of water, an example picked up by Engels (1940). See Rosser (2000a) for further discussion.
65. Deriving from the work on genetic algorithms is that on *articial life* (Langton, 1989). Epstein and Axtell (1996) provide general social science applications and Tesfatsion (1997) provides economics applications. The work of Albin with Foley (1998) is closely related.
66. For applications of the master equation in demography and migration models, see Weidlich and Haag (1983). Zhang (1991) provides a broader overview of synergetics applications in economics.

References

Aadland, David. 2004. "Cattle Cycles, Heterogeneous Expectations, and the Age Distribution of Capital." *Journal of Economic Dynamics and Control* 28, 1977–2002.

Abarbanel, Henry D.I. 1996. *Analysis of Observed Chaotic Data*. New York: Springer.

Abarbanel, Henry D.I., Reggie Brown, and Matthew B. Kennel. 1991. "Variation of Lyapunov Exponents on a Strange Attractor." *Journal of Nonlinear Science* 1, 175–199.

Abarbanel, Henry D.I., Reggie Brown, and Matthew B. Kennel. 1992. "Local Lyapunov Exponents Computed from Observed Data." *Journal of Nonlinear Science* 2, 343–365.

Abdel-Rahman, H.M. 1998. "Product Differentiation, Monopolistic Competition, and City Size." *Regional Science and Urban Economics* 18, 69–86.

Abraham, Ralph H. 1972. *Hamiltonian Catastrophes*. Lyons: Université Claude-Bernard.

Abraham, Ralph H. 1985a. "Chaostrophes, Intermittency, and Noise," in P. Fischer and William R. Smith, eds., *Chaos, Fractals, and Dynamics*. New York: Marcel Dekker, 3–22.

Abraham, Ralph H. 1985b. *On Morphodynamics*. Santa Cruz: Aerial Press.

Abraham, Ralph H., Laura Gardini, and Chrstian Mira. 1997. *Chaos in Discrete Dynamical Systems: A Visual Introduction in 2 Dimensions*. New York: Springer.

Acheson, James M. 1988. *The Lobster Gangs of Maine*. Durham: University Press of New England.

Ackerman, Frank, Elizabeth A. Stanton, and Ramón Bueno. 2010. "Fat Tails, Exponents, Extreme Uncertainty: Simulating Catastrophe in DICE." *Ecological Economics* 69, 1657–1665.

Akerlof, George. 1991. "Procrastination and Obedience." *American Economic Review* 81, 1–9.

Alavalapati, J.R.R., G.A. Stainback, and D.R. Carter. 2002. "Restoration of the Longleaf Pine Ecosystem on Private Lands in the US South." *Ecological Economics* 40, 411–419.

Albin, Peter S. 1982. "Reswitching: An Empirical Observation, A Theoretical Note, and an Environment Conjecture." *Mathematical Social Sciences* 3, 329–358.

Albin, Peter S., Edited and with an Introduction by Duncan K. Foley. 1998. *Barriers and Bounds to Rationality: Essays on Economic Complexity and Dynamics in Interactive Systems*. Princeton: Princeton University Press.

Alchian, Armen A. 1950. "Uncertainty, Evolution, and Economic Theory." *Journal of Political Economy* 58, 211–222.

Alchian, Armen A. 1952. *Economic Replacement Policy*. Santa Monica: RAND Corporation.

Alexander, D. 1979. "Catastrophic Misconception." *Area* 11, 228–229.

Alig, R.J., D.M. Adams, and B.A. McCarl. 1998. "Ecological and Economic Impacts of Forest Policies: Interactions across Forestry and Agriculture." *Ecological Economics* 27, 63–78.

Allee, W.C. 1931. *Animal Aggregations*. Chicago: University of Chicago Press.

Allen, R.C. 1997. "Agriculture and the Origins of the State in Ancient Egypt." *Explorations in Economic History* 34, 135–154.

Allen, J.C., W.M. Schaffer, and D. Rosko. 1993. "Chaos Reduces Species Extinction by Amplifying Local Population Noise." *Nature* 364, 229–232.

Allen, Peter M. 1978. "Dynamique des Centres Urbains." *Science et Techniques* 50, 15–19.

Allen, Peter M. 1983. "Self-Organization and Evolution in Urban Systems," in Robert W. Crosby, ed., *Cities and Regions as Nonlinear Decision Systems*. Boulder: Westview, 29–62.
Allen, Peter M., J.L. Denebourg, M. Sanglier, F. Boon, and A. de Palma. 1979. "Dynamic Urban Models." Report to Department of Transportation, USA, Contract TSC-1185, Cambridge.
Allen, Peter M., Guy Engelen, and Michele Sanglier. 1986. "Towards a General Dynamic Model of the Spatial Evolution of Urban Systems," in Bruce Hutchinson and Michael Batty, eds., *Advances in Urban Systems Modelling*. Amsterdam: North-Holland, 199–220.
Allen, Peter M. and Michele Sanglier. 1978. "Dynamic Models of Urban Growth." *Journal of Social and Biological Structures* 1, 265–280.
Allen, Peter M. and Michele Sanglier. 1979. "Dynamic Model for Growth in a Central Place System." *Geographical Analysis* 11, 256–272.
Allen, Peter M. and Michele Sanglier. 1981. "Urban Evolution, Self-Organization, and Decision Making." *Environment and Planning A* 13, 167–183.
Allen, Timothy F.H. and Thomas B. Starr. 1982. *Hierarchy: Perspectives for Ecological Complexity*. Chicago: University of Chicago Press.
Alonso, William. 1964. *Location and Land Use*. Cambridge: Harvard University Press.
Alonso, William. 1978. "A Theory of Movements," in Niles M. Hansen, ed., *Human Settlement Systems*. Cambridge: Ballinger, 197–211.
Amson, J.C. 1974. "Equilibrium and Catastrophic Models of Urban Growth," in E.L. Cripps, ed., *London Papers in Regional Science 4: Space-Time Concepts in Urban and Regional Models*. Londong: Pion, 108–128.
Amson, J.C. 1975. "Catastrophe Theory: A Contribution to the Study of Urban Systems?" *Environment and Planning B* 2, 177–221.
Anas, Alex. 1986. "From Physical to Economic Urban Models: The Lowry Framework Revisited," in Bruce Hutchinson and Michael Batty, eds., *Advances in Urban Systems Modelling*. Amsterdam: North-Holland, 163–172.
Anas, Alex. 1988. "Agglomeration and Taste Heterogeneity." *Regional Science and Urban Economic* 18, 7–35.
Anderson, L.G. 1973. "Optimum Economic Yield of a Fishery Given a Variable Price of Output." *Journal of the Fisheries Research Board of Canada* 30, 509–513.
Anderson, R.M. 1981. "Population Ecology of Infectious Disease Agents," in Robert M. May, ed., *Theoretical Ecology*, 2nd Edition. Sunderland: Sinauer Associates, Inc., 318–355.
Andersson, Åke E. 1986. "The Four Logistical Revolutions." *Papers of the Regional Science Association* 59, 1–12.
Andersson, Åke E. and G. Ferraro. 1982. "Accessibility and Density Distribution in Metropolitan Areas: Theory and Empirical Studies." Umeå Economic Papers 109, Umeå, Sweden.
Anderson, Simon, Andre de Palma, and Jacques-François Thisse. 1992. *Discrete Choice Theory of Product Differentiation*. Cambridge: MIT Press.
Andrews, Donald W.K. 1997. "A Simple Counterexample to the Bootstrap." Cowles Foundation Discussion Paper No. 1157, Yale University.
Andronov, A.A. 1929. "Les Cycles Limites de Poincaré et les Théories des Oscillations." *Comptes Rendus de l'Académie des Sciences de Paris* 189, 559–561.
Andronov, A.A. and L.S. Pontryagin. 1937. "Grubye Sistemy" ("Coarse Systems"). *Doklady Akademi Nauk SSSR* 14, 247–251.
Andronov, A.A., E.A. Leontovich, I.I. Gordon, and A.G. Maier. 1966. *Qualitative Theory of Second-Order Dynamic Systems*. Moscow: Nauka.
Antonelli, Cristiano. 1990. "Induced Adoption and Externalities in the Regional Diffusion Information Technology." *Regional Studies* 24, 31–40.
Armstrong, Jennifer and Andrew Johnson. 2009. "Seti: The Hunt for ET." *The Independent-Science*, September 27, http://www.independent.co.uk/news/science/seti-the-hunt-for-et-1793983.html
Arnol'd, Vladimir Igorevich. 1965. "Small Denominators. I. Mappings of the Circumference onto Itself." *American Mathematical Society Translations, Series 2* 46, 213–284.

Arnol'd, Vladimir Igorevich. 1968. "Singularities of Smooth Mappings." *Uspekhi Matemacheski Nauk* 23, 3–44.

Arnol'd, Vladimir Igorevich. 1992. *Catastrophe Theory*, 3rd Edition. Berlin: Springer.

Arnol'd, Vladimir Igorevich and A. Avez. 1968. *Ergodic Problems of Classical Mechanics*. New York: Benjamin.

Arnol'd, Vladimir Igorevich, S.M. Gusein-Zade, and A.N. Varchenko. 1985. *Singularities of Differentiable Mappings*. Boston: Birkhäuser.

Arrow, Kenneth J. and Anthony C. Fisher. 1974. "Environmental Preservation, Uncertainty, and Irreversibility." *Quarterly Journal of Economics* 88, 312–319.

Arthur, W. Brain. 1986. "Urban Systems and Historical Path Dependence." Report No. 0012, Stanford Food Research Institute.

Arthur, W. Brian. 1988. "Self-Reinforcing Mechanisms in Economics," in Philip W. Anderson, Kenneth J. Arrow, and David Pines, eds., *The Economy as an Evolving Complex System*. Redwood City: Addison-Wesley, 9–31 (reprinted as Chapter 7 in Arthur, 1994).

Arthur, W. Brian. 1989. "Competing Technologies, Increasing Returns, and Lock-In by Historical Events." *Economic Journal* 99, 116–131 (reprinted as Chapter 2 in Arthur, 1994).

Arthur, W. Brian. 1990. "Positive Feedbacks in the Economy." *Scientific American* 262 (February), 92–99 (reprinted as Chapter 1 in Arthur, 1994).

Arthur, W. Brian. 1994. *Increasing Returns and Path Dependence in the Economy*. Ann Arbor: University of Michigan Press.

Arthur, W. Brian, Steven N. Durlauf, and David A. Lane. 1997. "Introduction," in W. Brian Arthur, Steven N. Durlauf, and David A. Lane, eds., *The Economy as an Evolving Complex System II*. Reading: Addison-Wesley, 1–14.

Asheim, Geir B. 2008. "The Occurrence of Paradoxical Behavior in a Model Where Economic Activity has Environmental Effects." *Journal of Economic Behavior and Organization* 65, 529–546.

Astakhov, V., A. Shabunin, R. Kapitaniak, and V. Anishchenko. 1997. "Loss of Chaotic Synchronization through the Sequence of Bifurcations of Saddle Periodic Orbits." *Physical Review Letters* 79, 1014–1017.

Aston, P.J. and C.M. Bird. 1997. "Analysis of the Control of Chaos—Extending the Basin of Attraction." *Chaos, Solitons & Fractals* 8, 1413–1429.

Auerbach, Felix. 1913. "Das Gesetz der Bevölkerungskonzentration." *Petermans Mitteilungen* 59, 74–76.

Augustsson, T. and V. Ramanathan. 1977. "A Radiative-Convective Model of the CO_2-Climate Problem." *Journal of Atmospheric Science* 34, 448–451.

Awan, Akhtar A. 1986. "Marshallian and Schumpeterian Theories of Economic Evolution: Gradualism vs Punctualism." *Atlantic Economic Journal* 14, 37–49.

Axelrod, Robert. 1984. *The Evolution of Cooperation*. New York: Basic Books.

Ayres, Clarence E. 1932. *Huxley*. New York: Norton.

Ayres, Robert U. and Manaleer S. Sandilya. 1987. "Utility Maximization and Catastrophe Aversion: A Simulation Test." *Journal of Environmental Economics and Management* 14, 337–370.

Baas, N.A. 1997. "Self-Organization and Higher Order Structures," in Frank Schweitzer, ed., *Self-Organization of Complex Structures: From Individual to Collective Dynamics*. Amsterdam: Gordon and Breach, 71–81.

Bachelier, Louis. 1900. "Théorie de la Speculation." *Annales Scientifique de l'École Normale Supérieure* 3, 21–86.

Bachmura, Frank J. 1971. "The Economics of Vanishing Species." *Natural Resources Journal* 11, 674–692.

Bailey, Barbara A. 1996. "Local Lyapunov Exponents: Predictability Depends on Where You Are," in William A. Barnett, Alan P. Kirman, and Mark Salmon, eds., *Nonlinear Dynamics and Economics: Proceedings of the Tenth International Symposium in Economic Theory and Econometrics*. Cambridge: Cambridge University Press, 345–359.

Bailey, Martin J. 1959. "A Note on the Economics of Residential Zoning and Urban Renewal." *Land Economics* 35, 288–292.

Bak, Per. 1996. *How Nature Works: The Science of Self-Organized Criticality*. New York: Copernicus Press for Springer.

Bak, Per and Kan Chen. 1991. "Self-Organized Criticality." *Scientific American* 264, 46.

Bak, Per, Kan Chen, José Scheinkman, and Michael Woodford. 1993. "Aggregate Fluctuations from Independent Sectoral Shocks: Self-Organized Criticality in a Model of Production and Inventory Dynamics." *Ricerche Economiche* 47, 3–30.

Bak, Per, C. Tang, and K. Wiesenfeld. 1987. "Self-Organized Criticality: An Explanation of 1/f Noise." *Physical Review Letters* 59, 381–384.

Baker, A.R.H. 1978. "Settlement Pattern Evolution and Catastrophe Theory: A Comment." *Transactions, Institute of British Geographers*, New Series 4, 435–444.

Bala, Venkatesh and Mukul Majumdar. 1992. "Chaotic Tâtonnement." *Economic Theory* 2, 437–445.

Bala, Venkatesh, Mukul Majumdar, and Tapan Mitra. 1998. "A Note on Controlling a Chaotic Tâtonnement." *Journal of Economic Behavior and Organization* 33, 411–420.

Balasko, Yves. 1978. "Economic Equilibrium and Catastrophe Theory." *Econometrica* 46, 557–569.

Baldwin, Richard E. 1999. "Agglomeration and Endogenous Capital." *European Economic Review* 43, 253–280.

Baldwin, Richard E., Rikard Forslid, Philippe Martin, Gianmarco Ottaviano, and Frederic Robert-Nicoud. 2003. *Economic Geography and Public Policy*. Princeton: Princeton University Press.

Banks, J., J. Brooks, G. Cairns, G. Davis, and R. Stacey. 1992. "On Devaney's Definition of Chaos." *American Mathematical Monthly* 99, 332–334.

Banos, Arnaud. 2010. "Network Effects in Schelling's Model of Segregation: New Evidence from Agent-Based Simulation." Mimeo, Géographie-Cité, CNRS, Paris.

Barabási, Albert-László and Réka Albert. 1999. "Emergence of Scaling in Random Networks." *Science* 286, 509–512.

Barbier, Edward B. 2001. "The Economics of Tropical Deforestation and Land Use: An Introduction to the Special Issue." *Land Economics* 77, 155–171.

Barham, James. 1992. "From Enzymes to $E = mc^2$: A Reply to Critics." *Journal of Social and Evolutionary Systems* 15, 249–306.

Barnes, Trevor and Eric Sheppard. 1984. "Technical Choice and Reswitching in Space Economies." *Regional Science and Urban Economics* 14, 345–352.

Barnett, Harold J. 1979. "Scarcity and Growth Revisited," in V. Kerry Smith, ed., *Scarcity and Growth Reconsidered*. Baltimore: Johns Hopkins University Press, 163–196.

Barnett, Harold J. and Chandler Morse. 1963. *Scarcity and Growth: The Economics of Natural Resource Availability*. Baltimore: Johns Hopkins University Press for Resources for the Future.

Barnett, William A. and Ping Chen. 1988. "The Aggregation-Theoretic Monetary Aggregates are Chaotic and have Strange Attractors: An Econometric Application of Mathematical Chaos," in William A. Barnett, Ernst Berndt, and Halbert White, eds., *Dynamic Econometric Modelling: Proceedings of the Third International Symposium in Economic Theory and Econometrics*. Cambridge: Cambridge University Press, 199–246.

Barnett, William A., A. Ronald Gallant, Melvin J. Hinich, Jochen A. Jungeilges, Daniel T. Kaplan, and Mark J. Jensen. 1994. "Robustness of Nonlinearity and Chaos Tests to Measurement Error, Inference Method, and Sample Size." *Journal of Economic Behavior and Organization* 27, 301–320.

Barnett, William A., A. Ronald Gallant, Melvin J. Hinich, Jochen A. Jungeilges, Daniel T. Kaplan, and Mark J. Jensen. 1998. "A Single-Blind Controlled Competition among Tests for Nonlinearity and Chaos." *Journal of Econometrics* 82, 157–192.

Bascompte, Jordi and Ricard V. Solé. 1996. "Habitat Fragmentation and Extinction Thresholds in Spatially Explicit Metapopulation Models." *Journal of Animal Ecology* 65, 465–473.

Bask, Mikael. 1998. "Essays on Exchange Rates: Deterministic Chaos and Technical Analysis". Umeå Economic Studies No. 465, Umeå University, Sweden.
Bask, Mikael and Ramazan Gençay. 1998. "Testing Chaotic Dynamics via Lyapunov Exponents." *Physica D* 114, 1–2.
Batchelor, G.K. and A.A. Townsend. 1949. "The Nature of Turbulent Motion at High Wave Numbers." *Proceedings of the Royal Society of London A* 199, 238–255.
Batten, David. 2001. "Complex Landscapes of Spatial Interaction." *Annals of Regional Science* 35, 81–111.
Batten, David and Börje Johansson. 1987. "Dynamics of Metropolitan Change." *Geographical Analysis* 19, 189–199.
Batty, Michael, Paul A. Longley, and A. Stewart Fotheringham. 1989. "Urban Growth and Form: Scaling, Fractal Geometry, and Diffusion-limited Aggregation." *Environment and Planning A* 21, 1447–1472.
Baumol, William J. 1968. "On the Social Rate of Discount." *American Economic Review* 58, 788–802.
Baumol, William J. 1970. *Economic Dynamics*, 3rd Edition. New York: Macmillan.
Baumol, William J. 1986. "On the Possibility of Continuing Expansion of Finite Resources." *Kyklos* 39, 167–179.
Baumol, William J. and Jess Benhabib. 1989. "Chaos: Significance, Mechanism, and Economic Applications." *Journal of Economic Perspectives* 3, 77–105.
Bazykin, A.D., A.S. Khibnik, and E.A. Aponina. 1983. "A Model of Evolutionary Appearance of Dissipative Structure in Ecosystems." *Journal of Mathematical Biology* 18, 13–23.
Beaumont, J.R., M. Clarke, and A.G. Wilson. 1981a. "The Dynamics of Urban Spatial Structure: Some Exploratory Results Using Difference Equations and Bifurcation Theory." *Environment and Planning A* 13, 1472–1483.
Beaumont, J.R., M. Clarke, and A.G. Wilson. 1981b. "Charging Energy Parameteres and the Evolution of Urban Spatial Structure." *Regional Science and Urban Economics* 11, 287–316.
Becker, Gary S. 1957. *The Economics of Discrimination*. Chicago: University of Chicago Press.
Becker, Robert A. 1982. "Intergeneration Equity: The Capital-Environment Tradeoff." *Journal of Environmental Economics and Management* 9, 165–185.
Beckmann, Martin J. 1952. "A Continuous Model of Transportation." *Econometrica* 20, 643–660.
Beckmann, Martin J. 1953. "The Partial Equilibrium of a Continuous Space Market." *Weltwirtschaftliches Archiv* 71, 73–89.
Beckmann, Martin J. 1976. "Spatial Equilibrium in the Dispersed City," in Papageorgiou, G.J., ed., *Mathematical Land Use Theory*. Lexington: Heath.
Beckmann, Martin J. 1987. "Continuous Models of Spatial Dynamics," in David Batten, John Casti, and Börje Johanson, eds., *Economic Evolution and Structural Adjustment*. Berlin: Springer, 337–348.
Beckmann, Martin J. and Tönu Puu. 1985. *Spatial Economics: Density, Potential, and Flow*. Amsterdam: North-Holland.
Beddington, J.R.J., C.A. Free, and J.H. Lawson. 1975. "Dynamic Complexity in Predator-Prey Models Framed in Difference Equations." *Nature* 255, 58–60.
Beinhocker, Eric. 2006. *The Origin of Wealth*. London: Random House.
Belussi, Fiorenza and Katia Caldari. 2009. "At the Origin of the Industrial District: Alfred Marshall and the Cambridge School." *Cambridge Journal of Economics* 33, 335–355.
Bendixson, I. 1901. "Sur les courbes définies par des equations différentielle." *Acta Mathematica* 24, 1–88.
Benhabib, Jess and Richard H. Day. 1980. "Erratic Accumulation." *Economics Letters* 6, 113–117.
Berch, Peter. 1979. "Open Access and Extinction." *Econometrica* 47, 877–882.
Berck, Peter and Jeffrey M. Perloff. 1984. "An Open-Access Fishery with Rational Expectations." *Econometrica* 52, 489–506.
Berry, Brian J.L. 1964. "Cities as Systems within Systems of Cities." *Papers of the Regional Science Association* 13, 147–163.

Berry, Brian J.L. 1976. "Ghetto Expansion and Single Family Housing Prices: Chicago 1968–1972." *Journal of Urban Economics* 3, 397–423.

Berry, Brian J.L. 2010. "The Distribution of City Sizes," in Claudio Cioffi-Rivilla, ed., *Statistical, Mathematical, and Computational Emergence in Complex Social Systems*, forthcoming.

Berry, Christopher J. 1974. "Adam Smith's Considerations of Language." *Journal of the History of Ideas* 35, 130–138.

Berry, Michael V. 1976. "Waves and Thom's Theorem." *Advances in Physics* 25, 1–26.

Beverton, R.J.H. and S.V. Holt. 1957. *On the Dynamics of Exploiting Fish Populations*, Fisheries Investigations, Vol. 19, Section 2. London: Ministry of Agriculture, Fisheries and Food.

Biely, Andrey. 1913. *St. Petersbeurg* (English translation by Cournos, John, 1959, New York: Grove Press).

Binmore, Ken. 1987. "Modeling Rational Players I." *Economics and Philosophy* 3, 9–55.

Binmore, Ken and Larry Samuelson. 1999. "Evolutionary Drift and Equilibrium Selection." *Review of Economic Studies* 66, 363–393.

Binmore, Ken and Avner Shaked. 2010. "Experimental Economics: Where Next?" *Journal of Economic Behavior and Organization* 73, 87–100.

Birkhoff, George D. 1927. *Dynamical Systems*. Providence: American Mathematical Society.

Bitov, Andrei. 1995. *The Monkey Link: A Pilgrimage Novel* (translated from the Russian by Susan Brownsberger). New York: Farrar, Strauss, and Giroux.

Bjørndal, Trond and Jon M. Conrad. 1987. "The Dynamics of an Open Access Fishery." *Canadian Journal of Economics* 20, 74–85.

Blase, J.H. 1979. "Hysteresis and Catastrophe Theory: Empirical Identification in Transportation Modelling." *Environment and Planning A* 11, 675–688.

Blom, J.G., R. de Bruin, J. Grosman, and J.G. Verwer. 1981. "Forced Prey-Predator Oscillations." *Journal of Mathematical Biology* 12, 141–152.

Blum, Lenore, Felipe Cucker, Michael Shub, and Steve Smale. 1998. *Complexity and Real Computation*. New York: Springer.

Blume, Lawrence E. 1993. "The Statistical Mechanics of Strategic Interaction." *Games and Economic Behavior* 5, 387–424.

Blume, Lawrence E. 1997. "Population Games," in W. Brian Arthur, Steven N. Durlauf, and David A. Lane, eds., *The Economy as an Evolving Complex System II*. Reading: Addison-Wesley, 425–460.

Blumenthal, L.M. and Karl Menger. 1970. *Studies in Geometry*. San Francisco: W.H. Freeman.

Blythe, S.P., W.S.C. Gurney, and R. Nisbet. 1982. "Instability and Complex Dynamic Behavior in Population Models with Long Time Delays." *Theoretical Population Biology* 22, 147–176.

Bogdanov, Aleksandr A. 1922. *Tektologia: Vseobschaya Organizatsionnaya Nauka*, 3 Vols. Berlin: Z.I. Grschebin Verlag (English translation by George Gorelik, 1980, *Essays in Tektology: The General Science of Organization*. Seaside: Intersystems Publications).

Boisguilbert, Pierre le Pesant, Sieur de. 1695. *Le Détail de la France sous le Regne Présent*. Paris: NUC.

Boltzmann, Ludwig. 1886. *Der zaveite Hauptsetz der mechanischen Wirmtheori*. Vienna: Gerold.

Booth, G. Geoffrey and Peter E. Koveos. 1983. "Employment Fluctuations: An R/S Analysis." *Journal of Regional Science* 23, 19–47.

Bornholdt, Stefan. 2003. "The Dynamics of Large Biological Systems: A Statistical Physics View of Macroevolution," in James P. Crutchfield and Peter Schuster, eds., *Evolutionary Dynamics: Exploring the Interplay of Selection, Accident, Neutrality, and Function*. Oxford: Oxford University Press, 65–78.

Boschma, Ron. 2004. "Competitiveness of Regions from an Evolutionary Perspective." *Regional Studies* 38, 1001–1014.

Boschma, Ron and Ron Martin. 2007. "Constructing an Evolutionary Economic Geography." *Journal of Economic Geography* 7, 537–548.

Boulding, Kenneth E. 1966. "The Economics of the Coming Spaceship Earth," in Jarrett, H., ed., *Environmental Quality in a Growing Economy*. Baltimore: Johns Hopkins University Press.

Boulding, Kenneth E. 1978. *Ecodynamics: A New Theory of Societal Evolution*. Beverly Hills: Sage.
Boulding, Kenneth E. 1981. *Evolutionary Economics*. Beverly Hills: Sage.
Boulding, Kenneth E. 1989. "Economics as an Ecology of Commodities." Mimeo, University of Coloragdo.
Bowen, R. and David Ruelle. 1975. "The Ergodic Theory of Axiom A Flows." *Inventiones Mathematicae* 29, 181.
Bowes, Michael D. and John V. Krutilla. 1985. "Multiple Use Management of Public Forestlands," in Allen V. Kneese and James L. Sweeny, eds., *Handbook of Natural Resources and Energy Economics*. Amsterdam: Elsevier, 531–569.
Boyce, Ronald R. 1963. "Myth and Reality in Urban Planning." *Land Economics* 39, 241–251.
Boyd, Robert and Peter J. Richerson. 1985. *Culture and the Evolutionary Process*. Chicago: University of Chicago Press.
Boyd, Robert and Peter J. Richerson. 1992. "Punishment Allows the Evolution of Cooperation (or Anything Else) in Sizable Groups." *Ethology and Sociobiology* 13, 171–195.
Brander, James A. 1981. "Intra-Industry Trade in Identical Commodities." *Journal of International Economics* 11, 1–14.
Braudel, Fernand. 1967. *Civilization Matérielle et Capitalisme*. Paris: Librairie Armand Colin (English translation by Kochan, Miriam, 1973, *Capitalism and Material Life: 1400–1800*. New York: Harper and Row).
Braudel, Fernand. 1979. *Le Temps du Monde*. Paris: Librairie Armand Colin (English translation by Reynolds, Sian, 1984, *The Perspective of the World*. New York: Harper and Row).
Braudel, Fernand. 1986. *L'Identité de la France*. Paris: Librairie Armand Colin (English translation by Reynolds, Sian, 1988, *The Identity of France*. New York: Harper and Row).
Brauer, Fred. 1984. "Constant Yield Harvesting of Populations Systems," in Simon A. Levin and Thomas G. Hallam, eds., *Mathematical Ecology*. Berlin: Springer, 238–246.
Brauer, Fred. 1987a. "A Class of Volterra Integral Equations Arising in Delay Recruitment Population Models." *Natural Resource Modeling* 2, 259–277.
Brauer, Fred. 1987b. "Harvesting in Delayed-Recruitment Population Models." *Canadian Mathematical Society Conference Proceedings* 8, 317–327.
Brauer, Fred, David Rollins, and A.E. Soudack. 1988. "Harvesting in Population Models with Delayed Recruitment and Age-Dependent Mortality." *Natural Resourse Modeling* 3, 45–62.
Brauer, Fred and A.E. Soudack. 1979. "Stability Regions and Transition Phenomena for Harvested Predator-Prey Systems." *Journal of Mathematical Biology* 7, 319–337.
Brauer, Fred and A.E. Soudack. 1981. "Constant Rate Stocking of Predator-Prey Systems." *Journal of Mathematical Biology* 11, 1–14.
Brauer, Fred and A.E. Soudack. 1985. "Optimal Harvesting in Predator Prey Systems." *International Journal of Control* 41, 111–128.
Brigo, D., A. Pallavcini, and R. Torresetti. 2010. *Credit Models and the Crisis: A Journey into CDOs, Copulas, Correlations and Dynamic Models*. New York: Wiley.
Brindley, J. and T. Kapitaniak. 1991. "Existence and Characterization of Strange Nonchaotic Attractors in Nonlinear Systems." *Chaos, Solitons & Fractals* 1, 323–337.
Brock, William A. 1986. "Distinguishing Random and Deterministic Systmes: Abridged Version." *Journal of Economic Theory* 40, 168–195.
Brock, William A. 1993. "Pathways to Randomness in the Economy: Emergent Nonlinearity and Chaos in Economics and Finance." *Estudios Económicos* 8, 3–55.
Brock, William A. and Ehung G. Baek. 1991. "Some Theory of Statistical Inference for Nonlinear Science." *Review of Economic Studies* 58, 697–716.
Brock, William A. and Stephen R. Carpenter. 2006. "Variance as a Leading Indicator of Regime Shift in Ecosystem Services." *Ecology and Society* 11(2), 9.
Brock, William A. and W. Davis Dechert. 1991. "Non-Linear Dynamical Systems: Instability and Chaos in Economics," in Werner Hildenbrand and Hugo Sonnenschein, eds., *Handbook of Mathematical Economics*, Vol. IV. Amsterdam: North-Holland, 2209–2235.

Brock, William A., W. Davis Dechert, Blake LeBaron, and José A. Scheinkman. 1996. "A Test for Independence Based on the Correlation Dimension." *Econometric Reviews* 15, 197–235.

Brock, William A., W. Davis Dechert, and José A. Scheinkman. 1987. "A Test for Independence Based on the Correlation Dimension." SSRI Working Paper No. 8702, University of Wisconsin-Madison.

Brock, William A. and Aart de Zeeuw. 2002. "The Repeated Lake Game." *Economics Letters* 76, 109–114.

Brock, William A. and Steven N. Durlauf. 1995. "Discrete Choice with Social Interactions I: Theory." SSRI Working Paper No. 9521, University of Wisconsin-Madison (later version, *Review of Economic Studies* 68, 235–265).

Brock, William A. and Steven N. Durlauf. 1999. "Interactions-Based Models." SSRI Working Paper No. 9910, University of Wisconsin-Madison (also in James J. Heckman and Edward Leamer, eds., 2001, *Handbook of Econometrics 5*. Amsterdam: Elsevier).

Brock, William A. and Steven N. Durlauf. 2001a. "Discrete Choice with Social Interactions." *Review of Economic Studies* 68, 235–260.

Brock, William A. and Steven N. Durlauf. 2001b. "Interactions-Based Models," in James J. Heckman and Edward E. Leamer, eds., *Handbook of Econometrics*, Vol. 5. Amsterdam: North-Holland, 3297–3380

Brock, William A. and Steven N. Durlauf. 2002. "A Multinomial Choice Model with Neighborhood Effects." *American Economic Review, Papers and Proceedings* 92, 298–303.

Brock, William A. and Cars H. Hommes. 1997. "A Rational Route to Randomness." *Econometrica* 65, 1059–1095.

Brock, William A., David A. Hsieh, and Blake LeBaron. 1991. *Nonlinear Dynamics, Chaos, and Instability: Statistical Theory and Economic Evidence*. Cambridge: MIT Press.

Brock, William A. and Simon M. Potter. 1993. "Nonlinear Time Series and Macroeconometrics," in G.S. Maddala, C.B. Rao, and H.D. Vinod, eds., *Handbook of Statistics, Vol. II: Econometrics*. Amsterdam: North-Holland, 195–229.

Brock, William A. and Chera L. Sayers. 1988. "Is the Business Cycle Characterized by Deterministic Chaos?" *Journal of Monetary Economics* 22, 71–79.

Brock, William A. and David A. Starrett. 2003. "Managing Systems with Non-Convex Positive Feedback." *Environmental and Resource Economics* 26, 575–602.

Bromley, Daniel W. 1991. *Environment and Economy Property Rights and Public Policy*. Oxford: Basil Blackwell.

Broome, John. 1994. "Discounting the Future." *Philosophy and Public Affairs* 23, 128–156.

Brosnan, Sarah F. 2010. "An Evolutionary Perspective on Morality." *Journal of Economic Behavior and Organization*, 77, 23–30.

Brosnan, Sarah F., C. Freeman, and Frans B.M. van de Waal. 2006. "Partner's Behavior Not Reward Distribution, Determines Success in an Unequal Cooperative Task in Capuchin Monkeys." *American Journal of Primatology* 68, 713–724.

Brueckner, J.K. 1980a. "Residential Succession and Land-Use Dynamics in a Vintage Model of Urban Housing." *Regional Science and Urban Economics* 10, 225–240.

Brueckner, J.K. 1980b. "A Vintage Model of Urban Growth." *Journal of Urban Economics* 7, 389–402.

Brueckner, J.K. 1981a. "A Dynamic Model of Housing Production." *Journal of Urban Economics* 8, 1–14.

Brueckner, J.K. 1981b. "Testing a Vintage Model of Urban Growth." *Journal of Regional Science* 12, 197–210.

Brueckner, J.K. 1982. "Building Ages and Urban Growth." *Regional Science and Urban Economics* 10, 1–17.

Brueckner, J.K. and B. von Rabenau. 1980. "Dynamics of Land Use for a Closed City." *Regional Science and Urban Economics* 10, 1–17.

Brulhart, Marius and Federica Sbergami. 2009. "Agglomeration and Growth: Cross-Country Evidenc." *Journal of Urban Economics* 65, 48–63.

Brusco, S. 1989. *Piccolo Imprese e Distretti Industriali: Ima Racolta Saggi*. Turin: Rosenberg and Sellier.
Bryson, Reid A. 1974. "A Perspective on Climatic Change." *Science* 184, 753–760.
Bryson, Reid A. and Thomas J. Murray. 1977. *Climates of Hunger: Mankind and the World's Changing Weather*. Madison: University of Wisconsin Press.
Buchanan, James M. 1965. "An Economic Theory of Clubs." *Economica* 32, 1–14.
Buenstorf, Guido and Steven Kappler. 2009. "Heritage and Agglomeration: The Akron Tyre Cluster Revisited." *Economic Journal* 119, 705–733.
Bullard, James. 1994. "Learning Equilibria." *Journal of Economic Theory* 64, 468–485.
Bunow, Barry and George H. Weiss. 1979. "How Chaotic is Chaotic? Chaotic and Other 'Noisy' Dynamics in the Frequency Domain." *Mathematical Biosciences* 47, 221–237.
Burgess, Ernest W. 1925. "The Growth of the City," in E.W. Burgess and R.E. Park, eds., *The City*. Chicago: University of Chicago Press, 47–62.
Burkett, Paul. 1999. *Marx and Nature: A Red and Green Perspective*. New York: St. Martin's Press.
Burkhardt, R.W. 1977. *The Spirit of System: Lamarck and Evolutionary Biology*. Cambridge: Harvard University Press.
Burkhart, Judith, Ernst Fehr, Charles Efferson, and Carel van Schaik. 2007. "Other-Regarding Preferences in a Non-Human Primate: Common Marmosets Provision Food Altruistically." *Proceedings of the National Academy of Sciences of the United State of America* 104, 19762–19766.
Burness, Stuart, Ronald Cummings, Glenn Morris, and Inja Paik. 1980. "Thermodynamic and Economic Concepts as Related to Resource Use Policies." *Land Economics* 56, 1–9.
Butzer, K. 1976. *Early Hydraulic Civilization in Egypt*. Chicago: University of Chicago Press.
Byatt, Ian, Ian Castles, Indur M. Golkany, David Henderson, Nigel Lawson, Ross McKitrick, Julian Morris, Alan Peacock, Colin Richardson, and Robert Skidelsky. 2006. "The *Stern Review*: A Dual Critique: Part II: Economic Aspects." *World Economics* 7, 199–232.
Caldwell, Bruce. 2004. *Hayek's Challenge: An Intellectual Biography of F.A. Hayek*. Chicago: University of Chicago Press.
Camagni, Roberto, Lidia Diappi, and Giorgio Leonardi. 1986. "Urban Growth and Decline in a Hierarchical System." *Regional Science and Urban Economics* 16, 145–160.
Cantor, Georg. 1883. "Über unendliche, lineare Puntkmannigfaltigkeiten V." *Mathematische Annelen* 21, 545–591.
Caparrós, A. and F. Jacquemont. 2003. "Conflicts between Biodiversity and Carbon Sequestration." *Ecological Economics* 46, 143–157.
Carpenter, Stephen R. and Kathryn L. Cottingham. 2002. "Resilience and the Restoration of Lakes," in Lance H. Gunderson and Lowell Pritchard, Jr., eds., *Resilience and the Behavior of Large-Scale Systems*. Washington: Island Press, 51–70.
Carpenter, Stephen R., C.E. Kraft, R. Wright, X. He, P.A. Soranno, and J.R. Hodgson. 1992. "Resilience and Resistance of a Lake Phosphorus Cycle Before and After Food Web Manipulation." *American Naturalist* 140, 781–798.
Carpenter, Stephen R., Donald Ludwig, and William A. Brock. 1999. "Management of Eutrophication for Lakes Subject to Potentially Irrevsible Change." *Ecological Applications* 9, 751–771.
Carrier, David. 1993. "Will Chaos Kill the Auctioneer?" *Review of Political Economy* 5, 299–320.
Carroll, A.R. 1982. "National City Size Distributions: What Do We Know After 67 Years of Research?" *Progress in Human Geography* 6, 1–43.
Carter, Robert M., C.R. de Freitas, Indur M. Golkany, David Holland, and Richard S. Lindzen. 2006. "The *Stern Review*: A Dual Critique: Part I: The Science." *World Economics* 7, 167–198.
Cartwright, M.L. and J.E. Littlewood. 1945. "On nonlinear differential equations of the second order, I: the equation y + k(1-y^2)y + y = 6λcos(λt + a), k large." *Journal of the London Mathematical Society* 20, 180–189.
Casdagli, Martin, Stephen Eubank, J. Doyne Farmer, and John Gibson. 1991. "State Space Reconstruction in the Presence of Noise." *Physica D* 51, 52–98.

Casetti, Emilio. 1980. "Equilibrium Population Partitions between Urban and Agricultural Occupations." *Geographical Analysis* 12, 47–54.

Casetti, Emilio. 1982. "The Onset of Modern Economic Growth: Empirical Validation of a Catastrophe Model." *Papers of the Regional Science Association* 50, 9–20.

Casti, John L. 1979. *Connectivity, Complexity, and Catastrophe in Large-Scale Systems*. New York: Wiley-Interscience.

Casti, John L. 1989. *Alternate Realities: Mathematical Models of Nature and Man*. New York: Wiley-Interscience.

Casti, John L. and H. Swain. 1975. "Catastrophe Theory and Urban Processes." RM-75-14, IIASA, Laxenburg, Austria.

Cayley, Sir Arthur. 1879. "The Newton-Fourier Imaginary Problem." *American Journal of Mathematics* 2, 97.

Chakrabarti, Bikas K., Anirban Chakraborti, and Arnab Chatterjee, eds. 2006. *Econophysics and Sociophysics: Tends and Perspectives*. Weinheim: Wiley-VCH.

Charles, Anthony T. 1988. "Fishery Socioeconomics: A Survey." *Land Economics* 64, 276–295.

Charles, Anthony T. and Gordon R. Munro. 1985. "Irreversible Investment and Optimal Fisheries Management: A Stochastic Analysis." *Marine Resources Economics* 1, 247–264.

Chavas, Jean-Paul and Matthew T. Holt. 1991. "On Nonlinear Dynamics: The Case of the Pork Cycle." *American Journal of Agricultural Economics* 73, 819–828.

Chavas, Jean-Paul and Matthew T. Holt. 1993. "Market Instability and Nonlinear Dynamics." *American Journal of Agricultural Economics* 75, 113–120.

Chen, Zhiqi. 1997. "Can Economic Activity Lead to Climate Chaos?" *Canadian Journal of Economics* 30, 349–366.

Cheng, B. and H. Tong. 1992. "On Consistent Nonparametric Order Determination and Chaos." *Journal of the Royal Statistical Society B* 54, 427–449.

Chiarella, Carl. 1988. "The Cobweb Model: Its Instability and the Onset of Chaos." *Economic Modelling* 5, 377–384.

Chichilnisky, Graciela, Geoffrey Heal, and Andrea Beltratti. 1995. "The Green Golden Rule." *Economics Letters* 49, 175–179.

Childe, V. Gordon. 1936. *Man Makes Himself*. Harmondsworth: Penguin.

Childe, V. Gordon. 1942. *What Happened in History*. Harmondsworth: Penguin.

Chinitz, Benjamin. 1961. "Contrasts in Agglomeration: New York and Pittsburgh." *American Economic Review, Papers and Proceedings* 51, 279–289.

Chomsky, Noam. 1959. "On Certain Properties of Grammars." *Information and Control* 2, 137–167.

Christaller, Walter. 1933. *Die Zentralen Orte in Suddendeutschland*. Jena:Fischer (English translation by Baskin, C.W., 1966, *Central Places in Southern Germany*. Englewood Cliffs: Prentice-Hall).

Christensen, Paul P. 1989. "Historical Roots for Ecological Economics – Biophysical Versus Allocative Approaches." *Ecological Economics* 1, 17–36.

Christensen, Paul P. 2003. "Epicurean and Stoic Sources for Boisgiulbert's Physiological and Hippocratic Vision of Nature and Economics." *History of Political Economy* 35(Supplement), 103–128.

Cicchetti, Charles J. and A. Myrick Freeman III. 1971. "Option Demand and Consumer Surplus: Further Comment." *Quarterly Journal of Economics* 85, 528–539.

Ciriacy-Wantrup, Siegfried von. 1971. "The Economics of Environmental Policy." *Land Economics* 47, 36–45.

Ciriacy-Wantrup, Siegfried von, and Richard C. Bishop. 1975. "'Common Property' as a Concept in Natural Resources Policy." *Natural Resource Economics* 15, 713–727.

Clark, Colin W. 1973a. "Profit Maximization and the Extinction of Animal Species." *Journal of Political Economy* 81, 950–961.

Clark, Colin W. 1973b. "The Economics of Overexploitation." *Science* 181, 630–633.

Clark, Colin W. 1976. *Mathematical Bioeconomics*. New York: Wiley-Interscience.

Clark, Colin W. 1985. *Bioeconomic Modelling and Fisheries Management*. New York: Wiley-Interscience.
Clark, Colin W., F.H. Clarke, and G.R. Munro. 1979. "The Optimal Exploitation of Renewable Resource Stocks: Problems of Irreversible Investment." *Econometrica* 47, 25–49.
Clark, Colin W. and Marc Mangel. 1979. "Aggregation and Fishery Dynamics: A Theoretical Study of Schooling and the Purse Seine Tuna Fisheries." *Fisheries Bulletin* 77, 317–337.
Clark, Colin W. and Marc Mangel. 2000. *Dynamic State Variable Models in Ecology: Methods and Applications*. New York: Oxford University Press.
Clark, William A.V. 1992. "Residential Preferences and Neighborhood Racial Segregation: A Test of the Schelling Segregation Model." *Demography* 28, 1–19.
Clark, William A.V. and Mark Fossett. 2008. "Understanding the Social Context of the Schelling Segregation Model." *Proceedings of the National Academy of Sciences* 105, 4109–4114.
Clarke, M. and Alan G. Wilson. 1983. "The Dynamics of Urban Spatial Structure: Progress and Problems." *Journal of Regional Science* 23, 1–18.
Clements, Frederic E. 1916. *Plant Succession: Analysis of the Development of Vegetation*. Washington: Carnegie Institute.
Cline, William R. 1992. *The Economics of Global Warming*. Washington: Institute for International Economics.
Cobb, Loren. 1978. "Stochastic Catastrophe Models and Multimodal Distributions." *Behavioral Science* 23, 360–374.
Cobb, Loren. 1981. "Parameter Estimation for the Cusp Catastrophe Model." *Behavioral Science* 26, 75–78.
Cobb, Loren, P. Koppstein, and N.H. Chen. 1983. "Estimation and Moment Recursion Relationships for Multimodal Distributions of the Exponential Family." *Journal of the American Statistical Associations* 78, 124–130.
Cobb, Loren and Shelemyahu Zacks. 1985. "Applications of Catastrophe Theory for Statistical Modeling in the Biosciences." *Journal of the American Statistical Association* 80, 793–802.
Cobb, Loren and Shelemyahu Zacks. 1988. "Nonlinear Time Series Analysis for Dynamic Systems of Catastrophe Type," in R.R. Mohler, ed., *Nonlinear Time Series and Signal Processing*. Berlin: Springer-Verlag, 97–118.
Cochrane, John H. 2001. *Asset Pricing*. Princeton: Princeton University Press.
Coelho, José D. and Alan G. Wilson. 1976. "The Optimum Size and Location of Shopping Centers." *Regional Studies* 10, 413–421.
Collett, P. and Jean-Pierre Eckmann. 1980. *Iterated Maps on the Interval as Dynamical Systems*. Boston: Birkhäuser.
Commendatore, Pasquale, Martin Currie, and Ingrid Kubin. 2007. "Chaotic Footloose Capital." *Nonlinear Dynamics, Psychology, and Life Sciences* 11, 253–265.
Commendatore, Pasquale and Ingrid Kubin. 2010. "A Three-Regions New Economic Geography Model in Discrete Time." Mimeo, University of Naples "Federico II", Vienna University of Economics and Business Administration.
Commendatore, Pasquale, Ingrid Kubin, and Carmelo Petraglia. 2009. "Footloose Capital and Productive Public Services," in Neri Salvadori, Commendatore Pasquale, and Massimo Tamberi, eds., *Geography, Structural Change and Economic Development: Theory and Empirics*. Cheltenham: Edward Elgar, 3–28.
Conklin, James E. and William C. Kolberg. 1994. "Chaos for the Halibut?" *Marine Resource Economics* 9, 153–182.
Conlisk, John. 2007. "Comment on 'Markets Come to Bits: Evolution, Computation, and Markomata in Economic Science'." *Journal of Economic Behavior and Organization* 63, 243–246.
Conrad, Jon M. 1989. "Bioeconomics and the Bowhead Whale." *Journal of Political Economy* 97, 974–988.
Conrad, Jon M. 1997. "On the Option Value of Old-Growth Forests." *Ecological Economics* 22, 97–102.

Copes, Parzival. 1970. "The Backward-Bending Supply Curve of the Fishing Industry." *Scottish Journal of Political Economy* 17, 69–77.

Corsi, Pietro. 1988. *Science and Religion: Baden Powell and the Anglican Debate, 1800–1860*. Cambridge: Cambridge University Press.

Corsi, Pietro. 2005. "Before Darwin: Transformist Concepts in European Natural History." *Journal of the History of Biology* 38, 67–83.

Costanza, Robert, F. Andrade, P. Antunes, M. van den Belt, D. Boesch, D. Boersma, F. Catarino, S. Hanna, K. Limburg, B. Low, M. Molitor, J.G. Pereira, S. Rayner, R. Santos, J. Wilson, and M. Young. 1999. "Ecological Economics and Sustainable Governance of the Oceans." *Ecological Economics* 31, 171–187.

Cotogno, P. 2003. "Hypercomputation and the Physical Church-Turing Thesis." *British Journal for the Philosophy of Science* 54, 181–223.

Courant, Paul N. and John Yinger. 1977. "On Models of Racial Prejudice and Urban Spatial Structure." *Journal of Urban Economics* 4, 272–291.

Crank, J. 1974. "Chemical and Biological Problems," in J.R. Ockenden and E.A. Hodgkins, eds., *Moving Boundary Problems in Heat Flow and Diffusion*. Oxford: Oxford University Press, 62–70.

Crannell, Annalisa. 1995. "The Role of Transitivity in Devaney's Definition of Chaos." *American Mathematical Monthly* 102, 788–793.

Cronon, William. 1991. *Nature's Metropolis: Chicago and the Great West*. New York: W.W. Norton.

Cropper, Maureen L. 1976. "Regulating Activities with Catastrophic Environmental Effects." *Journal of Environmental Economics and Management* 3, 1–15.

Cropper, Maureen L. 1988. "A Note on the Extinction of Renewable Resources." *Journal of Environmental Economics and Management* 15, 64–70.

Cropper, Maureen L., Dwight R. Lee, and Sukkraj Dingh Pannu. 1979. "The Optimal Extinction of a Renewable Natural Resource." *Journal of Environment Economics and Management* 6, 341–349.

Crow, James F. 1955. "General Theory of Population Genetics: Synthesis." *Cold Spring Harbor Symposia on Quantitative Biology* 20, 54–59.

Crow, James F. and Kenichi Aoki. 1982. "Group Selection for a Polygenic Behavioral Trait: A Differential Proliferation Model." *Proceedings of the National Academy of Sciences of the United States of America* 79, 2628–2631.

Crow, James F. and Motoo Kimura. 1970. *An Introduction to Population Genetics Theory*. New York: Harper & Row.

Crutchfield, James P. 1994. "The Calculi of Emergence: Computation, Dynamics and Induction." *Physica D* 75, 11–54.

Crutchfield, James P. 2003. "When Evolution is Revolution – Origins of Innovation," in James P. Crutchfield and Peter Schuster, eds., *Evolutionary Dynamics: Exploring the Interplay of Selection, Accident, Neutralilty, and Function*. Oxford: Oxford University Press, 101–133.

Currie, Martin and Ingrid Kubin. 2006. "Chaos in the Core-Periphery Model." *Journal of Economic Behavior and Organization* 60, 252–275.

Cuvier, G. 1818. *An Essay on the Theory of the Earth* (Jameson translation). New York: Kirk & Mercein.

Cvitanovic, Predrag, ed. 1984. *Universality in Chaos*. Bristol: Adam Hilger.

Daly, Herman E. 1968. "Economics as a Life Science." *Journal of Political Economy* 76, 392–406.

Daly, Herman E. 1977. *Steady-State Economics*. San Francisco: W.H. Freeman.

Daly, Herman E. 1987. "The Economic Growth Debate: What Some Economists Have Learned But Many Have Not." *Journal of Environmental Economics and Management* 14, 323–336.

d'Arge, Ralph C., William D. Schulze, and David S. Brookshire. 1982. "Carbon Dioxide and Intergenerational Choice." *American Economic Review* 72, 251–256.

Darley, V.M. and Stuart A. Kauffman. 1997. "Natural Rationality," in W. Brian Arthur, Steven N. Durlauf, and David A. Lane, eds., *The Economy as an Evolving Complex System II*. Reading: Addison-Wesley, 45–80.

Darwin, Charles. 1859. *On the Origin of Species by Means of Natural Selection or the Preservation of Favored Races in the Struggle for Life*. London: John Murray.

Darwin, Charles. 1871. *The Descent of Man and Selection in Relation to Sex*. London: John Murray.

Darwin, Charles. 1872. *The Expression of Emotions in Man and Animal*. London: John Murray.

Darwin, Charles and Alfred Russel Wallace. 1858. "On the Tendency of Species to Form Varieties; and on the Perpetuation of Varieties and Species by Means of Natural Selection." *Journal of the Linnaean Society (Zoology)* 3, 45.

Darwin, Erasmus. 1794–1996. *Zoönomia: The Laws of Organic Life*, 3 Vols. London: J. Johnson.

Dasgupta, Partha A. and Geoffrey M. Heal. 1979. *Economic Theory and Exhaustible Resources*. Cambridge: Cambridge University Press.

Davidson, Julius. 1919. "One of the Physical Foundations of Economics." *Quarterly Journal of Economics* 33, 717–724.

Davidson, Paul. 1991. "Is Probability Theory Relevant for Uncertainty?" *Journal of Economic Perspectives* 5, 129–143.

Davidson, Paul. 1994. *Post Keynesian Macroeconomic Theory*. Aldershot: Edward Elgar.

Davidson, Paul. 1996. "Reality and Economic Theory." *Journal of Post Keynesian Economics* 18, 479–508.

Davies, Paul. 2003. "Complexity and the Arrow of Time," in Niels Henrik Gregersen, ed., *From Complexity to Life: On the Emergence of Life and Meaning*. Oxford: Oxford University Press, 72–92.

Davis, Donald R. 1998. "The Home Market, Trade and Industrial Structure." *American Economic Review* 88, 1264–1276.

Davis, Donald R. and David E. Weinstein. 1999. "Economic Geography and Regional Production Structure: An Empirical Investigation." *European Economic Review* 43, 379–407.

Davis, Donald and David Weinstein. 2002. "Bones, Bombs, and Breakpoints: The Geography of Economic Activity." *American Economic Review* 99, 1269–1289.

Davis, Harold J. 1941. *The Theory of Econometrics*. Bloomington: Indiana University Press.

Dawkins, Richard. 1976. *The Selfish Gene*. Oxford: Oxford University Press (2nd Edition, 1989).

Dawkins, Richard. 1983. "Universal Darwinism," in D.S. Bendall, ed., *Evolution from Molecules to Men*. Cambridge: Cambridge University Press, 403–425.

Day, Richard H. 1982. "Irregular Growth Cycles." *American Economic Review* 72, 406–414.

Day, Richard H. 1983. "The Emergence of Chaos from Classical Economic Growth." *Quarterly Journal of Economics* 98, 201–213.

Day, Richard H. 1986. "Unscrambling the Concept of Chaos Through Thick and Thin: Reply." *Quarterly Journal of Economics* 98, 201–213.

Day, Richard H. 1989. "Dynamical Systems, Adaptation and Economic Evolution." MRG Working Paper No. M8908, University of Southern California.

Day, Richard H. 1994. *Complex Economic Dynamics: An Introduction to Dynamical Systems and Market Mechanisms: Volume I*. Cambridge: MIT Press.

Day, Richard H., S. Dasgupta, S.K. Datta, and J.B. Nugent. 1987. "Instability in Rural-Urban Migration." *Economic Journal* 97, 940–950.

Day, Richard H. and Giulio Pianigiani. 1991. "Statistical Dynamics and Economics." *Journal of Economic Behavior and Organization* 16, 37–84.

Day, Richard H. and Jean-Luc Walter. 1989. "Economic Growth in the Very Long Run: On the Multiple Interaction of Population, Technology, and Social Infrastructure," in William A. Barnett, John Geweke, and Karl Shell, eds., *Economic Complexity: Chaos, Sunspots, Bubbles and Nonlinearity*. Cambridge: Cambridge University Press, 253–289.

Dechert, W. Davis and Ramazan Gençay, eds. 1996. *Chaos Theory in Economics: Methods, Models, and Evidence*. Cheltenham: Edward Elgar.

Dechert, W. Davis and Kazuo Nishimura. 1983. "A Complete Characterization of Optimal Growth Paths in an Aggregated Model with a Non-Concave Production Function." *Journal of Economic Theory* 31, 322–354.

Dechert, W. Davis and Sharon O'Donnell. 2006. "The Stochastic Lake Game: A Numerical Solution." *Journal of Economic Dynamics and Control* 30, 1569–1587.

De Canio, Stephen J. 2003. *Economic Models of Climate Change: A Critique*. Houndsmill: Palgrave-Macmillan.

de Lima, Pedro J.F. 1998. "Nonlinearities and Nonstationarities in Stock Returns." *Journal of Business and Economic Statistics* 16, 227–236.

De Vries, J. 1984. *European Urbanization 1500–1800*. Cambridge: Harvard University Press.

Dendrinos, Dimitrios S. 1978. "Urban Dynamics and Urban Cycles." *Environment and Planning A* 10, 43–49.

Dendrinos, Dimitrios S. 1979. "Slums in Capitalist Urban Settings: Some Insights from DDCatastrophe Theory." *Geographia Polonica* 42, 63–75.

Dendrinos, Dimitrios S. 1980a. "Dynamics of City Size and Structural Stability: The Case of a Single City." *Geographical Analysis* 12, 236–244.

Dendrinos, Dimitrios S. 1980b. "A Basic Model of Urban Dynamics Expressed as a Set of Volterra-Lotka Equations," in Dimitrios S. Dendrinos, ed., *Catastrophe Theory in Urban and Transport Analysis*, Report No. DOT/RSPA/DPB-25/80/20. Washington: US Department of Transportation.

Dendrinos, Dimitrios S. 1981. "Individual Lot and Neighborhood Competitive Equilibria: Some Extensions from the Theory of Structural Stability." *Journal of Regional Science* 21, 37–49.

Dendrinos, Dimitrios S. 1982. "On the Dynamic Stability of Interurban/Regional Labor and Capital Movements." *Journal of Regional Science* 22, 529–540.

Dendrinos, Dimitrios S. 1984a. "Regions, Antiregions, and their Dynamic Stability: The U.S. Case (1929–1979)." *Journal of Regional Science* 24, 65–83.

Dendrinos, Dimitrios S. 1984b. "The Structural Stability of the US Regions: Evidence and Theoretical Underpinnings." *Environment and Planning A* 16, 1433–1443.

Dendrinos, Dimitrios S. 1985. "Turbulence and Fundamental Urban/Regional Dynamics." Task Force on Dynamic Analysis of Spatial Development, IIASA, Laxenburg, Austria.

Dendrinos, Dimitrios S. 1989. "Growth Patterns of the Eight Regions in the People's Republic of China (1980–1985)." *Annals of Regional Science* 23, 213–222.

Dendrinos, Dimitrios S. and Gunter Haag. 1984. "Toward a Stochastic Dynamical Theory of Location: Empirical Evidence." *Geographical Analysis* 16, 287–300.

Dendrinos, Dimitrios S. and Henry Mulally. 1981. "Evolutionaly Patterns of Urban Populations." *Geographical Analysis* 13, 328–344.

Dendrinos, Dimitrios S. and Henry Mulally. 1983a. "Empirical Evidence of Volterra-Lotka Dynamics in United States Metropolitan Areas: 1940–1977," in Griffith, Daniel A. and Lea, Anthony C., eds., *Evolving Geographical Structures: Mathematical Models and Theories for Space-Time Processes*. The Hague: Martinus Nijhoff, 170–195.

Dendrinos, Dimitrios S. and Henry Mulally. 1983b. "Optimal Control in Nonlinear Ecological Dynamics of Metropolitan Areas." *Environment and Planning A* 15, 543–550.

Dendrinos, Dimitrios S. and Henry Mulally. 1984. "Interurban Population and Capital Accumulations and Structural Stability." *Applied Mathematics and Computation* 14, 11–24.

Dendrinos, Dimitrios S. and Henry Mulally. 1985. *Urban Evolution: Studies in the Mathematical Ecology of Cities*. Oxford: Oxford University Press.

Dendrinos, Dimitrios S. and J. Barkley Rosser, Jr. 1992. "Fundamental Issues in Nonlinear Urban Population Dynamics Models: Theory and a Synthesis." *Annals of Regional Science* 26, 135–145.

Dendrinos, Dimitrios S. and Michael Sonis. 1986. "Variational Principles and Conservation Conditions in Volterra's Ecology and in Urban Relative Dynamics." *Journal of Regional Science* 26, 359–377.

Dendrinos, Dimitrios S. and Michael Sonis. 1987. "The Onset of Turbulence in Discrete Relative Multiple Spatial Dynamics." *Applied Mathematics and Computation* 22, 25–44.

Dendrinos, Dimitrios S. and Michael Sonis. 1988. "Nonlinear Discrete Relative Population Dynamics of the U.S. Regions." *Applied Mathematics and Computation* 25, 265–285.

Dendrinos, Dimitrios S. and Michael Sonis. 1989. *Turbulence and Socio-Spatial Dynamics: Toward a Theory of Social Systems Evolution*. Berlin: Springer.
Dendrinos, Dimitrios S. and Michael Sonis. 1990. "Signatures of Chaos: Rules in Sequences of Spatial Stock Size Distributions for Discrete Relative Dynamics?" *Occasional Paper Series on Socio-Spatial Dynamics* 1, 57–73.
Desai, Meghnad. 1973. "Growth Cycles and Inflation in a Model of Class Struggle." *Journal of Economic Theory* 6, 527–545.
Devaney, Robert L. 1989. *An Introduction to Chaotic Dynamical Systems*, 2nd Edition. Redwood City: Addison-Wesley.
Diener, Marc and Tim Poston. 1984. "The Perfect Delay Convention, or The Revolt of the Slaved Variables," in Hermann Haken, ed., *Chaos and Order in Nature*, 2nd Edition. Berlin: Springer, 249–268.
Ding, Mingzhou, E-Jiang Ding, William L. Ditto, Bruce Gluckman, Visarath In, Jian-Hua Peng, Mark L. Spano, and Weiming Yang. 1997. "Control and Synchronization of Chaos in High Dimensional Systems: Review of Some Recent Results." *Chaos* 7, 644–652.
Ditto, William L., S.N. Rauseo, and Mark L. Spano. 1990. "Experimental Control of Chaos." *Physical Review Letters* 65, 3211–3214.
Ditto, William L., Mark L. Spano, and John F. Lindner. 1995. "Techniques for the Control of Chaos." *Physica D* 86, 198–211.
Dixit, Avinash K. and Joseph E. Stiglitz. 1977. "Monopolistic Competition and Optimum Product Diversity." *American Economic Review* 67, 297–308.
Dobkins, Linda H. and Yannis M. Ioannides. 2001. "Spatial Interactions among US Cities." *Regional Science and Urban Economics* 31, 701–731.
Dobzhansky, Theodosius. 1937. *Genetics and the Origin of Species*. New York: Columbia University Press.
Dobzhansky, Theodosius. 1940. "Catastrophism Versus Evolution." *Science* 92, 356–358.
Dodson, M.M. 1976. "Darwin's Law of Natural Selection and Thom's Theory of Catastrophes." *Mathematical Biosciences* 28, 243–274.
Domanski, R. and A.P. Wierzbiecki. 1983. "Self-Organization in Dynamic Settlement Systems." *Papers of the Regional Science Association* 51, 141–160.
Domowitz, Ian and Mahmoud A. El-Gamal. 1993. "A Consistent Test of Stationary Ergodicity." *Econometric Theory* 9, 589–601.
Done, Terry J. 1992. "Phase Shifts in Coral Reef Communities and Their Ecological Significance." *Hydrobiology* 247, 121–132.
Dopfer, Kurt, ed. 2005. *The Evolutionary Foundations of Economics*. Cambridge: Cambridge University Press.
Doveri, F., M. Scheffer, S. Rinaldi, S. Muratori, and Yu. A. Kuznetsov. 1993. "Seasonality and Chao in a Plankton-Fish Model." *Theoretical Population Biology* 43, 159–183.
Dressler, U. and G. Nitsche. 1991. "Controlling Chaos Using Time Delay Coordinates." *Physical Review Letters* 68, 1–4.
Duffing, G. 1918. *Erzwunge Schweingungen bei Veranderlicher Eigenfrequenz*. Braunschweig: F. Viewig u. Sohn.
Duncan, A.D. and B. Duncan. 1957. *The Negro Population of Chicago*. Chicago: University of Chicago Press.
Durlauf, Steven N. 1991. "Multiple Equilibria and Persistence in Aggregate Fluctuations." *American Economic Review Papers and Proceedings* 81, 70–74.
Durlauf, Steven N. 1997. "Statistical Mechanics Approaches to Socioeconomic Behavior," in W. Brian Arthur, Steven N. Durlauf, and David A. Lane, eds., *The Economy as an Evolving Complex System II*. Reading: Addison-Wesley, 81–104.
Durrenberger, E. Paul and Gísli Pálsson. 1987. "Ownership at Sea: Fishing Territories and Access to Sea Resources." *American Ethnologist* 14, 508–522.
Dutta, Prajit K. and Roy Radner. 2009. "A Strategic Analysis of Global Warming: Theory and Some Numbers." *Journal of Economic Behavior and Organization* 71, 187–209.

Eble, Gunther J. 2003. "Developmental Morphospaces and Evolution," in James P. Crutchfield and Peter Schuster, eds., *Evolutionary Dynamics: Exploring the Interplay of Selection, Accident, Neutrality, and Function*. Oxford: Oxford University Press, 33–63.

Eckmann, Jean-Pierre, S. Oliffson Kamphorst, David Ruelle, and S. Ciliberto. 1986. "Lyapunov Exponents from a Time Series." *Physical Review A* 34, 4971–4979.

Eckmann, Jean-Pierre and David Ruelle. 1985. "Ergodic Theory of Chaos and Strange Attractors." *Reviews of Modern Physics* 57, 617–656.

Eckmann, Jean-Pierre and David Ruelle. 1991. "Fundamental Limitations for Estimating Dimensions and Lyapunov Exponents in Dynamical Systems." *Physica D* 56, 117–119.

Edelson, Noel M. 1975. "The Developer's Problem, or How to Divide a Piece of Land Most Profitably." *Journal of Urban Economics* 2, 349–365.

Edgar, Gerald A. 1990. *Measure, Topology and Fractal Geometry*. New York: Springer.

Efron, Bradley. 1979. "Bootstrap Methods: Another Look at the Jacknife." *Annals of Statistics* 7, 1–26.

Eggleton, R.P. 1974. "Astrophysical Problems: A Moving Boundary Probliem in the Study of Stellar Interiors," in J.R. Ockenden and E.A. Hodgkins, eds., *Moving Boundary Problems in Heat Flow and Diffusion*. Oxford: Oxford University Press, 103–111.

Ehrlich, Paul R. and Peter H. Raven. 1964. "Butterflies and Plants: A Study of Coevolution." *Evolution* 18, 586–608.

Eigen, Manfred and Peter Schuster. 1979. *The Hypercycle: A Principle of Natural Self-Organization*. Berlin: Springer.

Ekman, P. 1992. *Telling Lies*. New York: Norton.

Eldredge, Niles J. and Stephen Jay Gould. 1972. "Punctuated Equilibria," in D.J.M. Schopf, ed., *Models in Paleobiology*. San Francisco: Freeman, Cooper, 82–115.

El-Gamal, Mahmoud A. 1991. "Non-Parametric Estimation of Deterministically Chaotic Systems." *Economic Theory* 1, 147–167.

Eliot, T.S. 1934. *Selected Poems*. New York: Harcourt, Brace, and World.

Ellis, R. 1985. *Entropy, Large Deviations and Statistical Mechanics*. New York: Springer.

Ellison, Glenn, Edward L. Glaeser, and Willam R. Kerr. 2010. "What Causes Industry Agglomeration? Evidence from Coagglomeration Patterns." *American Economic Review* 100, 1195–1213.

Ellner, Stephen and Peter Turchin. 1995. "Chaos in a Noisy World: New Methods and Evidence from Time Series Analysis." *American Naturalist* 145, 343–375.

El Naschie, M.S. 1994. "On Certain 'Empty' Cantor Sets and their Dimensions." *Chaos, Solitions & Fractals* 4, 293–296.

Elton, Charles S. 1924. "Periodic Fluctuatoins in the Number of Animals: Their Causes and Effects." *British Journal of Experimental Biology* 2, 119–163.

Elton, Charles S. 1942. *Voles, Mice, and Lemmings: Problems in Population Dynamics*. Oxford: Oxford University Press.

Elton, Charles S. 1958. *The Ecology of Invasions by Plants and Animals*. London: Methuen.

Elton, Charles S. 1966. *The Pattern of Animal Communities*. London: Methuen.

Embrechts, Paul, A.J. McNeil, and D. Staumann. 2002. "Correlation and Dependency in Risk Management: Properties and Pitfalls," in M. Dempster, ed., *Risk Management: Value at Risk and Beyond*. Cambridge: Cambridge University Press, 176–223.

Emerson, A.E. 1952. "The Supra-Organismic Aspects of Society." *Coloqques CNRS* 34, 333–353.

Engels, Friedrich. 1940. *The Dialectics of Nature*. New York: International Publishers.

Epstein, Joshua M. and Robert Axtell. 1996. *Growing Artificial Societies: Social Science from the Bottom Up*. Washington: Brookings Institution.

Erdös, Paul and Alfréd Renyi. 1959. "On Random Graphs I." *Publicationes Mathematicae Debreccen* 6, 290–297.

Erdös, Paul and Alfréd Renyi. 1960. "On the Evolution of Random Graphs." *Publications of the Mathematical Institute of the Hungarian Academy of Sciences* 5, 17–61.

Erdös, Paul and Joel H. Spencer. 1974. *Probabilistic Methods in Combinatorics*. New York: Academic Press.

Estes, James A. and D.O. Duggins. 1995. "Sea Otters and Kelp Forests in Alaska: Generality and Variation in a Community Ecological Paradigm." *Ecological Monographs* 65, 75–100.

Estigneev, Igor V. 1988. "Stochastic Extremal Problems and the Strong Markov Property of Random Fields." *Russian Mathematical Surveys* 43, 1–49.

Estigneev, Igor V. 1991. "Controlled Random Fields on Graphs and Stochastic Models of Economic Equilibrium," in V.V. Sazonov and T. Shervidze, eds., *New Trends in Probability and Statistics*. Utrecht: VSP, 391–412.

Fagiolo, Giorgio, Marco Valente, and Nicolaas J. Vriend. 2007. "Segregation in Networks." *Journal of Economic Behavior and Organizaion* 64, 316–336.

Falconer, Kenneth. 1990. *Fractal Geometry, Mathematical Foundations and Applications*. New York: Wiley

Farmer, J. Doyne. 1986. "Scaling in Fat Fractals," in G. Mayer-Kress, ed., *Dimensions and Entropies in Chaotic Systems: Quantification of Complex Behavior*. Berlin: Springer, 54–60.

Farmer, J. Doyne, Edward Ott, and James A. Yorke. 1983. "The Dimension of Chaotic Attractors." *Physica D* 7, 153–180.

Farzin, Y. Hossein. 1984. "The Effect of the Discount Rate on Depletion of Exhaustible Resources." *Journal of Political Economy* 92, 841–851.

Faustmann, Martin. 1849. "On the Determination of the Value which Forest Land and Immature Stands Possess for Forestry," (English edition, M. Gane, ed., 1968). *Martin Faustmann and the Evolution of Discounted Cash Flow*. Oxford University Paper 42.

Feigenbaum, Mitchell J. 1978. "Quantitative Universality for a Class of Nonlinear Transformations." *Journal of Statistical Physics* 19, 25–52.

Feigenbaum, Mitchell J. 1980. "Universal Behavior in Nonlinear Systems." *Los Alamos Science* 1, 4–27.

Fehr, Ernst and Klaus Schmidt. 1999. "A Theory of Fairness, Competition and Cooperation." *Quarterly Journal of Economics* 114, 817–868.

Fehr, Ernst and Klaus Schmidt. 2010. "On Inequity Aversion: A Reply to Binmore and Shaked." *Journal of Economic Behavior and Organization* 73, 101–108.

Fehr, Ernst and Simon Gächter. 2002. "Altruistic Punishment in Humans." *Nature* 415, 137–140.

Fisher, Anthony C. 1981. *Resource and Environmental Economics*. Cambridge: Cambridge University Press.

Fisher, Anthony C. and John V. Krutilla. 1974. "Valuing Long-Run Ecological Consequences and Irreversibilities." *Journal of Environmental Economics and Management* 1, 96–108.

Fisher, Irving. 1907. *The Rate of Interest*. New York: Macmillan.

Fisher, Irving. 1930. *The Theory of Interest*. New York: Augustus M. Kelly.

Fisher, Ronald A. 1930. *The Genetical Theory of Natural Selection*. Oxford: Oxford University Press.

Föllmer, Hans. 1974. "Random Economies with Many Interacting Agents." *Journal of Mathematical Economics* 1, 51–62.

Foroni, Ilaria, Laura Gardini, and J. Barkley Rosser, Jr. 2003. "Adaptive and Statistical Expectations in a Renewable Resource Market." *Mathematics and Computers in Simulation* 63, 541–567.

Forrester, Jay W. 1961. *Industrial Dynamics*. Cambridge: MIT Press.

Forrester, Jay W. 1969. *Urban Dynamics*. Cambridge: MIT Press.

Forrester, Jay W. 1971. *World Dynamics*. Cambridge: Wright-Allen.

Foster, Dean and H. Peyton Young. 1990. "Stochastic Evolutionary Game Dynamics." *Theoretical Population Biology* 38, 219–232.

Foster, John and J. Stanley Metcalfe, eds. 2001. *Frontiers of Evolutionary Economics: Competition, Self-Organization and Innovation Policy*. Cheltenham: Edward Elgar.

Foster, John Bellamy. 2000. *Marx's Ecology: Materialism and Nature*. New York: Monthly Review Press.

Fotheringham, A. Stewart, Michael Batty, and Paul A. Longley. 1989. "Diffusion-Limited Aggregation and the Fractal Nature of Urban Growth." *Papers of the Regional Science Association* 67, 55–69.

Fourier, F.M.C. 1840. *Le Nouveau Monde Industriel et Sociétaire*. Paris.

Frank, Murray Z. and Thanasios Stengos. 1988. "Chaotic Dynamics in Economic Time Series." *Journal of Economic Surveys* 2, 103–133.

Frank, Robert. 1988. *Passions with Reason: The Strategic Role of the Emotions*. New York: W.W. Norton.

Frank, Robert, T. Gilovich, and D.T. Regan. 1993. "The Evolution of One-Shot Cooperation in an Experiment." *Ethology and Sociobiology* 14, 247–256.

Frederickson, P., J.L. Kaplan, S.D. Yorke, and James A. Yorke. 1983. "The Liapunov Dimension of Strange Attractors." *Journal of Differential Equations* 49, 185–207.

French, David. 1986. "Confronting an Unsolvable Problem: Deforestation in Malawi." *World Development* 14, 531–540.

Frenken, Koen and Ron Boschma. 2007. "A Theoretical Framework for Evolutionary Economic Geography: Industrial Dynamics and Urban Growth as a Branching Process." *Journal of Economic Geography* 7, 635–649.

Friedman, Milton. 1953. *The Methodology of Positive Economics*. Chicago: University of Chicago Press.

Fujita, Masahisa. 1976a. "Towards a Dynamic Theory of Urban Land Use." *Papers of the Regional Science Association* 37, 133–165.

Fujita, Masahisa. 1976b. "Spatial Patterns of Urban Growth: Optimum and Market." *Journal of Urban Economics* 9, 22–52.

Fujita, Masahisa. 1981. "Spatial Patterns of Urban Growth: Optimum and Market," in Daniel A. Griffith and Ross D. MacKinnon, eds., *Dynamic Spatial Models*. Alphen van den Rijn: Sijthoof and Noordhoff, 404–439.

Fujita, Masahisa. 1988. "A Monopolistic Competition Approach to Spatial Agglomeration: A Differentiated Product Approach." *Regional Science and Urban Economics* 18, 87–124.

Fujita, Masahisa, Paul Krugman, and Anthony J. Venables. 1999. *The Spatial Economy: Cities, Regions, and International Trade*, Paperback edition. Cambridge: MIT Press.

Fujita, Masahisa, Paul Krugman, and Tomoya Mori. 1999. "On the Evolution of Hierarchical Urban Systems." *European Economic Review* 43, 209–257.

Fujita, Masahisa and Hideaki Ogawa. 1982. "Multiple Equilibria and Structural Transition of Non-Monocentric Urban Configurations." *Regional Science and Urban Economics* 12, 161–196.

Fujita, Masahisa and Jacques-François Thisse. 2002. *Economics of Agglomeration: Cities, Industrial Location, and Regional Growth*. Cambridge: Cambridge University Press.

Fujita, Masahisa and Jacques-François Thisse. 2010. "New Economic Geography: An Appraisal on the Occasion of Paul Krugman's 2008 Nobel Prize in Economic Sciences." *Regional Science and Urban Economics* 39, 109–119.

Fuller, R. Buckminster. 1975. *Synergetics*. New York: Macmillan.

Fuller, R. Buckminster. 1979. *Synergetics 2*. New York: Macmillan.

Fussbudget, H.J. and R.S. Snarler. 1979. "Sagacity Theory: A Critique." *Mathematical Intelligencer* 2, 56–59.

Futagami, Koichi and Kazuo Mino. 1995. "Public Capital and Patterns of Growth in the Presence of Threshold Externalities." *Journal of Economics* 61, 123–146.

Gabaix, Xavier. 1999. "Zipf's Law for Cities: An Explanation." *Quarterly Journal of Economics* 114, 739–768.

Gaffney, Mason. 1957. *Concepts of Financial Maturity of Timber and Other Assets*, Agricultural Economics Information Series 62. Raleigh: North Carolina State College, September.

Gallese, V., L. Fadiga, Leonardo Fogassi, and G. Rizzolati. 1996. "Action Recognition in the Premotor Cortex." *Brain* 119, 593–609.

Gardner, M.R. and W.R. Ashby. 1970. "Connectance of Large Dynamic (Cybernetic) Systems: Critical Values for Stablility." *Nature* 228, 784.

Garfinkel, Alan. 1987. "The Slime Mold *Dictosteliam* as a Model of Self-Organization in the Social Systems," in F. Eugene Yates, ed., *Self-Organizing Systems: The Emergence of Order*. New York: Plenum Press, 181–212.

Garreau, Joel R. 1981. *The Nine Nations of North America*. New York: Avon.

Gause, G.J. 1935. *La Théorie Mathématique de la Lutta Pour la Vie*. Paris: Hermann.

Gautieri, Giusseppe. 1805. *Slancio sulla Genealogica della Terra e sulla Construzione Dinamica della Organizzazione, Seguito da una Ricerca sull'Origine dei Vermi Abitanti le Interiora degli Animali*. Jena: Sassonia.

Gavrilets, Sergey. 2003. "Evolution and Speciation in a Hyperspace: The Roles of Neutrality, Selection, Mutation, and Random Drift," in James P. Crutchfield and Peter Schuster, eds., *Evolutionary Dynamics: Exploring the Interplay of Selection, Accident, Neutrality, and Function*. Oxford: Oxford University Press, 135–162.

Geddes, Patrick. 1915. *Cities in Evolution*. London: Williams and Norgate.

Geiger, Gerhard. 1983. "On the Dynamics of Evolutionary Discontinuities." *Mathematical Biosciences* 67, 59–79.

Gençay, Ramazan. 1996. "A Statistical Framework for Testing Chaotic Dynamics via Lyapunov Exponents." *Physica D* 89, 261–266.

Gençay, Ramazan and W. Davis Dechert. 1992. "An Algorithm for the N Lyapunov Exponents of an N-Dimensional Unknown Dynamical System." *Physica D* 59, 142–157.

Genest, C. and A.-C. Favre. 2007. "Everything You Always Wanted to Know about Copula Modeling but were Afraid to Ask." *Journal of Hydrological Engineering* 12, 347–368.

Gennotte, Gerard and Hayne Leland. 1990. "Market Liquidity, Hedging, and Crashes." *American Economic Review* 80, 999–1021.

Georgescu-Roegen, Nicholas. 1971. *The Entropy Law and the Economic Process*. Cambridge: Harvard University.

Georgescu-Roegen, Nicholas. 1979. "Comments on the Papers by Daly and Stiglitz," in V. Kerry Smith, ed., *Scarcity and Growth Reconsidered*. Baltimore: Johns Hopkins University Press, 95–105.

Gerelli, Emilio. 1985. "Entropy and the End of the World." *Ricerche Economiche* 34, 435–438.

Geweke, John. 1993. "Inference and Forecasting for Deterministic Nonlinear Time Series Observed with Measurement Error," in Richard H. Day and Ping Chen, eds., *Nonlinear Dynamics & Evolutionary Economics*. Oxford: Oxford University Press, 266–287.

Gibbon, Edward. 1788. *The Decline and Fall of the Roman Empire*. London: Methuen.

Gibbs, J.N. and R.S. Howell. 1972. "Dutch Elm Disease Survey, 1971." *Forest Record* No. 82.

Gibrat, R. 1931. *Les Inégalités Économiques*. Paris: Librairie de Recueil Sirey.

Gilmore, Claire G. 1993. "A New Test for Chaos." *Journal of Economic Behavior and Organization* 22, 209–237.

Gilmore, Robert. 1981. *Catastrophe Theory for Scientists and Engineers*. New York: Wiley.

Gilmore, Robert. 1998. "Topological Analysis of Chaotic Dynamical Systems." *Review of Modern Physics* 70, 1455–1529.

Gilpin, Michael E. 1979. "Spiral Chaos in a Predator Prey Model." *American Naturalist* 113, 306–308.

Gintis, Herbert. 2000. "Strong Reciprocity and Human Sociality." *Journal of Theoretical Biology* 206, 169–170.

Ginzburg, Lev and Mark Colyvan. 2004. *Ecological Orbits: How Planets Move and Populations Grow*. Oxford: Oxford University Press.

Gleick, James. 1987. *Chaos: The Making of a New Science*. New York: Viking.

Gödel, Kurt. 1931. "Über Formal Unentscheidbare satze der *Principia Mathematica* und Verwandter Systeme I." *Monatshefte fur Mathematik und Physik* 38, 173–198.

Godwin, William. 1820. *On Population*. London: Longman, Hurst, Orme, and Brown.

Goldschmidt, Richard. 1933. "Some Aspects of Evolution." *Science* 78, 539–547.

Goldschmidt, Richard. 1940. *The Material Basis of Evolution*. New Haven: Yale University Press.

Goldstein, Joshua S. 1988. *Long Cycles: War and Prosperity in the Modern Age*. New Haven: Yale University Press.

Gollub, Jerry P. and Harry L. Swinney. 1975. "Onset of Turbulence in a Rotating Fluid." *Physical Review Letters* 35, 927–930.

Golubitsky, Martin and John A. Guckenheimer. 1986. *Multiparameter Bifurcation Theory*. Providence: American Mathematical Society.
Golubitsky, Martin and Victor Guillemin. 1973. *Stable Mappings and Their Singularities*. Berlin: Springer.
Goodman, Paul and Percival Goodman. 1960. *Communitas*, 2nd Edition. New York: Vintage.
Goodwin, Brian. 1994. *How the Leopard Changed its Spots: The Evolution of Complexity*. New York: Simon & Schuster.
Goodwin, Philip B. 1977. "Habit and Hysteresis in Mode Choice." *Urban Studies* 14, 95–98.
Goodwin, Richard M. 1951. "The Nonlinear Accelerator and the Persistence of Business Cycles." *Econometrica* 19, 1–17.
Goodwin, Richard M. 1967. "A Growth Cycle," in C.H. Feinstein, ed., *Socialism, Capitalism and Economic Growth*. Cambridge: Cambridge University Press.
Goodwin, Richard M. 1978. "Wicksell and the Malthusian Catastrophe." *Scandinavian Journal of Economics* 80, 190–198.
Goodwin, Richard M. 1986. "The Economy as an Evolutionary Pulsator." *Journal of Economic Behavior and Organization* 7, 341–349.
Gordon, H. Scott. 1954. "Economic Theory of a Common-Property Resource: The Fishery." *Journal of Political Economy* 62, 124–142.
Gordon, Scott. 1989. "Darwin and Political Economy: The Connection Reconsidered." *Journal of the History of Biology* 22, 437–459.
Gould, J.R. 1972. "Extinction of a Fishery by Commercial Exploitation: A Note." *Journal of Political Economy* 80, 1031–1038.
Gould, Stephen Jay. 1987. "Is a New and General Theory of Evolution Emerging?," in F. Eugene Yates, ed., *Self-Organizing Systems: The Emergence of Order*. New York: Plenum Press, 113–130.
Gould, Stephen Jay. 2002. *The Structure of Evolutionary Theory*. Cambridge: Belknap Press of Harvard University Press.
Gowdy, John M., 1988. "Review of 'Entropy and Bioeconomics-The New Paradigm of Nicholas Georgescu-Roegen'." *International Journal of Social Economics* 15, 81–84.
Gowdy, John M. 1989. "The Entropy Law and Marxian Value Theory." *Review of Radical Political Economics* 20, 34–40.
Grafton, R. Quentin, Tom Kampas, and Pham Van Hu. 2009. "Cod Today and None Tomorrow: The Economic Value of a Marine Reserve." *Land Economics* 85, 454–469.
Gram, S. 2001. "Economic Valuation of Special Forest Products: An Assessment of Methodological Shortcomings." *Ecological Economics* 26, 109–117.
Grandmont, Jean-Michel. 1985. "On Endogenous Competitive Business Cycles." *Econometrica* 53, 995–1045.
Grandmont, Jean-Michel. 1988. "Expectations Formation and Stability in Large Socio-Economic Systems." *Econometrica* 66, 741–781.
Grassberger, Peter. 1986. "Do Climate Attractors Exist?" *Nature* 323, 609–612.
Grassberger, Peter. 1987. "Grassberger Replies." *Nature* 326, 524.
Grassberger, Peter and Itamar Procaccia. 1983a. "Measuring the Strangeness of Strange Attractors." *Physica D* 9, 189–208.
Grassberger, Peter and Itamar Procaccia. 1983b. "Estimation of the Kolmogorov Entropy from a Chaotic Signal." *Physical Review A* 28, 2591–2593.
Grebogi, Celso, Edward Ott, S. Pelikan, and James A. Yorke. 1984. "Strange Attractors that are Not Chaotic." *Physica D* 13, 261–268.
Grebogi, Celso, Edward Ott, and James A. Yorke. 1983. "Crises, Sudden Changes in Chaotic Attractors, and Transient Chaos." *Physica D* 7, 181–200.
Greiner, Alfred and Willi Semmler. 2005. "Economic Growth and Global Warming: A Model of Multiple Equilibria and Thresholds." *Journal of Economic Behavior and Organization* 57, 430–447.
Grossman, Gene and Elhanan Helpman. 1991. *Innovation and Growth in the World Economy*. Cambridge: MIT Press.

Gu, E.-G. and Y. Huang. 2006. "Global Bifurcations of Domains of Feasible Trajectories: An Analysis of a Discrete Predator-Prey Model." *International Journal of Bifurcations and Chaos* 16, 2601–2613.

Guastello, Stephen J. 1981. "Catastrophe Modeling of Equity in Organizations." *Behavioral Science* 26, 63–74.

Guastello, Stephen J. 1995. *Chaos, Catastrophe, and Human Affairs: Applications of Nonlinear Dynamics to Work, Organizations, and Social Evolution*. Mahwah: Lawrence Erlbaum Associates.

Guckenheimer, John H. 1973. "Bifurcation and Catastrophe," in Manuel M. Peixoto, ed., *Dynamical Systems*. New York: Academic Press, 111–128.

Guckenheimer, John H. 1978. "The Catastrophe Controversy." *Mathematical Intelligencer* 1, 15–20.

Guckenheimer, John H. and Philip Holmes. 1983. *Nonlinear Oscillations, Dynamical Systems, and Bifurcations of Vector Fields*. Berlin: Springer (1986, 2nd Printing, 1990, 3rd Printing).

Guckenheimer, John H., G. Oster, and A. Ipaktchi. 1977. "The Dynamics of Density Dependent Populations." *Journal of Mathematical Biology* 4, 101–147.

Guckenheimer, John H. and R.F. Williams. 1979. "Structural Stability of Lorenz Attractors." *Publications Mathématiques IHES* 50, 59–72.

Gunderson, Lance H., C.S. Holling, and Garry D. Peterson. 2002. "Surprises and Sustainability: Cycles of Renewal in the Everglades," in Lance H. Gunderson and C.S. Holling, eds., *Panarchy: Understanding Transformations in Human and Natural Systems*. Washington: Island Press, 293–313.

Gunderson, Lance H., C.S. Holling, Lowell Pritchard, Jr., and Garry D. Peterson. 2002. "Understanding Resilience: Theory, Metaphors, and Frameworks," in Lance H. Gunderson and Lowell Pritchard, Jr., eds., *Resilience and the Behavior of Large-Scale Systems*. Washington: Island Press, 3–20.

Gunderson, Lance H. and Carl J. Walters. 2002. "Resilience of Wet Landscapes in Southern Florida," in Lance H. Gunderson and Lowell Pritchard, Jr., eds., *Resilience and the Behavior of Large-Scale Systems*. Washington: Island Press, 165–182.

Haag, Günter and Dimitrios S. Dendrinos. 1983. "Toward a Stochastic Dynamical Theory of Location: A Nonlinear Migration Process." *Geographical Analysis* 15, 269–286.

Haag, Günter, Tilo Hagel, and Timm Sigg. 1997. "Active Stabilization of a Chaotic Urban System." *Discrete Dynamics in Nature and Society* 1, 127–134.

Haag, Günter and Wolfgang Weidlich. 1983. "A Non-Linear Dynamic Model for the Migration of Human Populations," in Daniel A. Griffith and Anthony C. Lea, eds., *Evolving Geographical Structures: Mathematical Models and Theories for Space-Time Processes*. The Hague: Martunus Nijhoff, 24–61.

Hadamard, Jacques S. 1898. "Les Surfaces à Coubures Opposées et leurs Lignes Géodésique." *Journal de Mathématique Pure et Appliquée* 4, 27–73.

Haeckel, Ernst. 1866. *Generelle Morphogi der Organismen*. Berlin: G. Reimer.

Haig, David. 2010. "Sympathy with Adam Smith and Reflexions on Self." *Journal of Economic Behavior and Organization* 77, 4–13.

Haken, Hermann. 1977. *"Synergetics," Nonequilibrium Phase Transitions and Social Measurement*, 3rd Edition. Berlin: Springer, 1983.

Haken, Hermann. 1996. "The Slaving Principle Revisited." *Physica D* 97, 95–103.

Haldane, J.B.S. 1932. *The Causes of Evolution*. London: Longmans and Green.

Haldane, J.B.S. 1940. Preface to Engels, Friedrich. *The Dialectics of Nature*. New York: International Publisher.

Hallegatte, Stéphane, Jean-Charles Hourcade, and Patrick Dumas. 2007. "Why Economic Dynamics Matter in Assessing Climate Change." *Ecological Economics* 62, 330–340.

Hamilton, W.D. 1964. "The Genetical Evolution of Social Behavior." *Journal of Theoretical Biology* 7, 1–52.

Hamilton, W.D. 1972. "Altruism and Related Phenomena, Mainly in the Social Insects." *Annual Review of Ecology and Systematics* 3, 192–232.

Hannesson, Rognvalder. 1975. "Fishery Dynamics: A North Atlantic Cod Fishery." *Canadian Journal of Economics* 8, 151–173.

Hannesson, Rognvalder. 1983. "Optimal Harvesting of Ecologically Interdependent Fish Species." *Journal of Environmental Economics and Management* 10, 329–345.

Hannesson, Rognvalder. 1987. "The Effect of the Discount Rate on the Optimal Exploitation of Renewable Resources." *Marine Resource Economics* 3, 319–329.

Hardin, Garrett. 1968. "The Tragedy of the Commons." *Science* 162, 1243–1248.

Harris, B., J.M. Choukroun, and A.G. Wilson. 1982. "Economics of Scale and the Existence of Supply Side Equilibria in a Production Constrained Spatial Interaction Model." *Environment and Planning A* 14, 823–837.

Harris, B. and A.G. Wilson. 1978. "Equilibrium Values and Dynamics of Attractiveness Terms in Production-Constrained Spatial-Interaction Models." *Environment and Planning A* 10, 371–388.

Harris, Chauncy D. and Edward L. Ullman. 1945. "The Nature of Cities." *Annals of the American Academy of Political and Social Science* 242, 7–17.

Harris, J.R. and M.P. Todaro. 1970. "Migration Unemployment and Development: A Two Sector Analysis." *American Economic Review* 60, 126–142.

Harrod, Roy F. 1948. *Towards a Dynamic Economics*. London: Macmillan.

Hartman, Richard. 1976. "The Harvesting Decision when a Standing Forest has Value." *Economic Inquiry* 14, 52–58.

Hartwick, John. 1976. "Intermediate Goods and the Spatial Integration of Land Uses." *Regional Science and Urban Economics* 6, 127–145.

Hartwick, John and Nancy D. Olewiler. 1986. *The Economics of Natural Resource Use*. New York: Harper and Row.

Harvey, L.D. Danny and Zhen Huang. 1995. "Evaluation of the Potential Impact of Methane Clathrate Destabilization on Future Global Warming." *Journal of Geophysical Research-Atmosphere* 100, 2905–2906.

Hasler, Arthur D. 1947. "Eutrophication of Lakes by Domestic Drainage." *Ecology* 28, 383–395.

Hassan, R. 1972. "Islam and Urbanization in the Medieval Middle East." *Ekistics* 33, 108.

Hassan, Rashid M. and Greg Hertzler. 1988. "Deforestation from the Overexploitation of Wood Resources as a Cooking Fuel." *Energy Economics* 10, 163–168.

Hassell, M.P., J.H. Lawton, and R.H. May 1976. "Patterns of Dynamical Behavior of Single-Species Populations." *Journal of Animal Ecology* 45, 471–486.

Hausdorff, Felix. 1918. "Dimension und äusseres Mass." *Mathematische Annalen* 79, 157–179.

Hausman, Jerry A. 1979. "Individual Discount Rates and the Purchase and Utilization of Consumer Durables." *Bell Journal of Economics* 10, 33–54.

Hayek, Friedrich A. 1948. *Individualism and Economic Order*. Chicago: University of Chicago Press.

Hayek, Friedrich A. 1952. *The Sensory Order: An Inquiry into the Foundations of Theoretical Psychology*. Chicago: University of Chicago Press.

Hayek, Friedrich A. 1967. "The Theory of Complex Phenomena," in *Studies in Philosophy, Politics, and Economics*. Chicago: University of Chicago Press, 22–42.

Hayek, Friedrich A. 1979. *The Counter-Revolution of Science: Studies on the Abuse of Reason*, 2nd Edition. Indianapolis: Liberty.

Hegel, George Wilhelm Friedrich. 1842. *Enzyclopdie der Philosophischen Wissenscheften im Grundrisse*, Part 1, Logik, Vol. VI. Berlin: Duncken und Humblot.

Heikkila, E., P. Gordon, J.I. Kim, R.B. Peiser, H.W. Richardson, and D. Dale-Johnson. 1989. "What Happened to the CBD-Distance Gradient?: Land Values in a Policentric City." *Environment and Planning A* 21, 221–232.

Helm, G. 1887. *Die Lehre von der Energie*. Leipzig: Felix.

Henderson-Sellers, Ann and K. McGuffie. 1987. *A Climate Modeling Primer*. New York: Wiley.

Henderson, Vernon. 1988. *Urban Development: Theory, Fact, and Illusion*. New York: Oxford University Press.

Hénon, Michel. 1976. "A Two-Dimensional Mapping with a Strange Attractor." *Communications in Mathematical Physics* 50, 69–77.

Henrich, Joseph. 2004. "Cultural Group Selection, Coevolutionary Processes and Large-Scale Cooperation." *Journal of Economic Behavior and Organization* 53, 3–35.

Henrich, Joseph and Robert Boyd. 1998. "The Evolution of Conformist Transmission and the Emergence of Between-Group Differences." *Evolution and Human Behavior* 19, 215–242.

Herfindahl, Orris C. and Allen V. Kneese. 1974. *Economic Theory of Natural Resources*. Columbus: Charles Merrill.

Hewitt, Charles Gordon. 1921. *The Conservation of the Wild Life of Canada*. New York: Charles Scribner's Sons.

Hicks, John R. 1950. *A Contribution to the Theory of the Trade Cycle*. Oxford: Oxford University Press.

Hilbert, David. 1891. "Über die stetige Abbildung einer Linie auf ein Flächenstück." *Mathematische Annalen* 38, 459–460.

Hinich, Melvin J. 1982. "Testing for Gaussianity and Linearity of a Stationary Time Series." *Journal of Time Series Analysis* 3, 169–176.

Hirsch, Werner Z. and Percival Goodman. 1972. "Is There an Optimum Size for a City?," in Matthew Edel and Jerome Rothenberg, eds., *Readings in Urban Economics*. New York: Macmillan, 398–406.

Hobbes, Thomas. 1651. *Leviathan*. London: Andrew Crooke.

Hodgson, Geoffrey M. 1993. *Economics and Evolution: Bringing Life Back into Economics*. Ann Arbor: University of Michigan Press.

Hodgson, Geoffrey M. 2006. *Economics in the Shadow of Darwin and Marx: Essays on Institutional and Evolutionary Themes*. Cheltenham: Edward Elgar.

Hodgson, Geoffrey M., ed. 2009. *Darwinism and Economics: The International Library of Critical Writings in Economics*. Cheltenham: Edward Elgar, 233.

Hodgson, Geoffrey M. and Thorbjørn Knudsen. 2006. "Why We Need a Generalized Darwinism and Why Generalized Darwinism is Not Enough." *Journal of Economic Behavior and Organization* 61, 1–19.

Hodgson, Geoffrey M. and Thorbjørn Knudsen. 2010. "Generative Replication and the Evolution of Complexity." *Journal of Economic Behavior and Organization* 75, 12–24.

Hofstadter, Douglas R. 1979. *Gödel, Escher, Bach: An Eternal Golden Braid*. New York: Basic Books.

Hofstadter, Richard. 1944. *Social Darwinism in American Thought*. Boston: Beacon Press.

Holland, John H. 1992. *Adaptation in Natural and Artificial Systems*, 2nd Edition. Cambridge: MIT Press.

Holling, C.S. 1965. "The Functional Response of Predators to Prey Density and its Role in Mimicry and Population Regulation." *Memorials of the Entomological Society of Canada* 45, 1–60.

Holling, C.S. 1973. "Resilience and Stability of Ecological Systems." *Annual Review of Ecology and Systematics* 4, 1–24.

Holling, C.S. 1986. "The Resilience of Terrestial Ecosystems: Local Surprise and Global Change," in W.C. Clark and R.E. Munn, eds., *Sustainable Development of the Biosphere*. Cambridge: Cambridge University Press, 292–317.

Holling, C.S. 1992. "Cross-Scale Morphology, Geometry, and Dynamics of Ecosystems." *Ecological Monographs* 62, 447–502.

Holling, C.S. and Lance H. Gunderson. 2002. "Resilience and Adaptive Cycles," in Lance H. Gunderson and C.S. Holling, eds., *Panarchy: Understanding Transformations in Human and Natural Systems*. Washington: Island Press, 25–62.

Holling, C.S., Lance H. Gunderson, and Garry D. Peterson. 2002. "Sustainability and Panarchies," in Lance H. Gunderson and C.S. Holling, eds., *Panarchy: Understanding Transformations in Human and Natural Systems*. Washington: Island Press, 63–102.

Holmes, Philip J. 1979. "A Nonlinear Oscillator with a Strange Attractor." *Philosophical Transactions of the Royal Society A* 292, 419–448.

Holyst, Janusz A., Tilo Hagel, Günter Haag, and Wolfgang Weidlich. 1996. "How to Control a Chaotic Economy." *Journal of Evolutionary Economics* 6, 31–42.

Hommes, Cars H. 1998. "On the Consistency of Backward-Looking Expectations: The Case of the Cobweb." *Journal of Economic Behavior and Organization* 33, 333–362.

Hommes, Cars H. and J. Barkley Rosser, Jr. 2001. "Consistent Expectations Equilibria and Complex Dynamics in Renewable Resource Markets." *Macroeconomic Dynamics* 5, 180–203.

Hommes, Cars H. and Gerhard Sorger. 1998. "Consistent Expectations Equilibria." *Macroeconomic Dynamics* 2, 287–321.

Hope, Chris. 2006. "The Marginal Impact of CO2 from PAGE2002: An Integrated Assessment Model Incorporating the IPCC's Five Reasons for Concern." *Integrated Assessment Journal* 6, 19–56.

Hopf, Eberhard. 1942. "Abzqeigung einer periodischen Losung von einer stationacen Losung eines differential-systems." *Berlin Math.-Phys. Klasse. Sachsiche Akad. Wissench* (Leipzig) 94, 1–22 (in English, 1976, "Bifurcation of a Periodic Solution from a Stationary Solution of a Differential System," in J.E. Marsden and E. McCracken, eds., *The Hopf Bifurcation and its Applications*, Vol. 19. Berlin: Springer, 163–193).

Horgan, John. 1995. "From Complexity to Perplexity." *Scientific American* 272 (June), 6, 104–109.

Horgan, John. 1997. *The End of Science: Facing the Limits of Knowledge in the Twilight of the Scientific Age*, Paperback edition. New York: Broadway Books.

Hotelling, Harold. 1929. "Stability in Competition." *Economic Journal* 39, 41–57.

Hotelling, Harold. 1931. "The Economics of Exhaustible Resources." *Journal of Political Economy* 39, 137–175.

Hoover, Edgar M. and Raymond Vernon. 1959. *Anatomy of a Metropolis: The Changing Distribution of People and Jobs within the New York Metropolitan Region*. Cambridge: Harvard University Press.

Howard, Ebenezer, 1902. *Garden Cities of Tomorrow*. London: Faber and Faber.

Hoyt, Homer. 1939. *Structure and Growth of Residential Neighborhoods*. Washington: Federal Housing Administration.

Huff, D. 1964. "Defining and Estimating a Trading Area." *Journal of Marketing* 28, 34–38.

Hughes, Terry P. 1994. "Catastrophes, Phase Shifts, and Large-Scale Degradation of a Caribbean Coral Reef." *Science* 265, 1547–1551.

Hume, David. 1779. *Dialogues Concerning Natural Religion*. Edinburgh: Pinter.

Hutchinson, G.E. 1948. "Circular Casual Systems in Ecology." *Annuals of the New York Academy of Science* 50, 221–246.

Hutchinson, G.E. 1959. "Homage to Santa Rosalia, or Why are There so Many Kinds of Animals?" *American Naturalist* 93, 145–159.

Intergovernmental Panel on Climate Change [IPCC]. 2007. *Climate-Change-2007 – IPCC Fourth Assessment Report*. Cambridge: Cambridge University Press.

Ioannides, Yannis M. 1990. "Trading Uncertainty and Market Form." *International Economic Review* 31, 619–638.

Ioannides, Yannis M. 1997. "Evolution of Trading Structures," in W. Brian Arthur, Steven N. Durlauf, and David A. Lane, eds., *The Economy as an Evolving Complex System II*. Reading: Addison-Wesley, 129–167.

Ioannides, Yannis M. and Henry G. Overman. 2003. "Zipf's Law for Cities: An Empirical Examination." *Regional Science and Urban Economics* 33, 127–137.

Isard, Peter. 1977. "How Far Can We Push the Law of One Price?" *American Economic Review* 67, 942–948.

Isard, Walter. 1956. *Location and Space-Economy*. Cambridge: Technology Press of MIT.

Isard, Walter. 1977. "Strategic Elements of a Theory of Major Structural Change." *Papers of the Regional Science Association* 38, 1–14.

Isard, Walter, Charles L. Choguli, John Kissin, Richard H. Seyforth, and Richard Tatlock. 1972. *Economic-Ecologic Analysis for Regional Development*. New York: Free Press.

Isard, Walter and Panagis Liossatos. 1977. "Models of Transition Processes." *Papers of the Regional Science Association* 39, 27–59.

Israel, Giorgio. 2005. "The Science of Complexity: Epistemological Implications and Perspectives." *Science in Context* 18, 1–31.

Iwasa, Yoh, Tomoe Uchida, and Hiroyushi Yokomizo. 2007. "Nonlinear Behavior of the Socio-Economic Dynamics for Lake Eutrophication Control." *Ecological Economics* 63, 219–229.

Jaditz, Ted and Chera L. Sayers. 1993. "Is Chaos Generic in Economic Data?" *International Journal of Bifurcations and Chaos* 3, 745–755.
Jansson, Bengt-Owe and AnnMari Jansson. 2002. "The Baltic Sea: Reversibly Unstable or Irreversibly Stable?," in Lance H. Gunderson and Lowell Pritchard, Jr., eds., *Resilience and the Behavior of Large-Scale Systems*. Washington: Island Press, 71–109.
Jantsch, Erich. 1979. *The Self-Organizing Universe: Scientific and Human Implications of the Emerging Paradigm of Evolution*. Oxford: Pergaman Press.
Jantsch, Erich. 1982. "From Self-Reference to Self-Transcendence: The Evolution of Self-Organization Dynamics," in William C. Schieve and Allen, Peter M., eds., *Self-Organization and Dissipative Structures*. Austin: University of Texas Press, 344–353.
Jeffers, John N.R. 1978. *An Introduction to Systems Analysis: With Ecological Applications*. London: Edward Arnold.
Joe, H. 1997. *Multivariate Models and Dependence Concepts*. London: Chapman & Hall.
Johnson, K.N., D.B. Jones, and B.M. Kent. 1980. *A User's Guide to the Forest Planning Model (FORPLAN)*. Fort Collins: USDA Forest Service, Land Management Planning.
Johnson, Ronald M. and Gary D. Libecap. 1982. "Contracting Problems and Regulations: The Case of the Fishery." *American Economic Review* 72, 1005–1022.
Jones, Dixon D. and Carl J. Walters. 1976. "Catastrophe Theory and Fisheries Regulation." *Journal of the Fisheries Resource Board of Canada* 33, 2829–2833.
Jones, Lamar B. 1989. "Schumpeter versus Darwin: re Malthus." *Southern Economic Journal* 56, 410–422.
Johnson, Ronald and Gary D. Libecap. 1980. "Agency Costs and the Assignment of Property Rights: The Case of Southwestern Indian Reservation." *Southern Economic Journal* 47, 332–347.
Jovanović, Miroslav N. 2009. *Evolutionary Economic Geography: Location of Production and the European Union*. London: Routledge.
Julia, Gaston. 1918. "Mémoire sur l'Itération des Fonctions Rationelles." *Journal de Mathématique Pure et Appliquée* 8, 47–245.
Kaas, Leo. 1998. "Stabilizing Chaos in a Dynamic Macroeconomic Model." *Journal of Economic Behavior and Organization* 33, 313–332.
Kac, Mark. 1968. "Mathematical Mechanisms of Phase Transitions," in M. Chrétien, E. Gross, and S. Deser, eds., *Statistical Physics: Transitions and Superfluidity*, Vol. 1. Brandeis, MA: Brandeis University Summer Institute in Theoretical Physics, 1966, 241–305.
Kahn, James and Alexandre Rivas. 2009. "The Sustainable Economic Development of Traditional Peoples," in Richard P.F. Holt, Steven Pressman, and Clive L. Spash, eds., *Post Keynesian and Ecological Economics: Confronting the Environmental Issues*. Cheltenham: Edward Elgar, 254–278.
Kaldor, Nicholas. 1970. "The Case for Regional Policies." *Scottish Journal of Political Economy* 17, 337–348.
Kalecki, Michal. 1935. "A Macrodynamic Theory of Business Cycles." *Econometrica* 3, 327–344.
Kaneko, Kunihiko. 1990. "Clustering, Coding, Switching, Hierarchical Ordering, and Control in a Network of Chaotic Elements." *Physica D* 41, 137–172.
Kaneko, Kunihiko. 1995. "Chaos as a Source of Complexity and Diversity in Evolution," in Christopher G. Langton, ed., *Artificial Life: An Overview*. Cambridge: MIT Press, 163–177.
Kaneko, Kunihiko and Ichiro Tsuda. 2000. *Complex Systems: Chaos and Beyond*. Berlin: Springer.
Kaneko, Kunihiko and Ichiro Tsuda. 2001. *Chaos and Beyond: A Constructive Approach with Applications in Life Sciences*. Berlin: Springer.
Kant, Shashi. 2000. "A Dynamic Approach to Forest Regimes in Developing Economies." *Ecological Economics* 32, 287–300.
Kantorovich, Leonid V. 1942. "On the Translocation of Masses." *Doklady Akademii Nauk SSSR* 37: translated into English in *Management Science* 5, 1–4.
Kaplan, Daniel T. 1994. "Exceptional Events as Evidence for Determinism." *Physica D* 73, 38–48.
Kauffman, Stuart A. 1993. *The Origins of Order: Self-Organization and Selection in Evolution*. Oxford: Oxford University Press.

Kauffman, Stuart A. 1995. *At Home in the Universe*. Oxford: Oxford University Press.
Kauffman, Stuart A. and Sonke Johnsen. 1991. "Coevolution to the Edge of Chaos: Coupled Fitness Landscapes, Poised States, and Coevolutionary Avalanches." *Journal of Theoretical Biology* 149, 467–505.
Keith, L.B. 1963. *Wildlife's Ten-Year Cycle*. Madison: University of Wisconsin Press.
Kennedy, Judy and James A. Yorke. 1991. "Basins of Wada." *Physica D* 51, 213–225.
Kermack, W.O. and A.G. MacKendrick. 1927. "Contributions to the Mathematical Theory of Epidemics." *Proceedings of the Royal Society A* 115, 700–721.
Keynes, John Maynard. 1921. *A Treatise on Probability*. London: Macmillan.
Khan, Ali M. and Adrianna Piazza. 2011. "Classical Turnpike Theory and the Economics of Forestry." *Journal of Economic Behavior and Organization*, in press.
Kim, Sukkoo. 1995. "Expansion of Markets and the Geographic Distribution of Economic Activities: The Trends in U.S. Regional Manufacturing Structure, 1860–1987." *Quarterly Journal of Economics* 110, 881–905.
Kimura, Motoo. 1968. "Evolutionary Rate at the Molocular Level." *Nature* 217, 624–626.
Kindleman, Pavel. 1984. "Stability vs. Complexity in Model Competition Communities," in Simon A. Levin and Thomas G. Hallam, eds., *Mathematical Ecology*. Berlin: Springer, 193–207.
Kirman, Alan. 2007. "The Basic Unit of Economic Analysis: Individuals or Markets? A Comment on 'Markets Come to Bits' by Phil Mirowski." *Journal of Economic Behavior and Organization* 63, 284–294.
Kirman, Alan P., Claude Oddou, and Shlomo Weber. 1986. "Stochastic Communication and Coalition Formation." *Econometrica* 54, 129–138.
Kiseleva, Tatiana and Florian O.O. Wagener. 2010. "Bifurcations of Optimal Vector Fields in the Shallow Lake Model." *Journal of Economic Dynamics and Control* 34, 825–843.
Knight, Frank H. 1921. *Risk, Uncertainty, and Profit*. Boston: Houghton Mifflin.
Kolata, Gina Bari. 1977. "Catastrophe Theory: The Emperor has no Clothes." *Science* 196 (April 15), 287.
Kolmogorov, Andrei N. 1936. "Sulla Teoria di Volterra della Lotta per l'Esistenza." *Giornale Instituto Italiani Attuari* 7, 74–80.
Kolmogorov, Andrei N. 1941. "Local Structure of Turbulence in an Incompressible Liquid for Very Large Reynolds Numbers." *Doklady Akademii Nauk SSSR* 30, 299–303.
Kolmogorov, Andrei N. 1958. "Novyi metritjeskij invariant tranzitivnych dinamitjeskich sistem I avtomorfizmov lebega." [A New Metric Invariant of Transient Dynamical Systems and Automorphisms in Lebesgue Spaces] *Doklady Akademii Nauk SSR* 119, 861–864.
Kolmogorov, Andrei N. 1962. "A Refinement of Previous Hypotheses Concerning the Local Structure of Turbulence in Viscous Incompressible Fluid at High Reynolds Number." *Journal of Fluid Mechanics* 13, 82–85.
Koopmans, Tjalling C. 1949. "Optimum Utilization of Transportation Systems." *Econometrica* 17, 136–146.
Kopel, Michael. 1997. "Improving the Performance of an Economic System: Controlling Chaos." *Journal of Evolutionary Economics* 7, 269–289.
Koppl, Roger and J. Barkley Rosser, Jr., 2002. "All I Have to Say Has Already Crossed Your Mind." *Metroeconomica* 53, 339–360.
Kosloff, R. and S.A. Rice. 1981. "Dynamical Correlations and Chaos in Classical Hamiltonian Systems." *Journal of Chemical Physics* 74, 1947–1956.
Kosobud, Richard F. and Thomas A. Daly. 1984. "Global Conflict or Cooperation over the CO_2 Climate Impact?" *Kyklos* 37, 638–659.
Krakover, S. 1998. "Testing the Turning Point Hypothesis in City-Size Distribution." *Urban Studies* 35, 2183–2196.
Krämer, Walter and Ralf Runde. 1997. "Chaos and the Compass Rose." *Economics Letters* 54, 113–118.
Kropotkin, Peter A. 1899. *Fields, Factories, and Workshops: Or Industry Combined with Agriculture, and Brainwork with Manual Work*. London: Freedom Press.
Kropotkin, Peter A. 1902. *Mutual Aid: A Factor of Evolution*. New York: McClure Phillips.

Krugman, Paul R. 1979. "Increasing Returns, Monopolistic Competition and International Trade." *Journal of International Economics* 9, 469–479.
Krugman, Paul R. 1980. "Scale Economies, Product Differentiation, and the Pattern of Trade." *American Economic Review* 70, 950–959.
Krugman, Paul R. 1991. "Increasing Returns and Economic Geography." *Journal of Political Economy* 99, 483–499.
Krugman, Paul R. 1993. *Geography and Trade*. Cambridge: MIT Press.
Krugman, Paul R. 1995. *Development, Geography, and Economic Theory*. Cambridge: MIT Press.
Krugman, Paul R. 1996. *The Self-Organizing Economy*. Cambridge: Blackwell.
Krugman, Paul R. 2009. "The Increasing Returns Revolution in Trade and Geography." *American Economic Review* 99, 561–574.
Kuznetsov, A.P., S.P. Kuznetsov, and I.R. Sataev. 1997. "A Variety of Period-Doubling Universality Classes in Multi-Parameter Analysis of Transition to Chaos." *Physica D* 109, 91–112.
Lagopoulos, A.P. 1971. "Rank-Size and Primate Distribution in Greece." *Ekistics* 32, 380–386.
Laibson, David. 1997. "Golden Eggs and Hyperbolic Discounting." *Quarterly Journal of Economics* 112, 443–477.
Lakshmanen, T.R. and W.G. Hansen. 1965. "A Retail Potential Model." *Journal of the American Institute of Planners* 31, 134–143.
Lamarck, Jean Baptiste de. 1809. *Philosophie Zoologique, ou Exposition des Considérations Relatives à l'Histoire Naturelle des Animaux*, 2 Vols. Paris: Dentu.
Landau, Lev D. 1944. "On the Problem of Turbulence." *Doklady Akademii Nauk SSSR* 44, 339–342.
Landau, Lev D. and E.M. Lifshitz. 1959. *Fluid Mechanics*. Oxford: Pergamon Press.
Langton, Chris G., ed. 1989. *Artificial Life*. Redwood City: Addison-Wesley.
Langton, Chris G. 1990. "Computation at the Edge of Chaos: Phase Transitions and Emergent Computation." *Physica D* 42, 12–37.
Laplace, Pierre Simon de. 1814. *Essai Philosophique sur le Fondemont des Probabilités*. Paris: Courcier.
Lasota, Andrzej and Michael C. Mackey. 1985. *Probabilistic Properties of Deterministic Systems*. Cambridge: Cambridge University Press.
Lauck, Tim, Colin W. Clark, Marc Mangel, and Gordon R. Munro. 1998. "Implementing the Precautionary Principle in Fisheries Management Through Marine Reserves." *Ecological Applications* 8, S72–S78.
Laurie, Alexander J. and Narendra K. Jaggi. 2003. "The Role of 'Vision' in Neighborhood Racial Segregation: A Variant of the Schelling Model." *Urban Studies* 40, 2687–2704.
Launhardt, Wilhelm. 1885. *Mathematische Begundung der Volkswirtschaftslehre*. Leipzig: B.G. Teubner.
Lavoie, Don. 1989. "Economic Chaos or Spontaneous Order? Implications for Political Economy of the New View of Science." *Cato Journal* 8, 613–635.
Lawson, R. 1984. *Economics of Fisheries Development*. London: Frances Pinter Publishers.
Lawson, Tony. 1997. *Economics and Reality*. London: Routledge.
LeBaron, Blake. 1994. "Chaos and Nonlinear Forecastibility in Economics and Finance." *Philosophical Transactions of the Royal Society of London A* 348, 397–404.
Leibniz, Gottfried Wilhelm von. 1695. "Letter to de l'Hôpital," reprinted in C.D. Gerhard, ed., 1849, *Mathematische Schriften* II, XXIV. Halle: H.W. Schmidt, 197.
Leonard, Thomas C. 2009. "Origins of the Myth of Social Darwinism: The Ambiguous Legacy of Richard Hofstadter's *Social Darwinism in American Thought*." *Journal of Economic Behavior and Organization* 71, 37–51.
Leonardi, Giorgio and John Casti. 1986. "Agglomerative Tendencies in the Distribution of Populations." *Regional Science and Urban Economics* 16, 43–56.
Leopold, Aldo. 1933. "The Conservation Ethic." *Journal of Forestry* 33, 636–637.
Lessinger, Jack. 1962. "The Case for Scatteration: Some Reflections of the National Capital Regional Plan for the Year 2000." *Journal of the American Institute of Planners* 24, 159–169.

Leung, Yee. 1987. "On the Imprecision of Boundaries." *Geographical Analysis* 19, 125–151.
Levi, M. 1981. "Qualitative Analysis of the Periodically Forced Relaxation Oscillation." *Memorials of the American Mathematical Society* 214, 1–147.
Levins, Richard A. 1968. *Evolution in Changing Environments*. Princton: Princeton University Press.
Levitt, Steven and Stephen J. Dubner. 2009. *Superfreakonomics: Global Cooling, Patriotic Prostitution, and Why Suicide Bombers Should Buy Life Insurance*. Chicago: University of Chicago Press.
Lewis, D. 1977. "Public Transport and Traffic Levels." *Journal of Transport Economics and Policy* 11, 155–168.
Lewis, T.R. and R. Schmalensee. 1977. "Nonconvexity and Optimal Exhaustion of Renewable Resources." *International Economic Review* 18, 535–552.
Lewontin, Richard C. 1974. *The Genetic Basis of Evolutionary Change*. New York: Columbia University Press.
Li, David X. 2001. "On Default Correlation: A Copula Function Approach." *Journal of Fixed Income* 9, 43–54.
Li, H. and G.S. Maddala. 1996. "Bootstrapping Time Series Models." *Econometric Reviews* 16, 115–195.
Li, Tien-Yien and James A. Yorke. 1975. "Period 3 Implies Chaos." *American Mathematical Monthly* 82, 985–992.
Libecap, Gary D. and Ronald Johnson. 1980. "Legislating Commons: The Navajo Tribal Council and the Navajo Range." *Economic Inquiry* 18, 69–86.
Liggett, T. 1985. *Interacting Particle Systems*. New York: Springer.
Lindgren, Kristian. 1997. "Evolutionary Dynamics in Game-Theoretic Models," in W. Brian Arthur, Steven N. Durlauf, and David A. Lane, eds., *The Economy as an Evolving Complex System II*. Reading: Addison-Wesley, 337–367.
Lindgren, Kristian and Johan Johansson. 2003. "Coevolution of Strategies in *n*-Person Prisoners' Dilemma," in James P. Crutchfield and Peter Schuster, eds., *Evolutionary Dynamics: Exploring the Interplay of Selection, Accident, Neutrality, and Function*. Oxford: Oxford University Press, 341–360.
Linnaeus, Carolus. 1751. "Specimen Academicum de Oeconomia Naturae." *Amoenitates Academicae* 2, 1–58.
Lisman, J.H.C. 1949. "Econometrics and Thermodynamics: A Remark on Davis's Theory of Budgets." *Econometrica* 17, 59–62.
Lomborg, Bjørn. 2001. *The Skeptical Environmentalist*. Cambridge: Cambridge University Press.
Lomborg, Bjørn, ed. 2004. *Global Crises, Global Solutions*. Cambridge: Cambridge University Press.
Lorenz, Edward N. 1963. "Deterministic Non-Periodic Flow." *Journal of Atmospheric Science* 20, 130–141.
Lorenz, Edward N. 1993. *The Essesnce of Chaos*. Seattle: University of Washington Press.
Lorenz, Hans-Walter. 1987a. "Goodwin's Nonlinear Accelerator and Chaotic Motion." *Zeitschrift für Nationalokonomie* 47, 413–418.
Lorenz, Hans-Walter. 1987b. "International Trade and the Possible Occurrence of Chaos." *Economics Letters* 23, 135–138.
Lorenz, Hans-Walter. 1987c. "International Trade and the Possible Occurrence of Chaos." *Economics Letters* 23, 135–138.
Lorenz, Hans-Walter. 1992. "Multiple Attractors, Complex Basin Boundaries, and Transient Motiion in Deterministic Economic Systems," in Gustav Feichtinger, ed., *Dynamic Economic Models and Optimal Control*. Amsterdam: North-Holland, 411–430.
Lorenz, Hans-Walter. 1993a. *Nonlinear Dynamical Economics and Chaotic Motion*, 2nd edition. Heidelberg: Springer (first edition, 1989).
Lorenz, Hans-Walter. 1993b. "Complex Transient Motion in Continuous-Time Economic Models," in Peter Nijkamp and Aura Reggiani, eds., *Nonlinear Evolution of Spatial Economic Systems*. Heidelberg: Springer, 112–137.

Lösch, August. 1940. *Die Raumlich Ordnumg der Wirtschaft*. Jena: Fischer (English translation by Woglom, W.G., 1954, *The Economics of Location*. New Haven: Yale University Press).
Lotka, Alfred J. 1920. "Analytical Notes on Certain Rhythmic Relations in Organic Systems." *Proceedings of the National Academy of Sciences, United States* 6, 410–415.
Lotka, Alfred J. 1925. *Elements of Physical Biology*. Baltimore: Williams and Wilkins.
Louçã, Francisco. 1997. *Turbulence in Economics: An Evolutionary Appraisal of Cycles and Complexity in Historical Processes*. Cheltenham: Edward Elgar.
Loury, Glenn C. 1978. "The Minimum Border Length Hypothesis Does Not Explain the Shape of Black Ghettos." *Journal of Urban Economics* 5, 147–153.
Low, B.S. 2000. *Why Sex Matters: A Darwinian Look at Human Behavior*. Princeton: Princeton University Press.
Lowry, Ira S. 1964. *A Model of Metropolis*. RM-4035-RC, Rand Corporation, Santa Monica.
Lucas, Robert E., Jr. 2001. "Externalities in Cities." *Review of Economic Dynamics* 4, 245–274.
Ludwig, Donald. 1978. "Optimal Harvesting of a Randomly Fluctuating Resource: I. Application or Perturbation Methods." *SIAM Journal of Applied Mathematics* 37, 166–184.
Ludwig, Donald., Dixon D. Jones, and C.S. Holling. 1978. "Quality Analysis of Insect Outbreak Systems: The Spruce Budworm and the Forest." *Journal of Animal Ecology* 47, 315–332.
Ludwig, Donald and J.M. Varah. 1979. "Optimal Harvesting of a Randomly Fluctuating Resource: II. Numerical Methods and Results." *SIAM Journal of Applied Mathematics* 37, 185–205.
Ludwig, Donald, Brian H. Walker, and C.S. Holling. 2002. "Models and Metaphors of Sustainability, Stability, and Resilience," in Lance H. Gunderson and Lowell Pritchard, Jr., eds., *Resilience and the Behavior of Large-Scale Systems*. Washington: Island Press, 21–48.
Lung, Yannick. 1988. "Complexity of Spatial Dynamics Modelling. From Catastrophe Theory to Self Organizing Process: A Review of the Literature." *Annals of Regional Science* 22, 81–111.
Lyapunov, Alexander Mikhailovich. 1892. [reprinted in 1950], *Obshchaya zadacha ob resto-ichivosti dvizheniya*, Moscow-Leningrad: Gosteklhizdat (English translation, 1947, *The General Stability of Motion*, Annals of Mathematical Studies No. 17. Princeton: Princeton University Press).
Lyell, Charles. 1830–1832. *The Principles of Geology; Or, The Modern Changes of the Earth and its Inhabitants as Illustrative of Geology*, 3 Vols. London: Murray.
MacArthur, R.H. 1955. "Fluctuations of Animal Populations, and Measure of Community Stability." *Ecology* 36, 533–536.
MacDonald, G. 1957. *The Epidemiology and Control of Malaria*. Oxford: Oxford University Press.
Mäler, Karl-Göran, Anastasios Xepapadeas, and Aart de Zeeuw. 2003. "The Economics of Shallow Lakes." *Environmental and Resource Economics* 26, 105–126.
Malgrange, Bernard. 1966. *Ideals of Differentiable Functions*. Oxford: Oxford University Press.
Malthus, Thomas Robert. 1798. *An Essay on the Principle of Population as it Affects the Future Improvement of Society with Remarks on the Speculations of Mr. Godwin M. Condorcet, and Other Writers*. London: J. Johnson (1817, 5th Edition).
Mandelbrot, Benoit B. 1963. "The Variation of Certain Speculative Prices." *Journal of Business* 36, 394–419.
Mandelbrot, Benoit B. 1965. "Very Long-Tailed Probability Distributions and the Empirical Distribution of City Sizes," in Fred Massarik and Philbun Ratoosh, eds., *Mathematical Exploration in Behavioral Science*. Homewood: L.R. Irwin, 322–332.
Mandelbrot, Benoit B. 1969. "Long-Run Linearity, Locally Gaussian Process, H-Spectra, and Infinite Variances." *International Economic Review* 10, 82–111.
Mandelbrot, Benoit B. 1972. "Statistical Methodology for Nonperiodic Cycles: From Covariance to R/S Analysis." *Annals of Economic and Social Measurement* 1, 259–290.
Mandelbrot, Benoit B. 1983. *The Fractal Geometry of Nature*. New York: W.H. Freeman.
Mandelbrot, Benoit B. 1988. "An Introduction to Multifractal Distribution Functions," in H. Eugene Stanley and Nicole Ostrowsky, eds., *Fluctuations and Pattern Formation*. Dordrecht: Kluwer Academic Publishers, 345–360.

Mandelbrot, Benoit B. 1990a. "Two Meanings of Multifractality, and the Notion of Negative Fractal Dimension," in David K. Campbell, ed., *Chaos/Xaoc: Soviet-American Perspectives on Nonlinear Science*. New York: American Institute of Physics, 79–90.

Mandelbrot, Benoit B. 1990b. "Negative fractal dimensions and multifractals." *Physica A* 163, 306–315.

Mandelbrot, Benoit B. 1997. *Fractals and Scaling in Finance: Discontinuity, Concentration, Risk*. New York: Springer.

Mandelbrot, Benoit B., Adlai Fisher, and Laurent Calvet. 1997. "A Multifractal Model of Asset Returns." Cowles Foundation Discussion Paper No. 1164, Yale University.

Mandel'shtam, L.I., N.D. Papaleski, A.A. Andronov, A.A. Vitt, G.S. Gorelik, and S.E. Khaikin. 1936. *Novge Isseldovaniya v Oblasti Nelineinykh Kolebanii* (New Research in the Field of Nonlinear Oscillations). Moscow: Radiozdat.

Manski, Charles F. 1993. "Identification of Endogenous Social Effects: The Reflection Problem." *Review of Economic Studies* 60, 531–542.

Manski, Charles F. 1995. *Identification Problems in the Social Sciences*. Cambridge: Harvard University Press.

Manski, Charles F. and Daniel McFadden. 1981. *Structural Analysis of Discrete Data with Econometric Applications*. Cambridge: MIT Press.

Mantegna, Rosario N. and H. Eugene Stanley. 2000. *An Introduction to Econophysics*. Cambridge: Cambridge University Press.

Marglin, Stephen A. 1963. "The Social Rate of Discount and the Optimal Rate of Investment." *Quarterly Journal of Economics* 77, 95–111.

Marsden, J.E. and M. McCracken. 1976. *The Hopf Bifurcation and its Applications*. Berlin: Springer.

Marshall, Alfred. 1920. *Principles of Economics*. London: Macmillan (1st Edition, 1890).

Marshall, Alfred. 1919. *Industry and Trade*. London: Macmillan.

Marshall, Alfred. 1923. *Money Trade and Commerce*. London: Macmillan.

Marshall, Alfred and M. Paley Marshall. 1879. *The Economics of Industry*. London: Macmillan.

Martin, Philippe and Gianmarco Ottaviano. 1999. "Growing Locations: Industry Location in a Model of Endogenous Growth." *European Economic Review* 43, 281–302.

Martin, Ron. 1999. "The New 'Geographical Turn' in Economics: Some Critical Reflections." *Cambridge Journal of Economics* 23, 65–91.

Marx, Karl. 1893. *Capital, Volume II*. Hamburg: Verlag Otto von Meissner, (English edition, 1967, New York: International Publishes).

Marx, Karl. 1952. *Theories of Surplus Value, Vol. II*. New York: International Publishers.

Marx, Karl and Friedrich Engels. 1848. *The Communist Manifesto*. London: Burghardt.

Marx, Karl and Friedrich Engels. 1942. *Selected Correspondence*. New York: International Publishers.

Mather, John N. 1968. "Stability of CPO Mapping III: Finitely Determined Map-germs." *Publications Mathématiques IHES* 35, 127–156.

Matsumoto, Akio. 1997. "Ergodic Cobweb Chaos." *Discrete Dynamics in Nature and Society* 1, 135–146.

Matsuyama, Kiminori. 1995. "Complementarities and Cumulative Processes in Models of Monopolistic Competition." *Journal of Economic Literature* 33, 701–729.

Maturana, Humberto R. and Francisco Varela. 1975. *Autopoietic Systems*. Report BCL 9.4. Urbana: Biological Computer Laboratory, University of Illinois.

May, Robert M. 1974. "Biological Populations with Non-Overlapping Generations: Stable Points, Stable Cycles, and Chaos." *Science* 186, 645–647.

May, Robert M. 1976. "Simple Mathematical Models with Very Complicated Dynamics." *Nature* 261, 459–467.

May, Robert M. 1977. "Thresholds and Breakpoints in Ecosystems with a Multiplicity of Stable States." *Nature* 269, 471–477.

May, Robert M. 1981a. "Models for Single Populations," in Robert M. May, ed., *Theoretical Ecology*, 2nd Edition. Sunderland: Sinauer Associates, 5–29.

May, Robert M. 1981b. "Models for Two Interacting Populations," in Robert M. May, ed., *Theoretical Ecology*, 2nd Edition. Sunderland: Sinauer Associates, 78–104.
May, Robert M. 1981c. "Patterns in Multi-Species Communities," in Robert M. May, ed., *Theoretical Ecology*, 2nd Edition. Sunderland, MA: Sinauer Associates, 197–227.
May, Robert M. and R.M. Anderson. 1983. "Epidemiology and Genetics in the Coevolution of Parasites and Hosts." *Philosophical Transactions of the Royal Society B* 219, 281–313.
May, Robert M. and George F. Oster. 1976. "Bifurcating and Dynamic Complexity in Simple Ecological Models." *American Naturalist* 110, 573–599.
Maynard Smith, John. 1972. "Game Theory and the Evolution of Fighting," in John Maynard Smith, ed., *On Evolution*. Edinburgh: Edinburgh University Press, 8–28.
Maynard Smith, John. 1998. "The Origin of Altruism." *Nature* 393, 639–640.
Maynard Smith, John and George R. Price. 1973. "The Logic of Animal Conflicts." *Nature* 246, 15–18.
Mayr, Ernst. 1942. *Systematics and the Origin of Species*. New York: Columbia University Press.
McCaffrey, Daniel F., Stephen Ellner, A. Ronald Gallant, and Douglas W. Nychka. 1992. "Estimating the Lyapunov Exponent of a Chaotic System with Nonparametric Regression." *Journal of the American Statistical Association* 87, 682–695.
McCallum, H.I. 1988. "Pulse Fishing May Be Superior to Selective Fishing." *Mathematical Biosciences* 89, 177–181.
McCauley, Joseph L. 2004. *Dynamics of Markets: Econophysics and Finance*. Cambridge: Cambridge University Press.
McCauley, Joseph L. 2005. "Making Mathematics Effective in Economics," in K. Vela Velupillai, ed., *Computability, Complexity and Constructivity in Economic Analysis*. Victoria: Blackwell, 51–84.
McClanahan, Tim R., Nicholas V.C. Polunin, and Terry J. Done. 2002. "Resilience of Coral Reefs," in Lance H. Gunderson and Lowell Pritchard, Jr., eds., *Resilience and the Behavior of Large-Scale Systems*. Washington: Island Press, 111–163.
McCloskey, Donald [Deirdre] N. 1991. "History, Differential Equations, and the Problem of Narration." *History and Theory* 30, 21–36.
McDonald, Steven W., Celso Grebogi, Edward Ott, and James A. Yorke. 1985. "Fractal Basin Boundaries." *Physica D* 17, 125–153.
McLaughlin, Bryan P. 1992. "The Rise and Fall of British Emergentism," in A. Beckerman, H. Flohr, and J. Kim, eds., *Emergence or Reduction? Essays on the Prospects of Nonreductive Physicalism*. Berlin: Walter de Gruyper, 49–93.
Meadows, Donella H., Dennis L. Meadows, Jørgen Randers, and William W. Behrens III. 1972. *The Limits to Growth*. New York: Universe Books.
Medio, Alfredo. 1984. "Synergetics and Dynamic Economic Models," in Richard M. Goodwin, M. Kruger, and Alessandro Vercelli, eds., *Nonlinear Models of Fluctuating Growth*. Berlin: Springer, 166–191.
Medio, Alfredo. 1994. "Reply to Dr. Nusse's review of 'Chaotic Dynamics: Theory and Applications to Economics.'" *Journal of Economics* 60, 335–338.
Medio, Alfredo. 1998. "Nonlinear Dynamics and Chaos Part I: A Geometrical Approach." *Macroeconomic Dynamics* 2, 505–532.
Medio, Alfredo and Giampolo Gallo. 1993. *Chaotic Dynamics: Theory and Applications to Economics*, Paperback edition. Cambridge: Cambridge University Press.
Meek, Ronald L. 1954. *Marx and Engels on Malthus*. New York: International Publishers.
Mees, Alistair I. 1975. "The Revival of Cities in Medieval Europe." *Regional Science and Urban Economics* 5, 403–425.
Mehre, R.K. 1981. "Choice of Input Signals," in P. Eykhoff, ed., *Trends and Progress in System Identification*. New York: Pergamon, 305–366.
Melèse, François and William Transue. 1986. "Unscrambling Chaos through Thick and Thin." *Quarterly Journal of Economics* 100, 419–423.
Mendelsohn, Robert O. 2006. "A Critique of the Stern Report." *Regulation* 29, 42–46.

Mendelsohn, Robert O., Wendy N. Morrison, Michael E. Schlesinger, and Natalia G. Andronova. 1998. "Country-Specific Market Impacts of Climate Change." *Climate Change* 45, 553–569.

Menger, Carl. 1892. "On the Origins of Money." *Economic Journal* 2, 239–255.

Menger, Karl. 1926. "Allgemeine Räume und charakteristische Räume, Zweite Mitteilung: Über umfassenste n-dimensionale Mengen." *Proceedings Academy Amsterdam* 29, 1125–1128.

Metcalfe, J. Stanley and John Foster, eds. 2004. *Evolution and Economic Complexity*. Cheltenham: Edward Elgar.

Metcalfe, J. Stanley and Ian Steedman. 1972. "Reswitching and Primary Input Use." *Economic Journal* 77, 140–157.

Metropolis, N., M.L. Stein, and P.R. Stein. 1973. "On Finite Limit Sets for Transformations on the Unit Interval." *Journal of Combinatorial Theory A* 15, 25–44.

Metzger, J.P and H. Décamps. 1997. "The Structural Connectivity Threshold: An Hypothesis in Conservation Biology at the Landscape Scale." *Acta Oecologica* 18, 1–12.

Michaels, Patrick J. 1989a. "The Science and Politics of the Greenhouse Effects: Collision Course?," in *Environmental Consequences of Energy Production*. Chicago: University of Illinois Press, 115–138.

Michaels, Patrick J. 1989b. "Crisis in Politics of Climate Change Looms on the Horizon." *Forum for Applied Research and Public Policy* 4, 14–23.

Michaels, Patrick J. 1992. *Sound and Fury: The Science and Politics of Global Warming*. Washington: Cato Institute.

Michaels, Patrick J. and Robert C. Balling. 2009. *Climate of Extremes: Global Warming Science They Don't Want You to Know*. Washington: Cato Institute.

Mill, John Stuart. 1843. *A System of Logic: Ratiocinative and Inductive*. London: Longmans Green.

Mill, John Stuart. 1859. *On Liberty*. London: Longman, Roberts, and Green.

Miller, J.R. 1981. "Irreversible Land Use and the Preservation of Endangered Species." *Journal of Environmental Economics and Management* 8, 19–26.

Millerd, Frank. 2007. "Early Attempts at Establishing Exclusive Rights in the British Columbia Salmon Fishery." *Land Economics* 83, 23–40.

Milliman, Scott R. 1986. "Optimal Fishery Management in the Presence of Illegal Activity." *Journal of Environmental Economics and Management* 13, 363–381.

Mills, Edwin S. 1967. "An Aggregative Model of Resource Allocation in a Metropolitan Area." *American Economic Review* 57, 197–210.

Milnor, John. 1985. "On the Concept of an Attractor." *Communication in Mathematical Physics* 102, 517–519.

Mindlin, Gabriel, Xin-Jun Hou, Hermán G. Solari, R. Gilmore, and N.B. Trufilaro. 1990. "Classification of Strange Attractors by Integers." *Physical Review Letters* 64, 2350–2353.

Mira, Christian. 1987. *Chaotic Dynamics: From the One-Dimensional Endomorphism to the Two-Dimensional Diffeomorphism*. Teaneck: World Scientific.

Mirowski, Philip. 1990. "From Mandelbrot to Chaos in Economic Theory." *Southern Economic Journal* 57, 289–307.

Mirowski, Philip. 2007. "Markets Come to Bits: Evolution, Computation and Markomata in Economic Science." *Journal of Economic Behavior and Organization* 63, 209–242.

Mishan, Ezra J. 1967. *Benefit-Cost Analysis*, 3rd Edition. London: Allen and Unwin.

Mitchell, John B.F. 1983. "The Seasonal Response to a General Circulation Model to Changes in CO_2 and Sea Temperature." *Quarterly Journal of the Royal Meteorological Society* 109, 113–152.

Mitra, Tapan and H.W. Wan. 1986. "On the Faustmann Solution to the Forest Management Problem." *Journal of Economic Theory* 40, 229–249.

Molnar-Szakacz, Istvan. 2010. "From Actions to Empathy and Morality – A Neural Perspective." *Journal of Economic Behavior and Organization*, 77, 76–85.

Monod, Jacques. 1971. *Chance and Necessity* (translated by A. Wainhouse). New York: Knopf.

Moon, F.C. and Philip J. Holmes. 1979. "A Magnetoelastic Strange Attractor." *Journal of Sound Vibrations* 65, 285–296.

Moore, Christopher. 1990. "Undecidability and Unpredictability in Dynamical Systems." *Physical Review Letters* 64, 2354–2357.

Moore, Christopher. 1991a. "Generalized Shifts: Undecidability and Unpredictability in Dynamical Systems." *Nonlinearity* 4, 199–230.

Moore, Christopher. 1991b. "Generalized One-Sided Shifts and Maps of the Interval." *Nonlinearity* 4, 727–745.

Morey, Edward R. 1985. "Desertification from an Economic Perspective." *Ricerche Economiche* 34, 550–560.

Morgan, C.L. 1923. *Emergent Evolution*. London: Williams and Norgate.

Morowitz, Harold J. 2003. "Emergence as Transcendance," in Niels Henrik Gregersen, ed., *From Complexity to Life: On the Emergence of Life and Meaning*. Oxford: Oxford University Press, 178–186.

Morse, Marston. 1931. "The Critical Points of a Function of n Variables." *Transactions of the American Mathematical Society* 33, 72–91.

Mosekilde, Erik, Steen Rasmussen, and Torben S. Sorensen. 1983. "Self-Organization and Stochastic Re-causalization in System Dynamics Models," in J.D.W. Morecroft, D.F. Andersen, and John D. Sterman, eds., *Proceedings of the 1983 International System Dynamics Conference*. Chestnut Hill: Pine Manor College, 128–160.

Mumford, Lewis. 1961. *The City in History*. New York: Harcourt Brace Jovanovich.

Muradian, Roldan. 2001. "Ecological Thresholds: A Survey." *Ecological Economics* 38, 7–24.

Murphy, G.I. 1967. "Vital Statistics of the Pacific Sardine." *Ecology* 48, 731–736.

Muth, John F. 1961. "Rational Expectations and the Theory of Price Movements." *Econometrica* 29, 315–335.

Muth, Richard F. 1969. *Cities and Housing*. Chicago: University of Chicago Press.

Myrberg, P.J. 1958. "Iteration der reellen Plynome zweiten Grades, I." *Annals Academca. Scientifica. Fennicae A* 256, 1–10; 1959, "[same title], II", [same journal] 268, 1–10; 1963, "[same title], III", [same journal] 336, 1–10.

Myrdal, Gunnar. 1957. *Economic Theory and Under-Developed Regions*. London: Duckworth.

Neary, J. Peter. 2001. "Of Hype and Hyperbolas: Introducing the New Economic Geography." *Journal of Economic Literature* 34, 536–561.

Nelson, Richard R. and Sidney G. Winter. 1974. "Neoclassical vs. Evolutionary Theories of Economic Growth." *Economic Journal* 84, 886–905.

Nelson, Richard R. and Sidney G. Winter. 1982. *An Evolutionary Theory of Economic Change*. Cambridge: Harvard University Press.

Nelson, Roger B. 1999. *An Introduction to Copulas*. New York: Springer.

Netting, R. 1976. "What Alpine Peasants have in Common: Observations on Communal Tenure in a Swiss Village." *Human Ecology* 4, 134–146.

Newman, M.E.J. 1997. "A Model of Mass Extinction." *Journal of Theoretical Biology* 189, 235–252.

Nicolis, John S. 1986. *Dynamics of Hierarchical Systems: An Evolutionary Approach*. Berlin: Springer.

Nicholson, A.J. 1933. "The Balance of Animal Populations." *Journal of Animal Ecology* 2, 131–178.

Nicholson, A.J. and V.A. Bailey. 1935. "The Balance of Animal Populations, Part I." *Proceedings of the Zoological Society of London*, 551–598.

Nicolis, C. and Grégoire Nicolis. 1984. "Is There a Climate Attractor?" *Nature* 311, 529–533.

Nicolis, C. and Grégoire Nicolis. 1987. "Evidence for Climatic Attractors." *Nature* 326, 523.

Nicolis, Grégoire and Ilya Prigogine. 1977. *Self-Organization in Nonequilibrium Systems: From Dissipative Structures to Order Through Fluctuations*. New York: Wiley-Interscience.

Nijkamp, Peter. 1983. "Technological Change, Policy Response and Spatial Dynamics," in Daniel A. Griffith and Anthony C. Lea, eds., *Evolving Geographical Structures: Mathematical Models and Theories for Space-Time Processes*. The Hague: Martinus Nijhoff, 75–98.

Nijkamp, Peter and Jacques Poot. 1987. "Dynamics of Generalized Spatial Interaction Models." *Regional Science and Urban Economics* 17, 367–390.

Nijkamp, Peter and Aura Reggiani. 1988. "Dynamic Spatial Interaction Models: New Directions." *Environment and Planning A* 20, 1449–1460.

Nishimura, Kazuo and M. Yano. 1996. "On the Least Upper Bound of Discount Factors that are Compatible with Optimal Period-Three Cycles." *Journal of Economic Theory* 69, 306–333.

Nordhaus, William D. 1988. "Entropy and Economic Growth." Paper presented at Allied Social Sciences Association Meetings, New York.

Nordhaus, William D. 1994. *Managing the Global Commons: The Economics of Climate Change*. Cambridge: MIT Press.

Nordhaus, William D. 2007. "A Review of the Stern Review on the Economics of Climate Change." *Journal of Economic Literature* 45, 686–702.

Nordhaus, William D. and Joseph Boyer. 2000. *Warming the World: Economic Models of Global Warming*. Cambridge: MIT Press.

Nordhaus, William D. and Zili Yang. 1996. "A Regional Dynamic General-Equilibrium Model of Alternative Climate-Change Strategies." *American Economic Review* 86, 741–765.

Norgaard, Richard B. 1984. "Coevolutionary Development Potential." *Land Economics* 60, 160–173.

Nowak, Martin A. and Karl Sigmund. 1998. "Evolution of Indirect Reciprocity by Image Scoring." *Nature* 393, 573–577.

Noy-Meir, I. 1973. "Desert Ecosystems: Environment and Producers." *Annual Review of Ecology and Systematics* 4, 353–364.

Nusse, Helena E. 1987. "Asymptotically Periodic Behavior in the Dynamics of Chaotic Mappings." *SIAM Journal of Applied Mathematics* 47, 498–515.

Nusse, Helena E. 1994a. "Review of Medio, A. (in collaboration with G. Gallo): Chaotic Dynamics, Theory and Applications to Economics." *Journal of Economics* 59, 106–113.

Nusse, Helena E. 1994b. "Rejoinder to Dr. Medio's Reply." *Journal of Economics* 60, 339–340.

Nusse, Helena E. and James A. Yorke. 1996. "Wada Basin Boundaries and Basin Cells." *Physica D* 90, 242–261.

Nychka, Douglas W., Stephen Ellner, A. Ronald Gallant, and Daniel F. McCaffrey. 1992. "Finding Chaos in Noisy Systems." *Journal of the Royal Statistical Society B* 54, 399–426.

Obukhov, A.M. 1962. "Some Specific Features of Atmospheric Turbulence." *Journal of Fluid Mechanics* 13, 82–85.

Ockenfels, Axel and Reinhard Selten. 2000. "An Experiment on the Hypothesis of Involunary Truth-Signaling in Bargaining." *Games and Economic Behavior* 33, 90–116.

Odland, J. 1978. "The Conditions for Multi-Center Cities." *Economic Geography* 54, 234–244.

Odum, Eugene P. 1953. *Fundamentals of Ecology*. Philadelphia: W.B. Saunders Company.

Ohlin, Bertil. 1933. *International and Interregional Trade*. Cambridge: Harvard University Press.

Ohls, James C. and David Pines. 1975. "Discontinuous Urban Development and Economic Efficiency." *Land Economics* 51, 224–234.

Oliva, T.A. and C.M. Capdeville. 1980. "Sussman and Zahler: Throwing the Baby Out with the Bath Water." *Behavioral Science* 25, 229–230.

Oliva, T.A., W.S. Desarbo, D.L. Day, and K. Jedidi. 1987. "GEMCAT: A General Multivariate Methodology for Estimating Catastrophe Models." *Behavioral Science* 32, 121–137.

O'Neill, William D. 1981. "Estimation of a Logistic Growth and Diffusion Model Describing Neighborhood Change." *Geographical Analysis* 13, 391–397.

Orishimo, Isao. 1987. "An Approach to Urban Dynamics." *Geographical Analysis* 19, 200–210.

Oseledec, V.I. 1968. "A Multiplicative Ergodic Theorem. Lyapunov Characteristic Numbers for Dynamical Systems." *Transactions of the Moscow Mathematical Society* 19, 197–231.

Ostrom, Elinor. 1990. *Governing the Commons*. Cambridge: Cambridge University Press.

Ostwald, W. 1908. *Die Energie*. Leipzig: Verlag Johann Ambrosius Barth.
O'Sullivan, Arthur. 2009. "Schelling's Model Revisited: Residential Sorting with Competitive Bidding for Land." *Regional Science and Urban Economics* 39, 397–408.
Ott, Edward, Celso Gebogi, and James A. Yorke. 1990. "Controlling Chaos." *Physical Review Letters* 64, 1196–1199.
Ott, Edward, Tim Sauer, and James A. Yorke, eds. 1994. *Coping with Chaos: Analysis of Chaotic Data and the Exploitation of Chaotic Systems*. New York: Wiley.
Paine, T.R. 1966. "Food Web Complexity and Species Diversity." *American Naturalist* 100, 65–75.
Palander, Tord F. 1935. *Beitrage zur Standortstheorie*. Uppsala: Almqvist & Wiksell.
Paley, William. 1802. *Natural Theology: Or Evidences of the Existence and Attributes of the Deity, Collected from the Appearances of Nature*. London: R. Faulder.
Palis, Jacob and Floris Takens. 1993. *Hyperbolicity and Sensitive Chaotic Dynamics at Homoclinic Bifurcations: Fractal Dimensions and Infinitely Many Attractors*. Cambridge: Cambridge University Press.
Pan, Shing and Fuliang Yin. 1997. "Using Chaos to Control Chaotic Systems." *Physics Letters A* 231, 173–178.
Pancs, Romans and Nicolaas J. Vriend. 2007. "Schelling's Spatial Proximity Model of Segregation Revisited." *Journal of Public Economics* 91, 1–24.
Papageorgiou, G.J. 1980. "On Sudden Urban Growth." *Environment and Planning A* 12, 1035–1050.
Papageorgiou, G.J. 1981. "Histories of Urbanization," in Daniel A. Griffith and R.D. MacKinnon, eds., *Dynamic Spatial Models*. Alphen aan den Rijn: Sitjhoff and Noordhoff.
Papageorgiou, Y.Y. and T.R. Smith. 1983. "Agglomeration as Local Instability of Spatially Uniform Steady-States." *Econometrica* 51, 1109–1119.
Pareto, Vilfredo. 1897. *Cours d'Économie Politique, Vol. II*. Lausanne: F. Rouge
Park, Thomas. 1992. "Early Trends toward Class Stratification: Chaos, Common Property, and Flood Recession Agriculture." *American Anthropologist* 94, 90–117.
Peano, Giuseppe. 1890. "Sur une Courbe, qui Remplit toute une Aire Plane." *Mathematische Annalen* 36, 157–160.
Pease, J.L., R.H. Vowles, and L.B. Keith. 1979. "Interaction of Snowshoe Hares and Woody Vegetation." *Journal of Wildlife Management* 43, 43–60.
Pecora, Louis M. and Thomas L. Carroll. 1990. "Synchronization in Chaotic Systems." *Physical Review Letters* 64, 821–824.
Peitgen, Heinz-Otto, Hartmut Jürgens, and Dietmar Saupe. 1992. *Chaos and Fractals: New Frontiers of Science*. New York: Springer.
Peixoto, Manuel M. 1962. "Structural Stability on Two-Dimensional Manifolds." *Topology* 1, 102–120.
Perelman, Michael S. 1979. "Marx, Malthus, and the Concept of Natural Resource Scarcity." *Antipode* 2, 80–91.
Perelman, Michael S. 1987. *Marx's Crises Theory: Scarcity, Labor, and Finance*. New York: Praeger.
Perelson, Alan S. and Evangelos A. Coutsias. 1986. "A Moving Boundary Model of Acrosomal Elogation." *Journal of Mathematical Biology* 23, 361–379.
Perez, J. and C. Jeffries. 1982. "Direct Observation of a Tangent Bifurcation." *Physical Letters A* 92, 82–84.
Perrin, Jean. 1906. "La Discontinuité de la Matière." *Revue de Mois* 1, 323–344.
Perrings, Charles. 1986. "Conservation of Mass and Instability in a Dynamic Economy-Environment System." *Journal of Environmental Economics and Management* 13, 199–211.
Perrings, Charles. 1989. "An Optimal Path to Extinction? Poverty and Resource Degradation in the Open Agrarian Economy." *Journal of Development Economics* 30, 1–244.
Perrings, Charles, Karl-Göran Mäler, Carl Folke, C.S. Holling, and Bengt-Owe Jansson, eds. 1995. *Biodiversity Loss: Economic and Ecological Issues*. Cambridge: Cambridge University Press.
Perroux, François. 1955. "Note sur la Croissance." *Économie Appliquée* 1–2, 307–320.

Petty, William. 1662. *A Treatise on Taxes & Contributions*. London: N. Brooke.
Pesin, Yahsa B. 1977. "Characteristic Lyapunov Exponents and Smooth Ergodic Theory." *Russian Mathematical Surveys* 32, 55–114.
Pimentel, David. 1968. "Population Regulation and Genetic Feedbacks." *Science* 159, 1432–1437.
Pirenne, Henri. 1925. *Medieval Cities* (English translation by F.D. Halsey). Princeton: Princeton University Press.
Plantinga, A.J. and J. Wu. 2003. "Co-Benefits from Carbon Sequestration in Forests: Evaluating Reductions in Agricultural Externalities from an Afforestation Policy in Wisconsin." *Land Economics* 79, 74–85.
Plourde, Charles and Richard Bodell. 1984. "Uncertainty in Fisheries Economics: The Role of the Discount Rate." *Marine Resource Economics* 1, 155–170.
Plykin, R. 1974. "Sources and Sinks for A-Diffeomorphims." *Mathematics of the USSR-Sbornik* 23, 233–253.
Pohjola, Matti T. 1981. "Stable, Cyclic and Chaotic Growth: The Dynamics of a Discrete Time Version of Goodwin's Growth Cycle Model." *Zeitschrift für Nationalekönomie* 41, 27–38.
Poincaré, Henri. 1880–1890. *Mémoire sur les Courbes Définies par les Équations Différentielles I-VI*, Oeuvre I. Paris: Gauthier-Villars.
Poincaré, Henri. 1890. "Sur les Équations de la Dynamique et le Problème de Trois Corps." *Acta Mathematica* 13, 1–270.
Poincaré, Henri. 1899. *Les Méthodes Nouvelles de la Mécanique Célèste*, 3 Vols. Paris: Gauthier-Villars.
Poincaré, Henri. 1908. *Science et Méthode*. Paris: Ernest Flammarion (English translation, 1952, *Science and Method*. New York: Dover Publications).
Pollicott, Mark and Howard Weiss. 2001. "The Dynamics of Schelling-Type Segregation Models and a Nonlinear Graph Laplacian Variational Problem." *Advances in Applied Mathematics* 27, 17–40.
Pomeau, Y. and P. Manneville. 1980. "Intermittent Transition to Turbulence in Dissipative Dynamical Systems." *Communications in Mathematical Physics* 74, 189–197.
Pope, J.G. 1973. "An Investigation into the Effects of Variable Rates of the Exploitation of Fishery Resources," in M.S. Barlett and R.W. Hiorns, eds., *The Mathematical Theory of Biological Populations*. New York: Academic Press, 23–34.
Porter, Richard C. 1982. "The New Approach to Wilderness through Benefit Cost Analysis." *Journal of Environmental Economics and Management* 9, 59–80.
Posner, Richard A. 2004. *Catastrophe: Risk and Response*. Oxford: Oxford University Press.
Possingham, Hugh and G. Tuck. 1997. "Application of Stochastic Dynamic Programming to Optimal Fire Management of a Spatially Structured Threatened Species," in A.D. McDonald and M. McAleer, eds., *Proceedings International Congress on Modelling and Simulation*, Vol. 2. Canberra: Modeling and Simulation Society of Australia.
Poston, Tim and Ian Stewart. 1978. *Catastrophe Theory and its Applications*. London: Pitman.
Poston, Tim and Alan G. Wilson. 1977. "Facility Size vs. Distance Travelled: Urban Services and the Fold Catastrophe." *Environment and Planning A* 9, 681–686.
Potts, Jason. 2000. *The New Evolutionary Microeconomics: Complexity, Competence and Adaptive Behaviour*. Cheltenham: Edward Elgar.
Pred, A. 1966. *The Spatial Dynamics of U.S. Urban-Industrial Growth*. Cambridge: MIT Press.
Price, George. 1970. "Selection and Covariance." *Nature* 227, 520–521.
Price, George. 1972. "Extensions of Covariance Selection Mathematics." *Annals of Human Genetics* 35, 485–490.
Prigogine, Ilya. 1980. *From Being to Becoming*. San Francisco: W.H. Freeman.
Prigogine, Ilya and Isabelle Stengers. 1984. *Order Out of Chaos*. New York: Bantam.
Prince, Raymond and J. Barkely Rosser, Jr., 1985. "Some Implications of Delayed Environmental Costs for Benefit Cost Analysis: A Study of Reswitching in the Western Coal Lands." *Growth and Change* 16, 18–25.
Pueyo, Salvador. 1997. "The Study of Chaotic Dynamics by Means of Very Short Time Series." *Physica D* 106, 57–65.

Puga, Diego. 1999. "The Rise and Fall of Regional Inequalities." *European Economic Review* 43, 303–334.

Pumain, D., Th. Saint-Julien, and L. Sanders. 1987. "Applications of a Dynamic Urban Model." *Geographical Analysis* 19, 152–166.

Puu, Tönu. 1979. "Regional Modelling and Structural Stability." *Environment and Planning A* 11, 1431–1438.

Puu, Tönu. 1981a. "Stability and Change in Two-Dimensional Flows," in Daniel A. Griffith and R.D. MacKinnon, eds., *Dynamic Spatial Models*. Alphen aan den Rijn: Sitjhoff and Noordhoff, 242–255.

Puu, Tönu. 1981b. "Structural Stability in Geographical Space." *Environment and Planning A* 13, 979–989.

Puu, Tönu. 1981c. "Catastrophic Structural Change in a Continuous Regional Model." *Regional Science and Urban Economics* 11, 317–333.

Puu, Tönu. 1982. "Outline of a Trade Cycle Model in Continuous Space and Time." *Geographical Analysis* 14, 19.

Puu, Tönu. 1986. "Multiple-Accelerator Models Revisited." *Regional Science and Urban Economics*16, 81–95.

Puu, Tönu. 1987. "Complex Dynamics in Continuous Models of the Business Cycle," in David Batten, John Casti, and Börje Johannson, eds., *Economic Evolution and Structural Adjustment*. Berlin: Springer, 227–259.

Puu, Tönu. 1989. *Nonlinear Economic Dynamics*. Berlin: Springer.

Puu, Tönu. 1990. "A Chaotic Model of the Business Cycle." *Occasional Paper Series on Socio-Spatial Dynamics* 1, 1–19.

Pyke, G.H., R. Saillard, and J. Smith. 1995. "Abundance of Eastern Bristlebirds in Relation to Habitat and Fire History." *Emu* 95, 106–110.

Quesnay, François. 1759. *Tableau Économique*. Paris.

Radzicki, Michael J. 1990. "Institutional Dynamics, Deterministic Chaos, and Self-Organizing Systems." *Journal of Economic Issues* 24, 57–102.

Ramsey, Frank P. 1928. "A Mathematical Theory of Saving." *Economic Journal* 38, 543–559.

Ramsey, James B., Chera L. Sayers, and Philip Rothman. 1990. "The Statistical Properties of Dimension Calculations Using Small Data Sets." *International Economic Review* 31, 991–1020.

Ramsey, James B. and Hsiao-Jane Yuan. 1989. "Bias and Error Bars in Dimension Calculations and Their Evaluation in Some Simple Models." *Physics Letters A* 134, 287–297.

Rand, David. 1976. "Threshold in Pareto Sets." *Journal of Mathematical Economics* 3, 139–154.

Rasmussen, D.R. and Erik Mosekilde. 1988. "Bifurcations and Chaos in a Generic Management Model." *European Journal of Operations Research* 35, 80–88.

Rawls, John. 1972. *A Theory of Justice*. Oxford: Clarendon.

Rayleigh, Lord J.W.S. 1880. "On the Resultant of a Large Number of Vibrations of the Same Pitch and Arbitrary Phase." *Philosophical Magazine* 10, 73.

Rayleigh, Lord J.W.S. 1916. "On Convective Currents in a Horizontal Layer of Fluid when the Higher Temperature is on the Under Side." *Philosophical Magazine* 32, 529–546.

Reed, W.J. and H.R. Clarke. 1990. "Harvest Decision and Asset Valuation for Biological Resources Exhibiting Size-Dependent Stochastic Growth." *International Economic Review* 31, 147–169.

Reilly, William J. 1931. *The Law of Retail Gravitation*. New York: Knickerbocker Press.

Richards, Robert. 1992. *The Meaning of Evolution: The Morphological Contruction and Ideological Reconstruction of Darwin's Theory*. Chicago: University of Chicago Press.

Richardson, Harry W. 1975. "Discontinuous Densities, Urban Spatial Structure and Growth: A New Approach." *Land Economics* 51, 305–312.

Richardson, Lewis Fry. 1922. *Weather Prediction by Numerical Process*. Cambridge: Cambridge University Press.

Richardson, Lewis Fry. 1926. "Atmospheric Diffusion Shown on a Distance-Neighbour Graph." *Proceedings of the Royal Society of London A* 110, 709–737.

Ricker, W.E. 1954. "Stock and Recruitment." *Journal of the Fisheries Research Board of Canada* 11, 559–623.

Rietschl, H. 1927. "Reine und Historische Dynamik des Standortes der Erzeungungszweige." *Schmollers Jahrbuch* 51, 813–870.

Rijk, F.J.A. and A.C.F. Vorst. 1983. "Equilibrium Points in an Urban Retail Model and Their Connection with Dynamical Systems." *Regional Science and Urban Economics* 13, 383–399.

Robbins, K.A. 1979. "Periodic Solutions and Bifurcation Structure at High r in the Lorenz Model." *SIAM Journal of Applied Mathematics* 36, 457–472.

Robinson, Abraham. 1966. *Nonstandard Analysis*. Princeton: Princeton University Press.

Rodriguez-Bachiller, Agustin. 1986. "Discontiguous Urban Growth and the New Urban Economics: A Review." *Urban Studies* 23, 79–104.

Rogers, Thomas D., Zhuo-Cheng Yang, and Lee Who Yip. 1986. "Complete Chaos in a Simple Epidemiological Model." *Journal of Mathematical Biology* 23, 263–268.

Rogerson, Peter A. 1985. "Disequilibrium Adjustment Processes and Chaotic Dynamics." *Geographical Analysis* 17, 185–198.

Romeiras, F.J., Celso Grebogi, Edward Ott, and W.P. Dayawansa. 1992. "Controlling Chaotic Dynamical Systems." *Physica D* 58, 165–192.

Rose-Ackerman, Susan. 1975. "Racism and Urban Structure." *Journal of Urban Economics* 2, 85–103.

Rosen, K.T. and M. Resnick. 1980. "The Size Distribution of Cities." *Journal of Urban Economics* 8, 165–186.

Rosenberg, Nathan. 1973. "Innovative Response to Materials Shortages." *American Economic Review, Papers and Proceedings* 63, 111–118.

Rosenstein, M.T., J.J. Collins, and C.J. De Luca. 1993. "A Practical Method for Calculating Largest Lyapunov Exponents from Small Data Sets." *Physica D* 65, 117–134.

Rosenstein-Rodan, Paul N. 1943. "Problems of Industrialization of Southern and South-Eastern Europe." *Economic Journal* 53, 202–211.

Rosenzweig, M. 1971. "Paradox of Enrichment: Destabilization of Exploitation Ecosystems in Ecological Time." *Science* 171, 385–387.

Ross, R. 1911. *The Prevention of Malaria*, 2nd Edition. London: Murray.

Rosser, J. Barkley, Jr. 1974. "A Review of Concepts Employed in Urban and Regional Economic Models." Institute for Environmental Studies Working Paper 15, University of Wisconsin-Madison.

Rosser, J. Barkley, Jr. 1976. "Essays Rlated to Spatial Discontinuities in Land Values at the Urban-Rural Margin." Ph.D. Dissertation, Department of Economics, University of Wisconsin-Madison.

Rosser, J. Barkley, Jr. 1978a. "The Theory and Policy Implications of Spatial Discontinuities in Land Values." *Land Economics* 54, 430–441.

Rosser, J. Barkley, Jr. 1978b. "A Reconsideration of Marx's Critique of Malthus's Principle of Population." *Virginia Social Science Journal* 13, 34–37.

Rosser, J. Barkley, Jr. 1980. "The Dynamics of Ghetto Boundary Movement and Ghetto Shape." *Urban Studies* 17, 235–321.

Rosser, J. Barkley, Jr. 1982. "A Catastrophe Model of White Flight." Mimeo, James Madison Universtiy.

Rosser, J. Barkley, Jr. 1990a. "Approaches to the Analysis of the Morphogenesis of Regional Systems." *Occasional Paper Series on Socio-Spatial Dynamics* 1(2), 75–102.

Rosser, J. Barkley, Jr. 1990b. "The Economics of Species Extinction." *Proceedings of the 8th International IFOAM Conference: Socio-Economics of Organic Agriculture*. Bonn: Deutsche Stiftung für Internationale Entwicklung DSE.

Rosser, J. Barkley, Jr. 1992 [1991]. "The Dialogue Between the Economic and the Ecologic Theories of Evolution." *Journal of Economic Behavior and Organization* 17, 195–215.

Rosser, J. Barkley, Jr. 1994. "Dynamics of Emergent Urban Hierarchy." *Chaos, Solitons & Fractals* 4, 553–562.

Rosser, J. Barkley, Jr. 1995. "Systemic Crises in Hierarchical Ecological Economies." *Land Economics* 71, 163–172.

Rosser, J. Barkley, Jr. 1996. Book Review of Paul Krugman's *Development, Geography, and Economic Theory*. *Journal of Economic Behavior and Organization* 31, 450–454.

Rosser, J. Barkley, Jr. 1998. "Coordination and Bifurcation in Growing Spatial Economies." *Annals of Regional Science* 32, 133–143.

Rosser, J. Barkley, Jr. 1999a. "The Prehistory of Chaotic Economic Dynamics," in Murat R. Sertel, ed., *Proceedings of the Eleventh World International Economic Association Congress, Tunis. Volume 4: Contemporary Economic Issues*. London: Macmillan, 207–224.

Rosser, J. Barkley, Jr. 1999b. "On the Complexities of Complex Economic Dynamics." *Journal of Economic Perspectives* 13(4), 169–192.

Rosser, J. Barkley, Jr. 2000a. "Aspects of Dialectics and Nonlinear Dynamics." *Cambridge Journal of Economics* 24, 311–324.

Rosser, J. Barkley, Jr. 2000b. *From Catastrophe to Chaos: A General Theory of Economic Discontinuities: Mathematics, Microeconomics, Macroeconomics, and Finance*, 2nd Edition, Vol. I. Boston: Kluwer Academic Publishers.

Rosser, J. Barkley, Jr. 2000c. "Self-Fulfilling Chaotic Mistakes: Some Examples and Implications." *Discrete Dynamics in Nature and Society* 4, 29–37.

Rosser, J. Barkley, Jr. 2001a. "Complex Ecologic-Economic Dynamics and Environmental Policy." *Ecological Economics* 37, 23–37.

Rosser, J. Barkley, Jr. 2001b. "Alternative Keynesian and Post Keynesian Perspectives on Uncertainty and Expectations." *Journal of Post Keynesian Economics* 23, 545–566.

Rosser, J. Barkley, Jr. 2002. "Complex Coupled System Dynamics and the Global Warming Policy Problem." *Discrete Dynamics in Nature and Society* 7, 93–100.

Rosser, J. Barkley, Jr. 2005. "Complexities of Dynamic Forest Management Problems," in Shashi Kant and R. Albert Berry, eds., *Economics, Sustainability, and Natural Resources: Economics of Sustainable Forest Management*. Dordrecht: Springer, 191–206.

Rosser, J. Barkley, Jr. 2009a. "Introduction," in J. BarkleyRosser, Jr., ed., *Handbook of Research on Complexity*. Cheltenham: Edward Elgar, 3–11.

Rosser, J. Barkley, Jr. 2009b. "Computational and Dynamic Complexity in Economics," in J. Barkley Rosser, Jr., ed., *Handbook of Research on Complexity*. Cheltenham: Edward Elgar, 22–35.

Rosser, J. Barkley, Jr. 2009c. "Theoretical and Policy Issues in Complex Post Keynesian Ecological Economics," in Richard P.F. Holt, Steven Pressman, and Clive L. Spash, eds., *Post Keynesian and Ecological Economics: Confronting Environmental Issues*. Cheltenham: Edward Elgar, 221–236.

Rosser, J. Barkley, Jr. 2009d. "Chaos Theory Before Lorenz." *Nonlinear Dynamics, Psychology, & Life Sciences* 11, 746–760.

Rosser, J. Barkley, Jr. 2010a. "Is a Transdisciplinary Perspective on Economic Complexity Possible?" *Journal of Economic Behavior and Organization* 75, 3–11.

Rosser, J. Barkley, Jr. 2010b. "Constructivist Logic and Emergent Evolution in Economic Complexity," in Stefano Zambelli, ed., *Computable, Constructive and Behavioural Economic Dynamics: Essays in Honour of Kumaraswamy (Vela) Velupillai*. London: Routledge, 184–197.

Rosser, J. Barkley, Jr. 2011. "Post Keynesian Perspectives and Complex Ecologic-Economic Systems." *Metroeconomica* 62, 96–121.

Rosser, J. Barkley, Jr., Carl Folke, Folke Günther, Heikki Isomäki, Charles Perrings, and Tönu Puu. 1994. "Discontinuous Change in Multilevel Hierarchical Systems." *Systems Research* 11, 77–94.

Rosser, J. Barkley, Jr., Richard P.F. Holt, and David Colander. 2010. *European Economics at a Crossroads*. Cheltenham: Edward Elgar.

Rosser, J. Barkley, Jr. and Marina V. Rosser. 2006. "Institutional Evolution of Environmental Management under Economic Growth." *Journal of Economic Issues* 40, 421–429.

Rosser, J. Barkley, Jr. and Richard G. Sheehan. 1995. "A Vector Autoregressive Model of Saudi Arabian Inflation." *Journal of Economics and Business* 47, 79–90.

Rössler, Otto E. 1976. "An Equation for Continuous Chaos." *Physics Letters A* 57, 397–398.
Rössler, Otto E. 1998. *Endophysics: The World as an Interface*. Singapore: World Scientific.
Rössler, Otto E. and J.L. Hudson. 1989. "Self-Similarity in Hyperchaotic Data," in E. Basar and T.H. Bullock, eds., *Springer Series in Brain Dynamics 2*. Berlin: Springer, 113–121.
Rotenberg, Manuel. 1988. "Mappings of the Plane that Simulate Predator-Prey Systems." *Journal of Mathematical Biology* 26, 169–191.
Ruelle, David. 1979. "Sensitive Dependence on Initial Condition and Turbulent Behavior of Dynamical Systems," in O. Gurel and Otto E. Rössler, eds., *Bifurcation Theory and Applications in Scientific Disciplines*. New York: New York Academy of Sciences, 408–446.
Ruelle, David. 1980. "Strange Attractors." *Mathematical Intelligencer* 2, 126–137.
Ruelle, David. 1990. "Deterministic Chaos: The Science and the Fiction." *Proceedings of the Royal Society of London A* 427, 241–248.
Ruelle, David. 1991. *Chance and Chaos*. Princeton: Princeton University Press.
Ruelle, David and Floris Takens. 1971. "On the Nature of Turbulence." *Communications in Mathematical Physics* 20, 167–192.
Ruse, Michael. 1980. "Charles Darwin and Group Selection." *Annals of Science* 37, 615–630.
Ruse, Michael. 2009. "Charles Darwin on Human Evolution." *Journal of Economic Behavior and Organization* 71, 10–19.
Russell, Bertrand. 1945. *History of Western Philosophy*. New York: Simon & Shuster.
Sakai, H. and H. Tokumaru. 1980. "Autocorrelations of a Certain Chaos." *IEEE Transactions on Acoustics, Speech and Signal Processing* 28, 588–590.
Sakai, Kenshi. 2001. *Nonlinear Dynamics and Chaos in Agricultural Systems*. Amsterdam: Elsevier.
Salo, S. and O. Tahvonen. 2002. "On Equilibrium Cycles and Normal Forests in Optimal Harvesting of Tree Villages." *Journal of Environmental Economics and Management* 44, 1–22.
Salo, S. and O. Tahvonen. 2003. "On the Economics of Forest Vintages." *Journal of Economic Dynamics and Control* 27, 1411–1435.
Samuelson, Paul A. 1939. "Interactions between the Multiplier Analysis and the Principle of Acceleration." *Review of Economics and Statistics* 21, 75–78.
Samuelson, Paul A. 1942. "The Stability of Equilibrium: Linear and Nonlinear Systems." *Econometrica* 10, 1–25.
Samuelson, Paul A. 1947. *The Foundations of Economic Analysis*. Cambridge: Harvard University Press.
Samuelson, Paul A. 1952. "Spatial Price Equilibrium and Linear Programming." *American Economic Review* 42, 283–303.
Samuelson, Paul A. 1967. "A Universal Cycle?," in R. Henn, ed., *Methods of Operations Research III*. Muhlgasse: Verlag Anton Hain, 170–183.
Samuelson, Paul A. 1971. "Generalized Predator-Prey Oscillations in Ecological and Economic Equilibrium." *Proceedings of the National Academy of Sciences* 68, 980–983.
Samuelson, Paul A. 1972. "Maximum Principles in Analytical Economics." *American Economic Review* 62, 2–17.
Samuelson, Paul A. 1976. "Economics of Forestry in an Evolving Society." *Economic Inquiry* 14, 466–491.
Sanglier, Michelle and Peter M. Allen. 1989. "Evolutionary Models of Urban Systems: An Applicaton to the Belgian Provinces." *Environment and Planning A* 21, 477–498.
Sapphores, J. 2003. "Harvesting a Renewable Resource under Uncertainty." *Journal of Economic Dynamics and Control* 28, 509–529.
Sardanyés, Josep and Ricard V. Solé. 2007. "Red Queen Strange Attractors in Host-Parasite Replicator Gene-for-Gene Coevolution." *Chaos, Solitons & Fractals* 32, 1666–1678.
Sauer, Tim, James A. Yorke, and Martin Casdagli. 1991. "Embedology." *Journal of Statistical Physics* 65, 579–616.
Savit, Robert and M. Green. 1991. "Time Series and Dependent Variables." *Physica D* 50, 95–116.
Schaefer, M.B. 1957. "Some Considerations of Population Dynamics and Economics in Relation to the Management of Marine Fisheries." *Journal of the Fisheries Research Board of Canada* 14, 669–681.

Schaffer, W.M. 1984. "Stretching and Folding in Lynx Fur Returns: Evidence for a Strange Attractor in Nature?" *American Naturalist* 124, 796–820.

Scheinkman, José and Blake LeBaron. 1989. "Nonlinear Dynamics and Stock Returns." *Journal of Business* 62, 311–337.

Scheffer, Marten. 1989. "Alternative Stable States in Eutrophic, Shallow Freshwater Systems: A Minimal Model." *Hydrological Bulletin* 23, 73–83.

Scheffer, Marten. 1998. *Ecology of Shallow Lakes*. London: Chapman and Hall.

Scheffer, Marten, Frances Westley, William A. Brock, and Milena Holmgren. 2002. "Dynamic Interactions of Societies and Ecosystems – Linking Theories from Ecology, Economy, and Sociology," in Lance H. Gunderson and C.S. Holling, eds., *Panarchy: Understanding Transformations in Human and Natural Systems*. Washington: Island Press, 195–239.

Schelling, Thomas C. 1969. "Models of Segregation." *American Economic Review, Papers and Proceedings* 59, 488–493.

Schelling, Thomas C. 1971a. "Dynamic Models of Segregation." *Journal of Mathematical Sociology* 1, 143–186.

Schelling, Thomas C. 1971b. "On the Ecology of Micromotives." *The Public Interest* 25, 61–98.

Schelling, Thomas C. 1978. *Micromotives and Macrobehavior*. New York: W.W. Norton.

Schelling, Thomas C. 1992. "Some Economics of Global Warming." *American Economic Review* 82, 1–14.

Schindler, D.W. 1990. "Experimental Perturbations of Whole Lakes as Tests of Hypotheses Concerning Ecosystem and Structure and Function." *Oikos* 57, 25–41.

Schliesser, Eric. 2010. "Reading Adam Smith after Darwin: On the Evolution of Propensities, Institutions, and Sentiments." *Journal of Economic Behavior and Organization* 77, 14–22.

Schmid, A. Allen. 1968. *Converting Rural Land to Urban Uses*. Baltimore: John Hopkins University Press.

Schneider, Stephen H. 1975. "On the Carbon Dioxide Confusion." *Journal of Atmospheric Science* 32, 2060–2066.

Schneider, Stephen H. and S. Rasool. 1971. "Atmospheric Carbon Dioxide and Aerosols: Effect of Large Increases on Global Climate." *Science* 173, 138–141.

Schönhofer, Martin. 1999. "Chaotic Learning Equilibria." *Journal of Economic Theory* 89, 1–20.

Schönhofer, Martin. 2001. "Can Agents Learn Their Way Out of Chaos?" *Journal of Economic Behavior and Organization* 44, 363–382.

Schrödinger, Erwin. 1944. *What is Life?* Cambridge: Cambridge University Press.

Schumacher, E.F. 1973. *Small is Beautiful: Economics as if People Mattered*. New York: Harper and Row.

Schumpeter, Joseph A. 1911. *Theorie der Wirtschaftlichen Entwicklung*. Leipzig: Duncker & Humblot (English translation by Redvers Opie, 1934, *The Theory of Economic Development*. Cambridge: Harvard University Press).

Schumpeter, Joseph A. 1950. *Capitalism, Socialism, and Democracy*, 3rd Edition. New York: Harper and Row.

Schumpeter, Joseph A. 1954. *History of Economic Analysis*. Oxford: Oxford University Press.

Schwartz, Ira B. and Ioana Triandaf. 1996. "Sustaining Chaos by Using Basin Boundary Saddles." *Physical Review Letters* 77, 4740–4743.

Schweizer, U. and P. Varaiya. 1977. "The Spatial Structure of Production with a Leontief Technology-II: Substitute Techniques." *Regional Science and Urban Economics* 7, 293–320.

Scott, A.D. 1955. "The Fishery: The Objectives of Sole Ownership." *Journal of Political Economy* 63, 116–124.

Scott, A.J. 1979. "Commodity Production and the Dynamics of Land-Use Differentiation." *Urban Studies* 16, 95–104.

Selten, Reinhard. 1980. "A Note on Evolutionary Stable Strategies in Asymmetric Animal Conflict." *Journal of Theoretical Biology* 83, 93–101.

Seo, S. Niggol. 2007. "Is Stern Review Alarmist?" *Energy and Environment* 18, 521–523.

Sethi, Rajiv and Eswaran Somanathan. 1996. "The Evolution of Social Norms in Common Property Use." *American Economic Review* 86, 766–788.

Sethi, S.P. 1977. "Nearest Feasible Paths in Optimal Control Problems." *Journal of Optimization Theory and Applications* 29, 614–627.

Sharkovsky, Aleksandr N. 1964. "Coexistence of Cycles of a Continuous Map of a Line into Itself." *Ukrainskii Matemacheskii Zhurnal* 16, 61–71.

Sheppard, Eric. 1983. "Pasinetti, Marx and Urban Accumulation Dynamics," in Daniel A. Griffith and Anthony C. Lea, eds., *Evolving Geographical Structures: Mathematical Models and Theories for Space-Time Processes*. The Hague: Martinus Nijhoff, 293–322.

Sherrington, D. and S. Kirkpatrick. 1975. "Solvable Model of a Spin Glass." *Physical Review Letters* 35, 1792.

Sherwood, Steven C. and Matthew Huber. 2010. "An Adaptability Limit to Climate Damage due to Heat Stress." *Proceedings of the National Academy of Sciences* May 6 (www.pnas.org/cgi/doi/10.1073/pnas.0913352107).

Shibata, Tatsuo and Kunihiko Kaneko. 1998. "Tongue-like Bifurcation Structures of the Mean-Field Dynamics in a Network of Chaotic Elements." *Physica D* 124, 177–200.

Shilnikov, L.P. 1965. "A Case of the Existence of a Denumerable Set of Periodic Motions." *Doklady Matemacheskii SSSR* 6, 163–166.

Shinbrot, Troy, William L. Ditto, Celso Grebogi, Edward Ott, Mark L. Spano, and James A. Yorke. 1992. "Using the Sensitive Dependence of Chaos (the 'Butterfly Effect') to Direct Trajectories in an Experimental Chaotic System." *Physical Review Letters* 68, 2863–2866.

Shinbrot, Troy, Edward Ott, Celso Grebogi, and James A. Yorke. 1990. "Using Chaos to Direct Trajectories to Targets." *Physical Review Letters* 65, 3215–3218.

Sierpinski, Waclaw. 1915. "Sur une courbe don't tout point est un point de ramification." *Comptes Rendu de l'Académie Paris* 160, 302.

Sierpinski, Waclaw. 1916. "Sur une Courbe Cantorienne qui Contient une Image Biunivoquet et Continue detoute Courbe Donnée." *Comptes Rendu de l'Académie Paris* 162, 629–632.

Siljak, D.D. 1979. "Structure and Stability of Model Ecosystems," in Efrain Halfon, ed., *Theoretical Systems Ecology*. New York: Academic Press, 151–181.

Silverberg, Gerald, Giovanni Dosi, and Luigi Orsenigo. 1988. "Innovation, Diversity and Diffusion: A Self-Organization Model." *Economic Journal* 98, 1032–1054.

Simon, Herbert A. 1955. "On a Class of Skew Distributions." *Biometrika* 42, 425–445.

Simon, Herbert A. 1962. "The Architecture of Complexity." *Proceedings of the American Philosophical Society* 106, 467–482.

Simon, Julian L. 1981. *The Ultimate Resource*. Princeton: Princeton University Press.

Simpson, George G. 1944. *Tempo and Mode in Evolution*. New York: Columbia University Press.

Simpson, George G. 1947. *The Meaning of Evolution*. New York: Harcourt Brace & World.

Simpson, George G. 1949. "Rates of Evolution in Animals," in G.L. Jepson, Ernst Mayr, and George G. Simpson, eds., *Genetics Paleontology Evolution*. Princeton: Princeton University Press, 205–228.

Sinai, Yaha G. 1959. "O Ponjatiii Entropii Dinamitjeskoj Sistemy" [On the Concept of Entropy of a Dynamic System]. *Doklady Akademii Nauk SSSR* 124, 768–771.

Sinai, Yaha G. 1972. "Gibbs Measures in Ergodic Theory." *Uspekhi Matemacheskii Nauk* 27, 21.

Singer, H.W. 1936. "The 'Courbe des populations': A Parallel to Pareto's Law." *Economic Journal* 46, 254–263.

Singer, S. Fred and Dennis Avery. 2007. *Unstoppable Global Warming: Every 1500 Years*. New York: Rowman & Littlefield.

Sissenwine, M.P. 1984. "The Uncertain Environment of Fishery Scientists and Managers." *Marine Resource Economics* 1, 1–30.

Skiba, A.K. 1978. "Optimal Growth with a Convex-Concave Production Function." *Econometrica* 46, 527–539.

Sklar, A. 1959. "Fonctions de Répartition á *n* Dimensions et leurs Marges." *Publications de l'Institut de Statistique de L'Université de Paris* 8, 229–231.

Smale, Steve. 1963. "Diffeomorphisms with Many Periodic Points," in Stewart S. Cairns, ed., *Differential and Combinatorial Topology*. Princeton: Princeton University Press, 63–80.

Smale, Steve. 1967. "Differentiable Dynamical Systems." *Bulletin of the American Mathematical Society* 73, 747–817.
Smale, Steve. 1976. "On the Differential Equations of Species in Competition." *Journal of Mathematical Biology* 3, 5–7.
Smale, Steve. 1990. "Some Remarks on the Foundations of Numerical Analysis," in David K. Campbell, ed., *Chaos/Xaoc: Soviet-American Perspectives on Nonlinear Science*. New York: American Institute of Physics, 107–120.
Smale, Steve. 1991. "Dynamics Retrospective: Great Problems, Attempts that Failed." *Physica D* 51, 267–273.
Smith, Adam. 1759. *The Theory of Moral Sentiments*. London: Miller, Kincaid, and Bell.
Smith, Adam. 1767. "Considerations Concerning the First Formation of Languages." Appendix to *The Theory of Moral Sentiments*, 3rd Edition. London: Miller, Kincaid, and Bell.
Smith, Adam. 1776. *An Inquiry into the Nature and Causes of the Wealth of Nations*. London: Strahan and Cadell.
Smith, J. Barry. 1980. "Replenishable Resource Management under Uncertainty: A Reexamination of the US Northern Fishery." *Journal of Environmental Economics and Management* 7, 209–219.
Smith, T.R. 1977. "Continuous and Discontinuous Response to Smoothly Decreasing Effective Distance: An Analysis with Special Reference to 'Overbanking' in the 1920s." *Environment and Planning A* 9, 461–475.
Smith, Vernon L. 1968. "Economics of Production from Natural Resources." *American Economic Review* 58, 409–431.
Smith, Vernon L. 1975. "The Primitive Hunter Culture, Pleistocene Extinction, and the Rise of Agriculture." *Journal of Political Economy* 83, 727–756.
Smolensky, Eugene, Selwyn Becker, and Harvey Molotch. 1968. "The Prisoner's Dilemma and Ghetto Expansion." *Land Economics* 44, 420–430.
Sober, E. and David Sloan Wilson. 1998. *Do Unto Others: The Evolution and Psychology of Unselfish Behavior*. Cambridge: Harvard University Press.
Solé, Ricard V. and Jordi Bascompte. 2006. *Self-Organization in Complex Ecosystems*. Princeton: Princeton University Press.
Song, S. and K.H. Zhang. 2002. "Urbanization and City Size Distribution in China." *Urban Studies* 39, 2317–2327.
Sonis, Michael. 1981. "Diffusion of Competitive Innovations," in W. Bogt and N. Nickle, eds., *Modeling and Simulation* 12, 1037–1041.
Sonis, Michael. 1983. "Spatial-temporal Spread of Competitive Innovations: An Ecological Approach." *Papers of the Regional Science Association* 52, 159–174.
Sorger, Gerhard. 1998. "Imperfect Foresight and Chaos: An Example of a Self-Fulfilling Mistake." *Journal of Economic Behavior and Organization* 33, 363–383.
Sotomayer, J. 1973. "Generic Bifurcations of Dynamical Systems," in Manuel M. Peixoto, ed., *Dynamical Systems*. New York: Academic Press, 549–560.
Southgate, Douglas and Carlisle Runge. 1985. "Toward an Economic Model of Deforestation and Social Change in Amazonia." *Ricerche Economiche* 34, 561–567.
Sparrow, Colin. 1982. *The Lorenz Equations: Bifurcations, Chaos, and Strange Attractors*. Berlin: Springer.
Spence, Michael, 1975. "Blue Whales and Applied Control Theory," in H.W. Göttinger, ed., *Systems Approaches and Environmental Problems*. Göttingen: Vandenhoeck and Ruprecht.
Spencer, Herbert. 1852. "A Theory of Population, Deduced from the General Law of Animal Fertility." *Westminster Review* 57, 499–500.
Spencer, Herbert. 1864. *Principles of Biology*. London: Williams and Norgate.
Spencer, Herbert. 1893. "The Inadequacy of Natural Selection." *Contemporary Research* 64, 153–166, 434–456.
Spencer, Herbert. 1899. *Principles of Biology*, 2nd Edition. New York: D. Appleton.
Spitzer, Frank, 1971. *Random Fields and Interacting Particle Systems*. Providence: American Mathematical Society.

Sraffa, Piero. 1960. *Production of Commodities by Means of Commodities*. Cambridge: Cambridge University Press.

Stauffer, Dietrich and Sorin Solomon. 2007. "Ising, Schelling and Self-Organising Segregation." *European Physical Journal B* 57, 473–479.

Stefan, Johan. 1891. "Über die Theorie der Eisbildung im Polarmeere." *Annals of Physics and Chemistrie*, 269–281.

Stefanovska, Aneta, Sašo Strle, and Peter Krošelj. 1997. "On the Overestimation of the Correlation Dimension." *Physics Letters A* 235, 24–30.

Steinnes, D. 1977. "Alternative Models of Neighborhood Change." *Social Forces* 55, 1043–1058.

Stern, Nicholas. 2006. *The Economics of Climate Change: The Stern Review*. Cambridge: Cambridge University Press.

Stern, Nicholas. 2008. "The Economics of Climate Change." *American Economic Review, Papers and Proceedings* 98, 1–37.

Stern, Nicholas. 2010. "Imperfections in the Economics of Public Policy, Imperfections in Markets, and Climate Change." *Journal of the European Economic Association* 8, 253–288.

Stevens, Wallace. 1947. *Poems*. New York: Vintage.

Steward, Julian H. 1949. "Cultural Causality and the Law." *American Anthropologist* 51, 1–27.

Stewart, Ian. 1989. *Does God Play Dice? The Mathematics of Chaos*. Oxford: Basil Blackwell.

Stiglitz, Joseph E. 1979. "A Neoclassical Analysis of the Economics of Natural Resources," in V. Kerry Smith, ed., *Scarcity and Growth Reconsidered*. Baltimore: Johns Hopkins University Press, 36–66.

Stockfish, Jacob A. 1969. *Measuring the Opportunity Cost of Government Investments*. Washington: Institute for Defense Analysis.

Stokes, Kenneth M. 1992. *Man and the Biosphere: Toward a Coevolutionary Political Economy*. Armonk: M.E. Sharpe.

Stollery, Kenneth R. 1986. "A Short-Run Model of Capital Stuffing in the Pacific Halibut Fishery." *Marine Resource Economics* 3, 137–153.

Stollery, Kenneth R. 1987. "Cooperatives as an Alternative to Regulation in Commercial Fisheries." *Marine Resource Economics* 4, 289–304.

Strotz, Robert H. 1956. "Myopia and Inconsistency in Dynamic Utility Maximization." *Review of Economic Studies* 23, 165–180.

Strotz, Robert H., J.C. McAnulty, and Joseph B. Naines, Jr. 1953. "Goodwin's Nonlinear Theory of the Business Cycle: An Electro-Analog Solution." *Econometrica* 21, 390–411.

Stull, William J. 1974. "Land Use and Zoning in an Urban Economy." *American Economic Review* 63, 337–347.

Stutzer, Michael J. 1980. "Chaotic Dynamics and Bifurcation in a Macro Model." *Journal of Economic Dynamics and Control* 2, 353–376.

Sugihara, George and Robert M. May. 1990. "Nonlinear Forecasting as a Way of Distinguishing Chaos from Measurement Error in Time Series." *Nature* 344, 734–740.

Sussman, Hector J. and Raphael Zahler. 1978a. "Catastrophe Theory as Applied to the Social and Biological Sciences." *Synthèse* 37, 117–216.

Sussman, Hector J. and Raphael Zahler. 1978b. "A Critique of Applied Catastrophe Theory in the Applied Behavioral Sciences." *Behavioral Science* 23, 383–389.

Svirizhev, Y.M. and D.O. Logofet. 1983. *The Stability of Biological Communities* (translation by Alexey Voinov). Moscow: Mir.

Swallow, S.K., P.J. Parks, and D.N. Wear. 1990. "Policy-Relevant Nonconvexities in the Production of Multiple Forest Benefits." *Journal of Environmental Economics and Management* 19, 264–280.

Takens, Floris. 1981. "Detecting Strange Attractors in Turbulence," in David A. Rand and L.-S. Young, eds., *Dynamical Systems and Turbulence*. Berlin: Springer, 366–381.

Takens, Floris. 1996. "Estimation of Dimension and Order of Time Series," in H.W. Broer, S.A. van Gils, I. Hoveijn, and Floris Takens, eds., *Nonlinear Dynamical Systems and Chaos*. Basel: Birkhäuser, 405–422.

Taleb, Nassim Nicholas. 2010. *The Black Swan: The Impact of the Highly Improbable*, 2nd Edition. New York: Random House.

Teilhard de Chardin, Pierre. 1956. *Le Phénomène Humain*. Paris: Les Éditions du Seuil.

Tesfatsion, Leigh. 1997. "How Economists Can Get Alife," in W. Brian Arthur, Steven N. Durlauf, and David A. Lane, eds., *The Economy as an Evolving Complex System*. Reading: Addison-Wesley, 533–564.

Theiler, J., S. Eubank, A. Longtin, B. Galdrikian, and J. Farmer. 1992. "Testing for Nonlinearity in Time Series: The Method of Surrogate Data." *Physica D* 58, 77–94.

Thom, René. 1956. "Les Singularités des Applications Différentiables." *Annales Institute Fourier* (Grenoble) 6, 43–87.

Thom, René. 1972. *Stabilité Structurelle et Morphogenèse*. New York: Benjamin (English translation by D.H. Fowler, 1975, *Structural Stability and Morphogenesis*. Reading: Benjamin).

Thom, René with response by E. Christopher Zeeman. 1975. "Catastrophe Theory: Its Present State and Future Perspectives," in Anthony Manning, ed., *Dynamical Systems-Warwick 1974*. Lecture Notes in Mathematics No. 468. Berlin: Springer, 366–389.

Thom, René. 1983. *Mathematical Models of Morphogenesis*. Chichester: Ellis Harwood, Ltd.

Thompson, D'Arcy W. 1917. *On Growth and Form*. Cambridge: Cambridge University Press.

Thompson, Michael. 1979. *Rubbish Theory*. Oxford: Oxford University Press.

Thompson, J.M.T. 1982. *Instabilities and Catastrophes in Science and Engineering*. New York: Wiley.

Thompson, J.M.T. 1992. "Global Unpredictability in Nonlinear Dynamics: Capture, Dispersal and the Indeterminate Bifurcations." *Physica D* 58, 260–272.

Thompson, J.M.T. and G.W. Hunt. 1973. *A General Theory of Elastic Stability*. New York: Wiley.

Thompson, J.M.T. and G.W. Hunt. 1975. "Towards a Unified Bifurcation Theory." *Journal of Applied Mathematical Physics* 26, 581–603.

Thompson, J.M.T. and H.B. Stewart. 1986. *Nonlinear Dynamics and Chaos: Geometrical Methods for Engineers and Scientists*. New York: Wiley.

Thomsen, J.S. Erik Mosekilde and John D. Sterman. 1991. "Hyperchaotic Phenomena in Dynamic Decision Making," in M.G. Singh and L. Travé-Massuyès, eds., *Decision Support Systems and Qualitative Reasoning*. Amsterdam: North-Holland, 149–154.

Tiebout, Charles M. 1956. "The Pure Theory of Local Public Expenditures." *Journal of Political Economy* 64, 416–424.

Tilman, David, Robert May, Clarence Lehman, and Martin Nowak. 1994. "Habitat Destruction and the Extinction of Debt." *Nature* 371, 65–66.

Tol, Richard S.J. 2002. "Estimates of the Damage Costs of Climate Change." *Environmental and Resource Economics* 21, 139–160.

Tol, Richard S.J. and Gary W. Yohe. 2006. "A Review of the *Stern Review*." *World Economics* 7, 233–250.

Trivers, Robert L. 1971. "The Evolution of Reciprocal Altruism." *The Quarterly Review of Biology* 46, 34–57.

Trotman, David J.A. and E. Christopher Zeeman. 1976. "Classification of Elementary Catastrophes of Codimension ≤ 5," in Peter J. Hilton, ed., *Structural Stability, the Theory of Catastrophes and Applications in the Sciences*. Berlin: Springer, 263–327.

Tucotte, D.L. 1974. "Geophysical Problems with Moving Phase Change Boundaries and Heat Flow," in J.R. Ockenden and E.A. Hodgkins, eds., *Moving Boundary Problems in Heat Flow and Diffusion*. Oxford: Oxford University Press, 91–120.

Tullock, Gordon. 2004. "Comments." *Journal of Economic Behavior and Organization* 53, 117–120.

Turchin, Peter. 2003. *Complex Population Dynamics: A Theoretical/Empirical Synthesis*. Princeton: Princeton University Press.

Turing, Alan M. 1952. "The Chemical Basis of Morphogenesis." *Philosophical Transactions of the Royal Society B* 237, 37.

Turnbull, A.L. and D.A. Chang. 1961. "The Practice and Theory of Biological Control of Insects in Canada." *Canadian Journal of Zoology* 39, 697–753.

Ueda, Yoshisuke. 1980. "Explosion of Strange Attractors Exhibited by Duffing's Equation." *Annals of the New York Academy of Sciences* 357, 422–434.

Ueda, Yoshisuke. 1991. "Survey of Regular and Chaotic Phenomena in the Forced Duffing Oscillator." *Chaos, Solitons & Fractals* 1, 199–231.

Ulam, Stanislaw M. and John von Neumann. 1947. "On Combination of Stochastic and Deterministic Processes." *Bulletin of the American Mathematical Society* 53, 1120.

Umberger, D.K., G. Mayer-Kress, and E. Jen. 1986. "Hausdorff Dimensions for Sets with Broken Scaling Symmetry," in G. Mayer-Kress, ed., *Dimensions and Entropies in Chaotic Systems: Quantification of Complex Behavior*. Berlin: Springer, 42–53.

Valderarama, Diego and James L. Anderson. 2007. "Improving Utilization of the Atlantic Sea Scallop Resource: An Analysis of Rotational Management of Fishing Grounds." *Land Economics* 83, 86–103.

van der Pol, Balthasar. 1927. "Forced Oscillations in a Circuit with Nonlinear Resistance (Receptance with Reactive Triode)." *London, Edinburgh and Dublin Philosophical Magazine* 3, 65–80.

van der Pol, Balthasar and J. van der Mark. 1927. "Frequency Demultiplication." *Nature* 120, 363–364.

van Haller, Albrecht. 1739–1744. *Hermanni Boerhave Praelectiones Acadamicae in Pognias Institutions re: Medicae*, 7 Vols. Göttingen.

van Kooten, G. Cornelis. 2004. *Climate Change Economics: Why International Accords Fail*. Cheltenham: Edward Elgar.

van Moerbeke, P. 1974. "An Optimal Stopping Problem with Linear Reward." *Acta Mathematica* 132, 111–151.

Veblen, Thorstein B. 1898. "Why is Economics Not An Evolutionary Science?" *Quarterly Journal of Economics* 12, 373–397.

Veblen, Thorstein B. 1919. *The Place of Science in Modern Civilization and Other Essays*. New York: Huebsch.

Vela Velupillai K. 2011. "Nonlinear Dynamics, Complexity and Randomness: Algorithmic Foundations." *Journal of Economic Surveys* 25, 547–568.

Vellekoop, M. and R. Berglund. 1994. "On Intervals, Transitivity = Chaos." *American Mathematical Monthly* 101, 353–355.

Vellupillai, Kumaraswamy. 1978. "Some Stability Properties of Goodwin's Growth Cycle Model." *Zeitschrift für Nationalokönomie* 39, 245–257.

Velupillai, K. Vela. 2009. "A Computable Economist's Perspective on Computational Complexity," in J. Barkley Rosser, Jr., ed., *Handbook of Research on Complexity*. Cheltenham: Edward Elgar, 36–83.

Verhulst, P.F. 1838. "Notice sur la Loi que la Population Suit dans son Accroisement." *Correspondence Mathématique et Physique* 10, 113–121.

Vernadsky, Vladimir Ivanovich. 1945. "The Biosphere and the Noösphere." *Scientific American* 33(1), 1–12.

Viana, Marcelo. 1996. "Global Attractors and Bifurcations," in H.W. Broer, S.A. van Gils, I. Hoveijn, and Floris Takens, eds., *Nonlinear Dynamical Systems and Chaos*. Basel: Birkhäuser, 299–324.

Vincent, Jeffrey R. and Matthew D. Potts. 2005. "Nonlinearities, Biodiversity Conservation, and Sustainable Forest Management," in Shashi Kant and R. Albert Berry, eds., *Economics, Sustainability, and Natural Resources: Economics of Sustainable Forest Management*. Dordrecht: Springer, 207–222.

Vinković, Dejan and Alan Kirman. 2006. "A Physical Analogue of the Schelling Model." *Proceedings of the National Academy of Sciences* 103, 19261–19265.

Virey, Julien-Joseph. 1803. "Animal." *Nouveau Dictionaire d'Histoire Naturelle* 1, 419–466.

Viscusi, W. Kip and Richard J. Zeckhauser. 1976. "Environmental Policy Choice under Uncertainty." *Journal of Environmental Economics and Management* 3, 97–112.

Volterra, V. 1931. *Lecons sur la Théorie Mathématique de la Lutte pour la Vie*. Paris: Gauthier-Villars.

Volterra, V. 1937. "Principes de Biologia Mathématique." *Acta Biotheoretica* 3, 1–36.
von Bertalanffy, Ludwig. 1962. *General Systems Theory*. New York: George Braziller.
von Goethe, Johann Wolfgang. 1790. *Versuch der Metamorphose der Pflanzen zu Erklänen*. Gotha: Etting.
von Koch, H. 1904 "Sur une Courbe Continue sans Tangente, Obtennue par une Construction Géometrique Élémentaire." *Arkiv for Matematik, Astronomi, och Fysik* 1, 681–704.
von Neumann, John. 1937. "Über ein Okonomisches Gleichungssystem und eine Verallgemeinerung des Brouwerschen Fixpunkssatzes." *Ergebnisse eines mathematischen Kolloquims* 8, 73–83 (English translation, 1945, "A Model of General Equilibrium." *Review of Economic Studies* 13, 1–9).
von Neumann, John, edited and completed by Arthur W. Burks. 1966. *Theory of Self-Reproducing Automata*. Urbana: University of Illinois Press.
von Thünen, Johann Heinrich. 1826. *Der Isolierte Staat in Biechiezung auf Landwirtschaft und Nationaleckonomie*. Hamburg: Perthes (English translation by Wartenberg, C.M., 1966, *The Isolated State*. New York: Pergamon Press).
Waddington, D.H. 1940. *Organizers and Genes*. Cambridge: Cambridge University Press.
Wade, M. 1985. "Soft Selection, Hard Selection, Kin Selection, and Group Selection." *American Naturalist* 125, 61–73.
Wagener, Florian O.O. 2003. "Skiba Points and Heteroclinic Bifurcations with Applications to the Shallow Lake System." *Journal of Economic Dynamics and Control* 27, 1533–1561.
Wagener, Florian O.O. 2009. "Shallow Lake Economics Run Deep: Nonlinear Aspects of an Economic-Ecologic Conflict." Tinbergen Institute Discussion Paper 2009-033/1, Amsterdam.
Wagstaff, J.M. 1978. "A Possible Interpretation of Settlement Pattern Evolution in Terms of Catastrophe Theory." *Transactions, Institute of British Geographers*, New Series 3, 165–178.
Waldrop, M. Mitchell. 1992. *Complexity: The Emerging Science at the Edge of Order and Chaos*. New York: Simon & Schuster.
Wales, David J. 1990. "Calculating the Rate of Loss of Information from Chaotic Time Series Forecasting." *Nature* 350, 485–488.
Wallace, Alfred Russell. 1860. "On the Zoological Geography of the Malay Archipelago." *Journal of the Linnaean Society* 4, 172–184.
Wallace, Alfred Russel. 1876. *The Geographic Distribution of Animals*. London: Harper and Brothers.
Wallerstein, Immanuel. 1979. *The Capitalist World Economy*. Cambridge: Cambridge University Press.
Walters, Carl. 1986. *Adaptive Management of Renewable Resources*. New York: Macmillan.
Wang, Ar-Young and Kuo-Sheng Cheng. 1978. "Dynamic Analysis of a Commercial Fishing Model." *Journal of Environmental Economics and Management* 5, 113–127.
Watts, Duncan J. 1999. *Small Worlds*. Princeton: Princeton University Press.
Watts, Duncan J. 2003. *Six Degrees: The Science of a Connected Age*. New York: W.W. Norton.
Watts, Duncan J. and Steven H. Strogatz. 1998. "Collective Dynamics of Small-World Networks." *Nature* 393, 440–442.
Weber, Alfred. 1909. *Über den Standort der Industrien*. Tübingen: J.C.B. Mohr (English translation by C.J. Friedrich, 1929, *The Theory of the Location of Industries*. Chicago: University of Chicago Press).
Wegener, Michael. 1982. "Modelling Urban Decline: A Multi-Level Economic-Demographic Model of the Dortmund Region." *International Regional Science Review* 7, 21–41.
Wegener, Michael, Friedrich Gnad, and Michael Vannahme. 1986. "The Time Scale of Urban Change," in Bruce Hutchinson and Michael Batty, eds., *Advances in Urban Systems Modelling*. Amsterdam: North-Holland, 175–198.
Weidlich, Wolfgang. 1991. "Physics and Social Science – The Approach of Synergetics." *Physics Reports* 204, 1–163.
Weidlich, Wolfgang. 2002. *Sociodynamics: A Systematic Approach to the Mathematical Modelling in the Social Sciences*. London: Taylor & Francis.

Weidlich, Wolfgang and Martin Braun. 1992. "The Master Equation Approach to Nonlinear Economics." *Journal of Evolutionary Economics* 2, 233–265.

Weidlich, Wolfgang and Günter Haag. 1983. *Concepts and Models of a Quantitative Sociology. The Dynamics of Interaction Populations*. Berlin: Springer.

Weidlich, Wolfgang and Günter Haag. 1987. "A Dynamic Phase Transition Model for Spatial Agglomeration Processes." *Journal of Regional Science* 27, 529–569.

Weikart, Richard. 2009. "Was Darwin or Spencer the Father of Laissez-Faire Social Darwinism?" *Journal of Economic Behavior and Organization* 71, 20–28.

Weintraub, E. Roy. 2002. *How Economics Became a Mathematical Science*. Durham: Duke University Press.

Weisbrod, Burton A. 1964. "Collective-Consumption Services of Individual-Consumption Good." *Quarterly Journal of Economics* 78, 471–477.

Weitzman, Martin L. 2007. "A Review of *The Stern Review on the Economics of Climate Change*." *Journal of Economic Literature* 45, 703–724.

Weitzman, Martin L. 2009. "On Modeling and Interpreting the Economics of Catastrophic Climate Change." *Review of Economics and Statistics* 91, 1–19.

Weitzman, Martin L. 2010. "GHG Targets as Insurance Against Catastrophic Climate Damages." Mimeo, Department of Economics, Harvard University.

Wen, Kehong. 1996. "Continuous-Time Chaos in Stock Market Dynamics," in William A. Barnett, Alan P. Kirman, and Mark Salmon, eds., *Nonlinear Dynamics and Economics: Proceedings of the Tenth International Symposium in Economic Theory and Econometrics*. Cambridge: Cambridge University Press, 133–159.

Whang, Yoon-Jae and Oliver Linton. 1999. "The Asymptotic Distribution of Nonparametric Estimates of the Lyapunov Exponent for Stochastic Time Series." *Journal of Econometrics* 91, 1–42.

White, Halbert. 1989. "Some Asymptotic Results for Learning in Single Hidden-Layer Feedforward Network Models." *Journals of the American Statistical Association* 84, 1003–1013.

White, Michelle J. 1975. "The Effect of Zoning on the Size of Metropolitan Areas." *Journal of Urban Economics* 2, 217–283.

White, Michelle J. 1977. "Urban Models of Race Discrimination." *Regional Science and Urban Economics* 7, 217–232.

White, Roger W. 1985. "Transitions to Chaos with Increasing System Complexity: The Case of Regional Industrial Systems." *Environment and Planning A* 17, 387–396.

Whitney, Hassler. 1955. "Mappings of the Plane into the Plane." *Annals of Mathematics* 62, 374–410.

Wiener, Norbert. 1948. *Cybernetics: Or Control and Communication in the Animal and the Machine*. Cambridge, MA: MIT Press (2nd Edition, 1961, Cambridge: MIT Press).

Wiggins, Stephen. 1990. *Introduction to Applied Nonlinear Dynamical Systems and Chaos*. New York: Springer.

Willassen, Y. 1998. "The Stochastic Rotation Problem: A Generalization of Faustmann's Formula to Stochastic Forest Growth." *Journal of Economic Dynamics and Control* 22, 573–596.

Williams, G.C. 1966. *Adaptation and Natural Selection*. Princeton: Princeton University Press.

Wilson, Alan G. 1970. *Entropy in Urban and Regional Modelling*. London: Pion.

Wilson, Alan G. 1976. "Catastrophe Theory and Urban Modelling: An Application to Modal Choice." *Environment and Planning A* 8, 351–356.

Wilson, Alan G. 1981a. *Catastrophe Theory and Bifurcations: Applications to Urban Regional Systems*. London: Croom Helm.

Wilson, Alan G. 1981b. "Some New Sources of Instability and Oscillation in Dynamic Models of Shopping Centers and other Urban Structures." *Sitemi Urbani* 3, 391–401.

Wilson, Alan G. 1982. "Criticality and Urban Retail Structure: Aspects of Catastrophe Theory and Bifurcation," in William C. Schieve and Peter M. Allen, eds., *Self-Organization and Dissipative Structures*. Austin: University of Texas Press, 159–173.

Wilson, Edward O. 1975. *Sociobiology*. Cambridge: The Belknap Press Harvard University.
Wilson, James, Bobbi Low, Robert Costanza, and Elinor Ostrom. 1999. "Scale Misperceptions and the Spatial Dynamics of a Social-Ecological System." *Ecological Economics* 31, 243–257.
Winiarski, Léon. 1900. "Essai sur la Mécanique Sociale: L'Énergie Sociale et ses Mensurations, II." *Revue Philosophique* 49, 265–287.
Winterholder, B.P. 1980. "Canadian Fur Beaver Cycles and Cree-Ojibwa Hunting and Trapping Practices." *American Naturalist* 115, 870–879.
Wittfogel, Karl A. 1957. *Oriental Despotism: A Comparative Study of Total Power*. New Haven: Yale University Press.
Wold, H.O.A. 1938. *A Study in the Analysis of Stationary Time Series*. Uppsala: Almquist and Wiksell.
Wolf, Alan, Jack B. Swift, Harry L. Swinney, and John A. Vastano. 1985. "Determining Lyapunov Exponents from a Time Series." *Physica D* 16, 285–317.
Wolf, E.P. 1963. "The Tipping Point in Socially Changing Neighborhoods." *Journal of the American Institute of Planners* 29, 217–222.
Wolfram, Stephen. 1984. "Universality and Complexity in Cellular Automata." *Physica D* 10, 1–35.
Wolfram, Stephen, ed. 1986. *Theory and Applications of Cellular Automata*. Singapore: World Scientific.
Woodcock, Alexander and Monte Davis. 1978. *Catastrophe Theory*. New York: E.P. Dutton.
Woods, R.I. 1981. "Spatiotemporal Models of Ethnic Segregation and their Implications for Housing Policy." *Environment and Planning A* 13, 1415–1433.
Worster, Donald. 1977. *Nature's Economy: A History of Ecological Ideas*. Cambridge: Cambridge University Press.
Wright, Philip G. 1928. *The Tariff on Animal and Vegetable Oils*. New York: Macmillan.
Wright, Sewall. 1918. "On the Nature of Size Factors." *Genetics* 3, 367–374.
Wright, Sewall. 1921. "Correlation and Causation." *Journal of Agricultural Research* 20, 557–585.
Wright, Sewall. 1923. "The Theory of Path Coefficients: A Reply to Niles' Criticism." *Genetics* 8, 239–255.
Wright, Sewall. 1925. "Corn and Hog Correlations." USDA Bulletin No. 1300. Washington: GPO.
Wright, Sewall. 1931. "Evolution in Mendelian Populations." *Genetics* 16, 97–159.
Wright, Sewall. 1932. "The Roles of Mutation, Inbreeding, Crossbreeding, and Selection in Evolution." *Proceedings of 6th International Congress of Genetics* 1, 356–366.
Wright, Sewall. 1951. "The Genetical Theory of Populations." *Annals of Eugenics* 15, 323–354.
Wright, Sewall. 1978. *Evolution and the Genetics of Populations*, 4 Vols. Chicago: University of Chicago Press.
Wright, Sewall. 1988. "Surfaces of Selective Value Revisited." *American Naturalist* 131, 115–123.
Wynne-Edwards, V.C. 1962. *Animal Dispersion in Relation to Social Behavior*. Edinburgh: Oliver & Boyd.
Yakovenko, Victor and J. Barkley Rosser, Jr. 2009. "Colloquium: Statistical Mechanics of Money, Wealth, and Income." *Reviews of Modern Physics* 81, 1703–1725.
Yeomans, J. 1992. *Statistical Mechanics of Phase Transitions*. Oxford: Oxford University Press.
Yinger, John. 1976. "Racial Prejudice and Racial Residential Segregation in an Urban Model." *Journal of Urban Economics* 3, 383–396.
Yinger, John. 1979. "Estimating the Relationship between Location and the Price of Housing." *Journal of Regional Science* 21, 271–289.
Yoneyama, K. 1917. "Theory of Continuous Sets of Points." *Tohoku Mathematics Journal* 11–12, 43.
Young, H. Peyton. 1998. *Individual Strategy and Social Structure: An Evolutionary Theory of Institutions*. Princeton: Princeton University Press.
Young, Laurence C. 1969. *Lectures on the Calculus of Variations and Optimal Control Theory*. Philadelphia: W.B. Saunders.
Young, L.-S. 1982. "Dimension, Entropy and Lyapunov Exponents." *Ergodic Theory and Dynamical Systems* 2, 109–124.

Zahler, Raphael and Hector Sussman. 1977. "Claims and Accomplishments of Applied Catastrophe Theory." *Nature* 269, 759–763.

Zambelli, Stefano. 2007. "Comments on Phillip Mirowski's Article: Markets Come to Bits: Evolution, Computation and Markomata in Economic Science." *Journal of Economic Behavior and Organization* 63, 345–358.

Zeeman, E. Christopher. 1974. "On the Unstable Behavior of the Stock Exchanges." *Journal of Mathematical Economics* 1, 39–44.

Zeeman, E. Christopher. 1977. *Catastrophe Theory: Selected Papers, 1972–1977*. Reading: Addison-Wesley.

Zhang, Junfu. 2004a. "A Dynamic Model of Residential Segregation." *Journal of Mathematical Sociology* 28, 147–170.

Zhang, Junfu. 2004b. "Residential Segregation in an All-Integrationist World." *Journal of Economic Behavior and Organization* 54, 533–550.

Zhang, Wei-Bin. 1988. "The Pattern Formation of an Urban System." *Geographical Analysis* 20, 75–84.

Zhang, Wei-Bin. 1991. *Synergetic Economics: Time and Change in Nonlinear Economics*. Heidelberg: Springer.

Ziehmann, Christine, Leonard A. Smith, and Jürgen Kurths. 1999. "The Bootstrap and Lyapunov Exponents in Deterministic Chaos." *Physica D* 126, 49–59.

Zimmer, Carl. 1999. "Life after Chaos." *Science* 284, 83–86.

Zinkhan, F.C. 1991. "Option Pricing and Timberland's Land-Use Conversion Option." *Land Economics* 67, 317–325.

Zipf, George K. 1941. *National Unity and Disunity*. Bloomington: Principia Press.

Zipf, George K. 1949. *Human Behavior and the Principle of Least Effort*. Cambridge: Addison-Wesley.

Index

A
Abbasid caliphate, 97
Accumulation point, 240, 256
Adaptationism, 123
Adiabatic approximation, 78, 256
Advertising, 103
Agglomeration, 4–10, 12–14, 18, 20–23, 25, 27, 34, 36–37, 42, 61, 71, 102–103
  catastrophic, 34
Air holes, 238
Albedo, 206–207
Altruistic genes, 114, 130
Amenity values, 170
Anagenesis, 83, 102
Anarchism, 4, 126
Anorexia-bulimia, 223
Arbitrage, 118, 141, 215, 226, 235, 238–239, 243–244, 247
ARCH, 257
Asset substitutability, 210
Asymmetry, 34, 88
Attractor
  chaotic, 239, 242, 261
  global, 117
  Lorenz, 234–235
  Rössler, 119
  set, 118, 228
  strange, 68, 215, 218–219, 228–229, 231, 234, 237–239, 243, 249, 260
Austrian School, 127
Autopoiesis, 83

B
Baker, James A., 22
Basin of attraction, 132, 228, 242, 248
BDS statistic, 247
Benefit-cost analysis, 185
Bias factor, 16, 19, 223
Bifurcation
  amensal, 52
  commensal, 52
  Hopf, 69–70, 217, 229–230, 234, 238
  multiparameter, 261
  period-doubling, 37, 140–141, 229, 239–241, 256
  pitchfork, 217–218, 239
  point, 2–3, 6–7, 10–11, 34–35, 44, 46, 48, 51, 69, 72, 77, 79–80, 82, 113, 116, 216–218, 221, 256, 258
  self-similar cascade of, 215
  set, 8, 16, 57–58, 65, 221, 223
  tangential, 241, 258
  theory, 3, 46, 213–214, 216, 218–219, 225, 227–228, 256–257, 261
  transcritical, 217
  values, 9, 11, 37, 47, 79, 140–141
Bimodality, 222–223
Bioeconomics, 117, 128, 137, 147–151, 153, 160
Biogeochemical cycles, 185
Bionomic, base
  dynamics, 139–147
  equilibrium, 148, 150, 164
Black swans, 209
Blockbusting, 61
Blue whales, 146–147, 158, 161
Boreal forest, 182–183
Boswash, 96
Bronze Age, 22
Brownian motion, 96, 250
Brussels School, 2–3, 43–44, 48, 76, 83, 237, 254, 257
Buchanan club, 117
Buddhist economics, 196
Butterfly, effect, 16, 201, 209–210, 218, 223, 233, 243, 245, 260
  factor, 223

C
California sardine, 147
Cantor Set, 215, 230–231, 235–239, 250, 257, 259
  torus, 238
Capacity, 21, 65, 82, 139, 142–144, 154, 156, 161, 164, 181
Capital, mobility
  reversal, 36
  stock inertia, 152, 190
  stuffing, 156
  theory, controversies, 158–160, 169
    paradoxes, 159, 160, 185
Carbon dioxide (CO_2), 159, 199, 202, 206, 210
Carbon dioxide accumulation, 159
Carbon sequestration, 172
Carrying capacity, 82, 139, 142–144, 154, 161, 164, 181
Catastrophe
  butterfly, 2, 16, 223
  cusp, 2, 8–9, 44, 56–57, 72–73, 161, 222–223, 226, 229, 234, 258
  elementary, 220–221, 227, 250
  elliptic umbilic, 2, 65–66, 221, 223–224
  error, 116–117
  fold, 2, 18, 44–45, 178, 221–222
  function, 220
  generalized, 221, 249
  germ, 220
  hyperbolic umbilic, 2, 57–58, 65–66, 221, 223–224
  parabolic umbilic, 61, 221, 224
  swallowtail, 221
  theory, 2–3, 8, 22, 43, 46, 61, 77, 79–80, 113, 161, 178, 185, 213, 219–220, 224–229, 249, 256, 258, 261
  threshold, 116, 144
  ultraviolet, 214
Catastrophism, 121, 181, 188
Celestial mechanics, 214, 216, 229, 237, 258
Central place theory, 97
Chaos
  deterministic, 74–75, 82–83, 107, 112
  dynamics, 3, 20, 36–38, 44, 47, 68–69, 74–76, 82, 111–112, 114, 118–119, 140–141, 143, 145–146, 152, 155, 160, 164, 166–167, 184, 200, 202, 218, 228–229, 232–233, 235, 237, 240, 242–245, 247, 251, 254, 257–260
  Goodwin, 111, 140
  Malthusian, 82
  metastable, 234
  neoclassical, 3, 202, 260
  Old Keynesian, 118
  pure, 143
  Richardian, 237, 251, 259
  Samuelson, 111, 140
  theory, 22, 74, 77, 80, 209–210, 213–215, 220–221, 223, 228, 237, 244–247, 249, 252, 259–260
  trajectory, 155
  transition to, 47, 75, 80, 152, 215, 229, 238–241
Chartists, 227
Chattering solution, 153, 161
Chlorofluorocarbons, 188, 190
Circular causality, 34
City of the dead, 5
Clear-cuts, 173, 175–176
Climate–economic system, 199–201
Climate skeptics, 198
Climatology, 172–173, 188, 197–198
Club of Rome, 188–190, 194–196
Cobweb, 166–167, 188
  chaotic, 166
Coefficient of relative risk aversion, 205
Coevolution, 134, 137, 143, 161
Common property, 161, 185
Community matrix, 111, 145–146
Comparative advantage, 16–17, 50
Compensation, pure, 147–149
Complementarity, 132
Concave, indifference curves
  supply, 17, 149–150, 155, 163, 165–166, 184, 201
Congestion, 5–8, 11–12, 21, 47, 61, 69–70, 77
Connectance, 145–146
Connectivity index, 82
Consistent conjectures, 219
Consistent expectations equilibrium, 167
Continuous flow model, 63–69, 81
Control function, 235–236
  parameters, 71, 74, 200, 216, 220, 242, 248, 254, 257
  variables, 8, 16, 18, 50, 56, 58, 61, 65, 71, 79–80, 220–223, 226, 230, 256, 258
Conversion, 194
Cooperatives, 20, 126, 156
Copula, 208, 210–211
Core, 2, 14, 30, 34–37, 41, 112, 118, 129, 243
Core-periphery model, 30–38
Corn-hog cycle, 82, 137, 184
Crashes, v, 144, 161, 195, 209, 251, 257
  US stock market 1987, 209
Credit, 103, 117, 208, 257

Critical, economies
  points, 80, 149, 216, 219, 254, 257
  values, 37, 46, 50, 76, 111, 222
Critical realism, 40
Cumulative causation, 40
Cusp point, 74, 222–223, 257
  degenerate hexagonal, 65
Cycles, business
  chaotic, 184
  hare-lynx, 142, 161, 184
  limit, 68–70, 72, 111, 141, 143, 155, 161, 191, 229–230, 238, 245, 251
  period-doubling, 75
  predator-prey, 3, 69–74, 160, 184
  real, 118
  regional, 3, 69
  three-period, 140, 239–241, 260
  urban, 48, 72

D

Darwinism
  generalized, 122, 124
  Social, 111, 117, 124, 127, 137
  universal, 122, 129
Day–Rosser complexity, 138
Deforestation, 161, 185, 190
Degeneracy, 218
Deglomeration, 6, 19, 21
Delay convention, 221
Density dependence, 139, 141, 143
Depensation, 147–149, 157–158
  critical, 148
Depression, great, 22, 188
Desertification, 161, 190
De-urbanization, 19–21, 70
Dialectics, 43, 78, 108–109, 113, 118, 258
Diffusion-limited aggregation, 81
Dimension, correlation
  Euclidean, 231
  fractal, 80–82, 230–232, 239, 243, 249, 257, 259–260
  Hausdorff, 81, 230–231, 233, 246
Discontiguities, 57, 59–60
Discount rate, 20, 55, 57, 158–160, 162–164, 166, 168, 179–180, 184–185, 191, 201, 203–206, 210
Discrimination, 53–54, 56, 61, 88–89
Displacement, 111, 130
Dissipative structures, 77, 114
Divergence, 34, 36, 41, 64, 141, 162, 223, 231, 243, 245, 257
Dividend smoothing, 246
Dixit-Stiglitz model, 24–25, 28–30, 34, 40, 42, 98
Duffing oscillator, 229
Duopoly, 160
Dynamic Integrated model of Climate and Energy (DICE), 201–203, 205, 210

E

Eastern Europe, 118
Ecology, 3, 51, 69, 107, 110–112, 115, 117, 137, 181, 188, 206, 247
  succession, 110, 173, 181
Econobiology, 137
Economic base, 22, 26
Econophysics, 94, 133
Ecosystem
  complexity, 145–147
  multispecies, 145–147
  stability, 145–147, 161, 180–183
  tropical, 145
Emergence, 1, 8, 13, 21–22, 26, 30, 47, 74–76
Endogenous asymmetry, 34
Endogenous preferences, 201
Energy prices, 47
Entomology, 140
Entrainment, 68, 103–104, 116–117, 119
Entropy, 46, 71, 116, 187, 192–196, 245–246, 251, 260–261
Epidemiology, 143–144
Ergodicity, 133
Erie Canal, 103–104
Escape velocity, 216
Euler buckling, 224, 258
Euler conditions, 165
European Community, 117
Eutrophic, 177, 179
Eutrophication, 177–178, 185
Evolution
  co-, 134, 137, 146, 161
  punctuated, 124
Evolutionary economic geography, 40
Evolutionary stable strategy (ESS), 129
Evolutionary unfolding, 132
Excess demand function, 64, 67
Expectations, adaptive, 153, 167
  rational, 6, 153, 167, 227, 248
Exploitation, 21, 146–147, 156–157, 181, 210
Externality, 6–8, 11, 14, 53, 117, 147–148
Extinction, 115, 118, 121, 134, 136, 147–148, 156–159, 182, 184, 189–190, 195, 203, 205
  optimal, 156–158
Extraterritoriality, 56–57, 62

F
Fad, 115
Fat tails, 104, 205–209
Feedback mechanism, 139
Feigenbaum cascade, 83, 229, 241
Fire management, 174–175
Fisheries, 147, 151, 153, 155–156, 158–159, 161, 163, 166, 169, 183–184
  multi-cohort, 151
Fitness landscape, 124–125, 132, 137
Fixed point theorem, 218
Florida Everglades, 185
Fluid dynamics, 237
Footloose cities, 40
Forest management, 176
FORPLAN, 172–173
Fractal
  basin boundaries, 184, 215, 232
  geometry, 80–81, 213–214, 221, 231, 249–251
  multi, 231, 259
  set, 249, 259
Fractional derivatives, 214
Frequency entrainment, 103–104
Fundamentalists, 162, 227
Fundamentals, finanicial
  market, 94, 104, 208, 227
  misspecified, 58
Futures markets, 133
Fuzzy sets, 61

G
Game theory, 104, 128–129, 210
GARCH, 257
Garden cities, 4, 61
General equilibrium, 69, 110–111, 126, 214
General relativity, 214
Gentrification, 50–52
Geoengineering, 199
Global cooling, 197–198, 206
Global death temperature, 207
Global warming, 197–211
Golden Rule, 184, 206, 210
Gradient, 46, 53–54, 58, 60, 64, 81, 100, 220, 227, 229, 258
Gravity model, 75
Greater fool theory, 40
Great Lakes trout, 156–158
Greek settlement patterns, 2
Greenbelt, 4, 56–57
Greenhouse effect, 190
Greenhouse gases (GHGs), 198
Grey swans, 209
Growth pole, 67

H
Habit threshold, 45
Heather hen, 157
Hexagonal market areas, 63
Hierarchy, 14, 22, 47, 61, 63, 76, 78, 81, 93–95, 97–99, 102, 104–105, 123, 136–138, 182, 237, 252, 256, 262
Hilborn plan, 156
Home market effect, 30, 34–35, 42
Hookworm infections, 144
Hopeful monsters, 113
Hotelling theorem, 159
Human capital, 102
Hydraulic systems, 5
Hydrodynamics, 224, 258
Hyperbolicity, 184
Hypercycle, 116–118

I
Iceberg effect, 115
Imperfect competition, 23
Imperfect foresight model, 57
Imperialism, 157
Inaccessibility, 222
Incomplete markets, 204
Increasing returns to scale, 26–28
Industrial districts, 26–28, 40
Industrial, dynamics, 76
  production, 76
Inertia, 45, 152, 157, 184, 189–190, 209, 251
Infrastructure, 1, 18–21, 76, 80–82, 102–103, 105
Instability, 3, 5–13, 15, 17, 50, 115, 141, 145, 149, 161, 218–219, 236, 255
Institutionalism, 127
Insurance, 190, 206, 208, 211
Integrated assessment models (IAMs), 201, 204, 206, 210
Interest rates, 162, 169, 184
Intergovernmental Panel on Climate Change (IPCC), 199, 203, 209
Intermittency, 237, 241–242
International trade, 14, 24, 34, 82, 261
Invariant set, 235
Irreversibility, 157

K
Knightian–Keynesian, 208
Kolmogorov theorem, 143

Koonce's doughnut, 156, 158
Kurtosis, 104, 208

L
Labor market, 4, 22, 28, 30, 108, 200
Laissez-faire, 111, 119, 123
Lake dynamics, 176–180
La longue durée, 14
Lamarckian, 123–124, 127
Land use, 3, 43–44, 52, 56–61, 100, 172, 201
Laplace's demon, 214
Lattice case/structures, 86–87
Law of retail gravitation, 105
Lazy eight, 181–182
Learning to believe in chaos, 168
Learning processes, 114, 168
Lebesgue measure, 215, 244
Leeds School, 44, 48
Lemmings, 139, 184
Leviathan, 126
Light caustics, 224, 258, 261
Limits to growth, 187–196
Linearity, 12, 83
Linear programming, 63
Linnaean equilibrium, 110
Lobster gangs of Maine, 183
Local surprise, 184
Locational hysteresis, 34
Logistic function, revolutions, 18–19, 102
Long wave, 118
Lorenz model, 233, 235, 237
Lotka-Volterra system, 3, 48, 70, 74, 143, 161
Lyapunov, exponents, 245–246, 260
  theorem, 246

M
Malaria, 111, 144, 203
Malthusiantrap, 82
Manifold, 8, 44, 73, 113, 161, 220, 222, 228, 231, 234, 236, 244, 246, 248–249, 261
Margin, calls, 66
  requirements, 30
Market potential function, 98, 105
Mass suicide of lemmings, 184
Maxwell convention, 221
Medieval European cities, 13–14
Megalopolis, 105
Meme, 129
Mendelian genetics, 112, 118, 124, 127
Menger sponge, 215
Metaphysics, 108, 261
Methane, 198, 203, 206–207
Methodenstreit, 38
Migration, 3, 6, 8–12, 15, 17, 22, 37–39, 48, 61, 71–72, 75, 80, 130, 203, 262
Monocentric city, 98, 103
Monopolistic competition, 23–24, 28–30, 100
Monopoly, 56
Monstrous sets, 214
Moore neighborhood, 88–91
Morphogenesis, 21, 63–83, 115–117, 131, 134, 195, 219
Moscow, 83
Moving boundary problem, 55
Multi-level selection, 128–130, 132, 136
Multimodal density function, 227
Multiplier-accelerator model, 67–68
Muskrat, 139

N
Naked discontinuity, 70
Natural selection, 108, 111–112, 114, 116, 122–124, 131–136
"Natura non facit saltum", 112–113
Neighborhood, boundary, 52–53, 56
  tipping, 52
Neo-Darwinian synthesis, 123–124, 127–128, 130, 132, 134, 137
Neo-Ricardian, 59
Neo-Schumpeterians, 40, 126, 128
Network(s)
  analysis, 89–93
  fractal, 92
  scale-free, 92–93
  small-world, 91–92
  theory, 80, 90
  topologies, 90
New economic geography, 23–42
Newtonian, 110, 214, 216, 218, 251
Node, 10, 51, 65–66, 69–72, 90–92, 104, 217, 241
Non-directed graph, 90
Non-Gaussian distributions, 206, 208
Nonlinearity, 76, 82, 139, 200, 257
Nonmonotonic, 92
Noospheric(e), 134, 136, 211
Normal factor, 222–223
North Sea herring, 147, 161

O
Oligotrophic, 177–178, 180
Omega Point, 134, 136
Ontogeny recapitulates phylogeny, 122
Open access, 147–150, 155–157, 161–164, 166, 189

Open vs closed cities, 13–14
Optimal city size, 22
Optimal control theory, 2, 20, 60, 164, 180, 191
Optimal rotation, 169–170, 174–175
Option value, 172, 190
Orbits, heteroclinic, 218
homoclinic, 218, 236–237, 239, 242, 259
Order parameters, 78–80, 256
Oscillations, theory of, 14, 69–70, 75, 78, 82, 103, 108, 116, 118, 140–143, 146, 222–223, 229, 237, 249, 256, 258
Out-of-sample forecasts, 247
Outsiders, 156, 172, 183
Overexploitation, 147, 156–157
Overfishing, 148, 150–152, 190
Overlapping generations, 143

P
Pangenesis, 123
Paradox of enrichment, 143
Peano curve, 215
Perfect foresight equilibrium, 57
Permafrost, 203, 206
Pesticides, 145
Phase, diagram, 151
transition, 2, 4
nonequilibrium, 2, 4
Physiology, 224
Pirenne hypothesis, 14, 20
Pleistocene hunters, 157
Pocket of compromise, 223
Poincaré-Bendixson theorem, 218
Poincaré map, 218, 235–236
Polarization, 78
Pollution, 188–193
Polycentrism, 57–61
Positivism, 40
Potential function, 64–65, 89, 98, 100, 105, 220, 227
Poverty, 187, 195
Power law distributions, 94, 104, 210
Precautionary principle, 182, 208
Predator-prey modal, 52, 111, 142–143, 154, 161, 188
Prejudice, 53–56, 61, 88–89
Prison disturbances, 224
Prisoner's dilemma, 61, 115, 129, 135
Pulse fishing, 153, 161

Q
Quantum mechanics, 214, 224, 258

R
Radiative forcing, 202
Ramsey equation, 205
Random graphs, 90–92
Random, number generator, 259
Rank-size distribution, 95
Rate of exploitation, 181
Rate of social time preference, 201, 205
Rational morphology, 131
Rawlsian, 159, 162
Rayleigh number, 234
Reciprocal altruism, 131, 136
Regime switches, 114, 257
Regional, code
dynamics, 72
hierarchy, 63
systems, 2–3, 63–83, 86
trade, 41
Regional Integrated model of Climate and Energ (RICE), 201–203
Regional science, 3, 23–24, 39–40
Regularity, 91, 94, 230, 243, 249
Relative stock model, 74–75
Relativity theory, 214
Renormalization, 49
Repellor, 228–229
Rescaled range analysis, 81
Retail center size, 2
Return time, 139
Roman Empire, 116
Russian School, 218, 229, 250, 259

S
Saddle point, 10, 51, 64, 69, 111, 151, 155, 234, 248, 259
Saltationalism, 113–115, 118
Saudi Arabia, 162
Schelling model, 86–93, 104
Schumpeterian discontinuities, 40, 114, 118, 126, 128
Search for extra-terrestial intelligence (SETI), 211
Segregation, 44, 52, 61, 80, 86, 89–90, 104, 116, 226
Self-fulfilling prophecy, 55
Self-organization, 2–3, 116–117, 119, 131–136, 255
Semiotics, 224
Sensitive dependence on initial conditions, 167, 201, 210, 232–233, 238–239, 243, 245, 257
Separatix, 180, 228
Sewall Wright effect, 113, 124

Sewers, 5, 21–22, 62
Shallow lake system, 177–179
Sheep blowflies, 139
Sierpinski carpet, 92–93, 215
Simulation models, 2, 118
Singularity, 6, 66, 216, 219–221
Sink, 50, 69–70, 228, 234
Skiba points, 180, 210
Slave variables, 256
  revolt of, 256
Slums, 2, 50, 52, 61
Smale horseshoe, 234–239
Small sample bias, 259
Social supra-organismists, 119
Sociodynamics, 104
Sociophysics, 104
Solar energy, 193
Source, 5, 14, 23–24, 26–28, 64, 69, 82, 94–96, 98, 102–103, 114, 123, 130, 136, 149, 156, 160, 162, 180, 190, 193–194, 196, 198, 209, 228–229, 244
Soviet, 41, 116, 153, 181
Spatial, discontinuities
  discount factor, 11, 201
  dynamics, 2
Species, competitor
  invasions, 145
  K-adjusting, 140
  r-adjusting, 140
  single, 139–141, 145
  two, 142
Spectral analysis, 247
Splitting factor, 222–223
Spruce budworm, 144–145, 161, 169, 184
Spurious quantization, 226
Sraffa-von Neumann model, 195
Stability-resilience tradeoff, 140
Stag-hunt, 129
State variable, 8, 56, 58, 61, 65, 79, 188, 220–223, 226, 256, 258
Stationary state, 10, 110–111, 194
Steady state, 6, 22, 47, 69–70, 82, 136, 160, 162, 164, 194–195, 201, 217
  economy, 194–196
Stern Review, 203–204, 206–207, 210
Stochastically stable set, 89
Stochasticity, 48, 82–83
Stock market, 209, 228, 261
Strange container, 74–75
Structural, instability
  linguistics, 224, 250
  stability, 216, 218–219, 228, 234–235, 238, 250
Structuralism, 224
Suburb, 2, 48, 50–51, 70, 80
Sudden jumps, 222–223
Suicide, 184
"Surfing", 156, 158
Survival of the fittest, 110, 123
Sustainable yield, 148
  maximum, 153
Swiss alpine grazing commons, 185
Symbiosis, 144–145
Synergetics, 2–3, 61, 78–80, 82, 213, 256–257, 262

T
Tableau Economique, 111, 126
Tektology, 138
Teleology, 115, 122, 127, 134
Teleonomic, 137
Thermodynamics, 77, 110–111, 116, 192–196
  Second Law of, 111, 116, 192–194
Thermohaline circulation, 203
Thom's classification theorem, 219
Three-body problem, 216, 218
Tiebout hypothesis, 56
Timber, 169–170, 172–175, 189
Tit-for-tat, 131, 137
Tragedy of the commons, 185
Transfinite numbers, 215
Transformation problem, 194
Transportation mode, 2, 44–45, 67
Transversality, 220, 250, 258
Turbulence, 218, 221, 237–238
Turing machine, 133–134
Turnpike, 185

U
Uncertainty, 57, 147, 153, 155–156, 158, 160–161, 198, 205–209
Unemployment, 77, 79, 156
Uniformitarianism, 121
Unions, 41, 218, 228, 243
Universality, 94–95, 97, 240, 260
Urban, dynamics
  hierarchy, 93–97, 99
  infrastructure, 1
  property prices, 2
  and regional systems, 2–3, 69–76, 86
  -rural fringe, 56
  sudden growth, 4–13
  systems, 1, 43–62, 101, 249

Urban heat effect, 209
Urban hierarchy, 93–96

V
Van der Pol oscillator, 103
Vintage models, 58–59
Volatility, stock price, 250
Von Koch snowflake, 230
Von Neumann neighborhood, 88–89
Von Neumann ray, 88–91, 111

W
Wage-profit, curve
    frontier, 63
    -rent curve, 59
Watershed, 115, 228
Wave patterns, 67
Wealth effects, 169
Wedge-shaped ghetto, 54
Weierstrass function, 237
West German currency reform, 79
Wheel of perpetual motion, 86
World economy, 14
World system, 18

Y
Yield-effort curve, 147, 154

Z
Zeno's paradox, 214
Zipf's Law, 93–96
Zoning, 2, 56–57, 60

GPSR Compliance

The European Union's (EU) General Product Safety Regulation (GPSR) is a set of rules that requires consumer products to be safe and our obligations to ensure this.

If you have any concerns about our products, you can contact us on ProductSafety@springernature.com

In case Publisher is established outside the EU, the EU authorized representative is:

Springer Nature Customer Service Center GmbH
Europaplatz 3
69115 Heidelberg, Germany

Batch number: 10837188

Printed by Printforce, the Netherlands